Europe
Europa

Country	Code	Currency	SOS ☎ / 🚗	🛣	🚗	⚠	🏠	Toll	‰
Österreich / Austria	A	1 Euro (EUR) = 100 Cent	133 / 144	130	100	100	50	✓	0,5 ‰
Shqipëria / Albania	AL	1 Lek (ALL) = 100 Quindarka	129 /126	120	100	80	40		0,0 ‰
België/Belgique / Belgium	B	1 Euro (EUR) = 100 Cent	101 / 100	120	120	90	50		0,5 ‰
Bǎlgarija / Bulgaria	BG	1 Lew (BGN) = 100 Stótinki	166 / 150	130	90	90	50	✓	0,5 ‰
Bosna i Hercegovina / Bosnia and Herzegovina	BIH	Konvert. Marka (BAM) = 100 Fening	92 / 94	120	100	80	60		0,3 ‰
Schweiz/Suisse/Svizzera / Switzerland	CH	1 Franken (CHF) = 100 Rappen	117 / 144	120	100	80	50	✓	0,5 ‰
Kypros/Kibris / Cyprus	CY	1 Euro (EUR) = 100 Cent	199	100	80	80	50		0,5 ‰
Česká republika / Czech Republic	CZ	1 Koruna (CZK) = 100 Haliru	112 / 155	130	130	90	50	✓	0,0 ‰
Deutschland / Germany	D	1 Euro (EUR) = 100 Cent	110 / 112	⊘	⊘	100	50		0,5 ‰
Danmark / Denmark	DK	1 Krone (DKK) = 100 Øre	112	130	80	80	50		0,5 ‰
España / Spain	E	1 Euro (EUR) = 100 Cent	112	110	100	90	50	✓	0,5 ‰
Eesti / Estonia	EST	1 Euro (EUR) = 100 Cent	110 / 112	110	110	90	50		0,0 ‰
France / France	F	1 Euro (EUR) = 100 Cent	112	130	110	90	50	✓	0,5 ‰
Suomi/Finland / Finland	FIN	1 Euro (EUR) = 100 Cent	112	120	100	100	50		0,5 ‰
United Kingdom / United Kingdom	GB	1 Pound Sterling (GBP) = 100 Pence	999 / 112	70 mph (112)	70 mph (112)	60 mph (96)	30 mph (48)		0,8 ‰
Ellás (Hellás) / Greece	GR	1 Euro (EUR) = 100 Cent	100 / 166	120	110	90	50	✓	0,5 ‰
Magyarország / Hungary	H	1 Forint (HUF) = 100 Filler	112	130	110	90	50	✓	0,0 ‰
Hrvatska / Croatia	HR	1 Kuna (HRK) = 100 Lipa	112 / 94	130	110	90	50	✓	0,5 ‰
Italia / Italy	I	1 Euro (EUR) = 100 Cent	112 / 118	130	110	90	50	✓	0,5 ‰
Éire/Ireland / Ireland	IRL	1 Euro (EUR) = 100 Cent	999 / 112	120	100	60/100	50		0,5 ‰
Ísland / Iceland	IS	1 Krona (ISK) = 100 Aurar	112			80/90	50		0,0 ‰
Kosovo / Kosovo	RKS	1 Euro (EUR) = 100 Cent	112 / 92	130	110	80	50		0,5 ‰
Luxembourg / Luxembourg	L	1 Euro (EUR) = 100 Cent	113 / 112	130	90	90	50		0,5 ‰
Lietuva / Lithuania	LT	1 Litas (LTL) = 100 Centas	02 / 03 / 112	110	90	90	50		0,4 ‰
Latvija / Latvia	LV	1 Lats (LVL) = 100 Santīmi	02 / 03 / 112	110	90	90	50		0,5 ‰
Makedonija / Macedonia	MK	1 Denar (MKD) = 100 Deni	192 / 194	120	100	80	40/60	✓	0,5 ‰
Norge / Norway	N	1 Krone (NOK) = 100 Øre	112 / 113	90	90	80	50	✓	0,1 ‰
Nederland / Netherlands	NL	1 Euro (EUR) = 100 Cent	112	120	100	80	50		0,5 ‰
Portugal / Portugal	P	1 Euro (EUR) = 100 Cent	112	120	100	90	50	✓	0,5 ‰
Polska / Poland	PL	1 Zloty (PLN) = 100 Groszy	112 / 999	130/140	100/120	90/100	50	✓	0,2 ‰
România / Romania	RO	1 Leu (RON) = 100 Bani	112	130	100	90	50	✓	0,0 ‰
Rossija / Russia	RUS	1 Rubel (RUB) = 100 Kopeek	02 / 03	110	90	90	60		0,0 ‰
Sverige / Sweden	S	1 Krona (SEK) = 100 Öre	112	110	110/90	70/90	50		0,2 ‰
Srbija / Crna Gora / Serbia / Montenegro	SRB MNE	1 Dinar (CSM) = 100 Para ; Euro	92 / 94	120	100	80	60	✓	0,3 ‰
Slovenská republika / Slovakia	SK	1 Euro (EUR) = 100 Cent	112 / 155	130	90	90	50	✓	0,0 ‰
Slovenija / Slovenia	SLO	1 Euro (EUR) = 100 Cent	113 / 112	130	100	90	50	✓	0,5 ‰
Türkiye / Turkey	TR	1 Lira (TRY) = 100 Kurus	155 / 112	120	90	90	50	✓	0,5 ‰
Ukrajina / Ukraine	UA	1 Griwna (UAH) = 100 Kopijken	02 / 03	130	110	90	60		0,0 ‰

Table of contents/Inhaltsverzeichnis/Sommaire/Inhoud

Political map/Politische Karte/Carte politique/Politieke kaart   4-5
Distances/Enfernungen/Distances/Afstanden   6-7
Ferry routes/Fährverbindungen/Ferry routes/Veerdiensten   8-9
Legend/Zeichenerklärung/Légende/Legenda   10-12
Key to map pages/Kartenübersicht/Tableau d'assemblage/Kaartenoverzicht   13

Maps/Karten/Cartes/Kaarten   14-128
Index of place names/Ortsregister/Index des localités/Plaatsnamenregister   129-208

© Kunth Verlag GmbH & Co. KG 2013
Königinstraße 11, D-80539 München,
phone +49-89-458020-0, fax +49-89-458020-21
e-mail: info@kunth-verlag.de
www.kunth-verlag.de

© AA Media Limited 2013
Fanum House, Basing View,
Basingstoke, Hampshire RG21 4EA, UK
ISBN: 978-0-7495-7543-4
A05113

Hill shading 1:2 000 000 /1:4 000 000:
Produced using SRTM data from Heiner Newe,
GeoKarta, Altensteig

Printed in Slovakia

Reykjavik ♀ 319.575
☐ 103.125 km²

Norwe

AL ♀ 2.831.741
☐ 28.748 km²

MC ♀ 35.881
☐ 1,6 km²

AND ♀ 85.015
☐ 468 km²

MD ♀ 3.560.000
☐ 33.800 km²

BIH ♀ 4.621.598
☐ 51.129 km²

MK ♀ 2.057.284
☐ 25.713 km²

FL ♀ 36.476
☐ 160 km²

MNE ♀ 625.266
☐ 13.812 km²

HR ♀ 4.480.043
☐ 56.542 km²

RSM ♀ 32.284
☐ 61 km²

RKS ♀ 1.733.872
☐ 10.887 km²

SLO ♀ 2.057.660
☐ 20.253 km²

L ♀ 524.853
☐ 2.586 km²

V ♀ 836
☐ 0,44 km²

M ♀ 417.608
☐ 316 km²

North

IRL

♀ 4.581.269 Dublin GB
☐ 70.182 km²

♀ 61.792.000
☐ 244.820 km²

London Amsterdam

Brussel/Bruxelles

♀ 10.951.266 B
☐ 30.528 km²

Paris

F

♀ 62.793.432
☐ 543.965 km²

ATLANTIC OCEAN

♀ 10.602.000
☐ 92.212 km²

Andorra la Vella AND

P

Madrid

Lisboa

E

♀ 47.212.990
☐ 504.645 km²

Mediterranean

Al Jaza'ir
(Alger)

Ar-Ribat
(Rabat) MA DZ

gian S e a

Sea

Baltic Sea

Sea

Black Sea

↟ 5.404.956
☐ 338.432 km²

↟ 4.985.900
☐ 385.199 km²

↟ 9.514.406
☐ 450.295 km²

Helsinki

↟ 143.200.000
☐ 17.075.400 km²

Oslo

Tallinn (EST)

Stockholm

Moskva

↟ 1.340.021
☐ 45.227 km²

↟ 2.074.605
☐ 64.589 km²

(S)

(N)

(FIN)

Riga (LV)

(RUS)

↟ 5.475.791
☐ 43.094 km²

↟ 2.988.381
☐ 65.301 km²

(BY)

(DK)

(LT)

København

(RUS) **Vilnius**

Minsk

↟ 16.680.000
☐ 41.548 km²

↟ 9.457.000
☐ 207.595 km²

(NL)

Berlin

(PL)

Warszawa

↟ 81.903.000
☐ 357.121 km²

↟ 38.501.000
☐ 312.685 km²

Kyjiv

(L)

(D)

(CZ) **Praha**

(UA)

Luxembourg

↟ 10.526.685
☐ 78.866 km²

↟ 5.404.322
☐ 49.034 km²

↟ 45.665.281
☐ 603.700 km²

(SK) **Bratislava**

(A) **Wien**

(MD)

Bern **Vaduz**

(H) **Budapest**

(RO) **Chişinău**

(CH) (FL)

↟ 8.460.390
☐ 83.878 km²

↟ 10.005.000
☐ 93.036 km²

↟ 19.042.936
☐ 238.391 km²

↟ 7.952.600
☐ 41.285 km²

Ljubljana

(SLO)

Zagreb

Beograd

Bucureşti

(MC)

(RSM)

(HR)

(BIH)

↟ 7.120.666
☐ 77.474 km²

Monaco

San Marino

Sarajevo

(SRB)

(MNE) **Priština**

↟ 7.364.570
☐ 110.994 km²

(I)

Roma

Podgorica

(RKS)

Sofija (BG)

(V)

Skopje

Ankara

↟ 60.626.442
☐ 301.338 km²

Tiranë

(MK)

(AL)

(TR)

(GR)

↟ 74.724.269
☐ 814.578 km²

↟ 9.903.268
☐ 131.957 km²

Athína

(TN) **Tunis**

↟ 1.193.976
☐ 9.251 km²

(CY)

(A)	Österreich
(AL)	Shqipëria
(AND)	Andorra
(B)	België/Belgique
(BG)	Bâlgarija
(BIH)	Bosna i Hercegovina
(BY)	Belarus'
(MNE)	Crna Gora
(CH)	Schweiz/Suisse/Svizzera
(CY)	Kýpros
(CZ)	Česká Republika
(D)	Deutschland
(DK)	Danmark
(E)	España
(EST)	Eesti
(F)	France
(FIN)	Finland
(FL)	Liechtenstein
(GB)	United Kingdom
(GR)	Elláda
(H)	Magyarország
(HR)	Hrvatska
(I)	Italia
(IRL)	Éire/Ireland
(IS)	Ísland
(RKS)	Kosovo
(L)	Luxembourg
(LT)	Lietuva
(LV)	Latvija
(M)	Malta
(MC)	Monaco
(MD)	Moldova
(MK)	Makedonija
(N)	Norge
(NL)	Nederland
(P)	Portugal
(PL)	Polska
(RO)	România
(RSM)	San Marino
(RUS)	Rossija
(S)	Sverige
(SK)	Slovenská Republika
(SLO)	Slovenija
(SRB)	Srbija
(TR)	Türkiye
(UA)	Ukraïna
(V)	Città del Vaticano

	Amsterdam	Athína	Barcelona	Belfast	Beograd	Berlin	Bern	Birmingham	Bordeaux	Bratislava	Bruxelles/Brussel	Bucureşti	Budapest	Calais	Dublin	Edinburgh	Frankfurt a.M.	Genova	Hamburg	Helsinki	Istanbul	København	Köln	Kyjiv	Le Havre	Lisboa
Amsterdam		2827	1566	1286	1720	656	833	734	1082	1211	210	2267	1398	363	1125	1196	443	1216	466	1953	2693	788	263	1943	598	2241
Athína	2827		2612	3758	1106	2338	2010	3206	2682	1662	2598	1168	1466	2844	3598	3668	2386	1780	2627	3227	1094	2767	2568	2307	2744	3768
Barcelona	1566	2612		2280	1988	1877	915	1728	637	1894	1376	2574	1926	1365	2120	2190	1336	857	1776	3263	2961	2099	1383	3048	1251	1259
Belfast	1286	3758	2280		2800	1850	1745	594	1784	2349	1119	3415	2545	925	166	319	1521	2119	1676	3161	3773	1999	1331	3244	1191	2941
Beograd	1720	1106	1988	2800		1236	1334	2248	2031	560	1680	592	363	1877	2639	2709	1287	1159	1525	2125	979	1665	1469	1472	1971	3147
Berlin	656	2338	1877	1850	1236		956	1298	1632	683	774	1751	881	927	1689	1760	549	1177	289	1649	2320	434	576	1325	1148	2791
Bern	833	2010	915	1745	1334	956		1167	889	950	637	1920	1136	796	1564	1629	429	450	910	2397	2307	1232	583	2205	752	2044
Birmingham	734	3206	1728	594	2248	1298	1167		1232	1797	566	2794	1924	373	385	472	968	1567	1124	2609	3221	1447	779	2582	432	2233
Bordeaux	1082	2682	637	1784	2031	1632	889	1232		1936	891	2616	1967	869	1470	1540	1167	997	1483	2970	3003	1806	1065	2998	686	1162
Bratislava	1211	1662	1894	2349	560	683	950	1797	1936		1203	1071	201	1388	2151	2221	799	1063	968	1751	1640	1109	987	1256	1521	3052
Bruxelles/Brussel	210	2598	1376	1119	1680	774	637	566	891	1203		2227	1357	195	958	1028	402	1023	601	2088	2653	923	212	2163	406	2049
Bucureşti	2267	1168	2574	3415	592	1751	1920	2794	2616	1071	2227		874	2426	3196	3256	1833	1746	2035	2183	625	2175	2015	947	2585	3735
Budapest	1398	1466	1926	2545	363	881	1136	1924	1967	201	1357	874		1577	2315	2386	963	1094	1165	1776	1350	1305	1152	1123	1685	3083
Calais	363	2844	1365	925	1877	927	796	373	869	1388	195	2426	1577		764	777	600	1189	754	2241	2851	1077	410	2213	273	2025
Dublin	1125	3598	2120	166	2639	1689	1564	385	1470	2151	958	3196	2315	764		450	1326	1926	1480	2979	3578	1803	1136	2939	789	2616
Edinburgh	1196	3668	2190	319	2709	1760	1629	472	1540	2221	1028	3256	2386	777	450		1430	2021	1586	3071	3683	1909	1241	3043	894	2697
Frankfurt a.M.	443	2386	1336	1521	1287	549	429	968	1167	799	402	1833	963	600	1326	1430		808	496	1968	2261	818	189	1841	772	2306
Genova	1216	1780	857	2119	1159	1177	450	1567	997	1063	1023	1746	1094	1189	1926	2021	808		1244	2746	2123	1566	971	2210	1004	2013
Hamburg	466	2627	1776	1676	1525	289	910	1124	1483	968	601	2035	1165	754	1480	1586	496	1244		1502	2646	338	425	1603	997	2639
Helsinki	1953	3227	3263	3161	2125	1649	2397	2609	2970	1751	2088	2183	1776	2241	2979	3071	1968	2746	1502		3081	1173	1910	1546	2482	4125
Istanbul	2693	1094	2961	3773	979	2320	2307	3221	3003	1640	2653	625	1350	2851	3578	3683	2261	2123	2646	3081		2642	2442	1475	2944	4121
København	788	2767	2099	1999	1665	434	1232	1447	1806	1109	923	2175	1305	1077	1803	1909	818	1566	338	1173	2642		748	1744	1320	2962
Köln	263	2568	1383	1331	1469	576	583	779	1065	987	212	2015	1152	410	1136	1241	189	971	425	1910	2442	748		1947	580	2223
Kyjiv	1943	2307	3048	3244	1472	1325	2205	2582	2998	1256	2163	947	1123	2213	2939	3043	1841	2210	1603	1546	1475	1744	1947		2532	4183
Le Havre	598	2554	1251	1191	1971	1148	752	432	686	1521	406	2585	1685	273	789	894	772	1104	997	2482	2944	1320	580	2532		1845
Lisboa	2241	3768	1259	2941	3147	2791	2044	2233	1162	3052	2049	3735	3083	2025	2616	2697	2306	2013	2639	4125	4121	2962	2223	4183	1845	
Ljubljana	1234	1633	1462	2316	534	997	809	1764	1503	447	1156	1122	460	1382	2106	2183	801	623	1184	2126	1508	1390	984	1560	1437	2616
London	532	2952	1526	776	2046	1096	965	191	1030	1557	364	2592	1722	171	546	650	766	1364	922	2407	3019	1245	575	2379	298	2187
Luxembourg	360	2414	1180	1347	1500	743	453	795	995	1031	230	2077	1195	414	1145	1256	231	828	623	2106	2449	944	207	2048	531	2128
Lyon	923	2115	639	1672	1464	1238	305	1120	588	1368	732	2052	1399	759	1479	1582	700	475	1140	2625	2438	1463	746	2400	658	1742
Madrid	1770	3215	627	2474	2594	2320	1543	1768	691	2498	1578	3182	2529	1554	2146	2230	1835	1459	2169	3654	3567	2492	1752	3629	1374	626
Málaga	2321	3619	1031	3009	2998	2879	1947	2302	1242	2902	2129	3586	2933	2105	2717	2764	2341	1863	2720	4205	3971	3043	2303	4033	1925	683
Marseille	1235	2156	508	1983	1535	1549	573	1431	648	1439	1044	2122	1470	1070	1792	1893	1012	400	1452	2937	2508	1775	1058	2570	970	1662
Milano	1076	1691	978	2057	1036	1038	318	1498	1014	940	884	1624	971	1023	1751	1959	668	140	1109	2424	2009	1432	826	2071	1044	2132
Minsk	1768	2583	2989	2957	1480	1150	1992	2405	2744	1031	1884	1357	1132	2038	2770	2866	1663	2196	1428	882	2006	1104	1683	560	2261	3901
Moskva	2469	3283	3690	3601	2181	1850	2693	3108	3445	1902	2585	1790	1832	2738	3470	3569	2364	2897	2128	1107	2524	1786	2384	852	2962	4602
München	826	2039	1343	1856	940	588	433	1317	1276	490	737	1525	655	935	1677	1765	393	628	776	1974	1914	981	575	1749	1022	2430
Oslo	1268	3440	2578	2478	2338	1031	1723	1926	2285	1705	1403	2713	1901	1556	2288	2387	1308	2057	814	1019	3314	607	1224	2343	1802	3442
Paris	502	2554	1071	1206	1771	1053	561	654	586	1350	311	2356	1491	288	1019	1116	573	914	892	2387	2745	1215	485	2336	197	1743
Praha	883	1991	1715	2025	889	355	806	1460	1549	333	902	1399	529	1100	1826	1922	510	1081	646	1641	1866	785	692	1405	1230	2702
Riga	1873	2830	3093	3062	1728	991	2183	2608	2829	1353	1775	1786	1356	1929	2874	2971	1768	2348	1280	396	2569	912	1575	1045	2153	3793
Roma	1662	1267	1366	2551	1296	1518	903	2099	1506	1200	1549	1988	1231	1600	2438	1463	2342	2553	1254	522	1669	2879	1911	1411	1638	2520
Rotterdam	76	2834	1525	1226	1735	693	802	674	1039	1237	151	2288	1411	304	1030	893	456	1177	501	1986	2708	824	257	1977	540	2196
Sankt-Peterburg	2424	3381	3645	3601	2279	1711	2648	2913	3249	1904	2389	2366	1907	2543	3272	3375	2319	2899	1893	389	2948	1473	2138	1378	2715	4347
Sarajevo	1743	1175	2014	2864	305	1418	1271	2278	2059	723	1702	915	545	1905	2618	2682	1299	1068	1684	2334	1168	1832	1493	1652	2006	3175
Skopje	2155	701	2422	3241	439	1687	1767	2682	2463	1007	2113	690	810	2311	3040	3143	1721	1583	2104	2570	787	2117	1910	1645	2404	3576
Sofija	2113	798	2380	3193	398	1714	1726	2641	2422	1034	2072	383	769	2270	3033	3102	1680	1542	2063	2476	580	2144	1862	1320	2363	3530
Stockholm	1435	3415	2746	2647	2312	1082	1879	2095	2453	1756	1570	2764	1952	1724	2450	2556	1465	2213	985	517	3289	658	1392	1591	1970	3616
Strasbourg	602	2170	1130	1540	1314	753	238	988	964	893	434	1906	1067	617	1343	1450	223	613	703	2189	2287	1026	354	2003	688	2112
Tallinn	2183	3140	3450	3373	2038	1486	2320	2611	2944	1664	2094	2096	1666	2237	2969	3070	1882	2674	1588	88	2879	1139	1883	1461	2461	4107
Tiranë	2217	713	2360	3296	748	1967	1706	2730	2389	1316	2177	923	1119	2332	3101	3206	1785	1482	2170	2879	1015	2360	1967	1859	2432	3471
Vilnius	1665	2622	2886	2864	1520	1026	1943	2312	2641	1146	1781	1756	1148	1934	2672	2773	1560	2141	1324	689	2361	919	1580	751	2158	3795
Warszawa	1209	2343	2430	2401	1051	590	1448	1849	2185	684	1325	1338	687	1478	2204	2310	1104	1679	868	1062	1943	1009	1124	767	1702	3341
Wien	1148	1705	1829	2227	603	686	867	1675	1870	65	1107	1113	243	1305	2031	2137	715	991	976	1754	1580	1116	897	1343	1436	2981
Zagreb	1330	1493	1597	2405	395	1053	943	1853	1639	442	1289	982	344	1487	2213	2315	897	759	1280	2121	1368	1472	1079	1444	1580	2759

Ljubljana	London	Luxembourg	Lyon	Madrid	Málaga	Marseille	Milano	Minsk	Moskva	München	Oslo	Paris	Praha	Riga	Roma	Rotterdam	Sankt-Peterburg	Sarajevo	Skopje	Sofija	Stockholm	Strasbourg	Tallinn	Tiranë	Vilnius	Warszawa	Wien	Zagreb
…34	532	360	923	1770	2321	1235	1076	1768	2469	826	1268	502	883	1873	1662	76	2424	1743	2155	2113	1435	602	2183	2217	1665	1209	1148	1330
…33	2952	2414	2115	3215	3619	2156	1691	2583	3283	2039	3440	2554	1991	2830	1267	2834	3381	1175	701	798	3415	2170	3140	713	2622	2343	1705	1493
…62	1526	1180	639	627	1031	508	978	2989	3690	1343	2578	1071	1715	3093	1366	1525	3645	2014	2422	2380	2746	1130	3450	2360	2886	2430	1829	1597
…16	776	1347	1672	2474	3009	1983	2057	2957	3660	1856	2478	1206	2025	3062	2651	1226	3601	2864	3241	3193	2647	1540	3373	3296	2864	2401	2227	2405
…34	2046	1500	1464	2594	2998	1535	1036	1480	2181	940	2338	1771	889	1728	1296	1735	2279	305	439	398	2312	1314	2038	748	1520	1051	603	395
…97	1096	743	1238	2320	2879	1549	1038	1150	1850	588	1031	1053	355	991	1518	693	1711	1418	1687	1714	1082	753	1486	1967	1026	590	686	1053
…09	965	453	305	1543	1947	573	318	1992	2693	433	1723	561	806	2183	903	802	2648	1271	1767	1726	1879	338	2320	1706	1943	1448	867	943
…64	191	795	1120	1768	2302	1431	1498	2405	3108	1317	1926	654	1460	2608	2099	674	2913	2278	2682	2641	2095	988	2615	2730	2312	1849	1675	1853
…03	1030	995	588	691	1242	648	1014	2744	3445	1276	2285	586	1549	2829	1506	1039	3249	2059	2463	2422	2453	964	2944	2389	2641	2185	1870	1639
…47	1557	1031	1368	2498	2902	1439	940	1201	1902	490	1705	1350	333	1353	1200	1237	1904	723	1007	1034	1756	893	1664	1316	1146	684	65	442
…56	364	230	732	1578	2129	1044	884	1884	2585	737	1403	311	902	1775	1469	151	2389	1702	2113	2072	1570	434	2094	2177	1781	1325	1107	1289
…22	2592	2077	2052	3182	3586	2122	1624	1357	1790	1525	2713	2366	1399	1786	1884	2286	2366	915	690	383	2764	1906	2096	923	1756	1338	1113	982
…60	1722	1195	1399	2529	2933	1470	971	1132	1832	655	1901	1491	529	1356	1231	1411	1907	545	810	769	1952	1067	1666	1119	1148	687	273	344
…82	171	414	759	1554	2105	1070	1023	2038	2738	935	1556	288	1100	1929	1608	304	2543	1905	2311	2270	1724	617	2237	2332	1934	1478	1305	1487
…06	546	1145	1479	2146	2717	1792	1751	2770	3470	1677	2288	1019	1826	2874	2342	1030	3272	2618	3040	3033	2450	1343	2969	3101	2672	2204	2031	2213
…83	650	1256	1582	2230	2764	1893	1959	2866	3569	1765	2387	1116	1922	2971	2553	893	3375	2682	3143	3102	2556	1450	3070	3206	2773	2310	2137	2315
…1	766	231	700	1835	2341	1012	668	1663	2364	393	1308	573	510	1768	1254	456	2319	1299	1721	1680	1465	223	1882	1785	1560	1104	715	897
…3	1364	828	475	1459	1863	400	140	2196	2897	628	2057	914	1081	2348	522	1177	2899	1068	1583	1542	2213	613	2674	1482	2141	1679	991	759
…84	922	623	1140	2169	2720	1452	1109	1428	2128	776	814	892	646	1280	1669	501	1893	1684	2104	2063	985	703	1588	2170	1324	868	976	1280
…26	2407	2106	2625	3654	4205	2937	2424	882	1107	1974	1019	2387	1641	396	2879	1986	389	2334	2570	2476	517	2189	88	2879	689	1062	1754	2121
…08	3019	2449	2438	3567	3971	2508	2009	2006	2524	1914	3314	2745	1866	2569	1743	2708	2948	1168	787	580	3289	2287	2879	1015	2361	1943	1580	1368
…90	1245	944	1463	2492	3043	1775	1432	1104	1786	981	607	1215	785	912	1911	824	1473	1832	2117	2144	658	1026	1139	2360	919	1009	1116	1472
…4	575	207	746	1752	2303	1058	826	1683	2384	575	1224	485	692	1578	1411	257	2138	1493	1910	1862	1392	354	1883	1967	1580	1124	897	1079
…50	2379	2048	2480	3629	4033	2570	2071	560	852	1749	2343	2336	1405	1045	2331	1977	1378	1652	1645	1320	1591	2003	1461	1859	751	767	1343	1444
…37	298	531	658	1374	1925	970	1044	2261	2962	1022	1802	197	1230	2153	1638	540	2715	2006	2404	2363	1597	540	2461	2432	2158	1702	1436	1580
…16	2187	2128	1742	626	683	1662	2132	3901	4602	2430	3442	1743	2702	3793	2520	2196	4347	3175	3576	3535	3610	2118	4101	3474	3798	3342	2983	2751
	1538	942	939	2068	2472	1009	510	1588	2289	409	1999	1240	708	1741	770	1251	2245	554	965	924	2038	782	2051	949	1533	1072	383	140
…38		587	918	1720	2254	1229	1260	2202	2905	1120	1724	452	1270	2098	1897	472	2661	2067	2479	2438	1892	786	2098	2542	2109	1646	1473	1651
…2	587		517	1634	2158	829	669	1878	2579	523	1427	372	732	1788	1254	355	2352	1494	1906	1864	1595	219	2096	1969	1774	1319	938	1081
…9	918	517		1242	1646	317	448	2354	3044	751	943	468	1080	2265	983	849	2958	1473	1897	1856	2111	495	2573	1823	2251	1795	1304	1072
…68	1720	1634	1242		545	1105	1576	3434	4135	1941	2975	1275	2312	3538	1964	1728	3887	2605	3028	2987	3140	1733	3630	2923	3334	2871	2433	2200
…72	2254	2158	1646	545		1506	1977	3988	4689	2342	3577	1810	2713	4092	2365	2263	4596	2979	3420	3379	3677	2129	4206	3319	3884	3428	2828	2596
…09	1229	829	317	1105	1506		521	2577	3278	1010	2255	779	1382	2729	909	1160	3234	1544	1965	1924	2422	806	2884	1863	2522	2060	1372	1140
…0	1260	669	448	1576	1977	521		2077	2778	493	1921	853	865	2229	584	1041	2732	1045	1465	1423	2078	477	2365	1400	2022	1512	872	540
…88	2202	1878	2354	3434	3988	2577	2077		720	1627	1516	2159	1281	484	2338	1800	783	2447	1926	1744	1030	1791	794	2235	191	550	1213	1473
…39	2905	2579	3044	4135	4689	3278	2778	720		2362	1997	2863	1873	917	3041	2503	697	2382	2496	2265	1464	2570	1014	2938	908	1253	1916	2176
…9	1120	523	733	1941	2342	1010	493	1627	2362		1588	822	381	1608	928	824	2166	962	1374	1332	1627	364	1916	1435	1594	992	406	549
…99	1724	1427	1943	2975	3577	2255	1921	1516	1997	1588		1703	1382	1069	2507	1302	1341	2430	2713	2741	523	1516	986	2956	1331	1605	1712	2068
…40	452	372	468	1275	1810	779	853	2159	2863	822	1703		1030	2055	1445	458	2619	1805	2204	2163	1873	488	2363	2262	2061	1605	1237	1377
…8	1270	732	1080	2312	2713	1382	865	1281	1873	381	1382	1030		1282	1296	909	1777	1044	1334	1362	1427	606	1593	1542	1075	613	333	654
…41	2098	1788	2265	3538	4092	2729	2229	484	917	1608	1069	2055	1282		2482	1905	561	1916	2173	2078	547	1752	310	2482	291	664	1356	1723
…0	1897	1254	983	1964	2365	909	584	2338	3041	1296	2507	1445	1296	2482		1626	2993	892	1190	1686	2556	1062	2803	975	2284	1823	1135	903
…41	472	355	849	1728	2263	1160	1041	1800	2503	824	1302	458	909	1905	1626		2260	1757	2167	2126	1469	566	2002	2231	1699	1243	1161	1343
…45	2661	2352	2958	3887	4596	3234	2732	783	697	2166	1341	2619	1777	561	2993	2260		2447	2665	2571	899	2317	361	2975	714	1157	1849	2216
…4	2067	1494	1473	2605	2979	1544	1045	2447	2382	962	2430	1805	1044	1916	892	1757	2447		459	586	2482	1340	2249	498	1691	1250	759	414
…5	2479	1906	1897	3028	3420	1965	1465	1926	2496	1374	2713	2204	1334	2173	1190	2167	2665	459		229	2750	1747	2475	311	1957	1488	1040	828
…4	2438	1864	1856	2987	3379	1924	1423	1744	2265	1332	2741	2163	1362	2078	1686	2126	2571	586	229		2709	1706	2389	540	1916	1447	999	787
…82	1892	1595	2111	3140	3677	2422	2078	1030	1464	1627	523	1873	1427	547	2576	1469	899	2482	2750	2709		1674	482	3008	838	1198	1764	2120
…2	786	219	495	1733	2129	806	477	1791	2570	364	1516	488	606	1752	1062	566	2317	1340	1747	1706	1674		2090	1815	1767	1311	769	927
…1	2098	2096	2573	3630	4206	2884	2365	794	1014	1916	986	2363	1593	310	2803	2002	361	2249	2475	2389	482	2090		2793	602	975	1667	2034
…9	2542	1969	1823	2923	3319	1863	1400	2235	2938	1435	2956	2262	1542	2482	975	2231	2975	498	311	540	3008	1815	2793		2268	1799	1264	910
…3	2109	1774	2251	3334	3884	2522	2022	191	908	1594	1331	2061	1075	291	2284	1699	714	1691	1957	1916	838	1767	602	2268		466	1158	1525
…2	1646	1319	1795	2871	3428	2060	1512	550	1253	992	1605	1605	613	664	1823	1243	1157	1250	1488	1447	1198	1311	975	1799	466		689	1056
…3	1473	938	1304	2433	2828	1372	872	1213	1916	406	1712	1237	333	1356	1135	1161	1849	759	1040	999	1764	769	1667	1264	1158	689		376
…0	1651	1081	1072	2200	2596	1140	640	1473	2176	549	2068	1377	654	1723	903	1343	2216	414	828	787	2120	927	2034	910	1525	1056	376	

All distances in this chart are in kilometers and include any part of the route taken by ferry.

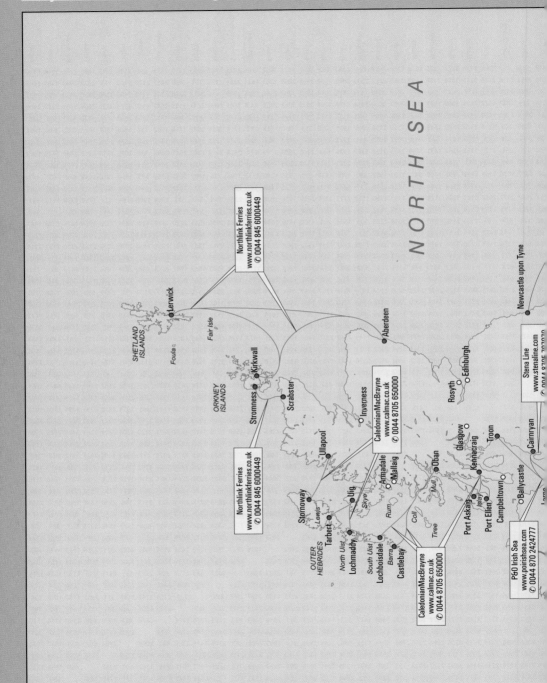

NORTH SEA

Northlink Ferries
www.northlinkferries.co.uk
© 0044 845 6000449

Northlink Ferries
www.northlinkferries.co.uk
© 0044 845 6000449

CaledonianMacBrayne
www.calmac.co.uk
© 0044 8705 650000

CaledonianMacBrayne
www.calmac.co.uk
© 0044 8705 650000

Stena Line
www.stenaline.com

P&O Irish Sea
www.poirishsea.com
© 0044 870 2424777

Lerwick
SHETLAND
ISLANDS
Foula
Fair Isle
Kirkwall
ORKNEY
ISLANDS
Stromness
Scrabster
Aberdeen
Inverness
Ullapool
Rosyth
Edinburgh
Glasgow
Newcastle upon Tyne
Troon
Cairnryan
Stornoway
Lewis
Tarbert
North Uist
Lochmaddy
South Uist
Lochboisdale
Barra
Castlebay
OUTER
HEBRIDES
Uig
Skye
Armadale
Mallaig
Rum
Mull
Oban
Coll
Tiree
Kennacraig
Islay
Port Askaig
Port Ellen
Campbeltown
Ballycastle

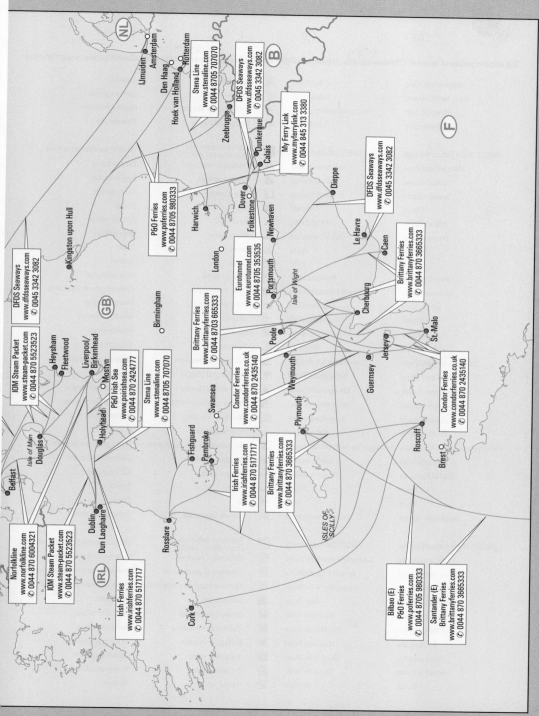

NL

IJmuiden
Amsterdam
Den Haag
Hoek van Holland
Rotterdam

Stena Line
www.stenaline.com
☎ 0044 8705 707070

DFDS Seaways
www.dfdsseaways.com
☎ 0045 3342 3082

B

Zeebrugge

Dunkerque

Calais

My Ferry Link
www.myferrylink.com
☎ 0044 845 313 3380

Dieppe

F

DFDS Seaways
www.dfdsseaways.com
☎ 0045 3342 3082

P&O Ferries
www.poferries.com
☎ 0044 8705 980333

Harwich

Dover
Folkestone
Newhaven

Le Havre
Caen

Brittany Ferries
www.brittanyferries.com
☎ 0044 870 3665333

Kingston upon Hull

DFDS Seaways
www.dfdsseaways.com
☎ 0045 3342 3082

London

Eurotunnel
www.eurotunnel.com
☎ 0044 8705 353535

Portsmouth
Isle of Wight

Cherbourg

Birmingham

GB

Heysham
Fleetwood

IOM Steam Packet
www.steam-packet.com
☎ 0044 870 5523523

Brittany Ferries
www.brittanyferries.com
☎ 0044 8703 665333

Poole

Weymouth

Jersey

St.-Malo

Condor Ferries
www.condorferries.co.uk
☎ 0044 870 2435140

Liverpool/
Birkenhead
Mostyn

P&O Irish Sea
www.poirishsea.com
☎ 0044 870 2424777

Stena Line
www.stenaline.com
☎ 0044 8705 707070

Condor Ferries
www.condorferries.co.uk
☎ 0044 870 2435140

Guernsey

Isle of Man

Holyhead

Douglas

Fishguard
Pembroke

Swansea

Plymouth

Roscoff

Brest

Belfast

Irish Ferries
www.irishferries.com
☎ 0044 870 517 1717

Brittany Ferries
www.brittanyferries.com
☎ 0044 870 3665333

Norfolkline
www.norfolkline.com
☎ 0044 870 6004321

IOM Steam Packet
www.steam-packet.com
☎ 0044 870 5523523

Dublin
Dun Laoghaire

IRL

Irish Ferries
www.irishferries.com
☎ 0044 870 517 1717

Rosslare

ISLES OF
SCILLY

Bilbao (E)
P&O Ferries
www.poferries.com
☎ 0044 8705 980333

Santander (E)
Brittany Ferries
www.brittanyferries.com
☎ 0044 870 3665333

Cork

9

GB D F NL

Significant points of interest · Herausragende Sehenswürdigkeiten · Curiosités remarquables · Opvallende bezienswaardigheden

GB	D		F	NL
Major tourist route	Autoroute		Autoroute	Autoroute
Major tourist railway	Bahnstrecke		Ligne ferroviaire	Spoorwegtraject
Highspeed train	Hochgeschwindigkeitszug		Train à Grande Vitesse	Hogesnelheidstrein
Shipping route	Schiffsroute		Itinéraire en bateau	Scheepsroute
UNESCO World Natural Heritage	UNESCO-Weltnaturerbe		Patrimoine naturel de l'humanité de l'UNESCO	UNESCO wereldnatuurerfgoed
Mountain landscape	Gebirgslandschaft		Paysage de montagne	Berglandschap
Rock landscape	Felslandschaft		Paysage rocheux	Rotslandschap
Ravine/canyon	Schlucht/Canyon		Gorge/canyon	Kloof/canyon
Glacier	Gletscher		Glacier	Gletsjer
Active volcano	Vulkan, aktiv		Volcan actif	Actieve vulkaan
Extinct volcano	Vulkan, erloschen		Volcan éteint	Dode vulkaan
Geyser	Geysir		Geyser	Geiser
Cave	Höhle		Grotte	Grotten
River landscape	Flusslandschaft		Paysage fluvial	Rivierlandschap
Waterfall/rapids	Wasserfall/Stromschnelle		Chute d'eau/rapide	Waterval/stroomversnelling
Lake country	Seenlandschaft		Paysage de lacs	Merenlandschap
Desert	Wüstenlandschaft		Désert	Woestijnlandschap
Fossil site	Fossilienfundstätte		Site fossile	Fossielenplaats
Nature park	Naturpark		Parc naturel	Natuurpark
National park (landscape)	Nationalpark (Landschaft)		Parc national (paysage)	Nationaal park (landschap)
National park (flora)	Nationalpark (Flora)		Parc national (flore)	Nationaal park (flora)
National park (fauna)	Nationalpark (Fauna)		Parc national (faune)	Nationaal park (fauna)
National park (culture)	Nationalpark (Kultur)		Parc national (site culturel)	Nationaal park (cultuur)
Biosphere reserve	Biosphärenreservat		Réserve de biosphère	Biosfeerreservaat
Wildlife reserve	Wildreservat		Réserve animale	Wildreservaat
Protected area for sea-lions/seals	Schutzgeb. für Seelöwen/Seehunde		Rés. naturelle d'otaries/de phoques	Besch. geb. v. zeeleeuwen/-honden
Zoo/safari park	Zoo/Safaripark		Zoo/parc de safari	Dierentuin/safaripark
Coastal landscape	Küstenlandschaft		Paysage côtier	Kustlandschap
Beach	Strand		Plage	Strand
Island	Insel		Île	Eiland
Underwater reserve	Unterwasserreservat		Réserve sous-marine	Onderwaterreservaat
UNESCO World Cultural Heritage	UNESCOWeltkulturerbe		Patrimoine culturel de l'humanité de l'UNESCO	UNESCO wereldcultuurerfgoed
Remarkable city	Außergewöhnliche Metropole		Métropole d'exception	Buitengewone metropolen
Pre-and early history	Vor- und Frühgeschichte		Préhistoire et protohistoire	Prehistorie en vroegste geschiedenis
Prehistoric rockscape	Prähistorische Felsbilder		Peintures rupestres préhistoriques	Prehistorische rotstekeningen
The Ancient Orient	Alter Orient		Ancien Orient	Oud-Oriënt
Minoan site	Minoische Kultur		Civilisation minoenne	Minoïsche cultuur
Phoenecian site	Phönikische Kultur		Civilisation phénicienne	Fenicische cultuur
Etruscan site	Etruskische Kultur		Civilisation étrusque	Etruskische cultuur
Greek antiquity	Griechische Antike		Antiquité grecque	Griekse oudheden
Roman antiquity	Römische Antike		Antiquité romaine	Romeinse oudheden
Vikings	Wikinger		Vikings	Vikingen

Significant points of interest · Herausragende Sehenswürdigkeiten · Curiosités remarquables · Opvallende bezienswaardigheden

GB	D	F	NL
Places of Jewish cultural interest	Jüdische Kulturstätte	Site juif	Joodse cultuurhist. plaatsen
Places of Christian cultural interest	Christliche Kulturstätte	Site chrétien	Christelijke cultuurhist. plaatsen
Places of Islamic cultural interest	Islamische Kulturstätte	Site islamique	Islamitische cultuurhist. plaatsen
Cultural landscape	Kulturlandschaft	Paysage culturel	Cultuurlandschap
Historical city scape	Historisches Stadtbild	Cité historique	Historisch stadsgezicht
Impressive skyline	Imposante Skyline	Gratte-ciel	Imposante skyline
Castle/fortress/fort	Burg/Festung/Wehranlage	Château/forteresse/remparts	Burcht/vesting/verdedigingswerk
Palace	Palast/Schloss	Palais	Paleis
Technical/industrial monument	Techn./industrielles Monument	Monument technique/industriel	Technisch/industrieel monument
Disused mine	Bergwerk geschlossen	Mine fermée	Mijn buiten bedrijf
Dam	Staumauer	Barrage	Stuwdam
Impressive lighthouse	Sehenswerter Leuchtturm	Très beau phare	Bezienswaardige vuurtoren
Notable bridge	Herausragende Brücke	Pont remarquable	Opvallende brug
Tomb/grave	Grabmal	Tombeau	Grafmonument
Monument	Denkmal	Monument	Monument
Memorial	Mahnmal	Mémorial	Gedenkteken
Theatre of war/battlefield	Kriegsschauplatz/Schlachtfeld	Champs de bataille	Strijdtoneel/slagvelden
Space telescope	Weltraumteleskop	Télescope astronomique	Ruimtetelescoop
Market	Markt	Marché	Markt
Caravanserai	Karawanserei	Caravansérail	Karavanserai
Festivals	Feste und Festivals	Fêtes et festivals	Feesten en festivals
Museum	Museum	Musée	Museum
Theatre	Theater	Théâtre	Theater
World exhibition/World Fair	Weltausstellung	Exposition universelle	Wereldtentoonstelling
Olympics	Olympische Spiele	Site olympique	Olympiade
Arena/stadium	Arena/Stadion	Arène/stade	Arena/stadion
Race track	Rennstrecke	Circuit automobile	Circuit
Golf	Golf	Golf	Golf
Horse racing	Pferdesport	Équitation	Paardensport
Skiing	Skigebiet	Station de ski	Skigebied
Sailing	Segeln	Voile	Zeilen
Wind surfing	Windsurfen	Planche à voile	Surfen
Surfing	Wellenreiten	Surf	Surfriding
Diving	Tauchen	Plongée	Duiken
Canoeing/rafting	Kanu/Rafting	Canoë/rafting	Kanoën/rafting
Waterskiing	Wasserski	Ski nautique	Waterskiën
Beach resort	Badeort	Station balnéaire	Badplaats
Mineral/thermal spa	Mineralbad/Therme	Station hydrothermale	Mineraalbad/thermen
Leisure park	Freizeitpark	Parc de loisirs	Recreatiepark
Casino	Spielcasino	Casino	Casino
Seaport	Seehafen	Port	Zeehaven

Legend/Zeichenerklärung/Légende/Legenda

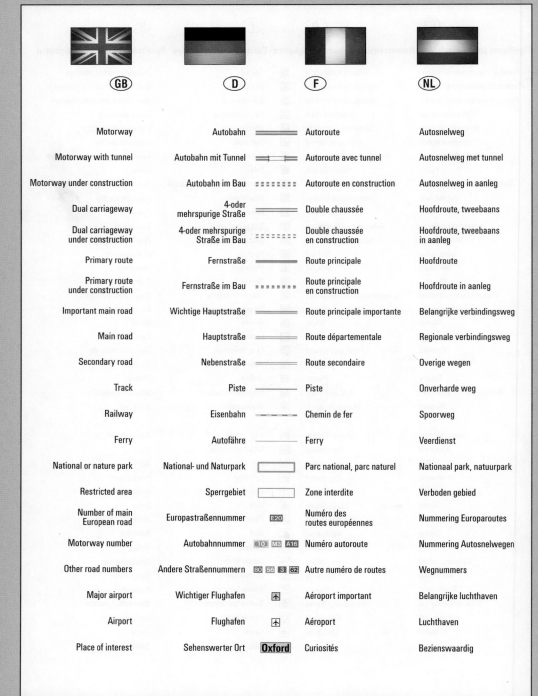

GB	D		F	NL
Motorway	Autobahn		Autoroute	Autosnelweg
Motorway with tunnel	Autobahn mit Tunnel		Autoroute avec tunnel	Autosnelweg met tunnel
Motorway under construction	Autobahn im Bau		Autoroute en construction	Autosnelweg in aanleg
Dual carriageway	4-oder mehrspurige Straße		Double chaussée	Hoofdroute, tweebaans
Dual carriageway under construction	4-oder mehrspurige Straße im Bau		Double chaussée en construction	Hoofdroute, tweebaans in aanleg
Primary route	Fernstraße		Route principale	Hoofdroute
Primary route under construction	Fernstraße im Bau		Route principale en construction	Hoofdroute in aanleg
Important main road	Wichtige Hauptstraße		Route principale importante	Belangrijke verbindingsweg
Main road	Hauptstraße		Route départementale	Regionale verbindingsweg
Secondary road	Nebenstraße		Route secondaire	Overige wegen
Track	Piste		Piste	Onverharde weg
Railway	Eisenbahn		Chemin de fer	Spoorweg
Ferry	Autofähre		Ferry	Veerdienst
National or nature park	National- und Naturpark		Parc national, parc naturel	Nationaal park, natuurpark
Restricted area	Sperrgebiet		Zone interdite	Verboden gebied
Number of main European road	Europastraßennummer	E20	Numéro des routes européennes	Nummering Europaroutes
Motorway number	Autobahnnummer	10 M3 A16	Numéro autoroute	Nummering Autosnelwegen
Other road numbers	Andere Straßennummern	80 56 3 62	Autre numéro de routes	Wegnummers
Major airport	Wichtiger Flughafen	✈	Aéroport important	Belangrijke luchthaven
Airport	Flughafen	✈	Aéroport	Luchthaven
Place of interest	Sehenswerter Ort	**Oxford**	Curiosités	Bezienswaardig

Key to map pages/Kartenübersicht/Tableau d'assemblage/Kaartenoverzicht

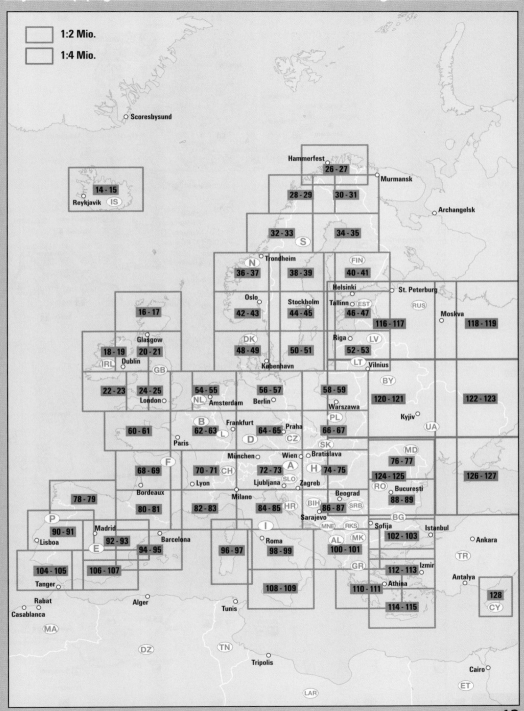

1:2 Mio.

1:4 Mio.

Scale 1:2 000 000

0 10 20 30 kilometres
0 10 20 miles

18

Bc   Bd   Ca

Listowel
Askeaton
Adare

Brandon Head
Tralee Bay
Dingle Bay
Dingle
Anascaul
Camp
Castleisland
Charleville
Knocklong
Tipperary
919
Galty Mts
Killenaule
Killarney
Cashel
Callan
Gowran Park
74

Killorglin
Glenbeigh
KFF
Farranfore
Valentia I.
Bray Head
Cahersiveen
Carrauntoohil 1038
Ring of Kerry
Muckross
Killarney
Kanturk
Mitchelstown
Caher
Fethard
Clonmel

Skellig Michael
Waterville
Sneem
837
Killarney N.P.
Rathmore
Mallow
Blackwater
Fermoy
Lismore
MB 77
Suir
63
Carrick-on-Suir

Caherdaniel
Kenmare River
Kenmare
Blarney Castle
Blarney
Dungarvan
New Ross
23

Dursey Island
Glengarriff
22
Macroom
Cork/ Corcaigh
Waterford
Arthurstown
126

Castletownbere
Bear Island
Bantry Bay
Bantry
87
Lee
Dunmanway
Fota Wildlife Park
Midleton
E30
25
Tramore
WAT

Ballydehob
Bandon
Cobh
Cork Harb.
Youghal
Mine Head
Hook Head

Mizen Head
Crookhaven
Roaringwater Bay
Skibbereen
Clonakilty
Kinsale
Charles Fort
Ringaskiddy
Youghal Bay
Waterford Harb.

Cape Clear
Drombeg Circle
Galley Head
Old Head of Kinsale

IRELAND / ÉIRE

99

87
Nymphe Bank

UNITED KINGDOM

C e l t i c

A T L A N T I C

62
Labadie Bank

S e a

O C E A N

73
Cockburn Bank

73
Jones Bank

Isles of Scilly
St. Mary's
ISC

Sennen
Land's End

25

26

27

28

Bc   Bd   Ca

Scale 1:2 000 000

0   10   20   30 kilometres
0   10   20 miles

NORWEGIAN

SEA

86   190

Hjelmsøya
Ingøya
Gunnarnes   Havøysund
Rolvsøya
Snøfjord
Akkerfjord   *Revsbotn*
HFT
Hammerfest
Storelv
Rypefjord   Struve Geodetic Arc
Sørvær   *Sørøya* 656   *Kvaløya*
Breivikbotn   94   60   Kvalsund
Hasvik   Eidvågeid
HAA   Seiland   Ska
1079   Saraby   E06

Lopphavet   Loppa
Loppa   *Silda*
Stjernøya   Storekorsnes   Nyvoll   88
Bukta
Årviksand   Leirvik   Øksfjord   Leirbotn   Stabbursdalen nasjonalpark
Fugløya   *Arnøy*   Sør-Tverrfjord   1204   Langfjordbotn   80   ALF
Nord-Kvaløy   Skardet   Halddetoppen   Alta
Vannareid   *Vanna*   1149   Struve Geodetic Arc
Helgøya   Skåningen   Storstein   Skjervøy   Burfjord   Altaelva
Mikkelvik   *Kågen*   Hamneidet   Hjemmeluft   93
Rebbenesøy   Hansnes   Russelv   *Uløya*   146   Sørstraumen   Sautso-canyon
Måsvik   Stakkvik   *Reinøya*   Sørkjosen   Reykfossen   *Jesja*
Ringvassøy   Skulgam   Storslett   Rieppe   Kvænangsbotn
Tromvik   1596   SOJ   1337
TOS   Oldervik   Djupvik
Vasstrand   Kaldfjord   Breidvikeidet   Svensby   Olderdalen   NORGE
Hillesøy   Tromsø   Forneset   Beahcegealhaldi   *Finnmark*
Laukvik   Larseng   Fagernes   Lyngseidet   Bilto   1326   Biedjovaggigruver   Masi
Kvaløya   1833   Kåfjordbotn   Mollisfossen   126   92   128
Vikran   E06   66   E06   Isfjellet   Mieriokki   *vidda*
Fjordgård   Furuflaten   1375   Skibotn   Halti   Reisa nasjonalpark   Lappoluobba
Lysnes   Stordalselv   42   1365   Struve Geodetic Arc
Gibostad   Eidet   Oteren   Skibotndalen   Kautokeino   Lavvooáivve
Silsand   Finnsnes   Balsfjord   44   Kilpisjärvi   622
Storsteinnes   52   1444   1029   Siebe   93
Sørreisa   Nordkjosbotn   E08
Moen   Skjold   21   Ropi
Andselv   BDU   Øvergård   Kummavuopio   115   945   106
Brøstadbotn   *Dividalen*   Råstojaure
Sjøvegan   Setermoen   *Nunjis*   Frihetsli   Palojärvi
Reife   82   1713   Markkina   Kaaresuvanto
Fossbakken   Øvre Dividal nasjonalpark   1102   Maunu   Karasavvon   Enontekiö Enkodak
Altevatnet   Struve Geodetic Arc

Gc   Gd   Ha
29

BARENTS SEA

260

nivskje-odden   Nordkapp
Kinnarodden
Magerøya   Skarsvåg
jesvær   31   HVG
Gamvik
MEH   Mehamn
Honningsvåg   Nordkinn-
Kåfjord   Kjøllefjord   halvøya
97   Sværholt-   BVG   Berlevåg
'orsanger-   Repvåg   halvøya   Raggonjargga
halvøya   E69   Store   Båtsfjord   BJF
    Veidnes   Bekkarfjord   Molvik   Sommersete
Russnes   Ytre Kjæs   Ifjord   673   Varanger-   Vardø
Olderfjord   Adamsfjord   Rusterfjelbma   725   halvøya   VAW
    Indre Billefjord   Leirpollskogen   Falkefjellet   Kiberg
    Børselv   Tana bru   545   77
LKL   Laksefjord-   Varangerbotn   Vestre   E75   VDS
    vidda   94   Jakobselv   Vadsø
    Lakselv   Nuorgam   Varangerfjorden   51
7   73   Porsangermoen   Polmak   Gandvik   Bugøynes   Kong Oscar II's Kapell   Pummank
    Rastigaissa   Vetsikko   11   Bjørnstad   Vajdaguba
Sápmi   1067   E06   Bugøyfjord   E06   KKN   Kirkenes   Liinahamari
    Lævvajokgiedde   Utsjoki   Skoltefossen   Bjørnevatn-   Pečenga
    101   E75   Skalltivaara   Näätämö   30   Zapoljarnyj
Karasjok   Patoniva   4   Ahmalahti   Salmijärvi   53   Luostar
    Nuvvus   Mierasłompolo   Sevettijärvi   Svanvik   Nikel   g.Kuorpukas
Kenttan   92   103   Iljärvi   Kobbfoss   650
    Iskaras   Petsikko   g.Šuort
    542   Karigasniemi   495
Jorgastak   Kaamasmukka   92   Nyrud   Prirečnyj
    85   Palomaa   ROSSIJA
    Koarvikodds   Sumuvuono   Øvre Pasvik
    590 Mutusjärvi   Kaamanen   Partakko   nasjonalpark
Gürbbeš   Inarijärvi   119   Rajakoski
587   Angeli   Inari   Virtaniemi   Nautsi
Øvre Anárjohka   Pyhäjärvi   Nellim
nasjonalpark   71   Koppelo   Vermelъjomsk
    FINLAND   Lotta   vo oraniliše
    Lemmenjoki   Ivalo   g.Čilta'd
    Menesjärvi   Törmänen   907
    Morgam-Viibus   Hammastunturi   IVL   g.Rastimuddar
    542   531   Lotta   646
Lemmenjoen   (valijoki)   Raja-
kansallispuisto   Jooseppi   g.Jonn-N'jugoaje
    63   Saariselkä   714   Javr
Nunnanen   Kuttura
Lisma   Repojoki   Urho Kekkosen kansallispuisto   Korvatunturi

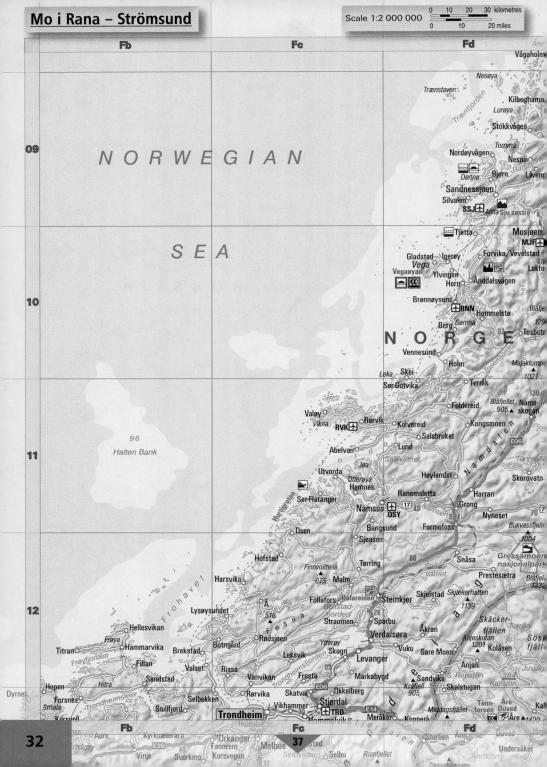

Scale 1:2 000 000

0   10   20   30 kilometres
0   10   20 miles

Ec   Ed   Fa

1460

N O R W E G I A N

S E A

Dyrnes

Tømmervåg
Kristiansund KS
Reinsvik 70 Frei
Averøya
Bud Eide
Elnesvågen Nordmøre
Steinshamn
Gossen Molde Hjelset E39
Austnes Molde MOL Kleive
AES Midsund Otrøy Solsnes
Vigra Brattvåg Vatne Åfarnes Eidsvåg Isfjorden
Godøy Ålesund Vestnes Åndalsnes
Atlanterhavsparken Runde Spjelkavik E136 Sjøholt Tresfjord Trolltindan Mardale
Langevåg Hareid Sykkylven Stordalen 60 1797 Øverdalen
Fosnavåg Ulsteinvik Vartdal Sunnmøre Stranda Linge Troll stigen Stugufläten
Stad Sandsøy Ørsta Sæbø Leknes Eidsdalen Puttega
Hurtigruten Arvik Volda HOV Kvitegga Sjusystre 1999 Geiranger
Leikanger Koparnes HOV 1691 Hellesylt Geirangerfjorden
Sildegåpet Folkestad Aheim Strynsvatn 73
Vågsøy Selje Stårheim Horning Stryn 15 Grotli
Raudeberg Måløy 52 Nordfjordeid dalsvatn 44 50
Bremangerlandet Oldeide Isane Videsæter
Frøya 52 Svelgen Staume N Sandane Olden O
Kalvåg Allottbreen 1385 59 SDN Byrkjelo Briksdal Sotasæter
Hovden Norddal 67 Jostedals- 1958 Fåberg
Skorpa Florø Eikefjord 5 Skei breen nasjonalpark Galdhøpigg 2469
Askrova FRO Naustdal 43 Bruheim Sognefjellsvegen Jotunheimen
Svanøy Nes Skjolden Jot
Ryggsteins-havet Askvoll Dale FDE Førde Norsk Bre museum Gaupne Urnes Øvre Årdal
Atløy Sande Fjærland 63 Lustrafjorden
Sula Vadheim E39 Høyanger Hella Leikanger Sogndal Kaupanger Ardalstangen 140
Krakhella Rysjedalsvika Balestrand Vangsnes SOG Lærdalsøyri Høgeset Øy
Ytre Sula Lavik 55 30 Høgeloft 1920
175 Rutledalen Sognefjorden 1308 Borlaug
Eivindvik Ytre Oppedal Ortnevik Viksøyri Store Hånos Borgund stavkirke
Leirvåg Halsund 162 13 1670 Nærøyfjorden Aurlands- 1836 52
Fedje Fosnøy Duesund Gudvangen 109 vangen
Lindås Masfjorden Nesheim Vinje Flåmsbana Flåm
Alvøy Radøy Manger 1412 Myrdal Bergensbanen
Blomøy Holsnøy Herdla Stamnes Evanger Finse
Toftøy Salhus Knarvik Lonevåg Dale Voss Ulvik Geilo Ho
Solsvik Kleppestø Ytre Arna 13 37 Granvin Kvanndal
Bryggen Bergen Indre Arna E16 60 Bergensbanen Eidfjord Haugastøl
291 BGO Espeland 137 Steinsdals- Alvik Brimnes Fossli 100 Dagali
Sotra Nesttun 7 fossen Norheimsund Kinsarvik Vøring- 7 Dyranut
Klokkarvik Fana E39 Hatrik 28 Strandebarm Utne fossen Lofthus
Korsfjorden Osøyro Fusa Jondal Hårteigen Hardanger-
Austevoll Skåvareid 1660 1690 Skrekken
Ec Huftarøy Gjermundshamn Ed Tyssedal Fa 1429
Tysnes Sandvikvåg Odda nasjonalpark
Selbjørnsfjorden strand

42

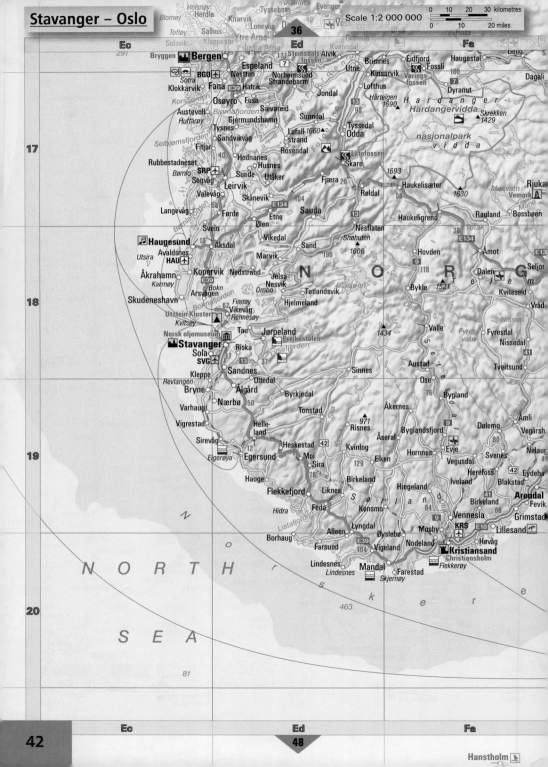

Ec
291
Ed
Fa
Gelo

Holsnøy
Herdla
Blomøy
Tyssebotn
Evanger
Knarvik
Lonevåg
Tyssebotn
Toftøy
Ytre Arna
Salhus
Kleppestø
Finse
Solsvik
Indre Arna
Granvin
Kvanndal

Bryggen Bergen
Steinsdals
fossen Alvik
Brimnes
Eidfjord
Haugastøl
Espeland
Utne
Kinsarvik
Vøringsfossen
Fossli
100
Dagali
Sotra BGO Nesttun Norheimsund
Strandebarm
Lofthus
Vøringsfossen
7
Klokkarvik Fana Hatrik
Jondal
Hårteigen
1690
Dyranut
Korsfjorden Osøyro Fusa
Sævareid
Hardanger-
Austevoll
Bjørnafjorden Gjermundshamn
Sunndal
13
98
Hardangervidda
Skrekken
1429
Huftarøy
Sandvikvåg
Løfall 1660
strand
Tyssedal
nasjonalpark
vidda

17
Tysnes Fitjar
Rosendal
Odda
Selbjørnsfjorden Hodnanes
Husnes
Latefossen
Rubbestadneset SRP
Skare
Haukelisæter
1693
Bømlo Sunde Utåker
Fjæra
20
1630
Rauland
Bossbøen
Segvåg Leirvik
Røldal
58
Mosvatn
Valevåg Skånevik
104
Haukeligrend
Vemork
Rjuka
Langevåg Førde
E134 Sauda
13
Rauland
A
Sveio Ølen Etne
38
Totak

Haugesund
Vikedal
Nesflaten
Snøhuten
Haukeligrend
E134
Åmot
18
Avaldsnes Aksdal
Sand
1606
Hovden
9
Seljord
E13
HAU
Marvik
196
118
Dalen
Utsira Kopervik Nedstrand
Jelsa
Bykle
1521
Kviteseid
Åkrahamn
Nesvik
Blåsjøen
R
Karmøy Arsvågen
Ombo
Vråd
Skudeneshavn Bokn
Finnøy
Tøtlandsvik
G
Nissedal
Bokhafjorden
62 Vikevåg
Hjelmeland
1434
Valle
Fyresdal
Utstein Kloster Rennesøy
Fyres
vatn
Nissedal
Kvitsøy Tau
Valle
41
Norsk oljemuseum Breikestolen
Austad
Tveitsund
Stavanger Riska Jørpeland
Sola Lysefjorden
Ose
SVG 17
13
Sinnes
76
Kleppe 37
Bygland
Revtangen Sandnes
Oltedal
Åkernes
Amli
Bryne Ålgård
Byrkjedal
Byglandsfjord
9
Dølemo
Varhaug Nærbø 50
Tonstad
Åseral
Evje
Vegårsh
Vigrestad
Stra
971
Risnes
Vegusdal
Svenes
Sirevåg Helle-
land
Heskestad 42
Kvinlog
Eiken
Hornnes
Herefoss
42
Eydeha
Eigerøya Egersund
Moi
Sira
129
Birkeland
Iveland
Blakstad
Hauge
78
Hægeland
64
Birkeland
Arendal
Flekkefjord Liknes
Konsmo
41
66
Fevik
Hidra Feda
Vennesla
Grimstad
Listafjorden
Lyngdal
Mosby
KRS
E18
Lillesand
Alleen
Øyslebø
Nodeland
Høvåg
Borhaug
Farsund E39 Vigeland
Kristiansand
104
Christiansholm
Lindesnes
Mandal
Flekkerøy
Lindesnes
Farestad
Skjernøy

NORTH

SEA
81

N
O
R
G
E

N
o
r
s
k
e
r
e

S
ø
r
l
a
n
d

463

Hanstholm

Marstrand
Skagens museum
Grenen
Skagen
Hirtshals
Tannis Bugt
Albæk
Hjørring
Sindal
Strandby
Frederikshavn
Fårup
Sommerland
Vrå
Gærum
Blokhus
Brønderslev
Sæby
Vesterø
Havn
Læsø
Aabybro
Pandrup
Hjallerup
Dronninglund
Vodskov
Lindholm Høje
AAL
Aalborg
Hals
Nibe
Storvorde
Aars
Støvring
Skørping
Øster Hurup
Aalborg Bugt
KATTEGAT
Np.Rebild Bakker
Arden
Als
Hadsund
Mariager
Hobro
Fyrkat
Mariager Fjord
Anholt
Spentrup
Holbæk
Viborg
Randers
Fjellerup
Kattegatcentret
Bjerringbro
Langå
Assentoft
Auning
Djurs
Hesselø
Hadsten
Hornslet
Grenaa
Fornæs
Trustrup
Aarhus
Ebeltoft
DANMARK
Skanderborg
Odder
Nordby
Samsø
Horsens
Hov
Brundby
Vejle
Juelsminde
Fredericia
Bogense
Kalundborg
Holbæk
KØBENHAVN
Middelfart
Otterup
Odense
Kolding
Søndersø
Svendborg
Nyborg
Korsør
Sjælland
Ringsted
Køge

SVERIGE
Göteborg
GOT
Kållered
Lindome
Kungsbacka
Säro
Rydet
Kinna
Fritsla
Limmared
Gislaved
Halmstad
Helsingborg
Lund
Malmö
Ystad

KØBENHAVN
CPH

Rügen
Stralsund

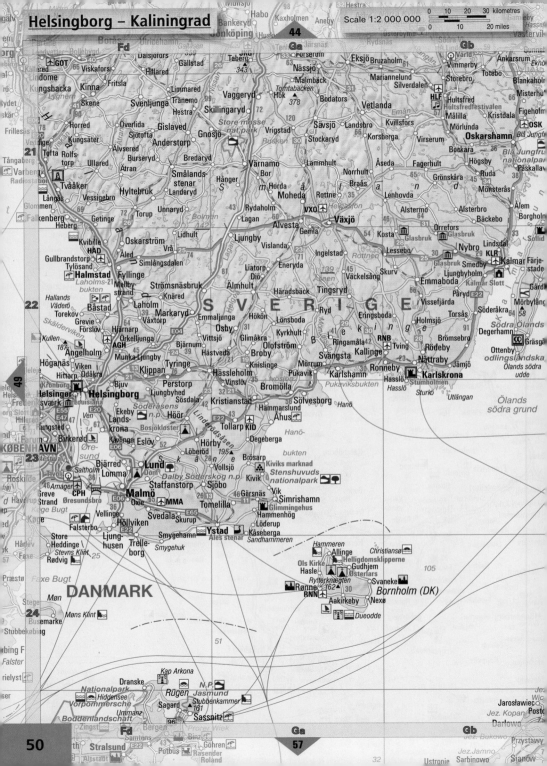

Gc

Kalisz

Wrocław

Opole

Częstochowa

Tarnowskie Góry

Bytom   Zabrze   Gliwice   Bytom

Katowice   Sosnowiec

Kraków

KRK

Rybnik

Ostrava

Olomouc

Bielsko-Biała

Žilina

Brno

Zakopane

Martin   Ružomberok

Banská Bystrica

Zvolen

S L O V E N S K O

29   30   65   31   32

A Coruña – Burgos

Scale 1:2 000 000

0 10 20 30 kilometres
0 10 20 miles

PORTUGAL

Major places: A Coruña / La Coruña, Ferrol, Betanzos, Santiago de Compostela, Lugo, Pontevedra, Vigo, Tui, Ourense / Orense, Ponferrada, Bragança, Braga, Guimarães, Porto, Vila Real, Viseu, Coimbra, Zamora, Salamanca.

78 | 91

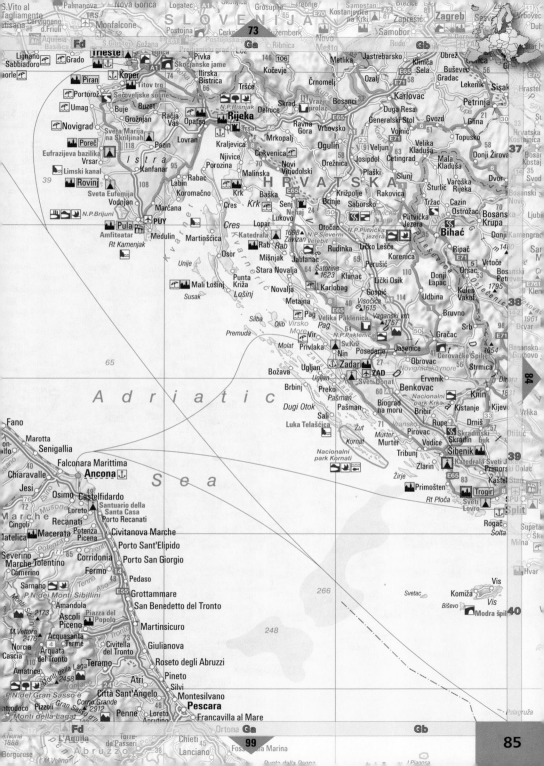

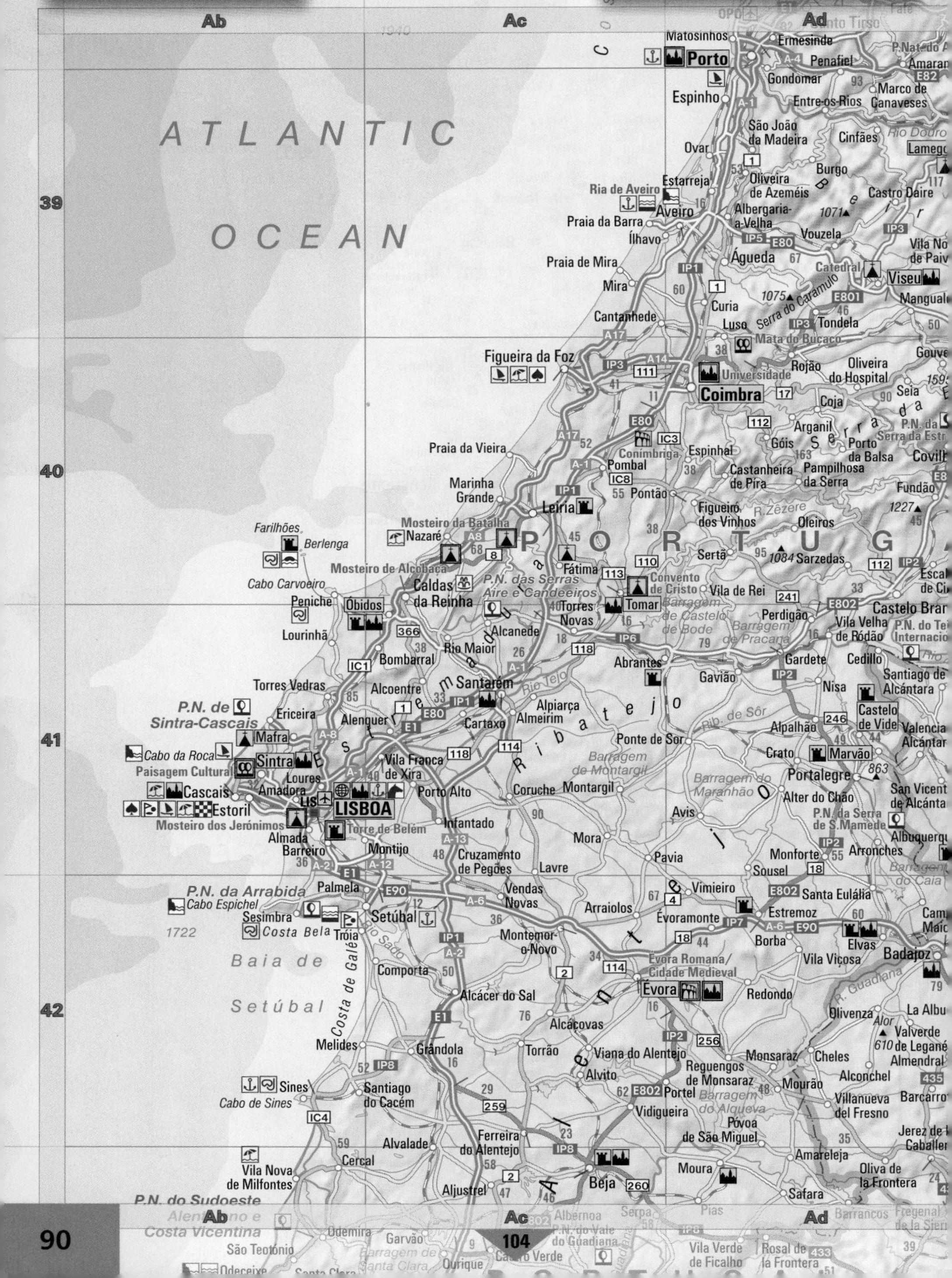
Scale 1:2 000 000
0 10 20 30 kilometres
0 10 20 miles
Ab
Ac
Ad
39
40
41
42
ATLANTIC
OCEAN
PORTUG
Matosinhos
Porto
Ermesinde
Penafiel
Amarante
Gondomar
Marco de Canaveses
Espinho
Entre-os-Rios
São João da Madeira
Cinfães
Rio Douro
Lamego
Ovar
Burgo
Estarreja
Oliveira de Azeméis
Castro Daire
Ria de Aveiro
Aveiro
Albergaria-a-Velha
Praia da Barra
Ílhavo
Vouzela
Vila Nova de Paiva
Praia de Mira
Águeda
Catedral
Viseu
Mira
Serra do Caramulo
Mangualde
Curia
Cantanhede
Luso
Tondela
Mata do Buçaco
Figueira da Foz
Rojão
Oliveira do Hospital
Universidade
Coimbra
Seia
Coja
Arganil
P.N. da Serra da Estrela
Praia da Vieira
Góis
Porto da Balsa
Covilhã
Conimbriga
Espinhal
Pombal
Castanheira de Pêra
Pampilhosa da Serra
Marinha Grande
Pontão
Fundão
Leiria
Figueiró dos Vinhos
R. Zêzere
Oleiros
Farilhões
Mosteiro da Batalha
Berlenga
Nazaré
Sertã
Sarzedas
Fátima
Mosteiro de Alcobaça
P.N. das Serras de Aire e Candeeiros
Convento de Cristo
Cabo Carvoeiro
Caldas da Reinha
Vila de Rei
Peniche
Óbidos
Torres Novas
Tomar
Barragem de Castelo de Bode
Perdigão
Castelo Branco
Barragem de Pracana
Vila Velha de Ródão
P.N. do Tejo Internacional
Lourinhã
Alcanede
Rio Maior
Abrantes
Bombarral
Gardete
Cedillo
Gavião
Santiago de Alcántara
Torres Vedras
Alcoentre
Santarém
Rio Tejo
Nisa
Alpiarça
P.N. de Sintra-Cascais
Ericeira
Alenquer
Almeirim
Castelo de Vide
Cartaxo
Alpalhão
Valencia de Alcántara
Mafra
Ponte de Sor
Cabo da Roca
Vila Franca de Xira
Crato
Marvão
Paisagem Cultural
Sintra
Barragem de Montargil
Portalegre
Loures
Amadora
Cascais
Porto Alto
Coruche
Montargil
Barragem do Maranhão
San Vicente de Alcántara
Estoril
LISBOA
Alter do Chão
Mosteiro dos Jerónimos
Infantado
Avis
P.N. da Serra de S.Mamede
Torre de Belém
Almada
Albuquerque
Barreiro
Montijo
Mora
Arronches
Cruzamento de Pegões
Pavia
Monforte
Lavre
Sousel
P.N. da Arrabida
Palmela
Vendas Novas
Vimieiro
Santa Eulália
Cabo Espichel
Arraiolos
Sesimbra
Setúbal
Évoramonte
Estremoz
Costa Bela
Tróia
Montemor-o-Novo
Borba
Elvas
Badajoz
Baia de Setúbal
Comporta
Évora Romana / Cidade Medieval
Vila Viçosa
Évora
Redondo
Costa de Galé
Alcácer do Sal
Olivenza
La Albuera
Alcáçovas
Valverde de Leganés
Melides
Grândola
Torrão
Viana do Alentejo
Monsaraz
Cheles
Almendral
Reguengos de Monsaraz
Alvito
Alconchel
Sines
Santiago do Cacém
Mourão
Cabo de Sines
Portel
Barragem do Alqueva
Villanueva del Fresno
Barcarrota
Vidigueira
Póvoa de São Miguel
Jerez de los Caballeros
Alvalade
Ferreira do Alentejo
Amareleja
Cercal
Vila Nova de Milfontes
Moura
Oliva de la Frontera
Aljustrel
Beja
Safara
P.N. do Sudoeste Alentejano e Costa Vicentina
Serpa
Pias
Barrancos
Albernoa
P.N. do Vale do Guadiana
Odemira
Garvão
São Teotónio
Barragem de Santa Clara
Ourique
Castro Verde
Vila Verde de Ficalho
Rosal de la Frontera
Ribatejo
Alentejo
Estremadura
Beira

104

Agramunt
Cardona
Prats de
Lluçanès
l'Escala
Torà
Súria
Sallent
Manresa
Navarcles
Montserrat 7236
Igualada
Monistir de
Montserrat
Terrassa
Sabadell
Martorell
Monestir de
Sant Cugat
L'Hospitalet
BCN
BARCELONA
Parc
Güell
Palau Güell
Castell-
defels
Tarragona
Vilanova
i la Geltrú
Sitges
el Vendrell
Vilafranca
del Penedès
Montblanc
Montseny 1706
Hostalric
Granollers
Calella
Matató
Arenys
de Mar
Badalona
Palau de la Música Catalana/
Hospital de Sant Pau
Caldes
de Montbui
Sant Celoni
Circuit de Catalunya
Sant Vicenç
Monistir
Santes Creus

Girona
la Bisbal
d'Empordà
Palafrugell
Palamós
Sant Feliu de Guixols
Lloret de Mar
Blanes
Malgrat de Mar

81
Da
Db
Dc

41

Costa Brava

Costa   Daurada

MEDITERRANEAN   SEA

2475

2132

1125

42

43

**ILLES BALEARS
(ISLAS BALEARES)**

Puig Major
1445
Sóller
Serra de Tramuntana
Valldemossa
Banyalbufar
I. Sa Dragonera
Andratx
La Seu
Santuari
de Lluc
Pollença
Port de
Pollença
Cap de Formentor
Alcúdia
Inca
Muro
Santa Maria
d.C.
Sineu
Artà
Cala Rajada
Pta. de Capdepera
Cala Millor
Coves del Drac
Portocristo
Cala Figuera
Cap de
Calvià
Palma
d.M.
PMI
S'Arenal
Montuïri
Llucmajor
Manacor
Felanitx
Campos
Badia Gran
Balears
Colònia de
Sant Jordi
Santanyí
Cap de
ses Salines
Mallorca
Serra de Llevant
Es Pla
Santuari de Sant Salvador

Menorca
Cap de
Cavalleria
Ciutadella
Es Mercadal
Fornells
Port
d'Addaia
Barranc d'Algendar
Tamarinda
El Toro
350
Maó (Mahón)
Cales Coves
Reserva de
Biosfera Menorca
S'Algar
MAH

78

**Parque Nacional
Terrestre-Marítimo
de Cabrera**
J. de Cabrera

93

281

1813

44

Da
Db
Dc

95

Scale 1:2 000 000

0   10   20   30 kilometres
0   10   20 miles

98
41
42

Toscana

Livorno

FRANCE

Corse (F)

Corse

Bastia

Ajaccio

Bonifacio

MEDITERRANEAN SEA

Olbia

Parco Nazionale dell'Arcipelago Toscano

Parco Nazionale dell'Asinara

ITALIA

Tyrrhenian Sea

Sardegna (I)

Sardegna

Sassari

Alghero

Capo Coda Cavallo
San Teodoro
Siniscola
Orosei
Golfo di Orosei
Capo di Monte Santu
Capo Bellavista
Arbatax
Capo Sterracavallo
Capo Ferrato
Villaputzu
Muravera
Villasimius
Capo Carbonara

Golfo di Cagliari

Capo Comino

Monti
M.Niedda
M.Rasu
Ozieri
Ottana
Nuoro
Bitti
Oliena
Dorgali
Orgosolo
Fonni
Baunei
Tortolì
Lanusei
P.ta Marteora
Sorgono
Tonara
Aritzo
Seui
Jerzu
Escalaplano
San Vito
Dolianova
Sinnai
Selargius
Quartu
Sant'Elena
Cagliari
CAG
Pula
Santa Margherita
Capo Spartivento
Teulada
Costa del Sud
Santadi
Carbonia
Iglesias
Fluminimaggiore
Portoscuso
Carloforte
Isola di San Pietro
Sant'Antioco
Isola di Sant'Antioco
Capo Sperone
Capo Pecora
Arbus
Guspini
San Gavino Monreale
Gonnosfanadiga
Villacidro
Domusnovas
Asseminí
Monastir
Senorbì
Mandas
Su Nuraxi
Laconi
Isili
Barumini
Sanluri
Terralba
Marrubiu
Arborea
Santa Giusta
Oristano
Cabras
San Giovanni di Sinis
Capo San Marco
Golfo di Oristano
Capo di Frasca
Capo Mannu
Santu Maragiu
Bosa
Capo Caccia
Grotta di Nettuno
Alghero
Porto Torres
Stintino
Fertilia
Ittiri
Thiesi
Mores
Ittireddu
Bono
Buddusò
Oschiri
S.Trinità di Saccargia
Sta Maria del Regno
Bonorva
Macomer
Abbasanta
Ghilarza
Santu Lussurgiu
M.Ferru

Tharros
Nuraghe Losa
Nuraghe Sta Cristina
Necropoli Sant'Andria Priu
Nuraghe Sant'Antine
Necropoli Anghelu Ruiu
Necropoli Santu Antine
Grotta di San Michele

Golfo di Orosei
P.N.del Golfo di Orosei e del Gennargentu
Gennargentu

Lago Omodeo
Lago Mulargia
Lago Posada

Museo Archeologico

Capo di Pula
Nora

Scale 1:2 000 000

0 10 20 30 kilometres
0   10   20 miles

88

Ja   Jb   Jc

Ja   Jb   Jc

112

SOFIJA

BĂLGARIJA

Plovdiv

Stara Zagora

Thessaloníki

E L L Á D A

Thássos

Áthos

Límnos

Samothráki

A e g e a n   S e

Thermaikós Kólpos

Pé_lagos

N.P. Pirin

Iztočni Rodo

Anatolikí

Thrakikó

101

102

40

41

42

43

89
Jd
Ka
Kb
BLACK
SEA
70
40
41
42
43
Sliven
Karnobat
Burgas
Pomorie
Sozopol
Djuni
Primorsko
Carevo
Ahtopol
Sinemorec
Rezovo
Beğendik
Malko Tărnovo
Zvezdec
Kondolovo
Jambol
Elhovo
Topolovgrad
Ustrem
Bălgarska Polyana
Radovec
Lalapaşa
Süleoğlu
Kırklareli
Kofças
Karacadağ
İğneada
Demirköy
Yıldız Dağları
1031
Kıyıköy
Edirne
Selimiye Camii
Svilengrad
Kyprinos
Orestiada
Ivajlovgrad
Didymoteicho
Lavara
Soufli
Rodhopi
Kornofolia
Havsa
Babaeski
İnece
Pınarhisar
Vize
Saray
Yalıköy
Karacaköy
Karaburun
Kumköy
Kilyos
Sarıyer
Kemerburgaz
Arnavutköy
Hadımköy
Topkapı Sarayı
Hagia Sophia
Çatalca
Büyükçekmece
IST
Selimpaşa
Gürpınar
İSTANBUL
Kartal
Büyük Ada
Silivri
Çerkezköy
Sinekli
Lüleburgaz
Sokollu Camii
Pehlivanköy
Hayrabolu
Dambaslar
Muratlı
Çorlu
Çatalca Yarımadası
Uzunköprü
Çöpköy
Hamidiye
Karapınar
Küplü
Sahin
Banarlı
Tekirdağ
Barbaros
Marmaraereğlisi
1355
Sea of Marmara
TÜRKIYE
Yalova
Çınarcık
Orhangazi
İpsala
Feres
Karpuzlu
Keşan
Malkara
Işıklar Dağı
924
Marmara Adası
İmralı Ad.
Armutlu
Gemlik Körfezi
Zeytinbağı
Mudanya
Loutros
Enez
Vakıf
Erikli
Mecidiye
İbrice
676
Evreşe
Mürefte
Marmara
Asmalı
Kapıdağı Yarımadası
Gakilköy
Şarköy
Türkeli
İlhanköy
Erdek
İnce Br.
Ortaköy
Saros Körfezi
Bolayır
Gelibolu
Fındıklı
Tayfur
Karabiga
Bozlar
Edincik
Bandırma
Karacabey
Görükle
Yeşil Camii
Çalı
Ulubat Gölü
Gümüşçay
Denizli
Bügdaylı
Kuş Gölü
Lapseki
Balıklıçeşme
Biga
Sarıköy
Kuşcenneti Milli Parkı
Mustafakemalpaşa
Gelibolu Yarımadası M.P.
Beyçayırı
Umurbey
719
Bakacak
Gönen
Şevketiye
Manyas
Susurluk
Çaltılıbük
Devecikonağı
Karatepe
Eceabat
Kilitbahir
Çimenlik
Çanakkale
Gökçeada
Biga Yarımadası
969
Can
Abide
Etili
877
İntepe
Salihler
Sakar Dağı
Pazarköy
Ilıca
Şamlı
1314
Kepsut
Durak
Kavacık
1391
Dursunbey
Kumkale
Truva
Hamdibey
Kaz Dağı Milli Parkı
Balya
Balıkesir
Yildirim Camii
BZI
Bozcaada
Bozcaada Kalesi
Geyikli
Ezine
Bayramiç
Evciler
1774
Kaz Dağı
Edremit
Ertuğrul
İvrindi
Çağış
Kireç
Alaçam Dağları
Gökçedağ
Uluköy
Ayvacık
672
Küçükkuyu
Zeytinli
Havran
Burhaniye
Korucu
Kayapa
Konakpınar
Savaştepe
Bademli
Bigadiç
1769
Düvertepe
Akdağ
Tavakli İsk.
Gülpınar
Behramkale
Assos
Edremit Körfezi
Gömeç
Karadere
1344
Gölcük
Sındırgı
Çaygören Brj.
Yeniköy
Gelenbe
Soma
Demirci
Kozak
Ayvalık
Mithimna
Mantamados
Petra
Antissa
Arisba
Sigri
Thermi
Mytilini
Altınova
Nebiler
Bergama
113
Poyracık
Kınık
Kırkağaç
Dağdere
E87
E80
E84
E90
E773
E85

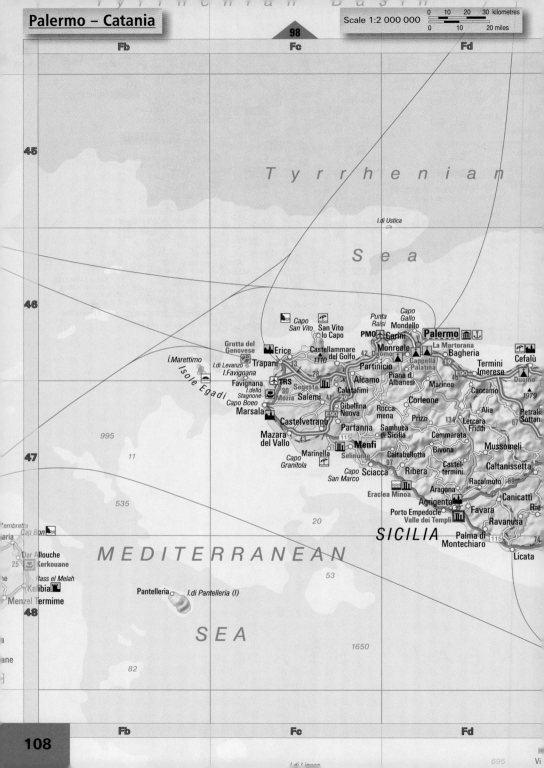

Scale 1:2 000 000

0　10　20　30 kilometres
0　　10　　20 miles

Fb　　　　Fc　　　　Fd

45

T y r r h e n i a n

I.di Ustica

S e a

46

Capo
San Vito

San Vito
lo Capo

Punta
Raisi

Capo
Gallo
Mondello

PMO

Carini

Palermo

Grotta del
Genovese

Erice

Castellammare
del Golfo

Monreale
Duomo

La Martorana

Bagheria

Cefalù

I.Marettimo

I.di Levanzo
I.Favignana

Trapani

42

1110

Partinicio

Cappella
Palatina

19

Termini
Imerese

Duomo

Isole Egadi

Favignana
I.dello
Stagnone
Capo Boeo

TRS

3

Segesta

28

Alcamo

Piana d'
Albanesi

Marineo

Caccamo

1979

Alia

Petralia
Sottan

Mozia

30

Salemi

41

Calatafimi

Rocca
mena

Corleone

Prizzi

134

Lercara
Friddi

67

Marsala

Castelvetrano

E90

Gibellina
Nuova

Sambuca
di Sicilia

Cammarata

Mussomeli

Mazara
del Vallo

115

43

Partanna

97

Menfi

Bivona

Castel
termini

Caltanissetta

Marinella

Selinunte

Caltabellotta

Racalmuto

69

Capo
Granitola

Sciacca

Ribera

Aragona

Canicatti

Rie

Capo
San Marco

Eraclea Minoa

Agrigento

Favara

995

11

Porto Empedocle
Valle dei Templi

Ravanusa

535

20

47

S I C I L I A

115

74

Palma di
Montechiaro

Licata

embretta
aria

Cap Bon

M E D I T E R R A N E A N

Dar Allouche
Kerkouane

25

Rass el Melah

53

Kelibia

Menzel Termime

48

a

ane

Pantelleria

I.di Pantelleria (I)

S E A

1650

82

I.di Linosa

695　Vi

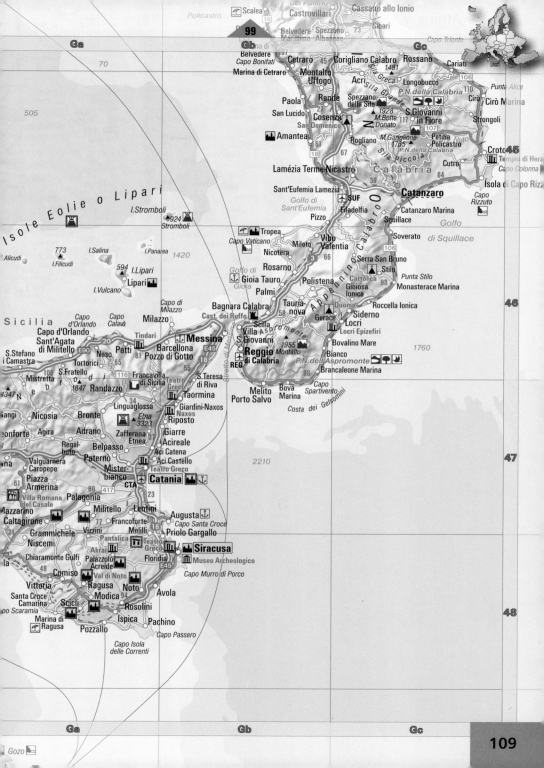

Policastro

Scalea

Castrovillari   Cassano allo Ionio

Belvedere   Spezzano   Sibari
Marittimo   Albanese

Capo Trionto

Belvedere
Capo Bonifati   Cetraro   Corigliano Calabro   Rossano   Cariati

Marina di Cetraro   Montalto
     Uffogo   1481   Longobucco

Paola   Acri   P.N.della Calabria

Rende   Spezzano   Cirò
         della Sila   Cirò Marina

San Lucido   Cosenza   1928   S.Giovanni
         San Domenico   M.Botte   in Fiore
              Donato   Strongoli

Amantea   Rogliano   M.Gariglione   Petilia
               1765   Policastro   Crotone
            P.N.della Calabria   Tempio di Hera

Lamézia Terme-Nicastro   Cutro   Capo Colonna
         Calàbria

Sant'Eufemia Lamezia   Ìsola di Capo Rizzuto
     Golfo di   SUF   Catanzaro   Capo
    Sant'Eufemia   Filadelfia   Catanzaro Marina   Rizzuto
        Pizzo   Squillace

      Tropea   Soverato   Golfo
Capo Vaticano   Vibo   di Squillace
    Nicotera   Mileto   Valentia

     Rosarno   Serra San Bruno
     Gioia Tauro   Stilo   Punta Stilo
Golfo di   Polistena   Cattòlica   Monasterace Marina
   Gioia   Palmi   Gioiosa   Ionica

   Bagnara Calabra   Tauria-   Roccella Ionica
    Cast. dei Ruffo   nova   Duomo
         Scilla   Gerace   Siderno
      Villa   S.Giovanni   Locri
     S.Giovanni   1955   Locri Epizefiri
     Reggio   Montalto   Bovalino Mare
   REG   di Calabria   Bianco
         P.N.dell'Aspromonte
      Melito   Bova   Brancaleone Marina
    Porto Salvo   Marina
         Capo
         Spartivento
       Costa dei   Gelsomini

Isole Eolie o Lipari

I.Stromboli   924   Stromboli

773   I.Salina   1420
I.Alicudi   I.Panarea
   I.Filicudi   594   I.Lipari
        Lipari
     I.Vulcano

Sicilia   Capo   Capo Calavà
     d'Orlando   Milazzo   Capo di
  Capo d'Orlando   Tindari   Milazzo
Sant'Agata   Patti   Messina
di Militello   Neso   Barcellona
S.Stefano   Tortorici   Pozzo di Gotto
i Camastra   S.Fratello   Francavilla   S.Teresa
  Mistretta   di Sicilia   di Riva
    1347   Randazzo   Taormina   Teatro Greco
     Nicosia   Bronte   Linguaglossa   Giardini-Naxos
        Adrano   Etna   Naxos
  Agira   Zafferana   Riposto
  Regal-   Belpasso   Etnea   Giarre
   buto   Paternò   Aci Catena
Valguarnera   Acireale
Caropepe   Mister-   Aci Castello
Piazza   bianco   Teatro Greco
Armerina   CTA   Catania
Villa Romana   Palagonia
del Casale   Militello   Lentini
Mazzarino   Caltagirone   Augusta
        Grammichele   Vizzini   Francoforte   Capo Santa Croce
   Niscemi   Melilli   Priolo Gargallo
       Pantalica
Chiaramonte Gulfi   Akrai   Teatro   Siracusa
    Palazzolo   Greco
Vittoria   Acreide   Floridia   Museo Archeologico
Comiso   Val di Noto   Capo Murro di Porco
Santa Croce   Ragusa   Noto
Camarina   Modica   Avola
  Scicli
Marina di   Rosolini
Ragusa   Ispica   Pachino
   Pozzallo   Capo Passero

Capo Isola
delle Correnti

Gozo

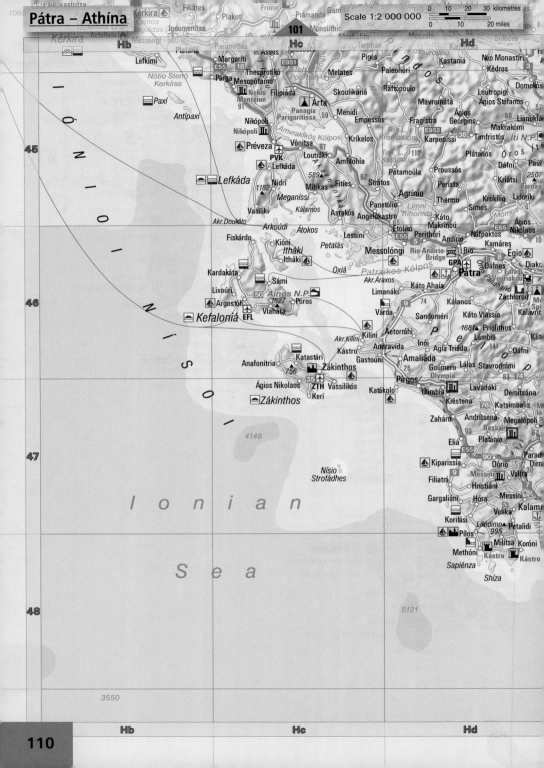

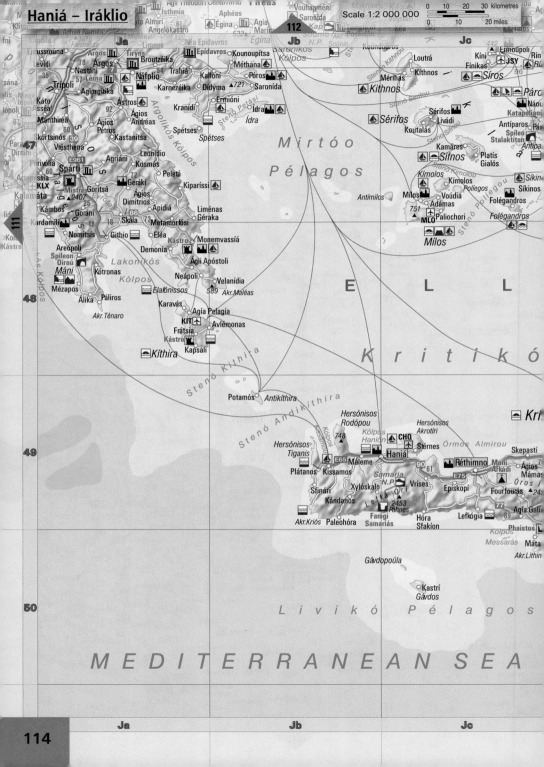

Charkiv – Volgograd

Scale 1:4 000 000

0 20 40 60 kilometres
0 20 40 miles

Ed

Fa

Fb

Juhnov Leninskij Gorelki Tula Novomoskovs Pica
Kimovs

Suhiniči Sosnenskij Plavsk Tovarkovskij Čaplygin 64 M6 Tatanov
Kirov Kozel'sk Teploe Dankov Kočetovka Tambov
Belev Starica Čern Silovo Lebedjan Dmitrievka Mičurinsk
Ljudinovo M3 216 Čern 163 Efremov Krasnoe Trubetčina Petrovskoe Volčki 214 Kotovsk
Djat'kovo Bolhov Mcensk Lipicy- Kuleši M4 Lipeck 136
ukova Fokino Zybino Stanovoe 96 Grjazi
han' Brjansk Karačev Orel Naryškino Zalegošč Ekaterinovka Zadonsk Borinskoe Dobrinka Mordovo
Kletnja BZK 128 Kromy Droskovo Livny Bol.Poljana Usman' Bol. Ertil' A144
Vygoniči Maloarhangel'sk Evlanovo Privalovka Anna 224
žel'kovo Navlja E101 Turiščevo Trosna Kolpny Terbuny Voronež Perelešinskij A38
Poček Lokot' Fatež Semiluki Rogačevka Talova
Unča Trubčevsk Železnogorsk E381 160 Ščigry Kšenskij Gremjač'e 157 Bobrov
rodhi 266 Pogar E105 Dmitriev- Besedino Tim Staryj Oskol Sinie Lipjagi 100 Buturlino
Elionka M3 L'govskij M2 182 Puzači Os'kino Liski M4
Desnjano Homutovka Kursk Gubkin Rep'evka Pešcanyj monastyr
Novhorod- Starogutskyj N.P. Drožba Prjamicyno Solncevo Volotovo Ostrogožsk Kamenka 100 Pavlovsk
Sivers'kyj M02 L'gov Medvenka 189 Skorodnoe Černjanka Alekseevka Podgorenskij
Šostka 422 Ryl'sk Obojan 137 Novyi Oskol Rossoš'
Avdijivka Hluchiv Salyhyne Korenevo 149 Koroča Ol'hovatka
Krolevec' Putyvl' Sudža Jakovlevo Zajač'e Volokonovka 70
Korop Vorožba Bilopillja Krasnaja Tomarovka EGO Vejdelevka 187 Mitrofanovka 117
Konotop Žovtneve Jaruga Belgorod Sebekino Valujki Roven'ki Kantemirovka
Bachmač Sumy Krasnopillja Borisovka 82 Vovčans'k Velykyj Pokrovs'ke Novopskov Markivka
Dmytrivka Nedryhajliv Stepivka Grajvoron 81 Lypci Burluk Bilokurakyne Starobil's'k
Nižyn Romny Lebedyn Velyka E105 Vasyl'eve 124
čnja 331 Trostjanec' Pysarivka Derhači Kup'jans'k Svatove
Sribne Ochtyrka Bohoduchiv CHARKIV Kup'jans'k- Sjeverodonec'k
Pryluky PO1 Varva Zin'kiv Krasnokuts'k HRK Cuhujiv Vuzlovyj Borova Lysyčans'k
jatyn Lypova 176 Vil'šany Merefa Sevčenkovo Kun'je Slov'jans'k Luhansk
Čornuchy Dolyna Kotel'va Vasyščeve M03 Izjum Stachanov
Hrebinka Lochvycja Opišnja M03 Zmijiv Lyman Balaklija Svjati Hory Lutuhy
Drabiv Lubny Romodan Myrhorod Dykan'ka Nova N.P. Zolote Alčevs'k
Oržycja Podil Poltava Krulila Vodolaha Pervomajs'kyj 135 E40 Debal'ceve Antra
Zolotonoša Chorol PLV hlosca M26 Krasnohrad Hrušuvacha Barvinkove Kramators'k Brjanka M03
Irklijiv Obolon Rešetylivka Karlivka 194 Krasnopavlivka Lozova Kostjantynivka Horlivka Krasnyj Ł
Čerkasy Hlobyne Oril' E105 Šandrivka Dobropillja Oleksandrivka Makijivka
Smila Svitlovods'k 115 Pereščepyne Jur'jivka Krasnoarmijs'k Jasynuvata 85 Jenakijeve
Čyhyryn Pavlyš PO17 Kobeljaky Mahdalynivka Hubynycha M04 Krasnohorivka DOK DONEC'K
am'janka Oleksandrivka Novomoskovs'k Petropavlivka E50 Havrylivka Dokučajevs'k
Novomyrhorod M04 Verchn'odniprovs'k DNK Pavlohrad 225 Krasnohorivka Tel'manove Novoazovs'k
Kirovohrad E577 Dnipro- M26 Synel'nykove Vasyl'kivka Vel.Novosilka E58
Znam'janka dzeržyns'k Solone Novomy Pokrovs'ke Ljubymivka P19
Kirovohrad M12 43 Pjatychatky DNIPRO- kolajivka Huljajpole Rozivka MPW Mariupol'
Novohrodka Žovti Vody PETROVS'K Novopokrovka 97 103 Polohy Kamjani Taganrog
Rivne Dolyns'ka 138 OZH Zaporižžja Orichiv Mohyly Berdjans'k
Kryvyj Rih KWG Ordžonikidze Chortycja Tomakivka vodoschovyšče Tokmak Petrivs'ka Dolžans'k
Apostolove Syroke Nikopol Enerhodar Myhajlivka fortec'a

Scale 1:4 000 000

| 0 | 20 | 40 | 60 kilometres |
| 0 | 20 | | 40 miles |

Ed
Fa
Fb

122

DNIPRO-PETROVS'K

Verchn'odniprovs'k
dzerzyns'k
Synel'nykovo
Vil'nohirs'k
Oleksandrija
Pjatychatky
Solone
Novomyrhorod
Novopokrovka
Vil'njans'k
Ljubymivka
Volnovacha
Tel'manove
Kirovohrad
Žovti Vody
Sofijivka
Zaporižžja
Huljajpole
Fedorivka
Novohorodka
Novopokrovka
Chortycja
Polohy
Novoazov
Rivne
Dolyns'ka
Tomakivka
Orichiv
Rozivka
Kryvyj Rih
KWG
Ordžonikidze
Marhanec'
Vasylivka
Kamjani Mohyly
MPW
Mariupol'
Bobrynec'
Kazanka
Apostolove
Nikopol'
Dniprorudne
Očeretuvate
Andrijivka
Osypenko
Petrivs'ka fortec'a
Ejs
Šyroke
Enerhodar
Tokmak
Zelenivka
Dolžansk
Užnoukrajins'k
Novyj Buh
Zelenodol's'k
Mychajlivka
Prymors'k
Berdjans'k
Jelanec'
Baštanka
Velyka Lepetycha
Vesela
Melitopol'
Berdjans'ka kosa
Voznesens'k
Nova Odesa
Bereznehuvate
Nyžni Torhaji
Pryazovs'ke
Azovo-Syvas'kyj N.P.
Veselynove
Snihurivka
Beryslav
Sirohozy
Obytična kosa
Berezanka
Mykolajiv
Kachovka
Ivanivka
NLV
Cherson
Nova Kachovka
Azovskoe More
Kominternivs'ke
Oleksandrivka
Cjurupyns'k
Novotrojic'ke
Heničes'k
Očakiv
Hola Prystan
Čaplynka
Novooleksijivka
Panticapaeum
Temrju
Sverdlove
Novomykolajivka
Kalančak
Kerč
Starotitarovskaja
ODESA
Novofedorivka
Skadovs'k
Armjans'k
Lenine
Anapa
ličivs'k
Krasnoperekops'k
Vojinka
Nyžn'ohirs'kyj
Zavitne
Rozdol'ne
Džankoj
Kirovs'ke
Čornomors'ke
Novoselivs'ke
Krasnohvardijs'ke
Feodosija
Olenivka
Džuma-Džami
Krymskij pivostriv
Bilohors'k
Koktebel'
Jevpatorija
Saky
Petrovskije Skaly
Sudak
Mykolajivka
Simferopol'
SIP
Chufut Kale
Alušta
Chansky Palac
Trolleybus
Bachčysaraj
Mankup Kale
Hurzuf
Sevastopol'
Alupka
Jalta
Chersonesus
Livadia Palac

B L A C K
2200
2243
2180

Nationál Dunării

İnce Burun
Sinop Burun
Sinop
Bafra Bu İkizte
Keremepe Burnu
İnebolu
Ayancık
Kabalı
Alacam
Cide
Ağlı
K ü r e
D a ğ l a r ı
Durağan
Yaralıgöz Dağı
Taşköprü
Boyabat
Vezirköprü
Seydiler
Bartın
Kastamonu
Merzifon

Ed
Fa
Fb

Zonguldak
Kozlu
Safranbolu
Tosya
Osmancik

The index explained

All of the places named on the maps in the atlas are listed in the atlas index. The place names are listed alpabetically. Special symbols and letters including accents and umlauts are ignored in the order of the index. For example, the letters Á, Ä, Â are all categorized under A, and Ž, Ż, ź are all treated as the standard Latin letter Z. Written characters consisting of two letters joined together (ligatures) are treated as two separate characters in the index: for example, words beginning with the character Æ would be indexed under A E.

The grid references for towns and cities identify the location of the place name on the map. The place names are followed by international vehicle registration codes and the page numbers of relevant maps as well as a number-letter combination indicating the area's location in the map. Letters indicate the east-west position and numbers the north-south position of an area.

International vehicle registration codes of Europe

AL	Albania	LV	Latvia
GBA	Alderney	FL	Liechtenstein
AND	Andorra	LT	Lithuania
A	Austria	L	Luxembourg
BY	Belarus'	MK	Macedonia
BY	Belgium	M	Malta
BIH	Bosnia and Herzegovina	MD	Moldova
BG	Bulgaria	MC	Monaco
HR	Croatia	MNE	Montenegro
CY	Cyprus	NL	Netherlands
CZ	Czech Republic	N	Norway
DK	Denmark	PL	Poland
EST	Estonia	P	Portugal
FIN	Finland	RO	Romania
F	France	RUS	Russia
D	Germany	RSM	San Marino
GBZ	Gibraltar	SRB	Serbia
GR	Greece	SK	Slovakia
GBG	Guernsey	SLO	Slovenia
H	Hungary	E	Spain
IS	Iceland	S	Sweden
IRL	Ireland	CH	Switzerland
GBM	Isle of Man	TR	Turkey
I	Italy	UA	Ukraine
GBJ	Jersey	GB	United Kingdom
RKS	Kosovo	V	Vatican City

A

Å N 32 Fc12
Aabenraa DK 48 Fa24
Aabybro DK 49 Fb21
Aachen D 63 Ec29
Aakirkeby DK 50 Ga24
Aalborg DK 49 Fb21
Aalen D 64 Fa32
Aalestrup DK 49 Fb22
Aalst B 62 Ea29
Aalter B 54 Ea28
Äänekoski FIN 40 Hc13
Aapua S 30 Ha08
Aarau CH 71 Ed34
Aareavaara S 30 Ha07
Aarhus DK 49 Fb22
Aars DK 49 Fb21
Aarschot B 63 Eb29
Aarup DK 49 Fb23
Aavasaksa FIN 34 Hb09
Abanilla E 107 Ca44
Abano Terme I 84 Fc37
Abarán E 107 Ca44
Abbadia San Salvatore I 84
  Fb40
Abbasanta I 97 Ec43
Abbeville F 62 Dc30
Abbeyfeale IRL 18 Bd24
Abbeyleix IRL 18 Ca24
Abbiategrasso I 83 Ed37
Abborrträsk S 34 Gd10
Abbotsbury GB 24 Cd28
Abejar E 79 Ca39
Abelvær N 32 Fc11
Abenójar E 106 Bc43
Abensberg D 64 Fc32
Aberaeron GB 23 Cc26
Aberdeen GB 17 Db20
Aberfeldy GB 17 Da20
Abergavenny GB 24 Cd26
Abergele GB 20 Cd24
Abersoch GB 23 Cc25
Aberystwyth GB 23 Cc25
Abetone I 84 Fb38
Abganerovo RUS 123 Fd14
Abide TR 103 Jd43
Abingdon GB 24 Da27
Abington GB 21 Da22
Abisko S 29 Gc06
Abjarovščyna BY 59 Hc27
Åbo FIN 40 Hb16
Abony H 74 Ha34
Aboyne GB 17 Db20
Abrantes P 90 Ac41
Abraur S 33 Gc09
Abrene RUS 47 Jb20
Abrud RO 75 Hd35
Åby S 44 Ga20
Åby S 44 Gb19
Åbyggeby S 39 Gc16
Åbyn S 34 Ha10
Åbytorp S 44 Ga18
A Cañiza E 78 Ad37
Acceglio I 83 Eb38

Acerenza I 99 Gb43
Achim D 56 Fa26
Achnasheen GB 17 Da19
Aci Castello I 109 Ga47
Aci Catena I 109 Ga47
Acireale I 109 Gb47
Acle GB 25 Dd26
A Coruña E 78 Ba36
Acqua Doria F 96 Ed41
Acquapendente I 84 Fb40
Acquasanta Terme I 85
  Fd40
Acquaviva delle Fonti I 99
  Gc43
Acqui Terme I 83 Ed37
Acri I 109 Gc45
Acsa H 74 Ha33
Ada SRB 75 Hb36
Adak S 33 Gc10
Ådalsbruk N 37 Fc16
Adámas GR 111 Jc47
Adamclisi RO 89 Ka37
Adamova BY 53 Jb22
Adamsfjord N 27 Hb03
Adamuz E 105 Bb44
Adare IRL 18 Bd24
Ademuz E 93 Cb42
Adenau D 63 Ec30
Adjud RO 77 Jd35
Adliswil CH 71 Ed34
Admjany BY 53 Ja24
Admont A 73 Ga34
Adolfsström S 33 Gb09
Adony H 74 Ha34
Adorf D 64 Fc30
Adra E 106 Bc46
Adrall E 81 Da40
Adrano I 109 Ga47
Adria I 84 Fc37
Adunații-Copăceni RO 88
  Jc37
Adutiškis LT 53 Ja23
Aegviidu EST 47 Hd18
A Estrada E 78 Ad37
Aetorráhi GR 110 Hd46
Äetsä FIN 40 Hb15
Afándou GR 115 Kc47
Åfarnes N 36 Fa14
Afétes GR 101 Ja44
Afumați RO 88 Jc37
Agápi GR 112 Jc46
Agapia RO 76 Jc34
Agde F 81 Dc39
Agen F 81 Da37
Agerbæk DK 48 Fa23
Agger DK 48 Fa21
Aggtelek H 75 Hb33
Aghireşu RO 75 Hd34
Agiá GR 101 Ja44
Agia Eirini CY 128 Gb18
Agía Galíni GR 114 Jc49
Agía Marína GR 112 Jb46
Agía Marína GR 112 Jb46
Agía Pelagía GR 111 Ja48
Agía Triáda GR 110 Hd46
Agía Varvára GR 115 Jd49

Agighiol RO 89 Ka36
Ágii Apóstoli GR 111 Ja48
Ágii Theódori GR 111 Ja46
Aginta RO 76 Ja35
Agiókambos GR 101 Ja44
Agiokambos GR 111 Ja45
Agiorgítika GR 111 Ja47
Ágios Andréas GR 111 Ja47
Agios Charalampos GR 102
  Jc42
Ágios Dimítrios GR 101
  Hd43
Ágios Dimítrios GR 111
  Ja47
Ágios Efstrátios GR 113
  Jc44
Ágios Geórgios GR 110
  Hd45
Ágios Kírikos GR 113 Jd46
Ágios Mámas GR 114 Jc49
Ágios Nikólaos GR 110
  Hc47
Ágios Nikólaos GR 110
  Hd46
Ágios Nikólaos GR 115 Jd49
Ágios Pétros GR 111 Ja47
Ágios Stéfanos GR 110
  Hd45
Agios Theódori GR 101
  Hc44
Agios Theodoros CY 128
  Gc18
Agira I 109 Ga47
Äglen BG 88 Jb39
Aglona LV 53 Ja22
Agnantiá GR 101 Hc44
Agnone I 99 Ga41
Ágordo I 72 Fc36
Agramunt E 81 Da40
Ágreda E 80 Cb39
Agreliá GR 101 Hd44
Agriáni GR 111 Ja47
Agrigento I 108 Fd47
Agrínio GR 110 Hd45
Agriovótano GR 111 Ja45
Agropoli I 99 Ga43
Ågskardet N 28 Ga08
A Guarda E 78 Ad37
A Gudiña E 78 Ba38
Agudo E 91 Bb42
Águeda P 78 Ad39
Aguilar E 105 Bb44
Aguilar de Campóo E 79
  Bd38
Águilas E 107 Ca45
Ahaus D 55 Ec28
Åheim N 36 Ed14
Ahırlı TR 128 Ga16
Ahladiá GR 102 Jb41
Ahladohóri GR 101 Ja42
Ahlainen FIN 40 Ha15
Ahlbeck D 57 Ga25
Ahlen D 55 Ed28
Ahmalahti RUS 27 Hd04
Ahmetli TR 113 Kb45
Ahmovaara FIN 35 Ja12

Ahrensbök D 56 Fb25
Ahrensburg D 56 Fb26
Ähtäri FIN 40 Hb14
Ahtme EST 47 Ja17
Ahtopol BG 103 Ka40
Ahtropovo RUS 118 Fb08
Ahtubinsk RUS 123 Ga14
Ahun F 69 Db35
Åhus S 50 Ga23
Ahvenselkä FIN 31 Hd07
Aibar E 80 Cc39
Aichach D 72 Fb33
Aigen A 65 Fd32
Aigen A 73 Ga34
Aigiáli GR 115 Jd47
Aigialousa CY 128 Gc18
Aigle CH 71 Ec35
Aignay-le-Duc F 70 Ea33
Aigre F 69 Da35
Aigrefeuille-d'Aunis F 68
  Cd34
Aiguebelle F 71 Eb36
Aigues-Mortes F 82 Dd38
Aiguilles F 83 Eb37
Aiguillon F 81 Da37
Aigurande F 69 Db34
Ailefroide F 83 Eb37
Ailly-sur-Noye F 62 Dc30
Ainaži LV 46 Hc20
Ainhoa F 80 Cc38
Ainsa E 80 Cd39
Airaines F 62 Dc30
Airasca I 83 Ec37
Aire-sur-l'Adour F 80 Cd37
Aire-sur-la-Lys F 62 Dd29
Airolo CH 71 Ed35
Airvault F 69 Da33
Aiud RO 76 Ja35
Aix-en-Othe F 62 Dd32
Aix-en-Provence F 82 Ea39
Aixe-sur-Vienne F 69 Db35
Aix-les-Bains F 71 Eb36
Aizenay F 68 Cd33
Aizkräukle LV 53 Hd21
Aizpute LV 52 Hb21
Ajaccio F 96 Ed41
Ajaureforsen S 33 Gb10
Ajka H 74 Gc35
Ajtos BG 89 Jd39
Äkäsjokisuu FIN 30 Ha07
Äkäslompolo FIN 30 Hb07
Akçaabat TR 127 Fd19
Akçaova TR 113 Kb46
Akçaşehir TR 128 Gc16
Akcjabrski BY 121 Eb13
Aken D 56 Fc28
Åkernes N 42 Fa19
Åkersberga S 45 Gc18
Åkersjön S 33 Ga12
Akhisar TR 113 Kb44
Akkerfjord N 26 Ha03
Akköy TR 113 Ka46
Akniste LV 53 Ja22
Akolica BY 53 Jb24
Akören TR 128 Ga15
Akova TR 128 Gb17

Åkran **N** 32 Fd12
Akranes **IS** 14 Bc06
Åkrestrømmen **N** 37 Fc15
Akrotiri **CY** 128 Gb19
Akrotíri **GR** 115 Jd48
Aksaj **RUS** 123 Fc15
Akşar **TR** 127 Ga19
Aksdal **N** 42 Ed18
Aksubaevo **RUS** 119 Ga09
Aktarsk **RUS** 123 Fd12
Akureyri **IS** 15 Ca06
Akyaka **TR** 128 Gb17
Ål **N** 37 Fb16
Ala **S** 39 Gc16
Alaçam **TR** 126 Fb19
Alacami **TR** 128 Ga17
Alacant (Alicante) **E** 107 Cb44
Alaçatı **TR** 113 Jd45
Aladağ **TR** 128 Gb16
Alaejos **E** 79 Bc39
Alagna Valesia **I** 71 Ec36
Alagón **E** 80 Cc40
Alahärmä **FIN** 40 Hb13
Alajärvi **FIN** 40 Hb13
Alakurtti **RUS** 31 Ja07
Alakylä **FIN** 30 Hb07
Alakylä **FIN** 35 Hc10
Alanäs **S** 33 Gb12
Älandsbro **S** 39 Gc14
Alange **E** 91 Ba42
Alanis **E** 105 Ba43
Alanta **LT** 53 Hd23
Alanya **TR** 128 Ga17
Alaraz **E** 91 Bc40
Alarcón **E** 92 Ca42
Alaşehir **TR** 113 Kb45
Ålåsen **S** 33 Ga12
Alassa **CY** 128 Gb19
Alassio **I** 83 Ec38
Alastaro **FIN** 40 Hb16
Alatri **I** 98 Fd42
Alatyr' **RUS** 119 Fd09
Alaveteli **FIN** 34 Hb12
Alavieska **FIN** 34 Hb11
Alavus **FIN** 40 Hb14
Alba **I** 83 Ec37
Albac **RO** 75 Hd35
Albacete **E** 92 Ca43
Alba de Tormes **E** 91 Bb40
Ålbæk **DK** 43 Fb20
Albaida **E** 107 Cb44
Alba Iulia **RO** 76 Ja35
Albalate del Arzobispo **E** 93 Cc41
Albalate de Zorita **E** 92 Ca41
Alban **F** 81 Db38
Albano Laziale **I** 98 Fc42
Albanyà **E** 81 Db40
Albarracín **E** 93 Cb41
Albena **BG** 89 Ka38
Albenga **I** 83 Ec38
Albentosa **E** 93 Cb42
Albergaria-a-Velha **P** 78 Ad39

Albernoa **P** 104 Ac43
Alberobello **I** 99 Gc43
Albersdorf **D** 56 Fa25
Albert **F** 62 Dd30
Albertville **F** 71 Eb36
Albești **RO** 77 Jd34
Albești **RO** 89 Ka38
Albi **F** 81 Db38
Albocàsser **E** 93 Cc42
Alborea **E** 93 Cb43
Albox **E** 106 Bd45
Albstadt **D** 71 Ed33
Albufeira **P** 104 Ac44
Albuñol **E** 106 Bc45
Albuquerque **E** 90 Ad41
Alcácer do Sal **P** 90 Ac42
Alcáçovas **P** 90 Ac42
Alcalá de Guadaira **E** 105 Ba44
Alcalá de Henares **E** 92 Bd41
Alcalá del Júcar **E** 93 Cb43
Alcalá de los Gazules **E** 105 Ba45
Alcalá del Río **E** 105 Ba44
Alcalà de Xivert **E** 93 Cc42
Alcalá la Real **E** 106 Bc44
Alcamo **I** 108 Fc46
Alcanar **E** 93 Cd42
Alcanede **P** 90 Ac41
Alcañices **E** 78 Bb38
Alcañiz **E** 93 Cc41
Alcántara **E** 91 Ba41
Alcantarilla **E** 107 Cb45
Alcaracejos **E** 105 Bb43
Alcarràs **E** 80 Cd40
Alcaudete **E** 106 Bc44
Alcaudete de la Jara **E** 91 Bc41
Alcázar de San Juan **E** 92 Bd42
Alcester **GB** 24 Da26
Alčevs'k **UA** 122 Fb15
Alcoba de los Montes **E** 91 Bc42
Alcoentre **P** 90 Ac41
Alcoi (Alcoy) **E** 107 Cb44
Alcolea del Pinar **E** 92 Ca40
Alconchel **E** 90 Ad42
Alcorisa **E** 93 Cc41
Alcoutim **P** 104 Ac43
Alcublas **E** 93 Cc42
Alcúdia **E** 95 Db43
Aldeadávila de la Ribera **E** 78 Bb39
Aldea del Rey **E** 92 Bc43
Aldeburgh **GB** 25 Dc27
Aldenueva del Codonal **E** 91 Bc40
Aldershot **GB** 24 Da28
Åled **S** 49 Fd22
Alëhovščina **RUS** 117 Eb08
Aleksandro Gaj **RUS** 123 Ga12
Aleksandrov **RUS** 118 Fa10
Aleksandrovac **SRB** 87 Hc38

Aleksandrovac **SRB** 87 Hc39
Aleksandrovskoe **RUS** 127 Ga16
Aleksandrów Kujawski **PL** 58 Gd27
Aleksandrów Łódzki **PL** 58 Ha28
Alekseevka **RUS** 122 Fb13
Alekseevka **RUS** 123 Fc12
Alekseevskaja **RUS** 123 Fc13
Alekseevskoe **RUS** 119 Ga09
Aleksin **RUS** 117 Ed11
Aleksinac **SRB** 87 Hc39
Alekšycy **BY** 59 Hd26
Ålem **S** 50 Gb21
Alemdar **TR** 128 Gb15
Ålen **N** 37 Fc13
Alençon **F** 61 Da31
Alenquer **P** 90 Ac41
Alès **F** 82 Dd38
Aleşd **RO** 75 Hc34
Alessandria **I** 83 Ed37
Ålesund **N** 36 Ed14
Alexándria **GR** 101 Hd43
Alexandria **RO** 88 Jb38
Alexandroupoli **GR** 102 Jc42
Alfaro **E** 80 Cb39
Alfarràs **E** 80 Cd40
Alfatar **BG** 89 Jd38
Alfeld **D** 56 Fb28
Alfonsine **I** 84 Fc38
Alford **GB** 17 Db19
Alford **GB** 25 Dc25
Alfta **S** 38 Gb16
Ålgård **N** 42 Ed19
Algeciras **E** 105 Ba46
Alghero **I** 97 Ec43
Algodonales **E** 105 Ba45
Alhama de Aragón **E** 80 Cb40
Alhama de Granada **E** 106 Bc45
Alhama de Murcia **E** 107 Ca45
Alhambra **E** 92 Bd43
Alhaurín el Grande **E** 105 Bb45
Alia **I** 108 Fd47
Aliaga **E** 93 Cc41
Aliağa **TR** 113 Ka44
Alíartos **GR** 111 Ja45
Alıbeyhüyüğü **TR** 128 Gb15
Alibunar **SRB** 87 Hb37
Alicante **E** 107 Cb44
Álika **GR** 111 Ja48
Alikí **GR** 102 Jb42
Alíko **GR** 115 Jd47
Alingsås **S** 43 Fd20
Aliseda **E** 91 Ba41
Alivéri **GR** 112 Jb45
Aljezur **P** 104 Ab43
Aljustrel **P** 104 Ac43

Alkmaar **NL** 55 Eb27
Allanche **F** 69 Dc36
Allariz **E** 78 Ba37
Allauch **F** 82 Ea39
Alleen **N** 42 Ed20
Allersberg **D** 64 Fb32
Allevard **F** 71 Eb36
Allinge **DK** 50 Ga24
Allo **E** 80 Cb39
Allones **F** 61 Da32
Allos **F** 83 Eb38
Almacelles **E** 80 Cd40
Almada **P** 90 Ab41
Almadén **E** 105 Bb43
Almagro **E** 92 Bc43
Almansa **E** 93 Cb43
Almanza **E** 79 Bc38
Almaraz **E** 91 Bb41
Almarza **E** 80 Cb39
Almazán **E** 92 Ca40
Almdalen **N** 33 Ga10
Almeida **P** 91 Ba40
Almeirim **P** 90 Ac41
Almelo **NL** 55 Ec27
Almenara **E** 93 Cc42
Almenar de Soria **E** 80 Cb40
Almendral **E** 90 Ad42
Almendralejo **E** 91 Ba42
Almere **NL** 55 Eb27
Almería **E** 106 Bd46
Almerimar **E** 106 Bd46
Al'met'evsk **RUS** 119 Ga08
Älmhult **S** 50 Ga22
Almiropótamos **GR** 112 Jb45
Almirós **GR** 101 Ja44
Almodôvar **P** 104 Ac43
Almodóvar del Campo **E** 92 Bc43
Almodóvar del Río **E** 105 Bb44
Almoharín **E** 91 Ba42
Almonte **E** 105 Ad44
Älmsta **S** 45 Gd17
Almudévar **E** 80 Cc40
Almuñécar **E** 106 Bc45
Almunge **S** 45 Gc17
Alnaši **RUS** 119 Ga08
Alness **GB** 17 Da19
Alnwick **GB** 21 Db22
Aloja **LV** 47 Hd20
Álora **E** 105 Bb45
Alpalhão **P** 90 Ad41
Alpera **E** 93 Cb43
Alphen a/d Rijn **NL** 55 Eb27
Alpiarça **P** 90 Ac41
Alpua **FIN** 35 Hc11
Alquézar **E** 80 Cd39
Als **DK** 49 Fb22
Alsasua **E** 80 Cb38
Alsfeld **D** 64 Fa29
Alsike **S** 45 Gc18
Alsterbro **S** 50 Gb21
Alstermo **S** 50 Gb21
Alta **N** 26 Ha04
Altamura **I** 99 Gc43

Altdorf CH 71 Ed35
Altdorf D 64 Fb31
Altea E 94 Cc44
Altenberg D 65 Fd30
Altenburg D 64 Fc29
Altenkirchen D 63 Ed29
Altenmarkt A 73 Fd34
Altenmarkt A 73 Ga34
Altensteig D 63 Ed32
Altentreptow D 57 Fd26
Alter do Chão P 90 Ad41
Altheim A 73 Fd33
Althofen A 73 Ga35
Alţina RO 76 Ja35
Altınova TR 113 Ka44
Altkirch F 71 Ec33
Altnaharra GB 17 Da18
Altn Bulg RUS 123 Ga14
Alton GB 24 Da28
Altötting D 72 Fc33
Altunhisar TR 128 Gc15
Altura E 93 Cc42
Alūksne LV 47 Ja20
Alunda S 45 Gc17
Alupka UA 126 Fa18
Alušta UA 126 Fa18
Alvalade P 90 Ac42
Älvängen S 43 Fc20
Alvdal N 37 Fc14
Älvdalen S 38 Ga16
Alvesta S 50 Ga21
Ålvho S 38 Ga15
Ålvik N 36 Ed16
Alvito P 90 Ac42
Älvkarleby S 45 Gc17
Älvros S 38 Fd15
Älvros S 38 Ga15
Älvsbyn S 34 Gd10
Älvsered S 49 Fd21
Alytus LT 53 Hd24
Alzey D 63 Ed31
Alzira E 93 Cc43
Ämådalen S 38 Ga16
Amadora P 90 Ab41
Åmål S 43 Fd19
Amalfi I 99 Ga43
Amaliáda GR 110 Hd46
Amandola I 85 Fd40
Amantea I 109 Gb45
Amara RO 89 Jd37
Amarante P 78 Ad38
Amărăştii de Jos RO 88 Ja38
Amareleja P 105 Ad43
Amárinthos GR 112 Jb45
Amaru RO 88 Jc37
Amatrice I 85 Fd40
Ambar TR 128 Gc15
Ambazac F 69 Db35
Ambelákia GR 101 Ja44
Ambelónas GR 100 Hb44
Ambelónas GR 101 Hd44
Amberg D 64 Fc31
Ambérieu-en-Bugey F 70 Ea35
Ambert F 70 Dd36

Ambjörby S 44 Fd17
Amble GB 21 Db22
Ambleside GB 21 Da23
Amboise F 69 Db33
Ameixial P 104 Ac43
Amelia I 84 Fc40
Amélie-les-Bains F 81 Db40
Amelinghausen D 56 Fb26
Amendolara I 99 Gc44
Amersfoort NL 55 Eb27
Amesbury GB 24 Da28
Amfíklia GR 111 Ja45
Amfilohía GR 110 Hc45
Ámfissa GR 111 Ja45
Amiens F 62 Dc30
Amilly F 62 Dc32
Amíndeo GR 101 Hd43
Åminne S 45 Gd20
Åmli N 42 Fa19
Amlwch GB 20 Cd24
Ämmänsaari FIN 35 Ja10
Ammarnäs S 33 Gb09
Ammochostos CY 128 Gc19
Amolianí GR 102 Jb43
Amorgós GR 115 Jd47
Åmot N 37 Fb16
Åmot N 42 Fa18
Åmot N 43 Fb17
Åmot S 38 Gb16
Åmotfors S 43 Fd18
Amou F 80 Cd38
Ampezzo I 72 Fc35
Amplepuis F 70 Dd35
Amposta E 93 Cd41
Åmsele S 34 Gd11
Amsterdam NL 55 Eb27
Amstetten A 73 Ga34
Amusquillo E 79 Bd39
Amzacea RO 89 Ka37
Anáfi GR 115 Jd48
Anafonitria GR 110 Hc46
Anagni I 98 Fd42
Anaharavi GR 100 Hb44
Anamur TR 128 Gb17
Anan'iv UA 77 Ka32
Anapa RUS 126 Fb17
Anascaul IRL 18 Bc24
Ånäset S 34 Ha11
Ance LV 46 Hb20
Ancenis F 68 Cd33
Ancerville F 62 Ea32
Ancona I 85 Fd39
Ancy-le-Franc F 70 Ea33
Åndalsnes N 36 Fa14
Ånddalsvågen N 32 Fd10
Andebu N 43 Fb18
Andelot F 63 Eb32
Andenes N 28 Gb05
Anderlecht B 62 Ea29
Andermatt CH 71 Ed35
Andernach D 63 Ec30
Andernos-les-Bains F 68 Cc36
Anderstorp S 49 Fd21
Andírio GR 110 Hd46
Andoain E 80 Cb38

Andocs H 74 Gd35
Andorra E 93 Cc41
Andorra la Vella AND 81 Da39
Andover GB 24 Da28
Andratx E 95 Da43
Andravída GR 110 Hc46
Andreapol' RUS 117 Ec10
Andria I 99 Gc42
Andrievo-Ivanivka MD 77 Kb32
Andrijevica MNE 87 Hb40
Andrijivka UA 126 Fb16
Andrítsena GR 110 Hd47
Ándros GR 112 Jc46
Andrušivka UA 121 Eb15
Andrychów PL 67 Ha31
Andselv N 26 Gc05
Andújar E 106 Bc44
Anduze F 82 Dd38
Aneby S 44 Ga20
Änge S 38 Ga13
Ånge S 38 Gb14
Ängelholm S 49 Fd22
Angeli FIN 27 Hb05
Angelókastro GR 110 Hc45
Angelókastro GR 111 Ja46
Ängelsberg S 44 Gb17
Angermünde D 57 Ga27
Angern A 74 Gc33
Angers F 69 Da33
Angerville F 62 Dc32
Anglès E 81 Db40
Angles F 68 Cd34
Anglure F 62 Dd32
Angoulême F 69 Da35
Angüés E 80 Cd40
Anguse EST 47 Ja18
Anina RO 87 Hc37
Anıtlı TR 128 Gb17
Anjalankoski FIN 41 Hd16
Anjan S 32 Fd12
Ankarsrum S 44 Gb20
Ankarvattnet S 33 Ga11
Anklam D 57 Fd26
Ånn S 38 Fd13
Anna RUS 122 Fb12
Annaberg-Buchholz D 65 Fd30
Annan GB 21 Da22
Anna Paulowna NL 55 Eb26
Annecy F 71 Eb36
Annemasse F 71 Eb35
Annino RUS 117 Ed08
Annonay F 70 Dd36
Annopol PL 67 Hc29
Annot F 83 Eb38
Áno Poróia GR 101 Ja42
Áno Vrondoú GR 101 Ja42
Anröchte D 55 Ed28
Ans B 63 Eb29
Ansbach D 64 Fb31
Ansnes N 36 Fa14
Antequera E 105 Bb45
Anthótopos GR 101 Ja44
Antibes F 83 Eb39
Antíparos GR 111 Jc47

Antnäs S 34 Ha10
Antonin PL 66 Gc29
Antonovo BG 88 Jc39
Antracyt UA 122 Fb15
Antrim GB 20 Cc22
Antrodoco I 98 Fd41
Antsla EST 47 Ja20
Anttis S 30 Ha07
Anttola FIN 41 Ja14
Antwerpen B 54 Ea28
Anykščiai LT 53 Hd23
Anzin F 62 Ea29
Anzio I 98 Fc42
Aoiz E 80 Cc38
Aosta I 71 Ec36
Apa TR 128 Ga16
Apagy H 75 Hc33
Apahida RO 76 Ja34
Apastovo RUS 119 Fd09
Apatin SRB 74 Ha36
Ape LV 47 Ja20
Apeldoorn NL 55 Ec27
Apen D 55 Ed26
Apidiá GR 111 Ja47
Apolda D 64 Fc29
Apólonas GR 115 Jd47
Apostolove UA 125 Ed16
Äppelbo S 44 Ga17
Appenzell CH 72 Fa34
Appingedam NL 55 Ed26
Appleby-in-Westmorland GB 21 Da23
Apricena I 99 Gb42
Aprīķi LV 52 Hb21
Aprilci BG 88 Jb39
Aprilia I 98 Fc42
Aprilovo BG 88 Jc39
Apšeronsk RUS 127 Fc17
Apšupe LV 52 Hc21
Apt F 82 Ea38
Aquileia I 73 Fd36
Aracena E 105 Ad43
Arad RO 75 Hc35
Aradippou CY 128 Gc19
Aragona I 108 Fd47
Aráhova GR 111 Ja45
Aralkı TR 127 Fd19
Aramits F 80 Cc38
Aranda de Duero E 79 Bd39
Aranda de Moncayo E 80 Cb40
Arandjelovac SRB 87 Hb38
Aranjuez E 92 Bd41
Arantzazu E 80 Cb38
Aras de Alpuente E 93 Cb42
Aravete EST 47 Hd18
Arbatax I 97 Ed44
Arboga S 44 Gb18
Arbois F 71 Eb34
Arborea I 97 Ec44
Årbostad N 28 Gb06
Arbrå S 38 Gb15
Arbroath GB 17 Db20
Arbus I 97 Ec44
Arbuzinka MD 77 Kb32
Arcachon F 68 Cc36

Arčadinskaja RUS 123 Fd13
Arc-en-Barrois F 70 Ea33
Arc-et-Senans F 71 Eb34
Archena E 107 Ca44
Archidona E 105 Bb45
Arcidosso I 84 Fb40
Arcis-sur-Aube F 62 Ea32
Arco I 72 Fb36
Arco de Baúlhe P 78 Ad38
Arcos de Jalón E 92 Ca40
Arcos de la Frontera E 105 Ba45
Arcyz UA 77 Ka35
Arcyz UA 125 Ec17
Ardahan TR 127 Ga18
Årdalstangen N 36 Fa15
Ardara IRL 18 Ca21
Ardatov RUS 118 Fb10
Ardee IRL 19 Cb23
Ardeluța RO 76 Jc34
Arden DK 49 Fb22
Ardentes F 69 Db34
Ardes F 69 Dc36
Ardeşen TR 127 Ga19
Ardgartan GB 16 Cd20
Ardino BG 102 Jc41
Ardisa E 80 Cc39
Ardres F 62 Dc29
Ardrossan GB 20 Cd21
Ardvasar GB 16 Cd19
Åre S 38 Fd13
Arefu RO 88 Jb36
Arenas de San Pedro E 91 Bc41
Arendal N 42 Fa19
Arendsee D 56 Fc27
Arenys de Mar E 95 Db41
Arenzano I 83 Ed38
Areópoli GR 111 Ja48
Arévalo E 91 Bc40
Arezzo I 84 Fc39
Argalastí GR 101 Ja44
Argamasilla de Alba E 92 Bd43
Argamasilla de Calatrava E 92 Bc43
Arganda E 92 Bd41
Arganil P 90 Ad40
Argelès-Gazost F 80 Cd38
Argelès-sur-Mer F 81 Dc40
Argenta I 84 Fc38
Argentan F 61 Da31
Argentat F 69 Db36
Argenteuil F 62 Dc31
Argenton-Château F 69 Da33
Argenton-sur-Creuse F 69 Db34
Argent-sur-Sauldre F 69 Dc33
Árgos GR 111 Ja46
Árgos Orestikó GR 101 Hc43
Argostóli GR 110 Hc46
Arguedas E 80 Cb39
Arhavi TR 127 Ga19

Arhéa Neméa GR 111 Ja46
Ariano Irpino I 99 Ga42
Aridéa GR 101 Hd42
Arieşeni RO 75 Hd35
Arıkören TR 128 Gb15
Arilje SRB 87 Hb39
Arinagour GB 16 Cc20
Ariniş RO 75 Hd34
Arinthod F 70 Ea35
Ariogala LT 52 Hc23
Arisaig GB 16 Cd19
Arisba GR 113 Jd44
Aritzo I 97 Ed44
Ariza E 80 Cb40
Årjäng S 43 Fd18
Arjeplog S 33 Gc09
Arjona E 106 Bc44
Arkadak RUS 123 Fc12
Arkássa GR 115 Kb48
Arkesíni GR 115 Jd47
Arkítsa GR 111 Ja45
Arklow IRL 23 Cb25
Arkösund S 45 Gc19
Ärla S 44 Gb18
Arlanc F 70 Dd36
Arles F 82 Dd38
Arlon B 63 Eb31
Árma GR 112 Jb45
Armagh GB 20 Cb22
Armavir RUS 127 Fd16
Armeniş RO 87 Hd37
Armentières F 62 Dd29
Armjans'k UA 126 Fa17
Armutlu TR 103 Kb42
Arnac-Pompadour F 69 Db36
Arnåsvall S 39 Gc13
Arnavutköy TR 103 Kb41
Arnay-le-Duc F 70 Ea34
Arnéa GR 101 Ja43
Arnedo E 80 Cb39
Årnes N 43 Fc17
Arnhem NL 55 Ec28
Árnissa GR 101 Hd42
Arnö S 45 Gc19
Arnsberg D 63 Ed29
Arnstadt D 64 Fb29
Arnstein D 64 Fa31
Arona I 71 Ed36
Arosa CH 72 Fa35
Årøysund N 43 Fb18
Arpajon la Norville F 62 Dc32
Arpaşu de Jos RO 88 Ja36
Arpela FIN 34 Hb09
Arpino I 98 Fd42
Arquata del Tronto I 85 Fd40
Arquillos E 106 Bc44
Arraiolos P 90 Ac42
Arras F 62 Dd29
Arreau F 80 Cd39
Arríondas E 79 Bd37
Arronches P 90 Ad41

Arroyo de la Luz E 91 Ba41
Ars-en-Ré F 68 Cd34
Arsk RUS 119 Fd08
Árskógssandur IS 15 Ca05
Arslanköy TR 128 Gc16
Årslev DK 49 Fb24
Årsunda S 44 Gb17
Arsvågen N 42 Ec18
Árta GR 110 Hc45
Artà E 95 Db43
Artemissía GR 110 Hd47
Artemivs'k UA 122 Fb15
Artenay F 62 Dc32
Artesa de Segre E 81 Da40
Arthurstown IRL 22 Ca25
Artvin TR 127 Ga19
Artziniega E 79 Ca38
Arundel GB 25 Db28
Arvidsjaur S 33 Gc10
Årvik N 36 Ed14
Arvika S 43 Fd18
Årviksand N 26 Gd04
Arvträsk S 33 Gc11
Arzachena I 96 Ed42
Arzamas RUS 119 Fc10
Arzfeld D 63 Ec30
Arzgir RUS 127 Ga16
Arzignano I 84 Fb37
Arzúa E 78 Ba36
Aš CZ 64 Fc30
Ås N 37 Fc13
Ås N 43 Fc18
Ås S 38 Ga13
Åsarna S 38 Ga14
Åsarp S 44 Fd20
Asby S 44 Ga20
Åsbyrgi IS 15 Cb06
Aschach A 73 Ga33
Aschaffenburg D 64 Fa31
Aschersleben D 56 Fc28
Ascó E 93 Cd41
Ascoli Piceno I 85 Fd40
Ascoli Satriano I 99 Gb42
Ascona CH 71 Ed36
Åseda S 50 Gb21
Åsele S 33 Gc12
Åselet S 34 Gd10
Åsen S 38 Ga16
Asenovgrad BG 102 Jb41
Åseral N 42 Fa19
Asfáka GR 101 Hc44
Ashburton GB 23 Cc28
Ashby-de-la-Zouch GB 24 Da25
Ashford GB 25 Dc28
Ashington GB 21 Db22
Asiago I 72 Fb36
Asikkala FIN 40 Hc15
Asipovičy BY 121 Eb13
Aska FIN 31 Hc07
Askeaton IRL 18 Bd24
Asker N 43 Fc17
Asker N 43 Fc17
Askersund S 44 Ga19
Åskiljeby S 33 Gc11
Askim N 43 Fc18

Askola FIN 41 Hd16
Äsköping S 44 Gb18
Askvoll N 36 Ed15
Asmalı TR 103 Ka42
Ašmjany BY 120 Ea12
Asmunti FIN 35 Hc09
Asnæs DK 49 Fc23
Asola I 84 Fa37
Asolo I 72 Fc36
Aspang Markt A 73 Gb34
Aspe E 107 Cb44
Aspeå S 39 Gc13
Aspet F 81 Da39
Aspö S 45 Gc18
As Pontes de García Rodríguez E 78 Ba36
Aspres-sur-Buëch F 82 Ea37
Asprógia GR 101 Hc43
Asprópirgos GR 112 Jb46
Aspsele S 33 Gc12
Assemini I 97 Ed45
Assen NL 55 Ec26
Assens DK 49 Fb23
Assentoft DK 49 Fb22
Assisi I 84 Fc40
Ássos GR 101 Hc44
Åstad N 28 Ga07
Astaffort F 81 Da37
Astakós GR 110 Hc45
Asten NL 55 Eb28
Asti I 83 Ec37
Astipálea GR 115 Ka47
Astorga E 78 Bb38
Astradamovka RUS 119 Fd10
Åsträsk S 34 Gd11
Astravec BY 53 Ja24
Ástros GR 111 Ja47
Astryna BY 59 Hd25
Astudillo E 79 Bd38
Asūne LV 53 Jb22
Asveja BY 53 Jb22
Aszód H 74 Ha34
Aszófő H 74 Gd35
Atarte E 106 Bc45
Ateca E 80 Cb40
Atessa I 99 Ga41
Ath B 62 Ea29
Atherstone GB 24 Da26
Athína GR 112 Jb46
Athlone IRL 18 Ca23
Athy IRL 19 Cb24
Atienza E 92 Ca40
Atjaševo RUS 119 Fc10
Atnbrua N 37 Fc15
Atnmoen N 37 Fc15
Ätran S 49 Fd21
Atri I 85 Fd40
Attleborough GB 25 Dc26
Åttonträsk S 33 Gc11
Åtvidaberg S 44 Gb20
Au D 72 Fc33
Aubagne F 82 Ea39
Aubange B 63 Eb31

Aubenas – Bagnara Calabra

Aubenas **F** 82 Dd37
Aubergenville **F** 62 Dc31
Auberive **F** 70 Ea33
Aubiet **F** 81 Da38
Aubigny-sur-Nère **F** 69 Dc33
Aubin **F** 81 Db37
Aubusson **F** 69 Dc35
Auce **LV** 52 Hc22
Auch **F** 81 Da38
Auchterarder **GB** 21 Da21
Audierne **F** 60 Cb31
Audincourt **F** 71 Ec34
Audru **EST** 46 Hc19
Audruicq **F** 62 Dd29
Aue **D** 65 Fd30
Auer **I** 72 Fb35
Auerbach **D** 64 Fc30
Auerbach **D** 64 Fc31
Aughnacloy **GB** 20 Cb22
Augsburg **D** 72 Fb33
Augusta **I** 109 Gb47
Augustów **PL** 59 Hc25
Aukštadvaris **LT** 53 Hd24
Auktsjaur **S** 34 Gd10
Aulla **I** 84 Fa38
Aullène **F** 96 Ed41
Aulnay **F** 68 Cd34
Ault **F** 62 Dc29
Aulum **DK** 48 Fa22
Aumale **F** 62 Dc30
Aumont-Aubrac **F** 81 Dc37
Aunay-sur-Odon **F** 61 Da31
Auneau **F** 62 Dc32
Auneuil **F** 62 Dc31
Auning **DK** 49 Fb22
Aups **F** 83 Eb39
Aura **FIN** 40 Hb16
Auray **F** 60 Cc32
Aurdal **N** 37 Fb16
Aure **N** 37 Fb13
Aurich **D** 55 Ed26
Aurillac **F** 69 Dc36
Auriol **F** 82 Ea39
Aurlandsvangen **N** 36 Fa16
Auronzo di Cadore **I** 72 Fc35
Aurora **RO** 89 Ka38
Austad **N** 42 Fa18
Austevoll **N** 42 Ec17
Austmarka **N** 43 Fd17
Austnes **N** 36 Ed13
Auterive **F** 81 Da38
Authon-du-Perche **F** 61 Db32
Auttoinen **FIN** 40 Hc15
Autun **F** 70 Dd34
Auvillar **F** 81 Da37
Auxerre **F** 70 Dd33
Auxi-le-Château **F** 62 Dc29
Auxonne **F** 70 Ea34
Auzances **F** 69 Dc35
Availles-Limouzine **F** 69 Da35
Avaldsnes **N** 42 Ec18
Avallon **F** 70 Dd33
Avaviken **S** 33 Gc10

Avdijivka **UA** 121 Ed13
Ávdira **GR** 102 Jc42
Avebury **GB** 24 Da27
A Veiga **E** 78 Bb38
Aveiro **P** 78 Ad39
Avellino **I** 99 Ga43
Aversa **I** 99 Ga43
Avesnes-sur-Helpe **F** 62 Ea30
Avesta **S** 44 Gb17
Avezzano **I** 98 Fd41
Avgustivka **UA** 77 Kb34
Aviemore **GB** 17 Da19
Avigliana **I** 83 Ec37
Avigliano **I** 99 Gb43
Avignon **F** 82 Dd38
Ávila **E** 91 Bc40
Avilés **E** 79 Bc36
Avinurme **EST** 47 Ja18
Avion **F** 62 Dd29
Avis **P** 90 Ad41
Avize **F** 62 Ea31
Avlémonas **GR** 111 Jb48
Avliotes **GR** 100 Hb44
Avlóna **GR** 112 Jb46
Avola **I** 109 Ga48
Avram Iancu **RO** 75 Hc35
Avram Iancu **RO** 75 Hd35
Avranches **F** 61 Cd31
Avrig **RO** 88 Ja36
Avrillé **F** 61 Da32
Ax-les-Thermes **F** 81 Db39
Axmarby **S** 39 Gc16
Axvall **S** 44 Fd19
Ayamonte **E** 104 Ac44
Ayancık **TR** 126 Fb19
Aydın **TR** 113 Kb45
Aydıncık **TR** 128 Gb17
Aydınlar **TR** 128 Gc16
Ayerbe **E** 80 Cc39
Aylesbury **GB** 25 Db27
Ayllón **E** 92 Ca40
Aylsham **GB** 25 Dc26
Ayora **E** 93 Cb43
Ayr **GB** 20 Cd21
Ayrancı **TR** 128 Gc16
Ayton **GB** 21 Db21
Aytré **F** 68 Cd34
Ayvacık **TR** 103 Jd43
Ayvalık **TR** 113 Ka44
Azaila **E** 80 Cc40
Azaryčy **BY** 121 Eb13
Azay-le-Rideau **F** 69 Da33
Aziory **BY** 59 Hd25
Aznakaevo **RUS** 119 Ga08
Azov **RUS** 123 Fc15
Azpeitia **E** 80 Cb38
Azuaga **E** 105 Ba43

B

Babadag **RO** 89 Ka36
Babaeski **TR** 103 Jd41
Babaevo **RUS** 117 Ec08
Babek **BG** 102 Jb40

Băbeni **RO** 88 Ja37
Babica **PL** 67 Hc30
Babilafuente **E** 91 Bc40
Babriškės **LT** 53 Hd24
Babrujsk **BY** 121 Eb13
Babtai **LT** 52 Hc24
Báč **SK** 74 Gc33
Bacău **RO** 76 Jc34
Baccarat **F** 63 Ec32
Băcești **RO** 76 Jc34
Bacharach **D** 63 Ed30
Bachčysaraj **UA** 126 Fa18
Bachmač **UA** 121 Ed14
Bachórz **PL** 67 Hc31
Bačina **SRB** 87 Hc39
Baciu **RO** 75 Hd34
Baciuty **PL** 59 Hc26
Bačka Palanka **SRB** 86 Ha37
Bačka Topola **SRB** 74 Ha36
Backe **S** 33 Gb12
Bäckebo **S** 50 Gb21
Bäckefors **S** 43 Fd19
Bäckhammar **S** 44 Ga18
Backnang **D** 64 Fa32
Bačko Novo Selo **SRB** 86 Ha37
Bad Aibling **D** 72 Fc33
Badajoz **E** 90 Ad42
Badalona **E** 95 Db41
Bad Arolsen **D** 64 Fa29
Bad Aussee **A** 73 Fd34
Bad Bederkesa **D** 56 Fa26
Bad Bentheim **D** 55 Ed27
Bad Bergzabern **D** 63 Ed32
Bad Berka **D** 64 Fb29
Bad Berleburg **D** 63 Ed29
Bad Bevensen **D** 56 Fb26
Bad Bibra **D** 64 Fc29
Bad Bramstedt **D** 56 Fb25
Bad Brückenau **D** 64 Fa30
Bad Camberg **D** 63 Ed30
Bad Doberan **D** 56 Fc25
Bad Driburg **D** 56 Fa28
Bad Düben **D** 57 Fd28
Bad Dürkheim **D** 63 Ed31
Bademli **TR** 103 Kb43
Baden **A** 73 Gb33
Baden **CH** 71 Ed34
Baden-Baden **D** 63 Ed32
Bad Endorf **D** 72 Fc33
Bad Fallingbostel **D** 56 Fa27
Bad Freienwalde **D** 57 Ga27
Bad Friedrichshall **D** 64 Fa31
Bad Gandersheim **D** 56 Fb28
Bad Gastein **A** 73 Fd34
Bad Gleichenberg **A** 73 Gb35
Bad Griesbach **D** 73 Fd33
Bad Hall **A** 73 Ga33
Bad Hersfeld **D** 64 Fa29
Bad Hofgastein **A** 73 Fd34
Bad Homburg **D** 63 Ed30
Bad Honnef **D** 63 Ec29

Badia Gran **E** 95 Db44
Bad Ischl **A** 73 Fd34
Bad Karlshafen **D** 56 Fa28
Bad Kissingen **D** 64 Fb30
Bad Kleinen **D** 56 Fc26
Bad Königshofen **D** 64 Fb30
Bad Kreuznach **D** 63 Ed31
Bad Krozingen **D** 71 Ec33
Bad Laasphe **D** 63 Ed29
Bad Langensalza **D** 64 Fb29
Bad Lausick **D** 65 Fd29
Bad Lauterberg **D** 56 Fb28
Bad Leonfelden **A** 73 Ga33
Bad Liebenwerda **D** 65 Fd29
Bad Mergentheim **D** 64 Fa31
Bad Münstereifel **D** 63 Ec30
Bad Muskau **D** 65 Ga29
Bad Nauheim **D** 64 Fa30
Bad Neuenahr-Ahrweiler **D** 63 Ec30
Bad Neustadt **D** 64 Fb30
Bad Oeynhausen **D** 56 Fa28
Bad Oldesloe **D** 56 Fb25
Badonviller **F** 63 Ec32
Bad Pyrmont **D** 56 Fa28
Bad Radkersburg **A** 73 Gb35
Bad Reichenhall **D** 73 Fd34
Bad Säckingen **D** 71 Ed33
Bad Salzuflen **D** 56 Fa28
Bad Salzungen **D** 64 Fb29
Bad Sankt Leonhard **A** 73 Ga35
Bad Saulgau **D** 72 Fa33
Bad Schönborn **D** 63 Ed31
Bad Schwalbach **D** 63 Ed30
Bad Schwartau **D** 56 Fb25
Bad Segeberg **D** 56 Fb25
Bad Sobernheim **D** 63 Ed31
Bad Sülze **D** 57 Fd25
Bad Tölz **D** 72 Fc34
Bad Urach **D** 64 Fa32
Bad Vöslau **A** 73 Gb33
Bad Waldsee **D** 72 Fa33
Bad Wildungen **D** 64 Fa29
Bad Wilsnack **D** 56 Fc27
Bad Windsheim **D** 64 Fb31
Bad Wünnenberg **D** 56 Fa28
Bad Wurzach **D** 72 Fa33
Bad Zwischenahn **D** 55 Ed26
Baena **E** 105 Bb44
Baeza **E** 106 Bc44
Bafra **TR** 126 Fb19
Bagà **E** 81 Da40
Bağarası **TR** 113 Kb46
Bağbaşı **TR** 128 Ga16
Bagenalstown **IRL** 19 Cb24
Bagenkop **DK** 49 Fb24
Bagheria **I** 108 Fd46
Bagienice **PL** 59 Hc26
Bagn **N** 37 Fb16
Bagnacavallo **I** 84 Fc38
Bagnara Calabra **I** 109 Gb46

Bagnères de-Bigorre **F** 80 Cd38
Bagnères-de-Luchon **F** 80 Cd39
Bagni Contursi **I** 99 Gb43
Bagno di Romagna **I** 84 Fc39
Bagnoles-de-l'Orne **F** 61 Da31
Bagnoli del Trigno **I** 99 Ga42
Bagnols-sur-Cèze **F** 82 Dd38
Bağyurdu **TR** 113 Kb45
Baia **RO** 89 Ka36
Baia de Aramă **RO** 87 Hd37
Baia de Arieş **RO** 75 Hd35
Baia Mare **RO** 75 Hd33
Baia Sprie **RO** 75 Hd33
Băicoi **RO** 88 Jc36
Băiculeşti **RO** 88 Jb37
Baiersbronn **D** 63 Ed32
Baigneux-les-Juifs **F** 70 Ea33
Baile Átha Cliath **IRL** 19 Cb24
Băile Felix **RO** 75 Hc34
Băile Govora **RO** 88 Ja37
Băile Herculane **RO** 87 Hd37
Bailén **E** 106 Bc44
Băile Olăneşti **RO** 88 Ja36
Băileşti **RO** 88 Ja38
Băile Tuşnad **RO** 76 Jb35
Bailleul **F** 62 Dd29
Baimaclia **MD** 77 Ka35
Bain-de-Bretagne **F** 61 Cd32
Bains-les-Bains **F** 71 Eb33
Baiona **E** 78 Ad37
Băişoara **RO** 75 Hd35
Baisogala **LT** 52 Hc23
Baja **H** 74 Ha36
Bajina Bašta **SRB** 86 Ha39
Bajmok **SRB** 74 Ha36
Bajovo Polje **MNE** 86 Ha40
Bajram Curr **AL** 100 Hb41
Bak **H** 74 Gc35
Bakacak **TR** 103 Ka43
Bakewell **GB** 24 Da25
Bakkafjörður **IS** 15 Cc06
Bakkagerði **IS** 15 Cc07
Bakketun **N** 33 Ga10
Bakko **N** 43 Fb17
Baklia **N** 37 Fb15
Bakonycsernye **H** 74 Gd34
Bakonyjákó **H** 74 Gc34
Bakša **UA** 77 Ka32
Baksan **RUS** 127 Ga17
Baktakék **H** 75 Hb33
Bala **GB** 24 Cd25
Balabanovo **RUS** 117 Ed11
Bălăceanu **RO** 89 Jd36
Balaguer **E** 80 Cd40
Balahna **RUS** 118 Fb09
Balaklija **UA** 122 Fa14

Balakovo **RUS** 119 Ga11
Balašiha **RUS** 118 Fa10
Balašov **RUS** 123 Fc12
Balassagyarmat **H** 74 Ha33
Balatonalmádi **H** 74 Gd35
Balatonbozsok **H** 74 Gd35
Balatonfüred **H** 74 Gd35
Balatonfűzfő **H** 74 Gd35
Balatonkeresztúr **H** 74 Gc35
Balatonlelle **H** 74 Gd35
Bălăuşeri **RO** 76 Ja35
Balazote **E** 92 Ca43
Balbriggan **IRL** 19 Cb23
Bălceşti **RO** 88 Ja37
Balçik **BG** 89 Ka38
Balcılar **TR** 128 Gb16
Baldone **LV** 53 Hd21
Balen **B** 63 Eb29
Balestrand **N** 36 Ed15
Bălgarene **BG** 88 Jb39
Bălgarska Polyana **BG** 103 Jd40
Balik **BG** 89 Jd38
Balıkesir **TR** 103 Kb43
Balıklıçeş **TR** 103 Ka42
Bälinge **S** 45 Gc17
Balingen **D** 71 Ed33
Ballachulish **GB** 16 Cd20
Ballaghaderreen **IRL** 18 Ca23
Ballangen **N** 28 Gb06
Ballantrae **GB** 20 Cd22
Ballater **GB** 17 Db20
Ballina **IRL** 18 Ca22
Ballinasloe **IRL** 18 Ca23
Balling **DK** 48 Fa22
Ballsh **AL** 100 Hb43
Ballstad **N** 28 Ga07
Ballybofey **IRL** 19 Cb22
Ballybunnion **IRL** 18 Bd24
Ballycastle **GB** 20 Cc21
Ballycastle **IRL** 18 Ca22
Ballyclare **GB** 20 Cc22
Ballydehob **IRL** 22 Bc25
Ballygawley **GB** 20 Cb22
Ballyhaunis **IRL** 18 Ca23
Ballymahon **IRL** 18 Ca23
Ballymena **GB** 20 Cc22
Ballymoney **GB** 20 Cc22
Ballysadare **IRL** 18 Ca22
Ballyshannon **IRL** 18 Ca22
Ballyvaughan **IRL** 18 Bd23
Balmaseda **E** 79 Ca37
Balmazújváros **H** 75 Hc34
Balneario de Panticosa **E** 80 Cd39
Baloži **LV** 52 Hc21
Balş **RO** 88 Ja38
Balşa **RO** 75 Hd35
Balsfjord **N** 26 Gc05
Bålsta **S** 45 Gc18
Balsthal **CH** 71 Ec34
Balta **UA** 77 Ka32
Balta **UA** 125 Ec16
Balta Albă **RO** 89 Jd36
Baltanás **E** 79 Bd39

Băltăteşti **RO** 76 Jc34
Bălti **MD** 77 Jd33
Baltijsk **RUS** 52 Ha24
Baltinava **LV** 53 Jb21
Balvi **LV** 47 Ja20
Balya **TR** 103 Ka43
Bamberg **D** 64 Fb31
Bampton **GB** 23 Cc27
Banarlı **TR** 103 Ka41
Banatski Karlovac **SRB** 87 Hc37
Banatsko Novo Selo **SRB** 87 Hb37
Banbridge **GB** 20 Cc22
Banbury **GB** 24 Da26
Banchory **GB** 17 Db20
Band **RO** 76 Ja35
Bande **E** 78 Ba38
Bandırma **TR** 103 Kb42
Bandol **F** 82 Ea39
Bandon **IRL** 22 Bd25
Bandurove **UA** 77 Ka32
Băneasa **RO** 88 Jc38
Băneasa **RO** 89 Jd37
Banff **GB** 17 Db19
Bangor **GB** 20 Cc22
Bangor **GB** 20 Cd24
Bangor **IRL** 18 Bd22
Bangsund **N** 32 Fc11
Banie **PL** 57 Ga27
Banja Luka **BIH** 86 Gc38
Bankeryd **S** 44 Ga20
Bankja **BG** 102 Ja40
Bannalec **F** 60 Cb31
Baños de Benasque **E** 80 Cd39
Bánovce nad Bebravou **SK** 66 Gd32
Banovci Dunav **SRB** 87 Hb37
Banovići **BIH** 86 Gd38
Bansin **D** 57 Ga25
Banská Bystrica **SK** 67 Ha32
Banská Štiavnica **SK** 74 Gd33
Bansko **BG** 101 Ja41
Banstead **GB** 25 Db28
Bantry **IRL** 22 Bc25
Banyalbufar **E** 95 Da43
Banyoles **E** 81 Db40
Bapaume **F** 62 Dd30
Bar **MNE** 100 Ha41
Bar **UA** 121 Eb15
Bara **RO** 75 Hc36
Bâra **RO** 76 Jc34
Bărăganu **RO** 89 Jd36
Barajas de Melo **E** 92 Ca41
Barakaldo **E** 79 Ca37
Baranavičy **BY** 120 Ea13
Baranivka **UA** 121 Eb15
Baranów **PL** 59 Hc28
Baranów Sandomierski **PL** 67 Hb30
Baraolt **RO** 76 Jb35
Baraqueville **F** 81 Db37

Barbaros **TR** 103 Ka42
Barbastro **E** 80 Cd40
Barbate **E** 105 Ad45
Bärbele **LV** 53 Hd22
Barbezieux **F** 68 Cd35
Bârca **RO** 88 Ja38
Barca de Alva **P** 78 Ba39
Barcarrota **E** 90 Ad42
Barcellona Pozzo di Gotto **I** 109 Gb46
Barcelona **E** 95 Db41
Barcelonnette **F** 83 Eb38
Barcelos **P** 78 Ad38
Bárcena de Pie de Concha **E** 79 Bd37
Barcin **PL** 58 Gc27
Barcs **H** 74 Gc36
Barczewo **PL** 58 Ha25
Bardejov **SK** 67 Hb31
Bardi **I** 84 Fa38
Bardonecchia **I** 83 Eb37
Barentin **F** 61 Db30
Barfleur **F** 61 Da30
Barga **I** 84 Fa38
Bargteheide **D** 56 Fb26
Bari **I** 99 Gc42
Barjols **F** 82 Ea39
Barkava **LV** 53 Ja21
Bârlad **RO** 77 Jd35
Bar-le-Duc **F** 62 Ea32
Barletta **I** 99 Gc42
Barlinek **PL** 57 Ga27
Barmouth **GB** 24 Cd25
Barnet **GB** 25 Db27
Barneveld **NL** 55 Eb27
Barneville-Carteret **F** 61 Cd30
Barnsley **GB** 21 Db24
Barnstaple **GB** 23 Cc27
Barnstorf **D** 56 Fa27
Barovo **MK** 101 Hd42
Barracas **E** 93 Cc42
Barrancos **P** 105 Ad43
Barranda **E** 107 Ca44
Barrax **E** 92 Ca43
Barreiro **P** 90 Ab41
Barrême **F** 83 Eb38
Barrow-in-Furness **GB** 21 Da23
Barruelo de Santullán **E** 79 Bd38
Barry **GB** 24 Cd27
Bar-sur-Aube **F** 62 Ea32
Bar-sur-Seine **F** 62 Ea32
Barth **D** 57 Fd25
Barton-upon-Humber **GB** 21 Db24
Bartoszyce **PL** 58 Ha25
Barun **RUS** 123 Ga14
Baruth **D** 57 Fd28
Barvas **GB** 16 Cd17
Barvinkove **UA** 122 Fb15
Barwice **PL** 57 Gb26
Baryš **RUS** 119 Fd10
Barysav **BY** 121 Eb12

135

Bârzava RO 75 Hc35
Bašaid SRB 75 Hb36
Basarabeasca MD 77 Ka34
Basarabi RO 89 Ka37
Bascov RO 88 Jb37
Basel CH 71 Ec34
Basi LV 52 Hb21
Basildon GB 25 Db27
Başin TR 128 Gc15
Basingstoke GB 24 Da28
Baška HR 85 Ga37
Bassano del Grappa I 72 Fc36
Bassella E 81 Da40
Bassum D 56 Fa27
Båstad S 49 Fd22
Baštanka UA 125 Ed16
Bastia F 96 Ed40
Bastogne B 63 Eb30
Bastuträsk S 34 Gd11
Băta BG 102 Jb40
Batajsk RUS 123 Fc15
Batak BG 102 Jb41
Batanovci BG 102 Ja40
Batăr RO 75 Hc35
Bátaszék H 74 Gd36
Batea E 93 Cd41
Bath GB 24 Cd27
Batina HR 74 Ha36
Batković BIH 86 Ha37
Batley GB 21 Db24
Bátonyterenye H 74 Ha33
Batovo BG 89 Ka38
Båtsfjord N 27 Hc03
Båtskärsnäs S 34 Hb09
Battenberg D 64 Fa29
Battipaglia I 99 Ga43
Battonya H 75 Hb35
Batuša SRB 87 Hc38
Batyrevo RUS 119 Fd09
Baud F 60 Cc32
Baugé F 69 Da33
Baume-les-Dames F 71 Eb34
Baunatal D 64 Fa29
Baunei I 97 Ed44
Bauska LV 52 Hc22
Băuțar RO 75 Hd36
Bautzen D 65 Ga29
Bavay F 62 Ea30
Bavella F 96 Ed41
Bawtry GB 25 Db25
Bayburt TR 127 Ga19
Bayeux F 61 Da30
Bayındır TR 113 Kb45
Bayon F 63 Eb32
Bayonne F 80 Cc37
Bayramiç TR 103 Jd43
Bayreuth D 64 Fc31
Baza E 106 Bd45
Bazarnye Mataki RUS 119 Ga09
Bazarnyi Karabulak RUS 119 Fd11
Bazas F 80 Cd37
Beasain E 80 Cb38
Beas de Segura E 106 Bd44

Beaucaire F 82 Dd38
Beaugency F 69 Db33
Beaujeu F 70 Ea35
Beaumont F 69 Da36
Beaumont-de-Lomagne F 81 Da37
Beaumont-Hague F 61 Cd29
Beaumont-le-Roger F 61 Db31
Beaumont-sur-Sarthe F 61 Da32
Beaune F 70 Ea34
Beaupréau F 68 Cd33
Beauraing B 63 Eb30
Beaurepaire F 70 Ea36
Beauvais F 62 Dc30
Beauvoir-sur-Mer F 68 Cc33
Beauvoir-sur-Niort F 68 Cd34
Bebra D 64 Fa29
Bebrene LV 53 Ja22
Bebri LV 53 Hd21
Beccles GB 25 Dd26
Bečej SRB 75 Hb36
Becerreá E 78 Bb37
Bechet RO 88 Ja38
Becilla de Valderaduey E 79 Bc38
Beckum D 55 Ed28
Beclean RO 76 Ja34
Bečov nad Teplou CZ 65 Fd31
Bédarieux F 81 Dc38
Bedekovčina HR 73 Gb36
Bedford GB 25 Db27
Beelitz D 57 Fd28
Beeskow D 57 Ga28
Bégard F 60 Cc30
Beğendik TR 103 Ka40
Beglež BG 88 Jb39
Begnadalen N 37 Fb16
Begovo BG 102 Jb40
Begunicy RUS 47 Jb17
Behramkale TR 113 Jd44
Beidaud RO 89 Ka36
Beilen NL 55 Ec26
Beilngries D 64 Fc32
Beisfjord N 29 Gc06
Beiuș RO 75 Hc35
Beja P 104 Ac43
Béjar E 91 Bb40
Békés H 75 Hb35
Békéscsaba H 75 Hb35
Bekkarfjord N 27 Hb03
Belaazërsk BY 120 Ea13
Bélâbre F 69 Db34
Bela Crkva SRB 87 Hc37
Belaja Kalitva RUS 123 Fc14
Belalcázar E 105 Bb43
Bela Palanka SRB 87 Hd39
Belarus BY 120 Ea12
Bełchatów PL 67 Ha29
Belchite E 80 Cc40
Belcoo GB 19 Cb22
Beldibi TR 128 Ga17
Beled H 74 Gc34

Belev RUS 121 Ed12
Belfast GB 20 Cc22
Belfir RO 75 Hc35
Belford GB 21 Db22
Belfort F 71 Ec33
Belgern D 65 Fd29
Belgodère F 96 Ed40
Belgorod RUS 122 Fa14
Belica MK 101 Hc42
Beli Izvor BG 88 Ja39
Beli Manastir HR 74 Gd36
Belin-Béliet F 68 Cd36
Beliş RO 75 Hd35
Belišće HR 74 Gd36
Beljanovo BG 88 Jc38
Belkaya TR 128 Gc15
Bel'ki BY 53 Jb23
Bel'kovo RUS 121 Ec12
Bellac F 69 Db35
Bellagio I 71 Ed36
Bellaria-Igea Marina I 84 Fc38
Bellegarde F 62 Dc32
Bellegarde-sur-Valserine F 71 Eb35
Bellême F 61 Db32
Belleville F 70 Ea35
Belleville-sur-Vie F 68 Cd33
Belley F 70 Ea36
Bellinzona CH 71 Ed36
Bellpuig E 81 Da40
Belluno I 72 Fc36
Bélmez E 105 Bb43
Belmonte E 92 Ca42
Belmonte P 91 Ba40
Belmullet IRL 18 Bd22
Beloci MD 77 Ka32
Belœil B 62 Ea29
Belogradčik BG 87 Hd39
Belorado E 79 Ca38
Belorečensk RUS 127 Fc17
Belören TR 128 Gb16
Beloslav BG 89 Ka39
Belotinci BG 87 Hd39
Belpasso I 109 Ga47
Belper GB 24 Da25
Belsay GB 21 Db22
Beltinci SLO 73 Gb35
Beltiug RO 75 Hd34
Belturbet IRL 19 Cb23
Belvedere Marittimo I 99 Gb44
Belvès F 69 Da36
Belyj RUS 117 Ec11
Belz UA 67 Hd30
Belzig D 57 Fd28
Bełżyce PL 67 Hc29
Benabarre E 80 Cd40
Benalup de Sidonia E 105 Ba45
Benamaurel E 106 Bd45
Benavente E 79 Bc38
Benavides E 79 Bc38
Benejama E 107 Cb44
Benešov CZ 65 Ga31
Benevento I 99 Ga42

Bengtsfors S 43 Fd19
Benicarló E 93 Cd42
Benicàssim (Benicasim) E 93 Cc42
Benidorm E 94 Cc44
Benifaió E 93 Cc43
Benkovac HR 85 Gb39
Bénodet F 60 Cb31
Bensheim D 63 Ed31
Beograd SRB 87 Hb37
Beograd-Surcin SRB 87 Hb37
Berat AL 100 Hb43
Berazino BY 53 Jb23
Berazino BY 121 Eb12
Berbinzana E 80 Cb39
Berceto I 84 Fa38
Berchtesgaden D 73 Fd34
Berck-Plage F 62 Dc29
Berdía E 78 Ba36
Berdjans'k UA 126 Fb16
Berdyčiv UA 121 Eb15
Berehomet UA 76 Jb32
Berehove UA 75 Hd33
Bereket TR 128 Gd15
Berendi TR 128 Gc16
Bere Regis GB 24 Cd28
Berestečko UA 120 Ea15
Berești RO 77 Jd35
Berettyóújfalu H 75 Hc34
Berezanka UA 125 Ec16
Berezanskaja RUS 127 Fc16
Berežany UA 120 Ea15
Berezivka MD 77 Kb33
Berezna UA 121 Ec13
Berezne UA 120 Ea14
Bereznehuvate UA 125 Ed16
Berg N 32 Fd10
Berga E 81 Da40
Bergama TR 113 Ka44
Bergamo I 72 Fa38
Bergara E 80 Cb38
Bergeforsen S 39 Gc14
Bergen D 56 Fb27
Bergen D 57 Fd25
Bergen N 36 Ed16
Bergen op Zoom NL 54 Ea28
Berger N 43 Fc18
Bergerac F 69 Da36
Bergheim D 63 Ec29
Bergö FIN 40 Ha13
Bergsfjord N 28 Gb05
Bergshamra S 45 Gd18
Bergsjö S 38 Gb15
Bergsviken S 34 Ha10
Bergues F 62 Dd29
Bergviken S 33 Gc09
Beringen B 63 Eb29
Berja E 106 Bd45
Berkåk N 37 Fc13
Berkovica BG 88 Ja39
Berkovici BIH 86 Gd40
Berlanga E 105 Ba43
Berlanga de Duero E 92 Ca40

Berlevåg **N** 27 Hc02
Berlin **D** 57 Fd27
Bermeo **E** 80 Cb37
Bermillo de Sayago **E** 78 Bb39
Bern **CH** 71 Ec34
Bernalda **I** 99 Gc43
Bernartice **CZ** 65 Ga32
Bernáti **LV** 52 Ha22
Bernau **D** 57 Fd27
Bernaville **F** 62 Dc30
Bernay **F** 61 Db31
Bernburg **D** 56 Fc28
Berndorf **A** 73 Gb33
Bernkastel-Kues **D** 63 Ec30
Bernsdorf **D** 65 Ga29
Beronovo **BG** 89 Jd39
Beroun **CZ** 65 Ga31
Berovo **MK** 101 Ja41
Berre-l'Étang **F** 82 Ea39
Beršaď **UA** 77 Ka32
Beršaď **UA** 125 Ec16
Bersenbrück **D** 55 Ed27
Berteştii de Jos **RO** 89 Jd36
Bertincourt **F** 62 Dd30
Bertrix **B** 63 Eb30
Berwick-upon-Tweed **GB** 21 Db21
Beryslav **UA** 125 Ed16
Berzence **H** 74 Gc36
Bērzpils **LV** 53 Ja21
Beşağil **TR** 128 Gb15
Besalú **E** 81 Db40
Besançon **F** 71 Eb34
Bešankovičy **BY** 117 Eb11
Besedino **RUS** 122 Fa13
Besenyszög **H** 75 Hb34
Best **NL** 55 Eb28
Bestwig **D** 63 Ed29
Betanzos **E** 78 Ba36
Bétera **E** 93 Cc43
Beteta **E** 92 Ca41
Béthune **F** 62 Dd29
Bettna **S** 44 Gb19
Bettola **I** 84 Fa37
Betton **F** 61 Cd31
Bettyhill **GB** 17 Da18
Betws-y-Coed **GB** 24 Cd25
Betzdorf **D** 63 Ed29
Beveren **B** 54 Ea28
Beverley **GB** 21 Db24
Beverstedt **D** 56 Fa26
Beverungen **D** 56 Fa28
Beyçayırı **TR** 103 Ka43
Beydağ **TR** 113 Kb45
Beykoz **TR** 103 Kb41
Bežanicy **RUS** 117 Eb10
Bezas **E** 93 Cb42
Bezdan **SRB** 74 Ha36
Bežeck **RUS** 117 Ed09
Bezenčuk **RUS** 119 Ga10
Béziers **F** 81 Dc39
Bez'va **RUS** 41 Jb19
Biała Piska **PL** 59 Hb26
Biała Podlaska **PL** 59 Hc28
Białka **PL** 67 Ha31

Białobrzegi **PL** 59 Hb28
Białobrzegi **PL** 67 Hc30
Białogard **PL** 57 Gb25
Białopole **PL** 67 Hd29
Białowieża **PL** 59 Hd27
Biały Bór **PL** 58 Gc25
Białystok **PL** 59 Hc26
Bianco **I** 109 Gb46
Biarritz **F** 80 Cc37
Biasca **CH** 71 Ed35
Bibbiena **I** 84 Fc39
Biberach **D** 72 Fa33
Bicaj **AL** 100 Hb41
Bicaz **RO** 76 Jb34
Bicaz-Chei **RO** 76 Jb34
Bicester **GB** 24 Da27
Bicske **H** 74 Gd34
Bideford **GB** 23 Cc27
Bie **S** 44 Gb19
Biecz **PL** 67 Hb31
Biedenkopf **D** 63 Ed29
Biedjovaggigruver **N** 26 Ha05
Biel **E** 80 Cc39
Biel/Bienne **CH** 71 Ec34
Bielawa **PL** 66 Gc30
Bielefeld **D** 56 Fa28
Bielice **PL** 58 Gd26
Biella **I** 71 Ec36
Bielsa **E** 80 Cd39
Bielsk **PL** 58 Ha27
Bielsko-Biała **PL** 66 Gd31
Bielsk Podlaski **PL** 59 Hc27
Bienenbüttel **D** 56 Fb26
Bieniów **PL** 57 Ga28
Bienne **CH** 71 Ec34
Bierdzany **PL** 66 Gd30
Biertan **RO** 76 Ja35
Bierutów **PL** 66 Gc29
Biescas **E** 80 Cd39
Biesiekierz **PL** 57 Gb25
Bièvre **B** 63 Eb30
Bieżuń **PL** 58 Ha27
Biga **TR** 103 Ka42
Bigadiç **TR** 103 Kb43
Biggar **GB** 21 Da21
Biggleswade **GB** 25 Db27
Bihać **BIH** 85 Gb38
Biharia **RO** 75 Hc34
Biharkeresztes **H** 75 Hc34
Biharnagybajom **H** 75 Hb34
Bihireşti **RO** 76 Jc34
Bijeljina **BIH** 86 Ha38
Bijelo Polje **MNE** 87 Hb40
Bila Cerkva **UA** 121 Ec15
Bilbao **E** 80 Cb37
Bilbo **E** 80 Cb37
Bilbor **RO** 76 Jb34
Bílčice **CZ** 66 Gc31
Bíldudalur **IS** 14 Bc04
Bileća **BIH** 86 Gd40
Biled **RO** 75 Hb36
Biłgoraj **PL** 67 Hc30
Bilgorod-Dnistrovs'kij **UA** 77 Kb34
Bílina **CZ** 65 Fd30

Bilisht **AL** 101 Hc43
Biljaivka **UA** 77 Kb34
Bilje **HR** 74 Ha36
Bilka **BG** 89 Jd39
Billdal **S** 43 Fc20
Billingsfors **S** 43 Fd19
Billom **F** 69 Dc35
Bilohors'k **UA** 126 Fa17
Bilokurakyne **UA** 122 Fb14
Bilopillja **UA** 121 Ed13
Bílovec **CZ** 66 Gd31
Bilovods'k **UA** 122 Fb14
Bilto **N** 26 Gd05
Binarowa **PL** 67 Hb31
Binche **B** 62 Ea29
Binéfar **E** 80 Cd40
Bingen **D** 63 Ed30
Bingham **GB** 25 Db25
Bingsjö **S** 38 Gb16
Binz **D** 57 Fd25
Bioča **MNE** 87 Hb40
Biograd na moru **HR** 85 Gb39
Birchiş **RO** 75 Hc36
Bircza **PL** 67 Hc31
Birgi **TR** 113 Kb45
Biri **N** 37 Fc16
Birkeland **N** 42 Ed19
Birkeland **N** 42 Fa19
Birkenfeld **D** 63 Ec31
Birkenhead **GB** 21 Da24
Birkerød **DK** 49 Fd23
Birmingham **GB** 24 Da26
Birr **IRL** 18 Ca24
Birsay **GB** 17 Db17
Birštonas **LT** 53 Hd24
Biruinţa **MD** 77 Jd33
Biržai **LT** 53 Hd24
Birži **LV** 53 Hd22
Bisaccia **I** 99 Gb43
Biscarrosse **F** 68 Cc36
Bisceglie **I** 99 Gc42
Bischofshofen **A** 73 Fd34
Bischofswerda **D** 65 Ga29
Bishop Auckland **GB** 21 Db23
Bishop's Stortford **GB** 25 Db27
Biskupiec **PL** 59 Hb25
Bismark **D** 56 Fc27
Bismo **N** 37 Fb15
Bispgården **S** 38 Gb13
Bistreţ **RO** 88 Ja38
Bistrica **BIH** 86 Gc38
Bistrica **MNE** 86 Ha40
Bistrica **SRB** 86 Ha39
Bistriţa **RO** 76 Ja34
Bisztynek **PL** 58 Ha25
Bitburg **D** 63 Ec30
Bitche **F** 63 Ec32
Bitola **MK** 101 Hc42
Bitonto **I** 99 Gc42
Bitterfeld **D** 56 Fc28
Bitti **I** 97 Ed43
Bivona **I** 108 Fd47
Bjahoml' **BY** 53 Jb23

Bjahoml' **BY** 120 Ea12
Bjala **BG** 88 Jc39
Bjala **BG** 89 Ka39
Bjala čerkva **BG** 102 Jb41
Bjala Slatina **BG** 88 Ja39
Bjalyničy **BY** 121 Eb12
Bjärnum **S** 49 Fd22
Bjaroza **BY** 120 Ea13
Bjarozavka **BY** 120 Ea13
Bjärred **S** 49 Fd23
Bjästa **S** 39 Gc13
Bjelovar **HR** 74 Gc36
Bjerkvik **N** 29 Gc06
Bjerringbro **DK** 49 Fb22
Björbo **S** 44 Ga17
Bjørkelangen **N** 43 Fc17
Björkliden **S** 29 Gc06
Björklinge **S** 45 Gc17
Björklund **S** 33 Gc10
Björköby **FIN** 40 Ha13
Björksele **S** 33 Gc11
Bjørn **N** 32 Fd09
Bjørna **N** 28 Gb06
Björna **S** 39 Gc13
Bjørneborg **S** 44 Ga18
Bjørnevatn **N** 27 Hd04
Bjørnstad **N** 27 Hd04
Bjurholm **S** 34 Gd12
Bjursås **S** 38 Gb16
Bjuv **S** 49 Fd23
Blace **SRB** 87 Hc39
Blackburn **GB** 21 Da24
Blackpool **GB** 21 Da24
Blaenavon **GB** 24 Cd26
Blagaj **BIH** 86 Gd40
Blagodarnyj **RUS** 127 Ga16
Blagoeve **MD** 77 Kb33
Blagoevgrad **BG** 101 Ja41
Blaiken **S** 33 Gb10
Blain **F** 61 Cd32
Blairgowrie **GB** 17 Da20
Blaj **RO** 76 Ja35
Błąkały **PL** 59 Hc25
Blakstad **N** 42 Fa19
Blåmont **F** 63 Ec32
Blandford Forum **GB** 24 Cd28
Blanes **E** 95 Db41
Blangy-sur-Bresle **F** 62 Dc30
Blankaholm **S** 50 Gb21
Blankenberge **B** 54 Dd28
Blankenburg **D** 56 Fb28
Blankenheim **D** 63 Ec30
Blanzac **F** 69 Da35
Blarney **IRL** 22 Bd25
Błaszki **PL** 58 Gd28
Blatnica **BIH** 86 Gd38
Blato **HR** 86 Gc40
Blaubeuren **D** 72 Fa33
Blaufelden **D** 64 Fa31
Blåvand **DK** 48 Fa23
Blaye **F** 68 Cd36
Blaževo **SRB** 87 Hc39
Blāzma **LV** 52 Hb21
Bleckede **D** 56 Fb26

Bled – Botoşani

Bled SLO 73 Ga35
Bleiburg A 73 Ga35
Bleik N 28 Gb05
Bleikvassli N 33 Ga09
Bléneau F 70 Dd33
Bleré F 69 Db33
Blerick NL 55 Ec28
Bletterans F 70 Ea34
Blieskastel D 63 Ec31
Blinisht AL 100 Hb41
Blizne PL 67 Hc31
Blois F 69 Db33
Blokhus DK 49 Fb21
Blombacka S 44 Ga18
Blönduós IS 14 Bd05
Błonie PL 58 Ha28
Błotno PL 57 Ga26
Bludenz A 72 Fa34
Blumau A 73 Gb35
Blumberg D 71 Ed33
Blyth GB 21 Db22
Bø N 43 Fb18
Boal E 78 Bb36
Boat of Garten GB 17 Da19
Bobâlna RO 75 Hd34
Bobbio I 83 Ed37
Bobigny F 62 Dc31
Bobingen D 72 Fb33
Böblingen D 64 Fa32
Bobolice PL 57 Gb25
Boboševo BG 101 Ja41
Bobovdol BG 102 Ja40
Bobr BY 121 Eb12
Bobrov RUS 122 Fb13
Bobrovycja UA 121 Ec14
Bobrowice PL 57 Ga28
Bobrynec' UA 125 Ed16
Bočac BIH 86 Gc38
Bochnia PL 67 Hb31
Bocholt D 55 Ec28
Bochum D 55 Ec28
Bockara S 50 Gb21
Bockenem D 56 Fb28
Bócki PL 59 Hc27
Bočkivci UA 76 Jb32
Bocşa RO 87 Hc37
Bocsig RO 75 Hc35
Bod RO 88 Jb36
Boda S 38 Ga16
Böda S 51 Gc21
Boðani SRB 86 Ha37
Bodators S 50 Ga21
Boden S 34 Ha09
Bodenwerder D 56 Fa28
Bodmin GB 23 Cb28
Bodø N 28 Ga08
Bodoc RO 76 Jb35
Bodrost BG 101 Ja41
Bodrum TR 115 Kb47
Bodsjö S 38 Ga14
Bodzentyn PL 67 Hb29
Boën F 70 Dd36
Bogarra E 107 Ca44
Bogatić SRB 86 Ha37
Bogatynia PL 65 Ga29
Boğaziçi TR 113 Kb45

Bogdana RO 77 Jd34
Bogë AL 100 Hb41
Böğecik TR 128 Gc16
Bogen D 64 Fc32
Bogen N 28 Gb06
Bogense DK 49 Fb23
Bogetići MNE 86 Ha40
Bognes N 28 Gb06
Bognor Regis GB 24 Da28
Bogny-sur-Meuse F 62 Ea30
Bogorodick RUS 118 Fa11
Bogorodsk RUS 118 Fb09
Bogova RO 87 Hd38
Bogučar RUS 123 Fc13
Bogutovac SRB 87 Hb39
Bohain-en-Vermandois F 62 Dd30
Bohdalov CZ 65 Gb31
Bohoduchiv UA 122 Fa14
Bohonal de Ibor E 91 Bb41
Böhönye H 74 Gc35
Bohorodčany UA 76 Ja32
Bohuslav UA 121 Ec15
Boiro E 78 Ad37
Bois-le-Roi F 62 Dd32
Boizenburg D 56 Fb26
Bojano I 99 Ga42
Bojanovo BG 103 Jd40
Bojanów PL 67 Hc30
Bojanowo PL 58 Gc28
Bøjden DK 49 Fb24
Bojnik SRB 87 Hc40
Boksjön S 33 Gb10
Bol HR 86 Gc40
Bol.Selo RUS 117 Ed09
Bolaños de Calatrava E 92 Bc43
Bolayır TR 103 Jd42
Bolbec F 61 Db30
Boldeşti Scăeni RO 88 Jc36
Bolechiv UA 67 Hd31
Bolesławiec PL 65 Gb29
Bolewicko PL 57 Gb27
Bolhó H 74 Gc36
Bolhov RUS 121 Ed12
Bolhrad UA 77 Ka35
Boliden S 34 Gd11
Bolintin-Vale RO 88 Jc37
Boljanići MNE 86 Ha39
Boljevac SRB 87 Hc39
Bolków PL 65 Gb29
Bollebygd S 43 Fd20
Bollène F 82 Dd38
Bollnäs S 38 Gb15
Bollstabruk S 39 Gc13
Bollullos del Condado E 105 Ad44
Bologna I 84 Fb38
Bologoe RUS 117 Ec09
Bologovo RUS 117 Eb10
Bol'šaja Ižora RUS 41 Jb16
Bol'šakovo RUS 52 Hb24
Bolsena I 84 Fc40
Bol'ševik RUS 123 Fd12
Bol'šinka RUS 123 Fc14
Bol'šoj Sabsk RUS 47 Jb18

Bol'šoj Taglino RUS 47 Jb17
Bolsward NL 55 Ec26
Boltaña E 80 Cd39
Bolton GB 21 Da24
Bolungarvík IS 14 Bc04
Bolzano I 72 Fb35
Bombarral P 90 Ac41
Boñar E 79 Bc37
Bonar Bridge GB 17 Da18
Bonäs S 38 Ga16
Bondeno I 84 Fb37
Bonifacio F 96 Ed42
Bonn D 63 Ec29
Bonnat F 69 Db34
Bonnétable F 61 Db32
Bonneval F 61 Db32
Bonneville F 71 Eb35
Bono I 97 Ed43
Bonorva I 97 Ec43
Bonyhád H 74 Gd36
Boo S 45 Gc18
Bopfingen D 64 Fb32
Boppard D 63 Ed30
Bor CZ 65 Fd31
Bor S 50 Ga21
Bor SRB 87 Hd38
Bor TR 128 Gd15
Borås S 43 Fd20
Borba P 90 Ad42
Borca RO 76 Jb34
Bordeaux F 68 Cd36
Bordeira P 104 Ab43
Bordesholm D 56 Fb25
Borðeyri IS 14 Bd05
Bordighera I 83 Ec39
Borek Wielkopolski PL 58 Gc28
Borensberg S 44 Gb19
Borga FIN 41 Hd16
Borgarnes IS 14 Bc06
Borger NL 55 Ec26
Borgholm S 50 Gb21
Borgomanero I 71 Ed36
Borgorose I 98 Fd41
Borgo San Dalmazzo I 83 Ec38
Borgo San Lorenzo I 84 Fb39
Borgosesia I 71 Ed36
Borgo Val di Taro I 84 Fa38
Borgo Valsugana I 72 Fb36
Borhaug N 42 Ed20
Borinskoe RUS 122 Fb12
Borisoglebsk RUS 123 Fc12
Borisovka RUS 122 Fa14
Borisovo RUS 117 Ed08
Borisovo-Sudskoe RUS 117 Ec08
Borja E 80 Cb40
Borkavičy BY 53 Jb22
Borken D 55 Ec28
Borlänge S 44 Gb17
Borlaug N 36 Fa16
Borlu TR 113 Kb44
Bormio I 72 Fa35
Borna D 64 Fc29

Bornheim D 63 Ec29
Boroaia RO 76 Jc33
Borobia E 80 Cb40
Borodinskoe RUS 41 Jb15
Borodjanka UA 121 Ec14
Borodyno UA 77 Ka34
Borova UA 122 Fb14
Borovan BG 88 Ja39
Borovany CZ 65 Ga32
Borovci BG 88 Ja39
Borovec BG 102 Ja40
Borovenka RUS 117 Ec09
Boroviči RUS 117 Ec09
Borovik RUS 47 Jb19
Borovsk RUS 117 Ed11
Borrisokane IRL 18 Ca24
Borşa RO 76 Ja33
Borščiv UA 76 Jb32
Borščiv UA 124 Ea16
Borsec RO 76 Jb34
Børselv N 27 Hb03
Borsh AL 100 Hb44
Bort-les-Orgues F 69 Dc36
Börtnan S 38 Ga14
Borup DK 49 Fc23
Borve GB 16 Cc18
Borvika UA 77 Jd32
Borynja UA 67 Hd32
Boryslav UA 67 Hd31
Boryspil' UA 121 Ec14
Borzna UA 121 Ec14
Borzysław PL 58 Gc25
Bosa I 97 Ec43
Bosanci HR 85 Gb37
Bosanska Dubica BIH 86 Gc37
Bosanska Gradiška BIH 86 Gc37
Bosanska Kostajnica BIH 86 Gc37
Bosanska Krupa BIH 85 Gb37
Bosanski Brod BIH 86 Gd37
Bosanski Kobaš BIH 86 Gd37
Bosanski Novi BIH 86 Gc37
Bosanski Petrovac BIH 86 Gc38
Bosanski Šamac BIH 86 Gd37
Bosansko Grahovo BIH 86 Gc38
Bosilegrad SRB 87 Hd40
Boskovice CZ 66 Gc31
Bossbøen N 42 Fa17
Boston GB 25 Db25
Bosut SRB 86 Ha37
Böszénfa H 74 Gd36
Bote S 39 Gc13
Boteşti RO 76 Jc34
Boteşti RO 88 Jb37
Botevgrad BG 102 Ja40
Boticas P 78 Ba38
Botiz RO 75 Hd33
Botngård N 32 Fc12
Botoşani RO 76 Jc33

Botsmark **S** 34 Gd12
Bottrop **D** 55 Ec28
Boueilho **F** 80 Cd38
Bouillon **B** 63 Eb30
Bouligny **F** 63 Eb31
Bouloc **F** 81 Dc37
Boulogne-Billancourt **F** 62
Dc31
Boulogne-sur-Gesse **F** 81
Da38
Boulogne-sur-Mer **F** 62
Dc29
Bouloire **F** 61 Db32
Bourbon-Lancy **F** 70 Dd34
Bourbon-l'Archambault **F**
69 Dc34
Bourbonne-les-Bains **F** 71
Eb33
Bourbriac **F** 60 Cc31
Bourdeaux **F** 82 Ea37
Bourganeuf **F** 69 Db35
Bourg-Argental **F** 70 Ea36
Bourg-en-Bresse **F** 70 Ea35
Bourges **F** 69 Dc34
Bourg-et-Comin **F** 62 Dd31
Bourg-Madame **F** 81 Db40
Bourgneuf-en-Retz **F** 68
Cc33
Bourgoin-Jallieu **F** 70 Ea36
Bourg-Saint-Andéol **F** 82
Dd37
Bourg-Saint-Maurice **F** 71
Eb36
Bournemouth **GB** 24 Da28
Boussac **F** 69 Dc34
Boussens **F** 81 Da38
Bouxwiller **F** 63 Ec32
Bovalino Mare **I** 109 Gb46
Bova Marina **I** 109 Gb47
Bovenden **D** 56 Fb28
Boves **F** 62 Dd30
Bovino **I** 99 Gb42
Bowes **GB** 21 Db23
Bowmore **GB** 20 Cc21
Boxberg **D** 65 Ga29
Boxholm **S** 44 Ga20
Boxmeer **NL** 55 Ec28
Boxtel **NL** 55 Eb28
Boyle **IRL** 18 Ca23
Božava **HR** 85 Ga38
Bozburun **TR** 115 Kb47
Bozcaada **TR** 103 Jd43
Bozdoğan **TR** 113 Kb46
Bozen **I** 72 Fb35
Bozioru **RO** 88 Jc36
Bozkir **TR** 128 Ga16
Bozlar **TR** 103 Ka42
Bozouls **F** 81 Dc37
Bozovici **RO** 87 Hc37
Bozyazı **TR** 128 Gb17
Bozzolo **I** 84 Fa37
Bra **I** 83 Ec37
Braås **S** 50 Ga21
Brabova **RO** 88 Ja38
Bracciano **I** 98 Fc41
Brachlewo **PL** 58 Gd25

Bräcke **S** 38 Gb14
Brackley **GB** 24 Da27
Brad **RO** 75 Hd35
Brădeni **RO** 76 Jb35
Bradford **GB** 21 Db24
Brædstrup **DK** 49 Fb23
Braemar **GB** 17 Da20
Braga **P** 78 Ad38
Bragadiru **RO** 88 Jc37
Bragança **P** 78 Bb38
Brăila **RO** 89 Jd36
Braine **F** 62 Dd31
Braintree **GB** 25 Dc27
Brake **D** 56 Fa26
Brakel **D** 56 Fa28
Brålanda **S** 43 Fd19
Brålos **GR** 111 Ja45
Bramming **DK** 48 Fa23
Brampton **GB** 21 Da22
Bramsche **D** 55 Ed27
Brånaberg **S** 33 Gb10
Branäs **S** 38 Fd16
Brancaleone Marina **I** 109
Gb46
Brandbu **N** 43 Fc17
Brande **DK** 48 Fa23
Brandenburg **D** 57 Fd27
Brand-Erbisdorf **D** 65 Fd30
Brändö **FIN** 46 Ha17
Brandon **GB** 25 Dc26
Brandval **N** 43 Fd17
Brandýs nad Labem-Stará
Boleslav **CZ** 65 Ga30
Braniewo **PL** 58 Ha25
Bränna **S** 43 Fd19
Brańsk **PL** 59 Hc27
Brantôme **F** 69 Da35
Braslav **BY** 53 Ja22
Brașov **RO** 88 Jb36
Brastad **S** 43 Fc19
Brąszewice **PL** 66 Gd29
Brataj **AL** 100 Hb43
Bratca **RO** 75 Hd34
Bratislava **SK** 74 Gc33
Bratovoești **RO** 88 Ja38
Bråttas **S** 34 Ha11
Brattmon **S** 38 Fd16
Brattvåg **N** 36 Fa14
Bratunac **BIH** 86 Ha38
Braunau **A** 73 Fd33
Braunfels **D** 63 Ed30
Braunlage **D** 56 Fb28
Braunschweig **D** 56 Fb28
Braunton **GB** 23 Cc27
Bray **IRL** 19 Cb24
Bray-sur-Seine **F** 62 Dd32
Bray-sur-Somme **F** 62 Dd30
Brazatortas **E** 106 Bc43
Brbinj **HR** 85 Ga39
Brčko **BIH** 86 Ha37
Breaza **RO** 76 Ja34
Breaza **RO** 88 Jc36
Brechin **GB** 17 Db20
Břeclav **CZ** 66 Gc32
Brecon **GB** 24 Cd26
Breda **NL** 55 Eb28

Bredaryd **S** 50 Ga21
Bredbyn **S** 39 Gc13
Bredstedt **D** 48 Fa24
Bree **B** 63 Eb29
Bregenz **A** 72 Fa34
Bregovo **BG** 87 Hd38
Bréhal **F** 61 Cd31
Breiðdalsvík **IS** 15 Cc08
Breidvikeidet **N** 26 Gc04
Breil-sur-Roya **F** 83 Ec38
Breisach **D** 71 Ec33
Breivika **N** 28 Gb06
Breivkbotn **N** 26 Gd03
Breja **RUS** 47 Jb18
Brejtovo **RUS** 117 Ed09
Brekken **N** 37 Fd14
Brekstad **N** 32 Fb12
Bremen **D** 56 Fa26
Bremerhaven **D** 56 Fa26
Bremervörde **D** 56 Fa26
Brem-sur-Mer **F** 68 Cc33
Breń **PL** 57 Gb27
Brenes **E** 105 Ba44
Brenna **N** 33 Ga10
Breno **I** 72 Fa36
Brescia **I** 72 Fa36
Bressanone **I** 72 Fc35
Bressuire **F** 69 Da33
Brëst **BY** 59 Hd27
Brest **F** 60 Cb31
Brestovac **SRB** 87 Hd38
Brestovo **BG** 88 Jb39
Brețcu **RO** 76 Jc35
Bretenoux **F** 69 Db36
Breteuil **F** 62 Dc30
Breteuil-sur-Iton **F** 61 Db31
Bretten **D** 63 Ed32
Breuil-Cervínia **I** 71 Ec36
Breza **BIH** 86 Gd38
Brežice **SLO** 73 Gb36
Breznik **BG** 87 Hd40
Brezno **SK** 67 Ha32
Brezoi **RO** 88 Ja36
Brezovo **BG** 102 Jb40
Briançon **F** 83 Eb37
Briare **F** 69 Dc33
Bribir **HR** 85 Gb39
Briceni **MD** 76 Jc32
Bricquebec **F** 61 Cd30
Bridge End **IRL** 19 Cb21
Bridgend **GB** 24 Cd27
Bridgnorth **GB** 24 Da26
Bridgwater **GB** 24 Cd27
Bridlington **GB** 21 Dc24
Bridport **GB** 24 Cd28
Briec **F** 60 Cb31
Brie-Comte-Robert **F** 62
Dc31
Brienne-le-Château **F** 62
Ea32
Brienz **CH** 71 Ed35
Briey **F** 63 Eb31
Brig **CH** 71 Ec35
Brighton **GB** 25 Db28
Brignogan-Plages **F** 60
Cb30

Brignoles **F** 82 Ea39
Brihuega **E** 92 Ca41
Briksdal **N** 36 Fa15
Brilon **D** 64 Fa29
Brimnes **N** 36 Fa16
Brindisi **I** 100 Gd43
Brinje **HR** 85 Ga37
Brinlack **IRL** 19 Cb21
Brintbodarna **S** 38 Ga16
Brionne **F** 61 Db31
Brioude **F** 69 Dc36
Briouze **F** 61 Da31
Brisighella **I** 84 Fb38
Bristol **GB** 24 Cd27
Brive-la-Gaillarde **F** 69 Db36
Briviesca **E** 79 Ca38
Brixen **I** 72 Fc35
Brixham **GB** 23 Cc28
Brjančaninovo **RUS** 47 Jb20
Brjanka **UA** 122 Fb15
Brjansk **RUS** 121 Ed12
Brka **BIH** 86 Ha37
Brnaze **HR** 86 Gc39
Brno **CZ** 66 Gc32
Bro **S** 45 Gd20
Broadford **GB** 16 Cd19
Broadstairs **GB** 25 Dc28
Broby **S** 50 Ga22
Broceni **LV** 52 Hb21
Brochów **PL** 58 Ha27
Brod **BIH** 86 Ha39
Brod **MK** 101 Hc42
Brod **MK** 101 Hc42
Brodaiži **LV** 53 Jb21
Brodarevo **SRB** 87 Hb39
Brodce **CZ** 65 Ga30
Brodec'ke **UA** 121 Eb15
Brodick **GB** 20 Cd21
Brodina de Jos **RO** 76 Jb33
Brodnica **PL** 58 Ha26
Brody **UA** 120 Ea15
Brojce **PL** 57 Gb25
Brokind **S** 44 Gb20
Brome **D** 56 Fb27
Bromölla **S** 50 Ga23
Brömsebro **S** 50 Gb22
Bromsgrove **GB** 24 Da26
Bromyard **GB** 24 Da26
Brønderslev **DK** 49 Fb21
Broni **I** 83 Ed37
Brønnøysund **N** 32 Fd10
Bronte **I** 109 Ga47
Broons **F** 61 Cd31
Brora **GB** 17 Da18
Brørup **DK** 48 Fa23
Brösarp **S** 50 Ga23
Brøstadbotn **N** 26 Gc05
Broșteni **RO** 87 Hd37
Broszków **PL** 59 Hc27
Broto **E** 80 Cd39
Brottby **S** 45 Gc18
Brou **F** 61 Db32
Brough **GB** 21 Da23
Broughton-in-Furness **GB**
21 Da23
Broumov **CZ** 65 Gb30

Broutzéika – Cagnano Varano

Broutzéika **GR** 111 Ja46
Brouwershaven **NL** 54 Ea28
Brovary **UA** 121 Ec14
Brovst **DK** 49 Fb21
Brozas **E** 91 Ba41
Brú **IS** 14 Bd05
Bruay-la-Buissière **F** 62 Dd29
Bruchsal **D** 63 Ed32
Bruck **A** 73 Fd34
Bruck **D** 64 Fc32
Bruck an der Leitha **A** 74 Gc33
Bruck an der Mur **A** 73 Gb34
Brüel **D** 56 Fc26
Brugg **CH** 71 Ed34
Brugge **B** 54 Dd28
Bruheim **N** 36 Fa15
Brûlon **F** 61 Da32
Brumath **F** 63 Ed32
Brumov-Bylnice **CZ** 66 Gd32
Brumunddal **N** 37 Fc16
Brundby **DK** 49 Fb23
Bruneck I 72 Fc35
Brunflo **S** 38 Ga13
Brunico I 72 Fc35
Brunsbüttel **D** 56 Fa25
Bruntál **CZ** 66 Gc31
Brus **SRB** 87 Hc39
Brusarci **BG** 87 Hd39
Brussel **B** 62 Ea29
Brüssow **D** 57 Ga26
Brusturoasa **RO** 76 Jc34
Bruvno **HR** 85 Gb38
Bruxelles **B** 62 Ea29
Bruyères **F** 71 Ec33
Bruz **F** 61 Cd32
Bruzaholm **S** 44 Ga20
Brvenik **SRB** 87 Hb39
Brwinow **PL** 59 Hb28
Bryne **N** 42 Ec19
Brzeg **PL** 66 Gc29
Brzeg Dolny **PL** 66 Gc29
Brześć Kujawski **PL** 58 Gd27
Brzesko **PL** 67 Hb31
Brzeszcze **PL** 67 Ha31
Brzeziny **PL** 58 Ha28
Brzostek **PL** 67 Hb31
Brzóza **PL** 59 Hb28
Brzozie Lubawskie **PL** 58 Ha26
Brzozów **PL** 67 Hc31
Buba **RO** 88 Jc36
Bubiai **LT** 52 Hc23
Buča **UA** 121 Ec14
Bučač **UA** 124 Ea16
Bucakkışia **TR** 128 Gb16
Buccino I 99 Gb43
Buceş **RO** 75 Hd35
Buchen **D** 64 Fa31
Buchholz **D** 56 Fb26
Buchloe **D** 72 Fb33
Buchs **CH** 72 Fa34

Buchy **F** 62 Dc30
Bučionys **LT** 53 Hd24
Buciumi **RO** 75 Hd34
Buckhaven **GB** 21 Da21
Bučovice **CZ** 66 Gc32
Bucşani **RO** 88 Jc37
Bucureşti **RO** 88 Jc37
Buczek **PL** 66 Gd29
Bud **N** 36 Fa13
Budaörs **H** 74 Ha34
Budapest **H** 74 Ha34
Buðardalur **IS** 14 Bc05
Buddusò I 97 Ed43
Bude **GB** 23 Cc27
Büdelsdorf **D** 56 Fb25
Budënnovsk **RUS** 127 Ga16
Budeşti **RO** 88 Ja37
Budeşti **RO** 88 Jc37
Buđevo **SRB** 87 Hb40
Büdingen **D** 64 Fa30
Budogošč' **RUS** 117 Eb08
Budrio I 84 Fb38
Budva **MNE** 100 Ha41
Budziszewice **PL** 58 Ha28
Budzyń **PL** 58 Gc27
Buenavista de Valdavia **E** 79 Bd38
Buendía **E** 92 Ca41
Bueu **E** 78 Ad37
Buftea **RO** 88 Jc37
Buğdaylı **TR** 103 Ka42
Bugeat **F** 69 Db35
Bugojno **BIH** 86 Gc39
Bugøyfjord **N** 27 Hd04
Bugøynes **N** 27 Hd04
Bugul'ma **RUS** 119 Ga09
Bühl **D** 63 Ed32
Buhovci **BG** 89 Jd39
Buhovo **BG** 102 Ja40
Buhuşi **RO** 76 Jc34
Builth Wells **GB** 24 Cd26
Buinsk **RUS** 119 Fd09
Buj **RUS** 118 Fa08
Bujalance **E** 105 Bb44
Bujanovac **SRB** 87 Hc40
Bujaraloz **E** 80 Cc40
Buje **HR** 85 Fd37
Bukanovskaja **RUS** 123 Fc13
Bukta **N** 26 Gd04
Buky **UA** 121 Ec15
Bülach **CH** 71 Ed34
Bulanlak **TR** 127 Fd19
Bulgar **RUS** 119 Fd09
Bullas **E** 107 Ca44
Bulle **CH** 71 Ec35
Bumbeşti-Jiu **RO** 88 Ja37
Bunclody **IRL** 23 Cb25
Buncrana **IRL** 19 Cb21
Bünde **D** 56 Fa27
Bundoran **IRL** 18 Ca22
Bunkris **S** 38 Fd15
Buñol **E** 93 Cb43
Bureå **S** 34 Ha11
Buren **NL** 55 Ec26
Burfjord **N** 26 Gd04

Burg **D** 56 Fc25
Burg **D** 56 Fc28
Burgas **BG** 89 Ka39
Burgdorf **CH** 71 Ec34
Burgdorf **D** 56 Fb27
Burgebrach **D** 64 Fb31
Burgess Hill **GB** 25 Db28
Burghausen **D** 73 Fd33
Burgillos del Cerro **E** 105 Ba43
Burglengenfeld **D** 64 Fc32
Burgo **P** 78 Ad39
Burgohondo **E** 91 Bc41
Burgos **E** 79 Ca38
Burgstädt **D** 65 Fd29
Burgsvik **S** 51 Gc21
Burgui **E** 80 Cc39
Burhaniye **TR** 103 Ka43
Burila Mare **RO** 87 Hd38
Burjassot **E** 93 Cc43
Burnham-on-Crouch **GB** 25 Dc27
Burnham-on-Sea **GB** 24 Cd27
Burnley **GB** 21 Da24
Burrel **RKS** 100 Hb42
Burriana **E** 93 Cc42
Burseryd **S** 49 Fd21
Bürstadt **D** 63 Ed31
Burton-upon-Trent **GB** 24 Da25
Burträsk **S** 34 Gd11
Burwick **GB** 17 Db17
Bury **GB** 21 Da24
Bury Saint Edmunds **GB** 25 Dc27
Busalla I 83 Ed38
Buşăuca **MD** 77 Ka33
Busca I 83 Ec38
Busemarke **DK** 49 Fd24
Buševec **HR** 73 Gb36
Busici **MK** 101 Hd41
Bus'k **UA** 120 Ea15
Busko-Zdrój **PL** 67 Hb30
Busovača **BIH** 86 Gd38
Buşteni **RO** 88 Jb36
Büsum **D** 56 Fa25
Butan **BG** 88 Ja39
Butrint **AL** 100 Hb44
Buttstädt **D** 64 Fc29
Buturlinovka **RUS** 122 Fb13
Butzbach **D** 63 Ed30
Bützow **D** 56 Fc25
Buxtehude **D** 56 Fb26
Buxton **GB** 24 Da25
Buxy **F** 70 Ea34
Büyükçekmece **TR** 103 Kb41
Buzançais **F** 69 Db34
Buzancy **F** 62 Ea31
Buzău **RO** 88 Jc36
Buzescu **RO** 88 Jb38
Buzet **HR** 85 Fd37
Buziaş **RO** 75 Hc36
Bychav **BY** 121 Eb12
Bychawa **PL** 67 Hc29

Byczyna **PL** 66 Gd29
Bydgoszcz **PL** 58 Gc26
Bygdeå **S** 34 Gd12
Bygdisheim **N** 37 Fb15
Bygdsiljum **S** 34 Gd11
Bygland **N** 42 Fa19
Byglandsfjord **N** 42 Fa19
Bykle **N** 42 Fa18
Bykovo **RUS** 123 Fd13
Byrkjedal **N** 42 Ed19
Byrkjelo **N** 36 Ed15
Byske **S** 34 Ha11
Bysław **PL** 58 Gc26
Bystrecovo **RUS** 47 Jb19
Bystřice nad Pernštejnem **CZ** 65 Gb31
Bystrycja **UA** 76 Ja32
Bystrzyca Kłodzka **PL** 66 Gc30
Byszyno **PL** 57 Gb25
Bytča **SK** 66 Gd32
Bytom **PL** 66 Gd30
Bytom Odrzański **PL** 57 Gb28
Bytoń **PL** 58 Gd27
Bytów **PL** 58 Gc25
Byxelkrok **S** 51 Gc21

C

Cabañaquinta **E** 79 Bc37
Cabanes **E** 93 Cc42
Cabeza del Buey **E** 105 Bb43
Cabezas Rubias **E** 105 Ad43
Cabezón de la Sal **E** 79 Bd37
Cabezuela del Valle **E** 91 Bb40
Cabourg **F** 61 Da30
Cabra **E** 105 Bb44
Cabras I 97 Ec44
Čačak **SRB** 87 Hb39
Caccamo I 108 Fd47
Cacela Velha **P** 104 Ac44
Cáceres **E** 91 Ba41
Čačërsk **BY** 121 Ec13
Čačëvicy **BY** 121 Eb12
Cachopo **P** 104 Ac43
Čadca **SK** 66 Gd31
Cadenet **F** 82 Ea38
Cadillac **F** 68 Cd36
Cádiz **E** 105 Ad45
Caen **F** 61 Da30
Caernarfon **GB** 20 Cd24
Caerphilly **GB** 24 Cd27
Caersws **GB** 24 Cd25
Čaevo **RUS** 117 Ed08
Cagan Aman **RUS** 123 Ga14
Cagan-Nur **RUS** 123 Ga14
Çağış **TR** 103 Kb43
Cagli I 84 Fc39
Cagliari I 97 Ed45
Cagnano Varano I 99 Gb41

140

Cagnes-sur-Mer **F** 83 Eb39
Čagoda **RUS** 117 Ec08
Caher **IRL** 22 Ca25
Caherdaniel **IRL** 22 Bc25
Cahersiveen **IRL** 22 Bc25
Cahors **F** 81 Db37
Cahul **MD** 77 Jd35
Căinari **MD** 77 Ka34
Căinarii Vechi **MD** 77 Jd32
Câineni **RO** 88 Ja36
Cairnryan **GB** 20 Cd22
Cairo Montenotte **I** 83 Ec38
Cajarc **F** 81 Db37
Čajniče **BIH** 86 Ha39
Čakino **RUS** 123 Fc12
Çakırbeyli **TR** 113 Kb46
Çakmak **TR** 128 Gc15
Čakovec **HR** 74 Gc35
Calaceite **E** 93 Cd41
Calaf **E** 81 Da40
Calafat **RO** 87 Hd38
Calahorra **E** 80 Cb39
Calais **F** 54 Cd28
Cala Millor **E** 95 Db43
Calamocha **E** 93 Cd41
Călan **RO** 75 Hd36
Calañas **E** 105 Ad43
Calanda **E** 93 Cc41
Calangianus **I** 96 Ed42
Cala Rajada **E** 95 Db43
Călăraşi **MD** 77 Jd33
Călăraşi **RO** 89 Jd37
Calasparra **E** 107 Ca44
Calatafimi **I** 108 Fc47
Calatañazor **E** 79 Ca39
Calatayud **E** 80 Cb40
Calau **D** 57 Ga28
Calbe **D** 56 Fc28
Caldaro **I** 72 Fb35
Caldas da Reinha **P** 90 Ac40
Caldas de Reis **E** 78 Ad37
Caldes de Montbui **E** 95 Db41
Calella **E** 95 Db41
Calenzana **F** 96 Ed40
Caleruega **E** 79 Ca39
Çalı **TR** 103 Kb42
Călimăneşti **RO** 88 Ja36
Callac **F** 60 Cc31
Callan **IRL** 22 Ca25
Callander **GB** 17 Da20
Callanish **GB** 16 Cd17
Callosa de Segura **E** 107 Cb44
Calp (Calpe) **E** 94 Cc44
Caltabellotta **I** 108 Fd47
Caltagirone **I** 109 Ga47
Caltanissetta **I** 108 Fd47
Çaltılıbük **TR** 103 Kb43
Călugăreni **RO** 88 Jc38
Calvi **F** 96 Ed40
Calvià **E** 95 Da43
Calw **D** 63 Gd37
Calzada de Calatrava **E** 92 Bc43

Camaiore **I** 84 Fa39
Camarasa **E** 80 Cd40
Camarès **F** 81 Dc38
Camaret-sur-Mer **F** 60 Cb31
Camas **E** 105 Ba44
Cambados **E** 78 Ad37
Cambo-les-Bains **F** 80 Cc38
Camborne **GB** 23 Cb28
Cambrai **F** 62 Dd30
Cambridge **GB** 25 Db26
Cambrils **E** 93 Cd41
Camelford **GB** 23 Cb28
Camenca **MD** 77 Jd32
Camerino **I** 85 Fd40
Camerota **I** 99 Gb44
Çamiçi **TR** 113 Kb46
Caminha **P** 78 Ad37
Caminreal **E** 93 Cb41
Çamlıca **TR** 128 Gb17
Çamliyayla **TR** 128 Gd16
Cammarata **I** 108 Fd47
Camp **IRL** 18 Bc24
Campanario **E** 91 Bb42
Campanas **E** 80 Cb38
Campbeltown **GB** 20 Cc21
Câmpeni **RO** 75 Hd35
Câmpia Turzii **RO** 76 Ja35
Campiglia Marittima **I** 84 Fa40
Campillo de Llerena **E** 105 Ba43
Campillos **E** 105 Bb45
Câmpina **RO** 88 Jc36
Campo **E** 80 Cd39
Campobasso **I** 99 Ga42
Campo de Criptana **E** 92 Bd42
Campo Ligure **I** 83 Ed38
Campo Maior **P** 90 Ad42
Camporrobles **E** 93 Cb42
Campos **E** 95 Db44
Campotéjar **E** 106 Bc45
Campo Tures **I** 72 Fc35
Câmpu lui Neag **RO** 75 Hd36
Câmpulung **RO** 88 Jb36
Câmpulung Moldovenesc **RO** 76 Jb33
Câmpuri **RO** 76 Jc35
Çan **TR** 103 Ka43
Canabal **E** 78 Ba37
Çanakkale **TR** 103 Jd43
Canale **I** 83 Ec37
Canals **E** 93 Cb43
Cañaveral **E** 91 Ba41
Cañaveras **E** 92 Ca41
Canazei **I** 72 Fc35
Cancale **F** 61 Cd31
Cancon **F** 81 Da37
Çandarlı **TR** 113 Ka44
Candé **F** 61 Cd32
Candeleda **E** 91 Bb41
Canelli **I** 83 Ed37
Cañete **E** 93 Cb42
Canet-Plage **F** 81 Dc39
Canfranc **E** 80 Cc39

Cangas **E** 78 Ad37
Cangas del Narcea **E** 78 Bb37
Cangas de Onís **E** 79 Bd37
Canicattì **I** 108 Fd47
Caniles **E** 106 Bd45
Cañizal **E** 79 Bc39
Canjáyar **E** 106 Bd45
Cannes **F** 83 Eb39
Cannobio **I** 71 Ed36
Canosa di Puglia **I** 99 Gb42
Cantalejo **E** 92 Bd40
Cantalpino **E** 91 Bc40
Cantanhede **P** 90 Ac39
Cantavieja **E** 93 Cc41
Cantemir **MD** 77 Jd35
Canterbury **GB** 25 Dc28
Cantillana **E** 105 Ba44
Cantoria **E** 106 Bd45
Caorle **I** 73 Fd36
Capaccio **I** 99 Ga43
Čapaevskij **RUS** 119 Ga10
Caparroso **E** 80 Cb39
Capbreton **F** 80 Cc37
Cap d'Agde **F** 81 Dc39
Capdenac-Gare **F** 81 Db37
Capel'ka **RUS** 47 Jb19
Cap Ferret **F** 68 Cc36
Capidava **RO** 89 Ka37
Capinha **P** 91 Ba40
Čaplina **BIH** 86 Gd40
Čaplygin **RUS** 118 Fb11
Čaplynka **UA** 126 Fa17
Capo d'Orlando **I** 109 Ga46
Capri **I** 99 Ga43
Captieux **F** 80 Cd37
Capua **I** 99 Ga42
Caracal **RO** 88 Jb38
Caraman **F** 81 Db38
Caranga de Abajo **E** 79 Bc37
Caransebeş **RO** 75 Hc36
Carantec **F** 60 Cb30
Caravaca de la Cruz **E** 107 Ca44
Carballiño **E** 78 Ba37
Carballo **E** 78 Ba36
Carboneras **E** 107 Ca46
Carboneras de Guadazaón **E** 93 Cb42
Carbonia **I** 97 Ec45
Carbonne **F** 81 Da38
Carcans **F** 68 Cc36
Carcans-Plage **F** 68 Cc35
Carcassonne **F** 81 Db39
Carcastillo **E** 80 Cc39
Carcelén **E** 93 Cb43
Cardeña **E** 106 Bc43
Cardiff **GB** 24 Cd27
Cardigan **GB** 23 Cc26
Cardona **E** 81 Da40
Carei **RO** 75 Hc33
Carentan **F** 61 Da30
Carevo **BG** 103 Ka40
Cargèse **F** 96 Ed41
Carhaix-Plouguer **F** 60 Cb31

Cariati **I** 99 Gc44
Carignan **F** 63 Eb31
Cariñena **E** 80 Cb40
Carini **I** 108 Fd46
Car Kalojan **BG** 88 Jc38
Cârlibaba **RO** 76 Jb33
Carlisle **GB** 21 Da22
Carloforte **I** 97 Ec45
Carlow **IRL** 19 Cb24
Carloway **GB** 16 Cd17
Carmagnola **I** 83 Ec37
Carmanova **MD** 77 Ka33
Carmarthen **GB** 23 Cc26
Carmaux **F** 81 Db37
Cármenes **E** 79 Bc37
Carmona **E** 105 Ba44
Carnac **F** 60 Cc32
Carndonagh **IRL** 19 Cb21
Carnew **IRL** 23 Cb25
Carnforth **GB** 21 Da23
Carnikava **LV** 52 Hc21
Čarnjany **BY** 59 Hd28
Carnoustie **GB** 17 Db20
Carolinensiel **D** 55 Ed25
Carpen **RO** 88 Ja38
Carpentras **F** 82 Ea38
Carpi **I** 84 Fb37
Carquefou **F** 68 Cd33
Carrara **I** 84 Fa38
Carrascosa del Campo **E** 92 Ca42
Carrbridge **GB** 17 Da19
Carrickfergus **GB** 20 Cc22
Carrickmacross **IRL** 19 Cb23
Carrick-on-Shannon **IRL** 18 Ca23
Carrick-on-Suir **IRL** 22 Ca25
Carrión de los Condes **E** 79 Bd38
Carrouges **F** 61 Da31
Carryduff **GB** 20 Cc22
Çarşamba **TR** 127 Fc19
Cartagena **E** 107 Cb45
Cartaxo **P** 90 Ac41
Cartaya **E** 105 Ad44
Cărvarica **BG** 101 Hd41
Carvin **F** 62 Dd29
Casacalenda **I** 99 Ga42
Casa de Juan Núñez **E** 93 Cb43
Casalbordino **I** 99 Ga41
Casale Monferrato **I** 83 Ed37
Casalmaggiore **I** 84 Fa37
Casalpusterlengo **I** 84 Fa38
Casamassima **I** 99 Gc43
Casamozza **F** 96 Ed40
Casarano **I** 100 Gd44
Casas de Lázaro **E** 92 Ca43
Casas del Puerto **E** 107 Cb44
Casas-Ibáñez **E** 93 Cb43
Casavieja **E** 91 Bc41
Cascais **P** 90 Ab41

Cascante **E** 80 Cb39
Cascia **I** 85 Fd40
Casciana Terme **I** 84 Fa39
Cascina **I** 84 Fa39
Căscioarele **RO** 88 Jc38
Caselle Torinese **I** 83 Ec37
Caserta **I** 99 Ga42
Cashel **IRL** 18 Ca24
Casimcea **RO** 89 Ka36
Casinos **E** 93 Cb42
Čáslav **CZ** 65 Gb31
Čašniki **BY** 121 Eb12
Casoli **I** 99 Ga41
Casoria **I** 99 Ga43
Caspe **E** 93 Cc41
Cassano allo Ionio **I** 99 Gc44
Cassel **F** 62 Dd29
Cassino **I** 98 Fd42
Cassis **F** 82 Ea39
Castagneto Carducci **I** 84 Fa40
Castañar de Ibor **E** 91 Bb41
Castanheira de Píra **P** 90 Ad40
Castejón de Valdejasa **E** 80 Cc40
Castel di Sangro **I** 99 Ga42
Castelfidardo **I** 85 Fd39
Castelfranco Emilia **I** 84 Fb38
Castelfranco Veneto **I** 72 Fc36
Casteljaloux **F** 80 Cd37
Castellabate **I** 99 Ga43
Castellammare del Golfo **I** 108 Fc46
Castellane **F** 83 Eb38
Castellaneta **I** 99 Gc43
Castellaneta Marina **I** 99 Gc43
Castellar de Santiago **E** 92 Bd43
Castell' Arquato **I** 84 Fa37
Castelldans **E** 80 Cd40
Castelldefels **E** 95 Da41
Castell de Ferro **E** 106 Bc46
Castelló de la Plana **E** 93 Cc42
Castelnaudary **F** 81 Db38
Castelnau-de-Médoc **F** 68 Cd36
Castelnau-Magnoac **F** 80 Cd38
Castelnovo ne'Monti **I** 84 Fa38
Castelnuovo di Garfagnana **I** 84 Fa38
Castelo Branco **P** 90 Ad40
Castelo de Vide **P** 90 Ad41
Castel San Giovanni **I** 84 Fa37
Castel San Pietro Terme **I** 84 Fb38
Castelsardo **I** 96 Ec42
Castelsarrasin **F** 81 Da37

Casteltermini **I** 108 Fd47
Castelvetrano **I** 108 Fc47
Castets **F** 80 Cc37
Castiglioncello **I** 84 Fa39
Castiglione della Pescaia **I** 84 Fb40
Castiglione delle Stiviere **I** 84 Fa37
Castiglione sul Lago **I** 84 Fc40
Castiglion Fiorentino **I** 84 Fc39
Castilblanco **E** 91 Bb42
Castillejo de Martín Viejo **E** 91 Ba40
Castillon-en-Couserans **F** 81 Da39
Castillonnès **F** 69 Da36
Castlebar **IRL** 18 Bd22
Castlebay **GB** 16 Cc19
Castleblayney **IRL** 19 Cb23
Castle Douglas **GB** 20 Cd22
Castleisland **IRL** 18 Bd24
Castlepollard **IRL** 19 Cb23
Castlerea **IRL** 18 Ca23
Castletown **GB** 17 Db18
Castletown **GBM** 20 Cd23
Castletownbere **IRL** 22 Bc25
Castres **F** 81 Db38
Castricum **NL** 55 Eb27
Castril **E** 106 Bd44
Castrocaro Terme **I** 84 Fc38
Castro Daire **P** 78 Ad39
Castro del Río **E** 105 Bb44
Castrojeriz **E** 79 Bd38
Castropol **E** 78 Bb36
Castro-Urdiales **E** 79 Ca37
Castro Verde **P** 104 Ac43
Castrovillari **I** 99 Gb44
Castuera **E** 91 Bb42
Çatak **TR** 128 Gc17
Çatalca **TR** 103 Kb41
Catania **I** 109 Ga47
Catanzaro **I** 109 Gc45
Catanzaro Marina **I** 109 Gc45
Cateraggio **F** 96 Ed41
Cattolica **I** 84 Fc39
Căuaş **RO** 75 Hd34
Caudry **F** 62 Dd30
Caumont-l'Éventé **F** 61 Da30
Caunes-Minervois **F** 81 Db38
Cauro **F** 96 Ed41
Căuşeni **MD** 77 Ka34
Caussade **F** 81 Db37
Cauterets **F** 80 Cd39
Cava de'Tirreni **I** 99 Ga43
Cavaillon **F** 82 Ea38
Cavalaire-sur-Mer **F** 83 Eb39
Cavalese **I** 72 Fb35
Cavan **IRL** 19 Cb23
Căvăran **RO** 75 Hc36
Cavnic **RO** 76 Ja33

Cavour **I** 83 Ec37
Cavtat **HR** 86 Gd40
Čavusy **BY** 121 Ec12
Çayağzı **TR** 103 Kb41
Çayeli **TR** 127 Ga19
Cayeux-sur-Mer **F** 62 Dc29
Çayhan **TR** 128 Gc15
Çayırova **CY** 128 Gc18
Caylus **F** 81 Db37
Cazalla de la Sierra **E** 105 Ba43
Cazaubon **F** 80 Cd37
Cazin **BIH** 85 Gb37
Čazma **HR** 74 Gc36
Cazorla **E** 106 Bd44
Cea **E** 79 Bc38
Ceadâr-Lunga **MD** 77 Ka35
Ceanu Mare **RO** 76 Ja35
Ceatalchioi **RO** 89 Ka36
Čeboksary **RUS** 119 Fc09
Cebreros **E** 91 Bc41
Cebrikove **MD** 77 Kb33
Čečava **BIH** 86 Gd38
Ceccano **I** 98 Fd42
Cece **H** 74 Gd35
Čečel'nyk **UA** 77 Ka32
Čečel'nyk **UA** 125 Ec16
Čechtice **CZ** 65 Ga31
Cecina **I** 84 Fa39
Cedeira **E** 78 Ba36
Cedillo **E** 90 Ad41
Cedrillas **E** 93 Cc41
Cée **E** 78 Ad36
Cefalù **I** 108 Fd46
Cegléd **H** 74 Ha34
Ceglie Messapica **I** 100 Gd43
Cehegín **E** 107 Ca44
Čehov **RUS** 118 Fa11
Cehu Silvaniei **RO** 75 Hd34
Čejč **CZ** 66 Gc32
Čekiškė **LT** 52 Hc23
Celano **I** 98 Fd41
Celanova **E** 78 Ba37
Celbridge **IRL** 19 Cb24
Čelebići **BIH** 86 Ha39
Čelić **BIH** 86 Ha38
Celina **RUS** 123 Fd15
Čelinac Donji **BIH** 86 Gc38
Celjachany **BY** 120 Ea13
Celje **SLO** 73 Gb36
Cella **E** 93 Cb41
Celldömölk **H** 74 Gc34
Celle **D** 56 Fb27
Celle Ligure **I** 83 Ed38
Celorico da Beira **P** 78 Ba39
Čel'ovce **SK** 67 Hc32
Cemerno **BIH** 86 Ha40
Cenovo **BG** 88 Jc38
Centelles **E** 81 Db40
Cento **I** 84 Fb38
Čepigovo **MK** 101 Hc42
Čepin **RO** 86 Gd37
Cer **MK** 101 Hc42
Cerachovka **BY** 121 Ec13
Cerbère **F** 81 Dc40

Cercal **P** 104 Ab43
Čerdakly **RUS** 119 Fd09
Cerdeira **P** 91 Ba40
Čerencovo **RUS** 117 Eb08
Čerepovec **RUS** 117 Ed08
Čereševo **BG** 88 Jc38
Ceresole Reale **I** 71 Ec36
Céret **F** 81 Db40
Cerezo de Abajo **E** 92 Bd40
Cerfontaine **B** 62 Ea30
Cerignola **I** 99 Gb42
Cérilly **F** 69 Dc34
Cerizay **F** 68 Cd33
Čerkasovo **RUS** 41 Ja16
Čerkasy **UA** 121 Ed15
Čerkessk **RUS** 127 Fd17
Çerkezköy **TR** 103 Ka41
Cerknica **SLO** 73 Ga36
Cermei **RO** 75 Hc35
Čern' **RUS** 122 Fa12
Cerna **HR** 86 Gd37
Cerna **RO** 89 Ka36
Cerna-Sat **RO** 87 Hd37
Černava **RUS** 118 Fa11
Černava **RUS** 122 Fa12
Cernavodă **RO** 89 Ka37
Cernay **F** 71 Ec33
Černěvo **RUS** 47 Jb18
Cernica **RO** 88 Jc37
Černihiv **UA** 121 Ec14
Cernivci **UA** 76 Jb32
Černivci **UA** 124 Ea16
Černjachiv **UA** 121 Eb14
Černjahovsk **RUS** 52 Hb24
Černjanka **RUS** 122 Fa13
Černovice **CZ** 65 Ga32
Černyškovskij **RUS** 123 Fd14
Cerovica **SRB** 87 Hd39
Cerrigydrudion **GB** 24 Cd25
Cërrik **RKS** 100 Hb42
Certaldo **I** 84 Fb39
Čertíže **SK** 67 Hc31
Čertkovo **RUS** 123 Fc14
Čerusti **RUS** 118 Fa10
Červen' **BY** 121 Eb12
Červená Skala **SK** 67 Ha32
Červená Voda **CZ** 66 Gc31
Červen Brjag **BG** 88 Ja39
Cervera **E** 81 Da40
Cervera del Río Alhama **E** 80 Cb39
Cervera de Pisuerga **E** 79 Bd37
Cerveteri **I** 98 Fc41
Cervia **I** 84 Fc38
Cervignano del Friuli **I** 73 Fd36
Červonoarmijs'ke **UA** 77 Ka35
Červonohrad **UA** 67 Hd30
Červonoznam'janka **MD** 77 Kb33
Čërykav **BY** 121 Ec12
Cesena **I** 84 Fc38

Cesenatico I 84 Fc38
Cēsis LV 47 Hd20
Česká Kamenice CZ 65 Ga30
Česká Lípa CZ 65 Ga30
České Budějovice CZ 65 Ga32
České Velenice CZ 65 Ga32
Český Brod CZ 65 Ga31
Český Dub CZ 65 Ga30
Český Krumlov CZ 65 Ga32
Český Těšín CZ 66 Gd31
Çeşme TR 113 Jd45
Cesvaine LV 53 Ja21
Cetatea de Baltă RO 76 Ja35
Cetăţeni RO 88 Jb36
Cetingrad HR 85 Gb37
Cetinje MNE 100 Ha41
Cetraro I 99 Gb44
Ceuta E 105 Ba46
Ceva I 83 Ec38
Cewice PL 58 Gc25
Chabanais F 69 Da35
Chabeuil F 82 Ea37
Chablis F 70 Dd33
Chabovičy BY 59 Hd27
Chabris F 69 Db33
Chagny F 70 Ea34
Chaillé-les-Marais F 68 Cd34
Chalais F 69 Da36
Chalamera E 80 Cd40
Chalamont F 70 Ea35
Châlette-sur-Loing F 62 Dc32
Challans F 68 Cc33
Châlons-en-Champagne F 62 Ea31
Chalon-sur-Saône F 70 Ea34
Châlus F 69 Da35
Cham CH 71 Ed34
Cham D 64 Fc32
Chambéry F 71 Eb36
Chambley F 63 Eb31
Chambly F 62 Dc31
Chamonix-Mont-Blanc F 71 Eb36
Champagne-Mouton F 69 Da35
Champagnole F 71 Eb34
Champlitte-et-le-Prélot F 71 Eb33
Chantada E 78 Ba37
Chantelle F 69 Dc35
Chantilly F 62 Dc31
Chantonnay F 68 Cd33
Chaource F 70 Ea33
Charkiv UA 122 Fa14
Charleroi B 62 Ea29
Charlestown IRL 18 Ca22
Charleville IRL 18 Bd24
Charleville-Mézières F 62 Ea30
Charlieu F 70 Dd35
Charlottenberg S 44 Fd17

Charmes F 63 Eb32
Charny F 70 Dd33
Charolles F 70 Dd35
Charost F 69 Dc34
Chartres F 62 Dc32
Château-Arnoux F 82 Ea38
Châteaubourg F 61 Cd32
Châteaubriant F 61 Cd32
Château-Chinon F 70 Dd34
Château-du-Loir F 61 Da32
Châteaudun F 61 Db32
Châteaugiron F 61 Cd32
Château-Gontier F 61 Da32
Château-Landon F 62 Dc32
Château-la-Vallière F 69 Da33
Château-l'Evêque F 69 Da36
Châteaulin F 60 Cb31
Châteaumeillant F 69 Dc34
Châteauneuf-de-Randon F 82 Dd37
Châteauneuf-du-Faou F 60 Cb31
Châteauneuf-en-Thymerais F 61 Db31
Châteauneuf-la-Forêt F 69 Db35
Châteauneuf-sur-Charente F 69 Da35
Châteauneuf-sur-Cher F 69 Dc34
Châteauneuf-sur-Loire F 62 Dc32
Châteauneuf-sur-Sarthe F 61 Da32
Châteauponsac F 69 Db35
Château-Porcien F 62 Ea31
Château-Renault F 69 Db33
Châteauroux F 69 Db34
Château-Salins F 63 Ec32
Château-Thierry F 62 Dd31
Châteauvillain F 70 Ea33
Châtelaillon-Plage F 68 Cd34
Châtel-Censoir F 70 Dd33
Châtelet B 62 Ea30
Châtelguyon F 69 Dc35
Châtellerault F 69 Da34
Châtelus-Malvaleix F 69 Db35
Châtenois F 63 Eb32
Chatham GB 25 Db28
Châtillon I 71 Ec36
Châtillon-Coligny F 70 Dd33
Châtillon-en-Bazois F 70 Dd34
Châtillon-sur-Chalaronne F 70 Ea35
Châtillon-sur-Indre F 69 Db33
Châtillon-sur-Loire F 69 Dc33
Châtillon-sur-Marne F 62 Ea31
Châtillon-sur-Seine F 70 Ea33

Chaudes-Aigues F 81 Dc37
Chauffailles F 70 Dd35
Chaumergy F 70 Ea34
Chaumont F 70 Ea33
Chauny F 62 Dd30
Chauvigny F 69 Da34
Chaves P 78 Ba38
Chazelles-sur-Lyon F 70 Dd36
Cheadle GB 24 Da25
Cheb CZ 64 Fc31
Chęciny PL 67 Ha29
Chef-Boutonne F 69 Da34
Cheia RO 88 Jc36
Cheles E 90 Ad42
Chełm PL 67 Hd29
Chełmno PL 58 Gd26
Chelmsford GB 25 Dc27
Chełmża PL 58 Gd26
Cheltenham GB 24 Da26
Chelva E 93 Cb42
Chemillé F 68 Cd33
Chemnitz D 65 Fd30
Chénerailles F 69 Dc35
Chenôve F 70 Ea34
Cheptow GB 24 Cd27
Cherbourg-Octeville F 61 Cd30
Chéroy F 62 Dd32
Cherson UA 125 Ed16
Cheste E 93 Cb43
Chester GB 24 Da25
Chesterfield GB 25 Db25
Chevanceaux F 68 Cd35
Chianciano Terme I 84 Fb40
Chiaramonte Gulfi I 109 Ga48
Chiaravalle I 85 Fd39
Chiari I 72 Fa36
Chiaromonte I 99 Gb44
Chiavari I 83 Ed38
Chiavenna I 72 Fa35
Chichester GB 24 Da28
Chiclana de la Frontera E 105 Ad45
Chieri I 83 Ec37
Chieti I 99 Ga41
Chigwell GB 25 Db27
Chimay B 62 Ea30
Chinchilla de Monte Aragón E 92 Ca43
Chinchón E 92 Bd41
Chinon F 69 Da33
Chioggia I 84 Fc37
Chiojdu RO 88 Jc36
Chipiona E 105 Ad45
Chippenham GB 24 Da27
Chipping Norton GB 24 Da27
Chiprana E 93 Cc41
Chirivel E 106 Bd45
Chişinău MD 77 Ka33
Chişlaz RO 75 Hc34
Chiusa I 72 Fb35
Chiusi I 84 Fc40
Chiva E 93 Cb43

Chivasso I 83 Ec37
Chłudowo PL 58 Gc27
Chlumec nad Cidlinou CZ 65 Gb30
Chmel'nyc'kyj UA 121 Eb15
Chmielnik PL 67 Hb30
Chmil'nyk UA 121 Eb15
Chocianów PL 65 Gb29
Chociwel PL 57 Gb26
Chodoriv UA 120 Ea15
Chodová Planá CZ 65 Fd31
Chodzież PL 58 Gc27
Chojna PL 57 Ga27
Chojnice PL 58 Gc26
Chojniki BY 121 Eb13
Chojnów PL 65 Gb29
Cholet F 68 Cd33
Chomutov CZ 65 Fd30
Chorol UA 121 Ed14
Choroszcz PL 59 Hc26
Chorzele PL 59 Hb26
Chorzów PL 66 Gd30
Choszczno PL 57 Gb26
Chotilsko CZ 65 Ga31
Chotyn UA 76 Jc32
Chr'aščevka RUS 119 Ga10
Chrisí Ammoudiá GR 102 Jb42
Christchurch GB 24 Da28
Christiansfeld DK 49 Fb23
Chrudim CZ 65 Gb31
Chrystynivka UA 121 Ec15
Chrzanów PL 67 Ha30
Chur CH 72 Fa35
Church Stretton GB 24 Cd26
Chust UA 75 Hd33
Chvaletice CZ 65 Gb31
Chwałowice PL 67 Hc29
Chwaszczyno PL 58 Gd25
Chynów PL 59 Hb28
Chyriv UA 67 Hc31
Ćićevac SRB 87 Hc39
Ciechanów PL 58 Ha27
Ciechanowiec PL 59 Hc27
Ciechocinek PL 58 Gd27
Ciemnik PL 57 Gb26
Ciemnoszyje PL 59 Hc26
Čierny Balog SK 67 Ha32
Cieszanów PL 67 Hd30
Cieszyn PL 66 Gd31
Cieza E 107 Ca44
Ciężkowice PL 67 Ha29
Çiftehan TR 128 Gd15
Cifuentes E 92 Ca41
Cigel'ka SK 67 Hb31
Cigliano I 83 Ec37
Cilibia RO 89 Jd36
Cillas E 93 Cb41
Cilleros E 91 Ba40
Čil'na RUS 119 Fd09
Cimljansk RUS 123 Fd15
Cimoszki PL 59 Hc25
Çınarcık TR 103 Kb42
Çine TR 113 Kb46
Ciney B 63 Eb30

Cinfães P 78 Ad39
Cingoli I 85 Fd39
Cintei RO 75 Hc35
Cioara MD 77 Jd34
Ciocăneşti RO 76 Jb33
Ciochina RO 89 Jd37
Cioclovina RO 75 Hd36
Ciolacu Nou MD 77 Jd33
Ciorani RO 88 Jc37
Ciorăşti RO 89 Jd36
Cirencester GB 24 Da27
Cirey-sur-Vezouze F 63 Ec32
Ciriè I 83 Ec37
Ciripcău MD 77 Jd32
Cirò I 109 Gc45
Cirò Marina I 109 Gc45
Čirpan BG 102 Jc40
Cislău RO 88 Jc36
Cismişlia MD 77 Ka34
Cisterna di Latina I 98 Fc42
Cistierna E 79 Bc37
Čitluk BIH 86 Gd40
Cittadella I 72 Fc36
Città della Pieve I 84 Fc40
Città di Castello I 84 Fc39
Città Sant'Angelo I 98 Fd41
Ciucea RO 75 Hd34
Ciucurova RO 89 Ka36
Ciudad Real E 92 Bc43
Ciudad Rodrigo E 91 Ba40
Ciuperceni RO 87 Hd37
Ciutadella E 95 Dc43
Ciuteşti MD 77 Jd33
Cividale del Friuli I 73 Fd36
Civil'sk RUS 119 Fc09
Civita Castellana I 98 Fc41
Civitanova Marche I 85 Fd39
Civitavecchia I 98 Fb41
Civitella del Tronto I 85 Fd40
Civitella Roveto I 98 Fd41
Civray F 69 Da34
Cjurupyns'k UA 125 Ed17
Čkalovsk RUS 118 Fb09
Clacton-on-Sea GB 25 Dc27
Clamecy F 70 Dd33
Claonaig GB 20 Cd21
Claremorris IRL 18 Ca23
Clausthal-Zellerfeld D 56 Fb28
Cleethorpes GB 25 Dc25
Clejani RO 88 Jc37
Clelles F 82 Ea37
Clermont F 62 Dc31
Clermont-en-Argonne F 62 Ea31
Clermont-Ferrand F 69 Dc35
Clermont-l'Hérault F 81 Dc38
Clerval F 71 Eb34
Clervaux L 63 Eb30
Cles I 72 Fb35
Clevedon GB 24 Cd27

Cleveleys GB 21 Da24
Clifden IRL 18 Bd23
Clisson F 68 Cd33
Clitheroe GB 21 Da24
Cloghan IRL 18 Ca24
Clogherhead IRL 19 Cb23
Clonakilty IRL 22 Bd25
Clones IRL 19 Cb22
Clonmel IRL 22 Ca25
Cloppenburg D 55 Ed27
Clovelly GB 23 Cc27
Cloyes-sur-le-Loir F 61 Db32
Cluj-Napoca RO 75 Hd34
Cluny F 70 Ea35
Cluses F 71 Eb35
Clusone I 72 Fa36
Clydebank GB 20 Cd21
Coarnele Caprei RO 76 Jc33
Cobadin RO 89 Ka37
Cobh IRL 22 Bd25
Coburg D 64 Fb30
Coca E 91 Bc40
Cochem D 63 Ec30
Cockermouth GB 21 Da23
Codigoro I 84 Fc37
Codlea RO 88 Jb36
Codogno I 84 Fa37
Codroipo I 73 Fd36
Codru MD 77 Ka33
Coesfeld D 55 Ed28
Coevorden NL 55 Ec27
Cognac F 68 Cd35
Cogne I 71 Ec36
Cogolin F 83 Eb39
Coimbra P 90 Ad40
Coín E 105 Bb45
Coja P 90 Ad40
Colchester GB 25 Dc27
Colditz D 65 Fd29
Coldstream GB 21 Db22
Colera E 81 Dc40
Coleraine GB 20 Cc21
Colfontaine B 62 Ea29
Colibiţa RO 76 Ja34
Colico I 72 Fa36
Colintraive GB 20 Cd21
Collado-Villalba E 92 Bd40
Collecchio I 84 Fa37
Colle di Val d'Elsa I 84 Fb39
Colleferro I 98 Fc42
Colmar F 71 Ec33
Colmars F 83 Eb38
Colmenar E 105 Bb45
Colmenar Viejo E 92 Bd40
Colombey-les-Belles F 63 Eb32
Colombey-les-Deux-Églises F 62 Ea32
Colònia de Sant Jordi E 95 Db44
Colunga E 79 Bd37
Colwyn Bay GB 20 Cd24
Comacchio I 84 Fc38
Comandău RO 76 Jc35

Comăneşti RO 76 Jc35
Comarnic RO 88 Jb36
Combeaufontaine F 71 Eb33
Combles F 62 Dd30
Combourg F 61 Cd31
Comiso I 109 Ga48
Commentry F 69 Dc35
Commercy F 63 Eb32
Como I 71 Ed36
Compiègne F 62 Dd31
Comporta P 90 Ac42
Comps-sur-Artuby F 83 Eb39
Comrat MD 77 Ka34
Concarneau F 60 Cb31
Conches-en-Ouche F 61 Db31
Condat F 69 Dc36
Condé-en-Brie F 62 Dd31
Condé-sur-Noireau F 61 Da31
Condom F 81 Da37
Conegliano I 72 Fc36
Confolens F 69 Da35
Congaz MD 77 Ka35
Congleton GB 24 Da25
Congostrina E 92 Ca40
Conil de la Frontera E 105 Ad45
Connah's Quay GB 24 Cd25
Connel GB 16 Cd20
Connerré F 61 Db32
Conques F 81 Db37
Conquista E 106 Bc43
Conselice I 84 Fc38
Constanţa RO 89 Ka37
Constantina E 105 Ba43
Consuegra E 92 Bd42
Contadero E 106 Bc43
Conteşti RO 88 Jc37
Contin GB 17 Da19
Contres F 69 Db33
Contrexéville F 71 Eb33
Conversano I 99 Gc43
Cookstown GB 20 Cb22
Cootehill IRL 19 Cb23
Copălău RO 76 Jc33
Copalnic-Mănăstur RO 75 Hd33
Cope E 107 Ca45
Copertino I 100 Gd43
Çöpköy TR 103 Jd41
Copparo I 84 Fc37
Copşa Mică RO 76 Ja35
Corabia RO 88 Jb38
Corato I 99 Gc42
Corbeil-Essonnes F 62 Dc32
Corbie F 62 Dd30
Corbigny F 70 Dd34
Corbridge GB 21 Db23
Corby GB 25 Db26
Corcaigh IRL 22 Bd25
Cordes F 81 Db37
Córdoba E 105 Bb44

Corella E 80 Cb39
Corestăuţi MD 76 Jc32
Coria E 91 Ba41
Corigliano Calabro I 99 Gc44
Cork IRL 22 Bd25
Corlay F 60 Cc31
Corleone I 108 Fd47
Corleto Perticara I 99 Gb43
Çorlu TR 103 Ka41
Corna UA 77 Ka33
Cornea RO 87 Hd37
Corneşti MD 77 Jd33
Corneşti RO 88 Jc37
Cornimont F 71 Ec33
Čornobyl' UA 121 Ec14
Čornomors'ke UA 125 Ed17
Čornuchy UA 121 Ed14
Cornudilla E 79 Ca38
Cornu Luncii RO 76 Jb33
Çorovodë AL 100 Hb43
Corporales E 78 Bb38
Corps F 83 Eb37
Corral de Almaguer E 92 Bd42
Corral de Calatrava E 92 Bc43
Corrales E 78 Bb39
Correggio I 84 Fb37
Corridonia I 85 Fd40
Corsicana F 96 Ed41
Corte F 96 Ed41
Cortemilia I 83 Ec38
Cortijos Nuevos E 106 Bd44
Cortina d'Ampezzo I 72 Fc35
Čortkiv UA 124 Ea16
Cortona I 84 Fc40
Coruche P 90 Ac41
Corund RO 76 Jb35
Corwen GB 24 Cd25
Cosenza I 109 Gc45
Coşeşti RO 88 Jb37
Cosmeşti RO 88 Jb38
Cosne-Cours-sur-Loire F 69 Dc33
Cosne-d'Allier F 69 Dc34
Cossato I 71 Ed36
Costeşeşti RO 88 Jb37
Costeşti MD 77 Jc33
Costeşti RO 88 Jc36
Costineşti RO 89 Ka37
Coswig D 56 Fc28
Coteana RO 88 Jb38
Cotofăneşti RO 76 Jc35
Cottbus D 57 Ga28
Coudekerque-Branche F 54 Dd28
Couflens F 81 Da39
Couhé F 69 Da34
Couiza F 81 Db39
Coulommiers F 62 Dd31
Coulonges-sur-l'Autize F 68 Cd34
Coupar Anguse GB 17 Da20
Courchevel F 71 Eb36

Courmayeur I 71 Ec36
Cournon-d'Auvergne F 69 Dc35
Coursan F 81 Dc39
Courseulles-sur-Mer F 61 Da30
Cours-la Ville F 70 Dd35
Courtenay F 62 Dd32
Courtomer F 61 Db31
Coutances F 61 Cd30
Coutras F 68 Cd36
Couvin B 62 Ea30
Covaleda E 79 Ca39
Covasna RO 76 Jc35
Coventry GB 24 Da26
Covilhã P 90 Ad40
Cowes GB 24 Da28
Cózar E 92 Bd43
Cozes F 68 Cd35
Crăieşti RO 76 Ja34
Craignure GB 16 Cd20
Crail GB 21 Db21
Crailsheim D 64 Fa32
Craiova RO 88 Ja38
Craiva RO 75 Hc35
Cranbrook GB 25 Db28
Craon F 61 Cd32
Craponne-sur-Arzon F 70 Dd36
Crasna RO 75 Hd34
Crasnoe MD 77 Kb34
Crathie GB 17 Db20
Crato P 90 Ad41
Craven Arms GB 24 Cd26
Crawley GB 25 Db28
Creagorry GB 16 Cc18
Crediton GB 23 Cc28
Creil F 62 Dc31
Crema I 84 Fa37
Crémieu F 70 Ea36
Cremona I 84 Fa37
Créon F 68 Cd36
Crepaja SRB 87 Hb37
Crépy-en-Valois F 62 Dd31
Cres HR 85 Ga37
Crest F 82 Ea37
Créteil F 62 Dc31
Creußen D 64 Fc31
Creutzwald F 63 Ec31
Creuzburg D 64 Fb29
Crèvecœur-le-Grand F 62 Dc30
Crevillente E 107 Cb44
Crewe GB 24 Da25
Crewkerne GB 24 Cd28
Crianlarich GB 16 Cd20
Crickhowell GB 24 Cd26
Cricova MD 77 Ka33
Crieff GB 17 Da20
Crikvenica HR 85 Ga37
Crimmitschau D 64 Fc30
Crişan RO 89 Kb36
Čristopol' RUS 119 Ga08
Cristuru Secuiesc RO 76 Jb35
Criuleni MD 77 Ka33

Crivitz D 56 Fc26
Crna Bara SRB 75 Hb36
Črnomelj SLO 85 Gb37
Crocq F 69 Dc35
Croissilles F 62 Dd30
Cromarty GB 17 Da19
Cromer GB 25 Dc26
Crookhaven IRL 22 Bc25
Cross Hands GB 23 Cc26
Crotone I 109 Gc45
Crozon F 60 Cb31
Črtil' RUS 122 Fb12
Crucea RO 76 Jb34
Crucea RO 89 Ka37
Cruden Bay GB 17 Dc19
Cruzamento de Pegões P 90 Ac41
Csakvár H 74 Gd34
Csánytelek H 75 Hb35
Csaroda H 75 Hc33
Csátalja H 74 Ha36
Csenger H 75 Hd33
Csesznek H 74 Gd34
Csongrád H 75 Hb35
Csorna H 74 Gc34
Csorvás H 75 Hb35
Csót H 74 Gc34
Cubel E 80 Cb40
Čučkovo RUS 118 Fb11
Cucoara MD 77 Jd35
Cudillero E 79 Bc36
Čudniv UA 121 Eb15
Čudovo RUS 117 Eb09
Čudzin BY 120 Ea13
Cuéllar E 79 Bd39
Cuenca E 92 Ca42
Cuers F 82 Ea39
Cuerva E 91 Bc42
Cuevas del Almanzora E 107 Ca45
Cugir RO 75 Hd36
Cugnaux F 81 Da38
Čuhloma RUS 118 Fa08
Cuhneşti MD 76 Jc33
Čuhujiv UA 122 Fa14
Cuijk NL 55 Ec28
Cuiseaux F 70 Ea35
Cuisery F 70 Ea35
Çukurkuyu TR 128 Gc15
Culan F 69 Dc34
Culemborg NL 55 Eb28
Cúllar-Baza E 106 Bd45
Cullen GB 17 Db19
Cullera E 93 Cc43
Cullompton GB 23 Cc28
Culoz F 71 Eb36
Cumbernauld GB 21 Da21
Čumić SRB 87 Hb38
Cumnock GB 20 Cd21
Çumra TR 128 Gb15
Cunicea MD 77 Jd32
Cunlhat F 70 Dd36
Cuorgnè I 71 Ec36
Cupar GB 21 Da21
Cupcini MD 76 Jc32

Ćuprija SRB 87 Hc38
Curia P 78 Ad39
Curtea de Argeş RO 88 Jb36
Curtici RO 75 Hc35
Cusset F 70 Dd35
Čuteevo RUS 119 Fd09
Čutove UA 122 Fa14
Cutro I 109 Gc45
Cuxhaven D 56 Fa25
Cwmcarn GB 24 Cd27
Cybinka PL 57 Ga28
Čyhyryn UA 121 Ed15
Czaplinek PL 57 Gb26
Czarna PL 67 Hc31
Czarna Białostocka PL 59 Hc26
Czarna Dąbrówka PL 58 Gc25
Czarnków PL 57 Gb27
Czarny Dunajec PL 67 Ha31
Czechowice-Dziedzice PL 66 Gd31
Czekarzewice PL 67 Hb29
Czermno PL 67 Ha29
Czersk PL 58 Gc26
Czerwieńsk PL 57 Gb28
Czerwionka-Leszczyny PL 66 Gd30
Czerwony Dwór PL 59 Hb25
Częstochowa PL 66 Gd29
Człopa PL 57 Gb27
Człuchów PL 58 Gc26
Czyżew-Osada PL 59 Hc27

D

Dabas H 74 Ha34
Dąbie PL 57 Ga28
Dąbie PL 58 Gd28
Dabilja MK 101 Hd42
Dabravolja BY 59 Hd26
Dąbrowa Białostocka PL 59 Hc25
Dąbrowa Górnicza PL 67 Ha30
Dąbrowa Tarnowska PL 67 Hb30
Dabryn' BY 121 Eb14
Dăbuleni RO 88 Ja38
Dachau D 72 Fb33
Dačice CZ 65 Gb32
Dačne UA 77 Kb34
Dáfnes GR 110 Hd46
Dafni GR 102 Jb43
Dáfni GR 110 Hd46
Dáfni GR 110 Hd45
Dagali N 42 Fa17
Dagda LV 53 Jb22
Dağdere TR 113 Kb44
Dagomys RUS 127 Fd17
Dağpazarı TR 128 Gc16
Dahme D 57 Fd28
Dahn D 63 Ed31
Daimiel E 92 Bd43

Đakovica RKS 100 Hb41
Đakovo HR 86 Gd37
Dalarö S 45 Gc18
Dalbeattie GB 20 Cd22
Dălbok Dol BG 88 Jb39
Dălbok izvor BG 102 Jc40
Dale N 36 Ed16
Dale N 36 Ed15
Dalen N 42 Fa18
Dalfors S 38 Gb16
Dălghiu RO 88 Jc36
Dălgi Del BG 87 Hd39
Dălgopol BG 89 Jd39
Dalías E 106 Bd46
Dalj HR 86 Ha37
Dalkeith GB 21 Da21
Dalmally GB 16 Cd20
Dalmose DK 49 Fc24
Dalsbruk FIN 46 Hb17
Dalsjöfors S 44 Fd20
Dals Långed S 43 Fd19
Dalvík IS 15 Ca05
Dalwhinnie GB 17 Da20
Damaskiniá GR 101 Hc43
Dambaslar TR 103 Ka41
Dammartin-en-Goële F 62 Dd31
Damme D 55 Ed27
Damnica PL 58 Gc25
Dampierre-sur-Salon F 71 Eb33
Danasjö S 33 Gb10
Danilov RUS 118 Fa08
Danilovgrad MNE 86 Ha40
Danilovka RUS 123 Fd13
Dankov RUS 122 Fa12
Dannenberg D 56 Fc26
Darabani RO Fc32
Darány H 74 Gd36
Darbėnai LT 52 Hb22
Darda HR 74 Gd36
Dardesheim D 56 Fb28
Dardhë AL 101 Hc43
Darfo-Boario Terme I 72 Fa36
Dargosław PL 57 Gb25
Đarkavdčyna BY 53 Jb23
Darlington GB 21 Db23
Darłowo PL 57 Gb25
Dărmăneşti RO 88 Jc37
Darmstadt D 63 Ed31
Darney F 71 Eb33
Daroca E 93 Cb41
Dartford GB 25 Db28
Dartmouth GB 23 Cc28
Daruvar HR 74 Gc36
Darzininkai LT 53 Ja24
Dáski GR 101 Hd43
Dassel D 56 Fa28
Dassow D 56 Fb25
Datça TR 115 Kb47
Daudzeva LV 53 Hd21
Daugai LT 53 Hd24
Daugailiai LT 53 Ja23
Daugavpils LV 53 Ja22
Daun D 63 Ec30

Davhinava – Dolní Dvořiště

Davhinava **BY** 53 Jb24
Davor **BIH** 86 Gc37
Davos **CH** 72 Fa35
Davyd-Haradok **BY** 120 Ea14
Dax **F** 80 Cc37
Deal **GB** 25 Dc28
Deauville **F** 61 Db30
Debaľceve **UA** 122 Fb15
Debar **MK** 100 Hb42
Debelec **BG** 88 Jc39
Dębica **PL** 57 Gb25
Dębica **PL** 67 Hb30
Dęblin **PL** 59 Hb28
Dębnica Kaszubska **PL** 58 Gc25
Dębno **PL** 57 Ga27
Debrc **SRB** 87 Hb38
Debrecen **H** 75 Hc34
Debrznica **PL** 57 Ga28
Dečani **RKS** 87 Hb40
Decazeville **F** 81 Db37
Děčín **CZ** 65 Ga30
Decize **F** 70 Dd34
De Cocksdorp **NL** 55 Eb26
Deda **RO** 76 Jb34
Dedemsvaart **NL** 55 Ec27
Dedenevo **RUS** 117 Ed10
Dedoviči **RUS** 117 Eb10
Deftera **CY** 128 Gb19
Degeberga **S** 50 Ga23
Degerby **FIN** 46 Ha17
Degerfors **S** 44 Ga18
Degerhamn **S** 50 Gb22
Deggendorf **D** 65 Fd32
Değirmendere **TR** 113 Ka45
Degučiai **LT** 52 Hb23
Degučiai **LT** 53 Ja22
Deinze **B** 62 Ea29
Dej **RO** 76 Ja34
Deje **S** 44 Fd18
Dekélia **GR** 112 Jb46
De Koog **NL** 55 Eb26
Delbrück **D** 56 Fa28
Delčevo **MK** 101 Hd41
Delémont **CH** 71 Ec34
Delft **NL** 54 Ea27
Delfzijl **NL** 55 Ed26
Deligrad **SRB** 87 Hc39
Delitzsch **D** 64 Fc29
Delmenhorst **D** 56 Fa26
Delnice **HR** 85 Ga37
Delsbo **S** 38 Gb15
Delvin **IRL** 19 Cb23
Demidov **RUS** 117 Ec11
Demidovo **MD** 77 Kb33
Demirci **TR** 113 Kb44
Demir Kapija **MK** 101 Hd42
Demirköy **TR** 103 Ka40
Demirtaş **TR** 128 Ga17
Demitsána **GR** 110 Hd47
Demjansk **RUS** 117 Eb09
Demʼjas **RUS** 119 Ga11
Demmin **D** 57 Fd25
Demonía **GR** 111 Ja48
Demonte **I** 83 Ec38

Denain **F** 62 Dd29
Denbigh **GB** 24 Cd25
Den Burg **NL** 55 Eb26
Dendermonde **B** 62 Ea29
Den Haag **NL** 54 Ea27
Den Helder **NL** 55 Eb26
Denia **E** 94 Cc44
Deniz Kamp Yeri **TR** 113 Ka45
Denizli **TR** 103 Ka42
Den Oever **NL** 55 Eb26
Derbent **TR** 128 Ga15
Derby **GB** 24 Da25
Dereköy **TR** 113 Kb45
Dereli **TR** 127 Fd19
Dergači **RUS** 119 Ga11
Derhači **UA** 122 Fa14
Derry **GB** 20 Cb21
Derval **F** 61 Cd32
Derventa **BIH** 86 Gd37
Descartes **F** 69 Db33
Desenzano del Garda **I** 84 Fb37
Deskáti **GR** 101 Hd44
Despotovac **SRB** 87 Hc38
Despotovo **SRB** 86 Ha37
Dessau **D** 56 Fc28
Desvres **F** 62 Dc29
Deta **RO** 87 Hc37
Detkovo **RUS** 47 Jb18
Detmold **D** 56 Fa28
Detva **SK** 67 Ha32
Deurne **NL** 55 Eb28
Deutschfeistritz **A** 73 Gb34
Deutschkreuz **A** 74 Gc34
Deutschlandsberg **A** 73 Gb35
Deva **RO** 75 Hd36
Dévaványa **H** 75 Hb34
Devecikonağı **TR** 103 Kb43
Devecser **H** 74 Gc35
Deventer **NL** 55 Ec27
Devizes **GB** 24 Da27
Devnja **BG** 89 Ka39
Deza **E** 80 Cb40
Diafáni **GR** 115 Kb48
Diakoftó **GR** 110 Hd46
Diamante **I** 99 Gb44
Dianalund **DK** 49 Fc23
Diano Marina **I** 83 Ec39
Diavata **GR** 101 Ja42
Dichiseni **RO** 89 Jd37
Didam **NL** 55 Ec28
Didim **TR** 113 Ka46
Dídyma **GR** 111 Ja47
Didymoteicho **GR** 103 Jd41
Die **F** 82 Ea37
Dieburg **D** 64 Fa31
Diekirch **L** 63 Eb30
Diepholz **D** 56 Fa27
Dieppe **F** 62 Dc30
Dierdorf **D** 63 Ed30
Dieren **NL** 55 Ec28
Diest **B** 63 Eb29
Dietikon **CH** 71 Ed34
Dieulefit **F** 82 Ea37

Dieulouard **F** 63 Eb32
Dieuze **F** 63 Ec32
Dieveniškės **LT** 53 Ja24
Differdange **L** 63 Eb31
Digermulen **N** 28 Ga06
Digne-les-Bains **F** 83 Eb38
Digoin **F** 70 Dd35
Dijon **F** 70 Ea34
Dikanäs **S** 33 Gb10
Dikili **TR** 113 Ka44
Diksmuide **B** 54 Dd28
Diljatyn **UA** 76 Ja32
Diljatyn **UA** 124 Ea16
Dillenburg **D** 63 Ed29
Dillingen **D** 63 Ec31
Dillingen **D** 64 Fb32
Dílofo **GR** 101 Ja44
Dimitrie Cantemir **RO** 77 Jd34
Dimitrovgrad **BG** 102 Jc40
Dimitrovgrad **RUS** 119 Ga09
Dimitrovgrad **SRB** 87 Hd39
Dimovo **BG** 87 Hd39
Dinan **F** 61 Cd31
Dinant **B** 63 Eb30
Dinard **F** 61 Cd31
Dinek **TR** 128 Gb16
Dingle **IRL** 18 Bc24
Dingle **S** 43 Fc19
Dingolfing **D** 64 Fc32
Dingwall **GB** 17 Da19
Dinkelsbühl **D** 64 Fb32
Dinklage **D** 55 Ed27
Diö **S** 50 Ga22
Dioşti **RO** 88 Ja38
Dipkarpaz **CY** 128 Gc18
Dipótama **GR** 102 Jb41
Dippoldiswalde **D** 65 Fd29
Dirráhi **GR** 110 Hd47
Disentis **CH** 71 Ed35
Diss **GB** 25 Dc26
Dissen **D** 55 Ed28
Ditrău **RO** 76 Jb34
Divakë **RKS** 100 Hb42
Divčibare **SRB** 87 Hb38
Dívčice **CZ** 65 Ga32
Divnoe **RUS** 123 Ga15
Divonne **F** 71 Eb35
Djatʼkovo **RUS** 121 Ed12
Djulino **BG** 89 Ka39
Djuni **BG** 103 Ka40
Djúpivogur **IS** 15 Cb08
Djupvik **N** 26 Gd04
Djurås **S** 44 Ga17
Dmitrievka **RUS** 122 Fb12
Dmitriev-Lʼgovskij **RUS** 121 Ed13
Dmitrov **RUS** 117 Ed10
Dmytrivka **UA** 77 Ka35
Dmytrivka **UA** 121 Ed14
Dnestrovsc **MD** 77 Kb34
Dniprodzeržynsʼk **UA** 122 Fa15
Dnipropetrovsʼk **UA** 122 Fa15
Dniprorudne **UA** 126 Fa16

Dno **RUS** 117 Eb10
Dobbiaco **I** 72 Fc35
Dobczyce **PL** 67 Ha31
Dobele **LV** 52 Hc21
Döbeln **D** 65 Fd29
Dobiegniew **PL** 57 Gb27
Dobieszczyn **PL** 52 Ga26
Doboj **BIH** 86 Gd38
Dobra **PL** 57 Gb26
Dobra **RO** 75 Hd36
Dobra **SRB** 87 Hc37
Dobrá Niva **SK** 74 Ha33
Dobřany **CZ** 65 Fd31
Dobrcz **PL** 58 Gd26
Dobre **PL** 59 Hb27
Dobre Miasto **PL** 58 Ha25
Dobri **H** 74 Gc35
Dobrič **BG** 89 Ka38
Dobrinka **RUS** 122 Fb12
Dobříš **CZ** 65 Ga31
Dobrjanka **UA** 121 Ec13
Dobrjatino **RUS** 118 Fb10
Dobrodzień **PL** 66 Gd30
Dobromylʼ **UA** 67 Hc31
Dobropillja **UA** 122 Fb15
Dobro Polje **BIH** 86 Gd39
Dobrosyn **UA** 67 Hd30
Dobroteşti **RO** 88 Jb38
Dobrotič **BG** 89 Jd38
Dobrotica **BG** 89 Jd38
Dobrovolʼsk **RUS** 52 Hc24
Dobruči **RUS** 47 Ja18
Dobruš **BY** 121 Ec13
Dobrzeń Wielki **PL** 66 Gd30
Dobšiná **SK** 67 Hb32
Docksta **S** 39 Gc13
Doclin **RO** 87 Hc37
Doetinchem **NL** 55 Ec28
Doğanbey **TR** 113 Ka45
Doğanbey **TR** 128 Ga15
Doğankent **TR** 127 Fd19
Dogliani **I** 83 Ec38
Dojeviće **SRB** 87 Hb40
Dojrenci **BG** 88 Jb39
Dokka **N** 37 Fb16
Dokkum **NL** 55 Ec26
Doksy **CZ** 65 Ga30
Dokšycy **BY** 53 Jb23
Dokšycy **BY** 120 Ea12
Dokučajevsʼk **UA** 122 Fb15
Dol-de-Bretagne **F** 61 Cd31
Dole **F** 70 Ea34
Dolgellau **GB** 24 Cd25
Dolgorukovo **RUS** 59 Ha25
Dolianova **I** 97 Ed44
Dolišnij Šepit **UA** 76 Jb33
Doljani **BIH** 86 Gd39
Dolna Banja **BG** 102 Ja40
Dolna Mitropolija **BG** 88 Jb39
Dolna Orjahovica **BG** 88 Jc39
Dolní Bousov **CZ** 65 Ga30
Dolni Dăbnik **BG** 88 Jb39
Dolní Dvořiště **CZ** 65 Ga32

146

Dolni Lom **BG** 87 Hd39
Dolno Dupeni **MK** 101 Hc42
Dolný Kubín **SK** 67 Ha32
Dolo **I** 84 Fc37
Dolores **E** 107 Cb44
Dolyna **UA** 67 Hd32
Dolyna **UA** 67 Hd32
Dolyns'ka **UA** 125 Ed16
Dolyns'ke **UA** 77 Ka33
Dolžanskaja **RUS** 126 Fb16
Dolžicy **RUS** 47 Jb18
Domanivka **MD** 77 Kb32
Domaradz **PL** 58 Gc25
Domaradz **PL** 67 Hc31
Domažlice **CZ** 65 Fd31
Dombaj **RUS** 127 Ga17
Dombås **N** 37 Fb14
Dombóvár **H** 74 Gd35
Dombrád **H** 75 Hc33
Domeikava **LT** 52 Hc24
Domérat **F** 69 Dc35
Domfront **F** 61 Da31
Dömitz **D** 56 Fc26
Domme **F** 69 Da36
Domnești **RO** 88 Jb36
Domnovo **RUS** 59 Ha25
Domodedovo **RUS** 118 Fa10
Domodossola **I** 71 Ed36
Domokós **GR** 110 Hd45
Dompaire **F** 71 Eb33
Dompierre-sur-Besbre **F** 70 Dd34
Domusnovas **I** 97 Ec44
Domžale **SLO** 73 Ga36
Donaueschingen **D** 71 Ed33
Donauwörth **D** 64 Fb32
Don Benito **E** 91 Ba42
Doncaster **GB** 25 Db25
Dondușeni **MD** 76 Jc32
Donec'k **UA** 122 Fb15
Donegal **IRL** 19 Cb22
Donges **F** 60 Cc32
Donja Stubica **HR** 73 Gb36
Donji Dušnik **SRB** 87 Hd39
Donji Kamengrad **BIH** 86 Gc38
Donji Lapac **HR** 85 Gb38
Donji Miholjac **HR** 74 Gd36
Donjin Milanova **SRB** 87 Hd38
Donji Rujani **BIH** 86 Gc39
Donji Stajevac **SRB** 87 Hd40
Donji Striževac **SRB** 87 Hd39
Donji Tovarnik **SRB** 87 Hb37
Donji Vakuf **BIH** 86 Gc38
Donji Žirovac **HR** 85 Gb37
Donostia **E** 80 Cb38
Donoúsa **GR** 115 Jd47
Donskoe **RUS** 127 Fd16
Donzy **F** 70 Dd33
Dor **RUS** 118 Fa08
Đorče Petrov **MK** 101 Hc41
Dorchester **GB** 24 Cd28
Dordrecht **NL** 55 Eb28
Dorfen **D** 72 Fc33

Dorgali **I** 97 Ed43
Dório **GR** 110 Hd47
Dorking **GB** 25 Db28
Dormagen **D** 63 Ec29
Dormánd **H** 75 Hb34
Dormans **F** 62 Dd31
Dornbirn **A** 72 Fa34
Dornes **F** 70 Dd34
Dornoch **GB** 17 Da18
Dorohoi **RO** 76 Jc33
Dorohusk **PL** 67 Hd29
Doroslovo **SRB** 74 Ha36
Dorotea **S** 33 Gb12
Dörpen **D** 55 Ed26
Dorsten **D** 55 Ec28
Dortmund **D** 55 Ed28
Doruchów **PL** 66 Gd29
Dörzbach **D** 64 Fa31
Dos Hermanas **E** 105 Ba44
Dospat **BG** 102 Jb41
Douai **F** 62 Dd29
Douarnenez **F** 60 Cb31
Douchy-les-Mines **F** 62 Dd30
Doudeville **F** 61 Db30
Doué-la-Fontaine **F** 69 Da33
Douglas **GBM** 20 Cd23
Doullens **F** 62 Dd30
Dourdan **F** 62 Dc32
Dover **GB** 25 Dc28
Dovhe **UA** 67 Hd32
Dovre **N** 37 Fb15
Dovsk **BY** 121 Eb13
Downham Market **GB** 25 Dc26
Downpatrick **GB** 20 Cc23
Dowra **IRL** 18 Ca22
Drabiv **UA** 121 Ed14
Drachten **NL** 55 Ec26
Drag **N** 28 Gb07
Dragalj **MNE** 86 Ha40
Drăgănești **MD** 77 Jd33
Drăgănești **RO** 88 Jc37
Drăgănești-Olt **RO** 88 Jb38
Drăgănești-Vlașca **RO** 88 Jc38
Dragaš **RKS** 100 Hb41
Drăgășani **RO** 88 Ja37
Draginac **SRB** 86 Ha38
Draglica **SRB** 87 Hb39
Dragoș Vodă **RO** 89 Jd37
Dragsfjärd **FIN** 46 Hb17
Draguignan **F** 83 Eb39
Drăgușeni **RO** 77 Jd35
Drahičyn **BY** 120 Ea14
Drahovce **SK** 74 Gd33
Drahove **UA** 75 Hd33
Dralfa **BG** 88 Jc39
Dráma **GR** 102 Jb42
Drammen **N** 43 Fb18
Drangedal **N** 43 Fb18
Drangsnes **IS** 14 Bd05
Dranske **D** 50 Fd24
Drávafok **H** 74 Gd36
Drawsko Pomorskie **PL** 57 Gb26

Drebkau **D** 57 Ga28
Drégelypalánk **H** 74 Ha33
Drenovac **SRB** 87 Hd40
Drenovci **HR** 86 Ha37
Drenovo **MK** 101 Hd42
Dresden **D** 65 Fd29
Drëtun' **BY** 117 Eb11
Dretyň **PL** 58 Gc25
Dreux **F** 62 Dc31
Drevsjø **N** 37 Fd15
Drezdenko **PL** 57 Gb27
Drežnica **HR** 85 Ga37
Driebes **E** 92 Bd41
Driffield **GB** 21 Dc24
Drinjača **BIH** 86 Ha38
Drjanovo **BG** 88 Jc39
Drniš **HR** 85 Gb39
Drnje **HR** 74 Gc36
Drøbak **N** 43 Fc18
Drobeta-Turnu Severin **RO** 87 Hd37
Drobin **PL** 58 Ha27
Drochia **MD** 77 Jd32
Drogheda **IRL** 19 Cb23
Drohiczyn **PL** 59 Hc27
Drohobyč **UA** 67 Hd31
Droitwich **GB** 24 Da26
Drolshagen **D** 63 Ed29
Dromore **GB** 20 Cc22
Dronero **I** 83 Ec38
Dronninglund **DK** 49 Fb21
Dronten **NL** 55 Ec27
Droskovo **RUS** 122 Fa12
Drossáto **GR** 101 Ja42
Drosseró **GR** 101 Hc43
Drozdyn' **UA** 120 Ea14
Druja **BY** 53 Jb22
Drumcliff **IRL** 18 Ca22
Drummore **GB** 20 Cd22
Drumnadrochit **GB** 17 Da19
Druskininkai **LT** 59 Hd25
Druskininkai **LT** 59 Hd25
Drusti **LV** 47 Hd20
Druten **NL** 55 Eb28
Družba **UA** 121 Ed13
Družetići **SRB** 87 Hb38
Drvar **BIH** 86 Gc38
Drvenik **HR** 86 Gc40
Drwęczno **PL** 58 Ha25
Drygały **PL** 59 Hb25
Duas Igrejas **P** 78 Bb39
Dubăsari **MD** 77 Ka33
Dubău **MD** 77 Ka33
Dubienka **PL** 67 Hd29
Dubin **PL** 58 Gc28
Dub'jazy **RUS** 119 Fd08
Dublin **GB** 19 Cb24
Dubna **RUS** 117 Ed10
Dubna **RUS** 118 Fa11
Dub nad Moravou **CZ** 66 Gc31
Dubnica nad Váhom **SK** 66 Gd32
Dubno **UA** 120 Ea15
Dubova **RO** 87 Hd37
Dubove **UA** 76 Ja33

Dubovka **RUS** 123 Fd13
Dubovskoje **RUS** 123 Fd15
Dubovyj Ovrag **RUS** 123 Fd14
Dubrava **HR** 74 Gc36
Dubrivka **UA** 121 Eb15
Dubrovka **RUS** 53 Jb21
Dubrovka **RUS** 123 Fc12
Dubrovnik **HR** 86 Gd40
Dubrovcja **UA** 67 Hd30
Dubrovcja **UA** 120 Ea14
Ducey **F** 61 Cd31
Duchcov **CZ** 65 Fd30
Ducherow **D** 57 Fd26
Dudelange **L** 63 Eb31
Duderstadt **D** 64 Fb29
Dudley **GB** 24 Da26
Dueñas **E** 79 Bd39
Duesund **N** 36 Ed16
Dufftown **GB** 17 Db19
Duga Poljana **SRB** 87 Hb39
Duga Resa **HR** 85 Gb37
Dugo Selo **HR** 73 Gb36
Duhovnickoe **RUS** 119 Ga11
Duisburg **D** 55 Ec28
Dukat **AL** 100 Hb43
Dukla **PL** 67 Hc31
Dükštas **LT** 53 Ja23
Dülmen **D** 55 Ed28
Dulovo **BG** 89 Jd38
Dulverton **GB** 23 Cc27
Dumbarton **GB** 20 Cd21
Dumbrăveni **RO** 76 Ja39
Dumbrăveni **RO** 89 Ka38
Dumbrăvița **MD** 77 Jd33
Dumfries **GB** 21 Da22
Dumitrești **RO** 88 Jc36
Dunaföldvár **H** 74 Ha35
Dunaharaszti **H** 74 Ha34
Dunajivci **UA** 125 Eb16
Dunajská Streda **SK** 74 Gc33
Dunakeszi **H** 74 Ha34
Dunaszekcső **H** 74 Gd36
Dunaújváros **H** 74 Ha35
Dunbar **GB** 21 Db21
Dunblane **GB** 21 Da21
Dundaga **LV** 46 Hb20
Dundalk **IRL** 19 Cb23
Dundee **GB** 17 Db20
Dunfanaghy **IRL** 19 Cb21
Dunfermline **GB** 21 Da21
Dungannon **GB** 20 Cb22
Dungarvan **IRL** 22 Ca25
Dungiven **GB** 20 Cb22
Dunglow **IRL** 18 Ca21
Dunkeld **GB** 17 Da20
Dunkerque **F** 54 Dd28
Dunmanway **IRL** 22 Bd25
Dunnet **GB** 17 Db18
Dunoon **GB** 20 Cd21
Dunshaughlin **IRL** 19 Cb23
Dunstable **GB** 25 Db27
Dunster **GB** 24 Cd27
Dun-sur-Auron **F** 69 Dc34

Dun-sur-Meuse – Elvanlı

Dun-sur-Meuse **F** 63 Eb31
Dunvegan **GB** 16 Cd18
Dupnica **BG** 102 Ja40
Durak **TR** 103 Kb43
Duran **BG** 89 Jd38
Durango **E** 80 Cb38
Durankulak **BG** 89 Ka38
Duras **F** 69 Da36
Durbe **LV** 52 Hb22
Durbuy **B** 63 Eb30
Đurđenovac **HR** 86 Gd37
Đurđevac **HR** 74 Gc36
Düren **D** 63 Ec29
Durham **GB** 21 Db23
Durness **GB** 17 Da17
Durrës **AL** 100 Ha42
Durrow **IRL** 18 Ca24
Dursunbey **TR** 103 Kb43
Durtal **F** 61 Da32
Dusetos **LT** 53 Ja22
Dušinci **BG** 87 Hd40
Düsseldorf **D** 63 Ec29
Duved **S** 38 Fd13
Düvertepe **TR** 103 Kb43
Dvor **HR** 85 Gb37
Dvoriki **RUS** 118 Fa10
Dvůr Králové nad Labem **CZ** 65 Gb34
Dyce **GB** 17 Db20
Dydnia **PL** 67 Hc31
Dygowo **PL** 57 Gb25
Dykan'ka **UA** 121 Ed14
Dymer **UA** 121 Ec14
Dymniki **BY** 59 Hd27
Dynivci **UA** 76 Jb32
Dyranut **N** 42 Fa17
Dyrnes **N** 36 Fa13
Džalil' **RUS** 119 Ga08
Džankoj **UA** 126 Fa17
Dzelzava **LV** 53 Ja21
Dzeržinsk **RUS** 118 Fb09
Dziadkowice **PL** 59 Hc27
Działdowo **PL** 58 Ha26
Działoszyce **PL** 67 Ha30
Działoszyn **PL** 66 Gd29
Dziemiany **PL** 58 Gc25
Dzierzgoń **PL** 58 Gd25
Dzierżoniów **PL** 66 Gc30
Dzisna **BY** 53 Jb22
Dzivin **BY** 59 Hd28
Dzjarečyn **BY** 59 Hd26
Dzjaržynsk **BY** 120 Ea12
Dzjatlava **BY** 120 Ea13
Džubga **RUS** 127 Fc17
Džuryn **UA** 125 Eb16

E

Easingwold **GB** 21 Db24
Eastbourne **GB** 25 Db28
East Dereham **GB** 25 Dc26
East Grinstead **GB** 25 Db28
East Kilbride **GB** 20 Cd21
Eauze **F** 80 Cd37
Ebeleben **D** 64 Fb29

Ebeltoft **DK** 49 Fb22
Ebensee **A** 73 Fd34
Eberbach **D** 64 Fa31
Ebern **D** 64 Fb30
Ebersbach **D** 65 Ga29
Ebersberg **D** 72 Fc33
Eberswalde **D** 57 Fd27
Eboli **I** 99 Ga43
Ebreichsdorf **A** 73 Gb33
Eceabat **TR** 103 Jd43
Echternach **L** 63 Ec31
Écija **E** 105 Bb44
Eckernförde **D** 56 Fb25
Eckerö **FIN** 45 Gd17
Écommoy **F** 61 Da32
Ecouché **F** 61 Da31
Ecueillé **F** 69 Db33
Ed **S** 43 Fc19
Edam **NL** 55 Eb27
Edane **S** 43 Fd18
Ede **NL** 55 Eb27
Edebäck **S** 44 Fd17
Edefors **S** 34 Gd09
Edelény **H** 75 Hb33
Edemissen **D** 56 Fb27
Edenderry **IRL** 19 Cb24
Edesbyn **S** 38 Gb15
Édessa **GR** 101 Hd42
Edgeworthstown **IRL** 18 Ca23
Edinburgh **GB** 21 Da21
Edincik **TR** 103 Ka42
Edineţ **MD** 76 Jc32
Edirne **TR** 103 Jd41
Ēdole **LV** 52 Hb21
Edolo **I** 72 Fa36
Edremit **TR** 103 Ka43
Edsbro **S** 45 Gc17
Edsbruk **S** 44 Gb20
Edsele **S** 38 Gb13
Edsta **S** 38 Gb15
Eeklo **B** 54 Ea28
Eemshaven **NL** 55 Ed26
Efimovskij **RUS** 117 Ec08
Efkarpía **GR** 102 Jb42
Eforie **RO** 89 Ka37
Efremov **RUS** 122 Fa12
Egby **S** 51 Gc21
Egeln **D** 56 Fb28
Eger **H** 75 Hb33
Egersund **N** 42 Ed19
Eggedal **N** 43 Fb17
Eggenburg **A** 65 Gb32
Eggenfelden **D** 73 Fd33
Eggesin **D** 57 Ga26
Egilsstaðir **IS** 15 Cc07
Égina **GR** 112 Jb46
Egínio **GR** 101 Hd43
Égio **GR** 110 Hd46
Égletons **F** 69 Db36
Egmond aan Zee **NL** 55 Eb27
Egor'e **RUS** 117 Ed11
Egor'evsk **RUS** 118 Fa10
Egorlykskaja **RUS** 127 Fc16
Egósthena **GR** 111 Ja46

Egtved **DK** 48 Fa23
Egyed **H** 74 Gc34
Ehingen **D** 72 Fa33
Ehínos **GR** 102 Jc41
Ehrwald **A** 72 Fb34
Eibar **E** 80 Cb38
Eibiswald **A** 73 Gb35
Eichstätt **D** 64 Fb32
Eiðar **IS** 15 Cc07
Eide **N** 36 Fa13
Eidet **N** 26 Gc05
Eidfjord **N** 36 Fa16
Eidsdalen **N** 36 Fa14
Eidsvåg **N** 36 Fa13
Eidsvoll **N** 43 Fc17
Eidvågeid **N** 26 Ha03
Eijsden **NL** 63 Eb29
Eikefjord **N** 36 Ed15
Eiken **N** 42 Ed19
Eilenburg **D** 65 Fd29
Eìlgar **RUS** 123 Ga15
Eilsleben **D** 56 Fc28
Eina **N** 37 Fc16
Einbeck **D** 56 Fb28
Eindhoven **NL** 55 Eb28
Eisenach **D** 64 Fb29
Eisenberg **D** 64 Fc29
Eisenerz **A** 73 Ga34
Eisenhüttenstadt **D** 57 Ga28
Eisenstadt **A** 74 Gc34
Eisfeld **D** 64 Fb30
Eišiškės **LT** 59 Hd25
Eišiškės **LT** 59 Hd25
Eitorf **D** 63 Ed29
Eivindvik **N** 36 Ed16
Eivissa (Ibiza) **E** 94 Cd44
Ejea de los Caballeros **E** 80 Cc39
Ejsk **RUS** 126 Fb16
Ekaterinovka **RUS** 122 Fa12
Ekaterinovka **RUS** 123 Fc12
Ekeby **S** 49 Fd23
Ekenäs **FIN** 46 Hb17
Ekenäs **S** 44 Fd19
Ekerö **S** 45 Gc18
Ekimoviči **RUS** 121 Ec12
Ekshärad **S** 44 Fd17
Eksjö **S** 44 Ga20
Ekträsk **S** 34 Gd11
Ekzarh Antimovo **BG** 103 Jd40
Elabuga **RUS** 119 Ga08
Elan' **RUS** 123 Fd12
Elan'-Kolenovskij **RUS** 123 Fc13
El Arahal **E** 105 Ba44
Elassóna **GR** 101 Hd44
El Astillero **E** 79 Ca37
Elátia **GR** 111 Ja45
Elat'ma **RUS** 118 Fb10
Elatohóri **GR** 101 Hd44
Élatos **GR** 101 Hc43
El Barco de Ávila **E** 91 Bb40
Elbasan **RKS** 100 Hb42
Elbeuf **F** 61 Db30
Elbląg **PL** 58 Gd25

El Bonillo **E** 92 Ca43
El'brus **RUS** 127 Ga17
El Burgo de Osma **E** 92 Ca40
Elche **E** 107 Cb44
Elche de la Sierra **E** 107 Ca44
El Cubo de Tierra del Vino **E** 78 Bb39
Elda **E** 107 Cb44
Eléa **GR** 111 Ja48
Elec **RUS** 122 Fa12
Elefsína **GR** 112 Jb46
Eleftheroúpoli **GR** 102 Jb42
Eleja **LV** 52 Hc22
Èlektostal' **RUS** 118 Fa10
Elektrènai **LT** 53 Hd24
Elena **BG** 88 Jc39
Elgå **N** 37 Fd14
Elgin **GB** 17 Db19
El Grado **E** 80 Cd40
Elhovka **RUS** 119 Ga09
Elhovo **BG** 103 Jd40
Eliá **GR** 110 Hd47
Elimäki **FIN** 41 Hd16
Elin Pelin **BG** 102 Ja40
Elionka **RUS** 121 Ec13
Èlista **RUS** 123 Ga15
Ełk **PL** 59 Hc25
Ellon **GB** 17 Db19
Ellös **S** 43 Fc20
Ellwangen **D** 64 Fa32
El Molinillo **E** 91 Bc42
El Moral **E** 107 Ca44
Elmshorn **D** 56 Fb26
Elne **F** 81 Db39
Elnesvågen **N** 36 Fa13
El'nja **RUS** 117 Ec11
Elopía **GR** 111 Ja46
El Pedroso **E** 105 Ba43
El Pilar de la Mola **E** 94 Cd44
El Pobo de Dueñas **E** 93 Cb41
el Pont de Suert **E** 80 Cd39
El Puente del Arzobispo **E** 91 Bb41
El Puerto de Santa María **E** 105 Ad45
El Real de la Jara **E** 105 Ba43
El Real de San Vicente **E** 91 Bc41
El Rocío **E** 105 Ad44
El Rubio **E** 105 Bb44
El Saucejo **E** 105 Bb45
Elsfjord **N** 33 Ga09
Elsfleth **D** 56 Fa26
Elst **NL** 55 Ec28
Elsterwerda **D** 65 Fd29
Eltmann **D** 64 Fb31
Èl'ton **RUS** 123 Ga13
Eltville **D** 63 Ed30
Elva **EST** 47 Ja19
El Vacar **E** 105 Bb43
Elvanlı **TR** 128 Gc17

Elvas **P** 90 Ad42
Elven **F** 60 Cc32
el Vendrell **E** 95 Da41
Elverum **N** 37 Fc16
El Villar de Arnedo **E** 80 Cb39
El Viso **E** 105 Bb43
Elvkroken **N** 28 Gb07
Elx (Elche) **E** 107 Cb44
Ely **GB** 25 Dc26
Elze **D** 56 Fa28
Embrun **F** 83 Eb37
Embûte **LV** 52 Hb22
Emden **D** 55 Ed26
Emecik **TR** 115 Kb47
Emiralem **TR** 113 Ka45
Emirgazi **TR** 128 Gc15
Emlichheim **D** 55 Ec27
Emmaboda **S** 50 Gb22
Emmaljunga **S** 49 Fd22
Emmaste **EST** 46 Hb19
Emmeloord **NL** 55 Ec27
Emmen **NL** 55 Ec27
Emmendingen **D** 71 Ed33
Emmerich **D** 55 Ec28
Empessós **GR** 110 Hc45
Empoli **I** 84 Fb39
Emsdetten **D** 55 Ed27
Ëna **RUS** 31 Ja06
Enånger **S** 38 Gb15
Encekler **TR** 113 Kb44
Enciso **E** 80 Cb39
Encs **H** 75 Hb33
Enerhodar **UA** 126 Fa16
Eneryda **S** 50 Ga22
Enez **TR** 103 Jd42
Enge **N** 37 Fb13
Engelberg **CH** 71 Ed35
Engels **RUS** 123 Fd12
Enger **D** 56 Fa28
Engerneset **N** 37 Fd15
Engstingen **D** 72 Fa33
Enguera **E** 93 Cb43
Enguídanos **E** 93 Cb42
Engure **LV** 52 Hc21
Enisala **RO** 89 Ka36
Enkhuizen **NL** 55 Eb27
Enköping **S** 45 Gc18
Enna **I** 109 Ga47
Ennigerloh **D** 55 Ed28
Ennis **IRL** 18 Bd24
Enniscorthy **IRL** 23 Cb25
Enniskerry **IRL** 19 Cb24
Enniskillen **GB** 19 Cb22
Ennistimon **IRL** 18 Bd24
Enns **A** 73 Ga33
Eno **FIN** 41 Jb13
Enonkoski **FIN** 41 Ja14
Enontekiö Enkodak **FIN** 30 Ha06
Enschede **NL** 55 Ec27
Ensisheim **F** 71 Ec33
Entraygues-sur-Truyère **F** 81 Dc37
Entre-os-Rios **P** 78 Ad39
Entrevaux **F** 83 Eb38

Envermeu **F** 62 Dc30
Enviken **S** 38 Gb16
Épernay **F** 62 Ea31
Épila **E** 80 Cb40
Épinal **F** 71 Eb33
Epískopí **GR** 114 Jc49
Eppingen **D** 64 Fa32
Epsom **GB** 25 Db28
Eptahóri **GR** 101 Hc43
Équeurdreville-Hainneville **F** 61 Cd30
Erahtur **RUS** 118 Fb10
Erátira **GR** 101 Hc43
Erba **I** 71 Ed36
Erbach **D** 64 Fa31
Erbach **D** 72 Fa33
Erd **H** 74 Ha34
Erdek **TR** 103 Ka42
Erdemli **TR** 128 Gc17
Erdeven **F** 60 Cc32
Erding **D** 72 Fc33
Erdut **HR** 86 Ha37
Ereğli **TR** 128 Gc15
Eremivka **MD** 77 Kb33
Eremitu **RO** 76 Jb34
Erfurt **D** 64 Fb29
Ergli **LV** 53 Hd21
Ergolding **D** 72 Fc33
Ergoldsbach **D** 64 Fc32
Erice **I** 108 Fc46
Ericeira **P** 90 Ab41
Erikli **TR** 103 Jd42
Eringsboda **S** 50 Gb22
Erithrés **GR** 111 Ja46
Erka **N** 37 Fb14
Erkelenz **D** 63 Ec29
Erkner **D** 57 Fd27
Erla **E** 80 Cc39
Erlangen **D** 64 Fb31
Ermakovo **RUS** 119 Ga09
Ermenek **TR** 128 Gb17
Ermesinde **P** 78 Ad38
Ermióni **GR** 111 Jb47
Ermiš **RUS** 118 Fb10
Ermoúpoli **GR** 112 Jc46
Ernée **F** 61 Da31
Erquy **F** 60 Cc31
Erro **E** 80 Cc38
Ersekë **AL** 101 Hc43
Erši **RUS** 117 Ed11
Ersmark **S** 34 Gd12
Ersmark **S** 34 Gd11
Erstein **F** 63 Ec32
Ertuğrul **TR** 103 Ka43
Ervenik **HR** 85 Gb38
Ervy-le-Châtel **F** 70 Dd33
Erwitte **D** 55 Ed28
Erzurum **TR** 127 Ga19
Eržvilkas **LT** 52 Hc23
Esbjerg **DK** 48 Fa23
Esbo Fin **N** 46 Hc17
Escalada **E** 79 Ca38
Escalaplano **I** 97 Ed44
Escalona **E** 91 Bc41
Escalos de Cima **P** 90 Ad40
Escároz **E** 80 Cc38

Eschede **D** 56 Fb27
Eschenburg **D** 63 Ed29
Esch-sur-Alzette **L** 63 Eb31
Esch-sur-Sûre **L** 63 Eb30
Eschwege **D** 64 Fb29
Eschweiler **D** 63 Ec29
Esens **D** 55 Ed26
Eskifjörður **IS** 15 Cc07
Eskilstuna **S** 44 Gb18
Eslohe **D** 63 Ed29
Eslöv **S** 49 Fd23
Es Mercadal **E** 95 Dc43
Espalion **F** 81 Dc37
Espeland **N** 36 Ed16
Espiel **E** 105 Bb43
Espinama **E** 79 Bd37
Espinhal **P** 90 Ad40
Espinho **P** 78 Ad39
Espinosa de los Monteros **E** 79 Ca38
Espoo **FIN** 46 Hc17
Esposende **P** 78 Ad38
Esrange **S** 29 Gd07
Essen **B** 54 Ea28
Essen **D** 55 Ec28
Essentuki **RUS** 127 Ga17
Esslingen **D** 64 Fa32
Essoyes **F** 70 Ea33
Estaing **F** 81 Dc37
Estarreja **P** 78 Ad39
Estella **E** 80 Cb38
Estepa **E** 105 Bb44
Estepona **E** 105 Ba45
Estercuel **E** 93 Cc41
Esternay **F** 62 Dd32
Esterri d'Àneu **E** 81 Da39
Estissac **F** 62 Dd32
Estoril **P** 90 Ab41
Estremoz **P** 90 Ad42
Esztergom **H** 74 Gd34
Étain **F** 63 Eb31
Étampes **F** 62 Dc32
Étaples **F** 62 Dc29
Etili **TR** 103 Ka43
Etne **N** 42 Ed17
Etolikó **GR** 110 Hd46
Étrépagny **F** 62 Dc31
Étretat **F** 61 Db30
Etropole **BG** 102 Ja40
Ettelbruck **L** 63 Eb30
Ettenheim **D** 71 Ed33
Etten-Leur **NL** 55 Eb28
Ettlingen **D** 63 Ed32
Eu **F** 62 Dc30
Eupen **B** 63 Eb29
Eura **FIN** 40 Ha16
Eurajoki **FIN** 40 Ha15
Euskirchen **D** 63 Ec29
Eutin **D** 56 Fb25
Evanger **N** 36 Ed16
Evaux-les-Bains **F** 69 Dc35
Evciler **TR** 103 Ka43
Évdilos **GR** 113 Jd46
Evenskjer **N** 28 Gb06
Evergem **B** 54 Ea28
Evertsberg **S** 38 Ga16

Evesham **GB** 24 Da26
Évian-les-Bains **F** 71 Eb35
Evijärvi **FIN** 40 Hb13
Evisa **F** 96 Ed41
Evje **N** 42 Fa19
Evlanovo **RUS** 122 Fa12
Evolène **CH** 71 Ec35
Évora **P** 90 Ac42
Évoramonte **P** 90 Ad42
Evreşe **TR** 103 Jd42
Évreux **F** 61 Db31
Évron **F** 61 Da32
Évry **F** 62 Dc32
Éxarhos **GR** 111 Ja45
Exeter **GB** 23 Cc28
Extremo **P** 78 Ad38
Eydehavn **N** 42 Fa19
Eyemouth **GB** 21 Db21
Eygurande **F** 69 Dc35
Eymoutiers **F** 69 Db35
Eyrarbakki **IS** 14 Bc07
Ezcaray **E** 79 Ca39
Ezere **LV** 52 Hb22
Ežerėlis **LT** 52 Hc24
Ezernieki **LV** 53 Jb22
Ezine **TR** 103 Jd43

F

Faaborg **DK** 49 Fb24
Fåberg **N** 36 Fa15
Fåberg **N** 37 Fc16
Fábiánsebestyén **H** 75 Hb35
Fäboda **FIN** 34 Ha12
Fabriano **I** 84 Fc39
Fábricas de Riópar **E** 107 Ca44
Faenza **I** 84 Fc38
Fafe **P** 78 Ad38
Făgăraş **RO** 88 Jb36
Fågelsjö **S** 38 Ga15
Fagerås **S** 44 Fd18
Fagerhult **S** 43 Fc19
Fagerhult **S** 50 Gb21
Fagernes **N** 26 Gc05
Fagernes **N** 37 Fb16
Fagersta **S** 44 Gb17
Fäget **RO** 75 Hc36
Fagurhólsmýri **IS** 15 Ca08
Fakenham **GB** 25 Dc26
Fåker **S** 38 Ga13
Fakija **BG** 103 Jd40
Falaise **F** 61 Da31
Falconara Marittima **I** 85 Fd39
Falerum **S** 44 Gb20
Fălești **MD** 77 Jd33
Falkenberg **D** 65 Fd29
Falkenberg **S** 49 Fd21
Falkensee **D** 57 Fd27
Falkenstein **D** 64 Fc30
Falkirk **GB** 21 Da21
Falköping **S** 44 Fd20
Fällfors **S** 34 Gd10
Fälloheden **S** 33 Gc10

Falmouth – Forøya

Falmouth **GB** 23 Cb28
Falset **E** 93 Cd41
Falsterbo **S** 49 Fd23
Fälticeni **RO** 76 Jc33
Falun **S** 44 Gb17
Fameck **F** 63 Eb31
Fana **N** 42 Ed17
Fannrem **N** 37 Fc13
Fano **I** 85 Fd39
Fântânița **MD** 77 Jd32
Faraonivka **UA** 77 Kb34
Fărău **RO** 76 Ja35
Fărcașa **RO** 75 Hd33
Fârdea **RO** 75 Hc36
Fareham **GB** 24 Da28
Farestad **N** 42 Fa20
Färgelanda **S** 43 Fc19
Färila **S** 38 Gb15
Faringdon **GB** 24 Da27
Farini **I** 84 Fa38
Färjestaden **S** 50 Gb22
Farkadóna **GR** 101 Hd44
Fârliug **RO** 75 Hc36
Faro **P** 104 Ac44
Fårösund **S** 45 Gd20
Farranfore **IRL** 18 Bd24
Fársala **GR** 101 Hd44
Farsø **DK** 49 Fb21
Farsund **N** 42 Ed20
Farum **DK** 49 Fd23
Fasano **I** 100 Gd43
Fáskrúðsfjörður **IS** 15 Cc07
Fastiv **UA** 121 Ec15
Fatež **RUS** 122 Fa13
Fátima **P** 90 Ac40
Fatsa **TR** 127 Fc19
Faulquemont **F** 63 Ec32
Faura **E** 93 Cc43
Făurei **RO** 76 Jc34
Făurei **RO** 89 Jd36
Fauske **N** 28 Ga08
Fauville-en-Caux **F** 61 Db30
Fåvang **N** 37 Fc15
Favara **I** 108 Fd47
Faverges **F** 71 Eb36
Faversham **GB** 25 Dc28
Favignana **I** 108 Fc46
Favone **F** 96 Ed41
Faxe **DK** 49 Fc24
Fayence **F** 83 Eb39
Fayl-Billot **F** 71 Eb33
Fayón **E** 93 Cd41
Fay-sur-Lignon **F** 82 Dd37
Fécamp **F** 61 Db30
Feda **N** 42 Ed19
Fëdorovka **RUS** 122 Fb15
Fegyvernek **H** 75 Hb34
Fehérgyarmat **H** 75 Hc33
Fehring **A** 73 Gb35
Felanitx **E** 95 Db44
Feldbach **A** 73 Gb35
Feldberg **D** 57 Fd26
Feldkirch **A** 72 Fa34
Feldkirchen **A** 73 Ga35
Felixstowe **GB** 25 Dc27
Felletin **IS** 15 Cc07

Felletin **F** 69 Dc35
Fellingsbro **S** 44 Gb18
Felnac **RO** 75 Hc36
Felsőzsolca **H** 75 Hb33
Feltre **I** 72 Fc36
Fensmark **DK** 49 Fc24
Feodosija **UA** 126 Fb17
Fère-Champenoise **F** 62 Ea32
Fère-en-Tardenois **F** 62 Dd31
Ferentillo **I** 84 Fc40
Ferentino **I** 98 Fd42
Feres **GR** 103 Jd42
Ferlach **A** 73 Ga35
Fermo **I** 85 Fd40
Fermoselle **E** 78 Bb39
Fermoy **IRL** 22 Bd25
Ferrandina **I** 99 Gc43
Ferrara **I** 84 Fb37
Ferreira do Alentejo **P** 90 Ac42
Ferrette **F** 71 Ec34
Ferriere **I** 84 Fa38
Ferrol **E** 78 Ba36
Fertőszentmiklós **H** 74 Gc34
Festvåg **N** 28 Ga07
Fetești **RO** 89 Jd37
Fethard **IRL** 22 Ca25
Fetsund **N** 43 Fc17
Feuchtwangen **D** 64 Fb32
Feurs **F** 70 Dd36
Fevik **N** 42 Fa19
Ffestiniog **GB** 24 Cd25
Fibiș **RO** 75 Hc36
Fidenza **I** 84 Fa37
Fier **AL** 100 Hb43
Fierzë **AL** 100 Hb41
Fiesole **I** 84 Fb39
Figari **F** 96 Ed42
Figeac **F** 81 Db37
Figeholm **S** 50 Gb21
Figiás **GR** 112 Jb46
Figueira da Foz **P** 90 Ac40
Figueira de Castelo Rodrigo **P** 78 Ba39
Figueiró dos Vinhos **P** 90 Ad40
Figueres **E** 81 Db40
Filadelfia **I** 109 Gc45
Fil'akovo **SK** 74 Ha33
Filey **GB** 21 Dc24
Filiași **RO** 88 Ja37
Filiátes **GR** 100 Hb44
Filiatrá **GR** 110 Hd47
Filinskoe **RUS** 118 Fb10
Filipești **RO** 76 Jc34
Filipiáda **GR** 110 Hc45
Filipstad **S** 44 Ga18
Fillan **N** 32 Fb12
Filótas **GR** 101 Hd43
Filóti **GR** 115 Jd47
Finale Emilia **I** 84 Fb37
Finale Ligure **I** 83 Ed38
Finaña **E** 106 Bd45

Fındıklı **TR** 103 Jd42
Fındıkpınarı **TR** 128 Gd16
Fínikas **GR** 112 Jc46
Finnerödja **S** 44 Ga19
Finnøya **N** 28 Gb07
Finnsnes **N** 26 Gc05
Finnstad **N** 37 Fc14
Finse **N** 36 Fa16
Finspång **S** 44 Gb19
Finsterwalde **D** 57 Fd28
Fintown **IRL** 19 Cb21
Fionnphort **GB** 16 Cc20
Fiorenzuola d'Arda **I** 84 Fa37
Firenze **I** 84 Fb39
Firenzuola **I** 84 Fb38
Firminy **F** 70 Dd36
Firovo **RUS** 117 Ec09
Fishguard **GB** 23 Cc26
Fiskárdo **GR** 110 Hc46
Fiskebäckskil **S** 43 Fc20
Fiskebøl **N** 28 Ga06
Fismes **F** 62 Dd31
Fíties **GR** 110 Hc45
Fitjar **N** 42 Ed17
Fiuggi **I** 98 Fd41
Fiumicino **I** 98 Fc42
Fivizzano **I** 84 Fa38
Fjæra **N** 42 Ed17
Fjærland **N** 36 Fa15
Fjällbacka **S** 43 Fc19
Fjällnäs **S** 38 Fd14
Fjellerup **DK** 49 Fb22
Fjerritslev **DK** 49 Fb21
Fjordgård **N** 28 Gb05
Fjugesta **S** 44 Ga18
Fladungen **D** 64 Fb30
Flakaberg **S** 30 Ha08
Flakaträsk **S** 33 Gb10
Flakstad **N** 28 Ga07
Flåm **N** 36 Fa16
Flatøydegard **N** 37 Fb16
Fleetwood **GB** 21 Da24
Flekkefjord **N** 42 Ed19
Flen **S** 44 Gb19
Flensburg **D** 48 Fa24
Flers **F** 61 Da31
Flesberg **N** 43 Fb17
Flesnes **N** 28 Gb06
Fleurance **F** 81 Da37
Fleury-les-Aubrais **F** 62 Dc32
Flims **CH** 72 Fa35
Flisa **N** 37 Fd16
Flix **E** 93 Cd41
Flize **F** 62 Ea30
Floby **S** 44 Fd20
Flogny-la-Chapelle **F** 70 Dd33
Flöha **D** 65 Fd30
Florac **F** 81 Dc37
Florange **F** 63 Eb31
Florennes **B** 62 Ea30
Florenville **B** 63 Eb31
Florești **MD** 77 Jd32
Floridia **I** 109 Ga48

Flórina **GR** 101 Hc43
Florø **N** 36 Ed15
Florynka **PL** 67 Hb31
Flötningen **S** 38 Fd15
Fluberg **N** 37 Fc16
Flúðir **IS** 14 Bc07
Fluminimaggiore **I** 97 Ec44
Foča **BIH** 86 Ha39
Foça **TR** 113 Ka45
Fochabers **GB** 17 Db19
Focșani **RO** 77 Jd35
Foggia **I** 99 Gb42
Fohnsdorf **A** 73 Ga34
Foix **F** 81 Da39
Fojnica **BIH** 86 Gd39
Fokino **RUS** 121 Ed12
Foldereid **N** 32 Fd11
Folégandros **GR** 111 Jc47
Folelli **F** 96 Ed40
Foligno **I** 84 Fc40
Folkestad **N** 36 Ed14
Folkestone **GB** 25 Dc28
Follafors **N** 32 Fc12
Folldal **N** 37 Fc14
Follebu **N** 37 Fc16
Follingbo **S** 45 Gd20
Föllinge **S** 33 Ga12
Follonica **I** 84 Fb40
Foltești **RO** 77 Jd35
Fominki **RUS** 118 Fb09
Fondi **I** 98 Fd42
Fonni **I** 97 Ed43
Fonsagrada **E** 78 Bb37
Fontainebleau **F** 62 Dc32
Fontaine-Française **F** 70 Ea33
Fontanka **UA** 77 Kb34
Fontdepou **E** 80 Cd40
Fontenay-le-Comte **F** 68 Cd34
Fontenay-Trésigny **F** 62 Dd32
Fontevraud-l'Abbaye **F** 69 Da33
Fontiveros **E** 91 Bc40
Font-Romeu **F** 81 Db39
Fonyód **H** 74 Gc35
Foppolo **I** 72 Fa36
Forbach **F** 63 Ec31
Forcalquier **F** 82 Ea38
Forcarei **E** 78 Ba37
Forchheim **D** 64 Fb31
Førde **N** 36 Ed15
Førde **N** 42 Ed17
Forfar **GB** 17 Db20
Forges-les-Eaux **F** 62 Dc30
Forlì **I** 84 Fc38
Forlimpopoli **I** 84 Fc38
Formazza **I** 71 Ed35
Formby **GB** 21 Da24
Formia **I** 98 Fd42
Formofoss **N** 32 Fd11
Fornells **E** 95 Dc43
Forneset **N** 26 Gc05
Fornovo di Taro **I** 84 Fa38
Forøya **N** 28 Ga08

Forres GB 17 Da19
Fors S 44 Gb17
Forserum S 44 Ga20
Forshaga S 44 Fd18
Förslöv S 49 Fd22
Forsmark S 33 Gb10
Forsmo S 39 Gc13
Forsnäs S 33 Gc09
Forsnes N 37 Fb13
Forssa FIN 40 Hb16
Forst D 57 Ga28
Forsvik S 44 Ga19
Fort Augustus GB 17 Da19
Forte dei Marmi I 84 Fa39
Fort-Mahon-Plage F 62 Dc29
Fortrose GB 17 Da19
Fortuna E 107 Cb44
Fortunes-well GB 24 Cd28
Fort William GB 16 Cd20
Forvika N 32 Fd10
Fosnavåg N 36 Ed14
Fossacesia Marina I 99 Ga41
Fossano I 83 Ec38
Fossbakken N 29 Gc06
Fosses-la-Ville B 62 Ea30
Fossli N 36 Fa16
Fossombrone I 84 Fc39
Fos-sur-Mer F 82 Dd39
Fót H 74 Ha34
Fougères F 61 Cd31
Fourchambault F 70 Dd34
Fourfourás GR 114 Jc49
Fourmies F 62 Ea30
Fours F 70 Dd34
Foústani GR 101 Hd42
Fowey GB 23 Cb28
Foxford IRL 18 Ca22
Foynes IRL 18 Bd24
Foz E 78 Bb36
Foz de Odeleite P 104 Ac44
Frącki PL 59 Hc25
Fraga E 80 Cd40
Fragístra GR 110 Hd45
Framlev DK 49 Hb22
Frammersbach D 64 Fa30
Frampol PL 67 Hc29
Francardo F 96 Ed41
Francavilla al Mare I 99 Ga41
Francavilla di Sicilia I 109 Ga47
Francavilla Fontana I 100 Gd43
Francoforte I 109 Ga47
Franeker NL 55 Ec26
Frankenberg D 64 Fa29
Frankenthal D 63 Ed31
Frankfurt (Main) D 63 Ed30
Frankfurt (Oder) D 57 Ga28
Fränsta S 38 Gb14
Františkovy Lázně CZ 64 Fc30
Frascati I 98 Fc41
Fraserburgh GB 17 Db19

Frashër AL 100 Hb43
Frătăuţii Noi RO 76 Jb33
Frátsia GR 111 Ja48
Frauenfeld CH 71 Ed34
Frauenkirchen A 74 Gc34
Frecăţei RO 89 Ka36
Fredericia DK 49 Fb23
Frederikshavn DK 49 Fb21
Frederikssund DK 49 Fc23
Frederiksværk DK 49 Fc23
Fredrika S 33 Gc12
Fredriksberg S 44 Ga17
Fredrikstad N 43 Fc18
Fregenal de la Sierra E 105 Ad43
Freiberg D 65 Fd29
Freiburg D 71 Ed33
Freilassing D 73 Fd34
Freising D 72 Fc33
Freistadt A 73 Ga33
Freital D 65 Fd29
Fréjus F 83 Eb39
Frenštát pod Radhoštěm CZ 66 Gd31
Freren D 55 Ed27
Fresnay-sur-Sarthe F 61 Da32
Fresno-Alhándiga E 91 Bb40
Fresno de Caracena E 92 Ca40
Fretigney F 71 Eb34
Freudenberg D 63 Ed29
Freudenstadt D 63 Ed32
Frévent F 62 Dd29
Freyburg D 64 Fc29
Freyming-Merlebach F 63 Ec31
Freyung D 65 Fd32
Frí GR 115 Kb49
Fribourg CH 71 Ec35
Friedberg A 73 Gb34
Friedberg D 64 Fa30
Friedberg D 72 Fb33
Friedewald D 64 Fa29
Friedland D 57 Fd26
Friedland D 57 Ga28
Friedland D 64 Fb29
Friedrichshafen D 72 Fa34
Friedrichstadt D 56 Fa25
Friesach A 73 Ga35
Friesack D 57 Fd27
Friesoythe D 55 Ed26
Friggesund S 38 Gb15
Frihetsli N 29 Gc06
Frillesås S 49 Fc21
Friol E 78 Ba36
Fristad S 44 Fd20
Fritsla S 49 Fd21
Fritzlar D 64 Fa29
Friville-Escarbotin F 62 Dc30
Frjanovo RUS 118 Fa10
Frohnleiten A 73 Gb34
Frolovo RUS 123 Fd13
Frombork PL 58 Ha25

Frome GB 24 Cd27
Frómista E 79 Bd38
Frontignan F 81 Dc38
Frosinone I 98 Fd42
Frosta N 32 Fc12
Froussioúna GR 111 Ja46
Frövi S 44 Gb18
Fruges F 62 Dc29
Frunzivka UA 77 Ka33
Frunzivka UA 125 Ec16
Frutigen CH 71 Ec35
Frýdek-Místek CZ 66 Gd31
Frýdlant CZ 65 Ga29
Fuengirola E 105 Bb45
Fuensalida E 91 Bc41
Fuensanta E 107 Ca45
Fuente-Álamo E 107 Ca45
Fuente de Cantos E 105 Ba43
Fuente del Arco E 105 Ba43
Fuente el Fresno E 91 Bc42
Fuente Obejuna E 105 Bb43
Fuentesaúco E 79 Bc39
Fuentes de Ebro E 80 Cc40
Fügen A 72 Fc34
Fulda D 64 Fa30
Fulunäs S 38 Fd16
Fumay F 62 Ea30
Fumel F 81 Da37
Funäsdalen S 38 Fd14
Fundão P 90 Ad40
Fundulea RO 88 Jc37
Furculeşti RO 88 Jb38
Furmanov RUS 118 Fa09
Fürstenau D 55 Ed27
Fürstenberg D 57 Fd26
Fürstenfeld A 73 Gb35
Fürstenfeldbruck D 72 Fb33
Fürstenwalde D 57 Ga28
Furta H 75 Hc34
Fürth D 64 Fb31
Furth im Wald D 65 Fd32
Furtwangen D 71 Ed33
Furudal S 38 Ga16
Furuflaten N 26 Gd05
Furusund S 45 Gd18
Fusa N 42 Ed17
Fushë-Muhur AL 100 Hb41
Füssen D 72 Fb34
Fustiñana E 80 Cb39
Füzesabony H 75 Hb33
Füzesgyarmat H 75 Hb34
Fyllinge S 49 Fd22
Fynshav DK 49 Fb24
Fyresdal N 42 Fa18

G

Gabare BG 88 Ja39
Gabčíkovo SK 74 Gc33
Gabøl DK 48 Fa23
Gabrovo BG 88 Jc39
Gacé F 61 Db31
Gacko BIH 86 Gd40
Gäddede S 33 Ga11

Gadebusch D 56 Fc26
Gádor E 106 Bd46
Gærum DK 49 Fb21
Găeşti RO 88 Jb37
Gaeta I 98 Fd42
Gafsele S 33 Gc12
Gaggenau D 63 Ed32
Gagince SRB 87 Hc40
Gagino RUS 119 Fc09
Gagnef S 44 Ga17
Gaiķi LV 52 Hb21
Gaildorf D 64 Fa32
Gailey GB 24 Da25
Gaillac F 81 Db38
Gaillon F 62 Dc31
Gainsborough GB 25 Db25
Gairloch GB 16 Cd18
Gajutino RUS 117 Ed08
Gajvoron UA 77 Ka32
Gakilköy TR 103 Kb42
Gakkovo RUS 47 Ja17
Gäläbovo BG 102 Jc40
Galanta SK 74 Gd33
Galashiels GB 21 Da22
Galaţi RO 89 Jd36
Galatina I 100 Gd44
Galátista GR 101 Ja43
Galaxídi GR 111 Ja46
Galera E 106 Bd44
Galéria F 96 Ed40
Galgaguta H 74 Ha33
Gâlgău RO 76 Ja34
Galič RUS 118 Fa08
Gallarate I 71 Ed36
Gallipoli I 100 Gd44
Gällivare S 29 Gd08
Gallneukirchen A 73 Ga33
Gällö S 38 Ga13
Gällstad S 44 Fd20
Galtström S 39 Gc14
Galway IRL 18 Bd23
Gaming A 73 Ga33
Gamleby S 44 Gb20
Gammelbo S 44 Gb18
Gammelstaden S 34 Ha10
Gammertingen D 72 Fa33
Gamvik N 27 Hc02
Gan F 80 Cd38
Ganderkesee D 56 Fa26
Gandesa E 93 Cd41
Gandia E 94 Cc44
Gandvik N 27 Hc04
Ganges F 81 Dc38
Gangi I 109 Ga47
Gannat F 69 Dc35
Gap F 83 Eb37
Gara Hitrino BG 89 Jd38
Gara Läkatnik BG 88 Ja39
Garbatka-Letnisko PL 59 Hb28
Gârbou RO 75 Hd34
Garbów PL 67 Hc29
Garbsen D 56 Fa27
Garching D 72 Fc33
Garda I 72 Fb36
Gardanne F 82 Ea39

Gårdby – Gniechowice

Gårdby **S** 50 Gb22
Gardelegen **D** 56 Fc27
Gardermoen **N** 43 Fc17
Gardete **P** 90 Ad41
Gardíki **GR** 101 Hc44
Garding **D** 56 Fa25
Gärdnäs **S** 33 Ga12
Gardone Riviera **I** 72 Fb36
Gardone Val Trompia **I** 72 Fa36
Gárdony **H** 74 Gd34
Garður **IS** 14 Bb06
Garešnica **HR** 74 Gc36
Garessio **I** 83 Ec38
Gargaliáni **GR** 110 Hd47
Gargnäs **S** 33 Gc10
Gargżdai **LT** 52 Hb23
Garlasco **I** 83 Ed37
Garliava **LT** 52 Hc24
Gärljano **BG** 101 Hd41
Garmisch-Partenkirchen **D** 72 Fb34
Garoaia **RO** 77 Jd35
Garphyttan **S** 44 Ga18
Garrovillas **E** 91 Ba41
Garrucha **E** 107 Ca45
Gärsnäs **S** 50 Ga23
Gartz **D** 57 Ga26
Garvão **P** 104 Ac43
Garve **GB** 17 Da19
Garwolin **PL** 59 Hb28
Gasteiz **E** 80 Cb38
Gastoúni **GR** 110 Hc46
Gătaia **RO** 75 Hc36
Gatčina **RUS** 47 Jb17
Gatehouse of Fleet **GB** 20 Cd22
Gateshead **GB** 21 Db23
Gattinara **I** 71 Ed36
Gaucín **E** 105 Ba45
Gaupne **N** 36 Fa15
Gauting **D** 72 Fb33
Gavarnie **F** 80 Cd39
Gavião **P** 90 Ad41
Gävle **S** 39 Gc16
Gavorrano **I** 84 Fb40
Gavray **F** 61 Cd31
Gavrilov-Jam **RUS** 118 Fa09
Gávrio **GR** 112 Jc46
Gávros **GR** 101 Hc43
Gavry **RUS** 53 Jb21
Gaworzyce **PL** 57 Gb28
Gazimağusa **CY** 128 Gc19
Gazipaşa **TR** 128 Ga17
Gdańsk **PL** 58 Gd25
Gdov **RUS** 47 Ja18
Gdynia **PL** 58 Gd25
Gedser **DK** 49 Fc25
Geel **B** 63 Eb29
Geeste **D** 55 Ed27
Geesthacht **D** 56 Fb26
Gefell **D** 64 Fc30
Geilenkirchen **D** 63 Ec29
Geilo **N** 36 Fa16
Geiranger **N** 36 Fa14
Geiselhöring **D** 64 Fc32

Geisenfeld **D** 64 Fc32
Geisingen **D** 71 Ed33
Geislingen **D** 64 Fa32
Geithus **N** 43 Fb17
Gela **I** 109 Ga48
Geldern **D** 55 Ec28
Geldrop **NL** 55 Eb28
Geleen **NL** 63 Eb29
Gelenbe **TR** 113 Kb44
Gelendžik **RUS** 127 Fc17
Gelgaudiškis **LT** 52 Hc24
Gelibolu **TR** 103 Jd42
Gelnhausen **D** 64 Fa30
Gelsenkirchen **D** 55 Ec28
Gelting **D** 49 Fb24
Gelu **RO** 75 Hb36
Gembloux **B** 62 Ea29
Gemla **S** 50 Ga22
Gemona del Friuli **I** 73 Fd36
Gemünden **D** 64 Fa29
Gemünden **D** 64 Fa30
Gençay **F** 69 Da34
Generalski Stol **HR** 85 Gb37
General Toševo **BG** 89 Ka38
Genève **CH** 71 Eb35
Gengenbach **D** 63 Ed32
Genk **B** 63 Eb29
Genlis **F** 70 Ea34
Gennep **NL** 55 Ec28
Génolhac **F** 82 Dd37
Genova **I** 83 Ed38
Gent **B** 62 Ea29
Genthin **D** 56 Fc27
Genzano di Lucania **I** 99 Gb43
George Enescu **RO** 76 Jc32
Georgievsk **RUS** 127 Ga17
Gera **D** 64 Fc29
Geraardsbergen **B** 62 Ea29
Gerace **I** 109 Gc46
Gerakaroú **GR** 101 Ja43
Geráki **GR** 111 Ja47
Gerakiní **GR** 101 Ja43
Gérardmer **F** 71 Ec33
Gerena **E** 105 Ba44
Gérgal **E** 106 Bd45
Gergova **RO** 89 Ka36
Germencik **TR** 113 Kb45
Germering **D** 72 Fb33
Germersheim **D** 63 Ed31
Gernika **E** 80 Cb37
Gernsheim **D** 63 Ed31
Gerolstein **D** 63 Ec30
Gerolzhofen **D** 64 Fb31
Gersfeld **D** 64 Fa30
Gersthofen **D** 72 Fb33
Gescher **D** 55 Ec28
Gesunda **S** 38 Ga16
Gèsves **B** 63 Eb30
Geta **FIN** 45 Gd17
Getafe **E** 92 Bd41
Getinge **S** 49 Fd21
Gettorf **D** 56 Fb25
Getxo **E** 79 Ca37
Gevgelija **MK** 101 Hd42
Gex **F** 71 Eb35

Geyikli **TR** 103 Jd43
Ghedi **I** 84 Fa37
Gheorgheni **RO** 76 Jb34
Gherla **RO** 76 Ja34
Gherţa Mică **RO** 75 Hd33
Ghilarza **I** 97 Ed43
Ghimpaţi **RO** 88 Jc38
Ghisonaccia **F** 96 Ed41
Ghisoni **F** 96 Ed41
Gianitsá **GR** 101 Hd42
Giardini-Naxos **I** 109 Gb47
Giarmata **RO** 75 Hc36
Giarre **I** 109 Gb47
Gibellina Nuova **I** 108 Fc47
Gibostad **N** 26 Gc05
Gibraleón **E** 105 Ad44
Gibraltar **GBZ** 105 Ba46
Gibzde **LV** 52 Hb21
Gic **H** 74 Gd34
Gideå **S** 39 Gc13
Gideåkroken **S** 33 Gc11
Gieboldehausen **D** 56 Fb28
Gien **F** 69 Dc33
Giengen **D** 64 Fb32
Giens **F** 82 Ea39
Giera **RO** 87 Hb37
Gießen **D** 63 Ed30
Gieten **NL** 55 Ec26
Gietrzwałd **PL** 58 Ha26
Gifhorn **D** 56 Fb27
Gigant **RUS** 123 Fd15
Gighera **RO** 88 Ja38
Gignac **F** 81 Dc38
Gijón **E** 79 Bc36
Gilău **RO** 75 Hd35
Gilavë **AL** 100 Hb43
Gilleleje **DK** 49 Fd22
Gimåfors **S** 38 Gb14
Gimo **S** 45 Gc17
Gimone **F** 81 Da38
Ginduliai **LT** 52 Hb23
Ginosa **I** 99 Gc43
Gioia del Colle **I** 99 Gc43
Gioia Tauro **I** 109 Gb46
Gioiosa Ionica **I** 109 Gc46
Giraltovce **SK** 67 Hb32
Giresun **TR** 127 Fd19
Girne **CY** 128 Gb18
Giromagny **F** 71 Ec33
Girona **E** 81 Db40
Girvan **GB** 20 Cd22
Gisburn **GB** 21 Da24
Gislaved **S** 49 Fd21
Gisors **F** 62 Dc31
Githio **GR** 111 Ja48
Giulianova **I** 85 Fd40
Giulvăz **RO** 75 Hb36
Giurgeni **RO** 89 Jd37
Giurgiu **RO** 88 Jc38
Give **DK** 48 Fa23
Givet **F** 62 Ea30
Givors **F** 70 Ea36
Givry **F** 70 Ea34
Givry-en-Argonne **F** 62 Ea31
Giżałki **PL** 58 Gc28
Giżycko **PL** 59 Hb25

Gjermundshamn **N** 42 Ed17
Gjerstad **N** 43 Fb19
Gjersvik **N** 33 Ga11
Gjesvær **N** 27 Hb02
Gjirokastër **AL** 100 Hb44
Gjøra **N** 37 Fb14
Gjøvik **N** 37 Fc16
Gladenbach **D** 63 Ed29
Gladstad **N** 32 Fd10
Glamoč **BIH** 86 Gc39
Glamsbjerg **DK** 49 Fb24
Glandorf **D** 55 Ed28
Glarus **CH** 71 Ed34
Glasgow **GB** 21 Da21
Glastonbury **GB** 24 Cd27
Glavatičevo **BIH** 86 Gd39
Glavinica **BG** 89 Jd38
Głebokie **PL** 67 Hc29
Gleisdorf **A** 73 Gb34
Glenariff **GB** 20 Cc22
Glenarm **GB** 20 Cc22
Glenbeigh **IRL** 18 Bc24
Glencolumbkille **IRL** 18 Ca21
Glenfinnan **GB** 16 Cd19
Glengarriff **IRL** 22 Bc25
Glenluce **GB** 20 Cd22
Glenrothes **GB** 21 Da21
Glenties **IRL** 18 Ca21
Glífa **GR** 111 Ja45
Glifáda **GR** 100 Hb44
Glimåkra **S** 50 Ga22
Glina **HR** 85 Gb37
Glinojeck **PL** 58 Ha27
Gliwice **PL** 66 Gd30
Glodeanu-Siliştea **RO** 89 Jd37
Glodeni **MD** 76 Jc33
Gloggnitz **A** 73 Gb34
Glogovac **RKS** 87 Hc40
Głogów **PL** 57 Gb28
Głogówek **PL** 66 Gd30
Głogów Małopolski **PL** 67 Hc30
Glomfjord **N** 28 Ga08
Glommen **S** 49 Fd21
Glommersträsk **S** 34 Gd10
Glöte **S** 38 Fd15
Gloucester **GB** 24 Da27
Główczyce **PL** 51 Gc24
Głowno **PL** 58 Ha28
Głubczyce **PL** 66 Gd30
Glubokij **RUS** 123 Fc14
Głuchołazy **PL** 66 Gc30
Głuchowo **PL** 58 Gc28
Glücksburg **D** 49 Fb24
Glückstadt **D** 56 Fa25
Gluhove **RUS** 118 Fb10
Gmünd **A** 65 Ga32
Gmünd **A** 73 Fd35
Gmunden **A** 73 Fd33
Gnarp **S** 39 Gc15
Gnarrenburg **D** 56 Fa26
Gnesta **S** 45 Gc19
Gniazdowo **PL** 59 Hb26
Gniechowice **PL** 66 Gc29

152

Gniew **PL** 58 Gd25
Gniezno **PL** 58 Gc27
Gnjilane **RKS** 87 Hc40
Gnoien **D** 57 Fd25
Gnosjö **S** 50 Ga21
Gobesh **AL** 100 Hb43
Göçbeyli **TR** 113 Ka44
Goce Delčev **BG** 101 Ja41
Goce Delčev **BG** 101 Ja41
Goch **D** 55 Ec28
Göd **H** 74 Ha34
Godby **FIN** 45 Gd17
Godeanu **RO** 87 Hd37
Godeč **BG** 88 Ja39
Goderville **F** 61 Db30
Gödöllő **H** 74 Ha34
Goes **NL** 54 Ea28
Gogolin **PL** 66 Gd30
Göhren **D** 57 Fd25
Goián **E** 78 Ad37
Góis **P** 90 Ad40
Goito **I** 84 Fb37
Gójsk **PL** 58 Ha27
Gökçeada **TR** 103 Jd43
Gökçen **TR** 113 Kb45
Gökkuşağı **TR** 128 Gd16
Gol **N** 37 Fb16
Golce **PL** 57 Gb26
Gölcük **TR** 103 Kb43
Golčův Jeníkov **CZ** 65 Gb31
Golczewo **PL** 57 Ga26
Gołdap **PL** 59 Hb25
Goldberg **D** 56 Fc26
Göle **TR** 127 Ga19
Goleniów **PL** 57 Ga26
Golfo Aranci **I** 96 Ed42
Golica **BG** 89 Ka39
Golicyno **RUS** 117 Ed10
Gološeva **LV** 53 Jb21
Goljam Manastir **BG** 103 Jd40
Goljamo Kruševo **BG** 103 Jd40
Gölmarmara **TR** 113 Kb44
Gölören **TR** 128 Gc15
Golspie **GB** 17 Da18
Golßen **D** 57 Fd28
Golubac **SRB** 87 Hc37
Golub-Dobrzyń **PL** 58 Gd26
Gołymin-Ośrodek **PL** 59 Hb27
Gómara **E** 80 Cb40
Gömeç **TR** 113 Ka44
Gommern **D** 56 Fc28
Gomulin **PL** 67 Ha29
Goncelin **F** 71 Eb36
Gondomar **P** 78 Ad39
Gondrecourt-le-Château **F** 63 Eb32
Gönen **TR** 103 Ka43
Goniądz **PL** 59 Hc26
Goole **GB** 21 Db24
Goor **NL** 55 Ec27
Göppingen **D** 64 Fa32
Góra **PL** 57 Gb28
Góra **PL** 58 Ha27

Góra Kalwaria **PL** 59 Hb28
Goráni **GR** 111 Ja47
Goražde **BIH** 86 Ha39
Gorban **RO** 77 Jd34
Gördalen **S** 38 Fd15
Gördes **TR** 113 Kb44
Gorelki **RUS** 118 Fa11
Gorey **IRL** 23 Cb25
Gorica **BG** 89 Ka39
Goricë **AL** 101 Hc42
Goricy **RUS** 117 Ed09
Gorinchem **NL** 55 Eb28
Goritsá **GR** 111 Ja47
Gorizia **I** 73 Fd36
Gorjačij Ključ **RUS** 127 Fc17
Gorki **RUS** 47 Jb17
Gørlev **DK** 49 Fc23
Gorlice **PL** 67 Hb31
Görlitz **D** 65 Ga29
Gormanstown **IRL** 19 Cb23
Gorna Bešovica **BG** 88 Ja39
Gorna Orjahovica **BG** 88 Jc39
Gorni Okol **BG** 102 Ja40
Gornjackij **RUS** 123 Fc14
Gornja Radgona **SLO** 73 Gb35
Gornja Sabanta **SRB** 87 Hc38
Gornje Peulje **BIH** 86 Gc38
Gornji Jabolčište **MK** 101 Hc41
Gornji Milanovac **SRB** 87 Hb38
Gornji Vakuf-Uskoplje **BIH** 86 Gd39
Górno **PL** 67 Hb29
Gornyj **RUS** 119 Ga11
Gorodec **RUS** 118 Fb09
Gorodišče **RUS** 119 Fd11
Gorodovikovsk **RUS** 127 Fd16
Górowo Iławeckie **PL** 58 Ha25
Gorron **F** 61 Da31
Goršečnoe **RUS** 122 Fa13
Gort **IRL** 18 Bd24
Görükle **TR** 103 Kb42
Görvik **S** 38 Gb13
Gorzkowice **PL** 67 Ha29
Gorzków-Osada **PL** 67 Hc29
Gorzów Wielkopolski **PL** 57 Gb27
Gorzyń **PL** 57 Gb27
Gosau **A** 73 Fd34
Gościkowo Jordanowo **PL** 57 Gb27
Gosforth **GB** 21 Da23
Goslar **D** 56 Fb28
Gospić **HR** 85 Gb38
Gostilja **BG** 88 Ja39
Gostivar **MK** 101 Hc41
Göstling **A** 73 Ga34
Gostomia **PL** 57 Gb26
Gostyń **PL** 58 Gc28
Gostynin **PL** 58 Ha27

Göteborg **S** 43 Fc20
Götene **S** 44 Fd19
Gotha **D** 64 Fb29
Götlunda **S** 44 Gb18
Göttingen **D** 56 Fb28
Gottskär **S** 49 Fc21
Gouda **NL** 55 Eb27
Gouménissa **GR** 101 Hd42
Goúmero **GR** 110 Hd46
Gourdon **F** 69 Db36
Gourin **F** 60 Cb31
Gournay-en-Bray **F** 62 Dc30
Gouveia **P** 90 Ad40
Gouzon **F** 69 Dc35
Goveđari **HR** 86 Gc40
Gowidlino **PL** 58 Gc25
Gozdnica **PL** 65 Ga29
Gözne **TR** 128 Gd16
Grabarka **PL** 59 Hc27
Graben-Neudorf **D** 63 Ed32
Grabovica **SRB** 87 Hb38
Grabovica **SRB** 87 Hd38
Grabow **D** 56 Fc26
Grabów nad Prosną **PL** 66 Gd29
Grabowno **PL** 58 Gc26
Grabowo **PL** 59 Hb25
Gračac **HR** 85 Gb38
Gračanica **BIH** 86 Gd39
Gračanica **BIH** 86 Gd38
Gračanica **RKS** 87 Hc40
Graçay **F** 69 Dc33
Gračevka **RUS** 127 Fd16
Gradac **HR** 85 Gb37
Gradačac **BIH** 86 Gd37
Gradec **BG** 87 Hd38
Gradešnica **MK** 101 Hd42
Gradina **BG** 88 Jc39
Grădinari **RO** 87 Hc37
Gradište **HR** 86 Ha37
Grădiştea **RO** 89 Jd37
Grădiştea **RO** 88 Ja37
Grădiştea de Munte **RO** 75 Hd36
Gradnica **BG** 88 Jb39
Grado **I** 73 Fd36
Gradojević **SRB** 86 Ha38
Grafenau **D** 65 Fd32
Gräfenberg **D** 64 Fb31
Gräfenhainichen **D** 56 Fc28
Grafenwöhr **D** 64 Fc31
Graiguenamanagh **IRL** 23 Cb25
Grajduri **RO** 77 Jd34
Grajewo **PL** 59 Hc26
Grajvoron **RUS** 122 Fa14
Gram **DK** 48 Fa23
Gramat **F** 69 Db36
Grammichele **I** 109 Ga47
Gramsh **AL** 100 Hb43
Gramzow **D** 57 Ga26
Gran **N** 43 Fc17
Granada **E** 106 Bc45
Granard **IRL** 19 Cb23
Grandas de Salime **E** 78 Bb36

Grandcamp-Maisy **F** 61 Da30
Grândola **P** 90 Ac42
Grandrieu **F** 82 Dd37
Grandvillars **F** 71 Ec34
Grandvilliers **F** 62 Dc30
Grañén **E** 80 Cc40
Grangärde **S** 44 Ga17
Grangemouth **GB** 21 Da21
Grängesberg **S** 44 Ga17
Graniceşti **RO** 76 Jb33
Graninge **S** 38 Gb13
Granítis **GR** 102 Jb42
Grankullavik **S** 51 Gc21
Granliden **S** 33 Gb11
Gränna **S** 44 Ga20
Grannäs **S** 33 Gb10
Granö **S** 34 Gd12
Granollers **E** 95 Db41
Gransee **D** 57 Fd27
Granshered **N** 43 Fb18
Grantham **GB** 25 Db25
Grantown-on-Spey **GB** 17 Da19
Granville **F** 61 Cd31
Granvin **N** 36 Ed16
Grapska **BIH** 86 Gd38
Gräsgård **S** 50 Gb22
Grassano **I** 99 Gc43
Grassau **D** 72 Fc34
Grasse **F** 83 Eb39
Gråsten **DK** 49 Fb24
Grästorp **S** 43 Fd20
Gratwein **A** 73 Gb34
Graulhet **F** 81 Db38
Graus **E** 80 Cd40
Grávavencsellő **H** 75 Hc33
Gravberget **N** 37 Fd16
Gravedona **I** 72 Fa36
Gravelines **F** 54 Dd28
Gravesend **GB** 25 Db28
Graviá **GR** 111 Ja45
Gravina in Puglia **I** 99 Gc43
Gray **F** 71 Eb34
Graz **A** 73 Gb35
Gražiškiai **LT** 52 Hc24
Great Ayton **GB** 21 Db23
Great Malvern **GB** 24 Da26
Great Yarmouth **GB** 25 Dd26
Grebbestad **S** 43 Fc19
Grebenhain **D** 64 Fa30
Grębocin **PL** 58 Gd26
Greenlaw **GB** 21 Db21
Greenock **GB** 20 Cd21
Greenodd **GB** 21 Da23
Greetsiel **D** 55 Ed26
Greifenburg **A** 73 Fd35
Greifswald **D** 57 Fd25
Grein **A** 73 Ga33
Greiz **D** 64 Fc30
Gremjač'e **RUS** 122 Fb13
Grenaa **DK** 49 Fc22
Grenade **F** 81 Da38
Grenade-sur-l'Adour **F** 80 Cd37

Grenchen – Hainburg

Grenchen **CH** 71 Ec34
Grenivík **IS** 15 Ca05
Grenoble **F** 82 Ea37
Gressoney-la-Trinite **I** 71 Ec36
Gretna Green **GB** 21 Da22
Greve in Chianti **I** 84 Fb39
Greven **D** 55 Ed28
Grevená **GR** 101 Hc43
Grevenbroich **D** 63 Ec29
Grevenmacher **L** 63 Ec31
Grevesmühlen **D** 56 Fc25
Greve Strand **DK** 49 Fd23
Grevie **S** 49 Fd22
Greystones **IRL** 19 Cb24
Grgurnica **MK** 101 Hc41
Gribanovskij **RUS** 123 Fc12
Grieskirchen **A** 73 Fd33
Grigor'evskoe **RUS** 118 Fb08
Grigoriopol **MD** 77 Ka33
Grillby **S** 45 Gc18
Grimma **D** 65 Fd29
Grimmen **D** 57 Fd25
Grimsby **GB** 25 Dc25
Grimsey **IS** 15 Cb05
Grímsstaðir **IS** 15 Cb06
Grimstad **N** 42 Fa19
Grinăuți **MD** 77 Jd32
Grindavík **IS** 14 Bb07
Grindelwald **CH** 71 Ed35
Grindsted **DK** 48 Fa23
Grinkiškis **LT** 52 Hc23
Griškabūdis **LT** 52 Hc24
Grisolles **F** 81 Da38
Grisslehamn **S** 45 Gd17
Grivenskaja **RUS** 127 Fc16
Grivița **RO** 89 Jd37
Grjady **RUS** 117 Eb09
Grjazi **RUS** 122 Fb12
Grjazovec **RUS** 118 Fa08
Grobiņa **LV** 52 Ha22
Grocka **SRB** 87 Hb38
Gródek **PL** 59 Hd26
Gröditz **D** 65 Fd29
Gródki **PL** 58 Ha26
Gródki **PL** 67 Hc29
Grodków **PL** 66 Gc30
Grodziczno **PL** 58 Ha26
Grodzisk Mazowiecki **PL** 58 Ha28
Grodzisk Wielkopolski **PL** 57 Gb28
Groix **F** 60 Cb32
Grójec **PL** 59 Hb28
Grömitz **D** 56 Fb25
Gromnik **PL** 67 Hb31
Grong **N** 32 Fd11
Gröningen **D** 56 Fc28
Groningen **NL** 55 Ec26
Grönskåra **S** 50 Gb21
Gropeni **RO** 89 Jd36
Großenhain **D** 65 Fd29
Großenkneten **D** 55 Ed26
Grosseto **I** 84 Fb40
Grosseto Prugna **F** 96 Ed41

Groß-Gerau **D** 63 Ed31
Groß Gerungs **A** 73 Ga33
Großpetersdorf **A** 73 Gb34
Großräschen **D** 65 Ga29
Grosuplje **SLO** 73 Ga36
Grøtevær **N** 28 Gb05
Grotli **N** 36 Fa14
Grottaglie **I** 100 Gd43
Grottaminarda **I** 99 Ga42
Grottammare **I** 85 Fd40
Grov **N** 28 Gb06
Grövelsjön **S** 38 Fd14
Grožnjan **HR** 85 Fd37
Grubišno Polje **HR** 74 Gc36
Grudusk **PL** 58 Ha26
Grudziądz **PL** 58 Gd26
Grumento Nova **I** 99 Gb43
Grums **S** 44 Fd18
Grünberg **D** 64 Fa30
Grundarfjörður **IS** 14 Bb05
Grundträsk **S** 34 Ha09
Grünstadt **D** 63 Ed31
Grunwald **PL** 58 Ha26
Gruszka **PL** 67 Ha29
Gruža **SRB** 87 Hb39
Gruzdžiai **LT** 52 Hc22
Grybów **PL** 67 Hb31
Grycksbro **S** 38 Gb16
Gryfice **PL** 57 Ga25
Gryfino **PL** 57 Ga26
Gryfów Śląski **PL** 65 Gb29
Grykë **AL** 100 Ha43
Gryllefjord **N** 28 Gb05
Gryt **S** 44 Gb20
Grythyttan **S** 44 Ga18
Gstaad **CH** 71 Ec35
Guadalajara **E** 92 Bd41
Guadalcanal **E** 105 Ba43
Guadix **E** 106 Bc45
Gualdo Tadino **I** 84 Fc40
Guarda **P** 91 Ba40
Guardamar del Segura **E** 107 Cb45
Guardiagrele **I** 99 Ga41
Guardo **E** 79 Bd38
Guareña **E** 91 Ba42
Guastalla **I** 84 Fb37
Gubbio **I** 84 Fc39
Gubbträsk **S** 33 Gc10
Guben **D** 57 Ga28
Gubin **PL** 57 Ga28
Gubkin **RUS** 122 Fa13
Guča **SRB** 87 Hb39
Guderup **DK** 49 Fb24
Gudhjem **DK** 50 Ga24
Gudvangen **N** 36 Fa16
Guebwiller **F** 71 Ec33
Guémené-Penfao **F** 61 Cd32
Guémené-sur-Scorff **F** 60 Cc31
Guer **F** 61 Cd32
Guérande **F** 60 Cc32
Guéret **F** 69 Db35
Gueugnon **F** 70 Dd34
Gugești **RO** 89 Jd36
Guglionesi **I** 99 Ga41

Guijuelo **E** 91 Bb40
Guildford **GB** 25 Db28
Guillaumes **F** 83 Eb38
Guilvinec **F** 60 Cb31
Guimarães **P** 78 Ad38
Guimiliau **F** 60 Cb31
Guînes **F** 62 Dc29
Guingamp **F** 60 Cc31
Guipavas **F** 60 Cb31
Guisborough **GB** 21 Db23
Guiscard **F** 62 Dd30
Guise **F** 62 Ea30
Guissona **E** 81 Da40
Guitiriz **E** 78 Ba36
Gujan-Mestras **F** 68 Cc36
Gukovo **RUS** 123 Fc15
Gulbene **LV** 47 Ja20
Güldere **TR** 128 Gc16
Guljanci **BG** 88 Jb38
Guljanic'ke **MD** 77 Kb32
Gul'keviči **RUS** 127 Fd16
Gullbrandstorp **S** 49 Fd22
Gullesfjordbotn **N** 28 Gb06
Gullspång **S** 44 Ga19
Güllük **TR** 113 Kb46
Gülnar **TR** 128 Gb17
Gülpınar **TR** 113 Jd44
Gulsvik **N** 43 Fb17
Gumiel de Hizán **E** 79 Bd39
Gummersbach **D** 63 Ed29
Gümüldür **TR** 113 Ka45
Gümüşçay **TR** 103 Ka42
Gümüşhane **TR** 127 Fd19
Gundelfingen **D** 64 Fb32
Gündoğmuş **TR** 128 Ga16
Güneysınır **TR** 128 Gb16
Güneyyurt **TR** 128 Gb17
Gunnarn **S** 33 Gc11
Gunnarnes **N** 26 Ha03
Gunnarsbyn **S** 34 Ha09
Gunnebo **S** 44 Gb20
Gunnfarnes **N** 28 Gb05
Guntin de Pallares **E** 78 Ba37
Günzburg **D** 72 Fb33
Gunzenhausen **D** 64 Fb32
Gura Haitii **RO** 76 Jb34
Gurahonț **RO** 75 Hd35
Gura Humorului **RO** 76 Jb33
Gurasada **RO** 75 Hd36
Gur'evsk **RUS** 52 Ha24
Gurk **A** 73 Ga35
Gurkovo **BG** 102 Jc40
Gürpınar **TR** 103 Kb41
Gusev **RUS** 52 Hb24
Gus'-Hrustal'nyj **RUS** 118 Fa10
Gusinje **MNE** 87 Hb40
Guspini **I** 97 Ec44
Gusselby **S** 44 Ga18
Güssing **A** 73 Gb35
Gustavsberg **S** 45 Gc18
Güstrow **D** 56 Fc26
Gusum **S** 44 Gb20
Gus'-Železnyj **RUS** 118 Fb10
Gütersloh **D** 55 Ed28
Gützkow **D** 57 Fd25

Güzelbağ **TR** 128 Ga16
Güzelçamlı **TR** 113 Ka46
Güzeloluk **TR** 128 Gc16
Güzelsu **TR** 128 Ga16
Güzelyurt **CY** 128 Gb19
Gvardejsk **RUS** 52 Hb24
Gvarv **N** 43 Fb18
Gvozd **HR** 85 Gb37
Gy **F** 71 Eb34
Gyál **H** 74 Ha34
Gylien **S** 34 Ha09
Gyomaendrőd **H** 75 Hb35
Gyömrő **H** 74 Ha34
Gyöngyös **H** 74 Ha33
Győr **H** 74 Gc34
Győrtelek **H** 75 Hc33
Gysinge **S** 44 Gb17
Gyttorp **S** 44 Ga18
Gyula **H** 75 Hc35
Gżatsk **RUS** 117 Ed11

H

Häädemeeste **EST** 46 Hc19
Haag (Niederösterreich) **A** 73 Ga33
Haag am Hausruck **A** 73 Fd33
Haag in Oberbayern **D** 72 Fc33
Haaksbergen **NL** 55 Ec27
Haamstede **NL** 54 Ea28
Haapajärvi **FIN** 35 Hc12
Haapavesi **FIN** 35 Hc11
Haapsalu **EST** 46 Hc18
Haarlem **NL** 55 Eb27
Habay-la-Neuve **B** 63 Eb31
Habo **S** 44 Ga20
Hachenburg **D** 63 Ed29
Hackås **S** 38 Ga13
Haczów **PL** 67 Hc31
Hadamar **D** 63 Ed30
Haddington **GB** 21 Da21
Haderslev **DK** 49 Fb24
Hadım **TR** 128 Ga16
Hadımköy **TR** 103 Kb41
Hadjač **UA** 121 Ed14
Hadsten **DK** 49 Fb22
Hadsund **DK** 49 Fb22
Hadžići **BIH** 86 Gd39
Hægeland **N** 42 Fa19
Hafnarfjörður **IS** 14 Bc06
Hafnir **IS** 14 Bb06
Hagen **D** 63 Ed29
Hagenow **D** 56 Fc26
Hagetmau **F** 80 Cd37
Hagfors **S** 44 Ga17
Häggenås **S** 38 Ga13
Häggnäset **S** 33 Ga11
Hagondange **F** 63 Eb31
Haguenau **F** 63 Ed32
Hahót **H** 74 Gc35
Haiger **D** 63 Ed29
Hailuoto **FIN** 34 Hb10
Hainburg **A** 74 Gc33

Hainfeld **A** 73 Gb33
Hainichen **D** 65 Fd29
Hajdúböszörmény **H** 75 Hc33
Hajdúnánás **H** 75 Hc33
Hajdúsámson **H** 75 Hc34
Hajdúszoboszló **H** 75 Hc34
Hajnówka **PL** 59 Hd27
Hajós **H** 74 Ha35
Hajsyn **UA** 121 Ec15
Håkafot **S** 33 Ga11
Hakkas **S** 30 Ha08
Häkkilä **FIN** 40 Hc13
Halástra **GR** 101 Ja43
Halberstadt **D** 56 Fb28
Halden **N** 43 Fc18
Haldensleben **D** 56 Fc28
Halesworth **GB** 25 Dc27
Halič **UA** 124 Ea16
Halifax **GB** 21 Da24
Halikko **FIN** 40 Hb16
Haljala **EST** 47 Hd17
Halkapınar **TR** 128 Gc16
Halkída **GR** 112 Jb45
Halkirk **GB** 17 Db18
Hälla **S** 33 Gc12
Halle (Saale) **D** 64 Fc29
Hällefors **S** 44 Ga18
Hälleforsnäs **S** 44 Gb18
Hallein **A** 73 Fd34
Hällekis **S** 44 Fd19
Hallen **S** 38 Ga13
Hällesjö **S** 38 Gb13
Hall in Tirol **A** 72 Fb34
Hällnäs **S** 34 Gd11
Hallormsstaður **IS** 15 Cb07
Hallsberg **S** 44 Ga19
Hållsta **S** 44 Gb18
Hallstahammar **S** 44 Gb18
Hallstatt **A** 73 Fd34
Hallstavik **S** 45 Gc17
Hallviken **S** 33 Gb12
Halmstad **S** 49 Fd22
Hals **DK** 49 Fb21
Halsa **N** 37 Fb13
Hal'dany **BY** 53 Jc24
Hal'šany **BY** 120 Ea12
Halstead **GB** 25 Dc27
Halsteren **NL** 54 Ea28
Halsua **FIN** 34 Hb12
Halsvik **N** 36 Ed16
Haltern **D** 55 Ed28
Haltwhistle **GB** 21 Da22
Halvarsgårdarna **S** 44 Gb17
Ham **F** 62 Dd30
Hamar **N** 37 Fc16
Hamburg **D** 56 Fb26
Hamdibey **TR** 103 Ka43
Hämeenkyrö **FIN** 40 Hb15
Hämeenlinna **FIN** 40 Hc16
Hameln **D** 56 Fa28
Hamidiye **TR** 103 Jd41
Hamilton **GB** 21 Da21
Hamina **FIN** 41 Ja16
Hamm **D** 55 Ed28
Hammar **S** 44 Ga19

Hammarslund **S** 50 Ga23
Hammarstrand **S** 38 Gb13
Hammarvika **N** 32 Fb12
Hammel **DK** 49 Fb22
Hammelburg **D** 64 Fa30
Hammenhög **S** 50 Ga23
Hammerdal **S** 38 Ga13
Hammerfest **N** 26 Ha03
Hamminkeln **D** 55 Ec28
Hamneidet **N** 26 Gd04
Hamnes **N** 32 Fc11
Hamnvik **N** 28 Gb06
Håmojåkk **S** 29 Gd07
Hamyški **RUS** 127 Fd17
Hanak **TR** 127 Ga18
Hanau **D** 64 Fa30
Hâncăuţi **MD** 76 Jc32
Hancaviçy **BY** 120 Ea13
Hânceşti **MD** 77 Ka34
Handewitt **D** 48 Fa24
Handlová **SK** 66 Gd32
Hanestad **N** 37 Fc15
Haneviçy **BY** 53 Jb24
Hånger **S** 50 Ga21
Hangö **FIN** 46 Hb17
Haniá **GR** 114 Jc49
Haniótis **GR** 101 Ja43
Hankamäki **FIN** 35 Ja12
Hankasalmi **FIN** 41 Hd14
Hanko **FIN** 46 Hb17
Hann. Münden **D** 64 Fa29
Hannover **D** 56 Fa27
Hannut **B** 63 Eb29
Hanøy **N** 28 Ga06
Han Pijesak **BIH** 86 Ha38
Hansnes **N** 26 Gc04
Hanstholm **DK** 48 Fa21
Han-sur-Nied **F** 63 Ec32
Hanušovce nad Topl'ou **SK** 67 Hb32
Hanušovice **CZ** 66 Gc31
Haparanda **S** 34 Hb09
Haradok **BY** 117 Eb11
Harads **S** 34 Gd09
Häradsbäck **S** 50 Ga22
Haradzišča **BY** 120 Ea13
Hárakas **GR** 115 Jd49
Harasiuki **PL** 67 Hc30
Harbo **S** 45 Gc17
Harborg **N** 37 Fc14
Hardelot-Plage **F** 62 Dc29
Hardenberg **NL** 55 Ec27
Harderwijk **NL** 55 Ec27
Hardheim **D** 64 Fa31
Hareid **N** 36 Ed14
Haren (Ems) **D** 55 Ed27
Hargshamn **S** 45 Gc17
Harjavalta **FIN** 40 Ha15
Harkány **H** 74 Gd36
Hårlåu **RO** 76 Jc33
Hårlev **DK** 49 Fc24
Harlingen **NL** 55 Eb26
Harlow **GB** 25 Db27
Harlu **RUS** 41 Jb14
Harmånger **S** 39 Gc15
Härmänkyla **FIN** 35 Ja11

Harmanli **BG** 102 Jc41
Harnes **F** 62 Dd29
Härnösand **S** 39 Gc14
Haro **E** 79 Ca38
Harran **N** 32 Fd11
Harrogate **GB** 21 Db24
Harrsjö **S** 33 Gb11
Harrström **FIN** 40 Ha14
Harsefeld **D** 56 Fa26
Hârşova **RO** 89 Ka37
Harsovo **BG** 89 Jd38
Hårsovo **BG** 89 Jd38
Harsprånget **S** 29 Gd08
Harstad **N** 28 Gb06
Harsum **D** 56 Fb28
Harsvika **N** 32 Fc12
Harta **H** 74 Ha35
Hartberg **A** 73 Gb34
Hârtieşti **RO** 88 Jb36
Hartlepool **GB** 21 Db23
Hartola **FIN** 41 Hd15
Harwich **GB** 25 Dc27
Harzgerode **D** 56 Fb28
Haselünne **D** 55 Ed27
Haskovo **BG** 102 Jc41
Hasle **DK** 50 Ga24
Haslev **DK** 49 Fc24
Hasparren **F** 80 Cc38
Hassela **S** 38 Gb14
Hasselt **B** 63 Eb29
Haßfurt **D** 64 Fb30
Hässleholm **S** 49 Fd22
Hasslö **S** 50 Gb22
Hastings **GB** 25 Db28
Hästveda **S** 50 Ga22
Hasvik **N** 26 Gd03
Hateg **RO** 75 Hd36
Hatherleigh **GB** 23 Cc28
Hatip **TR** 128 Ga15
Hatrik **N** 42 Ed17
Hattfjelldal **N** 33 Ga10
Hattingen **D** 55 Ec28
Hattula **FIN** 40 Hc15
Hattuselkonen **FIN** 35 Ja12
Hattuvaara **FIN** 41 Jb12
Hatunsaray **TR** 128 Ga15
Hatvan **H** 74 Ha34
Haugastøl **N** 36 Fa16
Hauge **N** 42 Ed19
Hauho **FIN** 40 Hc15
Haukeligrend **N** 42 Fa17
Haukelisæter **N** 42 Fa17
Haukipudas **FIN** 35 Hc10
Haukivuori **FIN** 41 Hd14
Hausach **D** 71 Ed33
Hautajärvi **FIN** 31 Hd08
Hautefort **F** 69 Da36
Hautmont **F** 62 Ea30
Hauzenberg **D** 65 Fd32
Havant **GB** 24 Da28
Havdhem **S** 51 Gd21
Havdrup **DK** 49 Fc23
Havelberg **D** 56 Fc27
Haverfordwest **GB** 23 Cc26
Haverhill **GB** 25 Dc27
Håverud **S** 43 Fd19

Havířov **CZ** 66 Gd31
Havlíčkův Brod **CZ** 65 Gb31
Havneby **DK** 48 Fa24
Havøysund **N** 26 Ha03
Havran **TR** 103 Ka43
Havrylivka **UA** 122 Fb15
Havsa **TR** 103 Jd41
Hawick **GB** 21 Da22
Hayange **F** 63 Eb31
Hayrabolu **TR** 103 Ka41
Haywards Heath **GB** 25 Db28
Hazebrouck **F** 62 Dd29
Heanor **GB** 25 Db25
Heberg **S** 49 Fd21
Heby **S** 44 Gb17
Hechingen **D** 71 Ed33
Hedalen **N** 37 Fb16
Heddal **N** 43 Fb18
Hédé **F** 61 Cd31
Hede **S** 38 Fd14
Hedemora **S** 44 Gb17
Hedenäset **S** 34 Hb09
Hedensted **DK** 49 Fb23
Hedesunda **S** 44 Gb17
Hedeviken **S** 38 Ga14
Heek **D** 55 Ed28
Heerenveen **NL** 55 Ec26
Heerhugowaard **NL** 55 Eb27
Heerlen **NL** 63 Ec29
Hegyfalu **H** 74 Gc34
Heide **D** 56 Fa25
Heidelberg **D** 63 Ed31
Heidenau **D** 65 Fd29
Heidenheim **D** 64 Fa32
Heidenreichstein **A** 65 Ga32
Heikendorf **D** 56 Fb25
Heikkylä **FIN** 35 Ja09
Heilbronn **D** 64 Fa32
Heiligenblut **A** 73 Fd35
Heiligenhafen **D** 56 Fc25
Heiligenstadt **D** 64 Fb29
Heimaey **IS** 14 Bc08
Heimdal **N** 37 Fc13
Heinävesi **FIN** 41 Ja13
Heinola **FIN** 41 Hd15
Heinsberg **D** 63 Ec29
Heituinlahti **FIN** 41 Ja15
Heksem **N** 37 Fc13
Hel **PL** 51 Gd24
Heldrungen **D** 64 Fb29
Helechal **E** 105 Bb43
Helensburgh **GB** 20 Cd21
Heljulja **RUS** 41 Jb14
Hella **IS** 14 Bc07
Hella **N** 36 Ed15
Helleland **N** 42 Ed19
Hellesvikan **N** 32 Fb12
Hellesylt **N** 36 Fa14
Hellevoetsluis **NL** 54 Ea28
Hellín **E** 107 Ca44
Hellissandur **IS** 14 Bb05
Hellnar **IS** 14 Bb05
Helmond **NL** 55 Eb28
Helmsdale **GB** 17 Db18
Helmsley **GB** 21 Db24

Helmstedt D 56 Fb28
Helnessund N 28 Ga07
Hel'pa SK 67 Ha32
Helshan AL 100 Hb41
Helsingborg S 49 Fd23
Helsinge DK 49 Fc23
Helsingfors FIN 46 Hc17
Helsingør DK 49 Fd23
Helsinki FIN 46 Hc17
Helston GB 23 Cb28
Heltermaa EST 46 Hb19
Hemau D 64 Fc32
Hemavan S 33 Ga10
Hemel Hempstead GB 25 Db27
Hemer D 63 Ed29
Hemling S 33 Gc12
Hemmingsmark S 34 Ha10
Hemmoor D 56 Fa26
Hemnes N 43 Fc18
Hemnesberget N 33 Ga09
Hemse S 51 Gd21
Hemsedal N 37 Fb16
Hemsö S 39 Gc14
Henån S 43 Fc20
Hendaye E 80 Cb38
Hengelo NL 55 Ec27
Heničes'k UA 126 Fa17
Hénin-Beaumont F 62 Dd29
Hennan S 38 Gb15
Hennebont F 60 Cc32
Hennef D 63 Ec29
Hennigsdorf D 57 Fd27
Henningsvær N 28 Ga07
Henrichemont F 69 Dc33
Heradsbygd N 37 Fc16
Herbignac F 60 Cc32
Herborn D 63 Ed30
Herbrechtingen D 64 Fa32
Herbstein D 64 Fa30
Herby PL 66 Gd30
Herceg-Novi MNE 100 Ha41
Hercegszántó H 74 Ha36
Herdla N 36 Ec16
Hereford GB 24 Cd26
Herefoss N 42 Fa19
Herentals B 63 Eb29
Herford D 56 Fa28
Héricourt F 71 Ec33
Heringsdorf D 57 Ga25
Herisau CH 72 Fa34
Hérisson F 69 Dc34
Herl'any SK 67 Hb32
Herleshausen D 64 Fb29
Hermagor A 73 Fd35
Hermanaviči BY 53 Jb23
Hermannsburg D 56 Fb27
Hermsdorf D 64 Fc29
Herne D 55 Ed28
Herne Bay GB 25 Dc28
Herning DK 48 Fa22
Herónia GR 111 Ja45
Herrenberg D 63 Ed32
Herrera del Duque E 91 Bb42
Herrera de los Navarros E 80 Cc40

Herrera de Pisuerga E 79 Bd38
Herreruela E 91 Ba41
Herrestad S 43 Fc19
Herrljunga S 44 Fd20
Herrskog S 39 Gc13
Hersbruck D 64 Fc31
Herstal B 63 Eb29
Hertford GB 25 Db27
Hervás E 91 Bb40
Herzberg D 56 Fb28
Herzberg D 57 Fd28
Herzogenaurach D 64 Fb31
Herzogenburg A 73 Gb33
Hesdin F 62 Dc29
Hesel D 55 Ed26
Heskestad N 42 Ed19
Hessisch Lichtenau D 64 Fa29
Hestra S 44 Ga20
Hestra S 49 Fd21
Hetekylä FIN 35 Hc10
Hetényegyháza H 74 Ha35
Hettstedt D 56 Fc28
Heves H 75 Hb34
Hévíz H 74 Gc35
Hevlín CZ 65 Gb32
Hexham GB 21 Db23
Heyrieux F 70 Ea36
Heysham GB 21 Da24
Hickstead GB 25 Db28
Hidasnémeti H 67 Hb32
Hieflau A 73 Ga34
Hietapera FIN 35 Ja11
High Wycombe GB 25 Db27
Higueruela E 93 Cb43
Hiisijärvi FIN 35 Hd11
Híjar E 93 Cc41
Hijtola RUS 41 Jb15
Hildburghausen D 64 Fb30
Hilden D 63 Ec29
Hildesheim D 56 Fb28
Hillared S 44 Fd20
Hillerød DK 49 Fd23
Hillesøy N 26 Gc05
Hillosensalmi FIN 41 Hd15
Hilpoltstein D 64 Fb32
Hiltula FIN 41 Ja14
Hilvarenbeek NL 55 Eb28
Hilversum NL 55 Eb27
Himanka FIN 34 Hb12
Himki RUS 117 Ed10
Hinckley GB 24 Da26
Hinojosa del Duque E 105 Bb43
Híos GR 113 Jd45
Hirschaid D 64 Fb31
Hirson F 62 Ea30
Hirtshals DK 43 Fb20
Hirvas FIN 30 Hb08
Hirvensalmi FIN 41 Hd15
Hisarja BG 102 Jb40
Hisingen S 43 Fc20
Hislaviči RUS 121 Ec12
Hittarp S 49 Fd22
Hitzacker D 56 Fb26

Hjallerup DK 49 Fb21
Hjärnarp S 49 Fd22
Hjelmeland N 42 Ed18
Hjelset N 36 Fa13
Hjerkinn N 37 Fb14
Hjo S 44 Ga20
Hjørring DK 49 Fb21
Hjortkvarn S 44 Gb19
Hlevacha UA 121 Ec14
Hlinsko CZ 65 Gb31
Hlobyne UA 121 Ed15
Hlohovec SK 74 Gd33
Hluchiv UA 121 Ed13
Hlusk BY 121 Eb13
Hlybokae BY 53 Jb23
Hnivan' UA 121 Eb15
Hnjótur IS 14 Bb04
Höchstadt D 64 Fb31
Hódmező-Vásárhely H 75 Hb35
Hodnanes N 42 Ed17
Hodonín CZ 66 Gc32
Hoek van Holland NL 54 Ea27
Hof D 64 Fc30
Hof N 43 Fb18
Hofgeismar D 56 Fa28
Hofheim D 64 Fb30
Höfn IS 15 Cb08
Hofors S 44 Gb17
Hofsós IS 15 Ca05
Hofstad N 32 Fc12
Hofsvík IS 14 Bc06
Höganäs S 49 Fd22
Høgeset N 36 Fa16
Högland S 33 Gb11
Höglekardalen S 38 Ga13
Högsäter S 43 Fc19
Högsby S 50 Gb21
Högsjö S 44 Gb19
Hőgyész H 74 Gd35
Hohenau A 66 Gc32
Hohenems A 72 Fa34
Hohenwestedt D 56 Fb25
Hok S 50 Ga21
Hokksund N 43 Fb17
Hökmark S 34 Ha11
Hökön S 50 Ga22
Hol N 36 Fa16
Hola Prystan' UA 125 Ed17
Hólar IS 15 Ca05
Holasovice CZ 65 Gc31
Holbæk DK 49 Fb22
Holbæk DK 49 Fb23
Holbeach GB 25 Db26
Holešov CZ 66 Gc31
Holíč SK 66 Gc32
Höljes S 38 Fd16
Hollabrunn A 73 Gb33
Hollfeld D 64 Fb31
Hollókő H 74 Ha33
Hollola FIN 40 Hc15
Hollum NL 55 Ec26
Höllviken S 49 Fd23

Hollywood IRL 19 Cb24
Holm N 32 Fd10
Holm RUS 117 Eb10
Holm S 38 Gb14
Hólmavík IS 14 Bd05
Holmestrand N 43 Fb18
Holmsjö S 50 Gb22
Holmskij RUS 127 Fc17
Holmsund S 34 Gd12
Holmsveden S 38 Gb16
Holmudden S 45 Gd20
Holm-Žirkovskij RUS 117 Ec11
Hölö S 45 Gc19
Holovec'ke UA 67 Hd31
Holøydal N 37 Fc14
Holstebro DK 48 Fa22
Holsworthy GB 23 Cc27
Holwerd NL 55 Ec26
Holyhead GB 20 Cc24
Holywell GB 24 Cd25
Holywood GB 20 Cc22
Holzkirchen D 72 Fc33
Holzminden D 56 Fa28
Homberg (Efze) D 64 Fa29
Homberg (Ohm) D 64 Fa29
Homburg (Saar) D 63 Ec31
Homel' BY 121 Ec13
Hommelstø N 32 Fd10
Hommelvik N 37 Fc13
Homoroade RO 75 Hd33
Homorod RO 76 Jb35
Homps F 81 Db39
Homutovka RUS 121 Ed13
Hønefoss N 43 Fb17
Honfleur F 61 Db30
Høng DK 49 Fc23
Honiton GB 24 Cd28
Honkajoki FIN 40 Ha14
Honkilahti FIN 40 Ha16
Honningsvåg N 27 Hb03
Hönö S 43 Fc20
Hontianske Nemce SK 74 Ha33
Hontivka UA 77 Jd32
Hoogeveen NL 55 Ec27
Hoogezand-Sappemeer NL 55 Ec26
Hoogstraten B 55 Eb28
Höör S 49 Fd23
Hoorn NL 55 Eb27
Hopa TR 127 Ga19
Hopen N 37 Fb13
Hopfgarten A 72 Fc34
Hopseidet N 27 Hc03
Hóra GR 110 Hd47
Hóra TR 113 Ka46
Horasan TR 127 Ga19
Hóra Sfakíon GR 114 Jc49
Horb D 63 Ed32
Hörby S 49 Fd23
Horcajo de los Montes E 91 Bc42
Horcajo de Santiago E 92 Bd42
Horda S 50 Ga21

Horezu **RO** 88 Ja37
Horgen **CH** 71 Ed34
Horgoš **SRB** 75 Hb36
Horia **RO** 89 Ka36
Horki **BY** 121 Eb12
Horlivka **UA** 122 Fb15
Horn **A** 65 Gb32
Horn **N** 32 Fd10
Horn **S** 44 Gb20
Hornachos **E** 91 Ba42
Hornachuelos **E** 105 Bb44
Horncastle **GB** 25 Dc25
Horndal **S** 44 Gb17
Horneburg **D** 56 Fa26
Hörnefors **S** 34 Gd12
Horní Cerekev **CZ** 65 Gb32
Horní Lideč **CZ** 66 Gd32
Hørning **DK** 49 Fb22
Horní Planá **CZ** 65 Ga32
Hornnes **N** 42 Fa19
Hornsea **GB** 21 Dc24
Hörnsjö **S** 34 Gd12
Hornslet **DK** 49 Fb22
Horochiv **UA** 120 Ea15
Horodenka **UA** 76 Jb32
Horodenka **UA** 124 Ea16
Horodnja **UA** 121 Ec13
Horodnycja **UA** 121 Eb14
Horodok **UA** 67 Hd31
Horodok **UA** 120 Ea15
Horodyšče **UA** 121 Ec15
Hořovice **CZ** 65 Ga31
Hořovičky **CZ** 65 Fd30
Horred **S** 49 Fd21
Horsdal **N** 28 Ga08
Horse & Jockey **IRL** 18 Ca24
Horsens **DK** 49 Fb23
Horsham **GB** 25 Db28
Horslunde **DK** 49 Fc24
Horst **NL** 55 Ec28
Hörstel **D** 55 Ed27
Horten **N** 43 Fc18
Hortlax **S** 34 Ha09
Hortobágy **H** 75 Hb34
Horyniec **PL** 67 Hd30
Horyszów Ruski **PL** 67 Hd29
Hösbach **D** 64 Fa30
Hosio **FIN** 35 Hc09
Hossa **FIN** 35 Ja09
Hossegor **F** 80 Cc37
Hosszúhetény **H** 74 Gd36
Hosszúpereszteg **H** 74 Gc35
Hostalric **E** 95 Db41
Hostens **F** 68 Cd36
Hotagen **S** 33 Ga12
Hotamış **TR** 128 Gb15
Hoticy **RUS** 47 Jb19
Hoting **S** 33 Gb12
Houdan **F** 62 Dc31
Houeillès **F** 80 Cd37
Houffalize **B** 63 Eb30
Hourtin **F** 68 Cd35
Hourtin-Plage **F** 68 Cd35

Houton **GB** 17 Db17
Houtsklär **FIN** 46 Ha17
Hov **DK** 49 Fb23
Hova **S** 44 Ga19
Høvåg **N** 42 Fa20
Hovden **N** 42 Fa18
Hove **GB** 25 Db28
Hovsta **S** 44 Ga18
Howden **GB** 21 Db24
Howth **IRL** 19 Cc24
Höxter **D** 56 Fa28
Hoya **D** 56 Fa27
Høyanger **N** 36 Ed15
Hoyerswerda **D** 65 Ga29
Høylandet **N** 32 Fd11
Hoyos **E** 91 Ba40
Hoža **BY** 59 Hd25
Hradec Králové **CZ** 65 Gb30
Hradec nad Moravicí **CZ** 66 Gd31
Hrádek nad Nisou **CZ** 65 Ga30
Hradyz'k **UA** 121 Ed15
Hrafnagil **IS** 15 Ca06
Hrafnseyri **IS** 14 Bc04
Hranice **CZ** 64 Fc30
Hranice **CZ** 66 Gc31
Hraničné **SK** 67 Hb31
Hrasnica **BIH** 86 Gd39
Hrastelnica **HR** 86 Gc37
Hrastnik **SLO** 73 Ga36
Hrebinka **UA** 121 Ed14
Hredino **RUS** 47 Jb19
Hrísey **IS** 15 Ca05
Hrissoúpoli **GR** 102 Jb42
Hristiáni **GR** 110 Hd47
Hrodna **BY** 59 Hd25
Hronský Beňadik **SK** 74 Gd33
Hrubieszów **PL** 67 Hd29
Hrušuvacha **UA** 122 Fa14
Hrvatska Dubica **HR** 86 Gc37
Hrvatska Kostajnica **HR** 86 Gc37
Hubynycha **UA** 122 Fa15
Hucknall **GB** 25 Db25
Huddersfield **GB** 21 Da24
Hude **D** 56 Fa26
Hudiksvall **S** 39 Gc15
Huedin **RO** 75 Hd34
Huelgoat **F** 60 Cb31
Huelma **E** 106 Bc44
Huéneja **E** 106 Bd45
Huércal-Overa **E** 107 Ca45
Huesca **E** 80 Cc39
Huéscar **E** 106 Bd44
Huete **E** 92 Ca41
Huittinen **FIN** 40 Hb15
Hukanmaa **S** 30 Ha07
Hulín **CZ** 66 Gc32
Huljajpole **UA** 122 Fb15
Hulst **NL** 54 Ea28
Hultsfred **S** 50 Gb21
Hulubeşti **RO** 88 Jb37

Humanes **E** 92 Ca40
Humenné **SK** 67 Hc32
Humpolec **CZ** 65 Gb31
Humppila **FIN** 40 Hb16
Hundested **DK** 49 Fc23
Hundorp **N** 37 Fb15
Hundsjön **S** 34 Ha09
Hunedoara **RO** 75 Hd36
Hünfeld **D** 64 Fa30
Hungen **D** 64 Fa30
Hunnebostrand **S** 43 Fc19
Hunstanton **GB** 25 Dc26
Huntingdon **GB** 25 Db26
Huntly **GB** 17 Db19
Hurbanovo **SK** 74 Gd33
Hurdal **N** 43 Fc17
Hurezani **RO** 88 Ja37
Hurup **DK** 48 Fa21
Hurzuf **UA** 126 Fa18
Húsafell **IS** 14 Bc06
Husasău de Tinca **RO** 75 Hc35
Húsavík **IS** 15 Cb05
Huşi **RO** 77 Jd34
Husinec **CZ** 65 Ga32
Huskvarna **S** 44 Ga20
Husnes **N** 42 Ed17
Husum **D** 56 Fa25
Husum **S** 39 Gd13
Huuki **S** 30 Ha07
Huy **B** 63 Eb29
Hvaler **N** 43 Fc19
Hvalynsk **RUS** 119 Ga11
Hvammstangi **IS** 14 Bd05
Hvanneyri **IS** 14 Bc06
Hvar **HR** 86 Gc40
Hvastoviči **RUS** 121 Ed12
Hverageröi **IS** 14 Bc07
Hvide Sande **DK** 48 Fa22
Hvittingfoss **N** 43 Fb18
Hvolsvöllur **IS** 14 Bc07
Hvorostjanka **RUS** 119 Ga10
Hyères **F** 82 Ea39
Hyltebruk **S** 49 Fd21
Hyrynsalmi **FIN** 35 Hd10
Hyvinkää **FIN** 40 Hc16

I

Ía **GR** 115 Jd48
Ialoveni **MD** 77 Ka34
Ianca **RO** 89 Jd36
Iargara **MD** 77 Ka34
Iaşi **RO** 77 Jd33
Iásmos **GR** 102 Jc42
Iballë **AL** 100 Hb41
Ibbenbüren **D** 55 Ed27
Ibeas de Juarros **E** 79 Ca38
Ibi **E** 107 Cb44
Ibiza **E** 94 Cd44
Ibrice **TR** 103 Jd42
İçerіçumra **TR** 128 Gb15
Ichenhausen **D** 72 Fb33
Iclod **RO** 76 Ja34
Ičnja **UA** 121 Ec14

Idar-Oberstein **D** 63 Ec31
Idivuoma **S** 29 Ha06
Ídra **GR** 111 Jb47
Idre **S** 38 Fd15
Idrija **SLO** 73 Ga36
Idstein **D** 63 Ed30
Idvor **SRB** 87 Hb37
Iecava **LV** 52 Hc21
Ieper **B** 62 Dd29
Ierápetra **GR** 115 Jd49
Ierissós **GR** 102 Jb43
Iernut **RO** 76 Ja35
Ieud **RO** 76 Ja33
Ifjord **N** 27 Hb03
Igerøy **N** 32 Fd10
Iggesund **S** 39 Gc15
Ighiu **RO** 75 Hd35
Iglesias **I** 97 Ec44
Ignalina **LT** 53 Ja23
İğneada **TR** 103 Ka40
Igoumenítsa **GR** 100 Hb44
Igualada **S** 3 Da41
Igüeña **E** 78 Bb37
Iharosberény **H** 74 Gc35
Ihode **FIN** 40 Ha16
Ii **FIN** 35 Hc10
Iilvesi **FIN** 41 Hd13
Iisalmi **FIN** 35 Hd12
IJmuiden **NL** 55 Eb27
IJsselstein **NL** 55 Eb27
Ikaalinen **FIN** 40 Hb15
Ikast **DK** 48 Fa22
Ikškile **LV** 53 Hd21
Ilanz **CH** 72 Fa35
Ilava **SK** 66 Gd32
Iława **PL** 58 Ha26
Ilchester **GB** 24 Cd28
Il'ci **UA** 76 Ja33
Ildır **TR** 113 Ka45
Ilfeld **D** 56 Fb28
Ilfracombe **GB** 23 Cc27
İlhanköy **TR** 103 Ka42
Ílhavo **P** 90 Ac39
Ilıca **TR** 103 Ka43
Ilijaš **BIH** 86 Gd39
Il'ino **RUS** 117 Eb11
Il'insko- Zaborskoe **RUS** 118 Fb08
Iliokómi **GR** 102 Jb42
Ilirska Bistrica **SLO** 85 Ga37
Il'ja **BY** 53 Jb24
Illertissen **D** 72 Fa33
Illescas **E** 92 Bd41
Ille-sur-Têt **F** 81 Db39
Illičivs'k **UA** 77 Kb34
Illičivs'k **UA** 125 Ec17
Illiers-Combray **F** 61 Db32
Illkirch-Graffenstaden **F** 63 Ed32
Illueca **E** 80 Cb40
Illzach **F** 71 Ec33
Ilmajoki **FIN** 40 Hb13
Ilmenau **D** 64 Fb30
Il'men' Suvorovskij **RUS** 123 Fd14
Ilminster **GB** 24 Cd28

Ilok – Järva-Jaani

Ilok HR 86 Ha37
Ilomantsi FIN 41 Jb13
Ilükste LV 53 Ja22
Ilva Mare RO 76 Ja34
Iłża PL 67 Hb29
Imatra FIN 41 Ja15
Imavere EST 47 Hd18
Immenstadt D 72 Fa34
Immingham GB 25 Dc25
Imola I 84 Fb38
Imotski HR 86 Gc39
Imperia I 83 Ec39
Imphy F 70 Dd34
Imst A 72 Fb34
Inari FIN 27 Hc05
Inca E 95 Db43
Inchnadamph GB 17 Da18
Inciems LV 53 Hd21
Indal S 38 Gb14
Indija SRB 87 Hb37
Indre Arna N 36 Ed16
Indre Billefjord N 27 Hb03
Indura BY 59 Hd26
İnebolu TR 126 Fa19
İnece TR 103 Jd41
Ineu RO 75 Hc35
Infantado P 90 Ac41
Ingå FIN 46 Hc17
Ingelheim D 63 Ed30
Ingelstad S 50 Ga22
Ingolstadt D 64 Fb32
Inkoo FIN 46 Hc17
Innbygda N 37 Fd16
Inndyr N 28 Ga08
Innerleithen GB 21 Da21
Innfield IRL 19 Cb24
Innsbruck A 72 Fb34
Innset N 29 Gc06
Innset N 37 Fc14
Inói GR 110 Hd46
Inowłódz PL 58 Ha28
Inowrocław PL 58 Gd27
Insar RUS 119 Fc10
Insjön S 38 Ga16
Însurăței RO 89 Jd36
İntepe TR 103 Jd43
Interlaken CH 71 Ec35
Întorsura Buzăului RO 88 Jc36
Inveraray GB 16 Cd20
Invergarry GB 17 Da19
Invergordon GB 17 Da19
Invermoriston GB 17 Da19
Inverness GB 17 Da19
Inverurie GB 17 Db19
Inza RUS 119 Fd10
Inžavino RUS 123 Fc12
Ioánina GR 101 Hc44
Ion Roată RO 89 Jd37
Íos GR 115 Jd47
Ipatovo RUS 127 Fd16
İpsala TR 103 Jd42
Ipswich GB 25 Dc27
Iráklia GR 101 Ja42
Iráklia GR 115 Jd47
Iráklio GR 115 Jd49

Irbene LV 46 Hb20
Irečekovo BG 103 Jd40
Irklijiv UA 121 Ed15
Irmath RKS 100 Hb42
Ironbridge GB 24 Da25
Iršava UA 75 Hd33
Irsina I 99 Gb43
Irsta S 44 Gb18
Irun E 80 Cb38
Iruñea E 80 Cb38
Irurita E 80 Cc38
Irurzun E 80 Cb38
Irvine GB 20 Cd21
Irvinestown GB 19 Cb22
Isaba E 80 Cc38
Isaccea RO 89 Ka36
Ísafjörður IS 14 Bc04
Isaku EST 47 Ja18
Isane N 36 Ed14
Iscar E 79 Bc39
Ischgl A 72 Fa35
Ischia I 98 Fd43
Iseo I 72 Fa36
Iserlohn D 63 Ed29
Isernia I 99 Ga42
Isfjorden N 36 Fa14
Isigny-sur-Mer F 61 Da30
Isili I 97 Ed44
Islaz RO 88 Jb38
İslik TR 128 Gb15
İsmailli TR 113 Ka44
İsmıl TR 128 Gb15
Isny D 72 Fa34
Isojoki FIN 40 Ha14
Isokylä FIN 31 Hc08
Isokyrö FIN 40 Ha13
Isola F 83 Eb38
Isola 2000 F 83 Eb38
Isola del Liri I 98 Fd42
Ísola di Capo Rizzuto I 109 Gc45
Isperih BG 89 Jd38
Ispica I 109 Ga48
İspir TR 127 Ga19
Issoire F 69 Dc36
Issoudun F 69 Dc34
Is-sur-Tille F 70 Ea33
İstanbul TR 103 Kb41
Istiéa GR 111 Ja45
Istok RKS 87 Hb40
Istra RUS 117 Ed10
Istres F 82 Dd39
Istria RO 89 Ka37
Itéa GR 111 Ja45
Itháki GR 110 Hc46
Ittiri I 97 Ec43
Itzehoe D 56 Fa25
Ivacëvičy BY 120 Ea13
Ivajlovgrad BG 103 Jd41
Ivalo FIN 27 Hc05
Ivanava BY 120 Ea14
Ivančice CZ 65 Gb32
Ivanec HR 73 Gb36
Ivane-Puste UA 76 Jb32
Ivănești RO 77 Jd34
Ivangorod RUS 47 Ja17

Ivangrad MNE 87 Hb40
Ivanić Grad HR 74 Gc36
Ivanivci UA 76 Jc32
Ivanivka MD 77 Kb33
Ivanivka UA 126 Fa16
Ivanka pri Dunaji SK 74 Gc33
Ivankiv UA 121 Ec14
Ivankovo HR 86 Gd37
Ivano-Frankivs'k UA 76 Ja32
Ivano-Frankivs'k UA 124 Ea16
Ivano-Frankove UA 67 Hd30
Ivanovka RUS 119 Ga09
Ivanovo BG 88 Jc38
Ivanovo RUS 118 Fa09
Ivanovskoe RUS 118 Fb08
Ivanskaja BIH 86 Gc37
Ivarrud N 33 Ga10
Iveland N 42 Fa19
Ivești RO 77 Jd35
Ivjanec BY 120 Ea12
Ivje BY 120 Ea12
Ivrea I 71 Ec36
İvrindi TR 103 Ka43
Iyidere TR 127 Fd19
Izbica Kujawska PL 58 Gd27
Izbiceni RO 88 Jb38
Izbišča BY 53 Jb24
Izborsk RUS 47 Jb20
Izeda P 78 Bb39
Izernore F 70 Ea35
Izjum UA 122 Fb14
Izmajil UA 89 Ka36
İzmir TR 113 Ka45
Iznalloz E 106 Bc45
Izsák H 74 Ha35
Izvor BG 87 Hd40
Izvor MK 101 Hc42
Izvor SRB 87 Hc39
Izvoru Dulce RO 89 Jd36

J

Jaakonvaara FIN 41 Jb12
Jaala FIN 41 Hd15
Jablanac HR 85 Ga38
Jablanica BG 88 Jb39
Jablanica BIH 86 Gd39
Jablonec nad Nisou CZ 65 Ga30
Jablonica SK 66 Gc32
Jabłonka PL 67 Ha31
Jabłonowo Pomorskie PL 58 Gd26
Jabluniv UA 76 Ja32
Jablunkov CZ 66 Gd31
Jabugo E 105 Ad43
Jabukovac SRB 87 Hd38
Jabukovik SRB 87 Hd40
Jaca E 80 Cc39
Jädraås S 38 Gb16
Jadraque E 92 Ca40
Jaén E 106 Bc44

Jagare BIH 86 Gc38
Jagodina SRB 87 Hc38
Jahotyn UA 121 Ec14
Jajce BIH 86 Gc38
Jakabszállás H 74 Ha35
Jakalj SRB 87 Hb38
Jäkkvik S 33 Gb09
Jakobstad FIN 34 Ha12
Jakoruda BG 101 Ja41
Jakovlevo RUS 122 Fa13
Jalance E 93 Cb43
Jalasjärvi FIN 40 Hb14
Jalta UA 126 Fa18
Jambol BG 103 Jd40
Jämijärvi FIN 40 Hb15
Jäminkipohja FIN 40 Hc14
Jämjö S 50 Gb22
Jamkino RUS 47 Jb19
Jamnice CZ 65 Gb32
Jampil' UA 125 Eb16
Jämsä FIN 40 Hc14
Jämsänkoski FIN 40 Hc14
Janja BIH 86 Ha38
Janjina HR 86 Gd40
Jánoshalma H 74 Ha35
Jánosháza H 74 Gc34
Jánossomorja H 74 Gc34
Janów PL 59 Hc26
Janów PL 67 Ha30
Janów Lubelski PL 67 Hc29
Janowo PL 58 Ha26
Janów Podlaski PL 59 Hc27
Jånsmåssholmen S 33 Ga12
Jantarnyj RUS 52 Ha24
Jantra BG 88 Jc39
Janville F 62 Dc32
Janzé F 61 Cd32
Jäppilä FIN 41 Hd13
Jaraicejo E 91 Bb41
Jaraiz de la Vera E 91 Bb41
Jarandilla de la Vera E 91 Bb41
Jaransk RUS 119 Fc08
Järbo S 38 Gb16
Jarcevo RUS 117 Ec11
Jard-sur-Mer F 68 Cd34
Jaremča UA 76 Ja32
Jargeau F 69 Dc33
Jarhois S 30 Hb08
Järlåsa S 45 Gc17
Jarmen D 57 Fd25
Jarmolynci UA 121 Eb15
Järna S 44 Ga17
Järna S 45 Gc19
Jarnac F 68 Cd35
Jarny F 63 Eb31
Jarocin PL 58 Gc28
Jaroměř CZ 65 Gb30
Jaroměřice nad Rokytnou CZ 65 Gb32
Jaroslavl' RUS 118 Fa09
Jarosław PL 67 Hc30
Jarosławiec PL 57 Gb25
Järpen S 38 Fd13
Järpsnäs S 44 Ga20
Järva-Jaani EST 47 Hd18

158

Järvakandi **EST** 46 Hc18
Järvelä **FIN** 40 Hc16
Järvenpää **FIN** 40 Hc16
Järvsö **S** 38 Gb15
Jaryšiv **UA** 76 Jc32
Jasanova **AL** 87 Hb40
Jasa Tornič **SRB** 87 Hb37
Jaščera **RUS** 47 Jb17
Jasenice **HR** 85 Gb38
Jasenskaja **RUS** 127 Fc16
Jasienica **PL** 57 Gа28
Jasinja **UA** 76 Ja32
Jašiūnai **LT** 53 Hd24
Jaškul' **RUS** 123 Ga15
Jasło **PL** 67 Hb31
Jasná **SK** 67 Ha32
Jasna Poljana **BG** 103 Ka40
Jasnoe **RUS** 52 Hb24
Jasnogorsk **RUS** 118 Fa11
Jasov **SK** 67 Hb32
Jastarnia **PL** 51 Gd24
Jastrebarsko **HR** 73 Gb36
Jastrowie **PL** 58 Gc26
Jastrzębia Góra **PL** 51 Gd24
Jastrzębie-Zdrój **PL** 66 Gd31
Jasynuvata **UA** 122 Fb15
Jászalsószentgyörgy **H** 75 Hb34
Jászapáti **H** 75 Hb34
Jászárokszállás **H** 74 Ha34
Jászberény **H** 74 Ha34
Jättendal **S** 39 Gc15
Jaungulbene **LV** 53 Ja21
Jaunkalsnava **LV** 53 Hd21
Jaunpiebalga **LV** 47 Ja20
Jaunpils **LV** 52 Hc21
Javoriv **UA** 67 Hd30
Javorník **CZ** 66 Gc30
Jävre **S** 34 Ha10
Jawor **PL** 65 Gb29
Jawor Solecki **PL** 67 Hb29
Jaworzno **PL** 67 Ha30
Jazna **BY** 53 Jb23
Jebel **RO** 75 Hc36
Jedburgh **GB** 21 Da22
Jedlińsk **PL** 59 Hb28
Jednorożec **PL** 59 Hb26
Jędrzejów **PL** 67 Ha30
Jedwabne **PL** 59 Hc26
Jedwabno **PL** 58 Ha26
Jeesiö **FIN** 31 Hc07
Jēkabpils **LV** 53 Hd21
Jektvika **N** 33 Ga09
Jelanec' **UA** 125 Ed16
Jelcz-Laskowice **PL** 66 Gc29
Jelenia Góra **PL** 65 Gb29
Jelenino **PL** 57 Gb26
Jelgava **LV** 52 Hc21
Jelling **DK** 49 Fb23
Jelovac **SRB** 87 Hc38
Jelsa **N** 42 Ed18
Jemielno **PL** 65 Gb29
Jena **D** 64 Fc29

Jenakijeve **UA** 122 Fb15
Jenbach **A** 72 Fc34
Jennersdorf **A** 73 Gb35
Jepua **FIN** 40 Hb13
Jerez de la Frontera **E** 105 Ad45
Jerez de los Caballeros **E** 105 Ad43
Jergucat **AL** 100 Hb44
Jerichow **D** 56 Fc27
Jerka **PL** 58 Gc28
Jeršov **RUS** 119 Ga11
Jerzens **A** 72 Fb34
Jerzu **I** 97 Ed44
Jesenice **CZ** 65 Ga31
Jesenice **SLO** 73 Ga35
Jeseník **CZ** 66 Gc30
Jesi **I** 85 Fd39
Jesolo **I** 84 Fc37
Jessen **D** 57 Fd28
Jessheim **N** 43 Fc17
Jeumont **F** 62 Ea30
Jever **D** 55 Ed26
Jevnaker **N** 43 Fc17
Jevpatorija **UA** 126 Fa17
Jeziorany **PL** 58 Ha25
Jeżów **PL** 58 Ha28
Jeżowe **PL** 67 Hc30
Jibert **RO** 76 Jb35
Jibou **RO** 76 Hd34
Jičín **CZ** 65 Gb30
Jieznas **LT** 53 Hd24
Jihlava **CZ** 65 Gb31
Jilava **RO** 88 Jc37
Jiltjaur **S** 33 Gb10
Jimbolia **RO** 75 Hb36
Jimena de la Frontera **E** 105 Ba45
Jindřichov **CZ** 66 Gc30
Jindřichův Hradec **CZ** 65 Ga32
Jitia **RO** 88 Jc36
Joachimsthal **D** 57 Fd27
Jock **S** 30 Ha08
Jódar **E** 106 Bc44
Joensuu **FIN** 41 Jb13
Joesjö **S** 33 Ga10
Jõgeva **EST** 47 Hd18
Johanngeorgenstadt **D** 65 Fd30
John o'Groats **GB** 17 Db18
Johnstone **GB** 20 Cd21
Jõhvi **EST** 47 Ja17
Joigny **F** 70 Dd33
Joinville **F** 62 Ea32
Joița **RO** 88 Jc37
Jokikylä **FIN** 35 Hc12
Jokina Čuprija **SRB** 86 Ha39
Jokkmokk **S** 29 Gd08
Jöllen **S** 38 Ga15
Jomala **FIN** 45 Gd17
Jonava **LT** 53 Hd23
Jondal **N** 42 Ed17
Joniškis **LT** 52 Hc22
Joniškėlis **LT** 52 Hc22
Jönköping **S** 44 Ga20

Jonquières **F** 82 Dd38
Jonzac **F** 68 Cd35
Jordanów Śląski **PL** 66 Gc29
Jordbro **S** 45 Gc18
Jordet **N** 37 Fd15
Jorgastak **N** 27 Hb05
Jormvattnet **S** 33 Ga11
Jörn **S** 34 Gd10
Joroinen **FIN** 41 Ja14
Jørpeland **N** 42 Ed18
Jošanica **SRB** 87 Hc39
Jošanička Banja **SRB** 87 Hb39
Joseni **RO** 76 Jb34
Josenii Bârgăului **RO** 76 Ja34
Josipdol **HR** 85 Gb37
Joškar-Ola **RUS** 119 Fc08
Josselin **F** 60 Cc32
Joukokylä **FIN** 35 Hd10
Joure **NL** 55 Ec26
Joutsa **FIN** 41 Hd14
Joutseno **FIN** 41 Ja15
Joutsijärvi **FIN** 31 Hd08
Jovsa **SK** 67 Hc32
Józefów **PL** 59 Hb28
Józefów **PL** 67 Hc29
Józefów **PL** 67 Hc30
Juankoski **FIN** 35 Ja12
Jübek **D** 48 Fa24
Juchaviçy **BY** 53 Jb22
Juchnowiec Dolny **PL** 59 Hc26
Judenburg **A** 73 Ga34
Judin **RUS** 123 Fc14
Juelsminde **DK** 49 Fb23
Juhnov **RUS** 117 Ed11
Juillac **F** 69 Db36
Jukkasjärvi **S** 29 Gd07
Jule **N** 33 Ga12
Jülich **D** 63 Ec29
Jumaliskylä **FIN** 35 Ja10
Jumeaux **F** 69 Dc36
Jumilla **E** 107 Cb44
Juminen **FIN** 35 Hd12
Jumisko **FIN** 31 Hd08
Jumurda **LV** 53 Hd21
Jung **S** 44 Fd20
Junosuando **S** 30 Ha07
Junsele **S** 33 Gb12
Juntusranta **FIN** 35 Ja10
Juodkrantė **LT** 52 Ha23
Juoksengi **S** 30 Hb08
Juorkuna **FIN** 35 Hd10
Jurbarkas **LT** 52 Hc24
Jur'evec **RUS** 118 Fb08
Jur'ev-Pol'skij **RUS** 118 Fa09
Jüri **EST** 46 Hc18
Jurilovca **RO** 89 Ka36
Jur'jivka **UA** 122 Fa15
Jūrkalne **LV** 52 Ha21
Jūrmala **LV** 52 Hc21
Jurovo **RUS** 118 Fb08
Jurva **FIN** 40 Ha14
Juškino **RUS** 47 Ja18

Jussey **F** 71 Eb33
Justa **RUS** 123 Ga14
Juszkowy Gród **PL** 59 Hd26
Jüterbog **D** 57 Fd28
Juuka **FIN** 35 Ja12
Juuma **FIN** 31 Hd08
Juupajoki **FIN** 40 Hc15
Juva **FIN** 41 Ja14
Juža **RUS** 118 Fb09
Južnoukrains'k **MD** 77 Kb32
Južnoukrajins'k **UA** 125 Ec16
Južnyj **RUS** 52 Ha24
Južnyj **RUS** 123 Ga15
Juzufova **BY** 53 Jb24
Jyderup **DK** 49 Fc23
Jyrkänkoski **FIN** 31 Ja08
Jyrkkä **FIN** 35 Hd12
Jyväskylä **FIN** 40 Hc14
Jzobil'nyj **RUS** 127 Fd16

K

Kaamanen **FIN** 27 Hc05
Kaamasmukka **FIN** 27 Hb05
Kaansoo **EST** 47 Hd19
Kaaresuvanto Karasavvon **FIN** 30 Ha06
Kaarina **FIN** 40 Hb16
Kaavi **FIN** 41 Ja13
Kabalı **TR** 126 Fb19
Kåbdalis **S** 34 Gd09
Kabelvåg **N** 28 Ga06
Kabile **LV** 52 Hb21
Kablešovo **BG** 89 Ka39
Kabli **EST** 46 Hc20
Kačanovo **RUS** 47 Jb20
Kačerginė **LT** 52 Hc24
Kačergiškė **LT** 53 Ja23
Kachanaviçy **BY** 53 Jb22
Kachovka **UA** 126 Fa16
Kačurivka **UA** 77 Ka32
Kaczorów **PL** 65 Gb29
Kadrifakovo **MK** 101 Hd41
Kaduj **RUS** 117 Ed08
Kadyj **RUS** 118 Fb08
Kadzidło **PL** 59 Hb26
Kåfjord **N** 27 Hb03
Kåfjordbotn **N** 26 Gd05
Kåge **S** 34 Gd11
Kaharlyk **UA** 121 Ec15
Kahla **D** 64 Fc30
Käina **EST** 46 Hb19
Kaipiainen **FIN** 41 Hd15
Kaipola **FIN** 40 Hc14
Kairala **FIN** 31 Hc07
Kaiserslautern **D** 63 Ed31
Kaišiadorys **LT** 53 Hd24
Kaitum **S** 29 Gd07
Kajaani **FIN** 35 Hd11
Kajsackoe **RUS** 123 Ga12
Kakanj **BIH** 86 Gd38
Kakí **GR** 112 Jb46
Kąkol **PL** 58 Gd27
Kakopetria **CY** 128 Gb19

Kalač – Kascjukoviču

Kalač **RUS** 123 Fc13
Kalač- na-Donu **RUS** 123 Fd14
Kalajoki **FIN** 34 Hb11
Kalakoski **FIN** 40 Hb14
Kalamáki **GR** 101 Ja44
Kalamáta **GR** 110 Hd47
Kalambáka **GR** 101 Hd44
Kalambáki **GR** 102 Jb42
Kalana **EST** 46 Hb19
Kalančak **UA** 126 Fa17
Kalándra **GR** 101 Ja43
Kálanos **GR** 110 Hd46
Kalanti **FIN** 40 Ha16
Kälarne **S** 38 Gb13
Kalavárda **GR** 115 Kb47
Kalávrita **GR** 110 Hd46
Kalbe **D** 56 Fc27
Kaldfjord **N** 26 Gc05
Kaledibi **TR** 127 Ga19
Kalérgo **GR** 112 Jc46
Kálimnos **GR** 115 Ka47
Kalinina **RUS** 118 Fb08
Kaliningrad **RUS** 52 Ha24
Kalininsk **RUS** 123 Fd12
Kalinkaviču **BY** 121 Eb13
Kalinovik **BIH** 86 Gd39
Kalipéfki **GR** 101 Hd43
Kalisko **PL** 67 Ha29
Kalisz **PL** 58 Gd28
Kalisz Pomorski **PL** 57 Gb26
Kalithéa **GR** 101 Ja43
Kalitino **RUS** 47 Jb17
Kalivári **GR** 112 Jc46
Kalix **S** 34 Ha09
Kalixforsbron **S** 29 Gd07
Kaljazin **RUS** 117 Ed09
Kalkūne **LV** 53 Ja22
Kall **S** 38 Fd13
Kallaste **EST** 47 Ja18
Kållered **S** 43 Fc20
Kalli **EST** 46 Hc19
Kallinge **S** 50 Gb22
Kallithéa **GR** 101 Hd43
Kallmet **AL** 100 Hb41
Kalloní **GR** 111 Jb47
Kalmar **S** 50 Gb22
Kalmthout **B** 54 Ea28
Kalmykovskij **RUS** 123 Fd14
Kalna **SRB** 87 Hd39
Kalná nad Hronom **SK** 74 Gd33
Kalná Roztoka **SK** 67 Hc32
Kalnciems **LV** 52 Hc21
Kalocsa **H** 74 Ha35
Kalofer **BG** 102 Jb40
Kaló Horio **GR** 112 Jb45
Kalpáki **GR** 101 Hc44
Kalsdorf **A** 73 Gb35
Kaltanénai **LT** 53 Ja23
Kaltenkirchen **D** 56 Fb25
Kaltern **I** 72 Fb35
Kaluga **RUS** 117 Ed11
Kalugerovc **BG** 102 Jb40
Kalundborg **DK** 49 Fc23

Kaluš **UA** 124 Ea16
Kalvåg **N** 36 Ed15
Kalvarija **LT** 52 Hc24
Kälviä **FIN** 34 Hb12
Kalvitsa **FIN** 41 Hd14
Kalvola **FIN** 40 Hc15
Kalynivka **UA** 121 Eb15
Kamáres **GR** 110 Hd46
Kamáres **GR** 111 Jc47
Kamári **GR** 115 Jd48
Kamarino **RUS** 47 Jb19
Kambánis **GR** 101 Ja42
Kámbos **GR** 111 Ja47
Kamčija **BG** 89 Ka39
Kamen **D** 55 Ed28
Kamenec **RUS** 47 Jb18
Kamenica **SRB** 86 Ha38
Kamenice nad Lipou **CZ** 65 Ga32
Kamenka **RUS** 41 Jb16
Kamenka **RUS** 119 Fc11
Kamenka **RUS** 122 Fb13
Kamennogorsk **RUS** 41 Jb15
Kamenný Přívoz **CZ** 65 Ga31
Kameno **BG** 89 Jd39
Kamenskij **RUS** 123 Fd12
Kamensk- Šahtinskij **RUS** 123 Fc14
Kamenz **D** 65 Ga29
Kameškovo **RUS** 118 Fa09
Kamień **PL** 67 Ha29
Kamień Pomorski **PL** 57 Ga25
Kamin'-Kašyrs'kyj **UA** 120 Ea14
Kamyšlykuyu **TR** 128 Gc15
Kam'janec'-Podil's'kyj **UA** 76 Jc32
Kam'janec-Podil's'kyj **UA** 125 Eb16
Kamjaniec **BY** 59 Hd27
Kamjanjuki **BY** 59 Hd27
Kam'janka **UA** 77 Kb34
Kam'janka **UA** 121 Ed15
Kamjanka-Buz'ka **UA** 120 Ea15
Kam'jans'ke **UA** 77 Ka35
Kamlunge **S** 34 Ha09
Kamnik **SLO** 73 Ga36
Kampen **NL** 55 Ec27
Kamskoe Ust'e **RUS** 119 Fd09
Kamyšin **RUS** 123 Fd13
Kanaküla **EST** 47 Hd19
Kanaš **RUS** 119 Fd09
Kańczuga **PL** 67 Hc30
Kándanos **GR** 114 Jb49
Kandava **LV** 52 Hb21
Kandel **D** 63 Ed32
Kandersteg **CH** 71 Ec35
Kandila **GR** 111 Ja46
Kanepi **EST** 47 Ja19
Kanevskaja **RUS** 127 Fc16
Kanfanar **HR** 85 Fd37

Kangaslampi **FIN** 41 Ja14
Kangasniemi **FIN** 41 Hd14
Kangos **S** 30 Ha07
Kangosjärvi **FIN** 30 Ha07
Kaniv **UA** 121 Ec15
Kanjiža **SRB** 75 Hb36
Kankaanpää **FIN** 40 Hb15
Kankainen **FIN** 41 Hd14
Kanlıdivane **TR** 128 Gc17
Kannankoski **FIN** 40 Hc13
Kannus **FIN** 34 Hb12
Kantala **FIN** 41 Hd14
Kantemirovka **RUS** 122 Fb14
Kanturk **IRL** 22 Bd25
Kaolinovo **BG** 89 Jd38
Kaona **SRB** 87 Hb39
Kapandríti **GR** 112 Jb46
Kapellen **B** 54 Ea28
Kapfenberg **A** 73 Gb34
Kapitan Dimitrovo **BG** 89 Jd38
Kaplice **CZ** 65 Ga32
Kaposvár **H** 74 Gd35
Kappeln **D** 49 Fb24
Kappelshamn **S** 45 Gd20
Kappelskär **S** 45 Gd18
Kaprun **A** 72 Fc34
Kapsáli **GR** 111 Ja48
Kapsalos **CY** 128 Gc18
Kapuvár **H** 74 Gc34
Karabiga **TR** 103 Ka42
Karaburun **TR** 103 Kb41
Karaburun **TR** 113 Jd45
Karacabey **TR** 103 Kb42
Karacadağ **TR** 103 Ka40
Karačaevsk **RUS** 127 Ga17
Karacaköy **TR** 103 Kb41
Karačev **RUS** 121 Ed12
Karacva **TR** 113 Kb46
Karadere **TR** 113 Ka44
Karakaya **TR** 128 Gb15
Karakólithos **GR** 111 Ja45
Karali **RUS** 41 Jb13
Karaman **TR** 128 Gb16
Karamyševo **RUS** 47 Jb19
Karapelit **BG** 89 Jd38
Karapinar **TR** 103 Jd41
Karapınar **TR** 128 Gc15
Kararkút **H** 74 Gd36
Karasjok **N** 27 Hb04
Karatepe **TR** 103 Jd43
Karats **S** 29 Gc08
Karaurgan **TR** 127 Ga19
Karavás **GR** 111 Ja48
Karavómilos **GR** 111 Ja45
Karavostasi **CY** 128 Gb19
Kårböle **S** 38 Ga15
Karcag **H** 75 Hb34
Kardakáta **GR** 110 Hc46
Kardamíli **GR** 111 Ja47
Kardašova Řečice **CZ** 65 Ga32
Karditsa **GR** 101 Hd44
Kärdla **EST** 46 Hb18
Kardos **H** 75 Hb35

Kărdžali **BG** 102 Jc41
Kårehamn **S** 51 Gc21
Karesuando **S** 29 Ha06
Kärevete **EST** 47 Hd18
Kargıcak **TR** 128 Gc17
Kargowa **PL** 57 Gb28
Karhukangas **FIN** 35 Hc11
Karhula **FIN** 41 Hd16
Kariá **GR** 111 Ja46
Kariani **GR** 102 Jb42
Karigasniemi **FIN** 27 Hb05
Karijoki **FIN** 40 Ha14
Karine **TR** 113 Ka46
Karis **FIN** 46 Hc17
Káristos **GR** 112 Jc46
Karjaa **FIN** 46 Hc17
Karjala **FIN** 40 Ha16
Karjalohja **FIN** 46 Hc17
Karkkila **FIN** 40 Hc16
Karksi-Nuia **EST** 47 Hd19
Karleby **FIN** 34 Hb12
Karlholmsbruk **S** 45 Gc17
Karlino **PL** 57 Gb25
Karlivka **UA** 122 Fa14
Karlobag **HR** 85 Ga38
Karlovac **HR** 85 Gb37
Karlovássi **TR** 113 Ka46
Karlovice **CZ** 66 Gc31
Karlovka **RUS** 119 Ga11
Karlovo **BG** 102 Jb40
Karlovy Vary **CZ** 65 Fd30
Karlsborg **S** 44 Ga19
Karlshamn **S** 50 Ga22
Karlskoga **S** 44 Ga18
Karlskrona **S** 50 Gb22
Karlsruhe **D** 63 Ed32
Karlstad **S** 44 Fd18
Karlstadt **D** 64 Fa31
Kărnare **BG** 102 Jb40
Karnezéika **GR** 111 Ja47
Karnobat **BG** 89 Jd39
Kärpänkylä **FIN** 35 Ja09
Kárpathos **GR** 115 Kb48
Karpeníssi **GR** 110 Hd45
Karpuzlu **TR** 103 Jd42
Kärsämäki **FIN** 35 Hc12
Kārsava **LV** 53 Jb21
Kårsta **S** 45 Gc18
Karstädt **D** 56 Fc26
Karstula **FIN** 40 Hc13
Karsun **RUS** 119 Fd10
Kartal **TR** 103 Kb41
Karterés **GR** 101 Ja42
Karttula **FIN** 41 Hd13
Kartuzy **PL** 58 Gd25
Karungi **S** 34 Hb09
Karunki **FIN** 34 Hb09
Karup **DK** 48 Fa22
Kärväskylä **FIN** 35 Hc12
Karvia **FIN** 40 Hb14
Karviná **PL** 66 Gd31
Karvio **FIN** 41 Ja13
Karvoskylä **FIN** 35 Hc12
Kašary **RUS** 123 Fc14
Kascjaneviču **BY** 53 Jb24
Kascjukoviču **BY** 121 Ec12

Kascjukovka **BY** 121 Ec13
Kåseberga **S** 50 Ga23
Kasimov **RUS** 118 Fb10
Kašin **RUS** 117 Ed09
Kaşınhanı **TR** 128 Gb15
Kaskii **FIN** 41 Ja14
Kaskinen **FIN** 40 Ha14
Kaskö **FIN** 40 Ha14
Kassari **EST** 46 Hb19
Kassel **D** 64 Fa29
Kastaniá **GR** 101 Hc44
Kastaniá **GR** 101 Hd44
Kastanítsa **GR** 111 Ja47
Kastéli **GR** 115 Jd49
Kastellaun **D** 63 Ec30
Kaštel-Stari **HR** 86 Gc39
Kastl **D** 64 Fc31
Kastoriá **GR** 101 Hc43
Kastrí **GR** 114 Jc50
Kástro **GR** 110 Hc46
Kástro **GR** 111 Ja45
Katákolo **GR** 110 Hd47
Katápola **GR** 115 Jd47
Katastári **GR** 110 Hc46
Katerini **GR** 101 Hd43
Kathení **GR** 112 Jb45
Kathikas **CY** 128 Ga19
Katlanovska Banja **MK** 101 Hc41
Kato **CY** 128 Gb19
Káto Ahaía **GR** 110 Hd46
Káto Almirí **GR** 111 Ja46
Káto Asséa **GR** 111 Ja47
Kato Gialia **CY** 128 Ga19
Káto Makrinoú **GR** 110 Hd45
Káto Nevrokópi **GR** 102 Jb42
Káto Vlassía **GR** 110 Hd46
Katowice **PL** 66 Gd30
Katrineholm **S** 44 Gb19
Katsimbalis **GR** 110 Hd47
Kattavía **GR** 115 Kb48
Katthammarsvik **S** 51 Gd21
Katy Wrocławskie **PL** 66 Gc29
Kaufbeuren **D** 72 Fb33
Kaufungen **D** 64 Fa29
Kauhajoki **FIN** 40 Ha14
Kauhava **FIN** 40 Hb13
Kaukonen **FIN** 30 Hb07
Kaulsdorf **D** 64 Fc30
Kaunas **LT** 52 Hc24
Kaupanger **N** 36 Fa15
Kausala **FIN** 41 Hd16
Kauske **EST** 47 Ja18
Kaustinen **FIN** 34 Hb12
Kautokeino **N** 26 Ha05
Kavacık **TR** 103 Kb43
Kavadarci **MK** 101 Hd42
Kavajë **RKS** 100 Hb42
Kavaklıdere **TR** 113 Kb46
Kavála **GR** 102 Jb42
Kavarna **BG** 89 Ka38
Kavarskas **LT** 53 Hd23
Kävlinge **S** 49 Fd23
Kaxholmen **S** 44 Ga20

Kayaönü **TR** 128 Gc16
Kayapa **TR** 103 Ka43
Käylä **FIN** 31 Hd08
Kaymakçı **TR** 113 Kb45
Kaysersberg **F** 71 Ec33
Kazačka **RUS** 123 Fc12
Kazan' **RUS** 119 Fd08
Kazancı **TR** 128 Gb17
Kazanka **UA** 125 Ed16
Kazanlâk **BG** 102 Jc40
Kazanskaja **RUS** 123 Fc13
Kazıklı **TR** 113 Kb46
Kazimierza Wielka **PL** 67 Hb30
Kazimierz Dolny **PL** 67 Hc29
Kazımkarabekir **TR** 128 Gb16
Kazincbarcika **H** 75 Hb33
Kaz'jany **BY** 53 Ja23
Kazlų Rūda **LT** 52 Hc24
Kaznějov **CZ** 65 Fd31
Kcynia **PL** 58 Gc27
Kdyně **CZ** 65 Fd31
Kéa **GR** 112 Jc46
Kecskemét **H** 74 Ha35
Kėdainiai **LT** 52 Hc23
Kédros **GR** 101 Hd44
Kędzierzyn-Koźle **PL** 66 Gd30
Keel **IRL** 18 Bd22
Kéfalos **GR** 115 Ka47
Keflavík **IS** 14 Bb06
Kehl **D** 63 Ed32
Kehra **EST** 47 Hd18
Keighley **GB** 21 Da24
Keila **EST** 46 Hc18
Keipene **LV** 53 Hd21
Keitele **FIN** 41 Hd13
Keith **GB** 17 Db19
Kelankylä **FIN** 35 Hc09
Këlcyrë **AL** 100 Hb43
Kelheim **D** 64 Fc32
Kellaki **CY** 128 Gb19
Kellinghusen **D** 56 Fb25
Kello **FIN** 35 Hc10
Kellokoski **FIN** 40 Hc16
Kelloselkä **FIN** 31 Hd07
Kells **IRL** 19 Cb23
Kelmė **LT** 52 Hc23
Kelmis **B** 63 Eb29
Kelso **GB** 21 Db22
Kel'menci **UA** 76 Jc32
Kemalpaşa **TR** 113 Ka45
Kemalpaşa **TR** 127 Ga18
Kemerburgaz **TR** 103 Kb41
Kemerhısar **TR** 128 Gd15
Kemi **FIN** 34 Hb09
Kemijärvi **FIN** 31 Hc08
Kemilä **FIN** 35 Ja09
Keminmaa **FIN** 34 Hb09
Kemiö **FIN** 46 Hb17
Kemlja **RUS** 119 Fc10
Kemnath **D** 64 Fc31
Kempele **FIN** 35 Hc10
Kempten **D** 72 Fb34
Kendal **GB** 21 Da23

Kenderes **H** 75 Hb34
Kenmare **IRL** 22 Bc25
Kennacraig **GB** 20 Cd21
Kenttan **N** 27 Hb05
Kępno **PL** 66 Gd29
Kepsut **TR** 103 Kb43
Keramídi **GR** 101 Ja44
Keramotí **GR** 102 Jb42
Keratea **GR** 112 Jb46
Kerava **FIN** 40 Hc16
Kerč **UA** 126 Fb17
Kergu **EST** 46 Hc19
Kerí **GR** 110 Hc47
Kerimäki **FIN** 41 Ja14
Kérkira **GR** 100 Hb44
Kerkrade **NL** 63 Ec29
Kermen **BG** 103 Jd40
Kéros **GR** 115 Jd47
Kerpen **D** 63 Ec29
Kerteminde **DK** 49 Fb23
Keryneia **CY** 128 Gb18
Kesälahti **FIN** 41 Jb14
Keşan **TR** 103 Jd42
Kesh **GB** 19 Cb22
Kesteri **LV** 52 Hb22
Kestilä **FIN** 35 Hc11
Keswick **GB** 21 Da23
Keszthely **H** 74 Gc35
Ketčenery **RUS** 123 Ga14
Kettering **GB** 25 Db26
Keuruu **FIN** 40 Hc14
Kevastu **EST** 47 Ja19
Kevelaer **D** 55 Ec28
Kežmarok **SK** 67 Hb32
Kiáto **GR** 111 Ja46
Kibæk **DK** 48 Fa22
Kıbasan **TR** 128 Gb16
Kiberg **N** 27 Hd03
Kičevo **MK** 101 Hc42
Kicman' **UA** 76 Jb32
Kidderminster **GB** 24 Da26
Kidekša **RUS** 118 Fa09
Kiefersfelden **D** 72 Fc34
Kiekinkoski **FIN** 35 Ja11
Kiel **D** 56 Fb25
Kielce **PL** 67 Hb29
Kierinki **FIN** 30 Hb07
Kierspe **D** 63 Ed29
Kigyósgárgyán **H** 74 Ha35
Kihelkonna **EST** 46 Hb19
Kihlanki **FIN** 30 Ha07
Kihlanki **S** 30 Ha07
Kihniö **FIN** 40 Hb14
Kiikala **FIN** 40 Hb16
Kiikoinen **FIN** 40 Hb15
Kiiminki **FIN** 35 Hc10
Kiistala **FIN** 30 Hb07
Kijevo **HR** 86 Gc39
Kikerino **RUS** 47 Jb17
Kikinda **SRB** 75 Hb36
Kiknur **RUS** 119 Fc08
Kil **N** 43 Fb19
Kil **S** 44 Fd18
Kilafors **S** 38 Gb16
Kilbaha **IRL** 18 Bc24

Kilboghamn **N** 32 Fd09
Kilchoan **GB** 16 Cd19
Kilcolgan **IRL** 18 Bd23
Kildare **IRL** 19 Cb24
Kil'dinstroj **RUS** 31 Ja05
Kilija **UA** 77 Ka35
Kilingi-Nõmme **EST** 47 Hd19
Kílini **GR** 110 Hc46
Kilkee **IRL** 18 Bd24
Kilkeel **GB** 20 Cc23
Kilkenny **IRL** 18 Ca24
Kilkhampton **GB** 23 Cc27
Kilkís **GR** 101 Ja42
Killarney **IRL** 22 Bd25
Killbeggan **IRL** 18 Ca23
Killenaule **IRL** 18 Ca24
Killimer **IRL** 18 Bd24
Killin **GB** 17 Da20
Killinkoski **FIN** 40 Hb14
Killorglin **IRL** 18 Bc24
Killybegs **IRL** 18 Ca22
Kilmaine **IRL** 18 Bd23
Kilmarnock **GB** 20 Cd21
Kilmore Quay **IRL** 23 Cb25
Kilpisjärvi **FIN** 26 Gd05
Kilrush **IRL** 18 Bd24
Kilyos **TR** 103 Kb41
Kími **GR** 112 Jb45
Kimito **FIN** 46 Hb17
Kímolos **GR** 111 Jc47
Kimovsk **RUS** 118 Fa11
Kimry **RUS** 117 Ed09
Kinbrace **GB** 17 Da18
Kinel' **RUS** 119 Ga10
Kinešma **RUS** 118 Fb09
Kingisepp **RUS** 47 Jb17
Kingsbridge **GB** 23 Cc28
King's Lynn **GB** 25 Dc26
Kingston upon Hull **GB** 21 Dc24
Kingussie **GB** 17 Da19
Kíni **GR** 112 Jc46
Kınık **TR** 113 Ka44
Kinlochewe **GB** 16 Cd18
Kinna **S** 49 Fd21
Kinnarp **S** 44 Fd20
Kinnegad **IRL** 19 Cb23
Kinnula **FIN** 35 Hc12
Kinross **GB** 21 Da21
Kinsale **IRL** 22 Bd25
Kinsarvik **N** 42 Ed17
Kintore **GB** 17 Db20
Kinvarre **IRL** 18 Bd23
Kióni **GR** 110 Hc46
Kiparíssi **GR** 111 Ja47
Kiparissía **GR** 110 Hd47
Kipinä **FIN** 35 Hc10
Kipséli **GR** 101 Hc43
Kipséli **GR** 101 Ja44
Kipti **UA** 121 Ec14
Kirava **UA** 121 Ec14
Kiraz **TR** 113 Kb45
Kirchberg **D** 63 Ec30
Kirchdorf **A** 73 Ga33
Kirchhain **D** 64 Fa29
Kirchheim (Teck) **D** 64 Fa32

Kirchheimbolanden – Komsomol'skij

Kirchheimbolanden **D** 63 Ed31
Kirchschlag **A** 73 Gb34
Kireç **TR** 103 Kb43
Kiriáki **GR** 111 Ja45
Kirillovskoe **RUS** 41 Jb16
Kırkağaç **TR** 113 Ka44
Kirkby Lonsdale **GB** 21 Da23
Kirkcaldy **GB** 21 Da21
Kirkcudbright **GB** 20 Cd22
Kirkenær **N** 43 Fd17
Kirkenes **N** 27 Hd04
Kirke Såby **DK** 49 Fc23
Kirkjubæjarklaustur **IS** 14 Bd08
Kirkkonummi **FIN** 46 Hc17
Kirkkovo **RUS** 47 Ja17
Kırklareli **TR** 103 Jd41
Kirkliai **LT** 52 Hc23
Kirkwall **GB** 17 Db17
Kirn **D** 63 Ec31
Kirobasi **TR** 128 Gc17
Kirov **RUS** 121 Ed12
Kirovohrad **UA** 121 Ed15
Kirovsk **RUS** 117 Eb08
Kirovs'ke **UA** 126 Fa17
Kirriemuir **GB** 17 Db20
Kirsanov **RUS** 119 Fc11
Kiruna **S** 29 Gd07
Kiržač **RUS** 118 Fa10
Kisa **S** 44 Gb20
Kisbér **H** 74 Gd34
Kiseljak **BIH** 86 Gd39
Kiseljak **BIH** 86 Ha38
Kisielice **PL** 58 Gd26
Kiskkunmajsa **H** 74 Ha35
Kisko **FIN** 46 Hb17
Kisköre **H** 75 Hb34
Kiskőrös **H** 74 Ha35
Kiskunfélegyháza **H** 74 Ha35
Kiskunhalas **H** 74 Ha35
Kiskunlacháza **H** 74 Ha34
Kislovodsk **RUS** 127 Ga17
Kissamos **GR** 114 Jb49
Kisszentmiklós **H** 74 Ha35
Kist **D** 64 Fa31
Kistanje **HR** 85 Gb39
Kistelek **H** 75 Hb35
Kisvárda **H** 75 Hc33
Kitee **FIN** 41 Jb14
Kíthnos **GR** 111 Jc47
Kitkiöjoki **S** 30 Ha07
Kitros **GR** 101 Hd43
Kittelfjäll **S** 33 Gb10
Kittilä **FIN** 30 Hb07
Kitzbühel **A** 72 Fc34
Kitzingen **D** 64 Fb31
Kiuruvesi **FIN** 35 Hd12
Kiverci **UA** 120 Ea14
Kivesjärvi **FIN** 35 Hd11
Kivijärvi **FIN** 40 Hc13
Kivik **S** 50 Ga23
Kiviõli **EST** 47 Ja18
Kivotós **GR** 101 Hc43

Kıyıköy **TR** 103 Ka41
Kızılören **TR** 128 Ga15
Kizner **RUS** 119 Ga08
Kjeldebotn **N** 28 Gb06
Kjellerup **DK** 49 Fb22
Kjellmyra **N** 37 Fd16
Kjernmoen **N** 37 Fd16
Kjøllefjord **N** 27 Hb03
Kjøpsvik **N** 28 Gb07
Kjustendil **BG** 87 Hd40
Kladanj **BIH** 86 Ha38
Kladnica **SRB** 87 Hb39
Kladno **CZ** 65 Ga30
Kladovo **SRB** 87 Hd37
Klæbu **N** 37 Fc13
Klagenfurt **A** 73 Ga35
Klaipėda **LT** 52 Ha23
Klanac **HR** 85 Gb38
Kläppen **S** 34 Gd11
Klášterec nad Ohří **CZ** 65 Fd30
Klatovy **CZ** 65 Fd31
Klausen **I** 72 Fb35
Kłecko **PL** 58 Gc27
Kleive **N** 36 Fa13
Klembivka **UA** 77 Jd32
Klenovac **BIH** 86 Gc38
Kleppe **N** 42 Ec18
Kleppestø **N** 36 Ed16
Kleszczele **PL** 59 Hc27
Kletnja **RUS** 121 Ec12
Kletskij **RUS** 123 Fd13
Kleve **D** 55 Ec28
Klezevo **RUS** 47 Ja20
Kličav **BY** 121 Eb12
Kliczków **PL** 65 Gb29
Klimavičy **BY** 121 Ec12
Klimovo **RUS** 121 Ec13
Klimovsk **RUS** 117 Ed10
Klin **RUS** 117 Ed10
Klincovka **RUS** 119 Ga11
Klincy **RUS** 121 Ec13
Klingenthal **D** 64 Fc30
Klingnau **CH** 71 Ed34
Kliniča Sela **HR** 73 Gd36
Klintehamn **S** 51 Gc21
Klippan **S** 49 Fd22
Klissoúra **GR** 101 Hc44
Klisura **BG** 102 Jb40
Klitmøller **DK** 48 Fa21
Klitoría **GR** 110 Hd46
Kljajićevo **SRB** 74 Ha36
Kljascicy **BY** 53 Jb22
Kljavica **BY** 53 Ja24
Kljavino **RUS** 119 Ga09
Ključ **BIH** 86 Gc38
Kłobuck **PL** 66 Gd29
Kłodawa **PL** 58 Gd28
Kłodzko **PL** 66 Gc30
Kløfta **N** 43 Fc17
Klokkarvik **N** 42 Ec17
Kłomnice **PL** 67 Ha29
Klos **RKS** 100 Hb42
Kloštar Ivanić **HR** 74 Gc36
Kloster **CH** 72 Fa35
Klosterneuburg **A** 73 Gb33

Kloten **CH** 71 Ed34
Kloten **S** 44 Gb17
Klötze **D** 56 Fc27
Klövsjö **S** 38 Ga14
Kluczbork **PL** 66 Gd29
Klütz **D** 56 Fc25
Knäred **S** 49 Fd22
Knaresborough **GB** 21 Db24
Knarvik **N** 36 Ed16
Kneža **BG** 88 Ja39
Kneževici Sušica **SRB** 87 Hb39
Kneževi Vinogradi **HR** 74 Ha36
Knićanin **SRB** 87 Hb37
Knighton **GB** 24 Cd26
Knin **HR** 85 Gb39
Knislinge **S** 50 Ga22
Knittelfeld **A** 73 Ga34
Knivsta **S** 45 Gc18
Knjaževac **SRB** 87 Hd39
Knjaževo **RUS** 118 Fb08
Knocklong **IRL** 18 Bd24
Knokke-Heist **B** 54 Ea28
Knurów **PL** 66 Gd30
Knurowiec **PL** 59 Hb27
Knutsford **GB** 24 Da25
Knyszyn **PL** 59 Hc26
Kobarid **SLO** 73 Fd36
Kobbfoss **N** 27 Hd04
Kobeljaky **UA** 121 Ed15
København **DK** 49 Fd23
Koblenz **D** 63 Ed30
Kobona **RUS** 117 Eb08
Koboža **RUS** 117 Ec08
Kobryn **BY** 59 Hd27
Kobylin **PL** 58 Gc28
Kočani **MK** 101 Hd41
Koceljevo **SRB** 87 Hb38
Kočerin **BIH** 86 Gd39
Kočetovka **RUS** 122 Fb12
Kočevje **SLO** 73 Ga36
Kock **PL** 59 Hc28
Kočkarlej **RUS** 119 Fd10
Kocsola **H** 74 Gd35
Kócsújfalu **H** 75 Hb34
Kode **S** 43 Fc20
Kodeń **PL** 59 Hd28
Kodrąb **PL** 67 Ha29
Kodyma **UA** 77 Ka32
Kodyma **UA** 125 Ec16
Kofças **TR** 103 Jd40
Kofinou **CY** 128 Gb19
Köflach **A** 73 Ga35
Køge **DK** 49 Fc23
Kogula **EST** 46 Hb19
Kohila **EST** 46 Hc18
Kohma **RUS** 118 Fa09
Kohtlajärve **EST** 47 Ja17
Koilovci **BG** 88 Jb39
Koirakosk **FIN** 35 Hd12
Koivu **FIN** 34 Hb09
Koivulahti **FIN** 40 Ha13
Kojetín **CZ** 66 Gc31
Kökar **FIN** 46 Ha17
Kokemäki **FIN** 40 Hb15

Kokinombléa **GR** 111 Ja45
Kokkola **FIN** 34 Hb12
Koknese **LV** 53 Hd21
Kokotí **GR** 111 Ja45
Koktebel' **UA** 126 Fb17
Kola **RUS** 31 Ja05
Kołacze **PL** 59 Hd28
Kolari **FIN** 30 Hb07
Kolárovo **SK** 74 Gd33
Kolåsen **S** 32 Fd12
Kolašin **MNE** 86 Ha40
Kolbäck **S** 44 Gb18
Kolbu **N** 37 Fc16
Kolbudy Grn. **PL** 58 Gd25
Kolbuszowa **PL** 67 Hc30
Kol'čugino **RUS** 118 Fa10
Kolding **DK** 49 Fb23
Koler **S** 34 Gd10
Kölesd **H** 74 Gd35
Kolga-Jaani **EST** 47 Hd19
Kolgompja **RUS** 47 Ja17
Kolho **FIN** 40 Hc14
Koli **FIN** 35 Ja12
Kolín **CZ** 65 Ga31
Kolka **LV** 46 Hb20
Kolky **UA** 120 Ea14
Kölleda **D** 64 Fc29
Köln **D** 63 Ec29
Kolno **PL** 59 Hb26
Koło **PL** 58 Gd28
Kołobrzeg **PL** 57 Gb25
Koločava **UA** 67 Hd32
Kolokolčovka **RUS** 123 Fd12
Kolomna **RUS** 118 Fa10
Kolomyja **UA** 76 Ja32
Kolomyja **UA** 124 Ea16
Kolpino **RUS** 117 Eb08
Kolpny **RUS** 122 Fa12
Kolsva **S** 44 Gb18
Koluszki **PL** 58 Ha28
Kolvereid **N** 32 Fd11
Kolyčivka **UA** 121 Ec14
Kolyšlej **RUS** 119 Fc11
Komańcza **PL** 67 Hc31
Komárno **SK** 74 Gd34
Komarno **UA** 67 Hd31
Komárom **H** 74 Gd34
Komarówka Podlaska **PL** 59 Hc28
Koma tou Gialou **CY** 128 Gc18
Kominternivs'ke **MD** 77 Kb33
Kominternivs'ke **UA** 125 Ec17
Komiža **HR** 85 Gb40
Komló **H** 74 Gd36
Komniná **GR** 101 Hd43
Komorzno **PL** 66 Gd29
Komosomol'sk **RUS** 118 Fa09
Komotini **GR** 102 Jc42
Kompina **PL** 58 Ha28
Komsomol'sk **RUS** 52 Ha24
Komsomol'skij **RUS** 119 Fc10

Komsomol'sk Zap. **RUS** 52 Ha24
Kömürlimaný **TR** 102 Jc43
Konak **SRB** 87 Hb37
Konakovo **RUS** 117 Ed10
Konakpınar **TR** 103 Kb43
Konare **BG** 89 Ka38
Konarzyny **PL** 58 Gc26
Kondolovo **BG** 103 Ka40
Kondrovo **RUS** 117 Ed11
Köngas **FIN** 30 Hb07
Konginkangas **FIN** 40 Hc13
Kongsberg **N** 43 Fb18
Kongsmoen **N** 32 Fd11
Kongsvinger **N** 43 Fd17
Konice **CZ** 66 Gc31
Königsbrück **D** 65 Fd29
Königsbrunn **D** 72 Fb33
Königsee **D** 64 Fb30
Königstein **D** 63 Ed30
Königstein **D** 65 Ga29
Königswiesen **A** 73 Ga33
Königswinter **D** 63 Ec29
Königs Wusterhausen **D** 57 Fd28
Konin **PL** 58 Gd28
Kónitsa **GR** 101 Hc44
Köniz **CH** 71 Ec34
Konjic **BIH** 86 Gd39
Könnern **D** 56 Fc28
Konnevesi **FIN** 41 Hd13
Konopki **PL** 58 Ha27
Konotop **PL** 57 Gb28
Konotop **UA** 121 Ed14
Końskie **PL** 67 Ha29
Konsmo **N** 42 Fa19
Konstancin-Jeziorna **PL** 59 Hb28
Konstantin **BG** 88 Jc39
Konstantinovsk **RUS** 123 Fc15
Konstantinovy Lázně **CZ** 65 Fd31
Konstantynów **PL** 59 Hc27
Konstantynów Łódzki **PL** 58 Ha28
Konstanz **D** 72 Fa34
Kontiolahti **FIN** 41 Jb13
Kontiomäki **FIN** 35 Hd11
Konttajärvi **FIN** 30 Hb08
Konya **TR** 128 Gb15
Konz **D** 63 Ec31
Koosa **EST** 47 Ja19
Koparnes **N** 36 Ed14
Kópasker **IS** 15 Cb05
Kópavogur **IS** 14 Bc06
Koper **SLO** 85 Fd37
Kopidlno **CZ** 65 Gb30
Köping **S** 44 Gb18
Koplik i Poshtëm **AL** 100 Ha41
Köpmanholmen **S** 39 Gc13
Kopor'e **RUS** 47 Jb17
Koppang **N** 37 Fc15
Kopparberg **S** 44 Ga17
Koppelo **FIN** 27 Hc05

Kopperå **N** 37 Fd13
Koppom **S** 43 Fd18
Koprivna **BIH** 86 Gd37
Koprivnica **HR** 74 Gc36
Kopřivnice **CZ** 66 Gd31
Koprivštica **BG** 102 Jb40
Köprübaşı **TR** 113 Kb44
Köprülü **TR** 128 Ga16
Kopyčynci **UA** 124 Ea16
Korablino **RUS** 118 Fb11
Korbach **D** 64 Fa29
Korbeniči **RUS** 117 Ec08
Korçe **AL** 101 Hc43
Korčevka **RUS** 119 Fd10
Korčula **HR** 86 Gc40
Korec' **UA** 121 Eb14
Korenevo **RUS** 121 Ed13
Korenica **HR** 85 Gb38
Korenovsk **RUS** 127 Fc16
Korfantów **PL** 66 Gc30
Korgen **N** 33 Ga09
Koria **FIN** 41 Hd16
Korifási **GR** 110 Hd47
Korinós **GR** 101 Hd43
Kórinthos **GR** 111 Ja46
Korita **BIH** 86 Gd40
Korita **MNE** 86 Ha40
Korjukivka **UA** 121 Ec13
Körmen **TR** 115 Kb47
Körmend **H** 74 Gc35
Korneuburg **A** 73 Gb33
Kórnik **PL** 58 Gc28
Kornofolia **GR** 103 Jd41
Kornwestheim **D** 64 Fa32
Koroča **RUS** 122 Fa13
Koromačno **HR** 85 Ga37
Koróni **GR** 110 Hd48
Koronowo **PL** 58 Gc26
Korop **UA** 121 Ed13
Körösladány **H** 75 Hb34
Korosten' **UA** 121 Eb14
Korostyšiv **UA** 121 Eb15
Koroviha **RUS** 118 Fb08
Korpilahti **FIN** 40 Hc14
Korpilombolo **S** 30 Ha08
Korpiselkja **RUS** 41 Jb13
Korpo **FIN** 46 Ha17
Korppoo **FIN** 46 Ha17
Korsberga **S** 50 Ga21
Korskrogen **S** 38 Gb15
Korsnäs **FIN** 40 Ha13
Korsør **DK** 49 Fc24
Korsun'-Ševčenkivs'kyj **UA** 121 Ec15
Korsvegen **N** 37 Fc13
Korsvoll **N** 37 Fb13
Korsze **PL** 59 Hb25
Korten **BG** 102 Jc40
Kortesjärvi **FIN** 40 Hb13
Kórthio **GR** 112 Jc46
Kortrijk **B** 62 Dd29
Korucu **TR** 103 Ka43
Korvala **FIN** 31 Hc08
Koryčany **CZ** 66 Gc32
Korycin **PL** 59 Hc26
Korzybie **PL** 58 Gc25

Kós **GR** 115 Kb47
Kosaja Gora **RUS** 118 Fa11
Kosanica **MNE** 86 Ha40
Košarovce **SK** 67 Hc32
Kościan **PL** 58 Gc28
Kościelec **PL** 58 Gd28
Kościerzyna **PL** 58 Gc25
Kose **EST** 47 Hd18
Košice **SK** 67 Hb32
Košická Belá **SK** 67 Hb32
Kosihovce **SK** 74 Ha33
Kosiv **UA** 76 Ja32
Kosjerić **SRB** 87 Hb38
Koška **HR** 86 Gd37
Koskenpää **FIN** 40 Hc14
Koski **FIN** 40 Hb16
Koskolovo **RUS** 47 Ja17
Koskue **FIN** 40 Hb14
Koskullskulle **S** 29 Gd08
Kosmás **GR** 111 Ja47
Kosovska Mitrovica **RKS** 87 Hc40
Kosów Lacki **PL** 59 Hc27
Kosta **S** 50 Gb22
Kostanjevica na Krki **SLO** 73 Gb36
Kostelec nad Černými Lesy **CZ** 65 Ga31
Kostelec na Hané **CZ** 66 Gc31
Kostenec **BG** 102 Ja40
Kostinbrod **BG** 102 Ja40
Kostjantynivka **UA** 122 Fb15
Kostomłoty **PL** 66 Gc29
Kostomukša **RUS** 35 Ja10
Kostopil' **UA** 120 Ea14
Kostroma **RUS** 118 Fa08
Kostryna **UA** 67 Hc32
Kostrzyn **PL** 57 Ga27
Koszalin **PL** 57 Gb25
Kőszeg **H** 74 Gc34
Koszuty **PL** 58 Gc28
Kotel **BG** 89 Jd39
Kotel'nikovo **RUS** 123 Fd14
Kotel'skij **RUS** 47 Jb17
Kotel'va **UA** 121 Ed14
Köthen **D** 56 Fc28
Kotila **FIN** 35 Hd10
Kotka **FIN** 41 Hd16
Kotly **RUS** 47 Jb17
Kotor **MNE** 100 Ha41
Kotoriba **HR** 74 Gc35
Kotorsko **BIH** 86 Gd37
Kotor Varoš **BIH** 86 Gc38
Kotovo **RUS** 123 Fd12
Kotovsk **RUS** 122 Fb12
Kotovs'k **UA** 77 Ka32
Kotovs'k **UA** 125 Ec16
Kótronas **GR** 111 Ja48
Kötschach **A** 73 Fd35
Kötzting **D** 65 Fd32
Koufália **GR** 101 Hd42
Kouklia **CY** 128 Ga19
Kounávi **GR** 115 Jd49
Koúndouros **GR** 112 Jc46
Kounoupítsa **GR** 112 Jb46

Koutalás **GR** 111 Jc47
Kouvola **FIN** 41 Hd16
Kovačevci **BG** 102 Ja40
Kovačica **SRB** 87 Hb37
Kovdor **RUS** 31 Ja06
Kovel' **UA** 120 Ea14
Kovernino **RUS** 118 Fb08
Kovero **FIN** 41 Jb13
Kovrov **RUS** 118 Fa09
Kovylkino **RUS** 119 Fc10
Kowal **PL** 58 Gd27
Kowale Oleckie **PL** 59 Hc25
Kowary **PL** 65 Gb30
Kozac'ke **UA** 77 Kb34
Kozak **TR** 113 Ka44
Kozáni **GR** 101 Hd43
Kozel'sk **RUS** 117 Ed11
Koziegłowy **PL** 67 Ha30
Kozienice **PL** 59 Hb28
Kozjatyn **UA** 121 Eb15
Kozloduj **BG** 88 Ja38
Kozlovka **RUS** 119 Fd09
Kozłów **PL** 67 Ha30
Koźmin **PL** 58 Gc28
Koźminek **PL** 58 Gd28
Koźminiec **PL** 58 Gc28
Koz'modem'jansk **RUS** 119 Fc09
Kožuchów **PL** 57 Gb28
Kräckelbäcken **S** 38 Ga15
Kraddsele **S** 33 Gb10
Kragenæs **DK** 49 Fc24
Kragerø **N** 43 Fb19
Kragujevac **SRB** 87 Hc38
Krakhella **N** 36 Ec15
Kräklingbo **S** 51 Gd21
Krakovec' **UA** 67 Hd30
Kraków **PL** 67 Ha30
Krakow am See **D** 56 Fc26
Kraljevica **HR** 85 Ga37
Kraljevo **SRB** 87 Hb39
Kralovice **CZ** 65 Fd31
Král'ovský Chlmec **SK** 67 Hc32
Kralupy nad Vltavou **CZ** 65 Ga30
Kramators'k **UA** 122 Fb15
Kramfors **S** 39 Gc13
Kramjanica **BY** 59 Hd26
Kranidi **GR** 111 Ja47
Kranj **SLO** 73 Ga36
Kranjska Gora **SLO** 73 Fd35
Krapina **HR** 73 Gb36
Krapinske Toplice **HR** 73 Gb36
Krapkowice **PL** 66 Gd30
Kräslava **LV** 53 Ja22
Krasnae **BY** 53 Jb24
Krasnaja Gora **RUS** 121 Ec13
Krasnaja Jaruga **RUS** 122 Fa13
Krasnaja Poljana **RUS** 127 Fd17
Krásna nad Hornádom **SK** 67 Hb32

Kraśnik PL 67 Hc29
Krasni Okny UA 77 Ka33
Krasnoarmejsk RUS 118 Fa10
Krasnoarmejsk RUS 123 Fd12
Krasnoarmijs'k UA 122 Fb15
Krasnobród PL 67 Hd30
Krasnodar RUS 127 Fc17
Krasnodon UA 123 Fc15
Krasnoe RUS 52 Hb24
Krasnoe RUS 122 Fa12
Krasnogorodskoe RUS 53 Jb21
Krasnogvardejskoe RUS 127 Fd16
Krasnohorivka UA 122 Fb15
Krásnohorské Podhradie SK 67 Hb32
Krasnohrad UA 122 Fa14
Krasnohvardijs'ke UA 126 Fa17
Krasnojil's'k UA 76 Jb33
Krasnokuts'k UA 122 Fa14
Krasnomajskij RUS 117 Ec09
Krasnopavlivka UA 122 Fa15
Krasnoperekops'k UA 126 Fa17
Krasnopillja UA 122 Fa14
Krasnosielc PL 59 Hb26
Krasnoslobodsk RUS 119 Fc10
Krasnoslobodsk RUS 123 Fd14
Krasnotorovka RUS 52 Ha24
Krasnoznamensk RUS 52 Hc24
Krasnye Baki RUS 118 Fb08
Krasnyj Holm RUS 117 Ed09
Krasnyj Jar RUS 119 Ga10
Krasnyj Kut RUS 123 Ga12
Krasnyj Luč UA 122 Fb15
Krasnystaw PL 67 Hd29
Krastë RKS 100 Hb42
Krasti LV 53 Hd22
Krasyliv UA 121 Eb15
Kratovo MK 101 Hd41
Kražiai LT 52 Hc23
Krefeld D 55 Ec28
Krekenava LT 53 Hd23
Kremenčuk UA 121 Ed15
Kremenec' UA 120 Ea15
Kremidivka MD 77 Kb33
Kremmen D 57 Fd27
Kremna SRB 86 Ha39
Krems A 73 Fd35
Krems A 73 Gb33
Krepoljin SRB 87 Hc38
Krępsko PL 58 Gc26
Kreševo BIH 86 Gd39
Kresk-Królowa PL 59 Hc28
Kresna BG 101 Ja41
Krestcy RUS 117 Eb09

Kréstena GR 110 Hd47
Kretinga LT 52 Hb23
Kreuztal D 63 Ed29
Krëva BY 53 Ja24
Krëva BY 120 Ea12
Kriátsi GR 110 Hd45
Krieglach A 73 Gb34
Kriens CH 71 Ed34
Kríkelos GR 110 Hc45
Kríni GR 101 Hd44
Krinídes GR 102 Jb42
Kristdala S 50 Gb21
Kristiansand N 42 Fa20
Kristianstad S 50 Ga23
Kristiansund N 36 Fa13
Kristiinankaupunki FIN 40 Ha14
Kristineberg S 33 Gc11
Kristinehamn S 44 Ga18
Kristinestad FIN 40 Ha14
Kriva Feja SRB 87 Hd40
Kriva Palanka MK 101 Hd41
Krive Ozero MD 77 Kb32
Krivodol BG 88 Ja39
Krivolak MK 101 Hd41
Krivoroz'e RUS 123 Fc14
Kňžanov CZ 65 Gb31
Križevci HR 74 Gc36
Križpolje HR 85 Gb37
Krk HR 85 Ga37
Krnja MNE 86 Ha40
Krnov CZ 66 Gc31
Krobia PL 58 Gc28
Krøderen N 43 Fb17
Krokek S 44 Gb19
Krokílio GR 110 Hd45
Krokom S 38 Ga13
Króksfjarðarnes IS 14 Bc05
Krokvåg S 38 Gb13
Krolevec' UA 121 Ed13
Kroměříž CZ 66 Gc32
Kromy RUS 121 Ed12
Kronach D 64 Fb30
Kroņauce LV 52 Hc22
Kronshagen D 56 Fb25
Kronštadt RUS 41 Jb16
Kröpelin D 56 Fc25
Kropotkin RUS 127 Fd16
Krośnice PL 66 Gc29
Krośniewice PL 58 Gd28
Krosno PL 67 Hc31
Krosno Odrzańskie PL 57 Ga28
Krotoszyn PL 58 Gc28
Krško SLO 73 Gb36
Krstac MNE 86 Ha40
Krujë RKS 100 Hb42
Krukenyči UA 67 Hd31
Krukowo PL 59 Hb26
Krumbach D 72 Fb33
Krupa na Vrbasu BIH 86 Gc38
Krupanj SRB 86 Ha38
Krušari BG 89 Ka38
Krusedol Selo SRB 87 Hb37
Kruševac SRB 87 Hc39

Kruševo MK 101 Hc42
Krušovene BG 88 Jb39
Krušovica BG 88 Ja39
Kruszów PL 58 Ha28
Kruszwica PL 58 Gd27
Kruszyna PL 67 Ha29
Kruszyniany PL 59 Hd26
Kruunupyy FIN 34 Hb12
Kryčav BY 121 Ec12
Krylovo RUS 59 Hb25
Krymsk RUS 127 Fc17
Krynica PL 67 Hb31
Krynica Morska PL 58 Gd25
Krynki PL 59 Hd26
Krynyčne UA 77 Ka35
Kryve Ozero UA 125 Ec16
Kryvičy BY 53 Jb24
Kryvsk BY 121 Ec13
Kryvyj Rih UA 125 Ed16
Kryžopil' UA 77 Jd32
Kryžopil' UA 125 Eb16
Krzęcin PL 57 Gb27
Krzeczów PL 66 Gd29
Krzepice PL 66 Gd29
Krzeszyce PL 57 Ga27
Krzywa PL 65 Gb29
Kšenskij RUS 122 Fa13
Księżpol PL 67 Hc30
Kstovo RUS 118 Fb09
Ktísmata GR 100 Hb44
Kubrat BG 88 Jc38
Kučevište MK 101 Hc41
Kučevo SRB 87 Hc38
Kuchary PL 58 Gd28
Kućište RKS 87 Hb40
Küçükbahçe TR 113 Jd45
Küçükkuyu TR 103 Jd43
Kuczbork-Osada PL 58 Ha26
Kudirkos Naumiestis LT 52 Hc24
Kudowa-Zdrój PL 65 Gb30
Kuflew PL 59 Hb28
Kufstein A 72 Fc34
Kugej RUS 127 Fc16
Kuha FIN 35 Hc09
Kühlungsborn D 56 Fc25
Kuhmalahti FIN 40 Hc15
Kuhmo FIN 35 Ja11
Kuhmoinen FIN 40 Hc15
Kuimetsa EST 47 Hd18
Kuivaniemi FIN 34 Hb09
Kuivastu EST 46 Hc19
Kukës AL 100 Hb41
Kuklin PL 58 Ha26
Kukmor RUS 119 Fd08
Kukulje BIH 86 Gc37
Kula BG 87 Hd38
Kula SRB 74 Ha36
Kuldīga LV 52 Hb21
Kulebaki RUS 118 Fb10
Kulen Vakuf BIH 85 Gb38
Kuleši RUS 122 Fa12
Kulevča UA 77 Kb35
Kuliai LT 52 Hb23
Kulmbach D 64 Fc30

Kuloharju FIN 35 Hd09
Kumanovo MK 101 Hc41
Kumielsk PL 59 Hb26
Kumkale TR 103 Jd43
Kumköy TR 103 Kb41
Kumla S 44 Ga18
Kumlinge FIN 46 Ha17
Kummavuopio S 26 Gd05
Kunda EST 47 Hd17
Kungälv S 43 Fc20
Kungsäter S 49 Fd21
Kungsbacka S 49 Fc21
Kungshamn S 43 Fc19
Kungsör S 44 Gb18
Kunhegyes H 75 Hb34
Kun'je UA 122 Fb14
Kunmadaras H 75 Hb34
Kunowo PL 58 Gc28
Kunszentmárton H 75 Hb35
Kunszentmiklós H 74 Ha35
Künzelsau D 64 Fa31
Kuolajärvi RUS 31 Hd07
Kuolio FIN 35 Hd09
Kuopio FIN 41 Hd13
Kuortane FIN 40 Hb13
Kuortti FIN 41 Hd15
Kupiškis LT 53 Hd22
Kup'jans'k UA 122 Fb14
Kup'jans'k- Vuzlovyj UA 122 Fb14
Küplü TR 103 Jd42
Kuprava LV 47 Ja20
Kupres BIH 86 Gc39
Kurażyn UA 76 Jc32
Kurdžinovo RUS 127 Fd17
Kuremäe EST 47 Ja18
Kuressaare EST 46 Hb19
Kurganinsk RUS 127 Fd17
Kurgolovo RUS 47 Ja17
Kurikka FIN 40 Ha14
Kuřim CZ 66 Gc32
Kürkçü TR 128 Gd15
Kurkijoki RUS 41 Jb15
Kurlovskij RUS 118 Fa10
Kurovskoe RUS 118 Fa10
Kurów PL 59 Hc28
Kurowo PL 57 Gb25
Kurravaara S 29 Gd07
Kuršėnai LT 52 Hc22
Kursk RUS 122 Fa13
Kursu FIN 31 Hd08
Kuršumlija SRB 87 Hc39
Kurtakko FIN 30 Hb07
Kuru FIN 40 Hb14
Kurylavdčy BY 59 Hd26
Kuşadası TR 113 Ka45
Kušalino RUS 117 Ed09
Kuščevskaja RUS 127 Fc16
Kusel D 63 Ec31
Kušela RUS 47 Jb18
Kuševanda RUS 35 Ja09
Kušnin RKS 100 Hb41
Kusnyšča UA 59 Hd23
Kustavi FIN 40 Ha16
Kutina HR 86 Gc37
Kutjevo HR 86 Gd37

Kutlu-Bukaš **RUS** 119 Ga08
Kutná Hora **CZ** 65 Gb31
Kutno **PL** 58 Ha28
Kuttainen **S** 29 Ha06
Kuttura **FIN** 31 Hc06
Kúty **SK** 66 Gc32
Kuusalu **EST** 47 Hd18
Kuusamo **FIN** 35 Hd09
Kuusankoski **FIN** 41 Hd15
Kuusijärvi **S** 30 Ha08
Kuusjärvi **FIN** 41 Ja13
Kuvaskangas **FIN** 40 Ha15
Kuvšinovo **RUS** 117 Ec10
Kuyucak **TR** 113 Kb45
Kužiai **LT** 52 Hc22
Kuzneck **RUS** 119 Fd10
Kuznečnoe **RUS** 41 Jb15
Kuznecovs'k **UA** 120 Ea14
Kuźnica **PL** 59 Hc26
Kvænangsbotn **N** 26 Gd04
Kværndrup **DK** 49 Fb24
Kvalsund **N** 26 Ha03
Kvam **N** 37 Fb15
Kvanndal **N** 36 Ed16
Kvänum **S** 44 Fd20
Kvédarna **LT** 52 Hb23
Kvelde **N** 43 Fb18
Kvelia **N** 33 Ga11
Kvibille **S** 49 Fd22
Kvikkjokk **S** 29 Gc08
Kvilda **CZ** 65 Fd32
Kvillsfors **S** 50 Gb21
Kvinlog **N** 42 Ed19
Kvissleby **S** 39 Gc14
Kviteseid **N** 42 Fa18
Kwidzyn **PL** 58 Gd26
Kybartai **LT** 52 Hc24
Kyjiv **UA** 121 Ec14
Kyjov **CZ** 66 Gc32
Kyleakin **GB** 16 Cd19
Kyle of Lochalsh **GB** 16
  Cd19
Kylestrome **GB** 17 Da18
Kyprinos **GR** 103 Jd41
Kyritz **D** 56 Fc27
Kyrkhult **S** 50 Ga22
Kyrksæterøra **N** 37 Fb13
Kyrkslätt **FIN** 46 Hc17
Kyrksten **S** 44 Ga18
Kyrnyčky **UA** 125 Ec17
Kysucké Nové Mesto **SK** 66
  Gd31
Kyyjärvi **FIN** 40 Hc13

L

Laa an der Thaya **A** 65 Gb32
Laage **D** 56 Fc25
Laakajärvi **FIN** 35 Hd12
La Alberca **E** 91 Bb40
La Alberca de Záncara **E**
  92 Ca42
La Albuera **E** 90 Ad42
La Algaba **E** 105 Ba44
La Almarcha **E** 92 Ca42

La Almunia de Doña Godina
  E 80 Cb40
Laapinjärvi **FIN** 41 Hd16
Laatzen **D** 56 Fb27
La Bañeza **E** 79 Bc38
La Bassée **F** 62 Dd29
La Baule **F** 60 Cc32
Łabędzie **PL** 57 Gb26
Labenne **F** 80 Cc37
Labin **HR** 85 Ga37
Labinsk **RUS** 127 Fd17
la Bisbal d'Empordà **E** 81
  Db40
Labljane **RKS** 87 Hc40
Labouheyre **F** 80 Cc37
La Bourboule **F** 69 Dc36
La Bóveda de Toro **E** 79
  Bc39
Labrit **F** 80 Cd37
Labruguiere **F** 81 Db38
Lacanau **F** 68 Cd36
Lacanau-Océan **F** 68 Cc36
La Canourgue **F** 81 Dc37
La Capelle **F** 62 Ea30
La Carlota **E** 105 Bb44
La Carolina **E** 106 Bc44
Lacaune **F** 81 Db38
La Cavalerie **F** 81 Dc38
Lac de Tignes **F** 71 Eb36
La Chaise-Dieu **F** 70 Dd36
La Chapelle-en-Vercors **F**
  82 Ea37
La Charité-sur-Loire **F** 70
  Dd34
La Chartre-sur-le-Loir **F** 61
  Db32
La Châtaigneraie **F** 68 Cd34
La Châtre **F** 69 Db34
La Chaux-de-Fonds **CH** 71
  Ec34
Lachen **CH** 71 Ed34
La Chèze **F** 60 Cc31
Lachowo **PL** 59 Hb26
La Ciotat **F** 82 Ea39
La Clayette **F** 70 Dd35
La Clusaz **F** 71 Eb36
Lacock **GB** 24 Da27
Laconi **I** 97 Ed44
La Coruña **E** 78 Ba36
La Côte-Saint-André **F** 70
  Ea36
La Couronne **F** 69 Da35
La Courtine-le-Trucq **F** 69
  Dc35
Lacu Roşu **RO** 76 Jb34
Lad **H** 74 Gd36
Ląd **PL** 58 Gc28
Ladi **GR** 103 Jd41
Ladispoli **I** 98 Fc41
Laduškin **RUS** 52 Ha24
Ladvozero **RUS** 35 Ja10
Ladyžyn **UA** 125 Ec16
Lærdalsøyri **N** 36 Fa16
Láerma **GR** 115 Kb47
Lævvajokgiedde **N** 27 Hb04
La Fère **F** 62 Dd30

La Ferté-Bernard **F** 61 Db32
La Ferté-Gaucher **F** 62
  Dd31
La-Ferté-Macé **F** 61 Da31
La Ferté-Milon **F** 62 Dd31
La Ferté-Saint-Aubin **F** 69
  Dc33
La Ferté-Saint-Cyr **F** 69
  Db33
La Ferté-sous-Jouarre **F** 62
  Dd31
La Flèche **F** 61 Da32
la Font de la Figuera **E** 107
  Cb44
La Fuente de San Esteban **E**
  91 Bb40
La Gacilly **F** 60 Cc32
La Gallega **E** 79 Ca39
Lagan **S** 50 Ga21
Lage **D** 56 Fa28
La Gineta **E** 92 Ca43
Lagnieu **F** 70 Ea36
Lagny-sur-Marne **F** 62 Dd31
Lagoa **P** 104 Ab43
Lagolovo **RUS** 47 Jb17
Lagonegro **I** 99 Gb44
Lágos **GR** 102 Jc42
Lagos **P** 104 Ab43
Łagów **PL** 57 Gb28
Łagów **PL** 67 Hb29
la Granadella **E** 93 Cd41
La Grande-Motte **F** 82 Dd38
Laguardia **E** 80 Cb38
La Guardia **E** 92 Bd42
Laguarta **E** 80 Cd39
La Guerche-de-Bretagne **F**
  61 Cd32
La Guerche-sur-l'Aubois **F**
  69 Dc34
Laguiole **F** 81 Dc37
Laguna de Duero **E** 79 Bc39
Laguna de Negrillos **E** 79
  Bc38
La Haye-du-Puits **F** 61 Cd30
Lahdepoh'ja **RUS** 41 Jb14
Lahinch **IRL** 18 Bd24
Lahišyn **BY** 120 Ea13
Lahnajärvi **S** 30 Ha08
Lahnstein **D** 63 Ed30
Lahojsk **BY** 53 Jb24
Laholm **S** 49 Fd22
Lahr **D** 71 Ed33
Lahti **FIN** 41 Hd15
Laide **GB** 16 Cd18
L'Aigle **F** 61 Db31
Laignes **F** 70 Ea33
Laigueglia **I** 83 Ec38
L'Aiguillon-sur-Mer **F** 68
  Cd34
Laihia **FIN** 40 Ha13
Laiküla **EST** 46 Hc19
Laimoluokta **S** 29 Gd06
Lainio **S** 30 Ha07
Lairg **GB** 17 Da18
Laissac **F** 81 Dc37
Laisvall **S** 33 Gb09

Laitila **FIN** 40 Ha16
Lajkovac **SRB** 87 Hb38
la Jonquera **E** 81 Db40
Lakaträsk **S** 34 Gd09
Läki **BG** 102 Jb41
Lakinsk **RUS** 118 Fa10
Lakkí **GR** 113 Ka46
Lákkoma **GR** 102 Jc42
Lakselv **N** 27 Hb04
Laktaši **BIH** 86 Gc37
Lalapaşa **TR** 103 Jd41
Lálas **GR** 110 Hd46
l'Alcora **E** 93 Cc42
l'Alcúdia **E** 93 Cc43
Lalín **E** 78 Ba37
Lalinde **F** 69 Da36
La Línea de la Concepción **E**
  105 Ba46
Laloşu **RO** 88 Ja37
La Loupe **F** 61 Db32
La Louvière **B** 62 Ea29
L'Alpe-d'Huez **F** 83 Eb37
La Machine **F** 70 Dd34
la Maddalena **I** 96 Ed42
Lamarche **F** 71 Eb33
Lamastre **F** 82 Dd37
Lambach **A** 73 Fd33
Lamballe **F** 60 Cc31
Lambesc **F** 82 Ea38
Lámbia **GR** 110 Hd46
Lamego **P** 78 Ad39
l'Ametlla de Mar **E** 93 Cd41
Lamézia Terme-Nicastro **I**
  109 Gc45
Lamía **GR** 111 Ja45
Lammhult **S** 50 Ga21
Lammi **FIN** 40 Hc15
La Mothe-Achard **F** 68 Cd33
La Motte **F** 83 Eb38
Lamotte-Beuvron **F** 69 Dc33
Lampeland **N** 43 Fb17
Lampeter **GB** 23 Cc26
La Mure **F** 82 Ea37
Lana **I** 72 Fb35
Lanaja **E** 80 Cc40
Lanark **GB** 21 Da21
La Nava de Ricomalillo **E**
  91 Bc41
La Nava de Santiago **E** 91
  Ba42
Lancaster **GB** 21 Da24
Lanciano **I** 99 Ga41
Łańcut **PL** 67 Hc30
Landau **D** 63 Ed31
Landau **D** 64 Fc32
Landeck **A** 72 Fb34
Landerneau **F** 60 Cb31
Landeryd **S** 49 Fd21
Landete **E** 93 Cb42
Landivisiau **F** 60 Cb30
Landön **S** 38 Ga13
Landrecies **F** 62 Ea30
Landsberg **D** 72 Fb33
Landsbro **S** 50 Ga21
Landscheid **D** 63 Ec30

Landshut **D** 72 Fc33
Landskrona **S** 49 Fd23
Landvetter **S** 43 Fd20
Langå **DK** 49 Fb22
Långå **S** 38 Fd14
Langadás **GR** 101 Ja42
Langa de Duero **E** 79 Ca39
Långås **S** 49 Fd21
Langeac **F** 69 Dc36
Langeais **F** 69 Da33
Langedijk **NL** 55 Eb26
Längelmäki **FIN** 40 Hc15
Langen **D** 63 Ed30
Langenau **D** 64 Fa32
Langenhagen **D** 56 Fa27
Langenlois **A** 73 Gb33
Langenzenn **D** 64 Fb31
Langesund **N** 43 Fb19
Langevåg **N** 36 Ed14
Langevåg **N** 42 Ec17
Langfjordbotn **N** 26 Gd04
Langholm **GB** 21 Da22
Langnau **CH** 71 Ec34
Langogne **F** 82 Dd37
Langon **F** 68 Cd36
Langres **F** 70 Ea33
Långsele **S** 38 Gb13
Långshyttan **S** 44 Gb17
Långsjöby **S** 33 Gb11
Långträsk **S** 34 Gd10
Lanna **S** 44 Ga18
Länna **S** 45 Gc17
Lannavaara **S** 29 Ha06
Lannemezan **F** 80 Cd38
Lannion **F** 60 Cc30
Länsi-Aure **FIN** 40 Hb14
Lansjärv **S** 30 Ha08
Lanškroun **CZ** 66 Gc31
Lanslebourg-Mont-Cenis **F** 83 Eb37
Lanusei **I** 97 Ed44
Lány **CZ** 65 Ga30
Łany **PL** 66 Gd30
Lanzo Torinese **I** 83 Ec37
Laon **F** 62 Dd30
La Paca **E** 107 Ca45
La Pacaudière **F** 70 Dd35
Lapalisse **F** 70 Dd35
La Palma del Condado **E** 105 Ad44
Lapinlahti **FIN** 35 Hd12
La Plagne **F** 71 Eb36
La Pobla de Segur **E** 81 Da40
La Pola de Gordón **E** 79 Bc37
La Portera **E** 93 Cb43
Lapoş **RO** 88 Jc36
Lapovo **SRB** 87 Hc38
Lappajärvi **FIN** 40 Hb13
Läppe **S** 44 Gb18
Lappeenranta **FIN** 41 Ja15
Lappersdorf **D** 64 Fc32
Lappfjärd **FIN** 40 Ha14
Lappi **FIN** 40 Ha16
Lappohja **FIN** 46 Hb17

Lappoluobbal **N** 26 Ha05
Lappträsk **FIN** 41 Hd16
Lappträsk **S** 34 Hb09
Lappvattnet **S** 34 Gd11
Lappvik **FIN** 46 Hb17
Lapseki **TR** 103 Jd42
Laptevo **RUS** 53 Jb21
Lapua **FIN** 40 Hb13
La Puebla de Cazalla **E** 105 Ba44
La Puebla del Río **E** 105 Ba44
La Puebla de Montalbán **E** 91 Bc41
La Puebla de Valverde **E** 93 Cb42
Lăpuşna **MD** 77 Jd34
Lăpuşna **RO** 76 Jb34
Lapväärtti **FIN** 40 Ha14
Łapy **PL** 59 Hc26
L'Aquila **I** 98 Fd41
Laracha **E** 78 Ba36
Lara de los Infantes **E** 79 Ca39
Laragh **IRL** 19 Cb24
Laragne-Montéglin **F** 82 Ea38
L'Arbresle **F** 70 Ea36
Lärbro **S** 45 Gd20
Larderello **I** 84 Fb40
Laredo **E** 79 Ca37
La Réole **F** 68 Cd36
Largentière **F** 82 Dd37
L'Argentière-la Bessée **F** 83 Eb37
Largs **GB** 20 Cd21
Lárimna **GR** 111 Ja45
Larino **I** 99 Ga42
Lárissa **GR** 101 Hd44
Larkollen **N** 43 Fc18
Larmor-Plage **F** 60 Cb32
Larnaka **CY** 128 Gc19
Larne **GB** 20 Cc22
La Robla **E** 79 Bc37
La Roca de la Sierra **E** 91 Ba42
La Rochebeaucourt-et-Argentine **F** 69 Da35
La-Roche-Bernard **F** 60 Cc32
La Roche-Chalais **F** 69 Da36
La Roche-en-Ardenne **B** 63 Eb30
La Rochefoucauld **F** 69 Da35
La Rochelle **F** 68 Cd34
La Roche-Posay **F** 69 Db34
La Roche-sur-Foron **F** 71 Eb35
La Roche-sur-Yon **F** 68 Cd33
La Roda **E** 92 Ca43
La Roda de Andalucía **E** 105 Bb45
Larón **E** 78 Bb37
Laroquebrou **F** 69 Db36

Larseng **N** 26 Gc05
Laruns **F** 80 Cd38
Larvik **N** 43 Fb18
Laržanka **UA** 89 Ka36
La Salvetat-sur-Agout **F** 81 Db38
Las Cabezas de San Juan **E** 105 Ba44
la Sénia **E** 93 Cd41
La Seu d'Urgell **E** 81 Da40
La Seyne-sur-Mer **F** 82 Ea39
Łasin **PL** 58 Gd26
Łask **PL** 58 Gd28
Łaskarzew **PL** 59 Hb28
Laskowice **PL** 58 Gd26
Las Navas de la Concepción **E** 105 Ba43
Las Negras **E** 106 Bd46
Las Nieves **E** 105 Ba44
La Solana **E** 92 Bd43
La Souterraine **F** 69 Db35
Lasovo **SRB** 87 Hd39
Las Pedroñeras **E** 92 Ca42
La Spezia **I** 84 Fa38
Låstad **S** 44 Ga19
Lastovo **HR** 86 Gd40
La Suze-sur-Sarthe **F** 61 Da32
Las Ventas con Peña Aguilera **E** 91 Bc42
Las Viñas **E** 106 Bd45
Laterza **I** 99 Gc43
Lathen **D** 55 Ed27
Latheron **GB** 17 Db18
Latina **I** 98 Fc42
Latisana **I** 73 Fd36
Látky **SK** 67 Ha32
La Toba **E** 92 Ca42
La Tour du-Pin **F** 70 Ea36
La Tranche-sur-Mer **F** 68 Cd34
La Tremblade **F** 68 Cd35
La Trimouille **F** 69 Db34
La Trinité-Porhoët **F** 60 Cc31
Latronico **I** 99 Gb44
Lauchhammer **D** 65 Fd29
Lauda-Königshofen **D** 64 Fa31
Lauder **GB** 21 Da21
Laudio **E** 79 Ca38
Ļaudona **LV** 53 Ja21
Lauenburg **D** 56 Fb26
Lauf **D** 64 Fb31
Laufen **D** 73 Fd33
Lauffen (Neckar) **D** 64 Fa32
Laugar **IS** 15 Cb06
Laugarbakki **IS** 14 Bd05
Laugarvatn **IS** 14 Bc07
Laujar de Andarax **E** 106 Bd45
Laukaa **FIN** 40 Hc14
Lauker **S** 34 Gd10
Laukkala **FIN** 35 Hd12
Laukuva **LT** 52 Hb23
Laukvik **N** 26 Gc05

Laukvika **N** 28 Ga07
Launceston **GB** 23 Cc28
La Unión **E** 107 Cb45
Laupheim **D** 72 Fa33
Laurencekirk **GB** 17 Db20
Lauria **I** 99 Gb44
Lausanne **CH** 71 Eb35
Lautaporras **FIN** 40 Hc16
Lauterbach (Hessen) **D** 64 Fa30
Lauterecken **D** 63 Ed31
Lauwersoog **NL** 55 Ec26
Lauzerte **F** 81 Da37
Lavadáki **GR** 110 Hd47
Laval **F** 61 Da32
la Vall d'Uixó **E** 93 Cc42
Lavara **GR** 103 Jd41
Lavardac **F** 80 Cd37
Lavaur **F** 81 Db38
Lávdas **GR** 101 Hc44
Lavelanet **F** 81 Db39
Lavello **I** 99 Gb42
Låveng **N** 32 Fd09
Laveno **I** 71 Ed36
Lavia **FIN** 40 Hb15
La Vieille-Lyre **F** 61 Db31
Lavik **N** 36 Ed15
La Vila Joiosa (Villajoyosa) **E** 94 Cc44
La Voulte-sur-Rhône **F** 82 Ea37
Lavre **P** 90 Ac41
Lavrio **GR** 112 Jb46
Lavrovo **RUS** 117 Ed08
Lavry **RUS** 47 Ja20
Laxå **S** 44 Ga19
Laxbäcken **S** 33 Gb11
Laxford Bridge **GB** 17 Da18
Laž **RUS** 119 Fd08
Lazarevac **SRB** 87 Hb38
Lazarevskoe **RUS** 127 Fc17
Lazaropore **MK** 101 Hc42
Lazdijai **LT** 59 Hc25
Lazdijaī **LT** 59 Hc25
Lazuri de Beiuş **RO** 75 Hd35
Łeba **PL** 51 Gc24
Lebach **D** 63 Ec31
Lebane **SRB** 87 Hc40
Le Beausset **F** 82 Ea39
Lebedjan **RUS** 122 Fa12
Lebedyn **UA** 121 Ed14
Le Blanc **F** 69 Db34
Lębork **PL** 58 Gc25
Le Bourg-d'Oisans **F** 83 Eb37
Lebrija **E** 105 Ba44
Le Buisson-de-Cadouin **F** 69 Da36
Le Cateau-Cambrésis **F** 62 Dd30
Le Catelet **F** 62 Dd30
Le Caylar **F** 81 Dc38
Lecce **I** 100 Gd43
Lecco **I** 72 Fa36
Lécera **E** 93 Cc41

Lech **A** 72 Fa34
L'Echalp **F** 83 Eb37
Le Château-d'Oléron **F** 68 Cd34
Le Châtelet **F** 69 Dc34
Le Chesne **F** 62 Ea31
Le Cheylard **F** 82 Dd37
Lechinţa **RO** 76 Ja34
Leči **LV** 52 Hb21
Lecina **E** 80 Cd39
Leciñena **E** 80 Cc40
Leck **D** 48 Fa24
Le Conquet **F** 60 Cb31
Le Creusot **F** 70 Ea34
Le Croisic **F** 60 Cc32
Le Crotoy **F** 62 Dc29
Lectoure **F** 81 Da37
Łęczna **PL** 67 Hc29
Łęczyca **PL** 57 Ga26
Łęczyca **PL** 58 Gd28
Ledesma **E** 78 Bb39
Ledmore **GB** 17 Da18
Le Donjon **F** 70 Dd35
Le Dorat **F** 69 Db34
Lędyczek **PL** 58 Gc26
Leeds **GB** 21 Db24
Leek **GB** 24 Da25
Leek **NL** 55 Ec26
Leenane **IRL** 18 Bd23
Leer **D** 55 Ed26
Leerdam **NL** 55 Eb28
Leesi **EST** 47 Hd17
Leeuwarden **NL** 55 Ec26
Le Faou **F** 60 Cb31
Le Faouët **F** 60 Cb31
Lefkáda **GR** 110 Hc45
Lefkími **GR** 100 Hb44
Lefkógia **GR** 114 Jc49
Lefkónas **GR** 101 Ja42
Lefkoniko **CY** 128 Gc19
Lefkosia **CY** 128 Gb19
Leganés **E** 92 Bd41
Legden **D** 55 Ed28
Legé **F** 68 Cd33
Legionowo **PL** 59 Hb27
Legkovo **RUS** 117 Ed09
Legnago **I** 84 Fb37
Legnano **I** 71 Ed36
Legnica **PL** 65 Gb29
Legnickie Pole **PL** 65 Gb29
Legrad **HR** 74 Gc36
Le Grand-Lucé **F** 61 Db32
Le Grand-Quevilly **F** 61 Db30
Legutiano **E** 80 Cb38
Le Havre **F** 61 Db30
Lehliu-Gară **RO** 89 Jd37
Lehnin **D** 57 Fd28
Lehre **D** 56 Fb27
Lehrte **D** 56 Fb27
Lehtimäki **FIN** 40 Hb13
Leibnitz **A** 73 Gb35
Leicester **GB** 25 Db26
Leichlingen **D** 63 Ec29
Leiden **NL** 55 Eb27
Leie **EST** 47 Hd19

Leikanger **N** 36 Ed14
Leikanger **N** 36 Fa15
Leinefelde **D** 64 Fb29
Leipalingis **LT** 59 Hd25
Leipalingis **LT** 59 Hd25
Leipojärvi **S** 29 Gd08
Leipzig **D** 64 Fc29
Leira **N** 37 Fb16
Leira **N** 37 Fb13
Leirbotn **N** 26 Ha04
Leiria **P** 90 Ac40
Leirmoen **N** 28 Ga08
Leirpollskogen **N** 27 Hc03
Leirvåg **N** 36 Ec16
Leirvik **N** 26 Gd04
Leirvik **N** 42 Ed17
Leirvika **N** 33 Ga09
Leisi **EST** 46 Hb19
Leivonmäki **FIN** 41 Hd14
Leiza **E** 80 Cb38
Lejkowo **PL** 57 Gb25
Lekeitio **E** 80 Cb37
Lekenik **HR** 85 Gb37
Leknes **N** 28 Ga07
Leknes **N** 36 Fa14
Łęknica **PL** 65 Ga29
Leksand **S** 38 Ga16
Leksvik **N** 32 Fc12
Le Lavandou **F** 83 Eb39
Le Lion-d'Angers **F** 61 Da32
Lelis **PL** 59 Hb26
Le Locle **CH** 71 Eb34
Le Loroux-Bottereau **F** 68 Cd33
Le Lude **F** 61 Da32
Lelystad **NL** 55 Eb27
Le Malzieu-Ville **F** 81 Dc37
Le Mans **F** 61 Da32
Lembeye **F** 80 Cd38
Le Mêle-sur-Sarthe **F** 61 Db31
Le Merlerault **F** 61 Db31
Lemesos **CY** 128 Gb19
Lemförde **D** 55 Ed27
Lemgo **D** 56 Fa28
Lemland **FIN** 45 Gd17
Lemmenjoki **FIN** 27 Hb05
Lemmer **NL** 55 Ec26
Le Mont-Dore **F** 69 Dc36
Lempäälä **FIN** 40 Hb15
Le Muy **F** 83 Eb39
Lemvig **DK** 48 Fa22
Lena **N** 37 Fc16
Léndas **GR** 115 Jd50
Lendava **SLO** 74 Gc35
Le Neubourg **F** 61 Db31
Lengerich **D** 55 Ed27
Lenggries **D** 72 Fc34
Lengyeltóti **H** 74 Gd35
Lenhovda **S** 50 Gb21
Lenina **BY** 121 Ec13
Lenine **UA** 126 Fb17
Leninogorsk **RUS** 119 Ga09
Leninsk **RUS** 123 Ga13

Leninskij **RUS** 118 Fa11
Lenkivci **UA** 121 Eb15
Lennestadt **D** 63 Ed29
Lens **F** 62 Dd29
Lent'evo **RUS** 117 Ed08
Lenti **H** 74 Gc35
Lentiira **FIN** 35 Ja11
Lentini **I** 109 Ga47
Lentvaris **LT** 53 Hd24
Lenzen **D** 56 Fc26
Leoben **A** 73 Ga34
Leominster **GB** 24 Cd26
León **E** 79 Bc38
Leonding **A** 73 Ga33
Leonessa **I** 84 Fc40
Leonforte **I** 109 Ga47
Leonídio **GR** 111 Ja47
Leopoldsburg **B** 63 Eb29
Leorda **RO** 76 Jc33
Leova **MD** 77 Jd34
Le Palais **F** 60 Cc32
Lepassaare **EST** 47 Ja19
Lepe **E** 105 Ad44
Lepel' **BY** 121 Eb12
Lepoglava **HR** 73 Gb36
Le Pont-de-Beauvoisin **F** 70 Ea36
Le Porge **F** 68 Cd36
Le Portel **F** 62 Dc29
Leppävesi **FIN** 40 Hc14
Leppävirta **FIN** 41 Hd13
Lepşa **RO** 76 Jc35
Le Puy-en-Velay **F** 70 Dd36
Le Quesnoy **F** 62 Ea30
Lera **MK** 101 Hc42
Lerbäck **S** 44 Ga19
Lercara Friddi **I** 108 Fd47
Lerici **I** 84 Fa38
Lerín **E** 80 Cb39
Lerma **E** 79 Bd39
Lermontovo **RUS** 119 Fc11
Le Rozier-Peyreleau **F** 81 Dc37
Lerum **S** 43 Fd20
Lervik **N** 43 Fc18
Les **E** 81 Da39
Leş **RO** 75 Hc34
Les Aix-d'Angillon **F** 69 Dc33
Lešak **RKS** 87 Hb39
Les Andelys **F** 62 Dc31
Lešani **MK** 101 Hc42
Les Arcs **F** 71 Eb36
Le Sauze **F** 83 Eb38
les Borges Blanques **E** 80 Cd40
l'Escala **E** 81 Dc40
L'Escarène **F** 83 Ec39
Lescun **F** 80 Cc38
Les Deux-Alpes **F** 83 Eb37
Les Echelles **F** 70 Ea36
Les Essarts **F** 68 Cd33
Les Eyzies-de-Tayac **F** 69 Da36
Les Herbiers **F** 68 Cd33
Lesjöfors **S** 44 Ga17

Lesko **PL** 67 Hc31
Leskovac **SRB** 87 Hd40
Leskovik **AL** 101 Hc43
Lesneven **F** 60 Cb30
Lesnoe **RUS** 52 Ha24
Lesnoe **RUS** 117 Ec09
Lesnoj **RUS** 52 Ha24
Lesogorskij **RUS** 41 Ja15
Lesparre-Médoc **F** 68 Cd35
L'Esperou **F** 81 Dc38
Lespezi **RO** 76 Jc33
Les Ponts-de-Cé **F** 69 Da33
Les Riceys **F** 70 Ea33
Les Sables-d'Olonne **F** 68 Cc34
Lessay **F** 61 Cd30
Lessebo **S** 50 Gb22
Lessini **GR** 110 Hc46
Lestijärvi **FIN** 35 Hc12
Les Ulis **F** 62 Dc31
Leszno **PL** 58 Gc28
Létavértes **H** 75 Hc34
Letca **RO** 75 Hd34
Letchworth Garden City **GB** 25 Db27
Letea **RO** 89 Kb36
Le Teil **F** 82 Dd37
Letenye **H** 74 Gc35
Le Thillot **F** 71 Ec33
Letku **FIN** 40 Hb16
Le Touquet-Paris-Plage **F** 62 Dc29
Le Tréport **F** 62 Dc30
Letterfrack **IRL** 18 Bd23
Letterkenny **IRL** 19 Cb21
Letyčiv **UA** 121 Eb15
Leucate-Plage **F** 81 Dc39
Leukerbad **CH** 71 Ec35
Leutkirch **D** 72 Fa33
Leutkirch **D** 72 Fa33
Leuven **B** 63 Eb29
Levang **N** 43 Fb19
Levanger **N** 32 Fc12
Levanto **I** 84 Fa38
Leven **GB** 21 Dc24
Le Verdon-sur-Mer **F** 68 Cd35
Leverkusen **D** 63 Ec29
Levet **F** 69 Dc34
Levice **SK** 74 Gd33
Levico Terme **I** 72 Fb36
Levídi **GR** 111 Ja46
Levie **F** 96 Ed41
Levier **F** 71 Eb34
Le Vigan **F** 81 Dc38
Levoča **SK** 67 Hb32
Levroux **F** 69 Db34
Levski **BG** 88 Jb39
Lewes **GB** 25 Db28
Leyburn **GB** 21 Db23
Leżajsk **PL** 67 Hc30
Lezay **F** 69 Da34
Lezhë **AL** 100 Hb41
Lézignan-Corbières **F** 81 Db39
Lëzna **BY** 117 Eb11

Leźno **PL** 58 Gd25
Lezoux **F** 70 Dd35
L'gov **RUS** 121 Ed13
L'Hospitalet **E** 95 Da41
L'Hospitalet **F** 81 Da39
Lianokládi **GR** 110 Hd45
Liatorp **S** 50 Ga22
Liberec **CZ** 65 Ga30
Libiąż **PL** 67 Ha30
Libina **CZ** 66 Gc31
Libohovë **AL** 100 Hb44
Libourne **F** 68 Cd36
Libramont-Chevigny **B** 63 Eb30
Licata **I** 108 Fd48
Lich **D** 64 Fa30
Lichtenau **D** 56 Fa28
Lichtenfels **D** 64 Fb30
Lichtenvoorde **NL** 55 Ec28
Lički Osik **HR** 85 Gb38
Ličko Lešće **HR** 85 Gb38
Lida **BY** 120 Ea12
Liden **S** 38 Gb14
Lidhult **S** 49 Fd22
Lidingö **S** 45 Gc18
Lidköping **S** 44 Fd19
Lido di Jesolo **I** 84 Fc37
Lido di Metaponto **I** 99 Gc43
Lidoríki **GR** 110 Hd45
Lidsjöberg **S** 33 Ga12
Lidzbark **PL** 58 Ha26
Lidzbark Warmiński **PL** 58 Ha25
Liebenwalde **D** 57 Fd27
Lieberose **D** 57 Ga28
Liège **B** 63 Eb29
Lieksa **FIN** 35 Ja12
Lielauce **LV** 52 Hc22
Lielvärde **LV** 53 Hd21
Lienz **A** 72 Fc35
Liepāja **LV** 52 Ha22
Liepene **LV** 46 Hb20
Liepna **LV** 47 Ja20
Lier **B** 62 Ea29
Lierbyen **N** 43 Fb17
Liestal **CH** 71 Ec34
Lieto **FIN** 40 Hb16
Lievestuore **FIN** 41 Hd14
Liévin **F** 62 Dd29
Liezen **A** 73 Ga34
Liffol-le-Grand **F** 63 Eb32
Lifford **IRL** 19 Cb22
Lignano Sabbiadoro **I** 73 Fd36
Lignières **F** 69 Dc34
Ligny-en-Barrois **F** 63 Eb32
Ligny-le-Châtel **F** 70 Dd33
Ligueil **F** 69 Db33
Lihás **GR** 111 Ja45
Lihoslavl' **RUS** 117 Ed10
Lihovskoj **RUS** 123 Fc15
Lihula **EST** 46 Hc19
Liinahamari **RUS** 27 Hd04
Likenäs **S** 38 Fd16
Liknes **N** 42 Ed19

Likovskoe **RUS** 47 Jb18
Lilienfeld **A** 73 Gb33
Lilienthal **D** 56 Fa26
Liljendal **FIN** 41 Hd16
Lilla Edet **S** 43 Fd20
Lillärdal **S** 38 Ga15
Lille **F** 62 Dd29
Lillebonne **F** 61 Db30
Lillehammer **N** 37 Fc16
Lillers **F** 62 Dd29
Lillesand **N** 42 Fa19
Lillestrøm **N** 43 Fc17
Lilli **EST** 47 Hd19
Lillkågeträsk **S** 34 Gd11
Lillo **E** 92 Bd42
Lillselet **S** 30 Ha08
Lima **S** 38 Fd16
Limanáki **GR** 110 Hd46
Limanowa **PL** 67 Hb31
Limavady **GB** 20 Cb21
Limbaži **LV** 47 Hd20
Limburg **D** 63 Ed30
Liménas Géraka **GR** 111 Ja47
Liménas Hersoníssou **GR** 115 Jd49
Limerick **IRL** 18 Bd24
Liminka **FIN** 35 Hc10
Limmared **S** 49 Fd21
Límnes **GR** 111 Ja46
Límni **GR** 111 Ja45
Límni Vouliagménis **GR** 111 Ja46
Limoges **F** 69 Db35
Limone Piemonte **I** 83 Ec38
Limonlu **TR** 128 Gc17
Limoux **F** 81 Db39
Lin **AL** 101 Hc42
Linares **E** 106 Bc44
Linariá **GR** 112 Jc45
Lincoln **GB** 25 Db25
Lind **DK** 48 Fa22
Lindås **N** 36 Ed16
Lindau **D** 72 Fa34
Linde **LV** 53 Hd21
Lindelse **DK** 49 Fb24
Linden **D** 64 Fa30
Lindesberg **S** 44 Ga18
Lindesnes **N** 42 Ed20
Lindome **S** 49 Fc21
Lindos **GR** 115 Kc48
Lindoso **P** 78 Ad38
Lindow **D** 57 Fd27
Lindsdal **S** 50 Gb22
Linevo **RUS** 123 Fd12
Lingbo **S** 38 Gb16
Linge **N** 36 Fa14
Lingen (Ems) **D** 55 Ed27
Linghem **S** 44 Gb19
Linguaglossa **I** 109 Ga47
Linia **PL** 58 Gc25
Linköping **S** 44 Gb19
Linkuva **LT** 52 Hc22
Linlithgow **GB** 21 Da21
Linsell **S** 38 Ga14
Linz **A** 73 Ga33

Linz **D** 63 Ec30
Lipany **SK** 67 Hb32
Lipari **I** 109 Ga46
Lipcani **MD** 76 Jc32
Lipeck **RUS** 122 Fb12
Liperi **FIN** 41 Ja13
Lipiany **PL** 57 Ga27
Lipicy-Zybino **RUS** 122 Fa12
Lipik **HR** 86 Gc37
Lipka **PL** 58 Gc26
Lipki **RUS** 118 Fa11
Lipljan **RKS** 87 Hc40
Lipniak **PL** 59 Hc25
Lipnica **PL** 58 Gc25
Lipnica Murowana **PL** 67 Hb31
Lipník nad Bečvou **CZ** 66 Gc31
Lipno **PL** 58 Gd27
Lipolist **SRB** 86 Ha38
Lipova **RO** 75 Hc36
Lipoven'ke **MD** 77 Kb32
Lipovljani **HR** 86 Gc37
Lippstadt **D** 55 Ed28
Lipsk **PL** 59 Hc25
Lipsko **PL** 67 Hb29
Liptovský Hrádok **SK** 67 Ha32
Lisa Gora **MD** 77 Kb32
Lisboa **P** 90 Ab41
Lisburn **GB** 20 Cc22
Lisdoonvarna **IRL** 18 Bd23
Lisieux **F** 61 Db31
Liskeard **GB** 23 Cc28
Liski **RUS** 122 Fb13
L'Isle-Adam **F** 62 Dc31
L'Isle-en-Dodon **F** 81 Da38
L'Isle-Jourdain **F** 69 Da34
L'Isle-Jourdain **F** 81 Da38
L'Isle-sur-la-Sorgue **F** 82 Ea38
L'Isle-sur-le-Doubs **F** 71 Eb34
Lisma **FIN** 30 Hb06
Lismore **IRL** 22 Ca25
Lisnaskea **GB** 20 Cb22
Lišov **CZ** 65 Ga32
List **D** 48 Fa24
Listowel **IRL** 18 Bd24
Lit **S** 38 Ga13
Liteni **RO** 76 Jc33
Litl **GR** 101 Ja42
Litija **SLO** 73 Ga36
Litóhoro **GR** 101 Hd43
Litoměřice **CZ** 65 Ga30
Litomyšl **CZ** 65 Gb31
Litovel **CZ** 66 Gc31
Litvínov **CZ** 65 Fd30
Livada **RO** 75 Hd33
Livaderó **GR** 101 Hd43
Livaderó **GR** 102 Jb42
Livádi **GR** 111 Jc47
Livadiá **GR** 111 Ja45
Livadohóri **GR** 102 Jc43
Līvāni **LV** 53 Ja22
Livari **MNE** 100 Ha41

Livarot **F** 61 Db31
Livera **CY** 128 Gb18
Liverpool **GB** 21 Da24
Livezi **RO** 76 Jc35
Livigno **I** 72 Fa35
Livingston **GB** 21 Da21
Livizile **RO** 76 Ja35
Livno **BIH** 86 Gc39
Livny **RUS** 122 Fa12
Livo **FIN** 35 Hc09
Livorno **I** 84 Fa39
Livron-sur-Drôme **F** 82 Ea37
Liw **PL** 59 Hb27
Lixoúri **GR** 110 Hc46
Līzespasts **LV** 47 Ja20
Līzums **LV** 47 Ja20
Ljachavičy **BY** 120 Ea13
Ljady **RUS** 47 Jb18
Ljaplëvka **BY** 59 Hd28
Ljaskelja **RUS** 41 Jb14
Ljig **SRB** 87 Hb38
Ljørndalen **N** 37 Fd15
Ljuban' **BY** 121 Eb13
Ljuban' **RUS** 117 Eb08
Ljubar **UA** 121 Eb15
Ljubašivka **MD** 77 Kb32
Ljubešiv **UA** 120 Ea14
Ljubija **BIH** 86 Gc37
Ljubim **RUS** 118 Fa08
Ljubinje **BIH** 86 Gd40
Ljubiš **SRB** 87 Hb39
Ljubljana **SLO** 73 Ga36
Ljuboml' **UA** 67 Hd29
Ljubovija **SRB** 86 Ha38
Ljubuški **BIH** 86 Gd40
Ljubymivka **UA** 122 Fb15
Ljubytino **RUS** 117 Ec09
Ljudinovo **RUS** 121 Ed12
Ljugarn **S** 51 Gd21
Ljung **S** 44 Fd20
Ljunga **S** 44 Gb19
Ljungaverk **S** 38 Gb14
Ljungby **S** 50 Ga22
Ljungbyhed **S** 49 Fd23
Ljungbyholm **S** 50 Gb22
Ljungdalen **S** 38 Fd13
Ljunghusen **S** 49 Fd23
Ljungsbro **S** 44 Gb19
Ljungskile **S** 43 Fc20
Ljusdal **S** 38 Gb15
Ljusfallshammar **S** 44 Gb19
Ljustorp **S** 39 Gc14
Ljutomer **SLO** 73 Gb35
Llagostera **E** 81 Db40
Llanberis **GB** 24 Cd25
Llandeilo **GB** 23 Cc26
Llandovery **GB** 24 Cd26
Llandrindod-Wells **GB** 24 Cd26
Llandudno **GB** 20 Cd24
Llanelli **GB** 23 Cc26
Llanes **E** 79 Bd37
Llangollen **GB** 24 Cd25
Llangurig **GB** 24 Cd26
Llanidloes **GB** 24 Cd26
Llanrwst **GB** 24 Cd25

Llanwddyn **GB** 24 Cd25
Llanwrtyd Wells **GB** 24 Cd26
Lleida **E** 80 Cd40
Llerena **E** 105 Ba43
Llíria **E** 93 Cc43
Llivynci **UA** 76 Jc32
L'Ile-Rousse **F** 96 Ed40
Llodio **E** 79 Ca38
Lloret de Mar **E** 95 Db41
Llucena **E** 93 Cc42
Llucmajor **E** 95 Db43
Lnáře **CZ** 65 Fd31
Loano **I** 83 Ec38
Löbau **D** 65 Ga29
Lobcovo **RUS** 118 Fa09
Lobenstein **D** 64 Fc30
Löberöd **S** 49 Fd23
Łobez **PL** 57 Gb26
Lobonäs **S** 38 Gb15
Loburg **D** 56 Fc28
Łobżenica **PL** 58 Gc26
Locarno **CH** 71 Ed36
Lochaline **GB** 16 Cd20
Lochboisdale **GB** 16 Cc19
Lochearnhead **GB** 17 Da20
Lochem **NL** 55 Ec27
Loches **F** 69 Db33
Lochgilphead **GB** 16 Cd20
Lochinver **GB** 17 Da18
Lochmaddy **GB** 16 Cc18
Łochów **PL** 59 Hb27
Lochranza **GB** 20 Cd21
Lochvycja **UA** 121 Ed14
Lockerbie **GB** 21 Da22
Löcknitz **D** 57 Ga26
Locminé **F** 60 Cc32
Locri **I** 109 Gc46
Locronan **F** 60 Cb31
Loctudy **F** 60 Cb31
Löderup **S** 50 Ga23
Lodève **F** 81 Dc38
Lodi **I** 84 Fa37
Løding **N** 28 Ga08
Lødingen **N** 28 Gb06
Lodosa **E** 80 Cb39
Lödöse **S** 43 Fc20
Łódź **PL** 58 Ha28
Løfallstrand **N** 42 Ed17
Lofer **A** 72 Fc34
Lofsdalen **S** 38 Fd14
Loftahammar **S** 44 Gb20
Lofthus **N** 42 Ed17
Log **RUS** 123 Fd13
Logatec **SLO** 73 Ga36
Lögdeå **S** 34 Gd12
Lógos **GR** 111 Ja45
Logroño **E** 80 Cb39
Logrosán **E** 91 Bb42
Løgstør **DK** 49 Fb21
Løgumkloster **DK** 48 Fa24
Lohals **DK** 49 Fc24
Lohikoski **FIN** 41 Ja14
Lohiniva **FIN** 30 Hb07
Lohja **FIN** 46 Hc17
Lohmar **D** 63 Ec29
Lohne **D** 55 Ed27

Lohr **D** 64 Fa31
Lohtaja **FIN** 34 Hb12
Loimaa **FIN** 40 Hb16
Loitz **D** 57 Fd25
Loja **E** 105 Bb45
Løken **N** 43 Fc18
Lokeren **B** 62 Ea29
Lokka **FIN** 31 Hc06
Løkken **N** 37 Fb13
Loknja **RUS** 117 Eb10
Lőkösháza **H** 75 Hb35
Lokot' **RUS** 121 Ed13
Loksa **EST** 47 Hd17
Lollar **D** 64 Fa30
Lom **BG** 88 Ja38
Lom **N** 37 Fb15
Lombez **F** 81 Da38
Lomen **N** 37 Fb16
Łomianki **PL** 59 Hb27
Lomma **S** 49 Fd23
Lommel **B** 55 Eb28
Lom nad Rimavicou **SK** 67 Ha32
Lomonosov **RUS** 41 Jb16
Łomża **PL** 59 Hb26
London **GB** 25 Db27
Londonderry **GB** 20 Cb21
Lonevåg **N** 36 Ed16
Longarone **I** 72 Fc36
Longeau **F** 70 Ea33
Longford **IRL** 18 Ca23
Longobucco **I** 109 Gc45
Long Preston **GB** 21 Da24
Longtown **GB** 21 Da22
Longué-Jumelles **F** 69 Da33
Longuyon **F** 63 Eb31
Longwy **F** 63 Eb31
Löningen **D** 55 Ed27
Łoniów **PL** 67 Hb30
Lönsboda **S** 50 Ga22
Lons-le-Saunier **F** 70 Ea35
Lopar **HR** 85 Ga38
Lopătari **RO** 88 Jc36
Lopatino **RUS** 119 Fd11
Lopatovo **RUS** 47 Jb19
Loppa **N** 26 Gd04
Loppi **FIN** 40 Hc16
Lopuhinka **RUS** 47 Jb17
Lora del Río **E** 105 Ba44
Lorca **E** 107 Ca45
Lorch **D** 63 Ed30
Loreto **I** 85 Fd39
Lorgues **F** 83 Eb39
Lorient **F** 60 Cb32
Łórinci **H** 74 Ha34
Loriol-sur-Drôme **F** 82 Ea37
Lormes **F** 70 Dd33
Lörrach **D** 71 Ec34
Lorris **F** 69 Dc33
Los **S** 38 Ga15
Los Arcos **E** 80 Cb38
Los Barrios **E** 105 Ba46
Los Corrales de Buelna **E** 79 Ca37
Los Cortijos de Arriba **E** 91 Bc42

Losheim **D** 63 Ec31
Łosice **PL** 59 Hc27
Los Navalmorales **E** 91 Bc41
Løsning **DK** 49 Fb23
Los Palacios y Villafranca **E** 105 Ba44
Lossiemouth **GB** 17 Db19
Lostwithiel **GB** 23 Cb28
Los Yébenes **E** 92 Bd42
Løten **N** 37 Fc16
Lotošino **RUS** 117 Ed10
Lotta **RUS** 27 Hc05
Lottigna **CH** 71 Ed35
Löttorp **S** 51 Gc21
Lotyń **PL** 58 Gc26
Loudéac **F** 60 Cc31
Loudun **F** 69 Da33
Loué **F** 61 Da32
Loue **FIN** 34 Hb09
Loughborough **GB** 25 Db26
Loughrea **IRL** 18 Ca23
Louhans **F** 70 Ea35
Louisburgh **IRL** 18 Bd22
Loukíssia **GR** 112 Jd45
Loulé **P** 104 Ac44
Louny **CZ** 65 Fd30
Lourdes **F** 80 Cd38
Loures **P** 90 Ab41
Lourinhã **P** 90 Ab41
Louth **GB** 25 Dc25
Loutrá **GR** 112 Jc46
Loutrá Edipsoú **GR** 111 Ja45
Loutrá Eleftherón **GR** 102 Jb42
Loutráki **GR** 110 Hc45
Loutráki **GR** 111 Ja46
Loutropigí **GR** 110 Hd45
Loutros **GR** 103 Jd42
Louverné **F** 61 Da32
Louvie-Juzon **F** 80 Cd38
Louviers **F** 61 Db31
Louvigné-du-Désert **F** 61 Cd31
Lövånger **S** 34 Ha11
Lövberga **S** 33 Gb12
Loveč **BG** 88 Jb39
Lovere **I** 72 Fa36
Loviisa **FIN** 41 Hd16
Lovisa **FIN** 41 Hd16
Lovište **HR** 86 Gc40
Lövnäs **S** 38 Fd15
Lövnäsvallen **S** 38 Fd15
Lövő **H** 74 Gc34
Lovosice **CZ** 65 Ga30
Lovran **HR** 85 Ga37
Lovreć **HR** 86 Gc39
Lovrin **RO** 75 Hb36
Lövstabruk **S** 45 Gc17
Löwenberg **D** 57 Fd27
Lowestoft **GB** 25 Dd26
Łowicz **PL** 58 Ha28
Loxstedt **D** 56 Fa26
Lož **SLO** 73 Ga36
Loznica **BG** 89 Jd39
Loznica **SRB** 86 Ha38

Lozova **UA** 122 Fa15
Lozoyuela **E** 92 Bd40
Luanco **E** 79 Bc36
Luarca **E** 78 Bb36
Lubaczów **PL** 67 Hd30
Lubań **PL** 65 Gb29
Lubāna **LV** 53 Ja21
Lubartów **PL** 59 Hc29
Lubawa **PL** 58 Ha26
Lübbecke **D** 56 Fa27
Lübben (Spreewald) **D** 57 Ga28
Lübbenau (Spreewald) **D** 57 Ga28
Lübeck **D** 56 Fb25
Lubersac **F** 69 Db36
Lubiąż **PL** 65 Gb29
Lubień Kujawski **PL** 58 Gd27
Lubin **PL** 65 Gb29
Lubjaniki **RUS** 118 Fb10
Lublin **PL** 67 Hc29
Lubliniec **PL** 66 Gd30
Lubniewice **PL** 57 Gb27
Lubny **UA** 121 Ed14
Lubomino **PL** 58 Ha25
Luboń **PL** 58 Gc28
L'ubotín **SK** 67 Hb31
Lubsko **PL** 57 Ga28
Lubuczewo **PL** 58 Gc25
Lubycza Królewska **PL** 67 Hd30
Lübz **D** 56 Fc26
Luca Cernii de Jos **RO** 75 Hd36
Lucca **I** 84 Fa39
Lucena **E** 105 Bb44
Luc-en-Diois **F** 82 Ea37
Lučenec **SK** 74 Ha33
Lucera **I** 99 Gb42
Lüchow **D** 56 Fc27
Lučica **SRB** 87 Hc38
Luc'k **UA** 120 Ea15
Luckau **D** 57 Fd28
Luckenwalde **D** 57 Fd28
Luçon **F** 68 Cd34
Luc-sur-Mer **F** 61 Da30
Ludbreg **HR** 74 Gc36
Lüdenscheid **D** 63 Ed29
Lüdinghausen **D** 55 Ed28
Ludlow **GB** 24 Cd26
Ludomy **PL** 58 Gc27
Luduş **RO** 76 Ja35
Ludvika **S** 44 Ga17
Ludwigsburg **D** 64 Fa32
Ludwigsfelde **D** 57 Fd28
Ludwigshafen **D** 63 Ed31
Ludwigslust **D** 56 Fc26
Ludwigstadt **D** 64 Fc30
Ludza **LV** 53 Jb21
Lug **HR** 74 Ha36
Lugano **CH** 71 Ed36
Lugo **E** 78 Ba36
Lugo **I** 84 Fc38
Lugoj **RO** 75 Hc36
Luh **RUS** 118 Fb09

Luhamaa – Malmbäck

Luhamaa **EST** 47 Ja20
Luhanka **FIN** 40 Hc14
Luhans'k **UA** 122 Fb14
Luhovicy **RUS** 118 Fa10
Luidja **EST** 46 Hb18
Luikonlahti **FIN** 41 Ja13
Luino **I** 71 Ed36
Luizi Călugăra **RO** 76 Jc34
Luka **SRB** 87 Hd38
Lukavac **BIH** 86 Gd38
Lukiv **UA** 67 Hd29
Lukojanov **RUS** 119 Fc10
Lukovit **BG** 88 Jb39
Lukovnikovo **RUS** 117 Ec10
Lukovo **HR** 85 Ga37
Lukovo **MK** 101 Hc42
Łuków **PL** 59 Hc28
Łukta **PL** 58 Ha25
Luleå **S** 34 Ha10
Lüleburgaz **TR** 103 Ka41
Lumbier **E** 80 Cc39
Lumbrales **E** 78 Ba39
Lunca Corbului **RO** 88 Jb37
Lunca de Jos **RO** 76 Jb34
Lund **N** 32 Fd11
Lund **S** 49 Fd23
Lundamo **N** 37 Fc13
Lunde **N** 43 Fb18
Lunde **S** 39 Gc13
Lunderskov **DK** 48 Fa23
Lüneburg **D** 56 Fb26
Lunel **F** 82 Dd38
Lünen **D** 55 Ed28
Lunéville **F** 63 Ec32
Luninec **BY** 120 Ea13
Lunino **RUS** 119 Fc10
Lunna **BY** 59 Hd26
Luopioinen **FIN** 40 Hc15
Luostari **RUS** 27 Hd04
Lurcy-Lévis **F** 69 Dc34
Lure **F** 71 Eb33
Lurgan **GB** 20 Cc22
Lurnfeld **A** 73 Fd35
Lushnjë **RKS** 100 Hb42
Lusignan **F** 69 Da34
Lusigny-sur-Barse **F** 62 Ea32
Luso **P** 78 Ad39
Luspebryggan **S** 29 Gd08
Luss **GB** 20 Cd21
Lussac-les-Châteaux **F** 69 Da34
Lussan **F** 82 Dd38
Lütfiye **TR** 113 Kb44
Lutherstadt Eisleben **D** 64 Fc29
Lutherstadt Wittenberg **D** 57 Fd28
Lütjenburg **D** 56 Fb25
Luton **GB** 25 Db27
Lutuhyne **UA** 122 Fb15
Lututów **PL** 66 Gd29
Luumäki **FIN** 41 Ja15
Luusua **FIN** 31 Hc08
Luvia **FIN** 40 Ha15
Luxembourg **L** 63 Eb31

Luxeuil-les-Bains **F** 71 Eb33
Lužajka **RUS** 41 Ja15
Luzern **CH** 71 Ed34
Luzino **PL** 58 Gc25
Lużki **BY** 53 Jb23
Luz-Saint-Sauveur **F** 80 Cd39
Luzy **F** 70 Dd34
L'viv **UA** 67 Hd30
Lwówek Śląski **PL** 65 Gb29
Lychen **D** 57 Fd26
Lycksele **S** 33 Gc11
Lydney **GB** 24 Cd27
Lyman **UA** 77 Kb35
Lyman **UA** 122 Fa14
Lyme Regis **GB** 24 Cd28
Lymington **GB** 24 Da28
Lyngdal **N** 42 Ed19
Lyngseidet **N** 26 Gd05
Lynton **GB** 23 Cc27
Lyntupy **BY** 53 Ja23
Lyon **F** 70 Ea36
Lyons-la-Forêt **F** 62 Dc30
Lypci **UA** 122 Fa14
Lypova Dolyna **UA** 121 Ed14
Łyse **PL** 59 Hb26
Lysekil **S** 43 Fc20
Lysi **CY** 128 Gc19
Lyskovo **RUS** 119 Fc09
Lysnes **N** 26 Gc05
Lysøysundet **N** 32 Fc12
Lyss **CH** 71 Ec34
Lystrup **DK** 49 Fb22
Lysvik **S** 44 Fd17
Lysyčans'k **UA** 122 Fb14
Lysye Gory **RUS** 123 Fd12
Lytham Saint Anne's **GB** 21 Da24
Lyubimets **BG** 102 Jc41

M

Maam Cross **IRL** 18 Bd23
Maaninka **FIN** 35 Hd12
Maaninkavaara **FIN** 31 Hd08
Maanselkä **FIN** 35 Ja11
Maardu **EST** 46 Hc18
Maarianhamina **FIN** 45 Gd17
Maarja **EST** 47 Ja19
Maasbracht **NL** 63 Eb29
Maaseik **B** 63 Eb29
Maasmechelen **NL** 63 Eb29
Maastricht **NL** 63 Eb29
Mablethorpe **GB** 25 Dc25
Macclesfield **GB** 24 Da25
Macea **RO** 75 Hc35
Maceda **E** 78 Ba37
Macedo de Cavaleiros **P** 78 Ba39
Macerata **I** 85 Fd40
Machault **F** 62 Ea31
Machecoul **F** 68 Cd33
Machynlleth **GB** 24 Cd25
Maciejowice **PL** 59 Hb28
Măcin **RO** 89 Ka36

Macinaggio **F** 96 Ed40
Macomer **I** 97 Ec43
Mâcon **F** 70 Ea35
Macroom **IRL** 22 Bd25
Macugnaga **I** 71 Ec36
Madan **BG** 102 Jc41
Mädängsholm **S** 44 Ga20
Maddaloni **I** 99 Ga43
Maden **TR** 127 Ga19
Madesimo **I** 72 Fa35
Madliena **LV** 53 Hd21
Madona **LV** 53 Ja21
Madonna di Campiglio **I** 72 Fb36
Mădrec **BG** 102 Jc40
Madrid **E** 92 Bd41
Madridejos **E** 92 Bd42
Madrigal de las Altas Torres **E** 91 Bc40
Madrigalejo **E** 91 Bb42
Mădrino **BG** 89 Jd39
Madroñera **E** 91 Bb41
Maël-Carhaix **F** 60 Cc31
Maella **E** 93 Cd41
Mafra **P** 90 Ab41
Magdeburg **D** 56 Fc28
Magenta **I** 71 Ed36
Magganári **GR** 115 Jd47
Maghera **GB** 20 Cc22
Magherani **RO** 76 Jb35
Magione **I** 84 Fc40
Maglaj **BIH** 86 Gd38
Maglavit **RO** 87 Hd38
Maglie **I** 100 Gd44
Măgliž **BG** 102 Jc40
Magnetity **RUS** 31 Ja05
Magnor **N** 43 Fd17
Magny-en-Vexin **F** 62 Dc31
Mágocs **H** 74 Gd35
Maguiresbridge **GB** 20 Cb22
Măgura **RO** 88 Jc36
Măgurele **RO** 88 Jc36
Magyarkeszi **H** 74 Gd35
Mahdalynivka **UA** 122 Fa15
Mahilëv **BY** 121 Eb12
Mahón **E** 95 Dc43
Mahora **E** 92 Ca43
Maials **E** 93 Cd41
Măicăneşti **RO** 89 Jd36
Maïche **F** 71 Ec34
Maidenhead **GB** 25 Db27
Maidstone **GB** 25 Db28
Măieruş **RO** 76 Jb35
Mailly-le-Camp **F** 62 Ea32
Mainburg **D** 64 Fc32
Maintenon **F** 62 Dc31
Mainua **FIN** 35 Hd11
Mainz **D** 63 Ed30
Maïsiagala **LT** 53 Hd24
Majak Oktjabrja **RUS** 123 Ga13
Majaky **UA** 77 Ka33
Majdan **RUS** 119 Fd09
Majdan **UA** 67 Hd32
Majdanpek **SRB** 87 Hc38

Majilovac **SRB** 87 Hc37
Majkop **RUS** 127 Fd17
Majorskij **RUS** 123 Fd15
Makarovo **RUS** 123 Fc12
Makarska **HR** 86 Gc40
Makijivka **UA** 122 Fb15
Makó **H** 75 Hb35
Makov **SK** 66 Gd31
Makovo **MK** 101 Hc42
Mąkowarsko **PL** 58 Gc26
Maków Mazowiecki **PL** 59 Hb27
Makrakómi **GR** 110 Hd45
Makrany **BY** 59 Hd28
Makrigialós **GR** 115 Ka49
Makrinítsa **GR** 101 Ja44
Makriráhi **GR** 101 Ja44
Maksatiha **RUS** 117 Ed09
Malå **S** 33 Gc10
Malacky **SK** 74 Gc33
Maladzečna **BY** 53 Jb24
Maladzečna **BY** 120 Ea12
Málaga **E** 105 Bb45
Malagón **E** 91 Bc42
Mălăieşti **RO** 75 Hd36
Malaja Višera **RUS** 117 Eb09
Mala Kladuša **BIH** 85 Gb37
Malanów **PL** 58 Gd28
Malarrif **IS** 14 Bb05
Malaryta **BY** 59 Hd28
Mala Vyska **UA** 121 Ed15
Malax Maalahti **FIN** 40 Ha13
Malbork **PL** 58 Gd25
Malbuisson **F** 71 Eb34
Malcesine **I** 72 Fb36
Malchin **D** 57 Fd26
Malchow **D** 57 Fd26
Maldegem **B** 54 Ea28
Maldon **GB** 25 Dc27
Małdyty **PL** 58 Ha25
Malè **I** 72 Fb35
Małe Gacno **PL** 58 Gd26
Máleme **GR** 114 Jb49
Malente **D** 56 Fb25
Malesherbes **F** 62 Dc32
Malestroit **F** 60 Cc32
Malgrat de Mar **E** 95 Db41
Målilla **S** 50 Gb21
Mali Lošinj **HR** 85 Ga38
Maliniec **PL** 58 Gd28
Malinska **HR** 85 Ga37
Maliq **AL** 101 Hc43
Maljiševo **RKS** 87 Hc40
Malkara **TR** 103 Jd42
Malko Tărnovo **BG** 103 Ka40
Mal'kovo **RUS** 53 Jb21
Mallaig **GB** 16 Cd19
Mallaranny **IRL** 18 Bd22
Mallén **E** 80 Cb40
Malles Venosta **I** 72 Fb35
Mallnitz **A** 73 Fd35
Mallow **IRL** 22 Bd25
Mallwyd **GB** 24 Cd25
Malm **N** 32 Fc12
Malmbäck **S** 50 Ga21

Malmberget **S** 29 Gd08
Malmedy **B** 63 Eb30
Malmesbury **GB** 24 Da27
Malmköping **S** 44 Gb18
Malmö **S** 49 Fd23
Malmslätt **S** 44 Gb19
Malmyż **RUS** 119 Fd08
Maloarhangel'sk **RUS** 122 Fa12
Maloe **BY** 59 Hd25
Malojaroslavec **RUS** 117 Ed11
Małomice **PL** 65 Gb29
Måløy **N** 36 Ed14
Malpartida de Plasencia **E** 91 Bb41
Malpica de Bergantiños **E** 78 Ad36
Mālpils **LV** 53 Hd21
Mals im Vinschgau **I** 72 Fb35
Malta **LV** 53 Ja21
Malton **GB** 21 Db24
Małujowice **PL** 66 Gc30
Malung **S** 38 Ga16
Malungsfors **S** 38 Fd16
Maluszyn **PL** 67 Ha29
Malyn **UA** 121 Eb14
Mały Płock **PL** 59 Hb26
Malyševo **RUS** 118 Fb10
Mamadys **RUS** 119 Ga08
Mamaia **RO** 89 Ka37
Mamalyha **UA** 76 Jc32
Mamers **F** 61 Db32
Mamonovo **RUS** 59 Ha25
Mamykovo **RUS** 119 Ga09
Manacor **E** 95 Db43
Manamensalo **FIN** 35 Hd11
Mănăstirea **RO** 89 Jd37
Mancha Real **E** 106 Bc44
Manchester **GB** 21 Da24
Manching **D** 64 Fc32
Manciano **I** 84 Fb40
Mandal **N** 42 Fa20
Mandas **I** 97 Ed44
Mandráki **GR** 115 Kb47
Manduria **I** 100 Gd43
Manerbio **I** 84 Fa37
Manevyči **UA** 120 Ea14
Manfredonia **I** 99 Gb42
Mangalia **RO** 89 Ka38
Mangen **N** 43 Fc17
Manger **N** 36 Ed14
Mangualde **P** 78 Ad39
Maniago **I** 72 Fc36
Manisa **TR** 113 Ka44
Manises **E** 93 Cc43
Månkarbo **S** 45 Gc17
Manlleu **E** 81 Da40
Mannheim **D** 63 Ed31
Manningtree **GB** 25 Dc27
Manole **BG** 102 Jb40
Manoleasa **RO** 76 Jc32
Manorhamilton **IRL** 18 Ca22
Manosque **F** 82 Ea38
Manresa **E** 81 Da40

Mansfeld **D** 56 Fc28
Mansfield **GB** 25 Db25
Mansilla **E** 79 Bd38
Mansilla **E** 79 Ca39
Mansilla de las Mulas **E** 79 Bc38
Mansle **F** 69 Da35
Mantamádos **GR** 113 Jd44
Mantes-la-Jolie **F** 62 Dc31
Mantes-la-Ville **F** 62 Dc31
Manthiréa **GR** 111 Ja47
Mantorp **S** 44 Gb20
Mantova **I** 84 Fb37
Mäntsälä **FIN** 40 Hc16
Mänttä **FIN** 40 Hc14
Manturovo **RUS** 118 Fb08
Mäntyharju **FIN** 41 Hd15
Mäntyjärvi **FIN** 35 Hd09
Mäntyluoto **FIN** 40 Ha15
Manyas **TR** 103 Kb43
Manzanares **E** 92 Bd43
Maó (Mahón) **E** 95 Dc43
Maqueda **E** 91 Bc41
Maranello **I** 84 Fb38
Marans **F** 68 Cd34
Mărășești **RO** 77 Jd35
Mărașu **RO** 89 Ka36
Maratea **I** 99 Gb44
Marathónas **GR** 112 Jb46
Marazion **GB** 23 Cb28
Marbach **D** 64 Fa32
Marbella **E** 105 Bb45
Marburg **D** 64 Fa29
Marcali **H** 74 Gc35
Marcaltő **H** 74 Gc34
Marčana **HR** 85 Fd37
March **GB** 25 Db26
Marche-en-Famenne **B** 63 Eb30
Marchena **E** 105 Ba44
Marchenoir **F** 61 Db32
Marciac **F** 80 Cd38
Marciana Marina **I** 84 Fa40
Marcigny **F** 70 Dd35
Marcillac-la-Croisille **F** 69 Db36
Marcinkonys **LT** 59 Hd25
Marcinkonys **LT** 59 Hd25
Marck **F** 54 Dc28
Marco de Canaveses **P** 78 Ad39
Mardalen **N** 36 Fa14
Mårdsele **S** 34 Gd11
Marennes **F** 68 Cd35
Mareuil-sur-Lay **F** 68 Cd34
Mar'evka **RUS** 119 Ga10
Marevo **RUS** 117 Eb10
Margaríti **GR** 101 Hc44
Margaritove **RUS** 127 Fc16
Margate **GB** 25 Dc28
Mărgău **RO** 75 Hd35
Margecany **SK** 67 Hb32
Margherita di Savoia **I** 99 Gb42
Marghita **RO** 75 Hc34
Margone **I** 83 Ec37

Margonin **PL** 58 Gc27
Marhanec' **UA** 126 Fa16
Mariager **DK** 49 Fb22
Marialva **P** 78 Ba39
Mariannelund **S** 50 Gb21
Mariánské Lázně **CZ** 65 Fd31
Mariazell **A** 73 Gb34
Maribo **DK** 49 Fc24
Maribor **SLO** 73 Gb35
Mariefred **S** 45 Gc18
Mariehamn **FIN** 45 Gd17
Marielund **S** 33 Gc10
Marielyst **DK** 49 Fc24
Marienberg **D** 65 Fd30
Mariés **GR** 102 Jb42
Mariestad **S** 44 Ga19
Marignane **F** 82 Ea39
Marijampolė **LT** 52 Hc24
Marín **E** 78 Ad37
Marina di Belvedere **I** 99 Gb44
Marina di Carrara **I** 84 Fa38
Marina di Cetraro **I** 99 Gb44
Marina di Grosseto **I** 84 Fb40
Marina di Leuca **I** 100 Ha44
Marina di Pisa **I** 84 Fa39
Marina di Ragusa **I** 109 Ga48
Marina di Ravenna **I** 84 Fc38
Marine de Sisco **F** 96 Ed40
Marinella **I** 108 Fc47
Marineo **I** 108 Fd47
Maringues **F** 70 Dc35
Marinha Grande **P** 90 Ac40
Marinka **BG** 103 Ka40
Mariupol' **UA** 126 Fb16
Märjamaa **EST** 46 Hc18
Markabygd **N** 32 Fc12
Markaryd **S** 49 Fd22
Market Drayton **GB** 24 Da25
Market Harborough **GB** 25 Db26
Market Rasen **GB** 25 Db25
Market Weighton **GB** 21 Db24
Markivka **MD** 77 Kb33
Markivka **UA** 122 Fb14
Markkina **FIN** 30 Ha06
Markkleeberg **D** 64 Fc29
Markópoulo **GR** 112 Jb46
Markovo **BG** 89 Jd39
Marksewo **PL** 59 Hb26
Marktheidenfeld **D** 64 Fa31
Markt Indersdorf **D** 72 Fb33
Marktoberdorf **D** 72 Fb34
Marktredwitz **D** 64 Fc31
Marl **D** 55 Ec28
Marlborough **GB** 24 Da27
Marle **F** 62 Ea30
Marma **S** 38 Gb16
Marma **S** 45 Gc17
Marmande **F** 81 Da37
Marmara **TR** 103 Ka42

Marmaraereğlisi **TR** 103 Ka41
Mármaro **GR** 113 Jd45
Marnay **F** 71 Eb34
Marne **D** 56 Fa25
Marotta **I** 85 Fd39
Marovac **SRB** 87 Hc40
Marquise **F** 62 Dc29
Marradi **I** 84 Fb38
Marraskoski **FIN** 30 Hb08
Marsala **I** 108 Fc47
Maršavicy **RUS** 47 Jb20
Marsberg **D** 64 Fa29
Marsciano **I** 84 Fc40
Marseille **F** 82 Ea39
Marseille-en-Beauvaisis **F** 62 Dc30
Marsico Nuovo **I** 99 Gb43
Märsta **S** 45 Gc18
Marstal **DK** 49 Fb24
Marstrand **S** 43 Fc20
Martelange **B** 63 Eb30
Mártha **GR** 115 Jd49
Martigné-Ferchaud **F** 61 Cd32
Martigny **CH** 71 Ec35
Martigues **F** 82 Dd39
Martilla **FIN** 40 Hb16
Martin **SK** 66 Gd32
Martina Franca **I** 100 Gd43
Martinniemi **FIN** 35 Hc10
Martinšćica **HR** 85 Ga38
Martinsicuro **I** 85 Fd40
Martna **EST** 46 Hc18
Martonvaara **FIN** 35 Ja12
Martorell **E** 95 Da41
Martos **E** 106 Bc44
Martti **FIN** 31 Hd07
Marvão **P** 90 Ad41
Marvejols **F** 81 Dc37
Marvik **N** 42 Ed18
Maryport **GB** 21 Da23
Mas de las Matas **E** 93 Cc41
Masegoso de Tajuña **E** 92 Ca41
Masfjorden **N** 36 Ed16
Masi **N** 26 Ha05
Masku **FIN** 40 Hb16
Massa **I** 84 Fa38
Massafra **I** 99 Gc43
Massa Marittima **I** 84 Fb40
Massat **F** 81 Da39
Masseube **F** 81 Da38
Massiac **F** 69 Dc36
Mastihári **GR** 115 Ka47
Masty **BY** 59 Hd26
Masugnsbyn **S** 30 Ha07
Måsvik **N** 26 Gc04
Mátala **GR** 114 Jc50
Matamala de Almazán **E** 92 Ca40
Mataró **E** 95 Db41
Mätäsvaara **FIN** 35 Ja12
Matching Green **GB** 25 Db27
Matelica **I** 85 Fd40

Matera – Mézières-sur-Issoire

Matera I 99 Gc43
Mátészalka H 75 Hc33
Matfors S 38 Gb14
Matha F 68 Cd35
Matiši LV 47 Hd20
Matkaseľkja RUS 41 Jb14
Matosinhos P 78 Ad38
Mátraháza H 74 Ha33
Matrei A 72 Fc35
Mattersburg A 73 Gb34
Mattighofen A 73 Fd33
Matveev Kurgan RUS 123 Fc15
Matyli BY 59 Hd25
Maubeuge F 62 Ea30
Maubourguet F 80 Cd38
Mauléon F 68 Cd33
Mauléon-Licharre F 80 Cc38
Maunu S 29 Ha06
Maura N 43 Fc17
Maure-de-Bretagne F 61 Cd32
Mauriac F 69 Dc36
Mauron F 60 Cc31
Maurs F 81 Db37
Maurvangen N 37 Fb15
Mauterndorf A 73 Fd34
Mauthausen A 73 Ga33
Mauvezin F 81 Da38
Mauzé-sur-le-Mignon F 68 Cd34
Mauzé-sur-le-Mignon F 68 Cd34
Mavas S 28 Gb08
Mavréli GR 101 Hd44
Mavrománta GR 110 Hd45
Mavroúda GR 101 Ja42
Mavrovi Anovi MK 101 Hc41
Maybole GB 20 Cd22
Mayen D 63 Ec30
Mayenne F 61 Da31
Maynooth IRL 19 Cb24
Mayorga E 79 Bc38
Mayrhofen A 72 Fc34
Mazagón E 105 Ad44
Mazamet F 81 Db38
Mazara del Vallo I 108 Fc47
Mazarrón E 107 Ca45
Mažeikiai LT 52 Hb22
Mazières-en-Gâtine F 69 Da34
Mazilmäja LV 52 Hb22
Mazirbe LV 46 Hb20
Mazsalaca LV 47 Hd20
Mazyr BY 121 Eb13
Mazzarino I 109 Ga47
Mcensk RUS 122 Fa12
Meaux F 62 Dd31
Mechelen B 62 Ea29
Mecidiye TR 103 Jd42
Mečka BG 88 Jc38
Mede I 83 Ed37
Medele S 34 Gd11
Medemblik NL 55 Eb26
Medenyči UA 67 Hd31

Medevi S 44 Ga19
Medgidia RO 89 Ka37
Medgyesegyháza H 75 Hb35
Mediaş RO 76 Ja35
Medicina I 84 Fb38
Medinaceli E 92 Ca40
Medina del Campo E 79 Bc39
Medina de Pomar E 79 Ca38
Medina de Ríoseco E 79 Bc39
Medina Sidonia E 105 Ba45
Medininkai LT 53 Ja24
Medulin HR 85 Fd38
Međurečje SRB 87 Hb39
Međurijecje MNE 86 Ha40
Medvedja SRB 87 Hc40
Medvenka RUS 122 Fa13
Medyka UA 67 Hd31
Medze LV 52 Ha22
Medzilaborce SK 67 Hc31
Meerane D 64 Fc30
Megáli Panagia GR 102 Jb43
Megáli Stérna GR 101 Ja42
Megáli Vríssi GR 101 Ja42
Megalohóri GR 101 Hd44
Megálo Horío GR 115 Kb47
Megalópoli GR 110 Hd47
Mégara GR 112 Jb46
Megève F 71 Eb36
Mehamn N 27 Hc02
Mehikoorma EST 47 Ja19
Mehring D 63 Ec31
Mehun-sur-Yèvre F 69 Dc33
Meilen CH 71 Ed34
Meinersen D 56 Fb27
Meinhardt D 64 Fa32
Meiningen D 64 Fb30
Meira E 78 Bb36
Meiringen CH 71 Ed35
Meißen D 65 Fd29
Meitingen D 64 Fb32
Melá GR 112 Jc45
Melaje SRB 87 Hb40
Melalahti FIN 41 Ja13
Melates GR 110 Hc45
Melbu N 28 Ga06
Meldal N 37 Fb13
Meldorf D 56 Fa25
Melegnano I 83 Ed37
Melenci SRB 75 Hb36
Melenki RUS 118 Fb10
Melfi I 99 Gb43
Melfjorden N 33 Ga09
Melgar de Fernamental E 79 Bd38
Melhus N 37 Fc13
Melide E 78 Ba36
Melides P 90 Ab42
Melíki GR 101 Hd43
Melilli I 109 Ga47
Melineşti RO 88 Ja37
Mélissa GR 101 Ja44

Melitopol' UA 126 Fa16
Melito Porto Salvo I 109 Gb47
Melívia GR 101 Ja44
Melk A 73 Gb33
Mellakoski FIN 34 Hb09
Mellansel S 39 Gc13
Mellanström S 33 Gc10
Mellbystrand S 49 Fd22
Melle D 55 Ed27
Melle F 69 Da34
Mellerud S 43 Fd19
Mellrichstadt D 64 Fb30
Melnica SRB 87 Hc38
Melnik BG 101 Ja41
Mělník CZ 65 Ga30
Mel'nikovo RUS 41 Jb15
Melnsils LV 46 Hb20
Mels CH 72 Fa34
Melsungen D 64 Fa29
Meltaus FIN 30 Hb08
Melton Mowbray GB 25 Db26
Meltosjärvi FIN 30 Hb08
Melun F 62 Dc32
Melvich GB 17 Db18
Membrío E 91 Ba41
Memmingen D 72 Fa33
Mena UA 121 Ec13
Menaggio I 71 Ed36
Menai Bridge GB 20 Cd24
Mende F 81 Dc37
Mendeleevsk RUS 119 Ga08
Menden D 55 Ed28
Mendrisio CH 71 Ed36
Menemen TR 113 Ka45
Menen B 62 Dd29
Meneou CY 128 Gc19
Menesjärvi FIN 27 Hb05
Menfi I 108 Fc47
Mengen D 72 Fa33
Mengeš SLO 73 Ga36
Mengíbar E 106 Bc44
Menídi GR 110 Hc45
Mentana I 98 Fc41
Menton F 83 Ec39
Menzelinsk RUS 119 Ga08
Meppel NL 55 Ec27
Meppen D 55 Ed27
Mequinenza E 93 Cd41
Mer F 69 Db33
Meråker N 37 Fd13
Meran I 72 Fb35
Merano I 72 Fb35
Merasjärvi S 30 Ha07
Mercato Saraceno I 84 Fc39
Merdrignac F 60 Cc31
Merefa UA 122 Fa14
Merei RO 88 Jc36
Méribel F 71 Eb36
Meričleri BG 102 Jc40
Mérida E 91 Ba42
Mérignac F 68 Cd36
Mérihas GR 111 Jc47
Merijärvi FIN 34 Hb11
Merikarvia FIN 40 Ha15

Meri-Pori FIN 40 Ha15
Merkinė LT 59 Hd25
Merkinė LT 59 Hd25
Mernye H 74 Gd35
Mersch L 63 Eb31
Merseburg D 64 Fc29
Mersin TR 128 Gd16
Mērsrags LV 52 Hc21
Merthyr Tydfil GB 24 Cd26
Mértola P 104 Ac43
Méru F 62 Dc31
Měry BY 53 Jb22
Merzig D 63 Ec31
Mesagne I 100 Gd43
Meschede D 63 Ed29
Meselefors S 33 Gb11
Mesihovina BIH 86 Gc39
Meslay-du-Maine F 61 Da32
Mesohóri GR 101 Hd44
Mesopotamiá GR 101 Hc43
Mesopótamo GR 110 Hc45
Messaure S 29 Gd08
Messelt N 37 Fc15
Messina I 109 Gb46
Messini GR 110 Hd47
Messinó GR 111 Ja46
Meßkirch D 72 Fa33
Messolóngi GR 110 Hd46
Messongí GR 100 Hb44
Mesta BG 101 Ja41
Mestá GR 113 Jd45
Mestanza E 106 Bc43
Mesti GR 102 Jc42
Město Albrechtice CZ 66 Gc30
Město Touškov CZ 65 Fd31
Mestre I 84 Fc37
Mesvres F 70 Dd34
Metajna HR 85 Ga38
Metamorfósi GR 111 Ja47
Méthana GR 112 Jb46
Methóni GR 110 Hd48
Metković HR 86 Gd40
Metlika SLO 73 Gb36
Metóhi GR 112 Jb45
Metsäkylä FIN 35 Hd10
Metsküla EST 46 Hb19
Métsovo GR 101 Hc44
Mettlach D 63 Ec31
Metz F 63 Eb31
Metzingen D 64 Fa32
Meulan F 62 Dc31
Meuselwitz D 64 Fc29
Meydancik TR 127 Ga18
Meyenburg D 56 Fc26
Meymac F 69 Db36
Meyrueis F 81 Dc37
Meyzieu F 70 Ea36
Mézapos GR 111 Ja48
Mezdra BG 88 Ja39
Mężenin PL 59 Hc26
Mežica SLO 73 Ga35
Mézières-en-Brenne F 69 Db34
Mézières-sur-Issoire F 69 Da35

Mézin **F** 80 Cd37
Mezőberény **H** 75 Hb35
Mezőcsát **H** 75 Hb33
Mezőkovácsháza **H** 75 Hb35
Mezőkövesd **H** 75 Hb33
Mézos **F** 80 Cc37
Mežotne **LV** 52 Hc22
Mezőtúr **H** 75 Hb34
Miajadas **E** 91 Ba42
Miastko **PL** 58 Gc25
Michajlovskoe **RUS** 119 Fc09
Michalin **PL** 58 Gd27
Michalovce **SK** 67 Hc32
Michelstadt **D** 64 Fa31
Micleşti **RO** 77 Jd34
Mičurinsk **RUS** 122 Fb12
Mičurinskoe **RUS** 41 Jb16
Middelburg **NL** 54 Ea28
Middelfart **DK** 49 Fb23
Middelharnis **NL** 54 Ea28
Middlesbrough **GB** 21 Db23
Midhurst **GB** 24 Da28
Midleton **IRL** 22 Bd25
Midsund **N** 36 Fa13
Miechów **PL** 67 Ha30
Miedźno **PL** 66 Gd29
Międzychód **PL** 57 Gb27
Międzylesie **PL** 66 Gc30
Międzyrzec Podlaski **PL** 59 Hc28
Międzyrzecz **PL** 57 Gb27
Międzywodzie **PL** 57 Ga25
Międzyzdroje **PL** 57 Ga25
Miehikkälä **FIN** 41 Ja16
Miélan **F** 80 Cd38
Mielec **PL** 67 Hb30
Mieraslompolo **FIN** 27 Hc04
Miercurea-Ciuc **RO** 76 Jb35
Miercurea Sibiului **RO** 88 Ja36
Mieres **E** 79 Bc37
Mierojokki **N** 26 Ha05
Miesbach **D** 72 Fc34
Mieszków **PL** 58 Gc28
Mieszkowice **PL** 57 Ga27
Mietoinen **FIN** 40 Ha16
Mifol **AL** 100 Hb43
Migennes **F** 70 Dd33
Miglionico **I** 99 Gc43
Mihăeşti **RO** 88 Jb38
Mihail Kogălniceanu **RO** 89 Ka37
Mihailovca **MD** 77 Ka33
Mihailovca **MD** 77 Ka34
Mihajlov **RUS** 118 Fa11
Mihajlovka **RUS** 123 Fd13
Mihajlovo **BG** 88 Ja39
Mihalkovo **BG** 102 Jb41
Miheşu de Câmpie **RO** 76 Ja35
Mihnevo **RUS** 118 Fa10
Mikaševičy **BY** 121 Eb13
Mikaszówka **PL** 59 Hc25
Mikeļtornis **LV** 46 Hb20
Mikkeli **FIN** 41 Hd14

Mikkelvik **N** 26 Gc04
Mikolaivka **MD** 77 Kb32
Mikołajki **PL** 59 Hb25
Mikołów **PL** 66 Gd30
Míkonos **GR** 113 Jd46
Mikre **BG** 88 Jb39
Mikulov **CZ** 66 Gc32
Miladinovci **MK** 101 Hc41
Milagro **E** 80 Cb39
Miłakowo **PL** 58 Ha25
Milano **I** 71 Ed36
Milas **TR** 113 Kb46
Milazzo **I** 109 Gb46
Miléa **GR** 101 Hc44
Mileševo **SRB** 74 Ha36
Milestone **IRL** 18 Ca24
Mileto **I** 109 Gb46
Milevsko **CZ** 65 Ga31
Milford **GB** 25 Db28
Milford Haven **GB** 23 Cc26
Milići **BIH** 86 Ha38
Milicz **PL** 66 Gc29
Milín **CZ** 65 Ga31
Militello **I** 109 Ga47
Militsa **GR** 110 Hd48
Millas **F** 81 Db39
Millau **F** 81 Dc38
Millerovo **RUS** 123 Fc14
Millom **GB** 21 Da23
Milltown Malbay **IRL** 18 Bd24
Milmersdorf **D** 57 Fd27
Milna **HR** 86 Gc40
Mílos **GR** 111 Jc47
Milot **RKS** 100 Hb42
Milówka **PL** 67 Ha31
Miltenberg **D** 64 Fa31
Milton Keynes **GB** 25 Db27
Mimizan **F** 80 Cc37
Mimoň **CZ** 65 Ga30
Mina de São Domingos **P** 104 Ac43
Mindelheim **D** 72 Fb33
Minden **D** 56 Fa27
Minehead **GB** 23 Cc27
Mineral'nye Vody **RUS** 127 Ga16
Minervino Murge **I** 99 Gb42
Minglanilla **E** 93 Cb42
Mingorría **E** 91 Bc40
Minićevo **SRB** 87 Hd39
Minsk **BY** 120 Ea12
Mińsk Mazowiecki **PL** 59 Hb28
Mintlaw **GB** 17 Db19
Minturno **I** 98 Fd42
Miomo **F** 96 Ed40
Mionica **SRB** 87 Hb38
Mioveni **RO** 88 Jb37
Mira **E** 93 Cb42
Mira **I** 84 Fc37
Mira **P** 90 Ac39
Miramas **F** 82 Dd39
Mirambeau **F** 68 Cd35
Miramont-de-Guyenne **F** 69 Da36

Miranda de Ebro **E** 79 Ca38
Miranda do Douro **P** 78 Bb39
Mirande **F** 80 Cd38
Mirandela **P** 78 Ba39
Mirandola **I** 84 Fb37
Mirano **I** 84 Fc37
Mircze **PL** 67 Hd29
Mirebeau **F** 69 Da34
Mirebeau-sur-Bèze **F** 70 Ea34
Mirecourt **F** 63 Eb32
Mirepoix **F** 81 Db39
Mireşti **MD** 77 Jd34
Mírina **GR** 102 Jc43
Mirne **UA** 77 Kb34
Mirosławiec **PL** 57 Gb26
Mirotice **CZ** 65 Ga31
Mirovice **CZ** 65 Ga31
Mirow **D** 57 Fd26
Mírtos **GR** 115 Jd49
Mischii **RO** 88 Ja38
Misi **FIN** 31 Hc08
Miskolc **H** 75 Hb33
Mišnjak **HR** 85 Ga38
Misso **EST** 47 Ja20
Mistelbach **A** 74 Gc33
Misten **N** 28 Ga07
Misterbianco **I** 109 Ga47
Misterhult **S** 50 Gb21
Mistretta **I** 109 Ga47
Mitchelstown **IRL** 22 Bd25
Míthimna **GR** 113 Jd44
Mítikas **GR** 110 Hc45
Mitrašinci **MK** 101 Hd41
Mitrofanovka **RUS** 122 Fb14
Mitrovo **SRB** 87 Hc41
Mittådalen **S** 38 Fd14
Mittenwald **D** 72 Fb34
Mittersill **A** 72 Fc34
Mitterteich **D** 64 Fc31
Mittweida **D** 65 Fd29
Mizil **RO** 88 Jc36
Mjadzel **BY** 53 Jb23
Mjadzel **BY** 120 Ea12
Mjakiševo **RUS** 53 Jb21
Mjaksa **RUS** 117 Ed08
Mjölby **S** 44 Ga20
Mjönäs **S** 44 Fd17
Mjøndalen **N** 43 Fb18
Mladá Boleslav **CZ** 65 Ga30
Mladá Vožice **CZ** 65 Ga31
Mladenovac **SRB** 87 Hb38
Mława **PL** 58 Ha26
Mlebniko **RUS** 119 Fd08
Mlinište **BIH** 86 Gc38
Młodasko **PL** 57 Gb27
Młogoszyn **PL** 58 Ha28
Młynary **PL** 58 Ha25
Młynarze **PL** 59 Hb26
Mlyniv **UA** 120 Ea15
Mníšek nad Hnilcom **SK** 67 Hb32
Mo **N** 43 Fc17
Moacşa **RO** 76 Jc35
Moara Vlăsiei **RO** 88 Jc37

Moate **IRL** 18 Ca23
Mochy **PL** 57 Gb28
Mociu **RO** 76 Ja34
Möckern **D** 56 Fc28
Mockfjärd **S** 44 Ga17
Modane **F** 83 Eb37
Modena **I** 84 Fb38
Modica **I** 109 Ga48
Modigliana **I** 84 Fb38
Modliborzyce **PL** 67 Hc29
Mödling **A** 73 Gb33
Modriča **BIH** 86 Gd37
Modugno **I** 99 Gc42
Moelv **N** 37 Fc16
Moen **N** 26 Gc05
Moers **D** 55 Ec28
Moffat **GB** 21 Da22
Moftin **RO** 75 Hd33
Mogadouro **P** 78 Ba39
Mogili **RUS** 53 Jb21
Mogilno **PL** 58 Gc27
Mogliano Veneto **I** 72 Fc36
Mogosoaia **RO** 88 Jc37
Moguer **E** 105 Ad44
Mohács **H** 74 Gd36
Mohed **S** 38 Gb16
Moheda **S** 50 Ga21
Mohelnice **CZ** 66 Gc31
Möhnesee **D** 55 Ed28
Mohora **H** 74 Ha33
Mohyliv-Podil's'kyj **UA** 77 Jd32
Mohyliv-Podil's'kyj **UA** 125 Eb16
Moi **N** 42 Ed19
Moineşti **RO** 76 Jc35
Mo i Rana **N** 33 Ga09
Mõisaküla **EST** 47 Hd19
Moisiovaara **FIN** 35 Ja10
Moissac **F** 81 Da37
Mojácar **E** 107 Ca45
Mojados **E** 79 Bc39
Möklinta **S** 44 Gb17
Mokobody **PL** 59 Hc27
Mokre **PL** 58 Gc25
Mokren **BG** 89 Jd39
Mokrous **RUS** 119 Ga11
Mokšan **RUS** 119 Fc11
Mol **B** 63 Eb29
Mola di Bari **I** 99 Gc42
Mold **GB** 24 Cd25
Moldava nad Bodvou **SK** 67 Hb32
Molde **N** 36 Fa13
Molėtai **LT** 53 Hd23
Molfetta **I** 99 Gc42
Moliden **S** 39 Gc13
Molières **F** 81 Da37
Molina **E** 93 Cb41
Molina de Segura **E** 107 Cb44
Molinella **I** 84 Fb38
Molkom **S** 44 Ga18
Mollerussa **E** 80 Cd40
Mölln **D** 56 Fb26
Mölltorp **S** 44 Ga19

Molodi – Morskoj

Molodi RUS 47 Jb19
Mólos GR 111 Ja45
Moloskovicy RUS 47 Jb17
Molsheim F 63 Ec32
Molunat HR 100 Gd41
Mombuey E 78 Bb38
Momčilgrad BG 102 Jc41
Mommark DK 49 Fb24
Mon S 33 Ga11
Monaco MC 83 Ec39
Monaghan IRL 19 Cb22
Monaši UA 77 Kb34
Monasterace Marina I 109
   Gc46
Monastir I 97 Ed44
Monastyrščina RUS 121
   Ec12
Monastyryšče UA 121 Ec15
Monastyrys'ka UA 124 Ea16
Moncada E 93 Cc43
Moncalieri I 83 Ec37
Moncalvo I 83 Ed37
Monção P 78 Ad37
Mönchengladbach D 63
   Ec29
Monchique P 104 Ab43
Moncontour F 60 Cc31
Mondéjar E 92 Bd41
Mondello I 108 Fd46
Mondim de Basto P 78
   Ad38
Mondolfo I 85 Fd39
Mondoñedo E 78 Bb36
Mondoubleau F 61 Db32
Mondovì I 83 Ec38
Mondragone I 98 Fd42
Mondriz E 78 Bb36
Mondsee A 73 Fd33
Moneasa RO 75 Hc35
Monein F 80 Cd38
Monemvassiá GR 111 Ja48
Monesterio E 105 Ba43
Moneymore GB 20 Cb22
Monfalcone I 73 Fd36
Monforte P 90 Ad41
Monheim D 64 Fb32
Moniatis CY 128 Gb19
Mõniste EST 47 Ja20
Monistrol-d'Allier F 70 Dd36
Monistrol-sur-Loire F 70
   Dd36
Mońki PL 59 Hc26
Monmouth GB 24 Cd26
Monolíthio GR 101 Hc44
Monólithos GR 115 Kb48
Monopoli I 99 Gc43
Monóvar E 107 Cb44
Monreal del Campo E 93
   Cb41
Monreale I 108 Fd46
Monroy E 91 Ba41
Monroyo E 93 Cc41
Mons B 62 Ea29
Monsanto P 91 Ba40
Monsaraz P 90 Ad42
Monschau D 63 Ec29

Monselice I 84 Fc37
Mönsterås S 50 Gb21
Montagnac F 81 Dc38
Montagnana I 84 Fb37
Montaigu F 68 Cd33
Montalbán E 93 Cc41
Montalcino I 84 Fb40
Montalegre P 78 Ba38
Montalivet-les-Bains F 68
   Cd35
Montalto di Castro I 98 Fb41
Montalto Uffogo I 109 Gb45
Montamarta E 78 Bb39
Montana BG 88 Ja39
Montargil P 90 Ac41
Montargis F 62 Dc32
Montauban F 81 Da37
Montauban-de-Bretagne F
   61 Cd33
Montbard F 70 Ea33
Montbazon F 69 Db33
Montbéliard F 71 Ec34
Montblanc E 95 Da41
Montbrison F 70 Dd36
Montbron F 69 Da35
Montceau-les-Mines F 70
   Ea34
Montchanin F 70 Ea34
Montcuq F 81 Da37
Mont-Dauphin F 83 Eb37
Mont-de-Marsan F 80 Cd37
Montdidier F 62 Dd30
Montealegre del Castillo E
   93 Cb43
Monte Argentario-Porto San
   Stefano I 98 Fb41
Montebelluna I 72 Fc36
Montecatini Terme I 84
   Fb39
Montecchio Emilia I 84 Fa38
Montecchio Maggiore I 84
   Fb37
Montech F 81 Da37
Montefiascone I 84 Fc40
Monteforte de Lemos E 78
   Ba37
Montefrío E 106 Bc45
Montehermoso E 91 Ba40
Montélimar F 82 Dd37
Montella I 99 Ga43
Montellano E 105 Ba45
Montemor-o-Novo P 90
   Ac42
Montendre F 68 Cd35
Montepulciano I 84 Fb40
Montereau F 62 Dd32
Monteriggioni I 84 Fb39
Monterosso al Mare I 84
   Fa38
Monterotondo I 98 Fc41
Monte San Savino I 84 Fb39
Monte Sant' Angelo I 99
   Gb42
Montesilvano I 99 Ga41
Montesquieu-Volvestre F
   81 Da38

Montevarchi I 84 Fb39
Montfaucon-d'Argonne F
   63 Eb31
Montfaucon-en-Velay F 70
   Dd36
Montguyon F 68 Cd36
Monthey CH 71 Ec35
Monti I 97 Ed43
Montichiari I 84 Fa37
Monticiano I 84 Fb40
Montier-en-Der F 62 Ea32
Montignac F 69 Da36
Montigny F 63 Eb31
Montigny-le-Roi F 71 Eb33
Montigny-sur-Aube F 70
   Ea33
Montijo E 91 Ba42
Montijo P 90 Ac41
Montilla E 105 Bb44
Montivilliers F 61 Db30
Mont-Louis F 81 Db39
Montluçon F 69 Dc35
Montluel F 70 Ea36
Montmarault F 69 Dc35
Montmédy F 63 Eb31
Montmirail F 62 Dd31
Montmoreau-Saint-Cybard F
   69 Da35
Montmorency F 62 Dc31
Montmorillon F 69 Db34
Montoire-sur-le-Loir F 61
   Db32
Montón E 80 Cb40
Montoro E 106 Bc44
Montpellier F 81 Dc38
Montpon-Ménestérol F 69
   Da36
Montréjeau F 80 Cd38
Montreuil F 62 Dc29
Montreuil-Bellay F 69 Da33
Montreux CH 71 Ec35
Montrevel-en-Bresse F 70
   Ea35
Montrichard F 69 Db33
Montrond-les-Bains F 70
   Dd36
Montrose GB 17 Db20
Montroy E 93 Cb43
Mont-Saint-Aignan F 61
   Db30
Montsalvy F 81 Dc37
Montségur F 81 Db39
Montseny E 81 Bb40
Montsûrs F 61 Da32
Montuïri E 95 Db43
Monza I 71 Ed36
Monzón E 80 Cd40
Moosburg D 72 Fc33
Mór H 74 Gd34
Mora E 92 Bd42
Mora P 90 Ac41
Mora S 38 Ga16
Mora de Rubielos E 93
   Cc42
Morag PL 58 Ha25
Mórahalom H 74 Ha36

Morakovo MNE 86 Ha40
Morakowo PL 58 Gc27
Móra la Nova E 93 Cd41
Moral de Calatrava E 92
   Bd43
Moraleja E 91 Ba40
Morărești RO 88 Jb37
Moratalla E 107 Ca44
Moravița RO 87 Hc37
Morávka CZ 66 Gd31
Moravská Třebová CZ 66
   Gc31
Moravské Budějovice CZ
   65 Gb32
Moravské Lieskové SK 66
   Gd32
Moravský Beroun CZ 66
   Gc31
Moravský Krumlov CZ 65
   Gb32
Morawica PL 67 Hb29
Morbach D 63 Ec31
Mörbylånga S 50 Gb22
Morcenx F 80 Cc37
Morcone I 99 Ga42
Mordelles F 61 Cd32
Mordoğan TR 113 Ka45
Mordovo RUS 122 Fb12
Mordy PL 59 Hc27
Mor'e RUS 117 Eb08
Morecambe GB 21 Da24
Moreda E 106 Bc45
Morée F 61 Db32
Morella E 93 Cc41
Moreni RO 88 Jb37
Mores I 97 Ed43
Moreton-in-Marsh GB 24
   Da26
Moret-sur-Loing F 62 Dd32
Moreuil F 62 Dd30
Morez F 71 Eb35
Morfou CY 128 Gb19
Morges CH 71 Eb35
Morgins CH 71 Ec35
Morgongåva S 45 Gc17
Morgos RO 75 Hd35
Morhange F 63 Ec32
Moriani-Plage F 96 Ed41
Morjärv S 34 Ha09
Morki RUS 119 Fd08
Mörkret S 38 Fd15
Morlaàs F 80 Cd38
Morlaix F 60 Cb30
Mörlunda S 50 Gb21
Morón de Almazán E 92
   Ca40
Morón de la Frontera E 105
   Ba44
Morottaja FIN 31 Hd08
Morozeni MD 77 Jd33
Morozovsk RUS 123 Fc14
Morpeth GB 21 Db22
Mörrum S 50 Ga22
Moršansk RUS 118 Fb11
Mörsil S 38 Ga13
Morskoj RUS 52 Ha24

174

Mörskom FIN 41 Hd16
Morsovo RUS 118 Fb11
Mørsvik N 28 Gb07
Mortagne-au-Perche F 61 Db31
Mortagne-sur-Sèvre F 68 Cd33
Mortain F 61 Da31
Mortara I 83 Ed37
Mortrée F 61 Da31
Morzine F 71 Eb35
Morzyczyn PL 57 Ga26
Mosal'sk RUS 117 Ed11
Mosbach D 64 Fa31
Mosby N 42 Fa19
Mosfellsbær IS 14 Bc07
Moshófito GR 101 Hc44
Mosina PL 58 Gc28
Mosjøen N 32 Fd10
Mosko BIH 86 Gd40
Moskosel S 34 Gd09
Moskva RUS 117 Ed10
Moslavina Podravska HR 74 Gd36
Mosonmagyaróvár H 74 Gc33
Moss N 43 Fc18
Most CZ 65 Fd30
Mostar BIH 86 Gd39
Móstoles E 92 Bd41
Mostovskoj RUS 127 Fd17
Mosty PL 59 Hd28
Mostys'ka UA 67 Hd31
Mota del Cuervo E 92 Bd42
Mota del Marqués E 79 Bc39
Motala S 44 Ga19
Moţca RO 76 Jc33
Motherwell GB 21 Da21
Motilla del Palancar E 92 Ca42
Motril E 106 Bc45
Motru RO 87 Hd37
Moudon CH 71 Eb35
Moúdros GR 102 Jc43
Mougins F 83 Eb39
Mouhijärvi FIN 40 Hb15
Moulins F 70 Dd34
Mountain Ash GB 24 Cd26
Mount Bellew IRL 18 Ca23
Mountbenger GB 21 Da22
Mountmellick IRL 18 Ca24
Moura P 105 Ad43
Mourão P 90 Ad42
Mourenx F 80 Cc38
Mourmelon-le-Grand F 62 Ea31
Mouscron B 62 Dd29
Moustiers-Ste-Marie F 83 Eb38
Mouthe F 71 Eb35
Moutier CH 71 Ec34
Moûtiers F 71 Eb36
Moutsoúna GR 115 Jd47
Mouy F 62 Dc31
Mouzáki GR 101 Hd44

Mouzon F 63 Eb31
Movila Miresii RO 89 Jd36
Moviliţa RO 88 Jc37
Moyuela E 93 Cc41
Mozăceni RO 88 Jb37
Možajsk RUS 117 Ed10
Možga RUS 119 Ga08
Mozirje SLO 73 Ga36
Mozuli RUS 53 Jb21
Mragowo PL 59 Hb25
Mrčajevci SRB 87 Hb39
Mrežičko MK 101 Hd42
Mrkonjić Grad BIH 86 Gc38
Mrkopalj HR 85 Ga37
Mrzeżyno PL 57 Gb25
Mšanec' UA 67 Hc31
Mscislav BY 121 Ec12
Mšenélázně CZ 65 Ga30
Mučkapskij RUS 123 Fc12
Muckross IRL 22 Bd25
Mudanya TR 103 Kb42
Muel E 80 Cc40
Mügeln D 65 Fd29
Mühlacker D 63 Ed32
Mühldorf D 72 Fc33
Mühlhausen D 64 Fb29
Muhovo BG 102 Jb40
Mukačeve UA 67 Hd32
Mula E 107 Ca44
Mülheim (Ruhr) D 55 Ec28
Mulhos FIN 35 Hc10
Mulhouse F 71 Ec33
Müllheim D 71 Ec33
Mullingar IRL 19 Cb23
Müllrose D 57 Ga28
Mullsjö S 44 Ga20
Multia FIN 40 Hc14
Munaðarnes IS 14 Bd04
Münchberg D 64 Fc30
Müncheberg D 57 Ga27
München D 72 Fc33
Mundesley GB 25 Dd26
Mundford GB 25 Dc26
Munera E 92 Ca43
Mungia E 80 Cb37
Muniesa E 93 Cc41
Munka-Ljungby S 49 Fd22
Munkebo DK 49 Fb23
Munkedal S 43 Fc19
Munkfors S 44 Fd17
Münsingen D 72 Fa33
Münster CH 71 Ed35
Münster D 55 Ed28
Munster D 56 Fb27
Munster F 71 Ec33
Munteni RO 77 Jd35
Münzkirchen A 73 Fd33
Muodoslompolo S 30 Ha07
Muonio FIN 30 Ha07
Muradiye TR 113 Ka44
Murat F 69 Dc36
Muratlı TR 103 Ka41
Murato F 96 Ed40
Murau A 73 Ga34
Muravera I 97 Ed44
Murça P 78 Ba39

Murcia E 107 Cb45
Mur-de-Barrez F 81 Dc37
Mur-de-Bretagne F 60 Cc31
Mureck A 73 Gb35
Mürefte TR 103 Ka42
Muret F 81 Da38
Murgeni RO 77 Jd35
Murgia E 79 Ca38
Murighiol RO 89 Ka36
Murjek S 34 Gd09
Murmaši RUS 31 Ja05
Murnau D 72 Fb34
Muro E 95 Db43
Muro del Alcoy E 107 Cb44
Muro Lucano I 99 Gb43
Murom RUS 118 Fb10
Muros E 78 Ad36
Murrhardt D 64 Fa32
Murska Sobota SLO 73 Gb35
Mursko Središće HR 74 Gc35
Murten CH 71 Ec34
Murter HR 85 Gb39
Mürzzuschlag A 73 Gb34
Muša RUS 119 Fd08
Musorka RUS 119 Ga10
Musselburgh GB 21 Da21
Mussidan F 69 Da36
Mussomeli I 108 Fd47
Mussy-sur-Seine F 70 Ea33
Mustafakemalpaşa TR 103 Kb42
Mustér CH 71 Ed35
Mustjala EST 46 Hb19
Mustla EST 47 Hd19
Mustvee EST 47 Ja18
Muszyna PL 67 Hb31
Mut TR 128 Gb17
Mutovaara FIN 35 Ja09
Muurame FIN 40 Hc14
Muurasjärvi FIN 35 Hc12
Muurola FIN 30 Hb08
Muxía E 78 Ad36
Muzillac F 60 Cc32
Mychajlivka UA 126 Fa16
Myckelgensjö S 33 Gc12
Myczków PL 67 Hc31
Myjava SK 66 Gc32
Mykolajiv UA 67 Hd31
Mykolajiv UA 125 Ed16
Mykolajivka UA 126 Fa17
Myllykoski FIN 41 Hd16
Mynamäki FIN 40 Ha16
Myrdal N 36 Fa16
Myre N 28 Ga06
Myre N 28 Gb05
Myrhorod UA 121 Ed14
Myrland N 28 Gb06
Myrlandshaugen N 28 Gb06
Myrmoen N 37 Fd14
Myronivka UA 121 Ec15
Myrskylä FIN 41 Hd16
Myrtou CY 128 Gb18
Myrviken S 38 Ga13
Mysen N 43 Fc18

Myślenice PL 67 Ha31
Myślibórz PL 57 Ga27
Myslivka UA 67 Hd32
Mysovka RUS 52 Hb24
Myszków PL 67 Ha30
Myszyniec PL 59 Hb26
Mytilíni GR 113 Jd44
Mytišči RUS 117 Ed10
Mýtna SK 74 Ha33

N

Naantali FIN 40 Hb16
Naarva FIN 41 Jb12
Naas IRL 19 Cb24
Näätämö FIN 27 Hc04
Nabburg D 64 Fc31
Naberežny Čelny RUS 119 Ga08
Nabuvoll N 37 Fc14
Náchod CZ 65 Gb30
Nadarzyce PL 57 Gb26
Nådendal FIN 40 Hb16
Nadežda UA 77 Kb34
Nădlac RO 75 Hb36
Nadvirna UA 76 Ja32
Nadvirna UA 124 Ea16
Nærbø N 42 Ed19
Næstved DK 49 Fc24
Náfpaktos GR 110 Hd46
Náfplio GR 111 Ja47
Nagajbakovo RUS 119 Ga08
Naggen S 38 Gb14
Nagłowice PL 67 Ha30
Nagor'e RUS 117 Ed09
Nagu Nauvo FIN 46 Ha17
Nagyatád H 74 Gc36
Nagybajom H 74 Gc35
Nagyhalász H 75 Hc33
Nagyigmánd H 74 Gd34
Nagykanizsa H 74 Gc35
Nagykáta H 74 Ha34
Nagykőrös H 74 Ha34
Nagylak RO 75 Hb36
Nagyszénás H 75 Hb35
Nahačiv UA 67 Hd30
Naila D 64 Fc30
Nairn GB 17 Da19
Najac F 81 Db37
Nájera E 79 Ca39
Naklik PL 67 Hc30
Nakło nad Notecią PL 58 Gc26
Nakskov DK 49 Fc24
Nalbant RO 89 Ka36
Nal'čik RUS 127 Ga17
Nälden S 38 Ga13
Nałęczów PL 67 Hc29
Nálepkovo SK 67 Hb32
Näljänkä FIN 35 Hd10
Nalžovské Hory CZ 65 Fd32
Náměšť nad Oslavou CZ 65 Gb32
Námestovo SK 67 Ha31
Nämpnäs FIN 40 Ha14

Namsos **N** 32 Fc11
Namsskogan **N** 32 Fd11
Namur **B** 63 Eb29
Namystów **PL** 66 Gc29
Nancy **F** 63 Eb32
Nangis **F** 62 Dd32
Nanterre **F** 62 Dc31
Nantes **F** 68 Cd33
Nanteuil-le-Haudouin **F** 62 Dd31
Nantua **F** 70 Ea35
Nantwich **GB** 24 Da25
Náousa **GR** 115 Jd47
Náoussa **GR** 101 Hd43
Napoli **I** 98 Fd43
När **S** 51 Gd21
Narač **BY** 53 Ja23
Narač **BY** 53 Ja24
Narač **BY** 120 Ea12
Narberth **GB** 23 Cc26
Narbonne **F** 81 Dc39
Nardò **I** 100 Gd44
Narečenski bani **BG** 102 Jb41
Narew **PL** 59 Hc26
Narewka **PL** 59 Hd26
Narkaus **FIN** 35 Hc09
Narken **S** 30 Ha08
Narman **TR** 127 Ga19
Narni **I** 98 Fc41
Naro-Fominsk **RUS** 117 Ed10
Narovlja **BY** 121 Eb13
Närpes **FIN** 40 Ha14
Närpiö **FIN** 40 Ha14
Nartkala **RUS** 127 Ga17
Narva **EST** 47 Ja17
Narva-Jõesuu **EST** 47 Ja17
Närvijoki **FIN** 40 Ha14
Narvik **N** 28 Gb06
Naryškino **RUS** 121 Ed12
Nås **S** 44 Ga17
Năsăud **RO** 76 Ja34
Nasavrky **CZ** 65 Gb31
Nasbinals **F** 81 Dc37
Našice **HR** 86 Gd37
Nasielsk **PL** 59 Hb27
Naso **I** 109 Ga46
Nassau **D** 63 Ed30
Nässjö **S** 44 Ga20
Nastola **FIN** 41 Hd15
Näsviken **S** 38 Gb15
Natalinci **SRB** 87 Hb38
Nattavaara **S** 29 Gd08
Nättraby **S** 50 Gb22
Naturno **I** 72 Fb35
Naturns **I** 72 Fb35
Nauders **A** 72 Fb35
Nauen **D** 57 Fd27
Naujoji Akmenė **LT** 52 Hc22
Naumburg **D** 64 Fc29
Naumovskij **RUS** 123 Fd15
Naustdal **N** 36 Ed15
Nautijaur **S** 29 Gc08
Nautsi **RUS** 27 Hd05
Nava **E** 79 Bc37

Navacerrada **E** 92 Bd40
Navahermosa **E** 91 Bc42
Navahrudak **BY** 120 Ea13
Navalcarnero **E** 92 Bd41
Navalmanzano **E** 92 Bd40
Navalmanzano **E** 92 Bd40
Navalmoral de la Mata **E** 91 Bb41
Navalvillar de Pela **E** 91 Bb42
Navan **IRL** 19 Cb23
Navapolack **BY** 117 Eb11
Navarcles **E** 81 Da40
Navarrenx **F** 80 Cc38
Navarrés **E** 93 Cb43
Navascués **E** 80 Cc39
Navas del Madroño **E** 91 Ba41
Navasëlki **BY** 121 Eb13
Navašino **RUS** 118 Fb10
Nävekvarn **S** 44 Gb19
Navelgas **E** 78 Bb36
Navia **E** 78 Bb36
Navlja **RUS** 121 Ed12
Năvodari **RO** 89 Ka37
Navoloki **RUS** 118 Fa09
Náxos **GR** 115 Jd47
Nay **F** 80 Cd38
Nazaré **P** 90 Ac40
Nazilli **TR** 113 Kb45
Ndroq **RKS** 100 Hb42
Néa Aghíalos **GR** 101 Ja44
Néa Artáki **GR** 112 Jb45
Néa Epídavros **GR** 111 Ja46
Néa Fókea **GR** 101 Ja43
Néa Ionía **GR** 101 Ja44
Néa Kalikrátia **GR** 101 Ja43
Néa Mihanióna **GR** 101 Ja43
Néa Moudania **GR** 101 Ja43
Néa Péramos **GR** 102 Jb42
Neápoli **GR** 101 Hc43
Neápoli **GR** 111 Ja48
Neápoli **GR** 115 Jd49
Neath **GB** 23 Cc26
Néa Triglia **GR** 101 Ja43
Néa Zíhni **GR** 102 Jb42
Nebiler **TR** 113 Ka44
Nebolči **RUS** 117 Ec08
Neckargemünd **D** 63 Ed31
Neckarsulm **D** 64 Fa32
Nedelišće **HR** 73 Gb35
Nederweert **NL** 55 Eb28
Neðribær **IS** 14 Bc04
Nedryhajliv **UA** 121 Ed14
Nedstrand **N** 42 Ed18
Negotin **SRB** 87 Hd38
Negotino **MK** 101 Hd42
Negraşi **RO** 88 Jb37
Nègrepelisse **F** 81 Db37
Negreşti **RO** 77 Jd34
Negreşti-Oaş **RO** 75 Hd33
Negru Vodă **RO** 89 Ka38
Nehaevskij **RUS** 123 Fc13
Neja **RUS** 118 Fb08
Nekla **PL** 58 Gc27
Nekrasovskoe **RUS** 118 Fa09

Nelaug **N** 42 Fa19
Nelidovo **RUS** 117 Ec10
Nellim **FIN** 27 Hc05
Nelson **GB** 21 Da24
Neman **RUS** 52 Hb24
Nemenčinė **LT** 53 Ja24
Nemours **F** 62 Dc32
Nemšová **SK** 66 Gd32
Nemyriv **UA** 67 Hd30
Nemyriv **UA** 121 Eb15
Nenagh **IRL** 18 Ca24
Nenitoúria **GR** 113 Jd45
Néo Erásmio **GR** 102 Jc42
Neohóri **GR** 101 Hd44
Néo Monastíri **GR** 101 Hd44
Néo Petrítsi **GR** 101 Ja42
Néos Marmarás **GR** 102 Jb43
Néos Skopós **GR** 101 Ja42
Nepolje **RKS** 87 Hb40
Nepomuk **CZ** 65 Fd31
Neptun **RO** 89 Ka38
Nérac **F** 81 Da37
Neratovice **CZ** 65 Ga30
Nerehta **RUS** 118 Fa09
Nereju **RO** 76 Jc35
Neresheim **D** 64 Fb32
Nereta **LV** 53 Hd22
Nergnäset **S** 34 Ha10
Neringa-Nida **LT** 52 Ha23
Nerja **E** 106 Bc45
Nerl' **RUS** 117 Ed09
Nérondes **F** 69 Dc34
Nerpio **E** 107 Ca44
Nerušaj **UA** 77 Kb35
Nerva **E** 105 Ad43
Nervi **I** 83 Ed38
Nes **N** 36 Fa15
Nes **N** 37 Fb16
Nesbyen **N** 37 Fb16
Nesebăr **BG** 89 Ka39
Nesflaten **N** 42 Ed17
Nesheim **N** 36 Ed16
Nesjahverfi **IS** 15 Cb08
Neskaupstaður **IS** 15 Cc07
Neslandsvatn **N** 43 Fb19
Nesle **F** 62 Dd30
Nesna **N** 32 Fd09
Nesodden **N** 43 Fc18
Nestáni **GR** 111 Ja47
Nestavoll **N** 37 Fb14
Nesterov **RUS** 52 Hc24
Nestiary **RUS** 119 Fc09
Nesttun **N** 36 Ed16
Nesvik **N** 42 Ed18
Nettetal **D** 55 Ec28
Nettuno **I** 98 Fc42
Neubrandenburg **D** 57 Fd26
Neubukow **D** 56 Fc25
Neuburg an der Donau **D** 64 Fb32
Neuchâtel **CH** 71 Ec34
Neuenhagen **D** 57 Fd27
Neuenhaus **D** 55 Ec27
Neuenkirchen **D** 56 Fb26
Neuf-Brisach **F** 71 Ec33

Neufchâteau **B** 63 Eb30
Neufchâteau **F** 63 Eb32
Neufchâtel-en-Bray **F** 62 Dc30
Neufchâtel-sur-Aisne **F** 62 Ea31
Neuhaus **D** 56 Fb26
Neuhaus **D** 64 Fb30
Neuhof **D** 64 Fa30
Neuillé-Pont-Pierre **F** 69 Db33
Neukirchen **A** 72 Fc34
Neulengbach **A** 73 Gb33
Neum **BIH** 86 Gd40
Neumarkt **A** 73 Ga35
Neumarkt in der Oberpfalz **D** 64 Fc32
Neumarkt-Sankt Veit **D** 72 Fc33
Neumünster **D** 56 Fb25
Neunburg **D** 64 Fc31
Neung-sur-Beuvron **F** 69 Dc33
Neunkirchen **A** 73 Gb34
Neunkirchen **D** 63 Ec31
Neuruppin **D** 57 Fd27
Neusiedl **A** 74 Gc33
Neuss **D** 63 Ec29
Neustadt **D** 56 Fb25
Neustadt **D** 64 Fb30
Neustadt (Aisch) **D** 64 Fb31
Neustadt (Donau) **D** 64 Fc32
Neustadt (Orla) **D** 64 Fc30
Neustadt (Weinstraße) **D** 63 Ed31
Neustadt/Dosse **D** 56 Fc27
Neustadt am Rübenberg **D** 56 Fa27
Neustadt-Glewe **D** 56 Fc26
Neustift **A** 72 Fb34
Neustrelitz **D** 57 Fd26
Neutraubling **D** 64 Fc32
Neu-Ulm **D** 72 Fa33
Neuvic **F** 69 Dc36
Neuville-aux-Bois **F** 62 Dc32
Neuville-de-Poitou **F** 69 Da34
Neuville-sur-Saône **F** 70 Ea35
Neuvy-sur-Barangeon **F** 69 Dc33
Neuwied **D** 63 Ed30
Neveklov **CZ** 65 Ga31
Nevel' **RUS** 117 Eb11
Nevers **F** 70 Dd34
Nevesinje **BIH** 86 Gd40
Nevestino **BG** 87 Hd40
Nevinnomyssk **RUS** 127 Fd16
Nevlunghavn **N** 43 Fb19
Nevskoe **RUS** 52 Hc24
Newark-on-Trent **GB** 25 Db25
Newbridge **IRL** 19 Cb24
Newbury **GB** 24 Da27

Newcastle **GB** 20 Cc23
Newcastle-under-Lyme **GB** 24 Da25
Newcastle upon Tyne **GB** 21 Db23
Newcastle West **IRL** 18 Bd24
Newhaven **GB** 25 Db28
Newmarket **GB** 25 Dc27
Newport **GB** 24 Cd27
Newport **GB** 24 Da28
Newport **GB** 24 Da25
Newport Pagnell **GB** 25 Db26
Newquay **GB** 23 Cb28
New Romney **GB** 25 Dc28
New Ross **IRL** 22 Ca25
Newry **GB** 20 Cc23
Newton Abbot **GB** 23 Cc28
Newtonmore **GB** 17 Da19
Newton Stewart **GB** 20 Cd22
Newtown **GB** 24 Cd25
Newtownabbey **GB** 20 Cc22
Newtownards **GB** 20 Cc22
Newtown Saint Boswells **GB** 21 Da22
Newtownstewart **GB** 20 Cb22
Nexø **DK** 50 Ga24
Nezvys'ko **UA** 76 Jb32
Nianfors **S** 38 Gb15
Nibe **DK** 49 Fb21
Nicaj-Shalë **AL** 100 Hb41
Nice **F** 83 Eb39
Nicgale **LV** 53 Ja22
Nicosia **I** 109 Ga47
Nicotera **I** 109 Gb46
Niculiţel **RO** 89 Ka36
Nidda **D** 64 Fa30
Nidderau **D** 64 Fa30
Nidri **GR** 110 Hc45
Nidzica **PL** 58 Ha26
Niebüll **D** 48 Fa24
Niedalino **PL** 57 Gb25
Niederaula **D** 64 Fa29
Niederbronn-les-Bains **F** 63 Ec32
Niedrzwica Duża **PL** 67 Hc29
Nielisz **PL** 67 Hc29
Niemce **PL** 67 Hc29
Niemisel **S** 34 Ha09
Nienburg **D** 56 Fa27
Nierstein **D** 63 Ed31
Niesky **D** 65 Ga29
Nieuwegein **NL** 55 Eb27
Nieuwpoort **B** 54 Dd28
Niewegłosz **PL** 59 Hc28
Niezabyszewo **PL** 58 Gc25
Niğde **TR** 128 Gd15
Nigríta **GR** 101 Ja42
Nijar **E** 106 Bd46
Nijkerk **NL** 55 Eb27
Nijmegen **NL** 55 Ec28
Nijverdal **NL** 55 Ec27
Níkea **GR** 101 Hd44

Nikel' **RUS** 27 Hd04
Nikifóros **GR** 102 Jb42
Nikítas **GR** 102 Jb43
Nikkaluokta **S** 29 Gc07
Nikolaevka **RUS** 119 Fd10
Nikolaevo **BG** 102 Jc40
Nikolaevo **RUS** 47 Jb19
Nikolaevsk **RUS** 123 Fd13
Nikol'sk **RUS** 119 Fd10
Nikopol **BG** 88 Jb38
Nikopol' **UA** 126 Fa16
Nikópoli **GR** 110 Hc45
Nikšić **MNE** 86 Ha40
Nilivaara **S** 30 Ha08
Nilsiä **FIN** 35 Hd12
Nîmes **F** 82 Dd38
Nin **HR** 85 Ga38
Ninove **B** 62 Ea29
Niort **F** 68 Cd34
Niš **SRB** 87 Hc39
Nisa **P** 90 Ad41
Niscemi **I** 109 Ga48
Niška Banja **SRB** 87 Hd39
Nisko **PL** 67 Hc30
Nisou **CY** 128 Gb19
Nisporeni **MD** 77 Jd33
Nissedal **N** 42 Fa18
Nissi **EST** 46 Hc18
Nissilä **FIN** 35 Hd12
Nītaure **LV** 53 Hd21
Nitra **SK** 74 Gd33
Nitrianske Pravno **SK** 66 Gd32
Nittedal **N** 43 Fc17
Nittenau **D** 64 Fc32
Nivala **FIN** 35 Hc12
Nivelles **B** 62 Ea29
Nivenskoe **RUS** 52 Ha24
Nižná Boca **SK** 67 Ha32
Nižnekamsk **RUS** 119 Ga08
Nižnij Novgorod **RUS** 118 Fb09
Nižyn **UA** 121 Ec14
Nizza Monferrato **I** 83 Ed37
Njasviž **BY** 120 Ea13
Njivice **HR** 85 Ga37
Njurundabommen **S** 39 Gc14
Noailles **F** 62 Dc31
Noci **I** 99 Gc43
Nodeland **N** 42 Fa20
Nödinge-Nol **S** 43 Fc20
Nœux-les-Mines **F** 62 Dd29
Nogales **E** 91 Ba42
Nogarejas **E** 78 Bb38
Nogent **F** 71 Eb33
Nogent-le-Roi **F** 62 Dc31
Nogent-le-Rotrou **F** 61 Db32
Nogent-sur-Seine **F** 62 Dd32
Noginsk **RUS** 118 Fa10
Noguera **E** 93 Cb41
Nohfelden **D** 63 Ec31
Noia **E** 78 Ad36
Noirétable **F** 70 Dd35
Noirmoutier-en-l'Île **F** 68 Cc33

Nokia **FIN** 40 Hb15
Nola **I** 99 Ga43
Nolay **F** 70 Ea34
Nomeny **F** 63 Eb32
Nomitsís **GR** 111 Ja48
Nonancourt **F** 61 Db31
Nonantola **I** 84 Fb38
Nonza **F** 96 Ed40
Noordwijk aan Zee **NL** 55 Eb27
Noormarkku **FIN** 40 Ha15
Nora **S** 44 Ga18
Norberg **S** 44 Gb17
Norcia **I** 85 Fd40
Nordagutu **N** 43 Fb18
Nordborg **DK** 49 Fb24
Nordby **DK** 48 Fa23
Nordby **DK** 49 Fb23
Norddal **N** 36 Ed15
Norden **D** 55 Ed26
Nordenham **D** 56 Fa26
Norderstedt **D** 56 Fb26
Nordfjordeid **N** 36 Ed14
Nordfold **N** 28 Ga07
Nordhausen **D** 64 Fb29
Nordholz **D** 56 Fa25
Nordhorn **D** 55 Ed27
Nordingrå **S** 39 Gc13
Nordkjosbotn **N** 26 Gc05
Nördlingen **D** 64 Fb32
Nordmaling **S** 34 Gd12
Nordmark **S** 44 Ga18
Nordmela **N** 28 Gb05
Nordøyvågen **N** 32 Fd09
Nordre Osen **N** 37 Fc16
Nord-Sel **N** 37 Fb15
Noresund **N** 43 Fb17
Norheimsund **N** 36 Ed16
Norråker **S** 33 Gb11
Norra Tresund **S** 33 Gb11
Norrbäck **S** 33 Gc11
Nørre Aaby **DK** 49 Fb23
Nørre Alslev **DK** 49 Fc24
Nørre Nebel **DK** 48 Fa23
Nørre Vorupør **DK** 48 Fa21
Norrfjärden **S** 34 Ha10
Norrfors **S** 33 Gc12
Norrhult **S** 50 Ga21
Norrköping **S** 44 Gb19
Norrsundet **S** 39 Gc16
Norrtälje **S** 45 Gd18
Nors **DK** 48 Fa21
Norsholm **S** 44 Gb19
Norsjö **S** 34 Gd11
Northallerton **GB** 21 Db23
Northampton **GB** 25 Db26
North Berwick **GB** 21 Db21
Northeim **D** 56 Fb28
North Kessock **GB** 17 Da19
Northleach **GB** 24 Da27
North Walsham **GB** 25 Dd26
Nortorf **D** 56 Fb25
Nort-sur-Erdre **F** 61 Cd32
Norwich **GB** 25 Dc26
Nosivka **UA** 121 Ec14

Nosovo **RUS** 47 Jb20
Nossebro **S** 43 Fd20
Nössemark **S** 43 Fc18
Nossen **D** 65 Fd29
Noszolop **H** 74 Gc34
Noto **I** 109 Ga48
Notodden **N** 43 Fb18
Nottingham **GB** 25 Db25
Növa **EST** 46 Hc18
Nova Borova **UA** 121 Eb14
Nová Bystřice **CZ** 65 Ga32
Novačene **BG** 88 Ja39
Novaci **MK** 101 Hc42
Novaci **RO** 88 Ja37
Nova Crnja **SRB** 75 Hb36
Nova Gorica **SLO** 73 Fd36
Nova Gradiška **HR** 86 Gc37
Novaja Derevnja **RUS** 52 Hb24
Novaja Ladoga **RUS** 117 Eb08
Novaja Ruda **BY** 59 Hd25
Nova Kachovka **UA** 126 Fa16
Novalja **HR** 85 Ga38
Novalukoml' **BY** 121 Eb12
Nova Odesa **UA** 125 Ed16
Novara **I** 71 Ed36
Nova Topola **BIH** 86 Gc37
Nova Ušycja **UA** 125 Eb16
Nova Varoš **SRB** 87 Hb39
Nova Vodolaha **UA** 122 Fa14
Nova Zagora **BG** 102 Jc40
Nové Hrady **CZ** 65 Ga32
Novellara **I** 84 Fb37
Nové Město nad Metují **CZ** 65 Gb30
Nové Město na Moravě **CZ** 65 Gb31
Nové Zámky **SK** 74 Gd33
Novgorod **RUS** 117 Eb09
Novgorodka **RUS** 47 Jb20
Novhorodka **UA** 121 Ed15
Novhorod-Sivers'kyj **UA** 121 Ed13
Novi Bečej **SRB** 75 Hb36
Novi Bilokorovyči **UA** 121 Eb14
Novi Grad **BIH** 86 Gd37
Novigrad **HR** 85 Fd37
Novigrad-Podravski **HR** 74 Gc36
Novi Iskăr **BG** 102 Ja40
Novi Ligure **I** 83 Ed37
Novion-Porcien **F** 62 Ea31
Novi Pazar **BG** 89 Jd38
Novi Pazar **SRB** 87 Hb40
Novi Sad **SRB** 86 Ha37
Novi Sanžary **UA** 121 Ed15
Novi Vinodolski **HR** 85 Ga37
Novoaleksandrovsk **RUS** 127 Fd16
Novonanninskij **RUS** 123 Fc13
Novoarchanhel's'k **UA** 121 Ec15

Novoazovs'k **UA** 126 Fb16
Novočeboksarsk **RUS** 119 Fc09
Novočerkassk **RUS** 123 Fc15
Novocimljanskaja **RUS** 123 Fd14
Novofedorivka **UA** 125 Ed17
Novohrad-Volyns'kyj **UA** 121 Eb14
Novokašpirskij **RUS** 119 Ga10
Novokrasne **MD** 77 Kb32
Novokubansk **RUS** 127 Fd16
Novokujbyševsk **RUS** 119 Ga10
Novo Mesto **SLO** 73 Ga36
Novomičurinsk **RUS** 118 Fa11
Novomihajlovskij **RUS** 127 Fc17
Novomoskovsk **RUS** 118 Fa11
Novomoskovs'k **UA** 122 Fa15
Novomykolajivka **UA** 122 Fa15
Novomykolajivka **UA** 125 Ed17
Novomyrhorod **UA** 121 Ed15
Novonikolaevskij **RUS** 123 Fc13
Novooleksijivka **UA** 126 Fa17
Novopavlovsk **RUS** 127 Ga17
Novopokrovka **UA** 122 Fa15
Novopokrovskaja **RUS** 127 Fd16
Novopskov **UA** 122 Fb14
Novorossijsk **RUS** 127 Fc17
Novoržev **RUS** 117 Eb10
Novošahtinsk **RUS** 123 Fc15
Novoselci **BG** 103 Jd40
Novosel'e **RUS** 47 Jb19
Novoselec **BG** 102 Jc40
Novoselivs'ke **UA** 126 Fa17
Novo Selo **BG** 88 Jc39
Novo Selo **BG** 101 Hd41
Novo Selo **BIH** 86 Gd37
Novoselycja **UA** 76 Jb32
Novosokol'niki **RUS** 117 Eb10
Novotroickoe **RUS** 119 Fc10
Novotrojic'ke **UA** 126 Fa17
Novotulka **RUS** 123 Ga12
Novoukrajinka **UA** 125 Ed16
Novouljanovsk **RUS** 119 Fd10
Novouzensk **RUS** 123 Ga12
Novovolyns'k **UA** 67 Hd29
Novska **HR** 86 Gc37
Nový Bor **CZ** 65 Ga30
Novycja **UA** 76 Ja32
Novy Dvor **BY** 59 Hd26
Novy Dvor **BY** 59 Hd25
Novyi Oskol **RUS** 122 Fb13
Novyj Buh **UA** 125 Ed16
Nový Jičín **CZ** 66 Gd31
Novyj Rozdil **UA** 67 Hd31
Nowa Brzeźnica **PL** 66 Gd29

Nowa Cerekwia **PL** 66 Gd30
Nowa Dęba **PL** 67 Hc30
Nowa Karczma **PL** 58 Gd25
Nowa Ruda **PL** 65 Gb30
Nowa Słupia **PL** 67 Hb29
Nowa Sól **PL** 57 Gb28
Nowa Wieś **PL** 59 Hb26
Nowa Wieś Ełcka **PL** 59 Hc25
Nowa Wieś Lęborska **PL** 58 Gc25
Nowe Miasteczko **PL** 57 Gb28
Nowe Miasto **PL** 58 Ha27
Nowe Miasto nad Pilicą **PL** 58 Ha28
Nowe Warpno **PL** 57 Ga26
Nowinka **PL** 59 Hc25
Nowogard **PL** 57 Ga26
Nowogród **PL** 59 Hb26
Nowogród Bobrzański **PL** 57 Gb28
Nowo Miasto nad Wartą **PL** 58 Gc28
Nowosiółki **PL** 67 Hd30
Nowy Duninów **PL** 58 Ha27
Nowy Dwór **PL** 65 Gb29
Nowy Dwór Gdański **PL** 58 Gd25
Nowy Dwór Mazowiecki **PL** 59 Hb27
Nowy Korczyn **PL** 67 Hb30
Nowy Sącz **PL** 67 Hb31
Nowy Staw **PL** 58 Gd25
Nowy Targ **PL** 67 Ha31
Nowy Tomyśl **PL** 57 Gb28
Nowy Żmigród **PL** 67 Hb31
Noyant **F** 69 Da33
Noyers **F** 70 Dd33
Noyon **F** 62 Dd30
Nozay **F** 61 Cd32
Nucet **RO** 75 Hd35
Nudol' **RUS** 117 Ed10
Nudyže **UA** 59 Hd28
Nuenen **NL** 55 Eb28
Nufăru **RO** 89 Ka36
Nuijamaa **FIN** 41 Ja15
Nuits-Saint-Georges **F** 70 Ea34
Nules **E** 93 Cc42
Nummela **FIN** 40 Hc16
Nummi **FIN** 40 Hc16
Nummijärvi **FIN** 40 Hb14
Nuneaton **GB** 24 Da26
Nunnanen **FIN** 30 Hb06
Nuorgam **FIN** 27 Hc04
Nuoro **I** 97 Ed43
Núpsstaður **IS** 15 Ca08
Nurlat **RUS** 119 Ga09
Nurmes **FIN** 35 Ja12
Nurmijärvi **FIN** 35 Ja12
Nurmijärvi **FIN** 40 Hc16
Nurmo **FIN** 40 Hb13
Nürnberg **D** 64 Fb31
Nürtingen **D** 64 Fa32
Nușfalau **RO** 75 Hd34

Nusnäs **S** 38 Ga16
Nuupas **FIN** 35 Hc09
Nuvvus **FIN** 27 Hb04
Nyåker **S** 34 Gd12
Nybergsund **N** 37 Fd16
Nyborg **DK** 49 Fb24
Nyborg **S** 34 Ha09
Nybro **S** 50 Gb22
Nyékládháza **H** 75 Hb33
Nyergesújfalu **H** 74 Gd34
Nyhammar **S** 44 Ga17
Nyídalur **IS** 15 Ca07
Nyírábrány **H** 75 Hc34
Nyíradony **H** 75 Hc33
Nyírbátor **H** 75 Hc33
Nyírbéltek **H** 75 Hc33
Nyíregyháza **H** 75 Hc33
Nyírmada **H** 75 Hc33
Nyírtelek **H** 75 Hc33
Nykøbing F **DK** 49 Fc24
Nykøbing M **DK** 48 Fa21
Nykøbing S **DK** 49 Fc23
Nyköping **S** 45 Gc19
Nykroppa **S** 44 Ga18
Nykvarn **S** 45 Gc18
Nyland **S** 39 Gc13
Nymburk **CZ** 65 Ga30
Nynäshamn **S** 45 Gc19
Nyneset **N** 32 Fd11
Nyon **CH** 71 Eb35
Nyons **F** 82 Ea38
Nýřany **CZ** 65 Fd31
Nyrud **N** 27 Hd05
Nysa **PL** 66 Gc30
Nysäter **S** 43 Fd18
Nystad **FIN** 40 Ha16
Nysted **DK** 49 Fc24
Nyvoll **N** 26 Ha04
Nyžni Sirohozy **UA** 126 Fa16
Nyžni Torhaji **UA** 126 Fa16
Nyžni Vorota **UA** 67 Hd32
Nyžn'ohirs'kyj **UA** 126 Fa17

O

Oakham **GB** 25 Db26
Oban **GB** 16 Cd20
O Barco **E** 78 Bb37
Obbnäs **FIN** 46 Hc17
Obbola **S** 34 Gd12
Öbektaş **TR** 128 Gc15
Obeliai **LT** 53 Ja22
Oberammergau **D** 72 Fb34
Oberhausen **D** 55 Ec28
Oberkirch **D** 63 Ed32
Obernai **F** 63 Ec32
Obernburg **D** 64 Fa31
Oberndorf **A** 73 Fd33
Oberndorf **D** 71 Ed33
Oberpullendorf **A** 74 Gc34
Oberstdorf **D** 72 Fa34
Obertyn **UA** 76 Ja32
Oberviechtach **D** 64 Fc31
Oberwart **A** 73 Gb34
Óbidos **P** 90 Ac41

Obninsk **RUS** 117 Ed11
Obodivka **UA** 77 Ka32
Obojan' **RUS** 122 Fa13
Obolon' **UA** 121 Ed15
Oborniki **PL** 58 Gc27
Oborniki Śląskie **PL** 66 Gc29
Oborowo **PL** 58 Gd27
Obory **CZ** 65 Ga31
Obrenovac **SRB** 87 Hb38
Obrež **HR** 73 Gb36
Obrovac **HR** 85 Gb38
Obruk **TR** 128 Gc15
Obsza **PL** 67 Hc30
Obzor **BG** 89 Ka39
Obżyle **UA** 77 Ka32
Očakiv **UA** 125 Ed17
Ocaña **E** 92 Bd41
Očeretuvate **UA** 126 Fa16
Ochsenfurt **D** 64 Fa31
Ochsenhausen **D** 72 Fa33
Ochtrup **D** 55 Ed27
Ochtyrka **UA** 121 Ed14
Ocieka **PL** 67 Hb30
Ockelbo **S** 38 Gb16
Ocland **RO** 76 Jb35
Ocna Mureş **RO** 76 Ja35
Ocna Sibiului **RO** 88 Ja36
Ocnele Mari **RO** 88 Ja37
Ocnița **MD** 76 Jc32
Ocoliş **RO** 75 Hd35
Ödåkra **S** 49 Fd22
Odda **N** 42 Ed17
Odden Færgehavn **DK** 49 Fc23
Odder **DK** 49 Fb23
Odeceixe **P** 104 Ab43
Odemira **P** 104 Ab43
Ödemiş **TR** 113 Kb45
Odensbacken **S** 44 Gb18
Odense **DK** 49 Fb23
Oderzo **I** 72 Fc36
Odesa **UA** 77 Kb34
Odesa **UA** 125 Ec17
Odincovo **RUS** 117 Ed10
Odobasca **RO** 88 Jc36
Odobeşti **RO** 77 Jd35
Odolanów **PL** 66 Gc29
Odoorn **NL** 55 Ec27
Odorheiu Secuiesc **RO** 76 Jb35
Odry **CZ** 66 Gd31
Odrzywół **PL** 58 Ha28
Ødsted **DK** 49 Fb23
Odžaci **SRB** 86 Ha37
Odžak **BIH** 86 Gd37
Oebisfelde **D** 56 Fb27
Öekény **H** 74 Ha34
Oelsnitz **D** 64 Fc30
Oettingen **D** 64 Fb32
Oetz **A** 72 Fb34
Offenbach **D** 63 Ed30
Offenburg **D** 63 Ed32
Ogoşte **RKS** 87 Hc40
Ogre **LV** 53 Hd21
Ogrodniki **PL** 59 Hc25
Ogrodzieniec **PL** 67 Ha30

Ogulin **HR** 85 Gb37
Ohrid **MK** 101 Hc42
Öhringen **D** 64 Fa32
Oijärvi **FIN** 35 Hc09
Oikarainen **FIN** 31 Hc08
Oisemont **F** 62 Dc30
Oitti **FIN** 40 Hc16
Öja **FIN** 34 Hb12
Öje **S** 38 Ga16
Öjebyn **S** 34 Ha10
Ojos Negros **E** 93 Cb41
Ojrzeń **PL** 58 Ha27
Öjung **S** 38 Gb15
Okartowo **PL** 59 Hb25
Okehampton **GB** 23 Cc28
Okkelberg **N** 37 Fc13
Okovcy **RUS** 117 Ec10
Okrzeja **PL** 59 Hc28
Oksbøl **DK** 48 Fa23
Øksfjord **N** 26 Gd04
Okstad **N** 37 Fc13
Oktjabr'sk **RUS** 119 Ga10
Oktjabr'skij **RUS** 123 Fd14
Okučani **HR** 86 Gc37
Okulovka **RUS** 117 Ec09
Ólafsfjörður **IS** 15 Ca05
Ólafsvík **IS** 14 Bb05
Olaine **LV** 52 Hc21
Olargues **F** 81 Dc38
Oława **PL** 66 Gc29
Olbernhau **D** 65 Fd30
Olbia **I** 96 Ed42
Oldeide **N** 36 Ed14
Olden **N** 36 Fa15
Olden **S** 33 Ga12
Oldenburg **D** 55 Ed26
Oldenburg in Holstein **D** 56 Fb25
Oldenzaal **NL** 55 Ec27
Olderdalen **N** 26 Gd05
Olderfjord **N** 27 Hb03
Oldervik **N** 26 Gc04
Oldham **GB** 21 Da24
Oldmeldrum **GB** 17 Db19
Olecko **PL** 59 Hc25
Oleggio **I** 71 Ed36
Oleiros **P** 90 Ad40
Oleksandrija **UA** 121 Ed15
Oleksandrivka **MD** 77 Kb32
Oleksandrivka **UA** 121 Ed15
Oleksandrivka **UA** 121 Ed15
Oleksandrivka **UA** 122 Fb15
Oleksandrivka **UA** 125 Ed17
Ølen **N** 42 Ed17
Olenino **RUS** 117 Ec10
Olenivka **UA** 125 Ed17
Oleśnica **PL** 66 Gc29
Olesno **PL** 66 Gd29
Oleszno **PL** 67 Ha29
Oleszyce **PL** 67 Hd30
Olevs'k **UA** 121 Eb14
Olfen **D** 55 Ed28
Ølgod **DK** 48 Fa23
Olhão **P** 104 Ac44
Olhava **FIN** 35 Hc10
Ol'hi **RUS** 118 Fb11

Ol'hovatka **RUS** 122 Fb13
Ol'hovka **RUS** 123 Fd13
Oliena **I** 97 Ed43
Olimbía **GR** 110 Hd47
Olimp **RO** 89 Ka37
Olimpiáda **GR** 102 Jb42
Olite **E** 80 Cb39
Oliva **E** 94 Cc44
Oliva de la Frontera **E** 105 Ad43
Oliveira de Azeméis **P** 78 Ad39
Oliveira do Hospital **P** 90 Ad40
Olivenza **E** 90 Ad42
Olivet **F** 62 Dc32
Olkusz **PL** 67 Ha30
Ollerton **GB** 25 Db25
Olmedo **E** 79 Bc39
Olmeto **F** 96 Ed41
Olofström **S** 50 Ga22
Olomouc **CZ** 66 Gc31
Oloron-Sainte-Marie **F** 80 Cc38
Olot **E** 81 Db40
Olovo **BIH** 86 Gd38
Olpe **D** 63 Ed29
Ol'ša **RUS** 117 Ec11
Olsberg **D** 63 Ed29
Olshammar **S** 44 Ga19
Olszamy **PL** 59 Hb28
Olszanka **PL** 59 Hc25
Olsztyn **PL** 58 Ha25
Olsztynek **PL** 58 Ha26
Olszyna **PL** 57 Ga28
Oltedal **N** 42 Ed18
Olten **CH** 71 Ed34
Olteniţa **RO** 89 Jd38
Oltina **RO** 89 Jd37
Oltu **TR** 127 Ga19
Oltuš **BY** 59 Hd28
Olukpınar **TR** 128 Gb17
Olur **TR** 127 Ga19
Olustvere **EST** 47 Hd19
Ólvega **E** 80 Cb40
Olvera **E** 105 Ba45
Ólymbos **GR** 115 Kb48
Omagh **GB** 20 Cb22
Omalí **GR** 101 Hc43
Omarska **BIH** 86 Gc37
Omegna **I** 71 Ed36
Omiš **HR** 86 Gc39
Ommen **NL** 55 Ec27
Omurtag **BG** 89 Jd39
Onda **E** 93 Cc42
Ondarroa **E** 80 Cb37
Oneşti **RO** 76 Jc35
Onich **GB** 16 Cd20
Ontinyent **E** 107 Cb44
Ontojoki **FIN** 35 Ja11
Ontur **E** 107 Ca44
Onuškis **LT** 53 Hd22
Oostburg **NL** 54 Ea28
Oostende **B** 54 Dd28
Oosterend **NL** 55 Eb26
Oosterhout **NL** 55 Eb28

Oosterwolde **NL** 55 Ec26
Oostkapelle **NL** 54 Ea28
Oost-Vlieland **NL** 55 Eb26
Opaka **BG** 88 Jc38
Oparić **SRB** 87 Hc39
Opatija **HR** 85 Ga37
Opatów **PL** 66 Gd29
Opatów **PL** 67 Hb29
Opava **CZ** 66 Gd31
Ope **S** 38 Ga13
Opišnja **UA** 121 Ed14
Opličići **BIH** 86 Gd40
Opočka **RUS** 53 Jb21
Opoczno **PL** 67 Ha29
Opole **PL** 66 Gd30
Opol'e **RUS** 47 Jb17
Opole Lubelskie **PL** 67 Hc29
Opovo **SRB** 87 Hb37
Oppdal **N** 37 Fb14
Oppenheim **D** 63 Ed31
Opsa **BY** 53 Ja23
Opuzen **HR** 86 Gd40
Ora **I** 72 Fb35
Oradea **RO** 75 Hc34
Orahova **BIH** 86 Gc37
Orahovac **RKS** 87 Hb40
Orahovačko Polje **BIH** 86 Gd38
Orahovica **BIH** 86 Gd38
Orahovica **HR** 86 Gd37
Oraison **F** 82 Ea38
Orajärvi **FIN** 30 Hb08
Orange **F** 82 Dd38
Oranienburg **D** 57 Fd27
Oranmore **IRL** 18 Bd23
Orăştie **RO** 75 Hd36
Oraşu Nou **RO** 75 Hd33
Oravainen **FIN** 40 Ha13
Oraviţa **RO** 87 Hc37
Oravská Lesná **SK** 67 Ha31
Oravská Polhora **SK** 67 Ha31
Oravský Podzámok **SK** 67 Ha31
Orbassano **I** 83 Ec37
Orbeasca **RO** 88 Jb38
Orbec **F** 61 Db31
Orbetello **I** 98 Fb41
Örbyhus **S** 45 Gc17
Orce **E** 106 Bd45
Orchowo **PL** 58 Gd27
Orcières **F** 83 Eb37
Ordes **E** 78 Ba36
Ordu **TR** 127 Fc19
Orduña **E** 79 Ca38
Ordžonikidze **UA** 126 Fa16
Ordžonikidzevskij **RUS** 127 Ga17
Orea **E** 93 Cb41
Orebić **HR** 86 Gc40
Örebro **S** 44 Ga18
Oredež **RUS** 117 Eb09
Öregrund **S** 45 Gc17
Orehovno **RUS** 47 Jb18
Orehovo-Zuevo **RUS** 118 Fa10
Orel **RUS** 47 Ja18

Orel **RUS** 121 Ed12
Ören **TR** 113 Kb46
Orense **E** 78 Ba37
Orestiada **GR** 103 Jd41
Öreström **S** 33 Gc12
Orford **GB** 25 Dc27
Organyà **E** 81 Da40
Orgaz **E** 92 Bd42
Orgelet **F** 70 Ea35
Órgiva **E** 106 Bc45
Orgosolo **I** 97 Ed43
Orhei **MD** 77 Ka33
Orhomenós **GR** 111 Ja45
Oria **E** 106 Bd45
Orichiv **UA** 126 Fa16
Orihuela **E** 107 Cb44
Orijahovo **BG** 88 Ja38
Orimattila **FIN** 41 Hd16
Orio **GR** 112 Jb45
Oriolo **I** 99 Gc44
Orissaare **EST** 46 Hb19
Oristano **I** 97 Ec44
Öriszentpéter **H** 74 Gc35
Orivesi **FIN** 40 Hc15
Ørje **N** 43 Fc18
Orkanger **N** 37 Fc13
Örkelljunga **S** 49 Fd22
Orlea **RO** 88 Jb38
Orléans **F** 62 Dc32
Orleşti **RO** 88 Ja37
Orlivka **UA** 89 Ka36
Orlja **BY** 59 Hd25
Orlov Gaj **RUS** 123 Ga12
Orlovskij **RUS** 123 Fd15
Orly **F** 62 Dc31
Ormea **I** 83 Ec38
Órmos Panórmou **GR** 112 Jc46
Ormož **SLO** 73 Gb35
Ormskirk **GB** 21 Da24
Ornans **F** 71 Eb34
Ørnes **N** 28 Ga08
Orneta **PL** 58 Ha25
Örnsköldsvik **S** 39 Gc13
Oropesa **E** 91 Bb41
Orosei **I** 97 Ed43
Orosháza **H** 75 Hb35
Oroszlány **H** 74 Gd34
Orpesa **E** 93 Cc42
Orrefors **S** 50 Gb22
Orrliden **S** 38 Fd16
Orrviken **S** 38 Ga13
Orša **BY** 121 Eb12
Orsa **S** 38 Ga16
Orśac **BIH** 85 Gb38
Orşova **RO** 87 Hd37
Ørsta **N** 36 Ed14
Örsundsbro **S** 45 Gc18
Ortakaraören **TR** 128 Ga16
Ortakent **TR** 113 Kb46
Ortaklar **TR** 113 Kb45
Ortaköy **TR** 103 Jd42
Ortaköy **TR** 127 Ga19
Orta Nova **I** 99 Gb42
Orta San Giulio **I** 71 Ed36
Orte **I** 98 Fc41

Orthez – Páliros

Orthez **F** 80 Cc38
Ortigueira **E** 78 Ba36
Ortisei **I** 72 Fc35
Ortnevik **N** 36 Ed15
Orto **F** 96 Ed41
Ortona **I** 99 Ga41
Ortrand **D** 65 Fd29
Orvault **F** 68 Cd33
Orvieto **I** 84 Fc40
Orzesze **PL** 66 Gd30
Orzinuovi **I** 84 Fa37
Orživ **UA** 120 Ea14
Oržycja **UA** 121 Ed15
Orzysz **PL** 59 Hb25
Os **N** 37 Fc14
Osby **S** 50 Ga22
Oschatz **D** 65 Fd29
Oschersleben **D** 56 Fc28
Oschiri **I** 97 Ed43
Ose **N** 42 Fa18
Osečina **SRB** 86 Ha38
Osen **N** 32 Fc11
Osenovlag **BG** 88 Ja39
Osieczna **PL** 58 Gc28
Osieczno **PL** 57 Gb27
Osiek **PL** 58 Gd26
Osijek **HR** 74 Ha36
Osimo **I** 85 Fd39
Osinów **PL** 57 Ga27
Osjaków **PL** 66 Gd29
Osječenica **MNE** 86 Ha40
Oskarshamn **S** 50 Gb21
Oskarström **S** 49 Fd22
Os'kino **RUS** 122 Fb13
Oslo **N** 43 Fc17
Os'mino **RUS** 47 Jb18
Ösmo **S** 45 Gc19
Osmolda **UA** 76 Ja32
Osnabrück **D** 55 Ed27
Ośno Lubuskie **PL** 57 Ga27
Osor **HR** 85 Ga38
Osorno la Mayor **E** 79 Bd38
Osøyro **N** 42 Ed17
Oss **NL** 55 Eb28
Ossa de Montiel **E** 92 Bd43
Östansjö **S** 44 Ga19
Ostaškov **RUS** 117 Ec10
Ostatija **SRB** 87 Hb39
Östavall **S** 38 Gb14
Østby **N** 37 Fd16
Osterburg **D** 56 Fc27
Osterburken **D** 64 Fa31
Österbybruk **S** 45 Gc17
Österbymo **S** 44 Gb20
Österforse **S** 38 Gb13
Osterhofen **D** 65 Fd32
Osterholz-Scharmbeck **D** 56 Fa26
Øster Hurup **DK** 49 Fb21
Osterode **D** 56 Fb28
Östersund **S** 38 Ga13
Östervåla **S** 45 Gc17
Östhammar **S** 45 Gc17
Östmark **S** 44 Fd17
Ostra **RO** 76 Jb33
Ostrava **CZ** 66 Gd31

Ostren i madhë **RKS** 100 Hb42
Ostritz **D** 65 Ga29
Ostróda **PL** 58 Ha26
Ostrogožsk **RUS** 122 Fb13
Ostroh **UA** 120 Ea15
Ostrołęka **PL** 59 Hb26
Ostrov **CZ** 65 Fd30
Ostrov **RO** 89 Jd37
Ostrov **RO** 89 Ka36
Ostrov **RUS** 47 Jb20
Ostrowice **PL** 57 Gb26
Ostrowiec Świętokrzyski **PL** 67 Hb29
Ostrowieczno **PL** 58 Gc28
Ostrowite **PL** 58 Gd27
Ostrów Lubelski **PL** 59 Hc28
Ostrów Mazowiecka **PL** 59 Hb27
Ostrów Wielkopolski **PL** 58 Gc28
Ostrožac **BIH** 85 Gb37
Ostrzeszów **PL** 66 Gd29
Ostuni **I** 100 Gd43
Ostvik **S** 34 Gd11
Osuna **E** 105 Bb44
Oswestry **GB** 24 Cd25
Oświęcim **PL** 67 Ha30
Osypenko **UA** 126 Fb16
Otaci **MD** 77 Jd32
Otanmäki **FIN** 35 Hd11
Oţelu Roşu **RO** 75 Hd36
Otepää **EST** 47 Ja19
Oteren **N** 26 Gc05
Oteštii de Jos **RO** 88 Ja37
Otištić **HR** 86 Gc39
Otnes **N** 37 Fc15
Otok **HR** 86 Gc39
Otok **HR** 86 Ha37
Otorowo **PL** 57 Gb27
Otradnaja **RUS** 127 Fd17
Otradnyj **RUS** 119 Ga10
Otranto **I** 100 Ha44
Otrokovice **CZ** 66 Gc32
Otta **N** 37 Fb15
Ottenby **S** 50 Gb22
Otterbäcken **S** 44 Ga19
Otterburn **GB** 21 Db22
Otterndorf **D** 56 Fa25
Otterup **DK** 49 Fb23
Ottobrunn **D** 72 Fc33
Otwock **PL** 59 Hb27
Otynja **UA** 76 Ja32
Ouddorp **NL** 54 Ea28
Oudenaarde **B** 62 Ea29
Oude Pekela **NL** 55 Ed26
Oughterard **IRL** 18 Bd23
Ouistreham **F** 61 Da30
Oulainen **FIN** 35 Hc11
Oulu **FIN** 35 Hc10
Oulunsalo **FIN** 35 Hc10
Oundle **GB** 25 Db26
Ouranoúpoli **GR** 102 Jb43
Ourense **E** 78 Ba37
Ourique **P** 104 Ac43

Outakoski **FIN** 27 Hb04
Outokumpu **FIN** 41 Ja13
Ouzouer-sur-Loire **F** 69 Dc33
Ovacık **TR** 127 Ga19
Ovacık **TR** 128 Gc17
Ovada **I** 83 Ed38
Ovanåker **S** 38 Gb15
Ovar **P** 78 Ad39
Ovča **SRB** 87 Hb37
Overath **D** 63 Ec29
Øverdalen **N** 36 Fa14
Øvergård **N** 26 Gc05
Överhörnäs **S** 39 Gc13
Överkalix **S** 34 Ha09
Överlida **S** 49 Fd21
Övermark **FIN** 40 Ha14
Overpelt **B** 63 Eb29
Övertorneå **S** 34 Hb09
Överturingen **S** 38 Ga14
Överum **S** 44 Gb20
Ovidiopol' **UA** 77 Kb34
Ovidiopol' **UA** 125 Ec17
Ovidiu **RO** 89 Ka37
Oviedo **E** 79 Bc37
Øvre Årdal **N** 36 Fa15
Øvre Rendal **N** 37 Fc15
Övre Soppero **S** 29 Gd06
Ovruč **UA** 121 Eb14
Owińska **PL** 58 Gc27
Oxelösund **S** 45 Gc19
Oxford **GB** 24 Da27
Oxie **S** 49 Fd23
Øye **N** 36 Fa16
Oyonnax **F** 70 Ea35
Øyslebø **N** 42 Fa20
Oyten **D** 56 Fa26
Ozalj **HR** 85 Gb37
Ożarów **PL** 67 Hb29
Özbaşı **TR** 113 Kb46
Ózd **H** 75 Hb33
Ožďany **SK** 74 Ha33
Oženna **PL** 67 Hb31
Ožerel'e **RUS** 118 Fa11
Ozerki **RUS** 119 Fc09
Ozerki **RUS** 119 Fd10
Ozerki **RUS** 119 Fd11
Ozersk **RUS** 59 Ha25
Ozery **RUS** 118 Fa11
Ozieri **I** 97 Ed43
Ozimek **PL** 66 Gd30
Ozorków **PL** 58 Ha28

P

Paakkola **FIN** 34 Hb09
Paavola **FIN** 35 Hc11
Pabianice **PL** 58 Ha28
Pabradė **LT** 53 Ja23
Pačelma **RUS** 119 Fc11
Pachino **I** 109 Ga48
Pacov **CZ** 65 Ga31
Pacy-sur-Eure **F** 62 Dc31
Paczków **PL** 66 Gc30
Padarosk **BY** 59 Hd26

Padasjoki **FIN** 40 Hc15
Padej **SRB** 75 Hb36
Paderborn **D** 56 Fa28
Padina **RO** 89 Jd37
Padova **I** 84 Fc37
Padrón **E** 78 Ad36
Padstow **GB** 23 Cb28
Padsville **BY** 53 Jb23
Padul **E** 106 Bc45
Pafos **CY** 128 Ga19
Pag **HR** 85 Ga38
Pagégiai **LT** 52 Hb24
Pagelažiai **LT** 53 Hd23
Pagny-sur-Moselle **F** 63 Eb32
Pahraničny **BY** 59 Hd26
Paide **EST** 47 Hd18
Paignton **GB** 23 Cc28
Paimbœuf **F** 60 Cc32
Paimio **FIN** 40 Hb16
Paimpol **F** 60 Cc30
Paisley **GB** 20 Cd21
Paitasjärvi **S** 29 Ha06
Păiuşeni **RO** 75 Hc35
Pajala **S** 30 Ha08
Pajęczno **PL** 66 Gd29
Páka **H** 74 Gc35
Pakrac **HR** 86 Gc37
Pakruojis **LT** 52 Hc22
Paks **H** 74 Ha35
Palačany **BY** 53 Jb24
Palafrugell **E** 81 Dc40
Palagonia **I** 109 Ga47
Palaichori **CY** 128 Gb19
Palaiseau **F** 62 Dc31
Palamás **GR** 101 Hd44
Palamós **E** 81 Dc40
Palanga **LT** 52 Ha23
Palárikovo **SK** 74 Gd33
Palas de Rei **E** 78 Ba37
Palatna **RKS** 87 Hc40
Palau **I** 96 Ed42
Palazzolo Acreide **I** 109 Ga48
Palazzolo sull'Oglio **I** 72 Fa36
Paldiski **EST** 46 Hc18
Pale **BIH** 86 Gd39
Paleh **RUS** 118 Fb09
Palékastro **GR** 115 Ka49
Palencia **E** 79 Bd39
Paleohóra **GR** 114 Jb49
Paleohóri **GR** 101 Hd44
Paleokastrítsa **GR** 100 Hb44
Paleópoli **GR** 102 Jc42
Paleópoli **GR** 112 Jc46
Palermo **I** 108 Fd46
Palestrina **I** 98 Fc41
Pálháza **H** 67 Hc32
Paligrad **MK** 101 Hc41
Palin **H** 74 Gc35
Palinuro **I** 99 Gb44
Paliochori **GR** 111 Jc47
Palioúri **GR** 102 Jb43
Paliouriá **GR** 101 Hd44
Páliros **GR** 111 Ja48

Paliūniškis **LT** 53 Hd22
Pälkäene **FIN** 40 Hc15
Pålkem **S** 34 Ha09
Palkino **RUS** 47 Jb20
Palma Del Río **E** 105 Bb44
Palma de Mallorca **E** 95 Db43
Palma di Montechiaro **I** 108 Fd47
Palmanova **I** 73 Fd36
Palmela **P** 90 Ab42
Palmi **I** 109 Gb46
Palojärvi **FIN** 30 Ha06
Palojoensuu **FIN** 30 Ha06
Palokastër **AL** 100 Hb43
Palomaa **FIN** 27 Hc05
Palomas **E** 91 Ba42
Pålsboda **S** 44 Gb19
Paltamo **FIN** 35 Hd11
Paltaniemi **FIN** 35 Hd11
Pältiniş **RO** 75 Hc36
Pältiniş **RO** 88 Ja36
Pamiers **F** 81 Da39
Pampilhosa da Serra **P** 90 Ad40
Pampliega **E** 79 Bd39
Pamplona **E** 80 Cb38
Pamporovo **BG** 102 Jb41
Pamucak **TR** 113 Ka45
Pamūšis **LT** 52 Hc22
Panagia **CY** 128 Gb19
Panagía **GR** 101 Hc44
Panagjurište **BG** 102 Jb40
Pančarevo **BG** 102 Ja40
Pančevo **SRB** 87 Hb37
Pâncota **RO** 75 Hc35
Pandėlys **LT** 53 Hd22
Pandrup **DK** 49 Fb21
Panemunė **LT** 52 Hb24
Panes **E** 79 Bd37
Panetólio **GR** 110 Hd45
Panevėžys **LT** 53 Hd23
Paničkovo **BG** 102 Jc41
Pankakoski **FIN** 35 Jb12
Pannonhalma **H** 74 Gd34
Pano **CY** 128 Gb19
Pánormos **GR** 115 Ka47
Pantelleria **I** 108 Fb48
Panticeu **RO** 75 Hd34
Paola **I** 109 Gb45
Pápa **H** 74 Gc34
Pape **LV** 52 Ha22
Papenburg **D** 55 Ed26
Papernja **BY** 53 Jb24
Papilė **LT** 52 Hc22
Papilys **LT** 53 Hd22
Paraćin **SRB** 87 Hc39
Paradela **P** 78 Ba38
Paradísi **GR** 115 Kb47
Paradísia **GR** 110 Hd47
Parainen **FIN** 46 Hb17
Parakka **S** 29 Gd07
Paralía **GR** 111 Ja46
Paralía Porovítsis **GR** 111 Ja46
Paralimni **CY** 128 Gc19

Paramithiá **GR** 101 Hc44
Paranésti **GR** 102 Jb42
Pârău **RO** 88 Jb36
Paray-le-Monial **F** 70 Dd35
Parchim **D** 56 Fc26
Parczew **PL** 59 Hc28
Pardubice **CZ** 65 Gb31
Parečča **BY** 59 Hd25
Paredes de Nava **E** 79 Bd38
Parentis-en-Born **F** 68 Cc36
Párga **GR** 110 Hc45
Pargas **FIN** 46 Hb17
Pargolovo **RUS** 41 Jb16
Parikkala **FIN** 41 Jb14
Paris **F** 62 Dc31
Parkano **FIN** 40 Hb14
Parma **I** 84 Fa37
Pärnjõe **EST** 47 Hd19
Pärnu **EST** 46 Hc19
Pärnu-Jaagupi **EST** 46 Hc19
Páros **GR** 111 Jc47
Parres **E** 79 Bd37
Parsberg **D** 64 Fc32
Partakko **FIN** 27 Hc05
Partanna **I** 108 Fc47
Parthenay **F** 69 Da34
Partille **S** 43 Fc20
Partinicio **I** 108 Fc46
Partizánske **SK** 66 Gd34
Pärvomaj **BG** 102 Jc40
Paryčy **BY** 121 Eb13
Påryd **S** 50 Gb22
Paša **RUS** 117 Eb08
Paşcani **RO** 76 Jc33
Pasewalk **D** 57 Ga26
Pasiene **LV** 53 Jb21
Pasinler **TR** 127 Ga19
Paskalevo **BG** 89 Ka38
Påskallavik **S** 50 Gb21
Paškovskij **RUS** 127 Fc17
Pasłęk **PL** 58 Ha25
Pašman **HR** 85 Gb39
Passau **D** 73 Fd33
Pastavy **BY** 53 Ja23
Pastavy **BY** 120 Ea12
Pastrana **E** 92 Ca41
Pasvalys **LT** 53 Hd22
Pásztó **H** 74 Ha33
Pătârlagele **RO** 88 Jc36
Paternò **I** 109 Ga47
Patiška **MK** 101 Hc41
Patoniva **FIN** 27 Hc04
Pátra **GR** 110 Hd46
Patreksfjörður **IS** 14 Bc04
Patrickswell **IRL** 18 Bd24
Patti **I** 109 Ga46
Pattijoki **FIN** 34 Hb11
Pătulele **RO** 87 Hd38
Pau **F** 80 Cd38
Pauillac **F** 68 Cd35
Paulhaguet **F** 69 Dc36
Páuliani **GR** 110 Hd45
Pavel Banja **BG** 102 Jc40
Pavia **I** 83 Ed37
Pavia **P** 90 Ac41
Pavilly **F** 61 Db30

Pāvilosta **LV** 52 Ha21
Pavino Polje **MNE** 86 Ha40
Pavlikeni **BG** 88 Jb39
Pavlohrad **UA** 122 Fa15
Pavlovo **RUS** 118 Fb09
Pavlovsk **RUS** 122 Fb13
Pavlovskaja **RUS** 127 Fc16
Pavlovskij Posad **RUS** 118 Fa10
Pavlovskoe **RUS** 118 Fb09
Pavlyš **UA** 121 Ed15
Pavullo nel Frignano **I** 84 Fb38
Pavy **RUS** 47 Jb19
Pawłów **PL** 67 Hd29
Paymogo **E** 105 Ad43
Pazar **TR** 122 Ga19
Pazardžik **BG** 102 Jb40
Pazarić **BIH** 86 Gd39
Pazarköy **TR** 103 Ka43
Pazin **HR** 85 Fd37
Pčelarovo **BG** 102 Jc41
Pčelnik **BG** 89 Ka39
Peal de Becerro **E** 106 Bd44
Peć **RKS** 87 Hb40
Pécel **H** 74 Ha34
Pečenga **RUS** 27 Hd04
Pečenjevce **SRB** 87 Hd39
Pechea **RO** 77 Jd35
Pecica **RO** 75 Hb36
Pečki **RUS** 47 Jb19
Pečory **RUS** 47 Ja19
Pécs **H** 74 Gd36
Pedaso **I** 85 Fd40
Pedrafita do Cebreiro **E** 78 Bb37
Pedralba **E** 93 Cb43
Pedras Salgadas **P** 78 Ba38
Pedraza de la Sierra **E** 92 Bd40
Pedro Muñoz **E** 92 Bd42
Peebles **GB** 21 Da21
Peel **GBM** 20 Cd23
Péfkos **GR** 101 Hc43
Pegeia **CY** 128 Ga19
Pegnitz **D** 64 Fc31
Pego **E** 94 Cc44
Pehlivanköy **TR** 103 Jd41
Peine **D** 56 Fb27
Peiting **D** 72 Fb33
Peitz **D** 57 Ga28
Pektubaevo **RUS** 119 Fc08
Peletá **GR** 111 Ja47
Pelhřimov **CZ** 65 Gb31
Pelinei **MD** 77 Ka35
Pelkosenniemi **FIN** 31 Hc07
Pellinge **FIN** 41 Hd16
Pellinki **FIN** 41 Hd16
Pello **FIN** 30 Hb08
Pelplin **PL** 58 Gd25
Peltovuoma **FIN** 30 Hb06
Pélussin **F** 70 Dd36
Pembroke **GB** 23 Cc26
Pembroke Dock **GB** 23 Cc26

Peñacerrada **E** 80 Cb38
Peñafiel **E** 79 Bd39
Penafiel **P** 78 Ad38
Peñalén **E** 92 Ca41
Penamacor **P** 91 Ba40
Peñaranda de Bracamonte **E** 91 Bc40
Peñaranda de Duero **E** 79 Ca39
Penarth **GB** 24 Cd27
Peñas de San Pedro **E** 92 Ca43
Peñausende **E** 78 Bb39
Peniche **P** 90 Ab40
Penicuik **GB** 21 Da21
Peñíscola **E** 93 Cd42
Penkun **D** 57 Ga26
Penmarc'h **F** 60 Cb31
Penne **I** 98 Fd41
Penne-d'Agenais **F** 81 Da37
Peno **RUS** 117 Ec10
Penrith **GB** 21 Da23
Penryn **GB** 23 Cb28
Pentálofos **GR** 101 Hc43
Pentápoli **GR** 101 Ja42
Penza **RUS** 119 Fc11
Penzance **GB** 23 Cb28
Penzberg **D** 72 Fb34
Penzlin **D** 57 Fd26
Peqin **RKS** 100 Hb42
Perälä **FIN** 40 Ha14
Peraleda del Zaucejo **E** 105 Bb43
Perales del Alfambra **E** 93 Cb41
Pérama **GR** 101 Hc44
Peranka **FIN** 35 Hd09
Peranzanes **E** 78 Bb37
Perä-Posio **FIN** 31 Hd08
Peräseinäjoki **FIN** 40 Hb14
Perčunovo **MD** 77 Kb32
Perdasdefogu **I** 97 Ed44
Perdigão **P** 90 Ad41
Perečyn **UA** 67 Hc32
Perehins'ke **UA** 76 Ja32
Perehins'ke **UA** 124 Ea16
Perejaslav-Chmel'nyc'kyj **UA** 121 Ec14
Perekopka **RUS** 123 Fd13
Perelešinskij **RUS** 122 Fb12
Pereščepyne **UA** 122 Fa15
Peresecina **MD** 77 Ka33
Pereslavl'-Zalesskij **RUS** 118 Fa09
Perevalovo **RUS** 52 Hb24
Perevoz **RUS** 119 Fc09
Pergine Valsugana **I** 72 Fb36
Pergola **I** 84 Fc39
Perho **FIN** 40 Hb13
Periam **RO** 75 Hb36
Périers **F** 61 Cd30
Périgueux **F** 69 Da36
Perişoru **RO** 89 Jd37

Perísta – Pjaviņas

Perísta **GR** 110 Hd45
Perithóri **GR** 110 Hd46
Perivólia **GR** 111 Ja47
Perleberg **D** 56 Fc26
Perloja **LT** 59 Hd25
Perloja **LT** 59 Hd25
Pernik **BG** 102 Ja40
Perniö **FIN** 46 Hb17
Pernitz **A** 73 Gb33
Péronne **F** 62 Dd30
Perpignan **F** 81 Db39
Perros-Guirec **F** 60 Cc30
Persbo **S** 44 Ga17
Perstorp **S** 49 Fd22
Perth **GB** 17 Da20
Pertoúli **GR** 101 Hd44
Pertteli **FIN** 40 Hb16
Pertuis **F** 82 Ea38
Pertunmaa **FIN** 41 Hd15
Perugia **I** 84 Fc40
Perušić **HR** 85 Gb38
Pervomaisc **MD** 77 Kb34
Pervomajs'k **MD** 77 Kb32
Pervomajsk **RUS** 119 Fc10
Pervomajs'k **UA** 125 Ec16
Pervomajskij **RUS** 118 Fb11
Pervomajskoe **RUS** 41 Jb16
Pervomajskoe **RUS** 119 Ga11
Pervomajs'kyj **UA** 122 Fa14
Pesaro **I** 84 Fc39
Pesčanokopskoe **RUS** 127 Fd16
Pescara **I** 99 Ga41
Pescasseroli **I** 98 Fd41
Peschiera del Garda **I** 84 Fb37
Pescia **I** 84 Fb39
Pescina **I** 98 Fd41
Pesco Sannita **I** 99 Ga42
Peshkopi **AL** 100 Hb41
Pesiökylä **FIN** 35 Hd10
Pesmes **F** 71 Eb34
Pesočani **MK** 101 Hc42
Peso da Régua **P** 78 Ba39
Pessac **F** 68 Cd36
Peštera **BG** 102 Jb41
Peştişani **RO** 87 Hd37
Pestovo **RUS** 117 Ec09
Pestravka **RUS** 119 Ga10
Petäiskylä **FIN** 35 Ja12
Petäjäskoski **FIN** 34 Hb09
Petäjävesi **FIN** 40 Hc14
Petalax Petolahti **FIN** 40 Ha13
Petalidi **GR** 110 Hd47
Peterborough **GB** 25 Db26
Peterhead **GB** 17 Dc19
Peterlee **GB** 21 Db23
Petersfield **GB** 24 Da28
Petilia Policastro **I** 109 Gc45
Petín **E** 78 Bb37
Peťki **BY** 59 Hd27
Petkula **FIN** 31 Hc07
Petra **GR** 113 Jd44
Petralia-Sottana **I** 108 Fd47

Petran **AL** 100 Hb43
Petreni **MD** 77 Jd32
Petrič **BG** 101 Ja42
Petrila **RO** 88 Ja36
Petrinja **HR** 85 Gb37
Petrivka **MD** 77 Kb33
Petrivka **UA** 77 Ka34
Petrivka **UA** 121 Ec14
Petropavlivka **UA** 122 Fa15
Petropavlovka **RUS** 123 Fc13
Petroşani **RO** 88 Ja36
Petrova **RO** 76 Ja33
Petrovac **SRB** 87 Hc38
Petrovice **CZ** 65 Ga31
Petrovo **RUS** 117 Ec09
Petrovsk **RUS** 119 Fd11
Petrovskoe **RUS** 41 Jb15
Petrovskoe **RUS** 118 Fa09
Petrovskoe **RUS** 122 Fb12
Petrykav **BY** 121 Eb13
Petsikko **FIN** 27 Hc04
Petsmo **FIN** 40 Ha13
Petuški **RUS** 118 Fa10
Peuilly-sur-Claise **F** 69 Db34
Peurasuvanto **FIN** 31 Hc06
Peyrat-le-Château **F** 69 Db35
Peyrehorade **F** 80 Cc37
Pézenas **F** 81 Dc38
Pezens **F** 81 Db38
Pezinok **SK** 74 Gc33
Pfaffenhofen **D** 72 Fc33
Pfarrkirchen **D** 73 Fd33
Pforzheim **D** 63 Ed32
Pfronten **D** 72 Fb34
Pfullendorf **D** 72 Fa33
Pfungstadt **D** 63 Ed31
Phals-bourg **F** 63 Ec32
Philippeville **B** 62 Ea30
Piacenza **I** 84 Fa37
Piana di Albanesi **I** 108 Fd46
Pias **P** 105 Ad43
Piaseczno **PL** 59 Hb28
Piasek **PL** 66 Gd30
Piaski **PL** 67 Hc29
Piątek **PL** 58 Ha28
Piatra **RO** 88 Jd38
Piatra-Neamţ **RO** 76 Jc34
Piatra-Olt **RO** 88 Ja38
Piazza Armerina **I** 109 Ga47
Pičaevo **RUS** 118 Fb11
Pickering **GB** 21 Db24
Picquigny **F** 62 Dc30
Piedimonte Matese **I** 99 Ga42
Piedrabuena **E** 91 Bc42
Piedrahita **E** 91 Bb40
Piekary Śląskie **PL** 66 Gd30
Pieksämäki **FIN** 41 Hd14
Pielavesi **FIN** 35 Hd12
Pieniężno **PL** 58 Ha25
Pienza **I** 84 Fb39
Pierre-Buffière **F** 69 Db35
Pierre-de-Bresse **F** 70 Ea34
Pierrefonds **F** 62 Dd31

Pierrefort **F** 69 Dc36
Pierrelatte **F** 82 Dd37
Piešťany **SK** 66 Gd32
Pieszyce **PL** 66 Gc30
Pietarsaari **FIN** 34 Ha12
Pietrasanta **I** 84 Fa39
Pietroşani **RO** 88 Jc38
Pieve di Cadore **I** 72 Fc35
Pieve San Stefano **I** 84 Fc39
Pigés **GR** 101 Hc44
Pihtipudas **FIN** 35 Hc12
Piippola **FIN** 35 Hc11
Pikalevo **RUS** 117 Ec08
Pikasilla **EST** 47 Hd19
Piła **PL** 58 Gc26
Pilas **E** 105 Ad44
Pilawa **PL** 59 Hb28
Pilgrimstad **S** 38 Ga13
Pilis **H** 74 Ha34
Pilisvörösvár **H** 74 Ha34
Pílos **GR** 110 Hd47
Piltene **LV** 52 Hb21
Pilvíškiai **LT** 52 Hc24
Pilzno **PL** 67 Hb30
Pimpiö **S** 30 Ha08
Pınarbaşı **TR** 128 Gb16
Pınarcık **TR** 113 Kb46
Pinarello **F** 96 Ed41
Pınarhisar **TR** 103 Ka41
Pincehely **H** 74 Gd35
Pinczów **PL** 67 Hb30
Pinerolo **I** 83 Ec37
Pineto **I** 85 Fd40
Piney **F** 62 Ea32
Pingeyri **IS** 14 Bc04
Pinhão **P** 78 Ba39
Pinhel **P** 78 Ba39
Pinkafeld **A** 73 Gb34
Pinneberg **D** 56 Fb26
Pino **F** 96 Ed40
Pinoso **E** 107 Cb44
Pinos-Puente **E** 106 Bc45
Pinsk **BY** 120 Ea14
Pintamo **FIN** 35 Hd09
Pinto **E** 92 Bd41
Pioltikasvaara **S** 29 Gd07
Piombino **I** 84 Fa40
Pionerskij **RUS** 52 Ha24
Pionki **PL** 59 Hb28
Piotrków Trybunalski **PL** 67 Ha29
Pipiríg **RO** 76 Jb34
Pipriac **F** 61 Cd32
Piran **SLO** 85 Fd37
Pirčiupiai **LT** 53 Hd24
Pirdop **BG** 102 Jb40
Pireás **GR** 112 Jb46
Pirgadíkia **GR** 102 Jb43
Pirgí **GR** 100 Hb44
Pirgío **GR** 113 Jd45
Pírgos **GR** 110 Hd47
Pirin **BG** 101 Ja41
Pirki **BY** 121 Ec14
Pirkkala **FIN** 40 Hb15
Pirmasens **D** 63 Ec31
Pirna **D** 65 Ga29

Pirot **SRB** 87 Hd39
Pirovac **HR** 85 Gb39
Pirsógiani **GR** 101 Hc43
Pirttikoski **FIN** 31 Hc08
Pirttikylä **FIN** 40 Ha14
Pirttimäki **FIN** 35 Hd11
Pisa **I** 84 Fa39
Pišča **UA** 59 Hd28
Piščana **UA** 77 Ka32
Piščanka **UA** 77 Jd32
Pisciotta **I** 99 Gb44
Piscu **RO** 89 Jd36
Písek **CZ** 65 Ga32
Pisogne **I** 72 Fa36
Píso Livádi **GR** 115 Jd47
Pissos **F** 80 Cd37
Pissouri **CY** 128 Gb19
Pisticci **I** 99 Gc43
Pistoia **I** 84 Fb39
Pisz **PL** 59 Hb26
Piteå **S** 34 Ha10
Pitelino **RUS** 118 Fb10
Piteşti **RO** 88 Jb37
Pithiviers **F** 62 Dc32
Pitigliano **I** 84 Fb40
Pitkälahti **FIN** 41 Hd13
Pitkovo **RUS** 41 Jb15
Pitlochry **GB** 17 Da20
Pitomača **HR** 74 Gc36
Pitvaros **H** 75 Hb35
Pivka **SLO** 73 Ga36
Piwniczna-Zdrój **PL** 67 Hb31
Pižma **RUS** 119 Fc08
Pizzighettone **I** 84 Fa37
Pizzo **I** 109 Gb45
Pizzoli **I** 98 Fd41
Pjaozero **RUS** 35 Ja09
Pjatigorsk **RUS** 127 Ga17
P'jatychatky **UA** 121 Ed15
Plabennec **F** 60 Cb30
Pláka **GR** 102 Jc43
Plakotí **GR** 101 Hc44
Planá nad Labem **CZ** 65 Ga32
Plancoët **F** 61 Cd31
Plandište **SRB** 87 Hc37
Plan-du-Var **F** 83 Eb38
Pláš□ovce **SK** 74 Gd33
Plasencia **E** 91 Bb41
Plaški **HR** 85 Gb37
Platamónas **GR** 101 Ja43
Platamónas **GR** 102 Jb42
Plataniá **GR** 101 Ja44
Platánia **GR** 110 Hd47
Plátanos **GR** 110 Hd45
Plátanos **GR** 113 Jd49
Platariá **GR** 100 Hb44
Platís Gialós **GR** 111 Jc47
Platís Gialós **GR** 113 Jd46
Plattling **D** 65 Fd32
Plau **D** 56 Fc26
Plauen **D** 64 Fc30
Plav **MNE** 87 Hb40
Plavecký Mikuláš **SK** 74 Gc33
Pļaviņas **LV** 53 Hd21

Plavsk **RUS** 118 Fa11
Plélan-le-Grand **F** 61 Cd31
Pléneuf-Val-André **F** 60 Cc31
Pleščanicy **BY** 53 Jb24
Pleščanicy **BY** 120 Ea12
Plešin **SRB** 87 Hb39
Plešivec **SK** 67 Hb32
Plestin-les-Grèves **F** 60 Cc30
Pleszew **PL** 58 Gc28
Pleternica **HR** 86 Gd37
Pleven **BG** 88 Jb39
Pleyben **F** 60 Cb31
Plisa **BY** 53 Jb23
Pliska **BG** 89 Jd38
Plitvička Jezera **HR** 85 Gb37
Pljevlja **MNE** 86 Ha39
Pljussa **RUS** 47 Jb18
Ploče **HR** 86 Gd40
Plochingen **D** 64 Fa32
Płock **PL** 58 Ha27
Plodovoe **RUS** 41 Jb15
Ploemeur **F** 60 Cb32
Ploërmel **F** 60 Cc32
Plœuc-sur-Lié **F** 60 Cc31
Ploiești **RO** 88 Jc37
Plomári **GR** 113 Jd44
Plombières-les-Bains **F** 71 Eb33
Plön **D** 56 Fb25
Plonéour-Lanvern **F** 60 Cb31
Płońsk **PL** 58 Ha27
Plopana **RO** 76 Jc34
Plopeni **RO** 89 Ka37
Plopi **RO** 87 Hd37
Plopii-Slăvitești **RO** 88 Jb38
Plopșoru **RO** 88 Ja37
Ploske **UA** 67 Hd32
Ploski **PL** 59 Hc26
Ploskoš' **RUS** 117 Eb10
Płoty **PL** 57 Gb26
Plouagat **F** 60 Cc31
Plouay **F** 60 Cc31
Ploudalmézeau **F** 60 Cb30
Plouescat **F** 60 Cb30
Plougasnou **F** 60 Cb30
Plouguerneau **F** 60 Cb30
Plouha **F** 60 Cc31
Plovdiv **BG** 102 Jb40
Plozévet **F** 60 Cb31
Plungé **LT** 52 Hb23
Pluvigner **F** 60 Cc32
Plužine **MNE** 86 Ha40
Płużnica **PL** 58 Gd26
Plymouth **GB** 23 Cc28
Plzeň **CZ** 65 Fd31
Pniewy **PL** 57 Gb27
Pobedino **RUS** 52 Hc24
Pobiedziska **PL** 58 Gc27
Pobierowo **PL** 57 Ga25
Počep **RUS** 121 Ed12
Počinok **RUS** 121 Ec12
Počitelj **BIH** 86 Gd40

Pocking **D** 73 Fd33
Pocola **RO** 75 Hc35
Pocrovca **MD** 77 Jd32
Pocsaj **H** 75 Hc34
Podberez'e **RUS** 47 Jb20
Podberez'e **RUS** 117 Eb09
Podberez'e **RUS** 117 Eb10
Podbořanský Rohozec **CZ** 65 Fd30
Podbořany **CZ** 65 Fd30
Podborov'e **RUS** 47 Jb19
Podbožur **MNE** 86 Ha40
Poddor'e **RUS** 117 Eb10
Poděbrady **CZ** 65 Ga30
Podgora **HR** 86 Gc40
Podgorac **SRB** 87 Hc38
Podgorenskij **RUS** 122 Fb13
Podgorica **MNE** 100 Ha41
Podil **UA** 121 Ed14
Podil's'ke **UA** 76 Jc32
Podkova **BG** 102 Jc41
Podlesnoje **RUS** 119 Fd11
Podoleš'e **RUS** 47 Jb18
Podol'sk **RUS** 117 Ed10
Podrašnica **BIH** 86 Gc38
Podromanija **BIH** 86 Ha39
Podsnežnoe **RUS** 119 Fd11
Podu Iloaiei **RO** 76 Jc33
Podujevo **RKS** 87 Hc40
Podu Turcului **RO** 77 Jd35
Pogana **RO** 77 Jd35
Pogar **RUS** 121 Ed13
Poggibonsi **I** 84 Fb39
Poggio Mirteto **I** 98 Fc41
Pogoanele **RO** 89 Jd36
Pogradec **AL** 101 Hc42
Pohja **FIN** 46 Hb17
Pohjaslahti **FIN** 35 Hc09
Pohlois-li **FIN** 35 Hc10
Pohoarna **MD** 77 Jd32
Pohořelice **CZ** 66 Gc32
Pohrebyšče **UA** 121 Eb15
Poiana Lacului **RO** 88 Jb37
Poiana Largului **RO** 76 Jb34
Poiana Mare **RO** 87 Hd38
Poiana Mărului **RO** 75 Hd36
Poiana Stampei **RO** 76 Jb34
Poibrene **BG** 102 Ja40
Pöide **EST** 46 Hb19
Poienile de Sub Munte **RO** 76 Ja33
Poissy **F** 62 Dc31
Poitiers **F** 69 Da34
Poix-de-Picardie **F** 62 Dc30
Pojo **FIN** 46 Hb17
Pokka **FIN** 30 Hb06
Pokrov **RUS** 118 Fa10
Pokrovskaja Arčada **RUS** 119 Fc11
Pokrovs'ke **UA** 122 Fa15
Pokrovs'ke **UA** 122 Fb14
Polack **BY** 117 Eb11
Pola de Laviana **E** 79 Bc37
Pola de Lena **E** 79 Bc37
Pola de Siero **E** 79 Bc37
Pola de Somiedo **E** 79 Bc37

Połajewo **PL** 58 Gc27
Połaniec **PL** 67 Hb30
Polanów **PL** 58 Gc25
Połczyn-Zdrój **PL** 57 Gb26
Polesella **I** 84 Fb37
Polessk **RUS** 52 Hb24
Polgár **H** 75 Hb33
Polgárdi **H** 74 Gd35
Poliçan **AL** 100 Hb43
Police **PL** 57 Ga26
Polička **CZ** 65 Gb31
Policoro **I** 99 Gc44
Polidámio **GR** 101 Ja44
Polígiros **GR** 101 Ja43
Polignano a Mare **I** 99 Gc42
Poligny **F** 71 Eb34
Polihnítos **GR** 113 Jd44
Políkastro **GR** 101 Hd42
Polímilos **GR** 101 Hd43
Polis **CY** 128 Ga19
Polis'ke **UA** 121 Eb14
Polistena **I** 109 Gb46
Poljana **BG** 103 Jd40
Poljany **RUS** 41 Jb16
Poljice **BIH** 86 Gd38
Polkowice **PL** 65 Gb29
Polla **I** 99 Gb43
Pollença **E** 95 Db43
Polmak **N** 27 Hc04
Polna **RUS** 47 Jb19
Pologi **RO** 88 Jc37
Pologoe Zajmišče **RUS** 123 Ga13
Polohy **UA** 126 Fb16
Polom **SRB** 87 Hb38
Polonne **UA** 121 Eb15
Polovragi **RO** 88 Ja37
Polski Trämbeš **BG** 88 Jc39
Poltava **UA** 121 Ed14
Põltsamaa **EST** 47 Hd19
Põlva **EST** 47 Ja19
Polvijärvi **FIN** 41 Ja13
Polyantho **GR** 102 Jc42
Pomarance **I** 84 Fb39
Pomarkku **FIN** 40 Ha15
Pombal **P** 90 Ac40
Pomezia **I** 98 Fc42
Pomorie **BG** 89 Ka39
Pomos **CY** 128 Gb19
Pompey **F** 63 Eb32
Ponferrada **E** 78 Bb37
Poniatowa **PL** 67 Hc29
Ponikiew Mała **PL** 59 Hb27
Ponoarele **RO** 87 Hd37
Ponoševac **RKS** 100 Hb41
Pons **F** 68 Cd35
Pontacq **F** 80 Cd38
Pontailler-sur-Saône **F** 70 Ea34
Pont-à-Mousson **F** 63 Eb32
Pontão **P** 90 Ad40
Pontarion **F** 69 Db35
Pontarlier **F** 71 Eb34
Pontassieve **I** 84 Fb39
Pont-Audemer **F** 61 Db30
Pontaumur **F** 69 Dc35

Pontcharra **F** 71 Eb36
Pontchâteau **F** 60 Cc32
Pont-d'Ain **F** 70 Ea35
Pont-de-Roide **F** 71 Ec34
Pont-de-Vaux **F** 70 Ea35
Ponteareas **E** 78 Ad37
Pontecorvo **I** 98 Fd42
Ponte da Barca **P** 78 Ad38
Ponte de Lima **P** 78 Ad38
Pontedera **I** 84 Fa39
Ponte de Sor **P** 90 Ad41
Pontedeume **E** 78 Ba36
Pontefract **GB** 21 Db24
Ponte Leccia **F** 96 Ed40
Pontenova Villaodriz **E** 78 Bb36
Pont-en-Royans **F** 82 Ea37
Ponte Tresa **I** 71 Ed36
Pontevedra **E** 78 Ad37
Pontgibaud **F** 69 Dc35
Pontivy **F** 60 Cc31
Pont-l'Abbé **F** 60 Cb31
Pont-l'Evêque **F** 61 Db30
Pontoise **F** 62 Dc31
Pontokerasiá **GR** 101 Ja42
Pontorson **F** 61 Cd31
Pontremoli **I** 84 Fa38
Pontresina **CH** 72 Fa35
Ponts **E** 81 Da40
Pont-Sainte-Maxence **F** 62 Dd31
Pont-Saint-Esprit **F** 82 Dd38
Pont-Saint-Vincent **F** 63 Eb32
Pont-sur-Yonne **F** 62 Dd32
Pontypool **GB** 24 Cd27
Ponza **I** 98 Fc43
Poole **GB** 24 Cd28
Popčevo **MK** 101 Hd42
Pope **LV** 52 Hb21
Poperinge **B** 62 Dd29
Popești **RO** 75 Hc34
Popielów **PL** 66 Gc30
Popoli **I** 98 Fd41
Popovača **HR** 86 Gc37
Popovići **BIH** 86 Gd38
Popovo **BG** 88 Jc39
Popovyči **UA** 67 Hd31
Popów **PL** 58 Gd28
Poppi **I** 84 Fb39
Poprad **SK** 67 Hb32
Popsko **BG** 102 Jc41
Populonia **I** 84 Fa40
Porazava **BY** 59 Hd26
Porcuna **E** 106 Bc44
Pordenone **I** 72 Fc36
Pordim **BG** 88 Jb39
Porebeni **MD** 77 Ka33
Poreč **HR** 85 Fd37
Poreč'e **RUS** 47 Jb17
Porhov **RUS** 117 Eb10
Pori **FIN** 40 Ha15
Porjus **S** 29 Gd08
Porlákshöfn **IS** 14 Bc07
Pornic **F** 68 Cc33

Póros – Pryazovs'ke

Póros **GR** 110 Hc46
Póros **GR** 111 Jb47
Porozina **HR** 85 Ga37
Porpliđča **BY** 53 Jb23
Porras **FIN** 40 Hc16
Porrentruy **CH** 71 Ec34
Porretta Terme **I** 84 Fb38
Porriño **E** 78 Ad37
Porsangermoen **N** 27 Hb04
Porsgrunn **N** 43 Fb18
Þórshöfn **IS** 15 Cc06
Portadown **GB** 20 Cc22
Portaferry **GB** 20 Cc23
Portalegre **P** 90 Ad41
Portarlington **IRL** 19 Cb24
Port Askaig **GB** 20 Cc21
Portavadie **GB** 20 Cd21
Porta Westfalica **D** 56 Fa27
Port d'Addaia **E** 95 Dc43
Port-de-Bouc **F** 82 Dd39
Port de Pollença **E** 95 Db43
Port d'es Torrent **E** 94 Cd44
Portel **P** 90 Ad42
Port Ellen **GB** 20 Cc21
Port-en-Bessin **F** 61 Da30
Port Erin **GBM** 20 Cd23
Port Grimaud **F** 83 Eb39
Porthcawl **GB** 23 Cc27
Portimão **P** 104 Ab43
Portimo **FIN** 35 Hc09
Portinatx **E** 94 Cd44
Port-Joinville **F** 68 Cc33
Port-la-Nouvelle **F** 81 Dc39
Port Laoise **IRL** 18 Ca24
Port-Louis **F** 60 Cc32
Portmeirion **GB** 24 Cd25
Portnacroish **GB** 16 Cd20
Portnahaven **GB** 20 Cc21
Port-Navalo **F** 60 Cc32
Porto **F** 96 Ed41
Porto **P** 78 Ad38
Porto Alto **P** 90 Ac41
Porto Azzurro **I** 84 Fa40
Porto Cervo **I** 96 Ed42
Porto Cesareo **I** 100 Gd43
Portocristo **E** 95 Db43
Porto da Balsa **P** 90 Ad40
Porto do Son **E** 78 Ad36
Porto Empedocle **I** 108 Fd47
Portoferraio **I** 84 Fa40
Portofino **I** 83 Ed38
Port of Ness **GB** 16 Cd17
Portogruaro **I** 72 Fc36
Pórto Koufós **GR** 102 Jb43
Pörtom **FIN** 40 Ha14
Portomaggiore **I** 84 Fc38
Portomarín **E** 78 Ba37
Porto Recanati **I** 85 Fd39
Portorož **SLO** 85 Fd37
Porto San Giorgio **I** 85 Fd40
Porto Sant'Elipido **I** 85 Fd40
Portoscuso **I** 97 Ec45
Porto Tolle **I** 84 Fc37
Porto Torres **I** 96 Ec42
Porto Vecchio **F** 96 Ed42

Portovenere **I** 84 Fa38
Porto Viro **I** 84 Fc37
Portpatrick **GB** 20 Cd22
Portree **GB** 16 Cd19
Portrush **GB** 20 Cc21
Port-Saint-Louis-du-Rhône **F** 82 Dd39
Portsalon **IRL** 19 Cb21
Pörtschach **A** 73 Ga35
Portsmouth **GB** 24 Da28
Portsoy **GB** 17 Db19
Port-sur-Saône **F** 71 Eb33
Port Talbot **GB** 23 Cc27
Portugalete **E** 79 Ca37
Portumna **IRL** 18 Ca24
Port-Vendres **F** 81 Dc40
Porvoo **FIN** 41 Hd16
Porzuna **E** 91 Bc42
Posadas **E** 105 Bb44
Poschiavo **CH** 72 Fa35
Posedarje **HR** 85 Gb38
Pošehon'e **RUS** 117 Ed08
Posio **FIN** 35 Hd09
Positano **I** 99 Ga43
Posof **TR** 127 Ga18
Pößneck **D** 64 Fc30
Postojna **SLO** 73 Ga36
Postomino **PL** 58 Gc25
Posušje **BIH** 86 Gc39
Potamós **GR** 114 Jb49
Potamoúla **GR** 110 Hd45
Potcoava **RO** 88 Jb37
Potenza **I** 99 Gb43
Potenza Picena **I** 85 Fd39
Potes **E** 79 Bd37
Potsdam **D** 57 Fd27
Potworów **PL** 59 Hb28
Pouancé **F** 61 Cd32
Pouzauges **F** 68 Cd33
Považská Bystrica **SK** 66 Gd32
Póvoa de São Miguel **P** 90 Ad42
Póvoa de Varzim **P** 78 Ad38
Poyracık **TR** 113 Ka44
Poysdorf **A** 66 Gc32
Požarevac **SRB** 87 Hc38
Požega **HR** 86 Gd37
Požega **SRB** 87 Hb39
Pozezdrze **PL** 59 Hb25
Poznań **PL** 58 Gc27
Pozo Alcón **E** 106 Bd44
Pozoblanco **E** 105 Bb43
Pozo-Cañada **E** 92 Ca43
Pozohondo **E** 92 Ca43
Pozuelo de Alarcón **E** 92 Bd41
Pozzallo **I** 109 Ga48
Pozzuoli **I** 98 Fd43
Prača **BIH** 86 Ha39
Prachatice **CZ** 65 Ga32
Pradelles **F** 82 Dd37
Prades **E** 93 Cd41
Prades **F** 81 Db39
Pradła **PL** 67 Ha30
Prado del Rey **E** 105 Ba45

Pradoluengo **E** 79 Ca39
Præstø **DK** 49 Fc24
Praha **CZ** 65 Ga31
Prahovo **SRB** 87 Hd38
Praia a Mare **I** 99 Gb44
Praia da Barra **P** 90 Ac39
Praia da Vieira **P** 90 Ac40
Praia de Mira **P** 90 Ac39
Praid **RO** 76 Jb35
Pralognan **F** 71 Eb36
Pra-Loup **F** 83 Eb38
Prámanda **GR** 101 Hc44
Prastio **CY** 128 Gc19
Praszka **PL** 66 Gd29
Prato **I** 84 Fb39
Prats de Lluçanès **E** 81 Db40
Prats-de-Mollo **F** 81 Db40
Pravda **UA** 67 Hd29
Pravdinsk **RUS** 59 Hb25
Pravec **BG** 102 Ja40
Pravia **E** 79 Bc36
Prazaroki **BY** 53 Jb23
Prečistoe **RUS** 117 Ec11
Prečistoe **RUS** 118 Fa08
Predajane **SRB** 87 Hd40
Predazzo **I** 72 Fb35
Predeal **RO** 88 Jb36
Predeşti **RO** 88 Ja37
Pré-en-Pail **F** 61 Da31
Preetz **D** 56 Fb25
Pregarten **A** 73 Ga33
Preiļi **LV** 53 Ja22
Prejmer **RO** 88 Jb36
Preko **HR** 85 Ga39
Prelog **HR** 74 Gc36
Prémery **F** 70 Dd34
Premnitz **D** 56 Fc27
Prenzlau **D** 57 Fd26
Přerov **CZ** 66 Gc31
Preševo **SRB** 101 Hc41
Presjaka **MNE** 86 Ha40
Prešov **SK** 67 Hb32
Pressac **F** 69 Da35
Prestatyn **GB** 20 Cd24
Presteid **N** 28 Gb07
Prestesætra **N** 32 Fd12
Prestfoss **N** 43 Fb17
Přeštice **CZ** 65 Fd31
Preston **GB** 21 Da24
Prestwick **GB** 20 Cd21
Pretzsch **D** 57 Fd28
Préveza **GR** 110 Hc45
Priboj **BIH** 86 Ha38
Priboj **SRB** 86 Ha39
Priboj **SRB** 87 Hd40
Pribojska Goleša **SRB** 86 Ha39
Příbor **CZ** 66 Gd31
Pribovce **SK** 66 Gd32
Příbram **CZ** 65 Ga31
Přibyslav **CZ** 65 Gb31
Priego **E** 92 Ca41
Priego de Córdoba **E** 106 Bc44

Priekulė **LT** 52 Hb23
Priekule **LV** 52 Hb22
Prienai **LT** 53 Hd24
Prievidza **SK** 66 Gd32
Prigor **RO** 87 Hc37
Prijedor **BIH** 86 Gc37
Prijepolje **SRB** 86 Ha39
Prijutnoe **RUS** 123 Ga15
Prilep **BG** 89 Jd39
Prilep **MK** 101 Hc42
Prilike **SRB** 87 Hb39
Primorsk **RUS** 41 Ja16
Primorsk **RUS** 52 Ha24
Primorsk **RUS** 123 Fd13
Primors'ke **UA** 77 Kb35
Primorski Dolac **HR** 85 Gb39
Primorsko **BG** 103 Ka40
Primorsko- Ahtarsk **RUS** 127 Fc16
Primošten **HR** 85 Gb39
Prínos **GR** 101 Hd44
Priólithos **GR** 110 Hd46
Priolo Gargallo **I** 109 Gb48
Priozersk **RUS** 41 Jb15
Prirečnyj **RUS** 27 Hd05
Prisoje **BIH** 86 Gc39
Priština **RKS** 87 Hc40
Pritzwalk **D** 56 Fc26
Privas **F** 82 Dd37
Priverno **I** 98 Fd42
Privlaka **HR** 85 Ga38
Privolžsk **RUS** 118 Fa09
Prizren **RKS** 101 Hc41
Prizzi **I** 108 Fd47
Prjamicyno **RUS** 122 Fa13
Prnjavor **BIH** 86 Gd37
Probijnivka **UA** 76 Ja33
Prodănești **MD** 77 Jd33
Prokuplje **SRB** 87 Hc39
Proletarij **RUS** 117 Eb09
Proletarsk **RUS** 123 Fd15
Pronin **RUS** 123 Fc14
Propriano **F** 96 Ed41
Prosek AL 100 Hb41
Prossotsáni **GR** 102 Jb42
Prostějov **CZ** 66 Gc31
Proszowice **PL** 67 Ha30
Protivín **CZ** 65 Ga32
Proussós **GR** 110 Hd45
Provadija **BG** 89 Jd39
Provins **F** 62 Dd32
Provištip **MK** 101 Hd41
Prozor = Rama **BIH** 86 Gd39
Prrenjas **RKS** 100 Hb42
Pruchnik **PL** 67 Hc30
Prudentov **RUS** 123 Ga13
Prudnik **PL** 66 Gc30
Prüm **D** 63 Ec30
Prunete **F** 96 Ed41
Pruské **SK** 66 Gd32
Pruszcz Gdański **PL** 58 Gd25
Pruszków **PL** 59 Hb28
Pružany **BY** 59 Hd27
Pryazovs'ke **UA** 126 Fa16

Prylęk **PL** 67 Hb30
Pryluky **UA** 121 Ed14
Prymorsʻk **UA** 126 Fb16
Pryozerne **UA** 77 Ka35
Przasnysz **PL** 59 Hb26
Przechlewo **PL** 58 Gc26
Przedbórz **PL** 67 Ha29
Przemyśl **PL** 67 Hc31
Przeworsk **PL** 67 Hc30
Przewóz **PL** 65 Ga29
Przybiernów **PL** 57 Ga26
Przyborowice **PL** 58 Ha27
Przyłęki **PL** 58 Gc27
Przystawy **PL** 57 Gb25
Przysucha **PL** 67 Hb29
Przytoczno **PL** 59 Hc28
Przytuty **PL** 59 Hc26
Psahná **GR** 112 Jb45
Psará **GR** 113 Jd45
Psarádes **GR** 101 Hc42
Psári **GR** 111 Ja46
Psebaj **RUS** 127 Fd17
Pskov **RUS** 47 Jb19
Pszczyna **PL** 66 Gd31
Pszów **PL** 66 Gd31
Ptolemaída **GR** 101 Hd43
Ptuj **SLO** 73 Gb35
Ptujska Gora **SLO** 73 Gb36
Pučež **RUS** 118 Fb09
Púchov **SK** 66 Gd32
Pucioasa **RO** 88 Jb36
Pučišća **HR** 86 Gc39
Puck **PL** 51 Gd24
Puçol **E** 93 Cc43
Pudasjärvi **FIN** 35 Hc10
Puebla de Alcocer **E** 91 Bb42
Puebla de Don Fadrique **E** 106 Bd44
Puebla de Don Rodrigo **E** 91 Bc42
Puebla de Guzmán **E** 105 Ad43
Puebla de Lillo **E** 79 Bc37
Puebla de Sanabria **E** 78 Bb38
Puebla de Trives **E** 78 Ba37
Puente-Genil **E** 105 Bb44
Puente la Reina **E** 80 Cb38
Puente la Reina de Jaca **E** 80 Cc39
Puentelarrá **E** 79 Ca38
Puerto de San Vicente **E** 91 Bb42
Puertollano **E** 92 Bc43
Puerto Lumbreras **E** 107 Ca45
Puerto Real **E** 105 Ad45
Puerto Rey **E** 91 Bb42
Pufeşti **RO** 77 Jd35
Pugačev **RUS** 119 Ga11
Puget-Ville **F** 82 Ea39
Puhos **FIN** 35 Hd10
Puhos **FIN** 41 Jb14
Pui **RO** 75 Hd36
Puiatu **EST** 47 Hd19

Puieşti **RO** 77 Jd34
Puigcerdà **E** 81 Da40
Puig-reig **E** 81 Da40
Puiseaux **F** 62 Dc32
Pukalaidun **FIN** 40 Hb16
Pukavik **S** 50 Ga22
Pukë **AL** 100 Hb41
Pula **HR** 85 Fd37
Pula **I** 97 Ed45
Pulaj **AL** 100 Ha41
Puławy **PL** 67 Hc29
Pulju **FIN** 30 Hb06
Pulkkila **FIN** 35 Hc11
Pulkkinen **FIN** 34 Hb12
Pulpí **E** 107 Ca45
Pulsano **I** 100 Gd43
Pulsnitz **D** 65 Ga29
Pulsnitz **D** 65 Ga29
Pulsujärvi **S** 29 Gd06
Pułtusk **PL** 59 Hb27
Pumpėnai **LT** 53 Hd22
Punkaharju **FIN** 41 Jb14
Punta Križa **HR** 85 Ga38
Punta Umbría **E** 105 Ad44
Puokio **FIN** 35 Hd10
Puolanka **FIN** 35 Hd10
Puoltsa **S** 29 Gd07
Puottaure **S** 34 Gd09
Purchena **E** 106 Bd45
Purdoški **RUS** 119 Fc10
Purmerend **NL** 55 Eb27
Puškino **RUS** 123 Ga12
Puškinskie Gory **RUS** 47 Jb20
Püspökladány **H** 75 Hb34
Pustoška **RUS** 117 Eb11
Putbus **D** 57 Fd25
Putignano **I** 99 Gc43
Putlitz **D** 56 Fc26
Puttgarden **D** 56 Fc25
Putyvlʻ **UA** 121 Ed13
Puumala **FIN** 41 Ja15
Puurmani **EST** 47 Hd19
Puy lʻEvêque **F** 81 Da37
Puzači **RUS** 122 Fa13
Pwllheli **GB** 23 Cc25
Pyhäjärvi **FIN** 27 Hb05
Pyhäjärvi **FIN** 31 Hc07
Pyhäjärvi **FIN** 35 Hc12
Pyhäjoki **FIN** 34 Hb11
Pyhäkylä **FIN** 35 Hd10
Pyhäntä **FIN** 35 Hc11
Pyhäntä **FIN** 35 Hd11
Pyhäranta **FIN** 40 Ha16
Pyhäselkä **FIN** 41 Jb13
Pyhtää **FIN** 41 Hd16
Þykkvibær **IS** 14 Bc07
Pyla-sur-Mer **F** 68 Cc36
Pylkönmäki **FIN** 40 Hc13
Pynjany **UA** 67 Hd31
Þyrill **IS** 14 Bc06
Pyrjatyn **UA** 121 Ed14
Pyrzyce **PL** 57 Ga26
Pyskowice **PL** 66 Gd30
Pytalovo **RUS** 47 Jb20
Pyttis **FIN** 41 Hd16
Pyzdry **PL** 58 Gc28

Q

Qafëzez **AL** 101 Hc43
Quafmollë **RKS** 100 Hb42
Quakenbrück **D** 55 Ed27
Quarré-les-Tombes **F** 70 Dd33
Quarteira **P** 104 Ac44
Quartu SantʻElena **I** 97 Ed45
Quedlinburg **D** 56 Fb28
Querfurt **D** 64 Fc29
Quesada **E** 106 Bd44
Questembert **F** 60 Cc32
Quiberon **F** 60 Cc32
Quick born **D** 56 Fb26
Quillan **F** 81 Db39
Quimper **F** 60 Cb31
Quimperlé **F** 60 Cb31
Quingey **F** 71 Eb34
Quintana de Castillo **E** 79 Bc37
Quintana del Puente **E** 79 Bd39
Quintanar de la Orden **E** 92 Bd42
Quintanar del Rey **E** 92 Ca43
Quintin **F** 60 Cc31
Quinto **E** 80 Cc40
Quiroga **E** 78 Ba37

R

Raabs **A** 65 Gb32
Raahe **FIN** 34 Hb11
Rääkkylä **FIN** 41 Ja13
Raanujärvi **FIN** 30 Hb08
Raattama **FIN** 30 Hb06
Rab **HR** 85 Ga38
Rabac **HR** 85 Ga37
Rábafüzes **HR** 73 Gb35
Rábahidvég **H** 74 Gc35
Rabka-Zdroj **PL** 67 Ha31
Râbniţa **MD** 77 Ka32
Rača **SRB** 87 Hc40
Râcaciuni **RO** 76 Jc35
Racalmuto **I** 108 Fd47
Răcăşdia **RO** 87 Hc37
Racconigi **I** 83 Ec37
Rachiv **UA** 76 Ja33
Rachiv **UA** 124 Ea16
Raciąż **PL** 58 Ha27
Racibórz **PL** 66 Gd30
Raciȟy **BY** 59 Hc25
Rača Vas **HR** 85 Ga37
Racksund **S** 33 Gc09
Radakowice **PL** 66 Gc29
Radalj **SRB** 86 Ha38
Radaškovičy **BY** 53 Jb24
Radaškovičy **BY** 120 Ea12
Rădăuţi **RO** 76 Jb33
Rădăuţi-Prut **RO** 76 Jc32
Radeberg **D** 65 Fd29
Radebeul **D** 65 Fd29

Radeburg **D** 65 Fd29
Radechiv **UA** 67 Hd29
Radechiv **UA** 120 Ea15
Radenci **SLO** 73 Gb35
Radenthein **A** 73 Fd35
Radijovce **MK** 101 Hc41
Radilovo **BG** 102 Jb41
Radisne **MD** 77 Kb33
Radlje ob Dravi **SLO** 73 Gb35
Radnevo **BG** 102 Jc40
Radom **PL** 67 Hb29
Radomicko **PL** 57 Ga28
Radomir **BG** 102 Ja40
Radomsko **PL** 67 Ha29
Radomyšlʻ **UA** 121 Eb14
Radomyšl nad Sanem **PL** 67 Hc29
Radomyśl Wielki **PL** 67 Hb30
Radovan **RO** 88 Ja38
Radovec **BG** 103 Jd40
Radoviš **MK** 101 Hd41
Radovljica **SLO** 73 Ga36
Radstadt **A** 73 Fd34
Radunʻ **BY** 59 Hd25
Radviliškis **LT** 52 Hc23
Radymno **PL** 67 Hc30
Radzanów **PL** 58 Ha27
Radziejów **PL** 58 Gd27
Radzyń Chełmiński **PL** 58 Gd26
Radzyń Podlaski **PL** 59 Hc28
Raesfeld **D** 55 Ec28
Rafína **GR** 112 Jb46
Raftópoulo **GR** 110 Hd45
Ragaciems **LV** 52 Hc21
Ragusa **I** 109 Ga48
Rahačov **BY** 121 Eb13
Rahden **D** 56 Fa27
Raheste **EST** 46 Hc19
Rain **D** 64 Fb32
Raippaluoto **FIN** 40 Ha13
Raippo **FIN** 41 Ja15
Raisdorf **D** 56 Fb25
Raisio **FIN** 40 Hb16
Raivala **FIN** 40 Hb14
Raja-Jooseppi **FIN** 31 Hc06
Rajakoski **RUS** 27 Hd05
Rájec-Jestřebí **CZ** 66 Gc31
Rajec Poduchowny **PL** 59 Hb28
Rajgród **PL** 59 Hc25
Rajka **H** 74 Gc33
Rakaca **H** 75 Hb33
Rakkestad **N** 43 Fc18
Rakovica **BG** 87 Hd39
Rakovica **HR** 85 Gb37
Rakovník **CZ** 65 Fc31
Rakovski **BG** 102 Jb40
Rakvere **EST** 47 Hd18
Rama-Prozor **BIH** 86 Gd39
Rambervillers **F** 63 Ec32
Rambouillet **F** 62 Dc31
Rameški **RUS** 117 Ed09

Ramnäs – Rietschen

Ramnäs **S** 44 Gb18
Râmnicelu **RO** 89 Jd36
Râmnicu Sărăt **RO** 89 Jd36
Râmnicu Vâlcea **RO** 88 Ja37
Ramsele **S** 38 Gb13
Ramsey **GBM** 20 Cd23
Ramsgate **GB** 25 Dc28
Ramsjö **S** 38 Gb14
Ramstein **D** 63 Ec31
Ramvik **S** 39 Gc14
Ramygala **LT** 53 Hd23
Randalstown **GB** 20 Cc22
Randazzo **I** 109 Ga47
Rånddalen **S** 38 Fd14
Randers **DK** 49 Fb22
Randijaur **S** 29 Gc08
Randsverk **N** 37 Fb15
Råneå **S** 34 Ha09
Ranemsletta **N** 32 Fd11
Rankweil **A** 72 Fa34
Rannoch Station **GB** 17 Da20
Ransta **S** 44 Gb18
Rantasalmi **FIN** 41 Ja14
Rantsila **FIN** 35 Hc11
Ranua **FIN** 35 Hc09
Raon-l'Etape **F** 63 Ec32
Rapallo **I** 83 Ed38
Räpina **EST** 47 Ja19
Rapla **EST** 46 Hc18
Rapperswil **CH** 71 Ed34
Räsåker **S** 38 Gb13
Râșcani **MD** 76 Jc32
Rașcov **MD** 77 Jd32
Raseiniai **LT** 52 Hc23
Raška **SRB** 87 Hb39
Râșnov **RO** 88 Jb36
Rasova **RO** 89 Ka37
Rasovo **BG** 88 Ja39
Rasskazovo **RUS** 123 Fc12
Rastatt **D** 63 Ed32
Rastede **D** 55 Ed26
Rasti **FIN** 30 Hb07
Rätan **S** 38 Ga14
Ratasjärvi **FIN** 30 Hb08
Rathdrum **IRL** 19 Cb24
Rathenow **D** 56 Fc27
Rathfriland **GB** 20 Cc23
Rathmore **IRL** 22 Bd25
Rathnew **IRL** 19 Cb24
Ratíškovice **CZ** 66 Gc32
Ratne **UA** 59 Hd28
Ratne **UA** 120 Ea14
Ratten **A** 73 Gb34
Rättvik **S** 38 Ga16
Ratuș **MD** 77 Jd33
Ratzeburg **D** 56 Fb26
Raubling **D** 72 Fc34
Raudeberg **N** 36 Ed14
Raudlia **N** 33 Ga09
Raufarhöfn **IS** 15 Cc05
Raufoss **N** 37 Fc16
Rauland **N** 42 Fa17
Rauma **FIN** 40 Ha16
Rauna **LV** 47 Hd20
Râu Sadului **RO** 88 Ja36

Răuseni **RO** 76 Jc33
Rautalampi **FIN** 41 Hd13
Rautavaara **FIN** 35 Ja12
Rautjärvi **FIN** 41 Jb14
Ravanusa **I** 108 Fd47
Rava Rus'ka **UA** 67 Hd30
Ravenna **I** 84 Fc38
Ravensburg **D** 72 Fa33
Ravna Gora **HR** 85 Ga37
Ravnaja **SRB** 86 Ha38
Ravne na Koroškem **SLO** 73 Ga35
Ravno Bučje **SRB** 87 Hd39
Rawa Mazowiecka **PL** 58 Ha28
Rawicz **PL** 66 Gc29
Ražanka **BY** 59 Hd25
Războieni **RO** 76 Jc34
Razbojna **SRB** 87 Hc39
Razdol **BG** 101 Ja41
Răzeni **MD** 77 Ka34
Razgrad **BG** 89 Jd38
Razlog **BG** 101 Ja41
Reading **GB** 24 Da27
Réalmont **F** 81 Db38
Rebirechioulet **F** 81 Da38
Rebordelo **P** 78 Ba38
Recanati **I** 85 Fd39
Recaș **RO** 75 Hc36
Recea **RO** 88 Jb36
Recess **IRL** 18 Bd23
Recey-sur-Ource **F** 70 Ea33
Recklinghausen **D** 55 Ed28
Recoaro Terme **I** 72 Fb36
Rěčyca **BY** 121 Ec13
Recz **PL** 57 Gb26
Ręczno **PL** 67 Ha29
Reda **PL** 51 Gd24
Redange-sur-Attert **L** 63 Eb30
Redcar **GB** 21 Db23
Redditch **GB** 24 Da26
Redea **RO** 88 Ja38
Redkino **RUS** 117 Ed10
Redon **F** 60 Cc32
Redondela **E** 78 Ad37
Redondo **P** 90 Ad42
Redruth **GB** 23 Cb28
Rędzikowo **PL** 58 Gc25
Rędziny **PL** 67 Ha29
Rees **D** 55 Ec28
Regalbuto **I** 109 Ga47
Regen **D** 65 Fd32
Regensburg **D** 64 Fc32
Regenstauf **D** 64 Fc32
Reggio di Calabria **I** 109 Gb46
Reggio Nell'emilia **I** 84 Fb38
Reghin **RO** 76 Ja34
Reghiu **RO** 76 Jc35
Regínio **GR** 111 Ja45
Reguengos de Monsaraz **P** 90 Ad42
Rehau **D** 64 Fc30
Rehburg-Loccum **D** 56 Fa27
Reichenbach **D** 64 Fc30

Reichshoffen **F** 63 Ed32
Reife **N** 29 Gc06
Reigate **GB** 25 Db28
Reims **F** 62 Ea31
Reinach **CH** 71 Ed34
Reinbek **D** 56 Fb26
Reinberg **D** 57 Fd25
Reine **N** 28 Fd07
Reinheim **D** 64 Fa31
Reinosa **E** 79 Bd37
Reinsvik **N** 36 Fa13
Reinsvoll **N** 37 Fc16
Reisjärvi **FIN** 35 Hc12
Reit im Winkel **D** 72 Fc34
Rejmyre **S** 44 Gb19
Rejowiec **PL** 67 Hd29
Rejštejn **CZ** 65 Fd32
Rekavice **BIH** 86 Gc38
Relleu **E** 94 Cc44
Remagen **D** 63 Ec30
Remda **RUS** 47 Ja19
Remeskylä **FIN** 35 Hc12
Remiremont **F** 71 Ec33
Remontnoe **RUS** 123 Ga15
Remscheid **D** 63 Ec29
Rémuzat **F** 82 Ea37
Rena **N** 37 Fc16
Rencēni **LV** 47 Hd20
Renda **LV** 52 Hb21
Rende **I** 109 Gb45
Rendína **GR** 101 Ja42
Rendsburg **D** 56 Fb25
Reni **UA** 89 Ka36
Renko **FIN** 40 Hc16
Rennebu **N** 37 Fb13
Rennes **F** 61 Cd31
Renningen **D** 63 Ed32
Rensjön **S** 29 Gd07
Renträsk **S** 34 Gd10
Reola **EST** 47 Ja19
Rep'evka **RUS** 122 Fb13
Repojoki **FIN** 30 Hb06
Reposaari **FIN** 40 Ha15
Repvåg **N** 27 Hb03
Requena **E** 93 Cb43
Réquista **F** 81 Db38
Reșadiye **TR** 115 Kb47
Resen **MK** 101 Hc42
Rešetylivka **UA** 121 Ed15
Reșița **RO** 87 Hc37
Reszel **PL** 59 Hb25
Retford **GB** 25 Db25
Rethel **F** 62 Ea31
Rethem **D** 56 Fa27
Réthimno **GR** 114 Jc49
Retiers **F** 61 Cd32
Rétság **H** 74 Ha33
Retuerta del Bullaque **E** 91 Bc42
Retz **A** 65 Gb32
Reus **E** 93 Cd41
Reuterstadt Stavenhagen **D** 57 Fd26
Reutlingen **D** 64 Fa32
Reutte **A** 72 Fb34
Revel **F** 81 Db38

Revfülöp **H** 74 Gc35
Revigny-sur-Ornain **F** 62 Ea32
Revin **F** 62 Ea30
Řevnice **CZ** 65 Ga31
Revsnes **N** 28 Gb06
Revúca **SK** 67 Ha32
Reyðarfjörður **IS** 15 Cc07
Reykhólar **IS** 14 Bc05
Reykholt **IS** 14 Bc07
Reykholt **IS** 14 Bc06
Reykjadiskur **IS** 15 Ca05
Reykjahlíð **IS** 15 Cb06
Reykjanes **IS** 14 Bc04
Reykjavík **IS** 14 Bc06
Rezé **F** 68 Cd33
Rēzekne **LV** 53 Ja21
Rezovo **BG** 103 Ka40
Rgotina **SRB** 87 Hd38
Rhayader **GB** 24 Cd26
Rheda-Wiedenbrück **D** 55 Ed28
Rheinau **D** 63 Ed32
Rheine **D** 55 Ed27
Rheinfelden **D** 71 Ec34
Rheinsberg **D** 57 Fd27
Rheinstetten **D** 63 Ed32
Rhiconich **GB** 17 Da18
Rhinow **D** 56 Fc27
Rho **I** 71 Ed36
Rhondda **GB** 24 Cd27
Riákia **GR** 101 Hd43
Riala **S** 45 Gc18
Riaño **E** 79 Bd37
Rians **F** 82 Ea39
Riaza **E** 92 Bd40
Ribadavia **E** 78 Ba37
Ribadelago **E** 78 Bb38
Ribadeo **E** 78 Bb36
Ribadesella **E** 79 Bd37
Ribarica **BG** 102 Jb40
Ribarska Banja **SRB** 87 Hc39
Ribe **DK** 48 Fa23
Ribécourt **F** 62 Dd30
Ribera **I** 108 Fd47
Ribérac **F** 69 Da36
Ribnica **BIH** 86 Gd38
Ribnica **SLO** 73 Ga36
Ribnitz-Damgarten **D** 57 Fd25
Říčany **CZ** 65 Ga31
Riccia **I** 99 Ga42
Riccione **I** 84 Fc39
Richelieu **F** 69 Da33
Richmond **GB** 21 Db23
Richmond **GB** 25 Db27
Ricobayo **E** 78 Bb39
Ridderkerk **NL** 55 Eb28
Ried im Innkreis **A** 73 Fd33
Riedlingen **D** 72 Fa33
Riesa **D** 65 Fd29
Riesi **I** 108 Fd47
Rietavas **LT** 52 Hb23
Rieti **I** 98 Fc41
Rietschen **D** 65 Ga29

Rieumes **F** 81 Da38
Rieupeyroux **F** 81 Db37
Riez **F** 82 Ea38
Rīga **LV** 52 Hc21
Rignac **F** 81 Db37
Riguldi **EST** 46 Hc18
Riihikoski **FIN** 40 Hb16
Riihimäki **FIN** 40 Hc16
Rijeka **HR** 85 Ga37
Rijssen **NL** 55 Ec27
Riksgränsen **S** 29 Gc06
Rila **BG** 101 Ja41
Rimavská Sobota **SK** 74 Ha33
Rimbo **S** 45 Gc18
Rimforsa **S** 44 Gb20
Rimini **I** 84 Fc38
Rímnio **GR** 101 Hd43
Rindal **N** 37 Fb13
Rindbø **N** 28 Gb06
Ringamåla **S** 50 Ga22
Ringarum **S** 44 Gb20
Ringaskiddy **IRL** 22 Bd25
Ringe **DK** 49 Fb24
Ringebu **N** 37 Fc15
Ringkøbing **DK** 48 Fa22
Ringsted **DK** 49 Fc23
Ringwood **GB** 24 Da28
Rinia **GR** 112 Jc46
Rintala **RUS** 41 Jb15
Rinteln **D** 56 Fa28
Río **GR** 110 Hd46
Rio Frio **P** 78 Bb38
Riom **F** 69 Dc35
Rio Maior **P** 90 Ac41
Riom-ès-Montagnes **F** 69 Dc36
Rionero in Vulture **I** 99 Gb43
Rioz **F** 71 Eb34
Ripač **BIH** 85 Gb38
Ripanj **SRB** 87 Hb38
Ripky **UA** 121 Ec13
Ripoll **E** 81 Db40
Ripon **GB** 21 Db24
Riposto **I** 109 Gb47
Riquewihr **F** 71 Ec33
Risbäck **S** 33 Gb11
Riscle **F** 80 Cd38
Riska **N** 42 Ed18
Risnes **N** 42 Ed19
Risør **N** 43 Fb19
Risoul 1850 **F** 83 Eb37
Risøyhamn **N** 28 Gb05
Rissa **N** 32 Fc12
Rissna **S** 38 Gb13
Risti **EST** 46 Hc18
Ristiina **FIN** 41 Hd15
Ristijärvi **FIN** 35 Hd11
Ristilä **FIN** 41 Hd14
Ritsem **S** 28 Gb07
Ritterhude **D** 56 Fa26
Riumar **E** 93 Cd41
Riva del Garda **I** 72 Fb36
Rive-de-Gier **F** 70 Dd36
Rivesaltes **F** 81 Db39
Rivne **UA** 120 Ea14

Rivne **UA** 125 Ed16
Rivoli **I** 83 Ec37
Rize **TR** 127 Ga19
Rizokarpaso **CY** 128 Gc18
Rjabovskij **RUS** 123 Fc13
Rjazan' **RUS** 118 Fa11
Rjazanka **RUS** 123 Fc12
Rjažsk **RUS** 118 Fb11
Rjukan **N** 42 Fa17
Roa **E** 79 Bd39
Roa **N** 43 Fc17
Roanne **F** 70 Dd35
Röbäck **S** 34 Gd12
Röbel **D** 57 Fd26
Robertsfors **S** 34 Gd12
Robledo **E** 92 Ca43
Röblingen **D** 64 Fc29
Rocamadour **F** 69 Db36
Roccadaspide **I** 99 Gb43
Rocca Imperiale **I** 99 Gc44
Roccamena **I** 108 Fd47
Roccastrada **I** 84 Fb40
Roccella Ionica **I** 109 Gc46
Rochdale **GB** 21 Da24
Rochechouart **F** 69 Da35
Rochefort **B** 63 Eb30
Rochefort **F** 68 Cd34
Rocheservière **F** 68 Cd33
Rochester **GB** 25 Db28
Rochlitz **D** 65 Fd29
Ročov **CZ** 65 Fd30
Rocroi **F** 62 Ea30
Rødberg **N** 43 Fb17
Rødbyhavn **DK** 49 Fc24
Rödeby **S** 50 Gb22
Rødekro **DK** 48 Fa24
Rodel **GB** 16 Cc18
Roden **NL** 55 Ec26
Rodez **F** 81 Dc37
Rodi Garganico **I** 99 Gb41
Roding **D** 64 Fc32
Rodna **RO** 76 Ja33
Rodniki **RUS** 118 Fa09
Rodolívos **GR** 102 Jb42
Ródos **GR** 115 Kc47
Rødsjøen **N** 32 Fc12
Rødvig **DK** 49 Fd24
Roela **EST** 47 Hd18
Roermond **NL** 63 Ec29
Roeselare **B** 62 Dd29
Roești **RO** 88 Ja37
Roetgen **D** 63 Ec29
Rogač **HR** 85 Gb39
Rogačevka **RUS** 122 Fb13
Rogačica **SRB** 86 Ha38
Rogaška Slatina **SLO** 73 Gb36
Rogatica **BIH** 86 Ha39
Rogliano **I** 109 Gc45
Rognan **N** 28 Gb08
Rogne **N** 37 Fb16
Rogovo **RUS** 47 Jb20
Rogowo **PL** 58 Gc27
Rogoźniczka **PL** 59 Hc28
Rogoźno **PL** 58 Gc27
Rohan **F** 60 Cc31

Rohožník **SK** 74 Gc33
Rohrbach **A** 73 Ga33
Rohrbach-lès-Bitche **F** 63 Ec32
Rohuküla **EST** 46 Hc18
Rohuneeme **EST** 46 Hc17
Roismala **FIN** 40 Hb15
Roissy **F** 62 Dd31
Roja **LV** 46 Hb20
Rojão **P** 90 Ad40
Röjdåfors **S** 44 Fd17
Rokiciny **PL** 58 Ha28
Rokiškis **LT** 53 Hd22
Roknäs **S** 34 Gd10
Rokycany **CZ** 65 Fd31
Rokytne **UA** 121 Eb14
Røldal **N** 42 Ed17
Rolde **NL** 55 Ec26
Rolfs **S** 34 Ha09
Rolfstorp **S** 49 Fd21
Roma **I** 98 Fc41
Roma **S** 51 Gd21
Roman **BG** 88 Ja39
Roman **RO** 76 Jc34
Românești **RO** 76 Jc33
Romanshorn **CH** 72 Fa34
Romans-sur-Isère **F** 82 Ea37
Romilly-sur-Seine **F** 62 Dd32
Romny **UA** 121 Ec14
Romodan **UA** 121 Ed14
Romorantin-Lanthenay **F** 69 Db33
Romsey **GB** 24 Da28
Rönäs **S** 33 Ga10
Roncesvalles **E** 80 Cc38
Ronchamp **F** 71 Eb33
Ronciglione **I** 98 Fc41
Ronda **E** 105 Ba45
Rønde **DK** 49 Fb22
Ronehamn **S** 51 Gd21
Rõngu **EST** 47 Hd19
Rønne **DK** 50 Ga24
Ronneby **S** 50 Gb22
Ronnenberg **D** 56 Fa27
Rönnliden **S** 33 Gc10
Rönnöfors **S** 33 Ga12
Ronse **B** 62 Ea29
Roosendaal **NL** 54 Ea28
Ropczyce **PL** 67 Hb30
Ropotovo **MK** 101 Hc42
Roquefort **F** 80 Cd37
Roquesteron **F** 83 Eb38
Roquetas de Mar **E** 106 Bd46
Roquetes **E** 93 Cd41
Rore **BIH** 86 Gc38
Røros **N** 37 Fc14
Rorschach **CH** 72 Fa34
Rørvik **N** 32 Fc11
Rørvika **N** 37 Fc13
Ros' **BY** 59 Hd26
Rošal' **RUS** 118 Fa10
Rosal de la Frontera **E** 105 Ad43
Rosans **F** 82 Ea38
Rosarno **I** 109 Gb46

Roscales **E** 79 Bd38
Roščino **RUS** 41 Jb16
Roscoff **F** 60 Cb30
Roscommon **IRL** 18 Ca23
Roscrea **IRL** 18 Ca24
Rose **MNE** 100 Ha41
Rosendal **N** 42 Ed17
Rosengarten **D** 56 Fb26
Rosenheim **D** 72 Fc33
Roses **E** 81 Dc40
Roseto degli Abruzzi **I** 85 Fd40
Roșia **RO** 75 Hc35
Roșia de Secaș **RO** 76 Ja35
Roșia Nouă **RO** 75 Hd35
Rosica **BG** 89 Ka38
Rosice **CZ** 65 Gb32
Rosignano Marittimo **I** 84 Fa39
Rosignano Solvay **I** 84 Fa39
Roșiori **RO** 75 Hc34
Roșiori de Vede **RO** 88 Jb38
Roskilde **DK** 49 Fc23
Roslavl' **RUS** 121 Ec12
Rosolini **I** 109 Ga48
Rosoman **MK** 101 Hd42
Rosporden **F** 60 Cb31
Rossano **I** 99 Gc44
Rossija **RUS** 117 Ec11
Rosslare **IRL** 23 Cb25
Rosslare Harbour **IRL** 23 Cb25
Roßlau **D** 56 Fc28
Rossön **S** 33 Gb12
Ross-on-Wye **GB** 24 Cd26
Rossoš' **RUS** 122 Fb13
Rostock **D** 56 Fc25
Rostov **RUS** 118 Fa09
Rostov- na-Donu **RUS** 123 Fc15
Rostrenen **F** 60 Cc31
Røsvik **N** 28 Gb07
Rosvik **S** 34 Ha10
Rot **S** 38 Ga16
Rota **E** 105 Ad45
Rot am See **D** 64 Fa32
Rotenburg **D** 64 Fa29
Rotenburg (Wümme) **D** 56 Fa26
Roth **D** 64 Fb32
Rothenburg ob der Tauber **D** 64 Fb31
Rotherham **GB** 25 Db25
Rothesay **GB** 20 Cd21
Rothwell **GB** 21 Db24
Rotondella **I** 99 Gc44
Rottenburg **D** 63 Ed32
Rottenburg **D** 64 Fc32
Rotterdam **NL** 55 Eb27
Rottne **S** 50 Ga21
Rottneros **S** 44 Fd18
Rottweil **D** 71 Ed33
Rötz **D** 64 Fc31
Roubaix **F** 62 Dd29
Roudnice nad Labem **CZ** 65 Ga30

Rouen – Saint Anne

Rouen **F** 61 Db30
Rougemont **F** 71 Eb34
Rouillac **F** 69 Da35
Roulans **F** 71 Eb34
Roussillon **F** 70 Ea36
Roussilon **F** 82 Ea38
Rovaniemi **FIN** 31 Hc08
Rovato **I** 72 Fa36
Roveň **SK** 67 Hc32
Roven'ki **RUS** 122 Fb14
Rovereto **I** 72 Fb36
Roverud **N** 43 Fd17
Rovigo **I** 84 Fc37
Rovinari **RO** 87 Hd37
Rovinj **HR** 85 Fd37
Rovnoe **RUS** 123 Fd12
Rów **PL** 57 Ga27
Rowy **PL** 51 Gc24
Royal Tunbridge Wells **GB** 25 Db28
Royan **F** 68 Cd35
Roye **F** 62 Dd30
Røyken **N** 43 Fc18
Røyrvik **N** 33 Ga11
Royston **GB** 25 Db27
Roza **BG** 103 Jd40
Rožaj **MNE** 87 Hb40
Różan **PL** 59 Hb27
Rozay-en-Brie **F** 62 Dd32
Rozdil'na **UA** 125 Ec17
Rozdol'ne **UA** 126 Fa17
Rozdyl'na **MD** 77 Kb33
Rožencovo **RUS** 119 Fc08
Rozivka **UA** 126 Fb16
Rožmitál pod Třemšínem **CZ** 65 Fd31
Rožňava **SK** 67 Hb32
Rožnov pod Radhoštěm **CZ** 66 Gd31
Rozogi **PL** 59 Hb26
Rožok **RUS** 118 Fb09
Rozoy-sur-Serre **F** 62 Ea30
Rozprza **PL** 67 Ha29
Roztoky **CZ** 65 Ga30
Rožyšče **UA** 120 Ea14
Rrogozhinë **RKS** 100 Hb42
Rtiščevo **RUS** 119 Fc11
Ruba **BY** 117 Eb11
Rubbestadneset **N** 42 Ec17
Rubiás **E** 78 Bb36
Rucăr **RO** 88 Jb36
Rucava **LV** 52 Ha22
Ruciane-Nida **PL** 59 Hb26
Ruda **S** 50 Gb21
Ruda Śląska **PL** 66 Gd30
Rude **HR** 73 Gb36
Rüdersdorf **D** 57 Fd27
Rüdesheim **D** 63 Ed30
Rudilla **E** 93 Cc41
Rudinka **HR** 85 Ga38
Rūdiškės **LT** 53 Hd24
Rudkøbing **DK** 49 Fb24
Rudky **UA** 67 Hd31
Rudna Glava **SRB** 87 Hd38
Rudnik **BG** 89 Ka39
Rudnik **SRB** 87 Hb38

Rudniki **PL** 66 Gd29
Rudnja **RUS** 117 Eb11
Rudo **BIH** 86 Ha39
Rudolstadt **D** 64 Fc30
Rue **F** 62 Dc29
Rueda **E** 79 Bc39
Ruen **BG** 89 Jd39
Ruffec **F** 69 Da35
Rugāji **LV** 53 Ja21
Rugby **GB** 24 Da26
Rugles **F** 61 Db31
Ruguj **RUS** 117 Eb08
Ruhan' **RUS** 121 Ec12
Ruhland **D** 65 Fd29
Ruidera **E** 92 Bd43
Rūjiena **LV** 47 Hd20
Ruka **FIN** 31 Hd08
Ruma **SRB** 86 Ha37
Rumboci **BIH** 86 Gd39
Rumburk **CZ** 65 Ga29
Rumia **PL** 51 Gd24
Rumilly **F** 71 Eb36
Rumšiškės **LT** 53 Hd24
Runcorn **GB** 24 Da25
Rundfloen **N** 37 Fd16
Rundvik **S** 39 Gd13
Rungsted **DK** 49 Fd23
Runtuna **S** 45 Gc19
Ruokojärvi **FIN** 30 Hb07
Ruokolahti **FIN** 41 Ja15
Ruokto **S** 29 Gc08
Ruovesi **FIN** 40 Hb14
Rupe **HR** 85 Gb39
Rupea **RO** 76 Jb35
Ruse **BG** 88 Jc38
Rusele **S** 33 Gc11
Rushden **GB** 25 Db26
Ruskeala **RUS** 41 Jb14
Rusksele **S** 33 Gc11
Rusnė **LT** 52 Hb23
Rüsselsheim **D** 63 Ed30
Russelv **N** 26 Gd04
Russkij Kameškir **RUS** 119 Fd11
Russnes **N** 27 Hb03
Rust **A** 74 Gc34
Rusterfjelbma **N** 27 Hc03
Ruszów **PL** 65 Ga29
Rute **E** 105 Bb44
Rüthen **D** 55 Ed28
Ruthin **GB** 24 Cd25
Rutigliano **I** 99 Gc42
Rutka-Tartak **PL** 59 Hc25
Rutledalen **N** 36 Ed15
Ruukki **FIN** 35 Hc11
Ruuvaoja **FIN** 31 Hd07
Ruvo di Puglia **I** 99 Gc42
Ruza **RUS** 117 Ed10
Ruzaevka **RUS** 119 Fc10
Ružany **BY** 120 Ea13
Ružomberok **SK** 67 Ha32
Ry **DK** 49 Fb22
Rybačij **RUS** 52 Ha24
Rybczewice **PL** 67 Hc29
Rybinsk **RUS** 117 Ed09
Rybnik **PL** 59 Hc26

Rybnik **PL** 66 Gd30
Rybno **PL** 59 Hb25
Rybnoe **RUS** 118 Fa11
Rychłocice **PL** 66 Gd29
Rychnowo **PL** 58 Ha26
Rychtal **PL** 66 Gc29
Rychwał **PL** 58 Gd28
Ryd **S** 50 Ga22
Rydaholm **S** 50 Ga21
Ryde **GB** 24 Da28
Rydet **S** 49 Fc21
Rydsnäs **S** 44 Ga20
Rydzewo **PL** 59 Hb26
Rye **GB** 25 Dc28
Rykene **N** 42 Fa19
Ryki **PL** 59 Hc28
Ryl'sk **RUS** 121 Ed13
Rymań **PL** 57 Gb25
Rymanów **PL** 67 Hc31
Rýmařov **CZ** 66 Gc31
Rymättylä **FIN** 46 Ha17
Ryn **PL** 59 Hb25
Rypefjord **N** 26 Ha03
Rypin **PL** 58 Ha26
Rysjedalsvika **N** 36 Ed15
Rytinki **FIN** 35 Hd09
Rząśnik **PL** 59 Hb27
Rzecznica **PL** 58 Gc26
Rzepin **PL** 57 Ga28
Rzeszów **PL** 67 Hc30
Ržev **RUS** 117 Ec10
Ržyščiv **UA** 121 Ec15

S

Sääksjärvi **FIN** 40 Hb13
Saalfeld **D** 64 Fc30
Saalfelden am Steinernen Meer **A** 73 Fd34
Saarbrücken **D** 63 Ec31
Saarburg **D** 63 Ec31
Sääre **EST** 46 Hb20
Saari **FIN** 41 Jb14
Saarijärvi **FIN** 40 Hc13
Saariselkä **FIN** 31 Hc06
Saarivaara **FIN** 35 Ja10
Saarlouis **D** 63 Ec31
Saas Fee **CH** 71 Ec36
Šabac **SRB** 86 Ha37
Sabadell **E** 95 Da41
Šabany **RUS** 47 Jb20
Sabarat **F** 81 Da39
Sabatinivka **UA** 77 Ka32
Sabaudia **I** 98 Fc42
Sabbioneta **I** 84 Fa37
Sabile **LV** 52 Hb21
Sabiñánigo **E** 80 Cd39
Sabinov **SK** 67 Hb32
Šabla **BG** 89 Ka38
Sablé-sur-Sarthe **F** 61 Da32
Saborsko **HR** 85 Gb37
Sabres **F** 80 Cd37
Sabugal **P** 91 Ba40
Säby **S** 44 Ga20
Sacecorbo **E** 92 Ca41

Sacedón **E** 92 Ca41
Săcel **RO** 76 Ja33
Săcele **RO** 88 Jb36
Săcele **RO** 89 Ka37
Săceni **RO** 88 Jb38
Sacile **I** 72 Fc36
Šack **BY** 120 Ea13
Šack **RUS** 118 Fb11
Šac'k **UA** 59 Hd28
Sacoşu Turcesc **RO** 75 Hc36
Săcueni **RO** 75 Hc34
Sada **E** 78 Ba36
Sádaba **E** 80 Cc39
Sadala **EST** 47 Ja18
Sadova **RO** 88 Ja38
Sadovo **BG** 102 Jb40
Sadovoe **RUS** 123 Ga14
Sæbø **N** 36 Fa14
Sæby **DK** 49 Fb21
Săedinenie **BG** 102 Jb40
Săedinenie **BG** 102 Jc40
Saelices **E** 92 Ca42
Sævareid **N** 42 Ed17
Safara **P** 105 Ad43
Säffle **S** 43 Fd18
Saffron Walden **GB** 25 Db27
Safonovo **RUS** 117 Ec11
Sâg **RO** 75 Hd34
Sagadi **EST** 47 Hd17
Sagard **D** 57 Fd25
Sagone **F** 96 Ed41
Sagres **P** 104 Ab43
Sagunt (Sagunto) **E** 93 Cc43
Sagvåg **N** 42 Ed17
Sahagún **E** 79 Bc38
Saharna Nouă **MD** 77 Ka33
Sahechores **E** 79 Bc38
Sahin **TR** 103 Jd42
Šahty **RUS** 123 Fc15
Šahun'ja **RUS** 119 Fc08
Šahy **SK** 74 Ha33
Saija **FIN** 31 Hd07
Saillans **F** 82 Ea37
Saint-Affrique **F** 81 Dc38
Saint-Agrève **F** 82 Dd37
Saint-Aignan **F** 69 Db33
Saint Albans **GB** 25 Db27
Saint-Amand-en-Puisaye **F** 70 Dd33
Saint-Amand-les-Eaux **F** 62 Dd29
Saint-Amand-Montrond **F** 69 Dc34
Saint-Ambroix **F** 82 Dd38
Saint-Amé **F** 71 Ec33
Saint-Amour **F** 70 Ea35
Saint-André-de-Cubzac **F** 68 Cd36
Saint-André-de-l'Eure **F** 61 Db31
Saint-André-les-Alpes **F** 83 Eb38
Saint Andrews **GB** 21 Db21
Saint Anne **GBA** 61 Cd29

Saint-Antoine – Salamína

Saint-Antoine **F** 96 Ed41
Saint-Aubin-d'Aubigné **F** 61 Cd31
Saint-Aubin-du-Cormier **F** 61 Cd31
Saint Austell **GB** 23 Cb28
Saint-Avold **F** 63 Ec31
Saint-Beat **F** 81 Da39
Saint-Benoît-du-Sault **F** 69 Db34
Saint-Bertrand-de-Comminges **F** 80 Cd39
Saint-Bonnet **F** 83 Eb37
Saint-Brévin-les-Pins **F** 68 Cc33
Saint-Brice-en-Cógles **F** 61 Cd31
Saint-Brieuc **F** 60 Cc31
Saint-Calais **F** 61 Db32
Saint-CaSaint-le-Guildo **F** 61 Cd31
Saint-Céré **F** 69 Db36
Saint-Chamond **F** 70 Dd36
Saint-Chély-d'Apcher **F** 81 Dc37
Saint-Chinian **F** 81 Dc38
Saint-Claud **F** 69 Da35
Saint-Claude **F** 71 Eb35
Saint Clears **GB** 23 Cc26
Saint David's **GB** 23 Cb26
Saint-Denis **F** 62 Dc31
Saint-Dié-des-Vosges **F** 71 Ec33
Saint-Dizier **F** 62 Ea32
Saint-Doulchard **F** 69 Dc34
Sainte-Énimie **F** 81 Dc37
Sainte-Foy-la-Grande **F** 69 Da36
Sainte-Hermine **F** 68 Cd34
Sainte-Livrade-sur-Lot **F** 81 Da37
Saint-Eloy-les-Mines **F** 69 Dc35
Sainte-Maure de-Touraine **F** 69 Db33
Sainte-Maxime **F** 83 Eb39
Sainte-Menehould **F** 62 Ea31
Sainte-Mère-Église **F** 61 Da30
Saint-Émilion **F** 68 Cd36
Saintes **F** 68 Cd35
Sainte-Savine **F** 62 Ea32
Sainte-Sévère-sur-Indre **F** 69 Dc34
Saintes-Maries-de-la-Mer **F** 82 Dd39
Sainte-Suzanne **F** 61 Da32
Saint-Étienne **F** 70 Dd36
Saint-Étienne-de-Saint-Geoirs **F** 70 Ea36
Saint-Étienne-du-Rouvray **F** 61 Db30
Saint-Etienne-les-Orgues **F** 82 Ea38
Saint-Fargeau **F** 70 Dd33
Saint Fergus **GB** 17 Dc19

Saint-Florent **F** 96 Ed40
Saint-Florentin **F** 70 Dd33
Saint-Florent-sur-Cher **F** 69 Dc34
Saint-Flour **F** 69 Dc36
Saint-Fort-sur-Gironde **F** 68 Cd35
Saint-Gaudens **F** 81 Da38
Saint-Gaultier **F** 69 Db34
Saint-Geniez-d'Olt **F** 81 Dc37
Saint-Genix-sur-Guiers **F** 70 Ea36
Saint-Georges-de-Didonne **F** 68 Cd35
Saint-Germain-du-Bois **F** 70 Ea34
Saint-Germain-en-Laye **F** 62 Dc31
Saint-Germain-Laval **F** 70 Dd35
Saint-Gervais-d'Auvergne **F** 69 Dc35
Saint-Gervais-les-Bains **F** 71 Eb36
Saint-Gildas-des-Bois **F** 60 Cc32
Saint-Gilles **F** 82 Dd38
Saint-Gilles-Croix-de-Vie **F** 68 Cc33
Saint-Girons **F** 81 Da39
Saint-Girons-en-Marensin **F** 80 Cc37
Saint-Guénolé **F** 60 Cb31
Saint-Guilhem-le-Désert **F** 81 Dc38
Saint Helens **GB** 21 Da24
Saint Helier **GBJ** 61 Cd30
Saint-Hilaire-du-Harcouët **F** 61 Da31
Saint-Hippolyte **F** 71 Ec34
Saint-Hippolyte-du-Fort **F** 82 Dd38
Saint-Honoré-les-Bains **F** 70 Dd34
Saint-Hubert **B** 63 Eb30
Saint-Imier **CH** 71 Ec34
Saint Ives **GB** 23 Cb28
Saint Ives **GB** 25 Db26
Saint-James **F** 61 Cd31
Saint-Jean-Brévelay **F** 60 Cc32
Saint-Jean-d'Angely **F** 68 Cd35
Saint-Jean-de-Luz **F** 80 Cc38
Saint-Jean-de-Maurienne **F** 71 Eb36
Saint-Jean-de-Monts **F** 68 Cc33
Saint-Jean-Pied-de-Port **F** 80 Cc38
Saint-Jean-Poutge **F** 80 Cd38
Saint John's Town of Dalry **GB** 20 Cd22

Saint-Julien-en-Genevois **F** 71 Eb35
Saint-Junien **F** 69 Da35
Saint-Just-en-Chaussée **F** 62 Dd30
Saint-Just-en-Chevalet **F** 70 Dd35
Saint-Justin **F** 80 Cd37
Saint-Just-Saint-Rambert **F** 70 Dd36
Saint-Lary-Soulan **F** 80 Cd39
Saint-Laurent-de-la-Cabrerisse **F** 81 Db39
Saint-Laurent-de-la-Salanque **F** 81 Dc39
Saint-Laurent-en-Grandvaux **F** 71 Eb35
Saint-Léonard-de-Noblat **F** 69 Db35
Saint-Lô **F** 61 Da30
Saint-Loup-sur-Semouse **F** 71 Eb33
Saint-Maixent-l'École **F** 69 Da34
Saint-Malo **F** 61 Cd31
Saint-Marcellin **F** 70 Ea36
Saint-Mars-la-Jaille **F** 61 Cd32
Saint-Martin-de-Ré **F** 68 Cd34
Saint-Martin-Vésubie **F** 83 Ec38
Saint-Mathieu **F** 69 Da35
Saint-Maximin-la-Ste-Baume **F** 82 Ea39
Saint-Médard-en-Jalles **F** 68 Cd36
Saint-Méen-le-Grand **F** 61 Cd31
Saint-Michel **F** 62 Ea30
Saint-Mihiel **F** 63 Eb32
Saint-Nazaire **F** 60 Cc32
Saint Neots **GB** 25 Db26
Saint-Nicolas-de-Port **F** 63 Eb32
Saint-Omer **F** 62 Dd29
Saint-Paul-de-Fenouillet **F** 81 Db39
Saint-Paulien **F** 70 Dd36
Saint-Paul-lès-Dax **F** 80 Cc37
Saint-Péray **F** 82 Ea37
Saint-Père-en-Retz **F** 68 Cc33
Saint Peter-Port **GBG** 61 Cd30
Saint-Philbert-de-Grand-Lieu **F** 68 Cd33
Saint-Pierre **F** 81 Dc38
Saint-Pierre-de-Chignac **F** 69 Da36
Saint-Pierre-d'Oléron **F** 68 Cd34
Saint-Pierre-le-Moûtier **F** 69 Dc34

Saint-Pierre-sur-Dives **F** 61 Da31
Saint-Pol-de-Léon **F** 60 Cb30
Saint-Pol-sur-Mer **F** 54 Dd28
Saint-Pol-sur-Ternoise **F** 62 Dd29
Saint-Pons-de-Thomières **F** 81 Db38
Saint-Pourçain-sur-Sioule **F** 70 Dd35
Saint-Priest **F** 70 Ea36
Saint-Privat **F** 69 Db36
Saint-Quay-Portrieux **F** 60 Cc31
Saint-Quentin **F** 62 Dd30
Saint-Raphaël **F** 83 Eb39
Saint-Rémy-de-Provence **F** 82 Dd38
Saint-Renan **F** 60 Cb30
Saint-Saëns **F** 62 Dc30
Saint-Saulge **F** 70 Dd34
Saint-Sauveur-en-Puisaye **F** 70 Dd33
Saint-Sauveur-le-Vicomte **F** 61 Cd30
Saint-Sauveur-sur-Tinée **F** 83 Eb38
Saint-Savin **F** 69 Db34
Saint-Seine-l'Abbaye **F** 70 Ea33
Saint-Sever **F** 80 Cd37
Saint-Sulpice **F** 81 Db38
Saint-Thégonnec **F** 60 Cb31
Saint-Tropez **F** 83 Eb39
Saint-Vaast-la-Hougue **F** 61 Da30
Saint-Valéry-en-Caux **F** 61 Db30
Saint-Valery-sur-Somme **F** 62 Dc29
Saint-Vallier **F** 70 Ea36
Saint Vincent **I** 71 Ec36
Saint-Yorre **F** 70 Dd35
Saint-Yrieix-la-Perche **F** 69 Db35
Saissac **F** 81 Db38
Saittarova **S** 30 Ha07
Saivomuotka **S** 29 Ha06
Sajkaš **SRB** 87 Hb37
Sajósvámos **H** 75 Hb33
Saka **LV** 52 Ha21
Šakiai **LT** 52 Hc24
Säkilahti **FIN** 41 Ja14
Sakony **RUS** 118 Fb10
Sakskøbing **DK** 49 Fc24
Saky **UA** 126 Fa17
Sakyatan **TR** 128 Gb15
Säkylä **FIN** 40 Hb16
Sala **S** 44 Gb17
Šaľa **SK** 74 Gd33
Salacgriva **LV** 46 Hc20
Sala Consilina **I** 99 Gb43
Salakas **LT** 53 Ja23
Salamanca **E** 91 Bb40
Salamína **GR** 112 Jb46

189

Salantai **LT** 52 Hb22
Salas **E** 79 Bc36
Salas de los Infantes **E** 79 Ca39
Sălătrucu **RO** 88 Ja36
Salbris **F** 69 Dc33
Salcia **RO** 87 Hd38
Salcia **RO** 88 Jb38
Šalčininkai **LT** 53 Ja24
Sălcuţa **MD** 77 Ka34
Saldaña **E** 79 Bd38
Saldus **LV** 52 Hb21
Salemi **I** 108 Fc47
Sälen **S** 38 Fd16
Salerno **I** 99 Ga43
Salers **F** 69 Dc36
S'Algar **E** 95 Dc43
Salgótarján **H** 74 Ha33
Salhus **N** 36 Ed16
Sali **HR** 85 Ga39
Salihler **TR** 103 Jd43
Salihli **TR** 113 Kb45
Salihorsk **BY** 120 Ea13
Salins-les-Bains **F** 71 Eb34
Salisbury **GB** 24 Da28
Sălişte **RO** 88 Ja36
Salla **FIN** 31 Hd08
Sallanches **F** 71 Eb36
Sallent **E** 81 Da40
Salme **EST** 46 Hb20
Salmenkylä **FIN** 40 Hb14
Salmerón **E** 92 Ca41
Salmijärvi **RUS** 27 Hd04
Salò **I** 72 Fb36
Salo **FIN** 40 Hb16
Salon-de-Provence **F** 82 Ea38
Salonta **RO** 75 Hc35
Salsbruket **N** 32 Fd11
Salses-le-Château **F** 81 Db39
Sal'sk **RUS** 123 Fd15
Salsomaggiore Terme **I** 84 Fa37
Saltash **GB** 23 Cc28
Saltburn-by-the-Sea **GB** 21 Db23
Saltvik **FIN** 45 Gd17
Saluzzo **I** 83 Ec37
Salvatierra-Agurain **E** 80 Cb38
Salvatierra de los Barros **E** 91 Ba42
Šalyhyne **UA** 121 Ed13
Salzburg **A** 73 Fd34
Salzgitter **D** 56 Fb28
Salzkotten **D** 56 Fa28
Salzwedel **D** 56 Fc27
Samachvalavičy **BY** 120 Ea12
Samara **RUS** 119 Ga10
Samarína **GR** 101 Hc43
Sâmbăta **RO** 75 Hc35
Sambir **UA** 67 Hd31
Sambuca di Sicilia **I** 108 Fd47

Sámi **GR** 110 Hc46
Sämi **EST** 47 Hd17
Sămica **BG** 102 Jb41
Şamlı **TR** 103 Kb43
Samobor **HR** 73 Gb36
Samoëns **F** 71 Eb35
Samofalovka **RUS** 123 Fd13
Samokov **BG** 102 Ja40
Samolva **RUS** 47 Ja19
Samos **SRB** 87 Hb37
Sámos **TR** 113 Ka46
Samothráki **GR** 102 Jc42
Samro **RUS** 47 Jb18
Samsun **TR** 127 Fc19
Samtens **D** 57 Fd25
Sanadinovo **BG** 88 Jb39
Sânandrei **RO** 75 Hc36
Sanary-sur-Mer **F** 82 Ea39
San Bartolomé de la Torre **E** 105 Ad44
San Bartolomeo in Galdo **I** 99 Ga42
San Benedetto del Tronto **I** 85 Fd40
San Benedetto Po **I** 84 Fb37
San Cataldo **I** 100 Gd43
Sancerre **F** 69 Dc33
Sanchidrián **E** 91 Bc40
San Clemente **E** 92 Ca42
Sancoins **F** 69 Dc34
San Cristóbal de Entreviñas **E** 79 Bc38
Sancti-Spíritus **E** 91 Bb40
Sančursk **RUS** 119 Fc08
Sand **N** 42 Ed18
Sand **N** 43 Fc17
Sandane **N** 36 Ed15
San Daniele del Friuli **I** 73 Fd36
Sandanski **BG** 101 Ja41
Sandata **RUS** 127 Fd16
Sandbach **GB** 24 Da25
Sande **D** 55 Ed26
Sande **N** 36 Ed15
Sandefjord **N** 43 Fb18
Sandgerði **IS** 14 Bb06
Sand in Taufers **I** 72 Fc35
Sandnes **N** 42 Ed18
Sandnessjøen **N** 32 Fd09
Sandoméri **GR** 110 Hd46
Sandomierz **PL** 67 Hb29
Sândominic **RO** 76 Jb34
San Donà di Piave **I** 72 Fc36
Sandovo **RUS** 117 Ed09
Sandøysund **N** 43 Fb18
Šandrivka **UA** 122 Fa15
Sandsele **S** 33 Gc10
Sandstad **N** 32 Fb12
Sandvik **S** 51 Gc21
Sandvika **N** 32 Fd12
Sandvika **N** 33 Ga11
Sandviken **S** 38 Gb16
Sandvikvåg **N** 42 Ed17
Sandwich **GB** 25 Dc28
Sandy **GB** 25 Db27
San Elia a Pianisi **I** 99 Ga42

San Esteban de Gormaz **E** 79 Ca39
San Ferdinando di Puglia **I** 99 Gb42
San Fernando **E** 105 Ad45
San Fratello **I** 109 Ga46
Sangaste **EST** 47 Ja19
San Gavino Monreale **I** 97 Ec44
Sângeorgiu de Pădure **RO** 76 Jb35
Sângeorz-Băi **RO** 76 Ja34
Sângera **MD** 77 Ka34
Sângerei **MD** 77 Jd33
Sangerhausen **D** 64 Fc29
Sângeru **RO** 88 Jc36
San Gimignano **I** 84 Fb39
Sanginkylä **FIN** 35 Hc10
San Giovanni in Fiore **I** 109 Gc45
San Giovanni in Persiceto **I** 84 Fb38
San Giovanni Rotondo **I** 99 Gb42
San Giovanni Valdarno **I** 84 Fb39
Sangis **S** 34 Hb09
San Giuliano Terme **I** 84 Fa39
Sangla **EST** 47 Hd19
Sangüesa **E** 80 Cc39
San Javier **E** 107 Cb45
San José **E** 106 Bd46
Sankavak **TR** 128 Gc17
Sankt Andrä **A** 73 Ga35
Sankt Anna **S** 44 Gb19
Sankt Anton **A** 72 Fa34
Sankt Gallen **CH** 72 Fa34
Sankt Georgen **D** 71 Ed33
Sankt Gilgen **A** 73 Fd34
Sankt Goar **D** 63 Ed30
Sankt Ingbert **D** 63 Ec31
Sankt Jakob **A** 72 Fc35
Sankt Johann **A** 73 Fd34
Sankt Johann **A** 72 Fc34
Sankt Margrethen **CH** 72 Fa34
Sankt Michaelisdonn **D** 56 Fa25
Sankt Moritz **CH** 72 Fa35
Sankt-Peterburg **RUS** 41 Jb16
Sankt-Peterburg **RUS** 117 Eb08
Sankt Peter-Ording **D** 56 Fa25
Sankt Pölten **A** 73 Gb33
Sankt Ulrich **I** 72 Fc35
Sankt Valentin **A** 73 Ga33
Sankt Veit an der Glan **A** 73 Ga35
Sankt Vika **S** 45 Gc19
Sankt-Vith **B** 63 Ec30
Sankt Wendel **D** 63 Ec31
San Leonardo de Yagüe **E** 79 Ca39

San Lorenzo de Calatrava **E** 106 Bc43
San Lorenzo de El Escorial **E** 92 Bd40
San Lorenzo de la Parrilla **E** 92 Ca42
Sanlúcar de Barrameda **E** 105 Ad45
Sanlúcar de Guadiana **E** 104 Ac43
San Lucido **I** 109 Gb45
Sanluri **I** 97 Ed44
San Marco in Lamis **I** 99 Gb42
San Marino **RSM** 84 Fc39
Sânmartin **RO** 76 Jc35
San Martín del Pimpollar **E** 91 Bc41
San Martín de Montalbán **E** 91 Bc42
San Martín de Valdeiglesias **E** 91 Bc41
San Martino di Castrozza **I** 72 Fc36
San Miguel de Salinas **E** 107 Cb45
Sânmihaiu de Câmpie **RO** 76 Ja34
San Miniato **I** 84 Fb39
Sänna **EST** 47 Ja20
San Nicandro Garganico **I** 99 Gb41
Sânnicolau Mare **RO** 75 Hb36
Sanniki **PL** 58 Ha27
Sanok **PL** 67 Hc31
Šanovo **BG** 102 Jc40
San Pedro **E** 92 Ca43
San Pedro del Pinatar **E** 107 Cb45
San Pellegrino Terme **I** 72 Fa36
Sanquhar **GB** 21 Da22
San Quirico d'Orcia **I** 84 Fb40
Sanremo **I** 83 Ec39
San Roque **E** 105 Ba46
San Salvo **I** 99 Ga41
San Sebastián **E** 80 Cb38
San Sebastián de los Reyes **E** 92 Bd41
Sansepolcro **I** 84 Fc39
San Severino Marche **I** 85 Fd40
San Severo **I** 99 Gb42
Sanski Most **BIH** 86 Gc38
San Stefano di Camastra **I** 109 Ga46
Santa Amalia **E** 91 Ba42
Santa Bárbara de Casa **E** 105 Ad43
Santa Cesarea Terme **I** 100 Ha44
Santa Clara-a-Velha **P** 104 Ab43
Santa Coloma de Queralt **E** 95 Da41

Santa Comba E 78 Ad36
Santa Croce Camarina I 109 Ga48
Santa Cruz de Campezo E 80 Cb38
Santa Cruz de Mudela E 92 Bd43
Santadi I 97 Ec45
Santa Eufemia E 105 Bb43
Santa Eugenia (Ribeira) E 78 Ad37
Santa Eulalia E 93 Cb41
Santa Eulália P 90 Ad42
Santa Eulària des Riu E 94 Cd44
Santa Fé E 106 Bc45
Sant' Agata di Militello I 109 Ga46
Santa Margherita I 97 Ec45
Santa Maria CH 72 Fa35
Santa María de la Peña E 80 Cc39
Santa Maria del Calmí E 95 Db43
Santa María del Páramo E 79 Bc38
Santa María la Real de Nieva E 92 Bd40
Santa Marinella I 98 Fb41
Santa Marta E 91 Ba42
Santana da Serra P 104 Ac43
Santander E 79 Ca37
Sant'Andrea Frius I 97 Ed44
Sant'Angelo dei Lombardi I 99 Gb43
Sant'Angelo Lodigia I 84 Fa37
Sant'Antioco I 97 Ec45
Sant Antoni de Portmany E 94 Cd44
Sant'Antonio di Santadi I 97 Ec44
Santanyí E 95 Db44
Santa Olalla del Cala E 105 Ba43
Santa Pau E 81 Db40
Santa Pola E 107 Cb44
Sant' Arcangelo I 99 Gc44
Santarcangelo di Romagna I 84 Fc39
Santarém P 90 Ac41
Santa-Severa F 96 Ed40
Santa Teresa di Riva I 109 Gb47
Santa Teresa Gallura I 96 Ed42
Sant Carles de la Ràpita E 93 Cd42
Sant Carles de Peralta E 94 Cd44
Sant Celoni E 95 Db41
San Teodoro I 97 Ed43
Santeramo in Colle I 99 Gc43
Santesteban E 80 Cc38

Sant' Eufemia Lamezia I 109 Gc45
Sant Feliu de Guíxols E 95 Db41
Sant Francesc de Formentera E 94 Cd44
Santhià I 83 Ed37
Santiago de Alcántara E 90 Ad41
Santiago de Compostela E 78 Ad36
Santiago do Cacém P 90 Ab42
Santibáñez de la Sierra E 91 Bb40
Santillana del Mar E 79 Ca37
Santisteban del Puerto E 106 Bd44
Sant Joan d'Alacant E 107 Cb44
Sant Llorenç de Morunys E 81 Da40
Sant Mateu E 93 Cc42
Santo Domingo de la Calzada E 79 Ca38
Santo Domingo de Silos E 79 Ca39
Santoña E 79 Ca37
Santo Tirso P 78 Ad38
Santu Lussurgiu I 97 Ec43
San Vicente de Alcántara E 90 Ad41
San Vicente de la Barquera E 79 Bd37
San Vincenzo I 84 Fa40
San Vito I 97 Ed44
San Vito al Tagliamento I 73 Fd36
San Vito dei Normanni I 100 Gd43
San Vito lo Capo I 108 Fc46
Sanxenxo Sangenjo E 78 Ad37
Sanza I 99 Gb44
São Brás de Alportel P 104 Ac44
São João da Madeira P 78 Ad39
São Marcos da Serra P 104 Ac43
São Martinho de Angueira P 78 Bb39
Saorge F 83 Ec38
São Teotónio P 104 Ab43
Sápai GR 102 Jc42
Sapernoe RUS 41 Jb15
Sapri I 99 Gb44
Sara FIN 40 Hb14
Sarabikulovo RUS 119 Ga09
Saraby N 26 Ha03
Sarai RUS 118 Fb11
Säräisniemi FIN 35 Hd11
Saraiu RO 89 Ka37
Sarajärvi FIN 35 Hd09

Sarajevo BIH 86 Gd39
Sarakína GR 101 Hd43
Sarakína GR 101 Hd44
Sarakiní GR 101 Hd42
Saramon F 81 Da38
Saranci BG 102 Ja40
Sáránd H 75 Hc34
Sarandë AL 100 Hb44
Saransk RUS 119 Fc10
Sarantáporo GR 101 Hd43
Šarašova BY 59 Hd27
Sarata UA 77 Kb35
Sărăteni MD 77 Ka34
Saratov RUS 123 Fd12
Saray TR 103 Ka41
Sarbinowo PL 57 Gb25
Sárbogárd H 74 Gd35
Sardara I 97 Ec44
Šarečensk RUS 31 Ja07
S'Arenal E 95 Db43
Šarengrad HR 86 Ha37
Šarhorod UA 125 Eb16
Saria GR 115 Kb48
Sarıköy TR 103 Ka42
Sariñena E 80 Cd40
Sariveliler TR 128 Gb17
Sariyer TR 103 Kb41
Šar'ja RUS 117 Eb08
Šar'ja RUS 118 Fb08
Sarkadkeresztúr H 75 Hc35
Särkelä FIN 31 Hd07
Särkijarvi FIN 30 Ha07
Şarköy TR 103 Ka42
Sarlat-la-Canéda F 69 Da36
Sărmăşag RO 75 Hd34
Särna S 38 Fd15
Sarnaki PL 59 Hc27
Sarnano I 85 Fd40
Sarnen CH 71 Ed35
Sărnevo BG 102 Jc40
Sarnico I 72 Fa36
Sarno I 99 Ga43
Sarny UA 120 Ea14
Särö S 49 Fc21
Saronída GR 111 Jb47
Saronída GR 112 Jb46
Saronno I 71 Ed36
Sárosd H 74 Gd35
Sárospatak H 75 Hc33
Šarovce SK 74 Gd33
Sarpsborg N 43 Fc18
Sarralbe F 63 Ec32
Sarrebourg F 63 Ec32
Sarreguemines F 63 Ec32
Sarre-Union F 63 Ec32
Sarria E 78 Ba37
Sartène F 96 Ed42
Sárti GR 102 Jb43
Saruhanlı TR 113 Ka44
Sárvár H 74 Gc34
Särvsjön S 38 Fd14
Sarzana I 84 Fa38
Sarzeau F 60 Cc32
Sarzedas P 90 Ad40
Sa Savina E 94 Cd44
Sásd H 74 Gd36

Sasino PL 51 Gc24
Sasovo RUS 118 Fb10
Sassari I 97 Ec43
Sassnitz D 57 Fd25
Sassoferrato I 84 Fc39
Sasso Marconi I 84 Fb38
Sassuolo I 84 Fb38
Sástago E 80 Cc40
Šaštín-Stráže SK 66 Gc32
Såtenäs S 43 Fd19
Säter S 38 Ga14
Säter S 44 Gb17
Sātiņi LV 52 Hb22
Sátoraljaújhely H 75 Hc33
Satovče BG 102 Jb41
Sattanen FIN 31 Hc07
Satu Mare RO 75 Hd33
Šatura RUS 118 Fa10
Saucats F 68 Cd36
Sauclières F 81 Da38
Sauda N 42 Ed17
Sauðárkrókur IS 15 Ca05
Saue EST 46 Hc18
Saugues F 81 Dc37
Saujon F 68 Cd35
Sauland N 43 Fb18
Săuleşti RO 88 Ja37
Saulieu F 70 Dd34
Saulkrasti LV 52 Hc21
Sault F 82 Ea38
Saumur F 69 Da33
Saunajärvi FIN 35 Ja11
Sauveterre-de-Béarn F 80 Cc38
Sauveterre-de-Guyenne F 68 Cd36
Sauvo FIN 46 Hb17
Sauxillanges F 69 Dc36
Sauzé-Vaussais F 69 Da34
Sävar S 34 Gd12
Săvârşin RO 75 Hc36
Sävast S 34 Ha09
Savaştepe TR 103 Ka43
Savenay F 61 Cd32
Săveni RO 76 Jc33
Saverdun F 81 Da38
Saverne F 63 Ec32
Savigliano I 83 Ec37
Savignano sul Rubicone I 84 Fc38
Savikylä FIN 35 Ja12
Şaviri Vechi MD 77 Jd32
Savitaipale FIN 41 Ja15
Šavnik MNE 86 Ha40
Savona I 83 Ed38
Savonlinna FIN 41 Ja14
Savonranta FIN 41 Ja14
Savran UA 77 Ka32
Sävsjö S 50 Ga21
Savukoski FIN 31 Hd07
Sawin PL 67 Hd29
Saxmundham GB 25 Dc27
Saxnäs S 33 Ga11
Säyneinen FIN 35 Ja12
Scaër F 60 Cb31
Scăeşti RO 88 Ja38

Scalasaig **GB** 16 Cc20
Scalea **I** 99 Gb44
Scanno **I** 98 Fd41
Scansano **I** 84 Fb40
Scanzano Ionico **I** 99 Gc43
Scarborough **GB** 21 Dc24
Scarinish **GB** 16 Cc20
Scarriff **IRL** 18 Ca24
Ščekino **RUS** 118 Fa11
Schaffhausen **CH** 71 Ed33
Schagen **NL** 55 Eb26
Scharbeutz **D** 56 Fb25
Schärding **A** 73 Fd33
Scheeßel **D** 56 Fa26
Scheibbs **A** 73 Ga33
Scheifling **A** 73 Ga34
Scheßlitz **D** 64 Fb31
Scheveningen **NL** 54 Ea27
Schiermonnikoog **NL** 55 Ec26
Schiffdorf **D** 56 Fa26
Schiltach **D** 71 Ed33
Schio **I** 72 Fb36
Schirmeck **F** 63 Ec32
Schitu Duca **RO** 77 Jd34
Schitu Goleşti **RO** 88 Jb36
Schladming **A** 73 Fd34
Schlanders **I** 72 Fb35
Schleiden **D** 63 Ec30
Schleiz **D** 64 Fc30
Schleswig **D** 49 Fb24
Schleusingen **D** 64 Fb30
Schlieben **D** 57 Fd28
Schlitz **D** 64 Fa30
Schlüchtern **D** 64 Fa30
Schmalkalden **D** 64 Fb30
Schneverdingen **D** 56 Fb26
Schönberg **D** 56 Fb25
Schönberg **D** 56 Fb25
Schöne beck **D** 56 Fc28
Schongau **D** 72 Fb33
Schöningen **D** 56 Fb28
Schönsee **D** 64 Fc31
Schopfheim **D** 71 Ec33
Schörfling **A** 73 Fd33
Schorndorf **D** 64 Fa32
Schramberg **D** 71 Ed33
Schrobenhausen **D** 64 Fb32
Schruns **A** 72 Fa34
Schwaan **D** 56 Fc25
Schwabach **D** 64 Fb31
Schwäbisch Gmünd **D** 64 Fa32
Schwäbisch Hall **D** 64 Fa32
Schwabmünchen **D** 72 Fb33
Schwaigern **D** 64 Fa32
Schwalmstadt **D** 64 Fa29
Schwalmtal **D** 64 Fa30
Schwandorf **D** 64 Fc32
Schwanewede **D** 56 Fa26
Schwarmstedt **D** 56 Fa27
Schwarzenbek **D** 56 Fb26
Schwaz **A** 72 Fc34
Schwechat **A** 74 Gc33
Schwedt **D** 57 Ga27
Schweich **D** 63 Ec30

Schweinfurt **D** 64 Fb30
Schwerin **D** 56 Fc26
Schwerte **D** 55 Ed28
Schwetzingen **D** 63 Ed31
Schwyz **CH** 71 Ed34
Sciacca **I** 108 Fc47
Scicli **I** 109 Ga48
Ščigry **RUS** 122 Fa13
Scilla **I** 109 Gb46
Ścinawa **PL** 65 Gb29
Scoarţa **RO** 88 Ja37
Scorniceşti **RO** 88 Jb37
Ščors **UA** 121 Ec13
Scourie **GB** 17 Da18
Scrabster **GB** 17 Db18
Ščučyn **BY** 59 Hd25
Sculeni **MD** 77 Jd33
Scunthorpe **GB** 25 Db25
Scuol **CH** 72 Fa35
Scutaru **RO** 76 Jc35
Ščyrec' **UA** 67 Hd31
Seahouses **GB** 21 Db22
Seamer **GB** 21 Dc24
Šebekino **RUS** 122 Fa14
Sebeş **RO** 88 Ja36
Sebež **RUS** 53 Jb21
Sebiş **RO** 75 Hc35
Sebnitz **D** 65 Ga29
Secemin **PL** 67 Ha29
Sečenovo **RUS** 119 Fc09
Seclin **F** 62 Dd29
Secondigny **F** 69 Da34
Seda **LT** 52 Hb22
Sedan **F** 62 Ea30
Séderon **F** 82 Ea38
Sedini **I** 96 Ed42
Sedlčany **CZ** 65 Ga31
Šeduva **LT** 52 Hc23
Sędziszów **PL** 67 Ha30
Seefeld **A** 72 Fb34
Seehausen **D** 56 Fc27
Seelow **D** 57 Ga27
Sées **F** 61 Db31
Seferihisar **TR** 113 Ka45
Şegarcea **RO** 88 Ja38
Segorbe **E** 93 Cc42
Segovia **E** 92 Bd40
Segré **F** 61 Cd32
Segura **P** 91 Ba41
Segura de la Sierra **E** 106 Bd44
Segura de León **E** 105 Ba43
Seia **P** 90 Ad40
Şeica Mare **RO** 76 Ja35
Seilhac **F** 69 Db36
Seinäjoki **FIN** 40 Hb13
Seini **RO** 76 Hd33
Seirijai **LT** 59 Hd25
Seirijai **LT** 59 Hd25
Sejny **PL** 59 Hc25
Sękowa **PL** 67 Hb31
Šeksna **RUS** 117 Ed08
Sekulovo **BG** 89 Jd38
Selargius **I** 97 Ed45
Şelaru **RO** 88 Jb37
Selb **D** 64 Fc30

Selbekken **N** 37 Fc13
Selbitz **D** 64 Fc30
Selbu **N** 37 Fc13
Selby **GB** 21 Db24
Sel'co **RUS** 47 Jb19
Selçuk **TR** 113 Ka45
Selde **DK** 48 Fa21
Sélestat **F** 71 Ec33
Selet **S** 34 Gd10
Selevac **SRB** 87 Hb38
Selfoss **IS** 14 Bc07
Seligenstadt **D** 64 Fa30
Selimiye **TR** 113 Kb46
Selımpaşa **TR** 103 Kb41
Selište **SRB** 87 Hd38
Seližarovo **RUS** 117 Ec10
Seljaküla **EST** 46 Hc18
Seljatyn **UA** 76 Jb33
Seljatyn **UA** 124 Ea16
Selje **N** 36 Ed14
Seljebø **N** 37 Fb13
Seljord **N** 42 Fa18
Selkirk **GB** 21 Da22
Selles-sur-Cher **F** 69 Db33
Selongey **F** 70 Ea33
Selsjön **S** 39 Gc13
Seltjärn **S** 39 Gc13
Semenivka **UA** 121 Ec13
Semenov **RUS** 118 Fb09
Semënovka **RUS** 123 Fd13
Semerdžievo **BG** 88 Jc38
Semikarakorsk **RUS** 123 Fc15
Semiluki **RUS** 122 Fb13
Šemordan **RUS** 119 Fd08
Šempeter **SLO** 73 Ga36
Sempujärvi **FIN** 34 Hb09
Semur-en-Auxois **F** 70 Ea33
Senden **D** 72 Fa33
Şendreni **RO** 89 Jd36
Senec **SK** 74 Gc33
Senftenberg **D** 65 Ga29
Senica **SK** 66 Gc32
Senigallia **I** 85 Fd39
Senj **HR** 85 Ga37
Senkaya **TR** 127 Ga19
Senlis **F** 62 Dd31
Sennecey-le-Grand **F** 70 Ea34
Sennen **GB** 23 Ca28
Sennybridge **GB** 24 Cd26
Senohrad **SK** 74 Ha33
Senokos **BG** 89 Ka38
Senonches **F** 61 Db31
Senorbì **I** 97 Ed44
Senovo **BG** 88 Jc38
Sens **F** 62 Dd32
Senta **SRB** 75 Hb36
Separeva Banja **BG** 102 Ja40
Šepelevo **RUS** 41 Jb16
Šepetivka **UA** 121 Eb15
Sępólno Krajeńskie **PL** 58 Gc26
Sępopol **PL** 59 Hb25
Septemvri **BG** 102 Jb40

Sepúlveda **E** 92 Bd40
Serafimoviè **RUS** 123 Fd13
Seraing **B** 63 Eb29
Serdobsk **RUS** 119 Fc11
Serebrjanskij **RUS** 47 Jb18
Sereď **SK** 74 Gd33
Seredžius **LT** 52 Hc24
Seregno **I** 71 Ed36
Šeremet'evka **RUS** 119 Ga08
Séres **GR** 101 Ja42
Serfaus **A** 72 Fb34
Sergač **RUS** 119 Fc09
Sergiev Posad **RUS** 118 Fa10
Sergines **F** 62 Dd32
Sérifos **GR** 111 Jc47
Sermaize-les-Bains **F** 62 Ea32
Sermehin **MK** 101 Hd42
Sernancelhe **P** 78 Ba39
Sernur **RUS** 119 Fd08
Serock **PL** 59 Hb27
Serón **E** 106 Bd45
Serón de Nágima **E** 80 Cb40
Seròs **E** 80 Cd40
Serpa **P** 104 Ac43
Serpuhov **RUS** 117 Ed11
Serracapriola **I** 99 Ga41
Serra de Outes **E** 78 Ad36
Serradilla **E** 91 Bb41
Serra San Bruno **I** 109 Gc46
Serres **F** 82 Ea37
Serrières **F** 70 Ea36
Sertã **P** 90 Ad40
Sertolovo **RUS** 41 Jb16
Sérvia **GR** 101 Hd43
Sesimbra **P** 90 Ab42
Seskarö **S** 34 Hb09
Sessa Aurunca **I** 98 Fd42
Sestimo **BG** 102 Ja40
Sesto Fiorentino **I** 84 Fb39
Sesto San Giovanni **I** 71 Ed36
Sestriere **I** 83 Eb37
Sestri Levante **I** 83 Ed38
Sestroreck **RUS** 41 Jb16
Sesvete **HR** 73 Gb36
Setermoen **N** 29 Gc06
Setraki **RUS** 123 Fc14
Settimo Torinese **I** 83 Ec37
Settle **GB** 21 Da24
Setúbal **P** 90 Ac42
Seui **I** 97 Ed44
Seurre **F** 70 Ea34
Sevaster **AL** 100 Hb43
Sevastopol' **UA** 126 Fa18
Ševčenkove **UA** 122 Fa14
Sevenoaks **GB** 25 Db28
Séverac-le-Château **F** 81 Dc37
Sevettijarvi **FIN** 27 Hc04
Sevilla **E** 105 Ba44
Şevketiye **TR** 103 Ka43

Sevlievo **BG** 88 Jb39
Sevnica **SLO** 73 Gb36
Sevsk **RUS** 121 Ed13
Sevštari **BG** 89 Jd38
Seydişehir **TR** 128 Ga15
Seyðisfjörður **IS** 15 Cc07
Seyne **F** 83 Eb38
Seyssel **F** 71 Eb36
Sežana **SLO** 73 Fd36
Sézanne **F** 62 Dd32
Sezze **I** 98 Fd42
Sfáka **GR** 111 Ja45
Sfáka **GR** 115 Ka49
Sfântu Gheorghe **RO** 76 Jb35
Sfântu Gheorghe **RO** 89 Kb36
Sfinári **GR** 114 Jb49
's-Gravenhage **NL** 54 Ea27
Shaftesbury **GB** 24 Cd28
Shanklin **GB** 24 Da28
Shannon **IRL** 18 Bd24
Sheerness **GB** 25 Dc28
Sheffield **GB** 25 Db25
Shelcan **RKS** 100 Hb42
Shëmil **RKS** 100 Hb42
Shënmër **AL** 100 Hb41
Shepton Mallet **GB** 24 Cd27
Sherborne **GB** 24 Cd28
Sheringham **GB** 25 Dc26
's-Hertogenbosch **NL** 55 Eb28
Shëvasija **AL** 100 Hb44
Shiel Bridge **GB** 16 Cd19
Shieldaig **GB** 16 Cd19
Shinoúsa **GR** 115 Jd47
Shkodër **AL** 100 Ha41
Shrewsbury **GB** 24 Da25
Sianów **PL** 57 Gb25
Šiaulėnai **LT** 52 Hc23
Šiauliai **LT** 52 Hc22
Sibari **I** 99 Gc44
Sibbo **FIN** 40 Hc16
Šibenik **HR** 85 Gb39
Sibiu **RO** 88 Ja36
Şibot **RO** 75 Hd36
Sichnice **PL** 66 Gc29
Siciska **PL** 58 Ha28
Šid **SRB** 86 Ha37
Sideby **FIN** 40 Ha14
Sidensjö **S** 39 Gc13
Siderno **I** 109 Gc46
Sidirókastro **GR** 101 Ja42
Sidmouth **GB** 24 Cd28
Siebe **N** 26 Ha05
Siedlce **PL** 59 Hc27
Siegburg **D** 63 Ec29
Siegen **D** 63 Ed29
Sielpia Wielka **PL** 67 Ha29
Siemiatycze **PL** 59 Hc27
Siemień **PL** 59 Hc28
Siena **I** 84 Fb39
Sieniawa **PL** 67 Hc30
Šienlaukis **LT** 52 Hc23
Siennica **PL** 59 Hb28
Sieppijärvi **FIN** 30 Hb08

Sieradz **PL** 58 Gd28
Sieraków **PL** 66 Gd30
Sierentz **F** 71 Ec33
Sierpc **PL** 58 Ha27
Sierre **CH** 71 Ec35
Şieu **RO** 76 Ja34
Sieuleni **RO** 76 Jb35
Sievi **FIN** 34 Hb12
Sievin **FIN** 34 Hb12
Sigean **F** 81 Dc39
Siggerud **N** 43 Fc18
Sighetu Marmaţiei **RO** 76 Ja33
Sighişoara **RO** 76 Jb35
Siglufjörður **IS** 15 Ca05
Sigmaringen **D** 72 Fa33
Šigony **RUS** 119 Ga10
Sigrí **GR** 113 Jd44
Sigtuna **S** 45 Gc18
Sigüenza **E** 92 Ca40
Sigüés **E** 80 Cc39
Sigulda **LV** 53 Hd21
Šihany **RUS** 119 Fd11
Sihtuuna **FIN** 34 Hb09
Siikainen **FIN** 40 Ha15
Siikajoki **FIN** 34 Hb11
Siilinjärvi **FIN** 41 Hd13
Siipyy **FIN** 40 Ha14
Siivikko **FIN** 35 Hd10
Sikeå **S** 34 Gd12
Sikfors **S** 34 Gd10
Sikiés **GR** 101 Hd44
Síkinos **GR** 111 Jc47
Sikourió **GR** 101 Ja44
Sikovicy **RUS** 47 Jb19
Siksjö **S** 33 Gc11
Šilalė **LT** 52 Hb23
Silandro **I** 72 Fb35
Silbaš **SRB** 86 Ha37
Silene **LV** 53 Ja22
Siles **E** 106 Bd44
Silian **A** 72 Fc35
Silifke **TR** 128 Gc17
Silistra **BG** 89 Jd37
Silivaşu de Câmpie **RO** 76 Ja34
Silivri **TR** 103 Kb41
Siljan **N** 43 Fb18
Siljansnäs **S** 38 Ga16
Silkeborg **DK** 49 Fb22
Silla **E** 93 Cc43
Sillamäe **EST** 47 Ja17
Sille **TR** 128 Ga15
Silleda **E** 78 Ba37
Sillé-le-Guillaume **F** 61 Da32
Sillerud **S** 43 Fd18
Silloth **GB** 21 Da22
Silovo **RUS** 118 Fb11
Šilovo **RUS** 122 Fa12
Silsand **N** 26 Gc05
Šilutė **LT** 52 Hb23
Silvalen **N** 32 Fd09
Silván **E** 78 Bb38
Silverdalen **S** 50 Gb21
Silves **P** 104 Ab43
Silvi **I** 99 Ga41

Simakivka **UA** 121 Eb14
Simbach **D** 73 Fd33
Simbirsk **RUS** 119 Fd09
Simeria **RO** 75 Hd36
Simferopol' **UA** 126 Fa17
Sími **GR** 115 Kb47
Šimkaičiai **LT** 52 Hc23
Simlångsdalen **S** 49 Fd22
Şimleu Silvaniei **RO** 75 Hd34
Simmern **D** 63 Ed30
Simnas **LT** 52 Hc24
Simo **FIN** 34 Hb09
Símos **GR** 110 Hd45
Simrishamn **S** 50 Ga23
Simsk **RUS** 117 Eb09
Simuna **EST** 47 Hd18
Sinaia **RO** 88 Jb36
Sinalunga **I** 84 Fb40
Şinca Nouă **RO** 88 Jb36
Sindal **DK** 49 Fb21
Sindelfingen **D** 64 Fa32
Sindi **EST** 46 Hc19
Sındırgı **TR** 113 Kb44
Sinekli **TR** 103 Kb41
Sinemorec **BG** 103 Ka40
Sines **P** 90 Ab42
Sinettä **FIN** 30 Hb08
Sineu **E** 95 Db43
Singen **D** 71 Ed33
Singilej **RUS** 119 Fd10
Sinie Lipjagi **RUS** 122 Fb13
Siniscola **I** 97 Ed43
Sinj **HR** 86 Gc39
Sinjavka **BY** 120 Ea13
Sinnai **I** 97 Ed44
Sinnes **N** 42 Ed18
Sinodskoe **RUS** 119 Fd11
Sinop **TR** 126 Fb19
Sinsheim **D** 64 Fa31
Sintea Mare **RO** 75 Hc35
Sint-Niklaas **B** 54 Ea28
Sintra **P** 90 Ab41
Sint-Truiden **B** 63 Eb29
Sinzig **D** 63 Ec30
Siófok **H** 74 Gd35
Sion **CH** 71 Ec35
Šipka **BG** 102 Jc40
Sipoo **FIN** 40 Hc16
Šipovo **BIH** 86 Gc38
Sippola **FIN** 41 Hd16
Sira **N** 42 Ed19
Siracusa **I** 109 Gb48
Siret **RO** 76 Jb33
Sirevåg **N** 42 Ed19
Şiria **RO** 75 Hc35
Siriu **RO** 88 Jc36
Širjaeve **MD** 77 Kb33
Sirkka **FIN** 30 Hb07
Sirmione **I** 84 Fb37
Sirok **H** 75 Hb33
Široka läka **BG** 102 Jb41
Široké **SK** 67 Hb32
Široki Brijeg **BIH** 86 Gd39
Širvintos **LT** 53 Hd23
Sisak **HR** 85 Gb37

Sisante **E** 92 Ca42
Sissone **F** 62 Ea31
Şiştărovaţ **RO** 75 Hc36
Sisteron **F** 82 Ea38
Sitges **E** 95 Da41
Sitía **GR** 115 Ka49
Sitohóri **GR** 101 Ja42
Sittard **NL** 63 Eb29
Sittingbourne **GB** 25 Dc28
Sivac **SRB** 74 Ha36
Šivačevo **BG** 88 Jc39
Sivakka **FIN** 35 Ja11
Sivakka **FIN** 35 Ja11
Siverskij **RUS** 117 Eb09
Six-Fours-les-Plages **F** 82 Ea39
Sizun **F** 60 Cb31
Sjanno **BY** 121 Eb12
Sjas'stroj **RUS** 117 Eb08
Sjava **RUS** 119 Fc08
Sjenica **SRB** 87 Hb39
Sjeverodonec'k **UA** 122 Fb14
Sjoa **N** 37 Fb15
Sjøasen **N** 32 Fc12
Sjöbo **S** 49 Fd23
Sjøholt **N** 36 Fa14
Sjötofta **S** 49 Fd21
Sjötorp **S** 44 Ga19
Sjøvegan **N** 29 Gc06
Sjuntorp **S** 43 Fd20
Sjuvjaoro **RUS** 41 Jb14
Skadovs'k **UA** 125 Ed17
Skælskør **N** 49 Fc24
Skærbæk **DK** 48 Fa24
Skaftung **FIN** 40 Ha14
Skagaströnd **IS** 14 Bd05
Skagen **DK** 43 Fc20
Skagshamn **S** 39 Gd13
Skaidi **N** 26 Ha03
Skaill **GB** 17 Db17
Skaistgirys **LT** 52 Hc22
Skaistkalne **LV** 53 Hd22
Skaitekojan **N** 28 Gb07
Skaitekojan **S** 29 Gd08
Skála **GR** 111 Ja47
Skála **GR** 113 Ka46
Skała **PL** 67 Ha30
Skála Eressú **GR** 113 Jd44
Skála Marión **GR** 102 Jb42
Skála Oropoú **GR** 112 Jb45
Skala-Podil's'ka **UA** 124 Ea16
Skalica **BG** 103 Jd40
Skalica **SK** 66 Gc32
Skalltivaara **FIN** 27 Hc04
Skalmodal **S** 33 Ga10
Skaloti **GR** 102 Jb41
Skalstugan **S** 38 Fd13
Skandáli **GR** 102 Jc43
Skandawa **PL** 59 Hb25
Skanderborg **DK** 49 Fb23
Skånevik **N** 42 Ed17
Skåningen **N** 26 Gc04
Skänninge **S** 44 Ga19
Skansnäs **S** 33 Gb10

Skara – Sola

Skara **S** 44 Fd19
Skarberget **N** 28 Gb06
Skärblacka **S** 44 Gb19
Skardet **N** 26 Gd04
Skardet **N** 33 Ga09
Skare **N** 42 Ed17
Skåre **S** 44 Fd18
Skärhamn **S** 43 Fc20
Skarness **N** 43 Fc17
Skärplinge **S** 45 Gc17
Skärså **S** 39 Gc15
Skarsvåg **N** 27 Hb02
Skarvsjöby **S** 33 Gb11
Skaryszew **PL** 67 Hb29
Skarżysko-Kamienna **PL** 67 Hb29
Skattkärr **S** 44 Ga18
Skattungbyn **S** 38 Ga16
Skatval **N** 37 Fc13
Skaudvilė **LT** 52 Hc23
Skaulo **S** 29 Gd07
Skawina **PL** 67 Ha31
Skeby **S** 44 Fd19
Skeda **S** 44 Gb20
Skedshult **S** 44 Gb20
Skedsmokorset **N** 43 Fc17
Skee **S** 43 Fc19
Skegness **GB** 25 Dc25
Skei **N** 32 Fd10
Skei **N** 36 Ed15
Skei **N** 37 Fb13
Skellefteå **S** 34 Gd11
Skelleftehamn **S** 34 Ha11
Skender Vakuf **BIH** 86 Gc38
Skene **S** 49 Fd21
Skepastí **GR** 114 Jc49
Skerries **IRL** 19 Cb24
Ski **N** 43 Fc18
Skibbereen **IRL** 22 Bc25
Skibotn **N** 26 Gd05
Skidal' **BY** 59 Hd25
Skien **N** 43 Fb18
Skien **N** 43 Fb18
Skierbieszów **PL** 67 Hd29
Skierniewice **PL** 58 Ha28
Skillingaryd **S** 50 Ga21
Skinnskatteberg **S** 44 Gb18
Skipton **GB** 21 Da24
Skirmantiškė **LT** 52 Hc23
Skive **DK** 48 Fa22
Skjelstad **N** 32 Fd12
Skjern **DK** 48 Fa23
Skjervøy **N** 26 Gd04
Skjold **N** 26 Gc05
Skjolden **N** 36 Fa15
Skjønhaug **N** 43 Fc18
Šklov **BY** 121 Eb12
Skoczów **PL** 66 Gd31
Škofja Loka **SLO** 73 Ga36
Škofljica **SLO** 73 Ga36
Skógar **IS** 14 Bc08
Skoghall **S** 44 Fd18
Skogn **N** 32 Fc12
Skoki **PL** 58 Gc27
Skole **UA** 67 Hd31
Skollenborg **N** 43 Fb18

Skopiá **GR** 111 Ja45
Skopin **RUS** 118 Fa11
Skopje **MK** 101 Hc41
Skórcz **PL** 58 Gd26
Skorków **PL** 67 Ha29
Skorodnoe **RUS** 122 Fa13
Skorogoszcz **PL** 66 Gc30
Skoroszyce **PL** 66 Gc30
Skorovatn **N** 32 Fd11
Skørping **DK** 49 Fb21
Skortsinós **GR** 111 Ja47
Skotterud **N** 43 Fd17
Skoulikariá **GR** 110 Hc45
Skoúrta **GR** 112 Jb46
Skövde **S** 44 Ga19
Skrá **GR** 101 Hd42
Skrad **HR** 85 Ga37
Skradin **HR** 85 Gb39
Skreia **N** 37 Fc16
Skriveri **LV** 53 Hd21
Skrolsvika **N** 28 Gb05
Skrunda **LV** 52 Hb21
Skule **S** 39 Gc13
Skulgam **N** 26 Gc04
Skulsk **PL** 58 Gd27
Skulte **LV** 46 Hc20
Skultorp **S** 44 Ga20
Skultuna **S** 44 Gb18
Skuodas **LT** 52 Hb22
Skurup **S** 49 Fd23
Skurv **S** 50 Gb22
Skutari **AL** 100 Ha41
Skutskär **S** 39 Gc16
Skutvika **N** 28 Ga07
Skverbai **LT** 53 Hd22
Skvyra **UA** 121 Ec15
Skwierzyna **PL** 57 Gb27
Skyttmon **S** 38 Gb13
Skyttorp **S** 45 Gc17
Slabada **BY** 53 Jb24
Slagelse **DK** 49 Fc23
Slagnäs **S** 33 Gc10
Slănčev Briag **BG** 89 Ka39
Slancy **RUS** 47 Ja18
Slane **IRL** 19 Cb23
Slănic **RO** 88 Jc36
Slănic-Moldova **RO** 76 Jc35
Slano **HR** 86 Gd40
Slaný **CZ** 65 Ga30
Slatina **BIH** 86 Gc38
Slatina **HR** 74 Gd36
Slatina **RO** 88 Ja37
Slatina **SRB** 86 Ha38
Slatina-Timiş **RO** 87 Hd37
Slattum **N** 43 Fc17
Slavharad **BY** 121 Ec12
Slavičín **CZ** 66 Gd32
Slavikai **LT** 52 Hc24
Slavinja **SRB** 87 Hd39
Slavjansk na-Kubani **RUS** 127 Fc17
Slavkoviči **RUS** 47 Jb20
Slavonice **CZ** 65 Gb32
Slavonski Brod **HR** 86 Gd37
Slavonski Šamac **HR** 86 Gd37

Slavsk **RUS** 52 Hb24
Slavs'ke **UA** 67 Hd32
Slavuta **UA** 121 Eb15
Sławatycze **PL** 59 Hd28
Sławno **PL** 57 Gb25
Sleaford **GB** 25 Db25
Ślesin **PL** 58 Gd27
Slidre **N** 37 Fb16
Sligachan **GB** 16 Cd19
Sligo **IRL** 18 Ca22
Slisenvaara **RUS** 41 Jb14
Ślisselʹburg **RUS** 117 Eb08
Slite **S** 45 Gd20
Slivata **BG** 87 Hd38
Sliven **BG** 89 Jd39
Slivnica **BG** 102 Ja40
Slivo Pole **BG** 88 Jc38
Sloboda **LV** 53 Jb22
Slobozia **MD** 77 Kb34
Slobozia **RO** 89 Jd37
Slobozia Mare **MD** 77 Ka35
Słomniki **PL** 67 Ha30
Slonim **BY** 120 Ea13
Slovenj Gradec **SLO** 73 Ga35
Slovenska Bistrica **SLO** 73 Gb35
Slovenská L'upča **SK** 67 Ha32
Slovinka **RUS** 118 Fb08
Slov'jans'k **UA** 122 Fb15
Słubice **PL** 57 Ga28
Sluck **BY** 120 Ea13
Slunj **HR** 85 Gb37
Słupca **PL** 58 Gc28
Słupia **PL** 67 Hb30
Słupno **PL** 58 Ha27
Słupsk **PL** 58 Gc25
Slussfors **S** 33 Gb10
Smålandsstenar **S** 49 Fd21
Smalininkai **LT** 52 Hc24
Smaljanďca **BY** 59 Hd27
Smaljavičy **BY** 121 Eb12
Smârdioasa **RO** 88 Jc38
Smarhon' **BY** 53 Ja24
Smarhon' **BY** 120 Ea12
Šmarje pri Jelšah **SLO** 73 Gb36
Smeberg **S** 43 Fc19
Smedby **S** 50 Gb22
Smederevo **SRB** 87 Hb38
Smedjebacken **S** 44 Gb17
Śmierdnica **PL** 57 Ga26
Śmigiel **PL** 57 Gb28
Smila **UA** 121 Ed15
Smiltene **LV** 47 Hd20
Smjadovo **BG** 89 Jd39
Smogulec **PL** 58 Gc27
Šmojlovo **RUS** 47 Jb20
Smołdzino **PL** 51 Gc24
Smolenice **SK** 74 Gc33
Smolensk **RUS** 117 Ec11
Smoljan **BG** 102 Jb41
Smolnik **PL** 67 Hc31
Smolsko **BG** 102 Ja40

Smože **UA** 67 Hd32
Smygehamn **S** 49 Fd24
Šmykove **MD** 77 Kb32
Smyšljaevsk **RUS** 119 Ga10
Snåsa **N** 32 Fd12
Snedsted **DK** 48 Fa21
Sneek **NL** 55 Ec26
Sneem **IRL** 22 Bc25
Snihurivka **UA** 125 Ed16
Snillfjord **N** 37 Fb13
Snina **SK** 67 Hc32
Snjatyn **UA** 76 Jb32
Snjatyn **UA** 124 Ea16
Snøfjord **N** 26 Ha03
Soanlahti **RUS** 41 Jb13
Soave **I** 84 Fb37
Sobibór **PL** 59 Hd28
Sobinka **RUS** 118 Fa10
Sobolevo **RUS** 118 Fb11
Sobótka **PL** 67 Hb29
Sobra **HR** 86 Gd40
Sobrance **SK** 67 Hc32
Søby **DK** 49 Fb24
Sochaczew **PL** 58 Ha28
Soči **RUS** 127 Fd17
Socodor **RO** 75 Hc35
Socuéllamos **E** 92 Bd42
Sodankylä **FIN** 31 Hc07
Söderåkra **S** 50 Gb22
Söderbärke **S** 44 Gb17
Söderfors **S** 45 Gc17
Söderhamn **S** 39 Gc16
Söderköping **S** 44 Gb19
Södertälje **S** 45 Gc18
Södervik **S** 45 Gd18
Södra Sunderbyn **S** 34 Ha10
Södra Tresund **S** 33 Gb11
Södra Vi **S** 44 Gb20
Soest **D** 55 Ed28
Sofádes **GR** 101 Hd44
Sofija **BG** 102 Ja40
Sofijivka **UA** 121 Ed15
Šofjanga **RUS** 35 Ja09
Sögel **D** 55 Ed27
Sogndal **N** 36 Fa15
Sohós **GR** 101 Ja42
Soignies **B** 62 Ea29
Şoimi **RO** 75 Hc35
Soini **FIN** 40 Hb13
Soissons **F** 62 Dd31
Sokal' **UA** 67 Hd30
Sokal' **UA** 120 Ea15
Söke **TR** 113 Kb46
Sokna **N** 43 Fb17
Soknedal **N** 37 Fc13
Soko Banja **SRB** 87 Hc39
Sokol **RUS** 117 Ed08
Sokolac **BIH** 86 Ha39
Sokófka **PL** 59 Hc26
Sokołów Małopolski **PL** 67 Hc30
Sokołów Podlaski **PL** 59 Hc27
Sokoły **PL** 59 Hc26
Sokyrjany **UA** 76 Jc32
Sola **N** 42 Ec18

Solana del Pino **E** 106 Bc43
Solares **E** 79 Ca37
Solberg **S** 33 Gc12
Solca **RO** 76 Jb33
Sol'cy **RUS** 117 Eb09
Şoldăneşti **MD** 77 Ka32
Sölden **A** 72 Fb35
Solec Kujawski **PL** 58 Gd26
Solënoe **RUS** 123 Fd15
Solenzara **F** 96 Ed41
Solihull **GB** 24 Da26
Solingen **D** 63 Ec29
Sollebrunn **S** 43 Fd20
Sollefteå **S** 39 Gc13
Sollentuna **S** 45 Gc18
Sóller **E** 95 Db43
Sollihøgda **N** 43 Fc17
Solncevo **RUS** 122 Fa13
Solnečnogorsk **RUS** 117 Ed10
Solnice **CZ** 65 Gb30
Šolohovskij **RUS** 123 Fc14
Solone **UA** 122 Fa15
Solonţ **RO** 76 Jc34
Solothurn **CH** 71 Ec34
Solotvyn **UA** 76 Ja32
Solotvyna **UA** 76 Ja33
Sølsnes **N** 36 Fa14
Solsona **E** 81 Da40
Solsvik **N** 36 Ec16
Solt **H** 74 Ha35
Soltau **D** 56 Fb27
Soltvadkert **H** 74 Ha35
Solvarbo **S** 44 Gb17
Sölvesborg **S** 50 Ga23
Soly **BY** 53 Ja24
Sol y Nieve **E** 106 Bc45
Soma **TR** 113 Ka44
Somaén **E** 92 Ca40
Somain **F** 62 Dd29
Sombor **SRB** 74 Ha36
Şomcuta Mare **RO** 75 Hd34
Somero **FIN** 40 Hb16
Somianki **PL** 59 Hb27
Sömmerda **D** 64 Fb29
Sommersete **N** 27 Hd03
Sommesous **F** 62 Ea32
Sommières **F** 82 Dd38
Somogyvár **H** 74 Gd35
Somonino **PL** 58 Gd25
Sompolno **PL** 58 Gd27
Soncillo **E** 79 Ca38
Sondalo **I** 72 Fa35
Søndeled **N** 43 Fb19
Sønderborg **DK** 49 Fb24
Sønder Nissum **DK** 48 Fa22
Sønder Omme **DK** 48 Fa23
Sondershausen **D** 64 Fb29
Søndersø **DK** 49 Fb23
Søndervig **DK** 48 Fa22
Sondrio **I** 72 Fa36
Son en Breugel **NL** 55 Eb28
Sonkajärvi **FIN** 35 Hd12
Sonkovo **RUS** 117 Ed09
Sonneberg **D** 64 Fb30
Sonseca **E** 91 Bc42

Sonthofen **D** 72 Fa34
Sontra **D** 64 Fa29
Sopot **PL** 58 Gd25
Sopot **SRB** 87 Hb38
Sopotnica **MK** 101 Hc42
Sopron **H** 74 Gc34
Sora **I** 98 Fd42
Söråker **S** 39 Gc14
Sorano **I** 84 Fb40
Sorbas **E** 106 Bd45
Sörbygden **S** 38 Gb14
Sore **F** 80 Cd37
Søre Moen **N** 32 Fd12
Soresina **I** 84 Fa37
Sør-Flatanger **N** 32 Fc11
Sörforsa **S** 38 Gb15
Sorgono **I** 97 Ed44
Sorgues-l'Ouvèze **F** 82 Dd38
Sør-Gutvika **N** 32 Fd11
Soria **E** 79 Ca39
Sørkjosen **N** 26 Gd04
Sørland **N** 28 Fd07
Sørli **N** 33 Ga12
Sörmjöle **S** 34 Gd12
Sornac **F** 69 Db35
Sorø **DK** 49 Fc23
Soroca **MD** 77 Jd32
Soroč'i Gory **RUS** 119 Fd09
Sørreisa **N** 26 Gc05
Sorrento **I** 99 Ga43
Sørrollnes **N** 28 Gb06
Sorsakoski **FIN** 41 Hd13
Sorsele **S** 33 Gc10
Sorso **I** 97 Ec43
Sørstraumen **N** 26 Gd04
Sort **E** 81 Da39
Sortavala **RUS** 41 Jb14
Sortland **N** 28 Gb06
Sør-Tverrfjord **N** 26 Gd04
Sørumsand **N** 43 Fc17
Sørvær **N** 26 Gd03
Sørvågen **N** 28 Fd07
Sörvattnet **S** 38 Fd14
Sørvika **N** 37 Fd14
Sösdala **S** 49 Fd23
Sos del Rey Católico **E** 80 Cc39
Sosedka **RUS** 119 Fc11
Sosnenskij **RUS** 117 Ed11
Sosnicy **RUS** 47 Jb17
Sosnove **UA** 120 Ea14
Sosnovka **RUS** 118 Fb11
Sosnovka **RUS** 119 Fd08
Sosnovo **RUS** 41 Jb16
Sosnovyj Bor **RUS** 47 Jb17
Sosnowica **PL** 59 Hc28
Sosnowiec **PL** 67 Ha30
Sospel **F** 83 Ec39
Šoštanj **SLO** 73 Ga35
Šostka **UA** 121 Ed13
Sotasæter **N** 36 Fa15
Sotillo de la Adrada **E** 91 Bc41
Sotkamo **FIN** 35 Hd11
Soto del Barco **E** 79 Bc36

Sotogrande **E** 105 Ba46
Sottunga **FIN** 46 Ha17
Soufflenheim **F** 63 Ed32
Soufli **GR** 103 Jd41
Souillac **F** 69 Db36
Souilly **F** 63 Eb31
Soulac-sur-Mer **F** 68 Cd35
Soúli **GR** 111 Ja46
Soulópoulo **GR** 101 Hc44
Sourpi **GR** 111 Ja45
Sousceyrac **F** 69 Db36
Sousel **P** 90 Ad41
Soustons **F** 80 Cc37
Southampton **GB** 24 Da28
Southend-on-Sea **GB** 25 Dc27
South Molton **GB** 23 Cc27
Southport **GB** 21 Da24
South Shields **GB** 21 Db23
Southwold **GB** 25 Dd27
Souvigny **F** 69 Dc34
Sovata **RO** 76 Jb35
Soverato **I** 109 Gc46
Sovetsk **RUS** 52 Hb24
Sovetskaja **RUS** 123 Fc14
Sovetskaja **RUS** 127 Fd17
Sovetskij **RUS** 41 Ja16
Sovetskij **RUS** 119 Fd08
Sovetskoe **RUS** 127 Ga17
Sowczyce **PL** 66 Gd29
Sowia Góra **PL** 57 Gb27
Sozopol **BG** 103 Ka40
Spa **B** 63 Eb30
Spalding **GB** 25 Db26
Spálené Poříčí **CZ** 65 Fd31
Sparbu **N** 32 Fc12
Sparreholm **S** 44 Gb19
Spárti **GR** 111 Ja47
Spas-Klepiki **RUS** 118 Fa10
Spasovo **BG** 89 Ka38
Spassk- Rjazanskij **RUS** 118 Fb11
Spean Bridge **GB** 16 Cd19
Spentrup **DK** 49 Fb22
Spétses **GR** 111 Ja47
Speyer **D** 63 Ed31
Spezzano Albanese **I** 99 Gc44
Spezzano della Sila **I** 109 Gc45
Spiddle **IRL** 18 Bd23
Spiez **CH** 71 Ec35
Spijkenisse **NL** 54 Ea28
Spilimbergo **I** 73 Fd36
Spiljani **MNE** 87 Hb40
Spilsby **GB** 25 Dc25
Spinazzola **I** 99 Gb43
Špindlerův Mlýn **CZ** 65 Gb30
Spirovo **RUS** 117 Ec09
Spišská Belá **SK** 67 Hb32
Spittal an der Drau **A** 73 Fd35
Spitz **A** 73 Gb33
Spjelkavik **N** 36 Fa14
Split **HR** 86 Gc39

Splügen **CH** 72 Fa35
Spodsbjerg **DK** 49 Fb24
Špogi **LV** 53 Ja22
Špola **UA** 121 Ec15
Spoleto **I** 84 Fc40
Spotorno **I** 83 Ed38
Spremberg **D** 65 Ga29
Şpring **RO** 76 Ja35
Springe **D** 56 Fa28
Sproge **S** 51 Gc21
Spuž **MNE** 86 Ha40
Squillace **I** 109 Gc45
Squinzano **I** 100 Gd43
Srb **HR** 85 Gb38
Srbac **BIH** 86 Gc37
Srbica **RKS** 87 Hc40
Srbobran **SRB** 74 Ha36
Srbovac **RKS** 87 Hc40
Srdiečko **SK** 67 Ha32
Srebărna **BG** 89 Jd37
Srebrenica **BIH** 86 Ha38
Srebrenik **BIH** 86 Gd38
Sredec **BG** 102 Jc40
Sredec **BG** 103 Jd40
Śrem **PL** 58 Gc28
Sremska Mitrovica **SRB** 86 Ha37
Sremski Karlovci **SRB** 87 Hb37
Sribne **UA** 121 Ed14
Środa Wielkopolska **PL** 58 Gc28
Srokowo **PL** 59 Hb25
Stachanov **UA** 122 Fb15
Stachy **CZ** 65 Fd32
Staðarskáli **IS** 14 Bd06
Stade **D** 56 Fa26
Stadskanaal **NL** 55 Ed26
Stadthagen **D** 56 Fa27
Stadtlohn **D** 55 Ec28
Staffanstorp **S** 49 Fd23
Stafford **GB** 24 Da25
Stahnsdorf **D** 57 Fd27
Staicele **LV** 47 Hd20
Stakkvik **N** 26 Gc04
Stakliškės **LT** 53 Hd24
Stalbe **LV** 47 Hd20
Ställdalen **S** 44 Ga17
Staloluokta **S** 28 Gb08
Stalon **S** 33 Gb11
Stalowa Wola **PL** 67 Hc30
Stambolijski **BG** 102 Jb40
Stamford **GB** 25 Db26
Stamford Bridge **GB** 21 Db24
Stamnes **N** 36 Ed16
Stamsund **N** 28 Ga07
Stânceni **RO** 76 Jb34
Stånga **S** 51 Gd21
Stange **N** 37 Fc16
Stanhope **GB** 21 Db23
Stanica Bagaevskaja **RUS** 123 Fc15
Stanišić **SRB** 74 Ha36
Staňkov **CZ** 65 Fd31
Stanovoe **RUS** 122 Fa12

Stans CH 71 Ed34
Stanyčno- Luhans'ke UA 123 Fc14
Staphorst NL 55 Ec27
Stąporków PL 67 Hb29
Stara PL 67 Ha29
Stara Caryčanka UA 77 Kb34
Starachowice PL 67 Hb29
Staraja Russa RUS 117 Eb09
Stara Kiszewa PL 58 Gd25
Stara Moravica SRB 74 Ha36
Stara Novalja HR 85 Ga38
Stara Pazova SRB 87 Hb37
Stara Rečka BG 88 Jc39
Stara Reka BG 88 Jc39
Stara Ušycja UA 76 Jc32
Stara Vyživka UA 59 Hd28
Stara Zagora BG 102 Jc40
Stare Dolistowo PL 59 Hc26
Stare Jeżewo PL 59 Hc26
Stare Kiełbonki PL 59 Hb26
Stare Strącze PL 57 Gb28
Stargard Szczeciński PL 57 Ga26
Stårheim N 36 Ed14
Starica RUS 117 Ec10
Starica RUS 121 Ed12
Starigrad HR 86 Gc40
Starnberg D 72 Fb33
Starobil's'k UA 122 Fb14
Starobin BY 120 Ea13
Starodub RUS 121 Ec13
Starogard PL 57 Gb26
Starogard Gdański PL 58 Gd25
Starojur'evo RUS 118 Fb11
Starokostjantyniv UA 121 Eb15
Starominskaja RUS 127 Fc16
Staro Nagoričane MK 101 Hd41
Staro Petrovo Selo HR 86 Gd37
Starosel BG 102 Jb40
Staro Selo BG 88 Jc38
Starotitarovskaja RUS 126 Fb17
Starožilovo RUS 118 Fa11
Stary Dzierzgoń PL 58 Gd25
Staryi Oskol RUS 122 Fa13
Staryja Darohi BY 121 Eb13
Staryj Sambir UA 67 Hd31
Staßfurt D 56 Fc28
Staszów PL 67 Hb30
Stathelle N 43 Fb18
Staume N 36 Ed15
Stavanger N 42 Ed18
Stave SRB 86 Ha38
Stavelot B 63 Eb30
Stavern N 43 Fb19
Stavky UA 67 Hd29

Stavre S 38 Ga14
Stavrodrómi GR 110 Hd46
Stavropol' RUS 127 Fd16
Stavrós GR 101 Ja42
Stavroskiádi GR 101 Hc44
Stavroúpoli GR 102 Jb42
Stawiski PL 59 Hb26
Stawiszyn PL 58 Gd28
Steenbergen NL 54 Ea28
Steenvoorde F 62 Dd29
Steenwijk NL 55 Ec27
Stefan Karadža BG 89 Jd38
Ştefan-Vodă MD 77 Kb34
Steffisburg CH 71 Ec35
Stege DK 49 Fc24
Stegna PL 58 Gd25
Ştei RO 75 Hd35
Steķi LV 53 Ja21
Stein D 64 Fb31
Steinach A 72 Fb34
Steinach D 64 Fb30
Stein am Rhein CH 71 Ed34
Steinau D 64 Fa30
Steine N 28 Ga06
Steinfeld D 55 Ed27
Steinfurt D 55 Ed27
Steinhagen D 57 Fd25
Steinheim D 56 Fa28
Steinkjer N 32 Fc12
Steinshamn N 36 Fa13
Steinsstaðabyggð IS 15 Ca06
Stekenjokk S 33 Ga11
Stenay F 63 Eb31
Stendal D 56 Fc27
Stende LV 52 Hb21
Štěnovice CZ 65 Fd31
Stensele S 33 Gb11
Stenstorp S 44 Fd20
Stenträsk S 34 Gd09
Stenudden S 33 Gc09
Stenungsund S 43 Fc20
Stepanci MK 101 Hc42
Štepivka UA 121 Ed14
Stepnica PL 57 Ga26
Stepnoe Matjunico RUS 119 Fd10
Stepojevac SRB 87 Hb38
Sterdyń-Osada PL 59 Hc27
Sternberg D 56 Fc29
Šternberk CZ 66 Gc31
Stérnes GR 114 Jc49
Sterzing I 72 Fb35
Stęszew PL 58 Gc28
Stevenage GB 25 Db27
Steyr A 73 Ga33
Stężyca PL 58 Gc25
Stigen S 43 Fc19
Stigliano I 99 Gb43
Stigtomta S 44 Gb19
Stilida BG 111 Ja45
Stilo I 109 Gc46
Štimlje RKS 87 Hc40
Stinăpari RO 87 Hc37
Štip MK 101 Hd41
Stíra GR 112 Jb46

Stirling GB 21 Da21
Štítary CZ 65 Gb32
Štítnik SK 67 Hb32
Stjørdal N 37 Fc13
Stockach D 71 Ed33
Stockaryd S 50 Ga21
Stockbridge GB 24 Da28
Stockerau A 73 Gb33
Stockholm S 45 Gc18
Stockport GB 24 Da25
Stockton-on-Tees GB 21 Db23
Stoczek Lukowski PL 59 Hc28
Stod CZ 65 Fd31
Stöde S 38 Gb14
Stødi N 33 Ga09
Stöðvarfjörður IS 15 Cc08
Stoholm DK 48 Fa22
Stoke-on-Trent GB 24 Da25
Stokkseyri IS 14 Bc07
Stokkvågen N 32 Fd09
Stokmarknes N 28 Ga06
Stolac BIH 86 Gd40
Stolin BY 120 Ea14
Stollberg D 65 Fd30
Stöllet S 44 Fd17
Stoloiceni MD 77 Jd34
Stómio GR 110 Ja44
Stone GB 24 Da25
Stonehaven GB 17 Db20
Stonglandet N 28 Gb05
Stopnica PL 67 Hb30
Storå S 44 Ga18
Stora Blåsjön S 33 Ga11
Storberg S 33 Gc10
Storby FIN 45 Gd17
Stordalen N 36 Fa14
Stordalen S 29 Gc06
Stordalselv N 26 Gc05
Storebro S 50 Gb21
Store Heddinge DK 49 Fd24
Storekorsnes N 26 Ha04
Storelv N 26 Ha03
Store Molvik N 27 Hc03
Støren N 37 Fc13
Storfors S 44 Ga18
Storforshei N 33 Ga09
Storjola S 33 Ga11
Storjord N 28 Gb08
Storjorda N 28 Ga08
Storkow D 57 Ga28
Storlien S 38 Fd13
Stornoway GB 16 Cd18
Storožynec' UA 76 Jb32
Storožynec' UA 124 Ea16
Storslett N 26 Gd04
Storstein N 26 Gd04
Storsteinnes N 26 Gc05
Storuman S 33 Gb11
Storvorde DK 49 Fb21
Storvreta S 45 Gc17
Stöten S 38 Fd16
Stovbcy BY 120 Ea13
Støvring DK 49 Fb21
Stowięcino PL 58 Gc25

Stowmarket GB 25 Dc27
Stow-on-the-Wold GB 24 Da27
Strabane GB 20 Cb22
Stradella I 83 Ed37
Straelen D 55 Ec28
Strakonice CZ 65 Fd32
Straldža BG 103 Jd40
Stralki BY 53 Jb22
Stralsund D 57 Fd25
Strambino I 71 Ec36
Strâmtura RO 76 Ja33
Stranda N 36 Fa14
Strandby DK 49 Fb21
Strandebarm N 42 Ed17
Strangford GB 20 Cc23
Strängnäs S 45 Gc18
Strångsjö S 44 Gb19
Stranraer GB 20 Cd22
Strasbourg F 63 Ec32
Strasburg D 57 Fd26
Strǎşeni MD 77 Ka33
Straßwalchen A 73 Fd33
Stratford-upon-Avon GB 24 Da26
Stratínista GR 101 Hc44
Stratinska BIH 86 Gc38
Stratóni GR 102 Jb43
Strátos GR 110 Hc45
Stratton GB 23 Cc27
Straubing D 64 Fc32
Straumen N 26 Gc05
Straumen N 28 Ga08
Straumen N 28 Ga08
Straumen N 28 Gb08
Straumen N 32 Fc12
Straumsnes N 28 Ga06
Strausberg D 57 Ga27
Stražica BG 88 Jc39
Strážný CZ 65 Fd32
Štrba SK 67 Ha32
Štrbské Pleso SK 67 Ha32
Strečno SK 66 Gd32
Strehaia RO 87 Hd37
Strekov SK 74 Gd33
Strelča BG 102 Jb40
Strelkino RUS 47 Jb20
Strenči LV 47 Hd20
Stresa I 71 Ed36
Strezimirovci SRB 87 Hd40
Strezovce RKS 87 Hc40
Stříbro CZ 65 Fd31
Strilky UA 67 Hd31
Strimasund S 33 Ga09
Strimonikó GR 101 Ja42
Strmica HR 85 Gb38
Strofiliá GR 111 Ja45
Stromeferry GB 16 Cd19
Stromiec PL 59 Hb28
Stromness GB 17 Db17
Strömsbruk S 39 Gc15
Strömsnäsbruk S 49 Fd22
Strömstad S 43 Fc19
Strömsund S 33 Gb12
Strongoli I 109 Gc45
Strontian GB 16 Cd20
Stropkov SK 67 Hc31

Strošinci SRB 86 Ha37
Stroud GB 24 Da27
Stroumpi CY 128 Ga19
Struer DK 48 Fa22
Struga MK 101 Hc42
Strugi-Krasnye RUS 47 Jb19
Strumica MK 101 Hd42
Stryj UA 67 Hd31
Stryksele S 34 Gd11
Stryn N 36 Fa14
Strzegom PL 65 Gb29
Strzegowo-Osada PL 58 Ha27
Strzelce Krajeńskie PL 57 Gb27
Strzelce Opolskie PL 66 Gd30
Strzelin PL 66 Gc30
Strzelno PL 58 Gd27
Stubbekøbing DK 49 Fc24
Stubičke Toplice HR 73 Gb36
Stubline SRB 87 Hb38
Studenci HR 86 Gc39
Studénka CZ 66 Gd31
Studina RO 88 Jb38
Studzieniczna PL 59 Hc25
Stuguflåten N 36 Fa14
Stugun S 38 Gb13
Stuhr D 56 Fa26
Stupava SK 74 Gc33
Stupino RUS 118 Fa11
Stupnik HR 73 Gb36
Šturlić BIH 85 Gb37
Štúrovo SK 74 Gd33
Stuttgart D 64 Fa32
Stykkishólmur IS 14 Bc05
Subate LV 53 Ja22
Subiaco I 98 Fd41
Subotica SRB 74 Ha36
Suceava RO 76 Jc33
Suceviţa RO 76 Jb33
Sucha Beskidzka PL 67 Ha31
Suchań PL 57 Gb26
Suchorze PL 58 Gc25
Suchowola PL 59 Hc26
Suciu de Sus RO 76 Ja34
Sucuiu RO 88 Jc36
Sućuraj HR 86 Gc40
Sudak UA 126 Fa17
Súðavik IS 14 Bc04
Sudbury GB 25 Dc27
Suddesjaur S 33 Gc09
Süderbrarup D 49 Fb24
Sudislavl' RUS 118 Fa08
Sudogda RUS 118 Fa10
Sudova Vyšnja UA 67 Hd31
Suduragi TR 128 Gb16
Suðureyri IS 14 Bc04
Sudža RUS 121 Ed13
Sueca E 93 Cc43
Şugag RO 88 Ja36
Sugözü TR 128 Gb17
Suhindol BG 88 Jb39
Suhiniči RUS 117 Ed11

Suhl D 64 Fb30
Suhlendorf D 56 Fb27
Suhodol RUS 119 Ga09
Suho Polje BIH 86 Ha38
Suhopolje HR 74 Gc36
Suhostrel BG 101 Ja41
Šuica BIH 86 Gc39
Suippes F 62 Ea31
Suistamo RUS 41 Jb14
Šuja RUS 118 Fa09
Sukeva FIN 35 Hd12
Sükösd H 74 Ha35
Šula (Šunlja Stijena) MNE 86 Ha39
Sulechów PL 57 Gb28
Sulęcin PL 57 Ga27
Sulęczyno PL 58 Gc25
Sulejówek PL 59 Hb27
Süleoğlu TR 103 Jd41
Sulina RO 89 Kb36
Sulingen D 56 Fa27
Suliszewo PL 57 Gb26
Sulitjelma N 28 Gb08
Sulkava FIN 41 Ja14
Sully-sur-Loire F 69 Dc33
Sulmierzyce PL 58 Gc28
Sulmona I 98 Fd41
Sulzbach-Rosenberg D 64 Fc31
Sümeg H 74 Gc35
Šumen BG 89 Jd39
Šumerlja RUS 119 Fc09
Šumperk CZ 66 Gc31
Šumskas LT 53 Ja24
Sumy UA 121 Ed14
Sundborn S 38 Gb16
Sundby DK 48 Fa21
Sunde N 42 Ed17
Sunderland GB 21 Db23
Sundern D 63 Ed29
Sundnäs S 33 Gc09
Sundsbruk S 39 Gc14
Sundsvall S 39 Gc14
Sungurlare BG 89 Jd39
Sunja HR 86 Gc37
Sunndal N 42 Ed17
Sunndalsøra N 37 Fb14
Sunne S 44 Fd18
Sunnemo S 44 Ga17
Suntaži LV 53 Hd21
Suolahti FIN 40 Hc13
Suomenniemi FIN 41 Ja15
Suomusjärvi FIN 40 Hc16
Suomussalmi FIN 35 Hd10
Suonenjoki FIN 41 Hd13
Supetar HR 86 Gc39
Suplac RO 76 Ja35
Supraśl PL 59 Hc26
Surahammar S 44 Gb18
Šurany SK 74 Gd33
Suraž RUS 121 Ec12
Surdulica SRB 87 Hd40
Surgères F 68 Cd34
Súria E 81 Da40
Šurlane RKS 101 Hc41
Surma RUS 119 Fd08

Surovikino RUS 123 Fd14
Sursee CH 71 Ed34
Surskoe RUS 119 Fd10
Surviliškis LT 52 Hc23
Susa I 83 Ec37
Susēja LV 53 Hd22
Susek SRB 86 Ha37
Sušice CZ 65 Fd32
Suslonger RUS 119 Fd08
Susurluk TR 103 Kb43
Susz PL 58 Gd26
Suure-Jaani EST 47 Hd19
Suva Reka RKS 101 Hc41
Suvorov RUS 117 Ed11
Suvorove UA 77 Ka35
Suvorovo BG 89 Ka38
Suvorovskaja RUS 127 Ga17
Suwałki PL 59 Hc25
Suzdal' RUS 118 Fa09
Suzzara I 84 Fb37
Svabensverk S 38 Gb16
Svaljava UA 67 Hd32
Svanabyn S 33 Gb12
Svanberga S 45 Gd17
Svaneke DK 50 Ga24
Svängsta S 50 Ga22
Svanskog S 43 Fd18
Svanstein S 30 Hb08
Svanvik N 27 Hd04
Svappavaara S 29 Gd07
Svardsjö S 38 Gb16
Svarstad N 43 Fb18
Svartå S 44 Ga18
Svartbyn S 34 Ha09
Svartlå S 34 Gd09
Svartnäs S 38 Gb16
Svatá Kateřina CZ 65 Fd32
Svatove UA 122 Fb14
Svatsum N 37 Fb15
Svedala S 49 Fd23
Svėdasai LT 53 Hd23
Sveg S 38 Ga15
Sveio N 42 Ec17
Švėkšna LT 52 Hb23
Svelgen N 36 Ed15
Svelvik N 43 Fc18
Švenčionėliai LT 53 Ja23
Švenčionys LT 53 Ja23
Svendborg DK 49 Fb24
Svenes N 42 Fa19
Svenljunga S 49 Fd21
Svensby N 26 Gc05
Svenstavik S 38 Ga14
Sverdlove UA 126 Ed17
Sverdlovs'k UA 123 Fc15
Sveti Ivan Žabno HR 74 Gc36
Sveti Ivan Zelina HR 73 Gb36
Sveti Kostantin i Elena BG 89 Ka38
Sveti Nikola BG 89 Ka38
Sveti Nikole MK 101 Hd41
Sveti Stefan MNE 100 Ha41

Svetlahorsk BY 121 Eb13
Svetlice SK 67 Hc31
Svetlogorsk RUS 52 Ha24
Svetlograd RUS 127 Ga16
Svetlyi Jar RUS 123 Ga14
Svetlyj RUS 52 Ha24
Svetogorsk RUS 41 Ja15
Sviby EST 46 Hb18
Svidník SK 67 Hc31
Svilajnac SRB 87 Hc38
Svilengrad BG 103 Jd41
Svinndal N 43 Fc18
Svir BY 53 Ja24
Svislač BY 59 Hd26
Svislač BY 121 Eb12
Svitavy CZ 65 Gb31
Svitlovods'k UA 121 Ed15
Svobody RUS 127 Ga17
Svodna BIH 86 Gc37
Svoge BG 88 Ja39
Svoge BG 88 Ja39
Svolvær N 28 Ga06
Svorkmo N 37 Fb13
Svrljig SRB 87 Hd39
Svullrya N 43 Fd17
Swaffham GB 25 Dc26
Swanage GB 24 Cd28
Swansea GB 23 Cc26
Swarożyn PL 58 Gd25
Swarzędz PL 58 Gc27
Świdnica PL 65 Gb30
Świdnik PL 67 Hc29
Świdwin PL 57 Gb26
Świebodzice PL 65 Gb30
Świebodzin PL 57 Gb28
Świecie PL 58 Gd26
Świekatowo PL 58 Gd26
Świeradów-Zdrój PL 65 Gb29
Świerczów PL 66 Gc29
Świerzawa PL 65 Gb29
Święta Anna PL 67 Ha29
Świętajno PL 59 Hc25
Świętno PL 57 Gb28
Swindon GB 24 Da27
Swinford IRL 18 Ca22
Świnoujście PL 57 Ga25
Syčevka RUS 117 Ec10
Syców PL 66 Gc29
Sycowice PL 57 Gb28
Syke D 56 Fa27
Sykkylven N 36 Fa14
Synel'nykove UA 122 Fa15
Syötekylä FIN 35 Hd09
Şyrjajeve UA 125 Ec16
Šyroke UA 125 Ed16
Šyščycy BY 120 Ea13
Sysmä FIN 40 Hc15
Sysslebäck S 38 Fd16
Syston GB 25 Db26
Syväjärvi FIN 31 Hc07
Syzran' RUS 119 Ga10
Szabadszállás H 74 Ha35
Szadek PL 58 Gd28
Szamotuły PL 57 Gb27
Szarvas H 75 Hb35

Százhalombatta – Tenja

Százhalombatta **H** 74 Ha34
Szczawne **PL** 67 Hc31
Szczawnica **PL** 67 Hb31
Szczebrzeszyn **PL** 67 Hc29
Szczecin **PL** 57 Ga26
Szczecinek **PL** 58 Gc26
Szczekociny **PL** 67 Ha30
Szczerców **PL** 66 Gd29
Szczuczyn **PL** 59 Hc26
Szczurowa **PL** 67 Hb30
Szczytno **PL** 59 Hb26
Szécsény **H** 74 Ha33
Szederkény **H** 74 Gd36
Szeged **H** 75 Hb35
Székely **H** 75 Hc33
Székesfehérvár **H** 74 Gd34
Székkutas **H** 75 Hb35
Szekszárd **H** 74 Gd35
Szendrő **H** 75 Hb33
Szentendre **H** 74 Ha34
Szentes **H** 75 Hb35
Szentlőrinc **H** 74 Gd36
Szepietowo **PL** 59 Hc27
Szerencs **H** 75 Hb33
Szigetvár **H** 74 Gd36
Szilvásvárad **H** 75 Hb33
Szin **H** 67 Hb32
Szklarska Poręba **PL** 65 Gb30
Szolnok **H** 75 Hb34
Szombathely **H** 74 Gc34
Szprotawa **PL** 65 Gb29
Sztabin **PL** 59 Hc25
Sztum **PL** 58 Gd25
Szubin **PL** 58 Gc27
Szydłów **PL** 67 Hb30
Szydłowiec **PL** 67 Hb29
Szypliszki **PL** 59 Hc25

T

Taalintehdas **FIN** 46 Hb17
Tábara **E** 78 Bb38
Taberg **S** 44 Ga20
Tabernas **E** 106 Bd45
Tablate **E** 106 Bc45
Tábor **CZ** 65 Ga31
Tabuenca **E** 80 Cb40
Täby **S** 45 Gc18
Tachov **CZ** 64 Fc31
Tacinskij **RUS** 123 Fc14
Tafalla **E** 80 Cb39
Täfteå **S** 34 Gd12
Ţaga **RO** 76 Ja34
Tagaj **RUS** 119 Fd10
Taganrog **RUS** 123 Fc15
Taggia **I** 83 Ec39
Tagliacozzo **I** 98 Fd41
Tahkuna **EST** 46 Hb18
Tahta **RUS** 127 Fd16
Taicy **RUS** 47 Jb17
Tain **GB** 17 Da18
Tain-l'Hermitage **F** 82 Ea37
Tairove **UA** 77 Kb34
Taivalkoski **FIN** 35 Hd09
Taivassalo **FIN** 40 Ha16

Talačyn **BY** 121 Eb12
Talarrubias **E** 91 Bb42
Talavera de la Reina **E** 91 Bc41
Taldom **RUS** 117 Ed10
Talgarth **GB** 24 Cd26
Tallard **F** 83 Eb38
Tallåsen **S** 38 Gb15
Tällberg **S** 38 Ga16
Tallinn **EST** 46 Hc18
Talloires **F** 71 Eb36
Tallsjö **S** 33 Gc12
Talluskylä **FIN** 41 Hd13
Tălmaciu **RO** 88 Ja36
Talmont-Saint-Hilaire **F** 68 Cd34
Tal'ne **UA** 121 Ec15
Talovaja **RUS** 122 Fb13
Talsi **LV** 52 Hb21
Tamala **RUS** 119 Fc11
Tamames **E** 91 Bb40
Tamanhos **P** 78 Ba39
Tamarinda **E** 95 Dc43
Tamarite de Litera **E** 80 Cd40
Tamási **H** 74 Gd35
Tambov **RUS** 122 Fb12
Tammisaari **FIN** 46 Hb17
Tampere **FIN** 40 Hb15
Tamsalu **EST** 47 Hd18
Tamsweg **A** 73 Fd34
Tamworth **GB** 24 Da26
Tana bru **N** 27 Hc03
Ţăndărei **RO** 89 Jd37
Tandsbyn **S** 38 Ga15
Tandsjöborg **S** 38 Ga15
Tångaberg **S** 49 Fc21
Tangen **N** 37 Fc16
Tangerhütte **D** 56 Fc27
Tangermünde **D** 56 Fc27
Tanhua **FIN** 31 Hc07
Tankavaara **FIN** 31 Hc06
Tännäs **S** 38 Fd14
Tannay **F** 70 Dd33
Tänndalen **S** 38 Fd14
Tannila **FIN** 35 Hc10
Tanum **N** 43 Fc17
Tanumshede **S** 43 Fc19
Taormina **I** 109 Gb47
Tapa **EST** 47 Hd18
Tapia de Casariego **E** 78 Bb36
Tápiószele **H** 74 Ha34
Tapizё **RKS** 100 Hb42
Tapolca **H** 74 Gc35
Taraclia **MD** 77 Ka34
Taraclia **MD** 77 Ka35
Tarancón **E** 92 Bd42
Taranto **I** 99 Gc43
Tarare **F** 70 Dd35
Tarašča **UA** 121 Ec15
Tarascon **F** 82 Dd38
Tarascon-sur-Ariège **F** 81 Da39
Tarazona **E** 80 Cb39
Tarazona de la Mancha **E** 92 Ca43

Tarbert **GB** 16 Cd20
Tarbert **GB** 16 Cd18
Tarbert **GB** 20 Cd21
Tarbert **IRL** 18 Bd24
Tarbes **F** 80 Cd38
Tarcento **I** 73 Fd36
Tarczyn **PL** 59 Hb28
Tärendö **S** 30 Ha08
Târgovişte **RO** 88 Jb37
Targovište **BG** 89 Jd39
Târgu Bujor **RO** 77 Jd35
Târgu Cărbunești **RO** 88 Ja37
Târgu Frumos **RO** 76 Jc33
Târgu Gânguleşti **RO** 88 Ja37
Târgu Jiu **RO** 87 Hd37
Târgu Lăpuş **RO** 76 Ja34
Târgu Mureş **RO** 76 Ja35
Târgu-Neamţ **RO** 76 Jc34
Târgu Ocna **RO** 76 Jc35
Târgu Secuiesc **RO** 76 Jc35
Târguşor **RO** 89 Ka37
Tarifa **E** 105 Ba46
Târlişua **RO** 76 Ja34
Tarm **DK** 48 Fa23
Tärnaby **S** 33 Ga10
Tarna-lelesz **H** 75 Hb33
Tarna Mare **RO** 75 Hd33
Tärnamo **S** 33 Ga10
Târnăveni **RO** 76 Ja35
Tarnobrzeg **PL** 67 Hb30
Tarnogród **PL** 67 Hc30
Tarnov **SK** 67 Hb31
Târnova **RO** 75 Hc35
Tarnów **PL** 67 Hb30
Tarnowskie Góry **PL** 66 Gd30
Tärnsjö **S** 44 Gb17
Tårnvika **N** 28 Ga07
Tarporley **GB** 24 Da25
Tarquinia **I** 98 Fb41
Tarragona **E** 95 Da41
Tàrrega **E** 81 Da40
Tårs **DK** 49 Fc24
Tartas **F** 80 Cc37
Tărtăşeşti **RO** 88 Jc37
Tartaul de Salcie **MD** 77 Ka35
Tartu **EST** 47 Ja19
Tarusa **RUS** 117 Ed11
Tarutyne **UA** 77 Ka34
Tarvin **GB** 24 Da25
Tarvisio **I** 73 Fd35
Tåsjö **S** 33 Gb12
Taşkent **TR** 128 Ga16
Taşlâc **MD** 77 Ka33
Tăşnad **RO** 75 Hd34
Taşucu **TR** 128 Gc17
Tata **H** 74 Gd34
Tatabánya **H** 74 Gd34
Tătădrăştii de Jos **RO** 88 Jb37
Tataháza **H** 74 Ha36
Tatanovo **RUS** 118 Fb11
Tătăranu **RO** 89 Jd36

Tatarbunary **UA** 77 Kb35
Tatarbunary **UA** 125 Ec17
Tatarlı **TR** 128 Gc15
Tatiščevo **RUS** 123 Fd12
Tatlıkuyu **TR** 128 Gc15
Tau **N** 42 Ed18
Tauberbischofsheim **D** 64 Fa31
Taucha **D** 64 Fc29
Taufkirchen **D** 72 Fc33
Taulov **DK** 49 Fb23
Taunton **GB** 24 Cd27
Tauragė **LT** 52 Hb23
Taurianova **I** 109 Gb46
Taurisano **I** 100 Gd44
Tauste **E** 80 Cc40
Tavakli İsk. **TR** 103 Jd43
Tavelsjö **S** 34 Gd12
Tavernes de la Valldigna **E** 93 Cc43
Tavíkovice **CZ** 65 Gb32
Tavira **P** 104 Ac44
Tavistock **GB** 23 Cc28
Tayfur **TR** 103 Jd42
Tayinloan **GB** 20 Cc21
Tazlău **RO** 76 Jc34
Tczew **PL** 58 Gd25
Tczów **PL** 67 Hb29
Teaca **RO** 76 Ja34
Teano **I** 98 Fd42
Teba **E** 105 Bb45
Tebay **GB** 21 Da23
Teberda **RUS** 127 Ga17
Techirghiol **RO** 89 Ka37
Tecuci **RO** 77 Jd35
Tegelträsk **S** 33 Gc12
Tegernsee **D** 72 Fc34
Teignmouth **GB** 23 Cc28
Teiuş **RO** 76 Ja35
Tejkovo **RUS** 118 Fa09
Tekirdağ **TR** 103 Ka41
Telč **CZ** 65 Gb32
Telciu **RO** 76 Ja34
Teleneşti **MD** 77 Jd33
Telese **I** 99 Ga42
Telford **GB** 24 Da25
Telfs **A** 72 Fb34
Telgte **D** 55 Ed28
Tellejåkk **S** 34 Gd09
Tel'manove **UA** 122 Fb15
Telšiai **LT** 52 Hb22
Teltow **D** 57 Fd27
Tembleque **E** 92 Bd42
Temerin **SRB** 87 Hb37
Temmes **FIN** 35 Hc11
Tempio Pausania **I** 96 Ed42
Templemore **IRL** 18 Ca24
Templin **D** 57 Fd26
Temrjuk **RUS** 126 Fb17
Tenala **FIN** 46 Hb17
Tenby **GB** 23 Cc26
Tendilla **E** 92 Ca41
Tenec **RUS** 47 Jb20
Tenhola **FIN** 46 Hb17
Tenhult **S** 44 Ga20
Tenja **HR** 86 Ha37

Tenterden **GB** 25 Dc28
Teofipol' **UA** 120 Ea15
Teovo **MK** 101 Hc41
Tepasto **FIN** 30 Hb06
Tepelenë **AL** 100 Hb43
Teplice **CZ** 65 Fd30
Teploe **RUS** 118 Fa11
Tepsa **FIN** 30 Hb07
Terälahti **FIN** 40 Hb15
Teramo **I** 85 Fd40
Ter Apel **NL** 55 Ed26
Teratyn **PL** 67 Hd29
Terbuny **RUS** 122 Fa12
Terebovlja **UA** 120 Ea15
Teremia Mare **RO** 75 Hb36
Teren'ga **RUS** 119 Fd10
Tergnier **F** 62 Dd30
Terlizzi **I** 99 Gc42
Termachivka **UA** 121 Eb14
Terme **TR** 127 Fc19
Terme di Lurisia **I** 83 Ec38
Termini Imerese **I** 108 Fd46
Termoli **I** 99 Ga41
Terneuzen **NL** 54 Ea28
Terni **I** 84 Fc40
Ternitz **A** 73 Gb34
Ternopil' **UA** 120 Ea15
Terpnás **GR** 101 Hc44
Terracina **I** 98 Fd42
Terråk **N** 32 Fd11
Terralba **I** 97 Ec44
Terrassa **E** 95 Da41
Teruel **E** 93 Cb42
Tervakoski **FIN** 40 Hc16
Tervel **BG** 89 Jd38
Tervo **FIN** 41 Hd13
Tervola **FIN** 34 Hb09
Tešanj **BIH** 86 Gd38
Tešel **BG** 102 Jb41
Tešica **SRB** 87 Hc39
Teslić **BIH** 86 Gd38
Tét **H** 74 Gc34
Tetbury **GB** 24 Da27
Teterow **D** 57 Fd26
Teteven **BG** 88 Jb39
Tetijiv **UA** 121 Ec15
Tetovo **BG** 88 Jc38
Tetovo **MK** 101 Hc41
Teulada **I** 97 Ec45
Teulada-Moraira **E** 94 Cc44
Teuva **FIN** 40 Ha14
Tewkesbury **GB** 24 Da26
Thann **F** 71 Ec33
Thaon-les-Vosges **F** 71 Eb33
Thássos **GR** 102 Jb42
The Mumbles **GB** 23 Cc27
Theológos **GR** 111 Ja45
Thermo **GR** 110 Hd45
Thesprotikó **GR** 110 Hc45
Thessaloníki **GR** 101 Ja43
Thetford **GB** 25 Dc26
Thiene **I** 72 Fb36
Thiers **F** 70 Dd35
Thiesi **I** 97 Ec43
Thionville **F** 63 Eb31

Thíra **GR** 115 Jd48
Thirsk **GB** 21 Db24
Thisted **DK** 48 Fa21
Thíva **GR** 111 Ja45
Thiviers **F** 69 Da35
Thizy **F** 70 Dd35
Tholária **GR** 115 Jd47
Thonon-les-Bains **F** 71 Eb35
Thorne **GB** 21 Db24
Thornhill **GB** 21 Da22
Thorsminde **DK** 48 Fa22
Thouars **F** 69 Da33
Thrapston **GB** 25 Db26
Thueyts **F** 82 Dd37
Thuir **F** 81 Db39
Thun **CH** 71 Ec35
Thurles **IRL** 18 Ca24
Thursby **GB** 21 Da23
Thurso **GB** 17 Db18
Thury-Harcourt **F** 61 Da31
Thusis **CH** 72 Fa35
Thyborøn **DK** 48 Fa22
Ţibana **RO** 77 Jd34
Tibro **S** 44 Ga19
Tiča **BG** 89 Jd39
Tidaholm **S** 44 Ga20
Tidan **S** 44 Ga19
Tiel **NL** 55 Eb28
Tielt **B** 62 Ea29
Tienen **B** 63 Eb29
Tierp **S** 45 Gc17
Tigharry **GB** 16 Cc18
Tighina **MD** 77 Ka34
Tihoreck **RUS** 127 Fc16
Tihvin **RUS** 117 Eb08
Tikkakoski **FIN** 40 Hc14
Tilaj **H** 74 Gc35
Tilburg **NL** 55 Eb28
Tilbury **GB** 25 Db28
Til-Châtel **F** 70 Ea33
Tileagd **RO** 75 Hc34
Tillberga **S** 44 Gb18
Tilža **LV** 53 Ja21
Tim **RUS** 122 Fa13
Timaševsk **RUS** 127 Fc16
Timfristós **GR** 110 Hd45
Timişoara **RO** 75 Hc36
Timmele **S** 44 Fd20
Timohino **RUS** 117 Ec08
Timošino **RUS** 118 Fb08
Timrå **S** 39 Gc14
Tineo **E** 79 Bc36
Tinglev **DK** 48 Fa24
Tingsryd **S** 50 Ga22
Tingstäde **S** 45 Gd20
Tingvoll **N** 37 Fb13
Tinlot **B** 63 Eb30
Tínos **GR** 112 Jc46
Tinqueux **F** 62 Ea31
Tinténiac **F** 61 Cd31
Tinūži **LV** 53 Hd21
Tione di Trento **I** 72 Fb36
Tipasoja **FIN** 35 Ja11
Tipperary **IRL** 18 Ca24
Tiranë **RKS** 100 Hb42
Tirano **I** 72 Fa36

Tiraspol **MD** 77 Ka34
Tire **TR** 113 Kb45
Tirebolu **TR** 127 Fd19
Tirkšliai **LT** 52 Hb22
Tírnavos **GR** 101 Hd44
Tirrenia **I** 84 Fa39
Tirschenreuth **D** 64 Fc31
Tišća **BIH** 86 Ha38
Tišnov **CZ** 65 Gb31
Tisovec **SK** 67 Ha32
Tisvildeleje **DK** 49 Fc23
Tiszabecs **H** 75 Hd33
Tiszacsege **H** 75 Hb33
Tiszacsermely **H** 75 Hc33
Tiszadada **H** 75 Hb33
Tiszaföldvár **H** 75 Hb35
Tiszafüred **H** 75 Hb34
Tiszakécske **H** 75 Hb35
Tiszalúc **H** 75 Hb33
Tiszaújváros **H** 75 Hb33
Tiszavasvári **H** 75 Hb33
Titisee-Neustadt **D** 71 Ed33
Titran **N** 32 Fb12
Titu **RO** 88 Jb37
Tivat **MNE** 100 Ha41
Tiverton **GB** 23 Cc28
Tivoli **I** 98 Fc41
Tizzano **F** 96 Ed42
Tjaciv **UA** 75 Hd33
Tjæreborg **DK** 48 Fa23
Tjällmo **S** 44 Gb19
Tjåmotis **S** 29 Gc08
Tjautjas **S** 29 Gd07
Tjeldnes **N** 28 Gb06
Tjentište **BIH** 86 Ha39
Tjøtta **N** 32 Fd10
Tłuchowo **PL** 58 Ha27
Tłuszcz **PL** 59 Hb27
Tobarra **E** 107 Ca44
Tobercurry **IRL** 18 Ca22
Tobermory **GB** 16 Cd20
Toblach **I** 72 Fc35
Töcksfors **S** 43 Fc18
Todi **I** 84 Fc40
Todireşti **RO** 76 Jb33
Todorići **BIH** 86 Gc38
Todtnau **D** 71 Ed33
Tofta **S** 49 Fd21
Tofta **S** 51 Gc21
Tofte **N** 43 Fc18
Töftedal **S** 43 Fc19
Toftlund **DK** 48 Fa24
Tohmajärvi **FIN** 41 Jb13
Tohmo **FIN** 31 Hc08
Toholampi **FIN** 34 Hb12
Toijala **FIN** 40 Hb15
Toivakka **FIN** 41 Hd14
Toivala **FIN** 41 Hd13
Tokaj **H** 75 Hc33
Tokarevka **RUS** 122 Fb12
Tokmak **UA** 126 Fa16
Toledo **E** 91 Bc41
Tolentino **I** 85 Fd40
Tolfa **I** 98 Fc41
Tolga **N** 37 Fc14
Tol'jatti **RUS** 119 Ga10

Tollarp **S** 50 Ga23
Tolmezzo **I** 73 Fd35
Tolmin **SLO** 73 Fd36
Tolosa **E** 80 Cb38
Tolva **FIN** 31 Hd08
Tomakivka **UA** 126 Fa16
Tomar **P** 90 Ac40
Tomarovka **RUS** 122 Fa14
Tomaševac **SRB** 87 Hb37
Tomašpil' **UA** 77 Jd32
Tomašpil' **UA** 125 Eb16
Tomaszów Lubelski **PL** 67 Hd30
Tomaszów Mazowiecki **PL** 58 Ha28
Tomelilla **S** 50 Ga23
Tomelloso **E** 92 Bd43
Tomeşti **RO** 75 Hd36
Tomeşti **RO** 77 Jd33
Tomintoul **GB** 17 Db19
Tomislavgrad **BIH** 86 Gc39
Tømmerneset **N** 28 Gb07
Tømmervåg **N** 36 Fa13
Tompa **H** 74 Ha36
Tomrefjord **N** 36 Fa14
Tonara **I** 97 Ed44
Tonbridge **GB** 25 Db28
Tondela **P** 78 Ad39
Tønder **DK** 48 Fa24
Tongeren **B** 63 Eb29
Tongue **GB** 17 Da18
Tonkino **RUS** 119 Fc08
Tonnay-Boutonne **F** 68 Cd34
Tonnay-Charente **F** 68 Cd34
Tonneins **F** 81 Da37
Tonnerre **F** 70 Dd33
Tönning **D** 56 Fa25
Tonšaevo **RUS** 119 Fc08
Tønsberg **N** 43 Fb18
Tonstad **N** 42 Ed19
Tonya **TR** 127 Fd19
Topczewo **PL** 59 Hc27
Toplet **RO** 87 Hd37
Topli Do **SRB** 87 Hd39
Topliţa **RO** 76 Jb34
Topola **SRB** 87 Hb38
Topolčani **MK** 101 Hc42
Topol'čany **SK** 66 Gd32
Topolog **RO** 89 Ka36
Topoloveni **RO** 88 Jb37
Topolovgrad **BG** 103 Jd40
Topolovo **BG** 102 Jc41
Toponica **SRB** 87 Hb38
Toporu **RO** 88 Jc38
Topusko **HR** 85 Gb37
Torà **E** 81 Da40
Torbalı **TR** 113 Ka45
Tordesillas **E** 79 Bc39
Töre **S** 34 Ha09
Töreboda **S** 44 Ga19
Torekov **S** 49 Fd22
Torelló **E** 81 Db40
Toreno **E** 78 Bb37
Torfjanovka **RUS** 41 Ja16
Torgåsmon **S** 38 Fd16

Torgau **D** 65 Fd29
Torgelow **D** 57 Ga26
Torhout **B** 54 Dd28
Torigni-sur-Vire **F** 61 Da30
Torija **E** 92 Ca41
Toril **E** 93 Cb42
Torino **I** 83 Ec37
Tormac **RO** 75 Hc36
Törmänen **FIN** 27 Hc05
Tornal'a **SK** 75 Hb33
Torneträsk **S** 29 Gd06
Tornio **FIN** 34 Hb09
Tornjoš **SRB** 74 Ha36
Toro **E** 79 Bc39
Törökbalint **H** 74 Ha34
Törökszentmiklós **H** 75 Hb34
Torony **H** 74 Gc34
Toropec **RUS** 117 Eb10
Torošino **RUS** 47 Jb19
Torpo **N** 37 Fb16
Torpshammar **S** 38 Gb14
Torquay **GB** 23 Cc28
Torrão **P** 90 Ac42
Torre Annunziata **I** 99 Ga43
Torrebeleña **E** 92 Ca40
Torreblanca **E** 93 Cc42
Torrecampo **E** 105 Bb43
Torrecilla en Cameros **E** 79 Ca39
Torre de la Higuera **E** 105 Ad44
Torre del Greco **I** 99 Ga43
Torre de Moncorvo **P** 78 Ba39
Torre de'Passeri **I** 98 Fd41
Torredonjimeno **E** 106 Bc44
Torrejón de Ardoz **E** 92 Bd41
Torrelaguna **E** 92 Bd40
Torrelavega **E** 79 Ca37
Torremaggiore **I** 99 Gb42
Torremolinos **E** 105 Bb45
Torremormojón **E** 79 Bc39
Torrent **E** 93 Cc43
Torre-Pacheco **E** 107 Cb45
Torre Pellice **I** 83 Ec37
Torrequemada **E** 91 Ba41
Torres Novas **P** 90 Ac41
Torres Vedras **P** 90 Ab41
Torrevieja **E** 107 Cb45
Torri del Benaco **I** 72 Fb36
Torriglia **I** 83 Ed38
Torrijas **E** 93 Cb42
Torrijos **E** 91 Bc41
Tørring **DK** 49 Fb23
Tørring **N** 32 Fc12
Torrington **GB** 23 Cc27
Torroella de Montgrí **E** 81 Dc40
Torsåker **S** 44 Gb17
Torsås **S** 50 Gb22
Torsborg **S** 38 Fd14
Torsby **S** 44 Fd17
Torshälla **S** 44 Gb18
Tórtoles de Esgueva **E** 79 Bd39

Tortolì **I** 97 Ed44
Tortona **I** 83 Ed37
Tortorici **I** 109 Ga46
Tortosa **E** 93 Cd41
Torul **TR** 127 Fd19
Toruń **PL** 58 Gd27
Torup **S** 49 Fd21
Tõrva **EST** 47 Hd19
Toržok **RUS** 117 Ec10
Torzym **PL** 57 Ga28
Tosbotn **N** 32 Fd10
Toslak **TR** 128 Ga17
Tosno **RUS** 117 Eb08
Tõstamaa **EST** 46 Hc19
Tostedt **D** 56 Fb26
Totana **E** 107 Ca45
Totebo **S** 44 Gb20
Tôtes **F** 61 Db30
Tótkomlós **H** 75 Hb35
Tøtlandsvik **N** 42 Ed18
Totnes **GB** 23 Cc28
Toucy **F** 70 Dd33
Toul **F** 63 Eb32
Toulon **F** 82 Ea39
Toulon-sur-Arroux **F** 70 Dd34
Toulouse **F** 81 Da38
Tourcoing **F** 62 Dd29
Tourlaville **F** 61 Cd30
Tournai **B** 62 Dd29
Tournon-d'Agenais **F** 81 Da37
Tournon-sur-Rhône **F** 82 Ea37
Tournus **F** 70 Ea35
Tours **F** 69 Db33
Toury **F** 62 Dc32
Tovarkovskij **RUS** 118 Fa11
Tovarnik **HR** 86 Ha37
Tovste **UA** 76 Jb32
Töysä **FIN** 40 Hb13
Trabanca **E** 78 Bb39
Traben-Trarbach **D** 63 Ec30
Trabzon **TR** 127 Fd19
Tragacete **E** 93 Cb41
Trahiá **GR** 111 Ja47
Traiskirchen **A** 73 Gb33
Tralee **IRL** 18 Bc24
Tramore **IRL** 22 Ca25
Trän **BG** 87 Hd40
Tranås **S** 44 Ga20
Tranemo **S** 49 Fd21
Tranent **GB** 21 Da21
Trani **I** 99 Gc42
Tranøya **N** 28 Gb07
Transtrand **S** 38 Fd16
Trapani **I** 108 Fc46
Trasacco **I** 98 Fd41
Traun **A** 73 Ga33
Traunreut **D** 72 Fc33
Traunstein **D** 72 Fc33
Travemünde **D** 56 Fb25
Travnik **BIH** 86 Gd38
Travo **F** 96 Ed41
Trawniki **PL** 67 Hc29
Trbovlje **SLO** 73 Ga36

Trebbin **D** 57 Fd28
Třebíč **CZ** 65 Gb32
Trebinje **BIH** 86 Gd40
Trebisacce **I** 99 Gc44
Trebišov **SK** 67 Hc32
Treblinka **PL** 59 Hb27
Trebnje **SLO** 73 Ga36
Třeboň **CZ** 65 Ga32
Trecate **I** 83 Ed37
Treffurt **D** 64 Fb29
Tregaron **GB** 24 Cd26
Trégastel-Plage **F** 60 Cc30
Tréguier **F** 60 Cc30
Trehörningsjö **S** 33 Gc12
Treignac **F** 69 Db35
Trekljano **BG** 87 Hd40
Trélazé **F** 69 Da33
Trelleborg **S** 49 Fd24
Tremezzo **I** 71 Ed36
Tremp **E** 81 Da40
Trenčín **SK** 66 Gd32
Trento **I** 72 Fb36
Tresfjord **N** 36 Fa14
Trespaderne **E** 79 Ca38
Tretten **N** 37 Fc15
Treuchtlingen **D** 64 Fb32
Treuenbrietzen **D** 57 Fd28
Treviglio **I** 72 Fa36
Treviso **I** 72 Fc36
Tribunj **HR** 85 Gb39
Tricarico **I** 99 Gb43
Tricase **I** 100 Ha44
Tridubi **MD** 77 Kb32
Trieben **A** 73 Ga34
Trier **D** 63 Ec31
Trieste **I** 73 Fd36
Trie-sur-Baïse **F** 80 Cd38
Trifești **RO** 77 Jd33
Trignac **F** 60 Cc32
Trígono **GR** 101 Hc43
Tríkala **GR** 101 Hd44
Trikéri **GR** 111 Ja45
Trillo **E** 92 Ca41
Trim **IRL** 19 Cb23
Třinec **CZ** 66 Gd31
Trinitapoli **I** 99 Gb42
Trino **I** 83 Ed37
Triora **I** 83 Ec38
Trípoli **GR** 111 Ja47
Trivento **I** 99 Ga42
Trjavna **BG** 88 Jc39
Trnava **SK** 74 Gc33
Trnovo **BIH** 86 Gd39
Tročany **SK** 67 Hb32
Trödje **S** 39 Gc16
Troekurovo **RUS** 118 Fb11
Trofaiach **A** 73 Ga34
Trofors **N** 33 Ga10
Trogir **HR** 85 Gb39
Troglan Bara **SRB** 87 Hc38
Troia **I** 99 Gb42
Tróia **P** 90 Ab42
Troickaja **RUS** 127 Fc17
Troic'ke **MD** 77 Kb32
Troisdorf **D** 63 Ec29
Troița Nouă **MD** 77 Ka34

Trojaci **MK** 101 Hd42
Trojan **BG** 88 Jb39
Trollhättan **S** 43 Fd20
Tromsø **N** 26 Gc05
Tromvik **N** 26 Gc04
Trondheim **N** 37 Fc13
Troon **GB** 20 Cd21
Troøyen **N** 37 Fc13
Tropea **I** 109 Gb46
Trosa **S** 45 Gc19
Troškas **LV** 53 Ja21
Troškūnai **LT** 53 Hd23
Trosna **RUS** 121 Ed12
Trostan' **RUS** 121 Ec13
Trostberg **D** 72 Fc33
Trostjanec' **UA** 121 Ed14
Trostjanskij **RUS** 123 Fc13
Trouville-sur-Mer **F** 61 Db30
Trowbridge **GB** 24 Cd27
Troyes **F** 62 Ea32
Trsa **MNE** 86 Ha40
Tršće **HR** 85 Ga37
Trstenik **SRB** 87 Hc39
Trubčevsk **RUS** 121 Ed13
Trubetčino **RUS** 122 Fb12
Trud **BG** 102 Jb40
Trujillo **E** 91 Bb41
Trumieje **PL** 58 Gd26
Trun **F** 61 Da31
Truro **GB** 23 Cb28
Trușești **RO** 76 Jc33
Trustrup **DK** 49 Fc22
Trutnov **CZ** 65 Gb30
Tryškiai **LT** 52 Hb22
Tržac **BIH** 85 Gb37
Trzcianka **PL** 57 Gb27
Trzcianne **PL** 59 Hc26
Trzciel **PL** 57 Gb28
Trzebiatów **PL** 57 Gb25
Trzebień **PL** 65 Gb29
Trzebinia **PL** 67 Ha30
Trzebnica **PL** 66 Gc29
Trzemeszno **PL** 58 Gc27
Trzydnik Duży **PL** 67 Hc29
Tsepélovo **GR** 101 Hc44
Tsjernobyl **UA** 121 Ec14
Tuam **IRL** 18 Ca23
Tuapse **RUS** 127 Fc17
Tubbergen **NL** 55 Ec27
Tübingen **D** 64 Fa32
Tubize **B** 62 Ea29
Tuchan **F** 81 Db39
Tuchola **PL** 58 Gc26
Tuchów **PL** 67 Hb31
Tučovo **RUS** 117 Ed10
Tuczna **PL** 59 Hd28
Tuczno **PL** 57 Gb27
Tuczno **PL** 57 Gb26
Tudela **E** 80 Cb39
Tudela de Duero **E** 79 Bc39
Tudu **EST** 47 Ja18
Tudulinna **EST** 47 Ja18
Tuéjar **E** 93 Cb42
Tufeni **RO** 88 Jb37
Tugotino **RUS** 47 Jb19
Tuhala **EST** 46 Hc18

Tuhkala RUS 35 Ja09
Tui E 78 Ad37
Tuin MK 101 Hc41
Tûja LV 46 Hc20
Tukums LV 52 Hc21
Tula RUS 118 Fa11
Tulare SRB 87 Hc40
Tulcea RO 89 Ka36
Tul'čyn UA 125 Eb16
Tulgheş RO 76 Jb34
Tuliszków PL 58 Gd28
Tullamore IRL 18 Ca24
Tulle F 69 Db36
Tulln A 73 Gb33
Tullow IRL 19 Cb24
Tułowice PL 66 Gc30
Tulppio FIN 31 Hd06
Tulsk IRL 18 Ca23
Tuma RUS 118 Fb10
Tumba S 45 Gc18
Tunadal S 39 Gc14
Tungozero RUS 35 Ja09
Tunstall GB 21 Da23
Tuntsa FIN 31 Hd07
Tupicino RUS 47 Jb18
Turčianske Teplice SK 66 Gd32
Turda RO 76 Ja35
Turégano E 92 Bd40
Turek PL 58 Gd28
Tureni RO 76 Ja35
Turgutlu TR 113 Kb45
Turgutreıs TR 115 Kb47
Türi EST 47 Hd18
Turijs'k UA 120 Ea14
Turís E 93 Cb43
Turiščevo RUS 121 Ed12
Turka UA 67 Hd31
Türkeli TR 103 Ka42
Túrkeve H 75 Hb34
Turksad RUS 127 Ga16
Turku FIN 40 Hb16
Turnhout B 55 Eb28
Türnitz A 73 Gb33
Turnov CZ 65 Ga30
Turnu RO 75 Hc35
Turnu Măgurele RO 88 Jb38
Turoś PL 59 Hb26
Turriff GB 17 Db19
Turtel MK 101 Hd41
Turtola FIN 30 Hb08
Turzovka SK 66 Gd31
Tuscania I 98 Fb41
Tutaev RUS 118 Fa09
Tutin SRB 87 Hb40
Tutova RO 77 Jd35
Tutrakan BG 89 Jd38
Tuttlingen D 71 Ed33
Tuulos FIN 40 Hc15
Tuupovaara FIN 41 Jb13
Tuusniemi FIN 41 Ja13
Tuusula FIN 40 Hc16
Tuutisjärvi RUS 31 Ja08
Tuža RUS 119 Fc08
Tuzi MNE 100 Ha41
Tuzla BIH 86 Ha38

Tuzly UA 77 Kb35
Tuzly UA 125 Ec17
Tvååker S 49 Fd21
Tväråsund S 34 Gd12
Tvärdica BG 88 Jc39
Tvardiţa MD 77 Ka35
Tvedestrand N 43 Fb19
Tveitsund N 42 Fa18
Tver' RUS 117 Ed10
Tverrvika N 28 Ga08
Tving S 50 Gb22
Tvrdošín SK 67 Ha31
Twardogóra PL 66 Gc29
Twello NL 55 Ec27
Twistringen D 56 Fa27
Tychowo PL 57 Gb25
Tychy PL 66 Gd30
Tyczyń PL 67 Hc30
Tyfors S 44 Ga17
Tykocin PL 59 Hc26
Tylawa PL 67 Hc31
Tylkowo PL 58 Ha26
Tylösand S 49 Fd22
Tymkove MD 77 Ka32
Tyndrum GB 16 Cd20
Tynemouth GB 21 Db23
Tyngsjö S 44 Ga17
Tyniec PL 67 Ha31
Týniště nad Orlicí CZ 65 Gb30
Týn nad Vltavou CZ 65 Ga32
Tynset N 37 Fc14
Tyringe S 49 Fd22
Tyristrand N 43 Fb17
Tyrnävä FIN 35 Hc11
Tyrnyauz RUS 127 Ga17
Tyškivka UA 125 Ec16
Tysnes N 42 Ed17
Tyssebotn N 36 Ed16
Tyssedal N 42 Ed17
Tystberga S 45 Gc19
Tyszowce PL 67 Hd29
Tytuvėnai LT 52 Hc23
Tywyn GB 24 Cd25
Tzermiádo GR 115 Jd49

U

Ub SRB 87 Hb38
Úbeda E 106 Bc44
Überlingen D 72 Fa33
Ubieszyn PL 67 Hc30
Ubl'a SK 67 Hc32
Ubli MNE 86 Ha40
Ubrique E 105 Ba45
Ucero E 79 Ca39
Üçharman TR 128 Gc16
Uchte D 56 Fa27
Uckfield GB 25 Db28
Üçpınar TR 128 Ga16
Uda RO 88 Jb37
Udačnoe RUS 123 Ga14
Udbina HR 85 Gb38
Uddevalla S 43 Fc19
Uddheden S 44 Fd17

Uden NL 55 Eb28
Udine I 73 Fd36
Udomlja RUS 117 Ec09
Ueckermünde D 57 Ga26
Uelzen D 56 Fb27
Uetersen D 56 Fb26
Uetze D 56 Fb27
Uffenheim D 64 Fb31
Ugåle LV 52 Hb21
Ugao SRB 87 Hb40
Ugărčin BG 88 Jb39
Ugijar E 106 Bc45
Ugine F 71 Eb36
Uglič RUS 117 Ed09
Ugljan HR 85 Ga38
Ugra RUS 117 Ed11
Uherské Hradiště CZ 66 Gc32
Uherský Brod CZ 66 Gc32
Uhniv UA 67 Hd30
Uig GB 16 Cd18
Uimaharju FIN 41 Jb12
Uithuizen NL 55 Ec26
Uivar RO 75 Hb36
Ujeździec Mały PL 66 Gc29
Újfehértó H 75 Hc33
Ujma PL 58 Gd27
Ujście PL 58 Gc27
Ukiernica PL 57 Ga26
Ukmergė LT 53 Hd23
Ukrajina UA 121 Eb15
Ulan Ėrge RUS 123 Ga15
Ulanów PL 67 Hc30
Ulbroka LV 52 Hc21
Ulcinj MNE 100 Ha41
Ulefoss N 43 Fb18
Uleila del Campo E 106 Bd45
Ulfborg DK 48 Fa22
Úlibice CZ 65 Gb30
Ulieş RO 76 Jb35
Ul'janovka MD 77 Kb32
Ul'janovka MD 77 Kb32
Ul'janovka UA 125 Ec16
Uljanovo RUS 52 Hb24
Uljanovsk RUS 119 Fd09
Ullånger S 39 Gc13
Ullapool GB 17 Da18
Ullared S 49 Fd21
Ullatti S 30 Ha08
Ullava FIN 34 Hb12
Ulldecona E 93 Cd42
Ullerslev DK 49 Fb23
Ulm D 72 Fa33
Ulmu RO 89 Jd36
Ulricehamn S 44 Fd20
Ulrika S 44 Gb20
Ulriksfors S 33 Gb11
Ulsteinvik N 36 Ed14
Ulukışla TR 128 Gd15
Uluköy TR 103 Jd43
Ulvåker S 44 Ga19
Ulverston GB 21 Da23
Ulvik N 36 Fa16
Ulvila FIN 40 Ha15
Ulvsvåg N 28 Gb07

Umag HR 85 Fd37
Uman' UA 121 Ec15
Umbertide I 84 Fc40
Umčari SRB 87 Hb38
Umeå S 34 Gd12
Umgransele S 33 Gc11
Umka SRB 87 Hb38
Umurbey TR 103 Jd43
Umurga LV 47 Hd20
Umurlu TR 113 Kb45
Unari FIN 30 Hb07
Uncastillo E 80 Cc39
Undenäs S 44 Ga19
Undersåker S 38 Fd13
Uneča RUS 121 Ec13
Ungheni MD 77 Jd33
Ungheni RO 88 Jb37
Unguriņi LV 47 Hd19
Unichowo PL 58 Gc25
Uničov CZ 66 Gc31
Uniejów PL 58 Gd28
Unisław PL 58 Gd26
Unna D 55 Ed28
Unnaryd S 49 Fd21
Unterhaching D 72 Fc33
Ünye TR 127 Fc19
Upa EST 46 Hb19
Upinniemi FIN 46 Hc17
Upolokša RUS 31 Ja06
Upplands-Väsby S 45 Gc18
Uppsala S 45 Gc17
Ura-Vajgurore AL 100 Hb43
Urbania I 84 Fc39
Urbino I 84 Fc39
Uren RUS 119 Fc08
Urganlı TR 113 Kb45
Uria RO 76 Ja34
Uriž UA 67 Hd31
Urjala FIN 40 Hb16
Urjupinsk RUS 123 Fc13
Urk NL 55 Ec27
Urla TR 113 Ka45
Urlaţi RO 88 Jc36
Urlingford IRL 18 Ca24
Urmary RUS 119 Fd09
Uroševac RKS 101 Hc41
Ursviken S 34 Ha11
Urszulewo PL 58 Ha27
Urzędów PL 67 Hc29
Urziceni RO 88 Jc37
Uržum RUS 119 Fd08
Ušačy BY 117 Eb11
Usadišče RUS 117 Ec08
Usagre E 105 Ba43
Uschodni BY 120 Ea12
Usedom D 57 Ga26
Usingen D 63 Ed30
Usk GB 24 Cd27
Uskoplje (Gornji Vakuf) BIH 86 Gd39
Uslar D 56 Fa28
Usman' RUS 122 Fb12
Usovo RUS 119 Fc11
Ussel F 69 Dc36
Ust'Džeguta RUS 127 Fd17
Uster CH 71 Ed34

Ustibar – Varhaug

Ustibar **BIH** 86 Ha39
Ustikolina **BIH** 86 Ha39
Ústí nad Labem **CZ** 65 Ga30
Ústí nad Orlicí **CZ** 65 Gb31
Ustiprača **BIH** 86 Ha39
Ustjužna **RUS** 117 Ec08
Ustka **PL** 58 Gc25
Ust'-Labinsk **RUS** 127 Fc17
Ust'-Luga **RUS** 47 Ja17
Ustovo **BG** 102 Jb41
Ustrem **BG** 103 Jd40
Ustroń **PL** 66 Gd31
Ustronie Morskie **PL** 57 Gb25
Ustrzyki Dolne **PL** 67 Hc31
Ustyluh **PL** 67 Hd29
Usvjaty **RUS** 117 Eb11
Utajärvi **FIN** 35 Hc10
Utåker **N** 42 Ed17
Utansjö **S** 39 Gc14
Utena **LT** 53 Ja23
Utiel **E** 93 Cb43
Utne **N** 36 Ed16
Utrecht **NL** 55 Eb27
Utrera **E** 105 Ba44
Utsjoki **FIN** 27 Hc04
Uttoxeter **GB** 24 Da25
Utvin **RO** 75 Hc36
Utvorda **N** 32 Fc11
Uukuniemi **FIN** 41 Jb14
Uurainen **FIN** 40 Hc14
Uusikaarlepyy **FIN** 34 Ha12
Uusikaupunki **FIN** 40 Ha16
Úvaly **CZ** 65 Ga31
Uvarovo **RUS** 123 Fc12
Uvdal **N** 43 Fb17
Uzdowo **PL** 58 Ha26
Uzerche **F** 69 Db36
Uzès **F** 82 Dd38
Užhorod **UA** 67 Hc32
Užice **SRB** 87 Hb39
Uzlovaja **RUS** 118 Fa11
Užovka **RUS** 119 Fc10
Uzuncaburç **TR** 128 Gc17
Uzunköprü **TR** 103 Jd41
Uzunkuyu **TR** 128 Gb15
Uventis **LT** 52 Hc23
Uzyn **UA** 121 Ec15

V

Vääkio **FIN** 35 Hd10
Vaala **FIN** 35 Hd11
Vaalajärvi **FIN** 31 Hc07
Vaalimaa **FIN** 41 Ja16
Vaaraslahti **FIN** 35 Hd12
Vaasa **FIN** 40 Ha13
Vabalninkas **LT** 53 Hd22
Vabre **F** 81 Db38
Vác **H** 74 Ha34
Vacha **D** 64 Fb29
Väckelsång **S** 50 Ga22
Vadheim **N** 36 Ed15
Vadsø **N** 27 Hd03
Vadstena **S** 44 Ga19

Vadu Crişului **RO** 75 Hc34
Vaduz **FL** 72 Fa34
Vågaholmen **N** 28 Ga08
Vågåmo **N** 37 Fb15
Vaggeryd **S** 50 Ga21
Vagnhärad **S** 45 Gc19
Vägsele **S** 33 Gc11
Vähäkyrö **FIN** 40 Ha13
Vahto **FIN** 40 Hb16
Vaihingen (Enz) **D** 64 Fa32
Vailly-sur-Sauldre **F** 69 Dc33
Vainikkala **FIN** 41 Ja15
Vaiņode **LV** 52 Hb22
Vaison-la-Romaine **F** 82 Ea38
Vajszló **H** 74 Gd36
Vakfıkebir **TR** 127 Fd19
Vakıf **TR** 103 Jd42
Valaam **RUS** 41 Jb14
Vålådalen **S** 38 Fd13
Valandovo **MK** 101 Hd42
Valaská Belá **SK** 66 Gd32
Valašská Polanka **CZ** 66 Gd32
Valašské Meziříčí **CZ** 66 Gd31
Vålberg **S** 44 Fd18
Valbo **S** 38 Gb16
Valbonæ **AL** 100 Hb41
Vălčedrăm **BG** 88 Ja39
Vălčidol **BG** 89 Jd38
Valdagno **I** 72 Fb36
Valdahon **F** 71 Eb34
Valdaj **RUS** 117 Ec09
Valdefuentes **E** 91 Ba42
Valdelagua **E** 92 Bd41
Valdeltormo **E** 93 Cd41
Valdemārpils **LV** 52 Hb21
Valdemarsvik **S** 44 Gb20
Valdemeca **E** 93 Cb42
Valdemoro **E** 92 Bd41
Valdenoceda **E** 79 Ca38
Valdepeñas **E** 92 Bd43
Valdepeñas de Jaén **E** 106 Bc44
Valderas **E** 79 Bc38
Val de Reuil **F** 61 Db31
Valderrobres **E** 93 Cd41
Val d'Isère **F** 71 Eb36
Valdobbiadene **I** 72 Fc36
Valea Ierii **RO** 75 Hd35
Valea lui Mihai **RO** 75 Hc34
Valea Mare-Pravăţ **RO** 88 Jb36
Valea Mărului **RO** 77 Jd35
Valea Perjei **MD** 77 Ka34
Valea Sării **RO** 76 Jc35
Valea Ursului **RO** 76 Jc34
Valea Uzului **RO** 76 Jc35
Valejkiďki **BY** 53 Ja24
Valença do Minho **P** 78 Ad37
Valençay **F** 69 Db33
Valence **F** 81 Da37
Valence **F** 82 Ea37
Valence-sur-Baïse **F** 81 Da37

València **E** 93 Cc43
Valencia de Alcántara **E** 90 Ad41
Valencia de Don Juan **E** 79 Bc38
Valenciennes **F** 62 Ea29
Vălenii de Munte **RO** 88 Jc36
Valeni-Stânişoara **RO** 76 Jb33
Valensole **F** 82 Ea38
Valentano **I** 84 Fb40
Valenza **I** 83 Ed37
Våler **N** 37 Fc16
Valeria **E** 92 Ca42
Valevåg **N** 42 Ed17
Valga **EST** 47 Hd20
Valguarnera Caropepe **I** 109 Ga47
Valíra **GR** 110 Hd47
Vălişoara **RO** 75 Hd35
Văliug **RO** 87 Hc37
Valjevo **SRB** 87 Hb38
Valka **LV** 47 Hd20
Valkeakoski **FIN** 40 Hc15
Valkeala **FIN** 41 Hd15
Valkenswaard **NL** 55 Eb28
Valko **FIN** 41 Hd16
Valkom **FIN** 41 Hd16
Valky **UA** 122 Fa14
Valla **S** 44 Gb19
Valladolid **E** 79 Bc39
Vallargärdet **S** 44 Fd18
Valldemossa **E** 95 Db43
Valle **N** 42 Fa18
Valle de Cabuérniga **E** 79 Bd37
Vallentuna **S** 45 Gc18
Vallgrund **FIN** 40 Ha13
Vallon-Pont-d'Arc **F** 82 Dd37
Vallorbe **CH** 71 Eb35
Valls **E** 95 Da41
Vallsta **S** 38 Gb15
Vallvik **S** 39 Gc16
Valmanya **F** 81 Db39
Valmiera **LV** 47 Hd20
Valognes **F** 61 Cd30
Valøy **N** 32 Fc11
Valožyn **BY** 120 Ea12
Valpaços **P** 78 Ba38
Valpovo **HR** 74 Gd36
Valréas **F** 82 Ea37
Valset **N** 32 Fb12
Valsjöbyn **S** 33 Ga12
Val-Thorens **F** 71 Eb36
Valtimo **FIN** 35 Ja12
Valtournenche **I** 71 Ec36
Valujki **RUS** 122 Fb14
Valverde de Júcar **E** 92 Ca42
Valverde del Camino **E** 105 Ad43
Valverde de Leganés **E** 90 Ad42
Valverde del Fresno **E** 91 Ba40

Vama **RO** 76 Jb33
Vamberk **CZ** 65 Gb30
Vamdrup **DK** 48 Fa23
Våmhus **S** 38 Ga16
Vamlingbo **S** 51 Gc21
Vammala **FIN** 40 Hb15
Vampula **FIN** 40 Hb16
Vana-Kuuste **EST** 47 Ja19
Vânători **RO** 76 Jb35
Vânători **RO** 87 Hd38
Vändra **EST** 47 Hd19
Vändträsk **S** 34 Ha09
Vandžiogala **LT** 52 Hc23
Vāne **LV** 52 Hb21
Vänersborg **S** 43 Fd19
Vangazi **LV** 53 Hd21
Vängel **S** 33 Gb12
Vangsnes **N** 36 Ed15
Vänjaurträsk **S** 33 Gc12
Vânju Mare **RO** 87 Hd38
Vannareid **N** 26 Gc04
Vännäs **S** 34 Gd12
Vännäsberget **S** 34 Ha09
Vännäsby **S** 34 Gd12
Vannes **F** 60 Cc32
Vansbro **S** 44 Ga17
Vänsjö **S** 38 Ga15
Vanttauskoski **FIN** 31 Hc08
Vanvikan **N** 32 Fc12
Vara **S** 43 Fd20
Varades **F** 68 Cd33
Varakļāni **LV** 53 Ja21
Varallo **I** 71 Ed36
Vărăncău **MD** 77 Ka33
Varangerbotn **N** 27 Hc03
Varapaeva **BY** 53 Jb23
Varaždin **HR** 73 Gb36
Varaždinske Toplice **HR** 74 Gc36
Varazze **I** 83 Ed38
Varberg **S** 49 Fd21
Vărbica **BG** 89 Jd39
Várda **GR** 110 Hd46
Varde **DK** 48 Fa23
Vardø **N** 27 Hd03
Vårdö **FIN** 46 Ha17
Varekil **S** 43 Fc20
Varel **D** 55 Ed26
Varėna **LT** 59 Hd25
Varėna **LT** 59 Hd25
Varena I **LT** 59 Hd25
Varena I **LT** 59 Hd25
Varengeville-sur-Mer **F** 61 Db30
Varennes-en-Argonne **F** 62 Ea31
Varennes-sur-Allier **F** 70 Dd35
Vareš **BIH** 86 Gd38
Varese **I** 71 Ed36
Varese Ligure **I** 84 Fa38
Vârfu Câmpului **RO** 76 Jc33
Vârfurile **RO** 75 Hd35
Vårgårda **S** 43 Fd20
Vargön **S** 43 Fd19
Varhaug **N** 42 Ec19

Varilhes F 81 Da39
Váris GR 101 Hd43
Varkaus FIN 41 Ja14
Varmahlíð IS 15 Ca05
Värmlandsbro S 44 Fd18
Varna BG 89 Ka39
Värnamo S 50 Ga21
Varniai LT 52 Hb23
Varnja EST 47 Ja19
Varnjany BY 53 Ja24
Varnsdorf CZ 65 Ga29
Varoška Rijeka BIH 85 Gb37
Varpaisjärvi FIN 35 Hd12
Várpalota H 74 Gd34
Vărşag RO 76 Jb35
Vărşand RO 75 Hc35
Vărşec BG 88 Ja39
Vărşilo BG 103 Ka40
Vartdal N 36 Ed14
Vartius FIN 35 Ja10
Vârtop RO 88 Ja38
Värtsilä FIN 41 Jb13
Varva UA 121 Ed14
Varvara BG 102 Jb40
Varzi I 83 Ed37
Varzy F 70 Dd33
Vasa FIN 40 Ha13
Vasalemma EST 46 Hc18
Vásárosnamény H 75 Hc33
Vasil'evo RUS 47 Jb20
Vasil'evo RUS 119 Fd09
Vasilikí GR 110 Hc45
Vaškai LT 52 Hc22
Vaskelovo RUS 41 Jb16
Vaskivesi FIN 40 Hb14
Vasknarva EST 47 Ja18
Vaslui RO 77 Jd34
Vassilika GR 101 Ja43
Vassilikó GR 112 Jb45
Vassilikós GR 110 Hc47
Vasstrand N 26 Gc05
Västansjö S 33 Ga10
Västbacka S 38 Ga15
Västerås S 44 Gb18
Västerhaninge S 45 Gc18
Västervik S 44 Gb20
Vasto I 99 Ga41
Våstra S 45 Gc18
Västra Ämtervik S 44 Fd18
Vasvár H 74 Gc35
Vasylivka UA 126 Fa16
Vasyl'kiv UA 121 Ec15
Vasyl'kivka UA 122 Fa15
Vasyščeve UA 122 Fa14
Vața de Jos RO 75 Hd35
Vatan F 69 Db33
Váthi GR 101 Ja42
Vathí GR 115 Ka47
Vatla EST 46 Hc19
Vatne N 36 Fa14
Vatra MD 77 Ka33
Vatra Dornei RO 76 Jb34
Vatra Moldoviței RO 76 Jb33
Vättlax FIN 46 Hb17
Vatutine UA 121 Ec15

Vaucouleurs F 63 Eb32
Vaudrey F 71 Eb34
Vau i Dejës AL 100 Hb41
Vaukalata BY 53 Jb23
Vauvert F 82 Dd38
Väversunda S 44 Ga20
Vavkavysk BY 59 Hd26
Vaxholm S 45 Gc18
Växjö S 50 Ga21
Våxtorp S 49 Fd22
Vayrac F 69 Db36
Vechelde D 56 Fb28
Vechta D 55 Ed27
Vecinos E 91 Bb40
Veclaicene LV 47 Ja20
Vecpiebalga LV 53 Hd21
Vecses H 74 Ha34
Vecumnieki LV 53 Hd21
Veddige S 49 Fd21
Vedea RO 88 Jc38
Vedevåg S 44 Gb18
Vedjeön S 33 Gb12
Vedrovo RUS 118 Fb08
Veendam NL 55 Ec26
Veenendaal NL 55 Eb27
Veere EST 46 Hb19
Vegadeo E 78 Bb36
Vegarienza E 79 Bc37
Vegårshei N 42 Fa19
Veghel NL 55 Eb28
Veglie I 100 Gd43
Vegusdal N 42 Fa19
Vehmaa FIN 40 Ha16
Vehmersalmi FIN 41 Ja13
Vehu FIN 40 Hb15
Veidnes N 27 Hb03
Veisiejai LT 59 Hc25
Veisiejai LT 59 Hc25
Veitsiluoto FIN 34 Hb09
Vejdelevka RUS 122 Fb14
Vejen DK 48 Fa23
Vejer de la Frontera E 105 Ad45
Vejle DK 49 Fb23
Vejprty CZ 65 Fd30
Vekilski BG 89 Jd38
Vela Luka HR 86 Gc40
Velanídia GR 111 Jb48
Vel'aty SK 67 Hc32
Velbert D 63 Ec29
Velden A 73 Ga35
Veldhoven NL 55 Eb28
Velēna LV 47 Ja20
Velenje SLO 73 Ga36
Veles MK 101 Hd41
Velestino GR 101 Ja44
Vélez Blanco E 107 Ca45
Vélez-Málaga E 105 Bb45
Vélez Rubio E 107 Ca45
Velika GR 110 Hd47
Velika HR 86 Gd37
Velika Gorica HR 73 Gb36
Velika Kladuša HR 85 Gb37
Velika Plana SRB 87 Hc38
Velika Plana SRB 87 Hc39
Velika Slatina RKS 87 Hc40

Veliki Dal'nik UA 77 Kb34
Velikie Luki RUS 117 Eb10
Veliki Gradište SRB 87 Hc37
Veliki Grđevac HR 74 Gc36
Veliki Kupci SRB 87 Hc39
Veliki Preslav BG 89 Jd39
Veliki Radinci SRB 86 Ha37
Veliki Šiljegovac SRB 87 Hc39
Veliki Zdenci HR 74 Gc36
Veliko Tărnovo BG 88 Jc39
Velimlje MNE 86 Ha40
Velingrad BG 102 Jb41
Veliž RUS 117 Eb11
Veljun HR 85 Gb37
Velká Bíteš CZ 65 Gb32
Vel'ké Kapušany SK 67 Hc32
Velké Losiny CZ 66 Gc31
Velké Meziříčí CZ 65 Gb32
Velký Bor CZ 65 Fd31
Veľký Krtíš SK 74 Ha33
Veľký Šariš SK 67 Hb32
Velletri I 98 Fc42
Vellinge S 49 Fd23
Velventós GR 101 Hd43
Velyka Lepetycha UA 126 Fa16
Velyka Mychajlivka MD 77 Kb33
Velyka Pysarivka UA 122 Fa14
Velyki Dederkaly UA 120 Ea15
Velyki Mosty UA 67 Hd30
Velykoploske UA 77 Ka33
Velykyj Bereznyj UA 67 Hc32
Velykyj Burluk UA 122 Fa14
Vemb DK 48 Fa22
Vemdalen S 38 Ga14
Venafro I 98 Fd42
Venarey-les Laumes F 70 Ea33
Venčane SRB 87 Hb38
Vence F 83 Eb39
Venda Nova P 78 Ba38
Vendas Novas P 90 Ac42
Vendeuvre-sur-Barse F 62 Ea32
Vendôme F 61 Db32
Venec BG 89 Jd38
Veneheitto FIN 35 Hc11
Venev RUS 118 Fa11
Venezia I 84 Fc37
Vénissieux F 70 Ea36
Venjan S 38 Ga16
Venlo NL 55 Ec28
Vennesla N 42 Fa19
Vennesund N 32 Fd10
Venosa I 99 Gb43
Venray NL 55 Ec28
Venta LT 52 Hb22
Venta de Ballerías E 80 Cd40

Venta de Baños E 79 Bd39
Ventimiglia I 83 Ec39
Ventspils LV 52 Hb21
Vera E 107 Ca45
Verbania I 71 Ed36
Verbier CH 71 Ec35
Vercelli I 83 Ed37
Verchnjadzvinsk BY 53 Jb22
Verchnje Syn'ovydne UA 67 Hd31
Verchn'odniprovs'k UA 121 Ed15
Verdalsøra N 32 Fc12
Verden (Aller) D 56 Fa27
Verdun F 63 Eb31
Verdun-sur-le-Doubs F 70 Ea34
Vergato I 84 Fb38
Vergt F 69 Da36
Verhnetulomskij RUS 31 Ja05
Véria GR 101 Hd43
Verín E 78 Ba38
Verinsko BG 102 Ja40
Veriora EST 47 Ja19
Verl D 56 Fa28
Vermenton F 70 Dd33
Vernazza I 84 Fa38
Verneuil-sur-Avre F 61 Db31
Vernon F 62 Dc31
Vero F 96 Ed41
Verona I 84 Fb37
Versailles F 62 Dc31
Versmold D 55 Ed28
Vertelim RUS 119 Fc10
Vertijivka UA 121 Ec14
Vertjačij RUS 123 Fd14
Vertus F 62 Ea31
Verviers B 63 Eb29
Vervins F 62 Ea30
Vesanka FIN 40 Hc14
Vesanto FIN 41 Hd13
Ves'egonsk RUS 117 Ed08
Vesele UA 126 Fa16
Veselij Kut UA 77 Ka35
Veselí nad Lužnicí CZ 65 Ga32
Veselí nad Moravou CZ 66 Gc32
Veselynove UA 125 Ed16
Vešenskaja RUS 123 Fc13
Vesoul F 71 Eb33
Vessigebro S 49 Fd21
Vestby N 43 Fc18
Vesterli N 28 Ga08
Vesterø Havn DK 49 Fc21
Vestnes N 36 Fa14
Vestre Jakobselv N 27 Hc03
Veszprém H 74 Gd34
Vețel RO 75 Hd36
Veteli FIN 34 Hb12
Vetlanda S 50 Ga21
Vetluga RUS 118 Fb08
Vetrișoaia RO 77 Jd34
Větrný Jeníkov CZ 65 Gb31
Vetsikko FIN 27 Hc04

Veulettes-sur-Mer – Villeneuve

Veulettes-sur-Mer **F** 61 Db30
Veurne **B** 54 Dd28
Vevelstad **N** 32 Fd10
Vevey **CH** 71 Eb35
Vévi **GR** 101 Hd42
Veynes **F** 82 Ea37
Vézelay **F** 70 Dd33
Viadana **I** 84 Fa37
Viana **E** 80 Cb39
Viana de Bolo **E** 78 Ba38
Viana do Alentejo **P** 90 Ac42
Viana do Castelo **P** 78 Ad38
Vianden **L** 63 Eb30
Vianen **NL** 55 Eb27
Viareggio **I** 84 Fa39
Vias **F** 81 Dc39
Vibble **S** 45 Gc20
Viborg **DK** 49 Fb22
Vibo Valentia **I** 109 Gb46
Vibraye **F** 61 Db32
Vic **E** 81 Db40
Vicdessos **F** 81 Da39
Vic-en-Bigorre **F** 80 Cd38
Vicenza **I** 84 Fb37
Vichy **F** 70 Dd35
Vic-le-Comte **F** 69 Dc36
Vic-le-Fesq **F** 82 Dd38
Vico **F** 96 Ed41
Vicovu de Jos **RO** 76 Jb33
Vic-sur-Cère **F** 69 Dc36
Victoria **RO** 77 Jd33
Victoria **RO** 88 Jb36
Vičuga **RUS** 118 Fb09
Vidamlja **BY** 59 Hd27
Vidauban **F** 83 Eb39
Videbæk **DK** 48 Fa22
Videle **RO** 88 Jc38
Videsæter **N** 36 Fa15
Vidice **CZ** 65 Fd31
Vidigueira **P** 90 Ac42
Vidin **BG** 87 Hd38
Vidiškiai **LT** 53 Hd23
Vidsel **S** 34 Gd09
Vidzy **BY** 53 Ja23
Viechtach **D** 65 Fd32
Vieki **FIN** 35 Ja12
Viekšniai **LT** 52 Hb22
Vielha **E** 81 Da39
Vielsalm **B** 63 Eb30
Vienne **F** 70 Ea36
Vieremä **FIN** 35 Hd12
Viernheim **D** 63 Ed31
Viersen **D** 63 Ec29
Vierzon **F** 69 Dc33
Viesīte **LV** 53 Hd22
Vieste **I** 99 Gb41
Vietas **S** 29 Gc07
Vif **F** 82 Ea37
Vigeland **N** 42 Ed20
Vigevano **I** 83 Ed37
Vignola **I** 84 Fb38
Vigo **E** 78 Ad37
Vigrestad **N** 42 Ec19
Vihanti **FIN** 35 Hc11

Vihiers **F** 69 Da33
Vihtari **FIN** 41 Ja13
Vihti **FIN** 40 Hc16
Vīïaka **LV** 47 Jb20
Viiala **FIN** 40 Hb15
Viira **EST** 46 Hb19
Viisarimäki **FIN** 41 Hd14
Viişoara **RO** 76 Jc34
Viitasaari **FIN** 40 Hc13
Viitna **EST** 47 Hd17
Viivikonna **EST** 47 Ja17
Vík **IS** 14 Bd08
Vik **S** 50 Ga23
Vika **S** 38 Ga16
Vikajärvi **FIN** 31 Hc08
Vikanes **N** 36 Ed16
Vikarbyn **S** 38 Ga16
Vikedal **N** 42 Ed18
Viken **S** 49 Fd22
Vikersund **N** 43 Fb17
Vikevåg **N** 42 Ed18
Vikhammer **N** 37 Fc13
Vikno **UA** 76 Jb32
Vikran **N** 26 Gc05
Viksjö **S** 39 Gc14
Viksøyri **N** 36 Ed16
Vila de Rei **P** 90 Ad40
Vila do Bispo **P** 104 Ab43
Vila Flor **P** 78 Ba39
Vilafranca del Maestrat **E** 93 Cc42
Vilafranca del Penedès **E** 95 Da41
Vila Franca de Xira **P** 90 Ac41
Vilagarcía de Arousa **E** 78 Ad37
Vilalba **E** 78 Ba36
Vīļāni **LV** 53 Ja21
Vila Nova de Famalição **P** 78 Ad38
Vila Nova de Foz Côa **P** 78 Ba39
Vila Nova de Milfontes **P** 104 Ab43
Vila Nova de Paiva **P** 78 Ad39
Vilanova i la Geltrú **E** 95 Da41
Vila Pouca de Aguiar **P** 78 Ba38
Vilar **P** 78 Ba39
Vila Real **P** 78 Ba39
Vila-real (Villareal de los Infantes) **E** 93 Cc42
Vila Real de Santo Antonio **P** 104 Ac44
Vilar Formoso **P** 91 Ba40
Vila Velha de Ródão **P** 90 Ad41
Vila Verde de Ficalho **P** 105 Ad43
Vila Viçosa **P** 90 Ad42
Vilches **E** 106 Bc44
Vilejka **BY** 53 Jb24

Vilejka **BY** 120 Ea12
Vilhelmina **S** 33 Gb11
Viljandi **EST** 47 Hd19
Vilkaviškis **LT** 52 Hc24
Vilkija **LT** 52 Hc24
Villablino **E** 78 Bb37
Villacañas **E** 92 Bd42
Villacarillo **E** 106 Bd44
Villacarriedo **E** 79 Ca37
Villacastín **E** 91 Bc40
Villach **A** 73 Fd35
Villacidro **I** 97 Ec44
Villada **E** 79 Bc38
Villa del Río **E** 106 Bc44
Villadiego **E** 79 Bd38
Villafranca del Bierzo **E** 78 Bb37
Villafranca de los Barros **E** 91 Ba42
Villafranca de los Caballeros **E** 92 Bd42
Villafranca di Verona **I** 84 Fb37
Villafranco del Guadalquivir **E** 105 Ad44
Villaharta **E** 105 Bb43
Villahermosa **E** 92 Bd43
Villahoz **E** 79 Bd39
Villalba **E** 78 Ba36
Villalón de Campos **E** 79 Bc38
Villalpando **E** 79 Bc39
Villamalea **E** 93 Cb43
Villamanrique **E** 92 Bd43
Villamartín **E** 105 Ba45
Villamayor **E** 80 Cc40
Villamayor de Santiago **E** 92 Bd42
Villandraut **F** 68 Cd36
Villa Nova de Cerveira **P** 78 Ad37
Villanubla **E** 79 Bc39
Villanueva de Alcorón **E** 92 Ca41
Villanueva de Argaño **E** 79 Bd38
Villanueva de Córdoba **E** 105 Bb43
Villanueva de Gállego **E** 80 Cc40
Villanueva de la Fuente **E** 92 Bd43
Villanueva de la Jura **E** 92 Ca43
Villanueva de la Serena **E** 91 Bb42
Villanueva de la Sierra **E** 91 Ba40
Villanueva de las Torres **E** 106 Bd45
Villanueva del Campo **E** 79 Bc38
Villanueva del Fresno **E** 90 Ad42
Villanueva del Huerva **E** 80 Cc40

Villanueva de los Castillejos **E** 105 Ad43
Villanueva de los Infantes **E** 92 Bd43
Villanueva del Río y Minas **E** 105 Ba44
Villány **H** 74 Gd36
Villapalacios **E** 92 Bd43
Villaputzu **I** 97 Ed44
Villard-de-Lans **F** 82 Ea37
Villardeciervos **E** 78 Bb38
Villar de Domingo García **E** 92 Ca41
Villardefrades **E** 79 Bc39
Villar del Arzobispo **E** 93 Cb42
Villar del Rey **E** 91 Ba42
Villarejo de Fuentes **E** 92 Ca42
Villarejo de Salvanés **E** 92 Bd41
Villarente **E** 79 Bc38
Villarmayor **E** 78 Bb39
Villarrín de Campos **E** 79 Bc39
Villarrobledo **E** 92 Ca43
Villarroya de la Sierra **E** 80 Cb40
Villarrubia de los Ojos **E** 92 Bd42
Villars **CH** 71 Ec35
Villars-les-Dombes **F** 70 Ea35
Villarta de los Montes **E** 91 Bc42
Villasalto **I** 97 Ed44
Villasana de Mena **E** 79 Ca37
Villa San Giovanni **I** 109 Gb46
Villa Santa Maria **I** 99 Ga41
Villasimius **I** 97 Ed45
Villaviciosa **E** 79 Bc36
Villaviciosa de Córdoba **E** 105 Bb43
Villedieu-les-Poêles **F** 61 Da31
Villedieu-sur-Indre **F** 69 Db34
Villefort **F** 82 Dd37
Villefranche-de-Conflent **F** 81 Db39
Villefranche-de-Lauragais **F** 81 Db38
Villefranche-de-Rouergue **F** 81 Db37
Villefranche-du-Périgord **F** 81 Db37
Villefranche-sur-Cher **F** 69 Db33
Villefranche-sur-Mer **F** 83 Ec39
Villefranche-sur-Saône **F** 70 Ea35
Villena **E** 107 Cb44
Villeneuve **F** 81 Db37

Villeneuve-lès-Avignon F 82 Dd38
Villeneuve-sur-Lot F 81 Da37
Villeneuve-sur-Yonne F 62 Dd32
Villeréal F 69 Da36
Villers-Bocage F 61 Da30
Villers-Bocage F 62 Dd30
Villers-Bretonneux F 62 Dd30
Villers-Cotterêts F 62 Dd31
Villersexel F 71 Eb33
Villerupt F 63 Eb31
Villeurbanne F 70 Ea36
Villiers-Saint-Georges F 62 Dd32
Villingen-Schwenningen D 71 Ed33
Vilnius LT 53 Hd24
Vil'njans'k UA 122 Fa15
Vil'nohirs'k UA 121 Ed15
Vilppula FIN 40 Hc14
Vil'šanka UA 77 Jd32
Vil'šany UA 122 Fa14
Vilsbiburg D 72 Fc33
Vilshofen D 65 Fd32
Vimianzo E 78 Ad36
Vimieiro P 90 Ad42
Vimioso P 78 Bb39
Vimmerby S 44 Gb20
Vimoutiers F 61 Db31
Vimpeli FIN 40 Hb13
Vinac BIH 86 Gc38
Vinaròs E 93 Cd42
Vindeln S 34 Gd12
Vinderup DK 48 Fa22
Vindrej RUS 119 Fc10
Vinga RO 75 Hc36
Vingåker S 44 Gb19
Vinhais P 78 Ba38
Vinica MK 101 Hd41
Vinište BG 88 Ja39
Vinje N 36 Ed16
Vinje N 37 Fb13
Vinkovci HR 86 Ha37
Vinnycja UA 121 Eb15
Vinograd BG 88 Jc39
Vinon-sur-Verdon F 82 Ea38
Vinslöv S 50 Ga23
Vinsternes N 37 Fb13
Vinstra N 37 Fb15
Vipiteno I 72 Fb35
Vir HR 85 Ga38
Viranşehir TR 128 Gd17
Virbalis LT 52 Hc24
Vire F 61 Da31
Vireši LV 47 Ja20
Virginia IRL 19 Cb23
Virkby FIN 46 Hc17
Virkkala FIN 46 Hc17
Virklund DK 49 Fb22
Virojoki FIN 41 Ja16
Virolahden FIN 41 Ja16
Virovitica HR 74 Gc36
Virpazar MNE 100 Ha41

Virrat FIN 40 Hb14
Virsbo S 44 Gb17
Virserum S 50 Gb21
Virtaniemi FIN 27 Hc05
Virtasalmi FIN 41 Hd14
Virton B 63 Eb31
Virtsu EST 46 Hc19
Virttaa FIN 40 Hb16
Vis HR 85 Gb40
Visaginas LT 53 Ja23
Visalaukė LT 53 Hd23
Visby S 45 Gc20
Visé B 63 Eb29
Višegrad BIH 86 Ha39
Viseu P 78 Ad39
Vişeu de Sus RO 76 Ja33
Višgorodok RUS 47 Jb20
Vişina RO 88 Jb38
Viskafors S 43 Fd20
Vislanda S 50 Ga22
Viđneva BY 53 Ja24
Viso del Marqués E 106 Bc43
Visoki Dečani RKS 87 Hb40
Visoko BIH 86 Gd39
Visp CH 71 Ec35
Vissefjärda S 50 Gb22
Visselhövede D 56 Fa27
Vistabella del Maestrat E 93 Cc42
Vistheden S 34 Gd10
Vištytis LT 52 Hc24
Visuvesi FIN 40 Hb14
Vitberget S 34 Gd09
Vitebsk BY 117 Eb11
Viterbo I 98 Fd41
Vitez BIH 86 Gd38
Vithkuq AL 101 Hc43
Vitigudino E 78 Bb39
Vitina RKS 101 Hc41
Vitolište MK 101 Hd42
Vitoria E 80 Cb38
Vitré F 61 Cd32
Vitrolles F 82 Ea39
Vitry-le-François F 62 Ea32
Vitteaux F 70 Ea33
Vittel F 71 Eb33
Vittjärv S 34 Ha09
Vittoria I 109 Ga48
Vittorio Veneto I 72 Fc36
Vittsjö S 49 Fd22
Vitvattnet S 34 Ha09
Viù I 83 Ec37
Vivario F 96 Ed41
Viveiro E 78 Bb36
Viviers F 82 Dd37
Vivonne F 69 Da34
Vize TR 103 Ka41
Vizille F 82 Ea37
Viziru RO 89 Jd36
Vizovice CZ 66 Gd32
Vizzini I 109 Ga48
Vjalikija Matykaly BY 59 Hd27
Vjartsilja RUS 41 Jb13

Vjatskie Poljany RUS 119 Ga08
Vjatskoe RUS 118 Fa08
Vjaz'ma RUS 117 Ec11
Vjazniki RUS 118 Fb09
Vlădeni RO 76 Jc33
Vlădeni RO 76 Jc33
Vladimir MNE 100 Ha41
Vladimir RUS 118 Fa10
Vladimirovo BG 88 Ja39
Vlad Ţepeş RO 89 Jd37
Vlagtwedde NL 55 Ed26
Vlaháta GR 110 Hc46
Vlaháva GR 101 Hd44
Vlahiá GR 112 Jb45
Vlăhiţa RO 76 Jb35
Vlasenica BIH 86 Ha38
Vlašim CZ 65 Ga31
Vlaşin RO 88 Jc38
Vlasotince SRB 87 Hd40
Vlissingen NL 54 Ea28
Vlkolínec SK 67 Ha32
Vlorë AL 100 Hb43
Vlotho D 56 Fa28
Vöcklabruck A 73 Fd33
Vodice HR 85 Gb39
Vodňany CZ 65 Ga32
Vodnjan HR 85 Fd37
Vodskov DK 49 Fb21
Voerde D 55 Ec28
Vogatsikó GR 101 Hc43
Voghera I 83 Ed37
Vohburg D 64 Fc32
Vohenstrauß D 64 Fc31
Võhma EST 46 Hb19
Võhma EST 47 Hd19
Voikoski FIN 41 Hd15
Voineasa RO 88 Ja36
Voineasa RO 88 Ja38
Voineşti RO 88 Jb37
Voiron F 70 Ea36
Võiste EST 46 Hc19
Voiteg RO 75 Hc36
Voitsberg A 73 Ga35
Vojens DK 48 Fa23
Vojinka UA 126 Fa17
Vojnić HR 85 Gb37
Vojnica RUS 35 Ja10
Vojnika BG 103 Jd40
Vojnovo BG 89 Jd38
Vojutyči UA 67 Hd31
Voknavolok RUS 35 Ja10
Volary CZ 65 Fd32
Volčki RUS 122 Fb12
Volda N 36 Ed14
Volga RUS 117 Ed09
Volgodonsk RUS 123 Fd15
Volgograd RUS 123 Fd14
Volgorečensk RUS 118 Fa09
Volgsele S 33 Gb11
Volhov RUS 117 Eb08
Volintiri MD 77 Ka34
Volissós GR 113 Jd45
Volkach D 64 Fb31
Völkermarkt A 73 Ga35
Volkovo RUS 47 Jb20

Vollsjö S 49 Fd23
Volnovacha UA 122 Fb15
Voločaevskij RUS 123 Fd15
Voloçys'k UA 120 Ea15
Volodarka UA 121 Ec15
Volodarsk RUS 118 Fb09
Volodymyrec' UA 120 Ea14
Volodymyr-Volyns'kyj UA 67 Hd29
Vologda RUS 117 Ed08
Volokolamsk RUS 117 Ed10
Volokonovka RUS 122 Fb13
Vólos GR 101 Ja44
Vološča UA 67 Hd31
Volosjanka UA 67 Hd32
Volosovo RUS 47 Jb17
Volotovo RUS 122 Fb13
Volovec' UA 67 Hd32
Völs A 72 Fb34
Vol'sk RUS 119 Ga11
Volterra I 84 Fb39
Voltri I 83 Ed38
Voltti FIN 40 Hb13
Volvic F 69 Dc35
Volyně CZ 65 Fd32
Volžsk RUS 119 Fd09
Volžskij RUS 123 Fd13
Vonešta Voda BG 88 Jc39
Vónitsa GR 110 Hc45
Võnnu EST 47 Ja19
Vopnafjörður IS 15 Cc06
Vorbasse DK 48 Fa23
Vordingborg DK 49 Fc24
Vorey F 70 Dd36
Vormsele S 33 Gc11
Vorniceni RO 76 Jc33
Vorochta UA 76 Ja32
Voroneţ RO 76 Jb33
Voronež RUS 122 Fb13
Voronovo UA 121 Ed13
Vorsma RUS 118 Fb09
Võru EST 47 Ja20
Voshod RUS 123 Ga14
Voskresensk RUS 118 Fa10
Voskresenskoe RUS 117 Ed09
Voskresenskoe RUS 119 Fc08
Voss N 36 Ed16
Võsu EST 47 Hd17
Votice CZ 65 Ga31
Voúdia GR 111 Jc47
Vouillé F 69 Da34
Vouliagméni GR 112 Jb46
Vourkári GR 112 Jc46
Vouzela P 78 Ad39
Vouziers F 62 Ea31
Vovčans'k UA 122 Fa14
Voves F 62 Dc32
Voxna S 38 Gb15
Vöyri FIN 40 Ha13
Voznesens'k UA 125 Ed16
Voznesenskoe RUS 118 Fb10
Vrå DK 49 Fb21

Vrå **S** 49 Fd22
Vráble **SK** 74 Gd33
Vraca **BG** 88 Ja39
Vrácevšnica **SRB** 87 Hb38
Vrådal **N** 42 Fa18
Vradiivka **MD** 77 Kb32
Vradijivka **UA** 125 Ec16
Vranje **SRB** 87 Hd40
Vranov nad Topl'ou **SK** 67
 Hc32
Vrapce Polje **MNE** 87 Hb40
Vratěnin **CZ** 65 Gb32
Vratnica **MK** 101 Hc41
Vrbanja **BIH** 86 Gc38
Vrbanja **HR** 86 Ha37
Vrbovec **HR** 74 Gc36
Vrbovsko **HR** 85 Ga37
Vrchlabí **CZ** 65 Gb30
Vrésthena **GR** 111 Ja47
Vretstorp **S** 44 Ga19
Vrgorac **HR** 86 Gc40
Vrhnika **SLO** 73 Ga36
Vrhopolje **BIH** 86 Gc38
Vrigstad **S** 50 Ga21
Vríses **GR** 114 Jc49
Vrissohóri **GR** 101 Hc44
Vrlika **HR** 86 Gc39
Vrnjačka Banja **SRB** 87
 Hc39
Vrpolje **HR** 86 Gd37
Vršac **SRB** 87 Hc37
Vrsar **HR** 85 Fd37
Vrtoče **BIH** 85 Gb38
Vrulja **MNE** 86 Ha39
Vsetín **CZ** 66 Gd31
Vsevoložsk **RUS** 117 Eb08
Vučitrn **RKS** 87 Hc40
Vuka **N** 86 Gd37
Vukovar **HR** 86 Ha37
Vuku **N** 32 Fd12
Vulcan **RO** 75 Hd36
Vulcan **RO** 88 Jb36
Vulcăneşti **MD** 77 Ka35
Vultureni **RO** 75 Hd34
Vultureni **RO** 77 Jd34
Vulturu **RO** 77 Jd35
Vuoggatjålme **S** 33 Gb09
Vuohtomäki **FIN** 35 Hc12
Vuojärvi **FIN** 31 Hc07
Vuokatti **FIN** 35 Hd11
Vuolijoki **FIN** 35 Hd11
Vuollerim **S** 34 Gd09
Vuorijarvi **RUS** 31 Ja07
Vuostimo **FIN** 31 Hc08
Vuotso **FIN** 31 Hc06
Vuottas **S** 34 Ha09
Vurnary **RUS** 119 Fc09
Vyborg **RUS** 41 Ja16
Vygoniči **RUS** 121 Ed12
Vyksa **RUS** 118 Fb10
Vylkove **UA** 77 Kb35
Vynnyky **UA** 67 Hd30
Vynohradiv **UA** 75 Hd33
Vypolzovo **RUS** 117 Ec09
Vyra **RUS** 47 Jb17
Vyrica **RUS** 117 Eb08

Vyšgorodok **RUS** 47 Jb20
Vyšhorod **UA** 121 Ec14
Vyška **UA** 67 Hc32
Vyškov **CZ** 66 Gc32
Vyšné Nemecké **SK** 67
 Hc32
Vyšné Ružbachy **SK** 67
 Hb31
Vyšnij Voloček **RUS** 117
 Ec09
Vysock **RUS** 41 Ja16
Vysokaje **BY** 59 Hc27
Vysoké Mýto **CZ** 65 Gb31
Vysokovsk **RUS** 117 Ed10
Vyšší Brod **CZ** 65 Ga32
Vyžnycja **UA** 76 Jb32
Vyžnycja **UA** 124 Ea16

W

Waalre **NL** 55 Eb28
Waalwijk **NL** 55 Eb28
Wąbrzeźno **PL** 58 Gd26
Wąchock **PL** 67 Hb29
Wächtersbach **D** 64 Fa30
Wadebridge **GB** 23 Cb28
Wädenswil **CH** 71 Ed34
Wadlew **PL** 67 Ha29
Wadowice **PL** 67 Ha31
Wageningen **NL** 55 Eb28
Wagrain **A** 73 Fd34
Wągrowiec **PL** 58 Gc27
Waiblingen **D** 64 Fa32
Waidhaus **D** 64 Fc31
Waidhofen an der Thaya **A**
 65 Gb32
Waidhofen an der Ybbs **A**
 73 Ga33
Waimes **B** 63 Ec30
Wakefield **GB** 21 Db24
Wałbrzych **PL** 65 Gb30
Wałcz **PL** 57 Gb26
Waldbröl **D** 63 Ed29
Waldeck **D** 64 Fa29
Waldkirch **D** 71 Ed33
Waldkirchen **D** 65 Fd32
Waldkraiburg **D** 72 Fc33
Waldshut-Tiengen **D** 71
 Ed33
Wallasey **GB** 20 Cd24
Walldürn **D** 64 Fa31
Wallenfels **D** 64 Fc30
Wallingford **GB** 24 Da27
Walsall **GB** 24 Da26
Walsrode **D** 56 Fa27
Walton-on-the-Naze **GB** 25
 Dc27
Wangen **D** 72 Fa34
Wantage **GB** 24 Da27
Waplewo **PL** 58 Ha26
Warburg **D** 56 Fa28
Wardenburg **D** 55 Ed26
Waregem **B** 62 Ea29
Wareham **GB** 24 Cd28
Waremme **B** 63 Eb29

Waren **D** 57 Fd26
Warendorf **D** 55 Ed28
Warka **PL** 59 Hb28
Warlubie **PL** 58 Gd26
Warminster **GB** 24 Cd27
Warnemünde **D** 56 Fc25
Warrington **GB** 21 Da24
Warstein **D** 55 Ed28
Warszawa **PL** 59 Hb27
Warszkowo **PL** 58 Gc25
Warta **PL** 58 Gd28
Wartkowice **PL** 58 Gd28
Warwick **GB** 24 Da26
Washington **GB** 21 Db23
Wasilków **PL** 59 Hc26
Wąsosz **PL** 58 Gc27
Wąsosz **PL** 66 Gc29
Wassenaar **NL** 55 Eb27
Wasserburg **D** 72 Fc33
Wassy **F** 62 Ea32
Waterford **IRL** 22 Ca25
Waterloo **B** 62 Ea29
Waterville **IRL** 22 Bc25
Watford **GB** 25 Db27
Wattens **A** 72 Fc34
Wattwil **CH** 71 Ed34
Wavre **B** 62 Ea29
Wearhead **GB** 21 Da23
Węchadłów **PL** 67 Ha30
Wedel **D** 56 Fb26
Weener **D** 55 Ed26
Weert **NL** 63 Eb29
Węgliniec **PL** 65 Ga29
Węgorzewo **PL** 59 Hb25
Węgorzyno **PL** 57 Gb26
Węgrów **PL** 59 Hb27
Weida **D** 64 Fc30
Weiden **D** 64 Fc31
Weikersheim **D** 64 Fa31
Weil am Rhein **D** 71 Ec34
Weilburg **D** 63 Ed30
Weilheim **D** 72 Fb33
Weimar **D** 64 Fc29
Weingarten **D** 72 Fa33
Weinheim **D** 63 Ed31
Weißenburg **D** 64 Fb32
Weißenfels **D** 64 Fc29
Weißenhorn **D** 72 Fa33
Weißwasser **D** 65 Ga29
Weitra **A** 65 Ga32
Weiz **A** 73 Gb34
Wejherowo **PL** 51 Gd24
Wellingborough **GB** 25
 Db26
Wellington **GB** 24 Cd27
Wells **GB** 24 Cd27
Wells-next-the-Sea **GB** 25
 Dc26
Wels **A** 73 Ga33
Welshpool **GB** 24 Cd25
Welver **D** 55 Ed28
Welzheim **D** 64 Fa32
Wemyss Bay **GB** 20 Cd21
Werdohl **D** 63 Ed29
Werl **D** 55 Ed28
Werneck **D** 64 Fb31

Wernigerode **D** 56 Fb28
Wertheim **D** 64 Fa31
Wesel **D** 55 Ec28
Westbury **GB** 24 Cd27
Westerland **D** 48 Fa24
Westerstede **D** 55 Ed28
Weston-super-Mare **GB** 24
 Cd27
Westport **IRL** 18 Bd22
West-Terschelling **NL** 55
 Eb26
Wetherby **GB** 21 Db24
Wetlina **PL** 67 Hc31
Wetteren **B** 62 Ea29
Wetzikon **CH** 71 Ed34
Wetzlar **D** 63 Ed30
Wexford **IRL** 23 Cb25
Weyer Markt **A** 73 Ga33
Weymouth **GB** 24 Cd28
Whitby **GB** 21 Dc23
Whitchurch **GB** 24 Da25
Whitehaven **GB** 21 Da23
Whithorn **GB** 20 Cd22
Wiązów **PL** 66 Gc30
Wick **GB** 17 Db18
Wickede **D** 55 Ed28
Wicklow **IRL** 19 Cb24
Wicko **PL** 51 Gc24
Widminy **PL** 59 Hb25
Widuchowa **PL** 57 Ga26
Więcbork **PL** 58 Gc26
Wiehl **D** 63 Ed29
Wielbark **PL** 59 Hb26
Wieleń **PL** 57 Gb27
Wieliczka **PL** 67 Ha31
Wieluń **PL** 66 Gd29
Wien **A** 73 Gb33
Wiener Neustadt **A** 73 Gb34
Wieniawa **PL** 67 Hb29
Wieruszów **PL** 66 Gd29
Wierzbica **PL** 67 Hb29
Wierzchowo **PL** 57 Gb25
Wierzchucino **PL** 51 Gc24
Wierzchy **PL** 58 Gd28
Wiesbaden **D** 63 Ed30
Wieselburg **A** 73 Ga33
Wiesenburg **D** 56 Fc28
Wiesentheid **D** 64 Fb31
Wiesloch **D** 63 Ed31
Wiesmoor **D** 55 Ed26
Wigan **GB** 21 Da24
Wigston **GB** 25 Db26
Wigton **GB** 21 Da22
Wijchen **NL** 55 Eb28
Wikrowo **PL** 59 Hb25
Wil **CH** 71 Ed34
Wilchta **PL** 59 Hb28
Wilczęta **PL** 58 Ha25
Wildalpen **A** 73 Ga34
Wildeshausen **D** 56 Fa27
Wilga **PL** 59 Hb28
Wilhelmsburg **A** 73 Gb33
Wilhelmshaven **D** 55 Ed26
Williton **GB** 24 Cd27
Wilster **D** 56 Fa25
Wilton **GB** 24 Da28

Wiltz L 63 Eb30
Wimereux F 62 Dc29
Wincanton GB 24 Cd28
Winchester GB 24 Da28
Windermere GB 21 Da23
Windischgarsten A 73 Ga34
Windsbach D 64 Fb32
Winklern A 73 Fd35
Winnweiler D 63 Ed31
Winschoten NL 55 Ed26
Winsen D 56 Fb27
Winsen (Luhe) D 56 Fb26
Winsford GB 24 Da25
Wińsko PL 66 Gc29
Winsum NL 55 Ec26
Winterberg D 63 Ed29
Winterswijk NL 55 Ec28
Winterthur CH 71 Ed34
Wipperfürth D 63 Ed29
Wirges D 63 Ed30
Wisbech GB 25 Dc26
Wisła PL 66 Gd31
Wiślica PL 67 Hb30
Wismar D 56 Fc25
Wiśnice PL 59 Hc28
Wiśniowa PL 67 Hb31
Wissembourg F 63 Ed32
Wissen D 63 Ed29
Wisznia Mała PL 66 Gc29
Witham GB 25 Dc27
Withernsea GB 21 Dc24
Witkowo PL 58 Gc27
Witney GB 24 Da27
Witnica PL 57 Ga27
Witoszyce PL 57 Gb28
Witten D 55 Ed28
Wittenberge D 56 Fc27
Wittingen D 56 Fb27
Wittlich D 63 Ec30
Wittmund D 55 Ed26
Wittstock D 57 Fd26
Witzenhausen D 64 Fa29
Wiżajny PL 59 Hc25
Wizna PL 59 Hc26
Władysławowo PL 51 Gd24
Włocławek PL 58 Gd27
Włodawa PL 59 Hd28
Włodzimierzów PL 67 Ha29
Włoszakowice PL 57 Gb28
Włoszczowa PL 67 Ha29
Wodzisław Śląski PL 66 Gd31
Wohlen CH 71 Ed34
Woippy F 63 Eb31
Woking GB 25 Db28
Wola Uhruska PL 59 Hd28
Wolbrom PL 67 Ha30
Wołczyn PL 66 Gd29
Woldegk D 57 Fd26
Wolfen D 56 Fc28
Wolfenbüttel D 56 Fb28
Wolfratshausen D 72 Fb33
Wolfsberg A 73 Ga35
Wolfsburg D 56 Fb27
Wolgast D 57 Fd25
Wolhusen CH 71 Ed34

Wólka PL 67 Hc29
Wólka Kraśniczyńska PL 67 Hd29
Wolmirstedt D 56 Fc28
Wołosate PL 67 Hc32
Wołów PL 66 Gc29
Wolsztyn PL 57 Gb28
Wolvega NL 55 Ec26
Wolverhampton GB 24 Da26
Woodbridge GB 25 Dc27
Woodhall Spa GB 25 Db25
Woodstock GB 24 Da27
Wooler GB 21 Db22
Worb CH 71 Ec34
Worbis D 64 Fb29
Worcester GB 24 Da26
Wörgl A 72 Fc34
Workington GB 21 Da23
Worksop GB 25 Db25
Workum NL 55 Eb26
Worms D 63 Ed31
Wörth D 63 Ed32
Wörth D 64 Fa31
Worthing GB 25 Db28
Woziwoda PL 58 Gc26
Wrexham GB 24 Cd25
Wriezen D 57 Ga27
Wrocki PL 58 Gd26
Wrocław PL 66 Gc29
Wronki PL 57 Gb27
Września PL 58 Gc28
Wschowa PL 57 Gb28
Wunsiedel D 64 Fc31
Wunstorf D 56 Fa27
Wuppertal D 63 Ec29
Würzburg D 64 Fa31
Wurzen D 65 Fd29
Wygoda PL 58 Gd28
Wygoda PL 59 Hb26
Wygoda PL 66 Gd30
Wyk D 48 Fa24
Wylatowo PL 58 Gd27
Wymondham GB 25 Dc26
Wyrzysk PL 58 Gc26
Wysokie PL 59 Hc25
Wysokie PL 67 Hc29
Wysokie Mazowieckie PL 59 Hc26
Wyszków PL 59 Hb27
Wyszogród PL 58 Ha27

Xàbia (Jávea) E 94 Cc44
Xanten D 55 Ec28
Xánthi GR 102 Jb42
Xàtiva E 93 Cb43
Xert E 93 Cc42
Xerta E 93 Cd41
Xertigny F 71 Eb33
Xilókastro GR 111 Ja46
Xinzo de Limia E 78 Ba38
Xixona (Jijona) E 107 Cb44
Xylofagou CY 128 Gc19
Xylóskalo GR 114 Jb49

Yalıhüyük TR 128 Ga16
Yalıkavak TR 113 Kb46
Yalıköy TR 103 Kb41
Yarma TR 128 Gb15
Yarpuz TR 128 Ga16
Yatağan TR 113 Kb46
Yaylacık TR 128 Ga15
Ybbs A 73 Ga33
Yeadon GB 21 Db24
Yecla E 107 Cb44
Yenifoça TR 113 Ka44
Yeniköy TR 113 Ka44
Yeniköy TR 113 Kb44
Yenipazar TR 113 Kb45
Yeniyıldız TR 128 Gd16
Yenne F 70 Ea36
Yeovil GB 24 Cd28
Yepes E 92 Bd42
Yerville F 61 Db30
Yeşildere TR 128 Gc16
Yeste E 107 Ca44
Ylakiai LT 52 Hb22
Yläne FIN 40 Ha16
Ylihärmä FIN 40 Hb13
Yli-Ii FIN 35 Hc10
Yli-Kärppä FIN 35 Hc09
Ylikiiminki FIN 35 Hc10
Ylimarkku FIN 40 Ha14
Yli-Muonio FIN 30 Ha06
Ylistaro FIN 40 Ha13
Ylitornio FIN 34 Hb09
Ylivieska FIN 34 Hb11
Ylläsjärvi FIN 30 Hb07
Ylöjärvi FIN 40 Hb15
Ylvingen N 32 Fd10
York GB 21 Db24
Youghal IRL 22 Ca25
Ypäjä FIN 40 Hb16
Yppäri FIN 34 Hb11
Yset N 37 Fc14
Yssingeaux F 70 Dd36
Ystad S 50 Ga23
Ytre Arna N 36 Ed16
Ytre Kjæs N 27 Hb03
Ytre Oppedal N 36 Ed16
Ytterån S 38 Ga13
Ytterhogdal S 38 Ga14
Yttermalung S 44 Ga17
Yusufeli TR 127 Ga19
Yverdon CH 71 Eb35
Yvetot F 61 Db30

Zaanstad NL 55 Eb27
Žabalj SRB 87 Hb37
Zabalocce BY 121 Ec13
Zabierzów PL 67 Ha30
Žabinka BY 59 Hd27
Ząbkowice Śląskie PL 66 Gc30
Žabljak MNE 86 Ha40

Zabłudów PL 59 Hc26
Żabno PL 67 Hb30
Zabolova LV 47 Ja20
Zăbrani RO 75 Hc36
Zabrze PL 66 Gd30
Zabzuni RKS 100 Hb42
Zachlorou GR 110 Hd46
Zadar HR 85 Gb38
Zadonsk RUS 122 Fb12
Zadunajivka UA 77 Ka35
Zafferana Etnea I 109 Ga47
Zafra E 105 Ba43
Żagań PL 65 Gb29
Žagarė LT 52 Hc22
Zagnańsk PL 67 Hb29
Zagorje ob Savi SLO 73 Ga36
Zagórz PL 67 Hc31
Zagreb HR 73 Gb36
Žagubica SRB 87 Hc38
Zagvozd HR 86 Gc39
Zaháro GR 110 Hd47
Záhony H 67 Hc32
Zaidín E 80 Cd40
Zaimovo RKS 87 Hb40
Zainsk RUS 119 Ga08
Zaječar SRB 87 Hd38
Zákány H 74 Gc36
Zákinthos GR 110 Hc46
Zakliczyn PL 67 Hb31
Zakobjakino RUS 118 Fa08
Zakopane PL 67 Ha31
Zakroczym PL 58 Ha27
Zákros GR 115 Ka49
Zalaapáti H 74 Gc35
Zalabaska H 74 Gc35
Zalaegerszeg H 74 Gc35
Zalakomár H 74 Gc35
Zalamea de la Serena E 91 Bb42
Zalamea la Real E 105 Ad43
Zalaszentgrót H 74 Gc35
Zalău RO 75 Hd34
Zalegošč' RUS 122 Fa12
Zalesie PL 59 Hd28
Zališčyky UA 76 Jb32
Zališčyky UA 124 Ea16
Zalizci UA 120 Ea15
Zaltbommel NL 55 Eb28
Zaluč'e RUS 117 Eb09
Žaludok BY 59 Hd25
Zamárdi H 74 Gd35
Zamarte PL 58 Gc26
Zambrów PL 59 Hc26
Zamora E 78 Bb39
Zamość PL 67 Hd29
Zanarač BY 53 Ja24
Zandvoort NL 55 Eb27
Zanglivéri GR 101 Ja43
Zánka H 74 Gd35
Zaokskij RUS 118 Fa11
Zapadnaja Dvina RUS 117 Ec10
Zapfendorf D 64 Fb31
Zapoljarnyj RUS 27 Hd04

Zaporižžja – Żywiec

Zaporižžja **UA** 122 Fa15
Zaporožskoe **RUS** 41 Jb15
Zaprešić **HR** 73 Gb36
Zaprudnja **RUS** 117 Ed10
Zaprudy **BY** 59 Hd27
Zaragoza **E** 80 Cc40
Zarajsk **RUS** 118 Fa11
Zarasai **LT** 53 Ja22
Zarautz **E** 80 Cb38
Żardzjažža **BY** 53 Jb24
Żarki **PL** 67 Ha30
Zărneşti **RO** 88 Jb36
Žarnovica **SK** 74 Gd33
Žarošice **CZ** 66 Gc32
Zarrentin **D** 56 Fb26
Zarskoe Selo **RUS** 117 Eb08
Żary **PL** 65 Ga29
Zarza de Granadilla **E** 91 Bb40
Zasa **LV** 53 Ja22
Zašeek **RUS** 31 Ja08
Zasieki **PL** 57 Ga28
Žaškiv **UA** 121 Ec15
Zasos'e **RUS** 47 Jb18
Žatec **CZ** 65 Fd30
Zătreni **RO** 88 Ja37
Zatyšśja **UA** 77 Ka33
Zavala **BIH** 86 Gd40
Zavalinë **RKS** 100 Hb42
Zavet **BG** 89 Jd38
Zavetvoe **RUS** 123 Ga15
Zavidovići **BIH** 86 Gd38
Zavitne **UA** 126 Fb17
Zavoj **MK** 101 Hc42
Zavolž'e **RUS** 118 Fb09
Zawady **PL** 58 Ha28
Zawidów **PL** 65 Ga29
Zawiercie **PL** 67 Ha30
Zázrivá **SK** 67 Ha32
Zbaraž **UA** 120 Ea15
Zbąszyń **PL** 57 Gb28
Zbečno **CZ** 65 Ga31
Zbiroh **CZ** 65 Fd31
Zblewo **PL** 58 Gd25
Zbójna **PL** 59 Hb26
Zbójno **PL** 58 Gd27
Zboriv **UA** 120 Ea15
Zborov **SK** 67 Hb31
Zborowice **PL** 67 Hb31
Zbuczna **PL** 59 Hc28
Žd'ár **CZ** 65 Fd31
Žd'ár nad Sázavou **CZ** 65 Gb31
Ždírec nad Doubravou **CZ** 65 Gb31
Zdolbuniv **UA** 120 Ea15
Zdunje **MK** 101 Hc41
Zduńska Wola **PL** 58 Gd28
Zduny **PL** 58 Ha28
Zdzieszowice **PL** 66 Gd30
Żebrak **PL** 59 Hc28
Zebreira **P** 91 Ba41
Zeebrugge **B** 54 Dd28
Zehdenick **D** 57 Fd27
Žeimelis **LT** 52 Hc22
Žeimiai **LT** 52 Hc22

Zeist **NL** 55 Eb27
Zeitz **D** 64 Fc29
Żelazna **PL** 51 Gc24
Żelechów **PL** 59 Hb28
Zelenaja Rošča **RUS** 41 Jb16
Zelenčukskaja **RUS** 127 Fd17
Zelenivka **UA** 126 Fb16
Zelenodol'sk **RUS** 119 Fd09
Zelenodol's'k **UA** 125 Ed16
Zelenogirs'ke **UA** 77 Ka32
Zelenogorsk **RUS** 41 Jb16
Zelenograd **RUS** 117 Ed10
Zelenogradsk **RUS** 52 Ha24
Zelenokumsk **RUS** 127 Ga16
Železná Ruda **CZ** 65 Fd32
Železnodorožnyj **RUS** 59 Hb25
Železnogorsk **RUS** 121 Ed13
Željezovce **SK** 74 Gd33
Želju Vojoda **BG** 103 Jd40
Zella-Mehlis **D** 64 Fb30
Zell am See **A** 73 Fd34
Zell an der Pram **A** 73 Fd33
Zeltiņi **LV** 47 Ja20
Zeltweg **A** 73 Ga34
Zel'va **BY** 59 Hd26
Želva **LT** 53 Hd23
Zelzate **B** 54 Ea28
Žemaičių Kalvarija **LT** 52 Hb22
Žemaičių Naumiestis **LT** 52 Hb23
Zemblak **AL** 101 Hc43
Zemen **BG** 87 Hd40
Zemite **LV** 52 Hb21
Zemplénagárd **H** 75 Hc33
Zenica **BIH** 86 Gd38
Žepče **BIH** 86 Gd38
Žeravna **BG** 89 Jd39
Zerbst **D** 56 Fc28
Žerdevka **RUS** 123 Fc12
Žeredkove **UA** 77 Ka32
Zermatt **CH** 71 Ec36
Zernograd **RUS** 123 Fc15
Zerqan **RKS** 100 Hb42
Zetel **D** 55 Ed26
Zeulenroda **D** 64 Fc30
Zeven **D** 56 Fa26
Zevenaar **NL** 55 Ec28
Zevenbergen **NL** 55 Eb28
Zeytinbağı **TR** 103 Kb42
Zeytindağ **TR** 113 Ka44
Zeytinli **TR** 103 Ka43
Zgierz **PL** 58 Ha28
Zgniłoche **PL** 58 Ha26
Zgorzelec **PL** 65 Ga29
Zgozhd **RKS** 100 Hb42
Zguriţa **MD** 77 Jd32
Žiar nad Hronom **SK** 66 Gd32
Zicavo **F** 96 Ed41
Ziębice **PL** 66 Gc30

Zięby **PL** 58 Ha25
Ziēkas **LV** 52 Hb21
Zielona Góra **PL** 57 Gb28
Zierikzee **NL** 54 Ea28
Ziesar **D** 56 Fc28
Žiežmariai **LT** 53 Hd24
Žilina **SK** 66 Gd32
Žilino **RUS** 52 Hb24
Zilupe **LV** 53 Jb21
Zimbor **RO** 75 Hd34
Zimnicea **RO** 88 Jb38
Zimovniki **RUS** 123 Fd15
Zingst **D** 57 Fd25
Zin'kiv **UA** 121 Ed14
Zinnowitz **D** 57 Ga25
Zirc **H** 74 Gd34
Zirndorf **D** 64 Fb31
Zirnovsk **RUS** 123 Fd12
Žitište **SRB** 75 Hb36
Žitni Potok **SRB** 87 Hc40
Žitoradja **SRB** 87 Hc39
Zittau **D** 65 Ga29
Živinice **BIH** 86 Ha38
Zlarin **HR** 85 Gb39
Zlaté Moravce **SK** 74 Gd33
Zlatica **BG** 102 Jb40
Zlati Vojvoda **BG** 102 Jc40
Zlatna **RO** 75 Hd35
Zlatna Panega **BG** 88 Jb39
Zlatni Pjasăci **BG** 89 Ka38
Zlín **CZ** 66 Gc32
Žlobin **BY** 121 Eb13
Złocieniec **PL** 57 Gb26
Złoczew **PL** 66 Gd29
Złotniki Kujawskie **PL** 58 Gd27
Złotoryia **PL** 65 Gb29
Złotów **PL** 58 Gc26
Žlutice **CZ** 65 Fd31
Žmerynka **UA** 121 Eb15
Zmievka **RUS** 122 Fa12
Żmigród **PL** 66 Gc29
Zmijiv **UA** 122 Fa14
Zminica **MNE** 86 Ha40
Znamenka **BY** 59 Hd28
Znamensk **RUS** 52 Hb24
Znamenskoe **RUS** 121 Ed12
Znam'janka **UA** 121 Ed15
Žnin **PL** 58 Gc27
Znojmo **CZ** 65 Gb32
Žodzina **BY** 121 Eb12
Zoetermeer **NL** 55 Eb27
Zofingen **CH** 71 Ed34
Zohor **SK** 74 Gc33
Zollikofen **CH** 71 Ec34
Zoločiv **UA** 120 Ea15
Zolote **UA** 122 Fb14
Zolotonoša **UA** 121 Ed15
Żołynia **PL** 67 Hc30
Zonza **F** 96 Ed41
Żórawina **PL** 66 Gc29
Zörbig **D** 56 Fc28
Zorita **E** 91 Bb42
Zorleni **RO** 77 Jd35
Żory **PL** 66 Gd31
Zossen **D** 57 Fd28

Zovka **RUS** 47 Jb18
Žovkva **UA** 67 Hd30
Žovten' **MD** 77 Kb33
Žovti Vody **UA** 121 Ed15
Žovtneve **UA** 121 Ed14
Žovtyj Jar **UA** 77 Kb35
Zrenjanin **SRB** 87 Hb37
Zruč nad Sázavou **CZ** 65 Ga31
Zsadány **H** 75 Hc34
Zschopau **D** 65 Fd30
Zubcov **RUS** 117 Ec10
Zubova Poljana **RUS** 118 Fb11
Żubrówka **PL** 59 Hc25
Žuč **SRB** 87 Hc39
Zudaire **E** 80 Cb38
Zuera **E** 80 Cc40
Zug **CH** 71 Ed34
Zuidhorn **NL** 55 Ec26
Žukovka **RUS** 121 Ed12
Zülpich **D** 63 Ec29
Zumarraga **E** 80 Cb38
Zundert **NL** 55 Eb28
Županja **HR** 86 Ha37
Zürich **CH** 71 Ed34
Žuromin **PL** 58 Ha26
Zutphen **NL** 55 Ec27
Žužemberk **SLO** 73 Ga36
Zvenigorod **RUS** 117 Ed10
Zvenigovo **RUS** 119 Fd09
Zvenyhorodka **UA** 121 Ec15
Zvezdec **BG** 103 Ka40
Zvolen **SK** 67 Ha32
Zvonce **SRB** 87 Hd40
Zvornik **BIH** 86 Ha38
Zweibrücken **D** 63 Ec31
Zweisimmen **CH** 71 Ec35
Zwettl **A** 73 Ga33
Zwickau **D** 64 Fc30
Zwierzyniec **PL** 67 Hc29
Zwiesel **D** 65 Fd32
Zwijndrecht **NL** 55 Eb28
Zwoleń **PL** 67 Hb29
Zwolle **NL** 55 Ec27
Žychlin **PL** 58 Ha28
Žydačiv **UA** 120 Ea15
Żyrardów **PL** 58 Ha28
Żytkavičy **BY** 121 Eb13
Žytomyr **UA** 121 Eb15
Żywiec **PL** 67 Ha31